MELTDOWN

Inside

the

Fukushima

Nuclear

Crisis

MELTDOWN

YOICHI FUNABASHI

BROOKINGS INSTITUTION PRESS
Washington, D.C.

Copyright © 2021
THE BROOKINGS INSTITUTION
1775 Massachusetts Avenue, N.W.
Washington, D.C. 20036
www.brookings.edu

The Brookings Institution is a private nonprofit organization devoted to research,
education, and publication on important issues of domestic and foreign policy. Its
principal purpose is to bring the highest quality independent research and analysis
to bear on current and emerging policy problems. Interpretations or conclusions
in Brookings publications should be understood to be solely those of the authors.

Library of Congress Control Number: 2020952501
ISBN 9780815732594 (hc)
ISBN 9780815732600 (ebook)

9 8 7 6 5 4 3 2 1

Typeset in Sabon

Composition by Elliott Beard

Contents

Contents

Acknowledgments

SEIZE THE TRUTH WHILE IT'S HOT!

MARCH 11, 2011. When the Fukushima Daiichi Nuclear Power Station (NPS) accident took place, I listened to the news on TV with a feeling close to praying.

"Please let them reverse it."

A news bulletin came on.

"The news is that the power just came back on and the reactor is headed toward cooling."

Japan had beaten the nuclear crisis and had bounced back . . . For a time, I entertained the dream of a phoenix-like Japan. Turning the tables was Japan's rebirth strategy. I was convinced that at the end of the "lost decades," turning the tables was the only strategy if Japan was to be rebuilt.

However, there was no reversal. The game was over before we knew it. That fact was brought home on March 14. There was no way a reversal was possible.

This was a nuclear power plant accident waiting to happen. Was not the nature of the crisis in the government and Tokyo Electric Power Company (TEPCO) responses to the Fukushima Daiichi NPS accident the very nature of the crisis of Japan's "lost decades"? That was how it should be regarded.

As well as ashamed of my own ignorance, I was ensnared by the idea of investigating and verifying the background and cause of the accident.

At the end of March 2011, I learned that the government was going to set up a commission to investigate the accident. It was only to be expected that the government would look into the causes of the accident. Naturally, a government report would only be made from the standpoint of the government.

However, the citizens and people of Japan should not have lessons from the government imposed on us. We should be the principals, verifying the response to and the cause of the accident itself, extracting our own lessons to be learned, confronting the government with our findings, and monitoring the government.

I thought we needed an independent, private-sector investigation commission free from the government and the power industry, from politics and the nuclear village, a commission that could investigate and verify from an unfettered position.

To that end, I established, with a group of like-minded individuals, a think tank called the Rebuild Japan Initiative Foundation and launched a commission on the Fukushima Nuclear Accident, chaired by Professor Koichi Kitazawa. I was in charge of what would come to be known as the Independent Investigation Commission while serving as its program director.

As it moved forward with its investigations, the Independent Investigation Commission conducted interviews with more than three hundred people, including parliamentary members of the Kantei at the time of the accident.

We attacked the myth of safety that pervades nuclear power and the structure of the nuclear village, focusing mainly on the lead-up to the accident and the damage, the government and TEPCO responses, an analysis of historical and structural factors, and the global context.

The commission published its Survey/Investigation Report on February 28, 2012, and was disbanded. A revised English version of the report later became commercially available as *The Fukushima Daiichi Nuclear Power Station Disaster, Rebuild Japan Initiative Foundation (Routledge, 2014)*.[1]

As a matter of course, the report placed its emphasis on investigating the cause of the accident and analyzing its historical and structural background, but in the process, I became interested in the struggle of individuals to overcome the crisis. I wanted to get a hold on the truth of Japanese society—and human society—in a time of such crisis.

How did we face the fight when Big Technology and the absolute laws of physics became a lethal force capable of destroying human society and nature?

I would once again track the Fukushima Nuclear Power Station crisis, focusing on that cruel month of March 2011. I would portray this tragedy in the form of a detailed chronology of the origins of the severe nuclear accident and the crisis response. It is not only the nuclear reactors that are to be questioned. Both something and everything triggered an unexpected meltdown at that time. I want to delineate exactly how it happened.

After the report was published, I went back to being a reporter and started to interview. In the process, I was able to hear the stories of many people (the interview list can be found at the end of the book).

During the interviews, I asked whether memos existed, but only a few had written notes of the events. There was nothing for it but to get the parties involved to refresh their memories. I would re-create the situation and use that to trigger their recollections. Sometimes this involved a process of triangulation, cross-checking the memory of each person, which created a complex web, like *Rashomon,* to ascertain the facts.[2]

Statements within quotation marks were made at the time by the various parties. Text that is italicized represents the thoughts of the various parties. Of course, the italicized text is also based on the testimony of the parties and interviews I conducted. I learned at this time that in many cases people have a clearer recollection of their thoughts than of their actual words.

I also learned something else. In the eight months from March 2012, when I started interviewing for this book, the recollections of the parties involved changed slightly. As the investigation report of each ministry was announced, inconvenient truths that clashed with those reports faded away. I wondered whether a script was being written with an eye to countering trials and litigation, but after the release of these reports, they would start to be spoken of as the truth.

It is said, "Strike the iron while it's hot," but in this case, "Seize the truth while it's hot." This was brought home to me with a vengeance.

Countdown Meltdown (Japanese title of *Meltdown*) was awarded the Otoya Soichi Non-Fiction Award, given to Japan's best works of nonfiction. One of the committee members commented, "This is a war record of the Fukushima nuclear crisis."

Without intending to, I had written a war record. What covered the scene was not the fog of the battlefield, but the fog of crisis and its deep veils. I wanted to share with the people of the world the human, social drama that unfolded as the crisis developed in the depths of that fog. It was an unexpected pleasure when the Brookings Institution decided to publish an English version at this time.

I am indebted to former Brookings Institution president Strobe Talbott, as I was when I published *The Peninsula Question: A Chronicle of the Second Korean Nuclear Crisis,* after spending a year at the institution as a distinguished guest scholar. I would like to express my sincere thanks. I would also like to express my gratitude to Bill Finan, director of the Brookings Institution Press, for his hard and meticulous work.

The English version to be published at this time is a new revision of the Japanese version, incorporating new reports and materials announced later as well as subsequent interviews with many parties. The main new reports/materials that are referenced frequently throughout are as follows:

1) TEPCO, "A Summary of the Fukushima Nuclear Accident and Nuclear Safety Reform Plan," March 29, 2013[3]

TEPCO announced its *Fukushima Nuclear Accident Investigation Report* on June 20, 2012, but did not provide sufficient analytical overview of the reasons why the accident could not have been prevented. It was also criticized as an exercise in self-defense from start to finish. TEPCO then set up a new task force and published the above report, which compiled a Nuclear Safety Reform Plan based on its Reflections on the Fukushima Nuclear Accident. Here they acknowledged for the first time that the accident was "man-made" and that the fundamental problem was a matter of management.

2) Fukushima Nuclear Power Accident Record Team, Tomomi Miyazaki and Hideaki Kimura, *A Record of 49 Hours of TEPCO's Fukushima Nuclear Accident Videoconference* (Tokyo: Iwanami Shoten, 2013)

This is a document recording, in the wake of the accident, the real-time videoconferences from March 12, 11:59 p.m., to 12:06 a.m. on March 15, between TEPCO Head Office, Fukushima Daiichi, and Fukushima Daini Power Plants, among others.

3) Investigation Committee on the Accident at the Fukushima Nuclear Power Stations of Tokyo Electric Power Company (Government Investigation Commission), "Hearings Report" (also known as the Yoshida Testimony), July–November 2011[4]

This is a report of the thirteen interviews with (then) Site Supervisor Masao Yoshida, conducted by the Government Accident Investigation over a total of twenty-nine hours from the summer to the winter of 2011. In September 2014, the Japanese government released the full text of this transcript on the web, despite the interviews having been conducted on the premise of "non-disclosure." (Government Investigation Commission Hearing Records, online: https://www8.cao.go.jp/genshiryoku_bousai/fu_koukai/fu_koukai_2.html [Japanese only])

In this, Yoshida speaks frankly and in detail about his battle of life and death with the severe accident that "had no answer," caused by the total loss of power supply. This live account in Yoshida's voice—often confused and cloudy—is an irreplaceable testimony of human society's battle during a nuclear crisis. (In February 2015, RJIF published *Anatomy of the Yoshida Testimony: The Fukushima Nuclear Crisis as Seen through the Yoshida Hearings.*)[5]

In the aftermath of the Fukushima nuclear power plant accident, the Government Investigation's Interim Report, the Independent Investigation's Report, the Diet Investigation's Report, and the Government Investigation's Final Report were released in close succession.[6] There was no precedent for the government, Diet, and an independent investigation virtually competing with one another to draw lessons from Japan's national crisis and its response. I am proud that the Independent Investigation played a part.

The fruits of the joint research and serious discussion between members of the working group and the committee are impossible to measure. Without such valuable experience, this book would not have been possible. Once again, I would like to express my thanks to each and every one involved, including Lauren Altria, Takuya Matsuda, Patrick Madaj, Takuma Hirai, and Romeo Marcantuoni for their critical research support.

However, we were also touched by sadness. Professor Koichi Kitazawa, who was chairman of the Independent Investigation Commission, died in September 2014. He was seventy-one years old. Without the vision, insight, and leadership of Professor Kitazawa, a global scientist, the Independent Investigation would not have seen the light of day. I remember well his gentle but stern gaze when facing the truth. May he rest in peace.

Introduction

Fukushima is not yet over. The nuclear emergency declaration at the Fukushima Daiichi Nuclear Power Plant has still not been lifted even at the present juncture. Of the residents who evacuated in line with evacuation instructions issued four times within twenty-four hours of the accident (a peak of 164,865 people in May 2012), 43,022 are still unable to return to their homes (as of August 2020). There were no deaths due to direct exposure to radiation during the accident, but indirect deaths, due to the evacuation and subsequent stress, amounted to 3,739 (as of December 2019), according to the Reconstruction Agency.[1] Radiation in the plant near the nuclear reactor is still high, and the situation inside the nuclear reactors cannot be confirmed.

It is presumed that most of the highly radioactive "debris" resulting from the nuclear reactor core meltdowns is located at the bottom of the reactor containment vessels. The technology and plans for its removal have not yet been finalized.

Before the accident, fifty-four nuclear power plants were operating in Japan, but as of the end of October 2020, only nine reactors and five out of the twenty-seven plants that have applied to restart have been approved.

The total amount of damage caused by the accident was calculated at 22 trillion yen (US$204 billion) by the TEPCO Reform and 1F (Fukushima Daiichi nuclear plant) Problem Committee of the Ministry of Economy, Trade, and Industry (METI) in the "Proposal for TEPCO Reform" announced in 2016. In 2019, the Japan Economic Research Center, a private think tank, announced a trial calculation that the cost in managing the accident would rise to a maximum of 80 trillion yen (US$743 billion) over the course of forty years.

Fukushima is still not behind us.

However, the most symbolic indication that Fukushima is not yet over may be the fact that the investigation of the accident, its background, and responses to it are not yet complete. And, therefore, the essential question of what lessons can be drawn from Fukushima is yet to be answered.

MARCH 11, 2011. The Fukushima Daiichi Nuclear Power Plant accident happened due to a tsunami that came in the wake of an earthquake. The cause of this accident and crisis has been clarified to a considerable extent by research and investigations such as the Government Investigation, the Diet Investigation, the TEPCO Investigation, and the Independent Investigation.

The Independent Investigation Commission on the Fukushima Nuclear Accident produced by the Rebuild Japan Initiative Foundation made the following analysis. The accident was a "parallel chain nuclear disaster," in which Units 1, 2, and 3 went into meltdown one after another and Unit 4 caught fire, but was essentially a man-made disaster. The following factors can be cited as the structural background to the man-made disaster:

1. The trap of the myth of absolute safety
2. A failure in safety regulatory governance
3. The Galapagosization of safety regulations
4. The ambiguity of "national policy carried out by private entities"
5. A lack of leadership and crisis management during a national crisis

The myth of absolute safety is the perverted nuclear safety culture view that preparations for severe accidents in and of themselves cause anxiety among residents, concerning nuclear power. To put it another way, it is a belief system that embeds the social psychology of making risk a taboo in its superstructure, and the interests of the so-called nuclear village, which promotes nuclear power, in its sub-structure. The Japanese "nuclear village," politics, and government administration all fell into this trap.

Safety regulatory governance involved issues such as the duplicated and vertically compartmentalized nuclear administration of the Ministry of Economy, Trade, and Industry (METI) and the Ministry of Education, Culture, Sports, Science, and Technology (MEXT); the typical subservience of a regulatory body to the promoting body as seen with the Nuclear and Industrial Safety Agency located under METI and the Ministry of Resources and Energy; and the political dynamics of the "nuclear village," where the power company had stronger political power than the regulatory agency.

The Galapagosization of safety regulations refers to a belief and sense of superiority that Japanese safety regulations were excellent even in light of international standards. Nuclear safety regulations based on a "Japan-only

safety principle" equally took a backward stance on international cooperation concerning nuclear plant counterterrorism and making severe accident
measures mandatory.

National policy carried out by private entities is a system in which private enterprises are responsible for the "private" nuclear power generation
business under a "government policy" promoting the peaceful use of nuclear power. However, while this may have worked during normal times,
at a time of nuclear crisis, the system was revealed to not function at all.
National responsibility in the event of a severe accident and the role of the
responding forces at that time were not clear in the legal system. Who was
to make difficult decisions, as well as when and how, spanning both onsite
and offsite, such as evacuation or withdrawal from a nuclear power plant
at a time of rising radiation, remained obscure.

A severe nuclear accident inevitably brings about a national crisis. It is
also indicative that the Fukushima nuclear power plant accident caused a
crisis in the Japan-U.S. alliance. During this national crisis, the quality of
both the Japanese government and Japanese firms was called into question
in terms of both statecraft and strategy, and raised serious questions about
the nature of Japanese leadership.

Ultimately, the Fukushima nuclear power plant accident was a crisis
caused by human error. Of those preparations, the most important provision was governance, but this was inadequate. Fukushima was a tragic lack
of preparing for crisis governance.

In September 2012, the Nuclear Regulatory Commission (chaired by Shunichi Tanaka), a highly independent committee tasked with the mission of
ensuring safety in the use of nuclear energy, and its executing organization,
the Nuclear Regulatory Authority, were established. This has brought more
transparency and independence into decisions regarding safety regulations
and process. However, the public remains as yet unconvinced as to whether
the Nuclear Regulatory Authority is really different from the Nuclear and
Industrial Safety Agency and the former Science and Technology Agency,
which were riddled with members of the "nuclear village."

Certainly, each power company subsequently built tidal banks as a tsunami countermeasure, bought power supply trucks as an emergency power
supply measure, stockpiled a large amount of batteries, and purchased
several fire trucks. However, these provisions are all readily visible and
of a hardware-centric focus, so to speak. In contrast, software-based arrangements, such as organizing execution units as the "last bastion" during
extreme nuclear accidents, resident evacuation plans, health effects, and
radiation management are still inadequate.

Tokyo Electric Power Company has applied to reopen its Kashiwazaki-
Kariwa Nuclear Power Plant (No. 5 and 6) in Niigata Prefecture, the

world's largest nuclear complex, but Niigata Governor Ryuichi Yoneyama has stated that unless there is a thorough investigation of (1) the Fukushima nuclear accident, (2) the impact of a nuclear power plant accident on residents' health and lives, and (3) safe evacuation methods in the event of a nuclear accident, the debate on reopening cannot commence. And even nine years on from the accident, there is strong prefectural opposition along the lines of "restarting should not be allowed until they have investigated and learned their lessons."

For example, SPEEDI, a real-time damage prediction system for protecting residents from radiation exposure in a radiation accident, was not used for resident evacuation after the Fukushima nuclear power plant accident. The discussion as to what kind of lessons to draw from that is not yet over. Following a recommendation from the National Association of Governors to "use it effectively," the government decided "it would not prevent each municipality from using it at their own responsibility." However, opinions within related institutions are divided, with the Nuclear Regulatory Commission saying that SPEEDI "cannot and should not be used."

In terms of software, what we lack the most is perhaps imagination. Whether it is a tsunami, a large-scale compound disaster, a meltdown, or a worst-case scenario, the containment of one's imagination by defining them as "unexpected" can produce deadly results. This is the most important lesson learned from the Fukushima nuclear accident.

However, this does not mean that the Japanese people, nor Japanese society, inherently lack imagination. The root of the problem is that the political and administrative institutions have not imagined the possibility of "unexpected" events. National security and the safety of citizens can only be ensured through preparedness, prevention, and response by making the unexpected known among the public and disseminating information.

In addition, when a risk assessment exceeds the expectation of what can be managed and imposes excessive stress on business management or political systems, Japan has a political and organizational culture that tends to contain that assessment within an "expected range." A rigorous risk assessment is understood as causing "unnecessary anxiety and misunderstanding" among the public. Anything that falls outside of the "expected" range of risk, therefore, is driven away. The Independent Investigation Commission used the expression "prioritizing small reassurances and sacrificing greater security" to describe the costs of the psychological and political segregation of risk assessment and management.

After the Fukushima nuclear power plant accident, Japan redeveloped a new safety regulation system by proudly implementing "the world's strictest" safety measures. This enthusiasm deserves some praise, but to claim that it is "the world's strictest" simply serves the purpose of imposing "homework" for the companies and offering psychological reassurance to the public. As a result, a new "safety myth" is created, reproducing a regulatory culture that sacrifices safety.

After the accident, the number of reactors that have been slated for decommissioning stands at twenty-four, including those at TEPCO's Fukushima Daiichi.[2] As many nuclear power plants are forced to decommission or shut down operations, national opinion is also divided over the current back-end regime of stockpiling plutonium and the nuclear fuel cycle policy, any conclusion being continually put off. As James M. Acton argues in his piece, *Wagging the Plutonium Dog: Japanese Domestic Politics and Its International Security Implications*, Japan risks violating internationally recognized best practices by producing more plutonium than it can consume within a decade if policy procrastination continues.[3] And in the process of moving forward with reopening plants, other than the economic argument, the government still has not adequately considered the viewpoint of ethics, responsibility, and security, which is inevitably required when using nuclear power that carries with it the risk of destroying humanity from the roots.

After the Fukushima nuclear power plant accident, a paradigm shift away from nuclear power to renewable energy began in Germany, Taiwan, South Korea, and other countries. In such a setting, Japan has failed to provide a persuasive post-Fukushima energy policy or positioning of nuclear power plants.

This book is a record of the accident and crisis that began with the station blackout at Fukushima Daiichi Nuclear Power Plant on March 11, 2011. This is a story of the people who faced, dealt with, and sought to overcome the ordeal during the thick of this crisis. Rather than being a representation of problems peculiar to Japan, it is a universal challenge, something that could happen anywhere in the world when a civilized society fails to handle the unforgiving technology of nuclear power.

I, therefore, believe that the lessons learned from Fukushima should be shared with the world. It will be fortunate if this book can in some way contribute to a feedback mechanism for learning lessons from Fukushima.

May 25, 2020 (the day the Japanese government decided to lift the state of emergency for the coronavirus pandemic)

Yoichi Funabashi

Fukushima Disaster Response Timeline (Japan Standard Time)

MARCH 11, 2011

2:46 P.M. Great East Japan earthquake (Mw 9.0) occurs.

2:47 P.M. Unit 1 through 3 reactors automatically shut down (SCRAM).

2:48 P.M. Offsite AC power is lost; onsite emergency diesel generators automatically start up to provide AC power.

2:50 P.M. Earthquake response center is set up in the government.

2:52 P.M. Maritime SDF orders all operational ships to leave port.

3:14 P.M. Nuclear Emergency Response Headquarters set up in the Kantei.

3:27 P.M. First tsunami wave arrives at wave height meter.

3:36-3:37 P.M. Second (main) tsunami wave (height ~13 m) floods parts of plant.

3:37-3:41 P.M. Article 10 notification event occurs (loss of all plant power).

4:36 P.M. Article 15 emergency event occurs in Units 1 and 2 (loss of emergency core cooling system water injection sources).

5:00 P.M. TEPCO starts to use monitoring cars to measure radiation.

5:40 P.M. The first television report of station blackout at Fukushima Daiichi Units 1 and 2.

5:42 P.M. Banri Kaieda seeks approval from Naoto Kan for the declaration of a state of nuclear emergency.

5:55 P.M. Banri Kaieda instructs the venting of Units 1 and 2.

6:25 P.M. The operators close the IC valve of Unit 1.

6:50 P.M. Core damage in Unit 1.

7:00 P.M. The U.S. government informs the Japanese government about dispatching the USS *Ronald Reagan*.

7:03 P.M. The first Nuclear Emergency Response HQ (NERHQ) meeting takes place and the Japanese government declares a state of nuclear emergency.

7:19 P.M. Water level confirmed to be at 200 mm above top of active fuel in Unit 1.

7:30 P.M. Defense minister releases an order to dispatch the SDF to the nuclear disaster.

8:50 P.M. Fukushima Prefecture governor orders residents within a 2-kilometer radius of Daiichi to evacuate.

9:23 P.M. Japanese government expands evacuation radius for Daiichi to 3 kilometers.

9:30 P.M. The IC valve is opened in Unit 1.

9:51 P.M. The Unit 1 reactor building (RB) is put on "restricted access."

10:00 P.M. Workers enter Unit 2 reactor building to read the reactor pressure vessel water level (3,400 mm above top of active fuel).

11:50 P.M. Pressure of the dry well of Unit 1 is recorded to be 600 kPa (maximum working pressure is 427 kPa).

MARCH 12, 2011

12:15 A.M. Telephone conversation between President Barack Obama and Prime Minister Naoto Kan.

3:00 A.M. Power is restored to the offsite center.

5:44 A.M. Japanese government widens the evacuation radius for Daiichi to 10 kilometers.

5:46 A.M. Freshwater begins to be pumped into Unit 1.

6:14 A.M. Prime Minister Naoto Kan departs for Fukushima via helicopter.

6:50 A.M. Instructions to vent Units 1 and 2 are switched from an instruction to a formal order.

7:45 A.M. Japanese government sets evacuation radius for Daini to 10 kilometers.

9:04 A.M. Emergency Response Center issues the order to begin manual venting at Unit 1.

10:00 A.M. National Institute of Radiological Sciences (NIRS) doctors arrive at the offsite center.

10:47 A.M. Prime Minister Naoto Kan returns to the Kantei.

11:36 A.M. Reactor core isolation cooling system stops working in Unit 3.

2:30 P.M. Pressure containment vessel venting operations begin at Unit 1.

3:18 P.M. Masao Yoshida judges that radioactive material is being released from Unit 1 venting.

3:30 P.M. TEPCO begins making preparations to inject seawater into Unit 1.

3:36 P.M. Hydrogen explosion occurs in Unit 1 reactor building.

6:25 P.M. Japanese government widens the evacuation radius for Daiichi to 20 kilometers.

7:30 P.M. The SDF withdraws operations near Unit 1.

7:34 P.M. Seawater begins to be pumped into Unit 1.

MARCH 13, 2011

2:24 A.M. The high pressure coolant injection (HPCI) system of Units 3 and 4 is manually switched off.

5:10 A.M. Article 15 emergency event occurs in Unit 3 (loss of emergency core cooling system water injection sources).

7:00 A.M. TEPCO Procurement Group asks employees to donate their car batteries.

9:24 A.M. Reduction of pressure due to venting in Unit 3's dry well is noted.

9:25 A.M. Freshwater begins to be pumped into Unit 3.

10:40 A.M. Core damage in Unit 3.

1:12 P.M. Seawater begins to be pumped into Unit 3.

3:22 P.M. USAID team arrives at U.S. Misawa Air Base.

9:37 P.M. 3,200 microsieverts is measured at the front gate of Fukushima Daiichi.

MARCH 14, 2011

7:00 A.M. Motohisa Ikeda requests Central Special Weapons Protection Corps to inject water into Unit 3.

11:01 A.M. Hydrogen explosion occurs in Unit 3 reactor building.

1:20 P.M. Meeting is held at the Kantei, in which the permissible exposure level is raised to 250 millisieverts.

1:30 P.M. Reactor core isolation cooling system in Unit 2 stops operating.

2:58 P.M. TEPCO reports preparations to vent Unit 2 are complete.

3:30 P.M. Seawater begins to be pumped into Unit 3 again.

4:34 P.M. Central Control Room begins to try to open the safety relief (SR) valve of Unit 2.

5:00 P.M. The water level of Unit 2 reaches top of active fuel (TAF).

6:40 P.M. Yoshida calls Goshi Hosono to say "We may be finished" after pumping water into Unit 2 fails.

7:20 P.M. Core damage in Unit 2 and fire engines standing by Unit 2 run out of fuel.

7:57 P.M. The fire engines are refueled and water is pumped into Unit 2.

9:22 P.M. It is reported that Unit 2's water level has recovered to above top of active fuel (TAF).

MARCH 15, 2011

2:00 A.M. Tetsuro Ito is told that, in the worst case, Units 1 through 4 and possibly Units 5 and 6 would have to be abandoned.

3:30 A.M. "The Imperial Conference" meeting takes place.

4:17 A.M. TEPCO President Masataka Shimizu visits the Kantei and promises TEPCO will not pull out from the site.

5:26 A.M. Government-TEPCO Integrated Response Office is set up.

5:35 A.M. Kan leaves for TEPCO, where he makes a controversial ten-minute address.

6:14 A.M. Hydrogen explosion occurs in Unit 4 reactor building.

7:00 A.M. 650 people evacuate from Daiichi, leaving 70 or so workers.

8:11 A.M. Article 15 emergency event occurs in Unit 4 (abnormal release of radioactive materials).

11:00 A.M. Government announces a shelter-in-place order for residents between 20 and 30 kilometers from Fukushima Daiichi.

11:20 A.M. SDF helicopter takes off for monitoring but cancels due to fear of an explosion in Unit 4.

1:00 P.M. Miharu Town orders its people to take stable iodine.

2:00 P.M. Government reports that evacuation from 20-kilometer radius is completed.

6:00 P.M. Power trucks are sent from Fukushima Daini to Daiichi.

9:26 P.M. 330 microsieverts is recorded at Point 32 in Kawafusa in Namie Town.

MARCH 16, 2011

4:00 P.M. TEPCO employees board an SDF helicopter to take aerial shots of Unit 4.

4:30 P.M. Emperor's message broadcasts on all television stations.

5:20 P.M. Water drop operations at Unit 3 are suspended due to high air dose rate.

10:30 P.M. The testimony before U.S. Congress begins, in which Gregory Jaczko claims Unit 4 is dry.

MARCH 17, 2011

12:00 A.M. Detailed analysis of all the reactors and fuel pools delivered to the SDF.

8:56–10:01 A.M. Water is dropped by the SDF into Unit 3.

10:22 A.M. Telephone conference between Prime Minister Naoto Kan and President Barack Obama.

2:15 P.M. U.S. government orders 50-mile evacuation zone and recommendation for voluntary departure for families of U.S. government officials.

2:20 P.M. The riot police arrive at Fukushima Daiichi.

5:37 P.M. Five high-power water trucks to be used by the SDF arrive at Fukushima Daiichi.

7:00 P.M. The riot police sprays 44 tons of water into the spent-fuel pool at Unit 3.

7:35–8:09 P.M. SDF pumps water into the fuel pool at Unit 3.

8:00 P.M. Tokyo Mayor Shintaro Ishihara agrees to mobilize the Hyper Rescue Squad.

MARCH 18, 2011

12:50 A.M. Official instruction to mobilize the Hyper Rescue Squad.

3:30 A.M. Tokyo Fire Department's Hyper Rescue Squad mobilized.

4:30 A.M. President Obama holds a press conference about Fukushima after expressing condolences at the Japanese embassy.

MARCH 19, 2011

12:30–12:50 A.M. The Hyper Rescue Squad discharges 60 tons of water into Unit 3.

2:05–3:40 P.M. The Hyper Rescue Squad pumps 2,430 tons of water into Unit 3.

MARCH 20, 2011

8:21 A.M. Water begins to be pumped into Unit 4 by the SDF.

MARCH 21, 2011

9:00 A.M. *Kaiwo Maru* arrives at Onahama Port as a facility for plant workers and evacuees.

MARCH 22, 2011

1:00 P.M. First meeting of U.S.-Japan Joint Coordination Group on the Nuclear Emergency.

4:00 P.M. Prime Minister Kan asks heads of NSC, JAEC, and NISA to draw up a worst-case scenario.

5:17 P.M. Putzmeister's concrete boom, the Giraffe, pumps for water injection arrive onsite and spray water into Unit 4.

MARCH 23, 2011

7:00 A.M. SPEEDI calculation results arrive at the NSC.

2:30 P.M. NSC chairman briefs Prime Minister Naoto Kan about SPEEDI reverse estimation method and results.

MARCH 25, 2011

Shunsuke Kondo submits the worst-case scenario to Goshi Hosono.

The government sets a voluntary evacuation area (20–30 km from Fukushima Daiichi).

MARCH 27, 2011

12:34 A.M. Concrete boom Giraffe pumps begin to spray into Unit 3.

MARCH 29, 2011

1:03 P.M. Concrete boom Giraffe pumps begin to spray into Unit 1.

APRIL 2, 2011

9:30 A.M. A patrol finds that water in the pit near Unit 2 is more than 1,000 millisieverts per hour.

APRIL 5, 2011

3:17 P.M. TEPCO begins to inject glass water.

APRIL 6, 2011

5:38 A.M. TEPCO confirms that the outflow of highly contaminated water had stopped.

APRIL 22, 2011

The government releases the Planned Evacuation Area, which includes Iitate Village.

Source: National Research Council, "Lessons Learned from the Fukushima Nuclear Accident for Improving Safety of U.S. Nuclear Plants," July 24, 2014; core damage estimates are from TEPCO's Fukushima Nuclear Accident Report.

Principal Figures in the Fukushima Disaster Response

Position as of March 2011

TOKYO ELECTRIC POWER COMPANY (TEPCO)

Masataka Shimizu, *president*
Sakae Muto, *vice president*
Tsunehisa Katsumata, *chairman*
Akio Komori, *managing director*
Masao Yoshida, *Fukushima Daiichi site superintendent*
Ikuo Izawa, *Fukushima Daiichi Units 1 and 2 Central Control Room duty manager*
Naohiro Masuda, *Fukushima Daini site superintendent*
Ichiro Takekuro, *TEPCO fellow (liaison to the Kantei)*
Susumu Kawamata, *general manager for Nuclear Quality and Safety Management Department (liaison to the Kantei)*
Takeyuki Inagaki, *recovery team leader*
Hiroyuki Ogawa, *firefighting team chief*
Mari Sato, *Disaster Prevention Group leader*

THE PRIME MINISTER'S OFFICE (KANTEI)

Naoto Kan, *prime minister*
Yukio Edano, *chief cabinet secretary*
Tetsuro Fukuyama, *deputy chief cabinet secretary*
Tetsuro Ito, *deputy chief cabinet secretary for crisis management*
Goshi Hosono, *special adviser to the prime minister*
Manabu Terada, *special adviser to the prime minister*

Kenichi Shimomura, *counselor for public relations at the Cabinet Secretariat*

Satoshi Maeda, *executive assistant to the prime minister*

CABINET SECRETARIAT

Toshiso Kosako, *graduate school professor at the University of Tokyo, special adviser to the Cabinet Secretariat*

Oriza Hirata, *playwright, special adviser to the Cabinet Secretariat*

CABINET OFFICE

Koichiro Genba, *minister for national policy*

Kenkichi Hirose, *adviser to METI's permanent secretary until March 28, special adviser to the Cabinet Office from March 28*

MINISTRY OF ECONOMY, TRADE, AND INDUSTRY (METI)

Banri Kaieda, *minister*

Motohisa Ikeda, *senior vice minister (head of the local Nuclear Emergency Response Headquarters (NERHQ) until March 15)*

Tadahiro Matsushita, *senior vice minister (head of the local Nuclear Emergency Response Headquarters (NERHQ) from March 15)*

Kazuo Matsunaga, *permanent secretary*

Hiroyuki Fukano, *director general for commerce and distribution policy*

Masaya Yasui, *director general for the Energy Conservation and Renewable Energy Department*

METI'S NUCLEAR AND INDUSTRIAL SAFETY AGENCY (NISA)

Nobuaki Terasaka, *director general*

Eiji Hiraoka, *deputy director general*

Shinchi Kuroki, *deputy director general*

Hisanori Nei, *deputy director general*

Tetsuya Yamamoto, *chief of Inspection Unit*

Kazuma Yokota, *head of local inspectors at Fukushima Daiichi*

NUCLEAR SAFETY COMMISSION (NSC)

Haruki Madarame, *chairman*

Yutaka Kukita, *deputy chairman, acting chairman*

Akihiko Iwahashi, *secretary-general*

Shizuyo Kusumi, *commissioner*

JAPAN ATOMIC ENERGY COMMISSION (JAEC)

Shunsuke Kondo, *chairman*

Akira Omoto, *commissioner*

JAPAN ATOMIC ENERGY AGENCY (JAEA)

Masamichi Chino, *deputy director of the Nuclear Science and Engineering Directorate*

Toshimitsu Homma, *deputy director of the Nuclear Safety Research Center*

NATIONAL INSTITUTE OF RADIOLOGICAL SCIENCES (NIRS)

Takako Tominaga, *Radiation Emergency Medical Assistance Team (REMAT) doctor*

MINISTRY OF EDUCATION, CULTURE, SPORTS, SCIENCE, AND TECHNOLOGY (MEXT)

Kan Suzuki, *vice minister*

Yasutaka Moriguchi, *deputy director general*

MINISTRY OF DEFENSE (MOD)

Toshimi Kitazawa, *minister*

Hideo Suzuki, *deputy director general*

Ryoichi Oriki, *chief of staff of the Joint Staff, Japan Self-Defense Forces (SDF)*

Katsutoshi Kawano, *vice chief of staff of the Joint Staff, Japan Self-Defense Forces (SDF)*

Yoshifumi Hibako, *chief of staff, Japan Ground Self-Defense Forces (GSDF)*

Toshinobu Miyajima, *commanding general, Central Readiness Force (CRF)*

Masayuki Hironaka, *director of the Operations Department, Joint Staff Office*

Koichi Isobe, *director of the Defense Plans and Policy Department, Joint Staff Office*

MINISTRY OF INTERNAL AFFAIRS AND COMMUNICATIONS (MIC)

Yoshihiro Katayama, *minister*

MINISTRY OF FOREIGN AFFAIRS (MOFA)

Kenichiro Sasae, *vice minister*

EMBASSY OF JAPAN IN THE UNITED STATES OF AMERICA

Ichiro Fujisaki, *Japanese ambassador to the United States*

TOKYO FIRE DEPARTMENT

Yuji Arai, *fire chief*

FUKUSHIMA PREFECTURE

Katsunobu Sakurai, *mayor of Minamisoma City*
Tamotsu Baba, *mayor of Namie Town*
Yoshitaka Suzuki, *mayor of Miharu Town*
Norio Kanno, *mayor of Iitate Village*

NIIGATA PREFECTURE

Hirohiko Izumida, *governor*

U.S. NUCLEAR REGULATORY COMMISSION (NRC)

Gregory Jaczko, *chairman*
Charles Casto, *head of Japanese site support operations*

THE WHITE HOUSE

Barack Obama, *president*
Denis McDonough, *deputy national security adviser*
John Holdren, *assistant to the president for science and technology and director of the Office of Science and Technology Policy*
Richard Reed, *deputy assistant to the president for homeland security*

U.S. NATIONAL SECURITY COUNCIL (NSC)

Jeffrey Bader, *senior director for Asian affairs*
Daniel Russel, *director for Japan, South Korea, and North Korea*

U.S. NAVAL REACTORS

Kirk Donald, *director*

U.S. PACIFIC COMMAND (PACOM)

Robert Willard, *commander*

U.S. DEPARTMENT OF STATE

James Steinberg, *deputy secretary of state*
Kurt Campbell, *assistant secretary of state for East Asian and Pacific affairs*

U.S. EMBASSY IN JAPAN

John Roos, *U.S. ambassador to Japan*
James Zumwalt, *deputy chief of mission*
Ayako Kimura, *political specialist, Political-Military Affairs Unit*

MELTDOWN

ONE

Station Blackout

"WE'RE IN TROUBLE! WE'RE BEING INUNDATED WITH SEAWATER!"

2:46 P.M., MARCH 11, 2011. The Tokyo Electric Power Company (TEPCO) Fuku-shima Daiichi Nuclear Power Station.

At the time, there were twenty-four employees in the Central Control Room that managed the Unit 1 and Unit 2 reactors. The Central Control Room was the size of about two classrooms. The stainless steel, moss-green walls were crammed with instrumentation.

"460,000 kilowatts."

That number was displayed on a large digital panel on the Unit 1 side. It was the output generated by Unit 1.

The Central Control Room was situated in the Control Wing, which was attached in hinge-like fashion to the Unit 1 and Unit 2 turbine build-ings. Outside were the reactor buildings. Behind them were the radioactive waste treatment buildings for the Unit 1 and Unit 2 reactors.

There was not a single window connecting the room to the outside world. The instruments lining the wall shook with a creaking sound.

"Is that an earthquake?!"

The shaking became even stronger. The operations manual and doc-uments flew from the desk of Ikuo Izawa (age 52), the duty manager of Unit 1 and Unit 2 Central Control Room, and scattered all over the floor.

The operators could not remain on their feet. They held on to the levers attached to the control panel. The levers were mounted so that they could still be operated and not shaken loose by an earthquake. Some of the oper-ators sat down on the floor still clinging to the levers.

The shaking stopped after a little while. Red alarm lights started to flash. It was not just the red lights. White lights, orange lights, everything started to light up like a Christmas tree. Next came the fire alarm.

Izawa remembered an operator who worked in the control room of the TEPCO Kashiwazaki-Kariwa Station at the time of the 2007 Chuetsu earthquake, who said the fire alarm had been triggered by a mere flurry of dust in the control room.

"Try resetting it."

The alarm stopped ringing when one of the staff reset it. Apparently, there was no fire.

The loud voice of Izawa rang out, "Everyone, calm down! First, check the SCRAM! Don't operate the plant. Don't do anything until the quaking calms down."[1]

When an earthquake strikes, the first thing that has to be done is stopping the fission reaction of the reactor. If this is not stopped, the temperature in the reactor would rise, the fuel would melt, and a large amount of radioactive material would leak out.

In order to stop the fission reaction, rod-like devices called "control rods" were inserted into the reactor. Each control rod was about four meters long. They contained boron. They were inserted between the fuel rods in the reactor to allow the boron to absorb the neutrons and stop a nuclear fission chain reaction.

Following the assistant shift supervisor's instructions, the control panel workers started checking the situation in Units 1 and 2. They were able to ascertain that all control rods had been fully inserted and the two reactors had been automatically scrammed (SCRAM).

Finally, the tremors subsided. An alarm was ringing loudly. After a short time, one of the operators cried out, "Shift supervisor, we've lost external power!"

"Emergency power check." Izawa gave the instruction immediately.

The emergency power was a diesel generator (D/G) that ran on heavy fuel oil in an emergency. Nuclear power plants generated electricity, but several hundred of the devices in the facilities were powered by electricity provided by external transmission lines. This was what had been hit.

"The MSIV is off!"

"Roger, MSIV off!"

The main steam isolation valve (MSIV) was the valve that isolated the main steam going to the turbines from the reactors. Turning it off prevents any radioactive main steam from reaching the turbines and leaking.

Already a loss of electricity meant there was no external power coming in. An operator was soon heard to say, "We've started the D/G! Both A and B are firing up."

They felt a low reverberation inside the Central Control Room. The emergency diesel generator had started to operate. Up until this point, everything was going according to the operation manual. But it was a very short-lived moment of peace.

A young worker in the Central Control Room shouted out, "D/G trip!"

"What?"

"The D/G has tripped!"

The emergency diesel generator had gone offline. Alternating current (AC) power had already been lost from the quake. If the D/G was down, it meant that they had lost the power to cool the reactors down. If that was so, it meant the situation was hopeless.

One of the workers whispered, "The lights are flickering." The lights on the control room's power panel blinked, then, one by one, went out. The only light that remained was the emergency light for Unit 1. The alarms could no longer be heard and the room was enveloped in a bottomless silence.

The voice of Izawa, the duty manager, rang out, cutting the silence.

"SBO!"

Station blackout—that is, the total loss of AC power. One after the other, the workers all repeated, "SBO! SBO!"

Izawa placed a call to the operational manager at the Emergency Response Center.

"We have SBO. The D/G has failed. The emergency generator is down."

"This makes it a Special Measures [Act on Special Measures Concerning Nuclear Emergency Preparedness] article 10 event. We are currently checking what is functioning."

Izawa was surprised himself at how matter-of-fact he sounded when declaring an article 10 event.

I'm much calmer than during the training drill.

However, the person on the other end of the phone could not say anything but "Ahh!" He appeared to be thoroughly shaken and stunned.[2]

Immediately after that the four operators who had been outside to check the situation came back into the control room in two pairs, shouting at the top of their voices:

"We're in trouble! We're being flooded with seawater!"

"The basement of the turbine building is flooded up to around waist-height!"

"I heard a roaring growl from afar! I'd never heard such a noise before!"

"Seawater came flooding into the basement from the first floor! I managed to come up against the flow!"

All of them were soaked to the skin.

Is it a tsunami? Could a tsunami make it up to here?

This was something they had never imagined.[3]

The first tsunami hit the Fukushima Daiichi Station at 3:27 p.m., and the second and larger sometime between 3:35–3:37 p.m.[4] Ten and thirteen meter–high waves hit the reactor and turbine buildings. The emergency seawater pump installed at four meters above sea level was swallowed up.

The staff who went to see if the Service Building had electricity tried to enter the building, but were trapped in the entrance area. They tried to contact site security, but could not get through.

Water started seeping in from below. They thought it was all over, but an older member of the staff broke the glass from outside and they escaped with their lives just as the water was already up to their chins.

Staff who had gone to the site to restore the electric motor at Unit 2 ran up the stairs in a hurry. From below the ground came a roaring sound the likes of which they had never heard before. Water came suddenly pouring in from the entrance of the Service Building.

For some reason, the door connecting Units 1 and 2 closed, and one person could no longer open it; it required two people pushing on it. The moment it opened, a huge volume of water came surging in. They walked up to their waists in water.

That was when they realized for the first time: *It's a tsunami.*

Another member of the staff emerging from the Service Building saw a tsunami rolling in from the direction of the Unit 4 reactor. It was crashing violently into the steel plates of the water inlet in front of Unit 4, sending up columns of water. It looked like it was higher than ten meters. He froze in his tracks. Looking over to the sea, he saw the breakwaters tumbling down like a pack of dominoes. A construction crane was impaled on one of the pumps. He could hear the endless ringing of car horns below.

The Anti-Seismic Building and the various control rooms were separated by several hundred meters as the crow flies. The twenty- or thirty-meter flight of stairs linked to the Anti-Seismic Building, built on high ground, had been destroyed by a landslide and could not be used. Pipes above the ground had ruptured and water was spewing out in fountains.

The tsunami pounded in. It could well continue its attack. Izawa gathered the operators inside the Central Control Room. Only the emergency light on the Unit 1 side was dimly lit.

"Everyone, listen up. I have no idea what's happening onsite. From now on, we'll follow the rules when going to the site."

Izawa spoke looking them in the eye, one by one.

"You're to get my permission when going to the site, and I'm imposing a two-hour limit. You're not to go alone but in pairs; meaning, you're to move in twos. I want you to stick to this. If you're not back in two hours, I'll send out a rescue. Even if you don't make it to your destination, check the time, and if it looks like going over two hours, turn back then. And write on the whiteboard the time you set out."

Izawa then looked around at everyone and said, "If you don't follow these rules, then it's your lives on the line. So make sure of it. You've got that, right?"

"Roger that."

"Understood."[5]

Two of the workers headed to Unit 1 and another two to Unit 2 to check for damage to the emergency diesel generators in the turbine building basement. They took the stairs, but by the time they reached the first floor, another tsunami wave had hit. The workers just about managed to run back to the control room soaking wet. Two other young workers in the Unit 4 turbine buildings were not as lucky. They drowned as the waves came crashing in through the parking lot, seeping into all of the surrounding buildings.[6]

The Fukushima Daiichi Nuclear Power Station (NPS) had a two-stage structure from the sea level. The seawater intake and emergency seawater pumps were four meters above the sea level. The reactor buildings, turbine buildings, control buildings, and radioactive waste treatment buildings were located ten meters above sea level.

The operators called them the "4 disk" and "10 disk," respectively. They used to be called the "4M board" and the "10M board," but over time this had evolved into "disk."[7]

Site Superintendent Masao Yoshida had been in his onsite office. Although he could not stay on his feet when the quake struck, he thought, *The plant can withstand it*. He then ran immediately to the Anti-Seismic Building.[8]

The turbine buildings were on the seaside and the reactors toward the hillside. Units 1 through 4 on the Okuma site were painted blue in a seascape motif, while Units 5 and 6 on the Futaba site were decorated in a green mosaic. Blue represented the sea and green the hills. The sales pitch was: "A nuclear plant at one with its environment."

To the southern side of the Unit 4 reactor was a disposal complex for both handling radioactive liquid waste and incinerating solid waste. The entire station with its six reactor units was capable of generating 4.696 gigawatts of electricity (GWe).

There were two unit managers and three deputy site superintendents working under Masao Yoshida, the site superintendent. The operation of the reactor facilities was handled by the TEPCO shift supervisor. Shift supervisor was a career post. Training a full-fledged shift supervisor was said to cost 60 million yen. The shift supervisor acted something like the facility's pilot. Shift supervisors, who reported to the operational manager, were separated into those in charge of Units 1 and 2, 3 and 4, and 5 and 6. Each shift team consisted of eleven members: a shift supervisor, two assistant shift supervisors, two senior operators, one assistant senior operator, two main equipment shift operators, and four auxiliary equipment shift operators. There were five such teams rostered to operate the reactors around the clock. This meant a nucleus of fifty to fifty-five key personnel.

TEPCO had some 1,100 workers in operations at Fukushima Daiichi NPS. There were a further 2,000 workers from TEPCO-associated companies, who looked after plant manufacturing, fire protection, and site security. At the time of the quake, there was a total of 5,600 workers onsite, of whom 750 were TEPCO employees. The number of associated workers was so large because the quake coincided with a periodical inspection of Units 4, 5, and 6 reactors.

The emergency response center (ERC) was on the second floor of the Anti-Seismic Building. With the earthquake, the room's lights had gone out, only the glowing red light indicating the emergency exit. There were no windows overlooking the site in this room. There were no surveillance cameras, either.

3:37 P.M. One or two minutes had passed since the second tsunami hit.

A report came in via the hotline from the Units 1 and 2 Central Control Room.

"Both the Unit 1 emergency diesel generator and the DC power supply have stopped. We've lost all power! The tsunami is rapidly flooding the building."

Around 3:38 p.m., a hotline report was received, this time from the Units 3 and 4 Central Control Room.

"Both Units 3 and 4 have lost power!"

Around 3:41 p.m., emergency contact was again received from the Units 1 and 2 Central Control Room. A woeful voice reported:

"Unit 2 has also lost all power."[9] Four reactors had now all lost power.

Yoshida was at a loss for words.

What? The D/G is not working?

This is not good. This could be a severe accident. Isn't there any way to get the D/G to function properly again? If that is impossible, it might take hours for the IC and RCIC to cool. If we can't do that, what else can be done . . . ?

The DC power. We will be waiting eight hours for it. Even having said that, because DC power runs on batteries, there is only that capacity. When it does run out, will we be able to charge it? This could well fall under an article 15 for DC power.

Yoshida's thoughts spun around and around the possible scenarios that could unfold.[10]

The operators took out the emergency operating procedures manual that TEPCO had prepared in-house and started to read it by portable battery lights and LED torches.

"Event-based?"

"State-based?"

None of this corresponded to what they were directly facing. An outage of both AC and DC power had not been foreseen.

In the first place, the manuals all assumed that plant information could be ascertained via the instrumentation in the respective control rooms. But those very control rooms were currently in the dark. None of the instruments were showing anything.[11]

Still, the veteran shift supervisor and his team had a mental picture of where everything was on the power panel. They knew by instinct which meter was where even in the dark. In the words of a Toshiba engineer, "They were fellows who knew where even the mouse holes were."[12]

Even for such old hands as these, a total power outage was unimaginable. What's more, a total loss of DC power—also known as a station blackout—had never been conducted in training scenarios. The drills always ended before reaching such a severe point, with an instructor calling out, "Freeze!" Despite all the mayhem, one of the operators turned to Izawa and said, "Isn't this where the instructors say, 'Freeze'?" They both laughed.[13]

3:42 P.M. In accordance with section 1, article 10 of the Act on Special Measures Concerning Nuclear Emergency Preparedness (NEPA), Yoshida reported to the government that a specific event requiring notification (the total loss of all AC power sources) had occurred.[14] This measure was taken after receiving the report from Izawa in the Central Control Room. When Izawa called, he reported that the loss of power supplies and emergency core cooling systems mandated an article 15. Upon hearing this, the person on the other end of the phone in the ERC began to mumble and then fell speechless, Izawa recalls.[15] It had taken staff in the ERC somewhere between thirty minutes to an hour to decide whether to report an article 10 or 15, with article 15 representing the most serious condition: red. Although they had chosen to go with article 10, it was only one hour and three minutes later, at 4:45 p.m., that they would upgrade the incident to an article 15.[16]

By around 3:50 p.m., they were no longer able to read the reactor water level or pressure meters. What was happening inside the reactors? Was the cooling equipment working? They had lost their parameters for identifying this.

The control rooms had lost their five senses.

THE ISOLATION CONDENSER

2:52 P.M., MARCH 11. Let us turn back the clock an hour or so. Units 1 and 2 Central Control Room.

A loud voice reverberated.

"The IC is online."

Unit 1 was equipped with two isolation condenser systems (IC) as an emergency reactor cooling mechanism. This was an appendix-like object attached only to the early types of light-water boiling water reactors (BWR), but in Japan it had been left in Unit 1.

High temperature steam generated in the reactor was cooled by passing through a pipe coil in the IC's cooling water tank located on the fourth floor of the reactor building and condensed into a liquid, flowing back as water into the reactor. The fact that the IC had automatically started meant that steam could now be returned to the reactor as cool water.

After SCRAM took place, the cooling of the reactor core went smoothly. All the operators had to do now was keep switching the IC on and off to gradually lower the temperature of the reactor. The reason it was not left on was to avoid cooling the reactor too rapidly.

Keeping a close eye on the instrument indicating the temperature of the reactor, the operators kept opening and closing the valve of the IC using a lever. The reactor temperature began to fall slowly. Forty minutes after the reactor shutdown, the reactor temperature, which had been close to 300 degrees Celsius when operating, had dropped to about 180 degrees.

The operators were relieved.[17]

However, flooding by the tsunami changed everything. This was because it robbed the plant of both its AC and DC power.

The lever on the IC operation panel was designed to always return to a central position when released after operation. If the valve was open, a red light came on; if it was closed, a green light. Since they had to use the operation lever time and again, they determined its status by the different colored lights.

Those lights had disappeared.

Was the IC valve open or closed, which was it?

The operators could no longer remember. Was the IC working? What about it? Nobody knew.

We can't operate the valve without the display light.

The operators were completely shaken up.[18]

4:44 P.M. Izawa, duty manager in the Central Control Room, was contacted from the Anti-Seismic Building.

"There's steam coming out of the Pig's Nose."

"How much?"

"A puff."

"A puff?"

The Pig's Nose was the two exhaust pipes twenty meters high on the west wall of the Unit 1 Reactor Building. When the IC was working, part of its job was to discharge the steam generated from the IC outside.

Uncertain if the IC was working, Izawa had asked the ERC in the Anti-Seismic Building to check whether steam was coming out of the Pig's Nose. He had heard stories from older operators that when the IC was activated, white steam would gush out of the Pig's Nose.

A worker from the ERC's power generation team had gone out into the parking lot of the Anti-Seismic Building and confirmed steam was coming out of the Pig's Nose.

"The steam's coming out hazily." This was what he had reported.

The ERC interpreted this as "steam is coming out." But Izawa was adamant that the IC was *not* working, because he could not hear the release of steam, which, he had learned in training, was a crucial marker of a working IC. Regardless of this insight, Yoshida and personnel in the ERC were so engrossed in starting the water injection that the IC stoppage failed to catch their attention and remained uncommunicated to senior managers throughout the evening.[19]

The ERC continued to be at the center of communication problems that further strained onsite relations. Tasked with micromanaging onsite conditions and operations, the ERC demanded that all information be passed on to them. Izawa was simply overwhelmed with the sheer volume of data he now had to communicate to the ERC while managing reactor operations at the same time. At one point, an ERC worker questioned Izawa over the phone on how much battery power was left in the control room. "I f****** told you already that we don't have any batteries! I told you that we've lost electrical power! What's wrong with you?" Izawa shouted.[20]

4:56 P.M. The water level in the reactor fell down to 1.9 meters above the top of active fuel (TAF). Top of active fuel serves as the reference point for water-level readings in a reactor; it is the uppermost point in a fuel rod that contains uranium. A few minutes later, the water level gauge again was no longer visible. In the fifteen minutes that the water level gauge had been visible, this worked out to a sixty-centimeter drop.

At 5:15 p.m., in a videoconference connecting TEPCO's Tokyo Head Office and the Anti-Seismic Building, the voice of the person in charge of the technical crew rang out.

"If the Unit 1 drawdown continues at this pace, one hour to TAF!"

It was a shocking prediction. The exposed active fuel would melt, releasing radioactive material.

Is the information about steam coming out of the Pig's Nose a mistake?

Perhaps the IC isn't functioning.

It was only natural to harbor such doubts. However, it had only just been reported by workers from the power generation team that steam was coming out of the Pig's Nose. If steam was coming out, the IC was probably working. But they could not be sure. It was just a guess; it might be just barely working. That was the general conception. Yoshida shared this as well.[21]

No questions were asked about the status of the IC in the videoconference, and no links were made between the falling water level and the IC. Someone took the microphone and shouted, "Entering the Office Building is prohibited!"

Other officials interrupted in rapid succession.

"We can't go to help because seawater has flooded in as far as the seaside bus stop!"

"Suspected fire behind Unit 4 in the light water tank. Smoke has risen about five meters!"

Information on the drop in the water level at Unit 1 had been buried in the avalanche of other reports flooding in.[22]

Izawa sent operators to the field to check if the IC was working. Although he had received a report that steam was coming out of the Pig's Nose, he still was not convinced. It was at this time that the information on the decrease in the Unit 1 water level came in. The only way they could confirm whether the IC was working or not was to verify it directly.

The two ICs, A System and B System, were lined up together on the fourth floor of the reactor building. They decided to examine the water gauge attached to the side of the condensate tank to check the amount of cooling water to see whether it was sufficient. The door of the reactor building was a double door.

5:50 P.M. When the operators tried to open the door, the needle on their dosimeter went off the scale. It was over the 2.5 microsieverts (0.0025 millisieverts) maximum value. They had never seen this high a dose measured outside the double doors. Giving up on going inside, they returned to the Central Control Room.[23]

6:18 P.M. The operators had gathered in front of the control panel in the Central Control Room. The light indicating the status of the IC valve in Unit 1 was dimly lit up. For some reason, some of the batteries flooded by seawater had recovered and some of the instrumentation and lights were once again visible.

"Green."

"Closed."

The IC light was green. The valve was closed. If the valve in the IC piping was closed, that meant that the steam had stopped flowing and the IC was not moving.

"It's not moving. Can we start it up?" Izawa instructed the operator in charge to open the valve using the control panel lever.

"The valve is open. IsoCon startup confirmed."

"Roger that. The time is 18:18."

The operators here referred to the isolation condenser (IC) as IsoCon.

The light had changed from green to red. The IC to cool the Unit 1 reactor had at last started. Approximately two and a half hours had passed since the total power outage at 3:37 p.m.

Izawa ordered the operators to go outside and confirm whether steam was coming out of the Pig's Nose. The operators who had gone out to check came back in a hurry.

"It was billowing out at first, but started to peter out, then disappeared."

Apparently, the cooling water level in the IC tank had dropped and was not generating much steam. This was Izawa's assessment. When the cooling water in the tank ran out, it would fall into a boil-dry state, incurring a risk of damaging the IC piping and releasing radioactive material outside.

"Do you want to continue running the IC?"

After thinking a little, Izawa said:

"It can't be helped. Let's stop the IC. For now, let's close the 3A valve."

6:25 P.M. Izawa ordered the IC valve closed. The control panel light changed from red to green. After a mere seven minutes, the IC had been stopped again.[24]

However, the fact that they had closed the IC valve was not precisely transmitted to the ERC in the Anti-Seismic Building. From Site Superintendent Masao Yoshida down to senior managers in the ERC, even after this, they still believed that the IC was working and continued to respond to the emergency on that basis.

Why was there such a miscalculation? Why were mistakes made? What was happening onsite?

According to an investigation conducted by Niigata Prefecture, the operators and deputy director in charge of operating the IC in the Central Control Room understood that "the IC was not working." After all, electrical supply had been lost; they firmly believed they had closed the valves themselves; and with data up until that point lost from the power outage, their memory was the only gauge they could use.

In fact, the IC had not been working at that time, and their understanding was correct. However, when Izawa asked the onsite director about the condition of the IC, the answer was, "I don't know." The operator and the deputy director's understanding that the IC was not working had not been conveyed to the onsite director. Had Izawa asked the operator of the main reactor directly, he would have been aware of their assumptions on the condition of the IC. This was the first misunderstanding.

Later on, a second misunderstanding emerged as a result of this communication breakdown between the Central Control Room, the Anti-Seismic Building, and the Emergency Response Headquarters. Although Izawa made sure to constantly report to the power generation team leader in the Anti-Seismic Building, information on the condition of the IC had failed to reach Izawa himself, and therefore the Anti-Seismic Building, too. The power generation team leader continued to believe that "since we lost all power supply while the IC was running, it should still be working." In a chain of miscommunication, the fact that the IC had stopped working never reached Yoshida.

By 6:18 p.m., some of the power in the Central Control Room had been restored. The light showing the condition of the IC valves now indicated "closed." Izawa promptly reported this to the Anti-Seismic Building and began to operate the IC while the onsite director opened the valves. However, even this turn of events had been miscommunicated. The report was vague and simply indicated that "the IC is working" rather than communicating that it was working *because* "a valve had been opened that was closed before."

At 6:25 p.m., the onsite director judged that the effect of the IC had been limited and shut down the IC, but even this operation failed to reach the Anti-Seismic Building. By eleven p.m., however, the radiation dose in the turbine building of Unit 1 had risen, and the pressure on the storage container now exceeded the maximum that it was designed to endure. It was at this point that Yoshida became suspicious and realized that the IC might not actually be working. "The IC is working, the water level has a surplus, but something is strange. I started to realize that the situation inside is probably terrible," Yoshida recalled to the Government Investigation Commission.

The misunderstanding on whether the IC was working or not also appeared in TEPCO's official announcement. During the late evening hours of March 11 and early morning of March 12, TEPCO Head Office announced that they were "cooling the steam inside the nuclear reactor using the IC." But it was only after four a.m. on March 12 that TEPCO revealed that the IC had stopped working.

In domino-style, miscommunication had occurred at three different levels. First, between the operator in the Central Control Room and the onsite director; second, between the Central Control Room and the Anti-Seismic Building; and third, between the team leader and the director of the Anti-Seismic Building. This produced "a chain of misunderstanding." On this point, Yoshida later testified the following:

"As far as the IC is concerned, there was a certain water level being shown, so I was under the impression that the IC was still working. . . . That was because no mechanism had been set up for the shift supervisor to call me at that time. I know I should have made sure many times at that point whether the IC was really functional or not. . . . I've been intensely reflecting upon the fact that I didn't question that then, but at that time an SOS signal from the site had not reached me."[25]

To make matters worse, those at the Anti-Seismic Building, including Yoshida, and operators in the Central Control Room, including Izawa, did not accurately understand the IC itself. In theory, when power supply is lost, the system to detect failure in devices stops functioning and the IC automatically closes the valves. This is what is called "fail-safe function." If a common understanding of this function had existed, the misunderstanding that "the IC is still working" could have been avoided. Yoshida testified to the Government Investigation Commission on this point that "no one besides the onsite operators at Units 1 and 2 knew about it . . . the IC is an extremely unusual system, so, to be honest, I don't know myself."[26]

There was not a single operator onsite who had experience in actually operating the IC, including the operators at Units 1 and 2. According to a 2015 report that TEPCO submitted to Niigata Prefecture, the last time the IC had been operated at Fukushima Daiichi was on June 29, 1992.

However, it was not only the status of the IC that the ERC was wrong about. The water level gauge also fooled Yoshida. He was concerned that the water in the IC tank, which was the only means of cooling, would be gone, but it turned out that even after ten hours, it still contained water. After being stopped for three hours, the IC was restarted. However, at this point, the meltdown had already progressed to a state where the IC could no longer be cooled.[27]

THE WATER LEVEL GAUGE

4:46 P.M. Yoshida reported to the Nuclear and Industrial Safety Agency (NISA) and others that a specific event (inoperable emergency reactor core cooling equipment), as stipulated in Section 1, article 15 of the Act on Special Measures Concerning Nuclear Emergency Preparedness (NEPA), had taken place. At the time, he wrote: "We don't know what is happening with the cooling operations due to an inability to monitor the water levels in Units 1 and 2."

NINE MINUTES LATER, AT 4:55 P.M. This time, Yoshida contacted NISA to cancel his emergency report, because they had "recovered water level observation" in Unit 1. However, just before five p.m., the water level indicator once again could no longer be seen.

The Central Control Room was unable to confirm water levels in either Unit 1 or Unit 2. Nor could they confirm whether the isolation condenser (IC) in Unit 1 or the reactor core isolation cooling system (RCIC) in Unit 2 were working.

It was reported, "If the water level keeps dropping at this pace, the fuel rods in Unit 1 will start to be exposed by 6:15 p.m." Yoshida merely answered, "Roger that."

5:12 P.M. With just the aid of emergency lighting, the shift supervisor recorded the water level shown on the reactor water gauge (broadband = 1500 mm to −4000 mm). The water level was falling steadily. The time and measurement on the power panel next to the water indicator were recorded by hand, then reported to the station ERC. They were no longer able to use the Personal Handy-Phone System they had been using, so the power plant office at the Anti-Seismic Building and the shift supervisor at the control room were using a hotline. Yoshida once again filed a "state of emergency" to NISA.

Just when the Station Emergency Response Center received a report from onsite that "We are able to see the water level," they received another call, saying, "Once again we have lost the ability to assess the water level." Every time Yoshida received a figure, he checked with the reporting official, "Are those numbers really correct?" The answer he got was, "Umm, we aren't sure."[28]

At the mercy of the figures on the water level gauge, the site was in a state of utter disarray. Maintenance Manager Takeyuki Inagaki recalls that "we were quite doubtful about the IC status, but we hoped that the isolation condenser was still partially working on Unit 1. Because it was the only information we got after getting SBO, we wanted to believe the signal, though we knew the water level must be going down."[29] Ultimately, they were flying blind and wanted to believe any signal of hope.

QUITE SOME TIME AFTER SEVEN P.M. Staff from the control room reported that they could see, with a flashlight, billows of white steam on the far side of the glass of the double doors of the reactor building. It was also reported that radioactive material had been detected as far as outside of the control room and non-controlled areas.[30]

"It looks like there's a raw steam leak."

On hearing people whispering these words, one of the subcontracted workers in the Anti-Seismic Building thought to himself, *That's the end of nuclear power. TEPCO is finished.*[31]

In order to get the water indicator and other instruments back online, they needed to restore power via batteries or small generators, but Fukushima Daiichi NPS had nothing like this prepared at all.[32]

The restoration team at Response Headquarters stripped batteries from several buses onsite, delivering a total of five to the control room. Lining them up two abreast, they hooked them up to the water gauge on the power panel.[33]

9:19 P.M. The restoration team managed to reconnect the water gauge for

Unit 1 after four hours without it. They reported to the Tokyo Head Office, "We have confirmation of the reactor water level. TAF +200 via battery hookup."[34]

This meant the water was twenty centimeters above the top of active fuel. The report of TAF +200 shocked everyone in the ERC.

"It's awash."

"This isn't normal."

Takeyuki Inagaki, the recovery team leader, felt his body tremble.[35]

9:47 P.M. A report reconfirming the reactor water level was sent to the Tokyo Head Office. Around the same time, it was reported that the radiation dose in the Unit 1 Reactor Building had started to climb. The dosimeter of the TEPCO workers, who were entering the reactor building to check the water level, rose to 0.8 millisieverts in a short time.

9:51 P.M. The Unit 1 Reactor Building was put on "restricted access."[36]

It looked like the fuel had started to melt. Commensurately, a large volume of hydrogen was being generated and the pressure was mounting in the containment vessel. Radioactive material may have started to leak out of the containment vessel . . .

9:52 P.M. The power plant ERC reported to the authorities, concerned that the "water level is 450 mm from top of fuel," that the reactor water level was above top of active fuel (TAF).[37]

The water gauge continued to show the reactor water level was above TAF.

10:00 P.M. "TAF +550 mm."

10:35 P.M. "TAF +590 mm."[38]

The operators had started to realize, however, that "something's not right." They recorded the rising water level figures on a whiteboard in the control room, then scrawled next to them, "the water gauge is unreliable."[39]

Izawa sent two operators to the scene to check whether the IC was working. Yoshida was also thinking, *Something's up.* The first time he shook his head was when he received a report saying that the dose of Unit 1 reactor building had increased, before ten p.m.

The IC is moving, the water level is at a plus, why is the dosage going up? Something is wrong.

Is the water level wrong or is it a problem with something else?

At 11:50 p.m., the pressure of the dry well of Unit 1 was recorded to be at the high figure of 600 kPa. This exceeded the maximum working pressure of 427 kPa.

The cooling water must be missing.

Hasn't the IC stopped yet?[40]

With the reactor pressure now high, depressurizing the reactors was no longer an option. Their only strategy left was to cool the reactors through restoring high-pressure water systems.[41]

THE ANTI-SEISMIC BUILDING

Masao Yoshida (age 56) was in his ninth month as site superintendent at Fukushima Daiichi NPS. A graduate of mechanical physics at the Tokyo Institute of Technology, he had gone on to graduate school in nuclear power engineering at the same institution, and joined TEPCO in 1980. According to an old acquaintance, Yoshida had also been offered a position as a senior engineer by the Ministry of International Trade and Industry (MITI), but had chosen TEPCO.[42]

He had been transferred many times between the nuclear power stations at Fukushima Daiichi, Fukushima Daini, Kashiwazaki, and the Nuclear Energy Division at Head Office. He got married when working at Fukushima Daini NPS. Hamadori, the easternmost part of Fukushima Prefecture, was like a second home to him.

At 184 cm, Yoshida was tall for a Japanese. The first impression Charles Casto, the head of Japanese site support operations sent by the U.S. Nuclear Regulatory Commission (NRC), had of Yoshida was his height. "A slender gentleman" was his impression.

Getting Yoshida's permission, Casto took a commemorative photo. Yoshida was holding a bag of rice and a bottle of water. Yoshida told Casto, "This is enough for a meal."[43]

They were on the second floor of the Anti-Seismic Building. During the crisis, there was a round-the-clock video link with the emergency response team at Head Office. From the perspective of the Head Office video screen, Yoshida sat plumb in the middle-left seat at the round table, from morning till night and sometimes into the wee hours of the morning. He ran operations from there.

The Anti-Seismic Building had been newly built the previous year as a base for accident response. Based on the damage experienced from the 2007 Chuetsu earthquake, it was a robust design, built to withstand earthquakes of seismic intensity levels of 7 on the Japanese scale. The construction workers bragged, "It won't budge even if you fire missiles into it."[44]

The building had its own gas turbine generator, a videoconference system, and filtered ventilators. In order to prevent radioactive contamination, the entrance had double doors. The opening and closing of the doors operated on a round-the-clock system. When one door was opened, the other closed to prevent outside air infiltrating. When entering the Anti-Seismic Building from outside, workers removed their protective clothing in the space between the doors and immediately carried out contamination checks and decontamination.[45]

The Anti-Seismic Building was the command tower where Yoshida and the shift team set up camp. This was the only place onsite where protective masks could be removed.[46]

However, they were operating under atrocious conditions. The worst problem was inadequate filtering of radioactive material. Radioactive material was billowing out of the vents and core welding. Its entrance had been twisted by the force of the hydrogen explosion. Radioactive material was seeping into the Anti-Seismic Building from outside. After the explosion, radiation reached 120 microsieverts (0.12 millisieverts) per hour at one stage. They frantically decontaminated the mud on workers' boots.[47]

The radiation dose one of the female workers suffered was over the legal limit.[48] Late at night on March 12, the onsite safety team reported via videoconference link to TEPCO Head Office:

"For those people taking a rest, in order to minimize doses, the northwest corner of this room seems to have the lowest level . . . The room as a whole is about 70 microsieverts (0.07 millisieverts)."[49]

The occupational physicians at the Anti-Seismic Building had evacuated and were absent from March 11 until March 18. Resident physicians did not start examinations until March 19.[50]

Although they were inundated with problems, the Anti-Seismic Building was irreplaceable. It was here that the squad, composed of TEPCO workers under Yoshida's leadership, later on known as the "Fukushima 50," fought on to manage the situation.

After the tsunami warning sounded, Yoshida advised the workers of related companies to evacuate, and again, in the evening, gave the order, "Personnel who are not engaged in work, please evacuate." The allocation of cars began.[51] The workers of the associate companies began returning to their homes and hometowns.

In case of an emergency, there are twelve teams in place under the command of the director general (nuclear power plant site superintendent) of the power plant. Regardless of whether it was a holiday or midnight, the members of these teams had to gather. There were 406 such personnel. They fought night and day throughout the crisis in the Anti-Seismic Building.[52]

Yoshida told the deputy director general of defense, Hideo Suzuki, when Suzuki visited the site in the summer of 2011, "All of the glass shattered in the office building, but the Anti-Seismic Building escaped the impact of the earthquake. It was contaminated, but we decontaminated it. The hotline stayed up, and the videoconference link with Head Office continued to work. The Anti-Seistmic Building saved us. We would have been totally lost without it."[53]

Kazuma Yokota (age 40), head of the local NISA inspectors at the site, said exactly the same thing:

"It would have been total annihilation without it. I think there would have been six explosions. The quake had put the office building out of operation. If the Emergency Response Center had been in the office building, as before, we wouldn't have been able to use it. We couldn't have operated or issued directions. We were able to do that in the Anti-Seismic Building. Everyone says we were saved by the skin of our teeth."[54]

Unit 1 at Fukushima Daiichi NPS was the first nuclear power station TEPCO had built. Yokota remembers Yoshida saying, "It's small and problematic, but it's still a cute little unit."[55]

On that day, the cute little unit bared its fangs and went on the attack.

THE NUCLEAR SAFETY AGENCY INSPECTORS CUT AND RUN

The quake hit just after Yokota had finished an interview for the periodic inspection report in an office in the Training Building at Fukushima Daiichi NPS. Although he could barely stand, he made his way to the door, opened it, then hid under a desk. Someone had taught him that "the first thing to do in an earthquake is to open the door."

Yokota was the designated disaster expert. Under the Act on Special Measures Concerning Nuclear Emergency Preparedness, during the time of a nuclear emergency, it was a legal requirement to establish an offsite center (emergency response facility) to act as a base for measuring radiation levels and a collection point for all nuclear disaster information.[56]

The offsite center idea was born from the 1999 JCO criticality accident in Tokaimura, Naka District, Ibaraki Prefecture. This accident took place in the uranium reprocessing facility of JCO, a subsidiary of Sumitomo Metal Mining, and resulted in two deaths and one serious injury. Residents within a 350-meter radius from the conversion building were evacuated, an evacuation warning released for those within a 500-meter radius, and residents within a ten-kilometer radius were asked to remain indoors. The accident was classed as a Level 4 event (accident with local consequences) on the International Nuclear Event Scale (INES).

It was the need in hindsight for a government-wide, coordinated response, including resident evacuation and local accident response, which led to the promulgation of the Act on Special Measures Concerning Nuclear Emergency Preparedness (NEPA) and the requirement to establish an offsite center.

The offsite center had its own communications system, radiation measuring equipment, and a support system to respond to nuclear accidents, as well as a decontamination room in the case of radiation exposure. The joint offsite center for Fukushima Daiichi and Daini stations was set up in Okuma, Futaba District, Fukushima Prefecture. It was some five kilometers from Daiichi and twelve kilometers from Daini.[57]

At the time of the earthquake, all seven inspectors from the Fukushima Daiichi Nuclear Safety Inspectors' Office and one chief inspector from NISA in Tokyo were onsite, conducting their periodic inspection. After reporting an article 10 event, Yokota and three other inspectors headed to the offsite center. The remaining inspectors stayed behind in the Anti-Seismic Building to collect information and report to NISA.[58]

When Yokota and the others arrived at the offsite center, the local part-time worker minding the facility opened the doors for them. They were double doors.

"Are you all right?"

"Are you all right, too?"

After this kind of exchange with the woman, and learning that she had children, Yokota sent her home.

The entire building was in a blackout. Even the emergency power was not working. Communications were in a state of paralysis as well. There was one phone/fax line working, but nothing else. The mobile phone connections were down. There was no way to contact NISA in Tokyo. They could not videoconference, there was no water, and the toilets were out of order.

The first workers to arrive were from Kandenko, a TEPCO-affiliated company, and they immediately started trying to restore the emergency power. It had been decided with TEPCO that these workers should gather at the offsite center in case of an emergency. That night, the only people who had made it to the offsite center were six NISA inspectors, including Yokota (three from Daiichi, three from Daini), eight TEPCO employees, and a public servant from Okuma Town. (It was stipulated in the disaster plan that forty workers from thirteen ministries and agencies should gather there, but in reality only twenty-one from three ministries and agencies turned up.)[59]

A telephone and fax were connected to the Fukushima Prefectural Office, but it took an hour to send a fax over the line.

The four inspectors left behind onsite at Fukushima Daiichi were growing increasingly nervous. Radiation levels started climbing onsite in the early hours of March 12, and going in or out of the Anti-Seismic Building was becoming more restricted. At the time, they did not have any Tyvek suits or full-face masks. They were able to contact NISA in Tokyo via the satellite phone in the safety inspection's disaster vehicle parked outside, but it was becoming more difficult to exit the building, as radiation levels grew. At around five p.m. on March 12, they decided to evacuate from Fukushima Daiichi to the offsite center.[60]

Their reasoning was, "They gave us a room in the Anti-Seismic Building, but it was impossible to work with everyone coming and going."

In the evening of the same day, after the Kantei (the prime minister's office) had decided on seawater injection, Banri Kaieda, minister for the economy, trade, and industry, asked Eiji Hiraoka, deputy director general of NISA, "Doesn't NISA also need to directly witness the seawater injection onsite?"[61]

Kaieda was wondering, "What's happening on the ground? Aren't there any NISA inspectors there?" Upon checking with NISA, he learned, "There are none onsite."

"That's no good."

Kaieda had not been informed that the NISA inspectors had evacuated from Fukushima Daiichi. Hiraoka conveyed Kaieda's criticisms to Tetsuya Yamamoto, head of the NISA Inspection Division, who, as in a game of telephone, relayed the message to Yokota.

"Don't you think it's bad that no one is onsite? It's no good having all the inspectors at the offsite center. We want you to go back, all of you except the disaster expert."[62]

Around six a.m. on March 13, Yokota ordered four inspectors "to go to Fukushima Daiichi to observe operations, since they are going to start injecting seawater . . . I want the four of you to split up into two teams and contact the plant team with changes in the parameters every hour." Although he said "observe operations," no specific directives were issued.

"Do you mean go to the site and visually check if they are pumping the water in?"

"Contamination levels are high, so all you have to do is be at the Emergency Response Center checking the situation at the plant regularly and letting us know."[63]

The main point of the matter was to get the inspectors back onsite.

7:00 A.M., MARCH 13. Four inspectors left the offsite center and returned to the Anti-Seismic Building some forty minutes later. Their job was to "work twelve-hour shifts and make hourly reports on the plant data such as the reactor water."[64] Although they stayed on the job there until five p.m., they did not provide any live observations.

With the loss of power, the building was pitch-black. Instruments had to be read by the light of flashlights. In the end, all they did was receive plant status check sheets from TEPCO employees and convey their content via the in-house wireless phone system to the Local Nuclear Response Headquarters (NERHQ) in the offsite center.[65]

One of the four inspectors was a smoking buddy of Yoshida's. They were on easy speaking terms, but at this point everything was being dictated by the Kantei. They had a strong sense that "this isn't a situation for a lowly inspector to butt in."[66]

In the afternoon of March 14, one of them contacted Yokota via a TEPCO mobile phone.

"There's been a hydrogen explosion at Unit 3. I feel I'm in danger."

"I want you to hang in there somehow or other."

Yokota denied the request to leave, telling the four of them to work from the Emergency Response Center. The conversation by TEPCO workers at the Emergency Response Center roundtable could be overhead.

"If Unit 2 blows, this important [Anti-Seismic] Building won't escape either."

A short time later, another report came in.

"Site superintendent, if it does blow, it won't be safe here. There's a strong chance of Unit 2 exploding if pressure keeps mounting in the pressure vessel and venting operations don't make headway."

"Sir, the situation is critical. We can't stay here any longer. If there's trouble with the Unit 4 fuel pool, it'll undergo recriticality. If that happens, then no one here will be saved."

A specialist nuclear power engineer from the manufacturing side, who knew a lot about reactors, spoke up. With a quiet voice, he desperately appealed, "Please let us evacuate for the time being to the offsite center. I'll report the details to you at the offsite center."

He was ringing via mobile phone, but was probably surrounded by lots of workers from TEPCO and its associates. No doubt, they were all listening hard to what the inspectors were talking about with Yokota. He could not go into specifics. Nor was it easy to clearly say "come back" or "stay." The inspector at the end of the line said, "Chief, we're coming back."[67]

He could not say "fine," but then again, he could not say "don't." Yokota hung up with a simple "understood." The four inspectors returned to the offsite center in the disaster vehicle on the evening of March 14, 2011.[68]

THE OFFSITE CENTER

Motohisa Ikeda, senior vice minister of economy, trade, and industry, left the main building of the ministry at five p.m. on March 11. He got in the car with some disaster gear, hardhat, and boots in hand. He was heading to the offsite center in Okuma.

It was stipulated in article 17 of NEPA that a local nuclear response headquarters (NERHQ) should be set up at the offsite center in the case of a nuclear emergency. The vice minister (or the ministerial secretary) was designated to head NERHQ.

Shinichi Kuroki, NISA deputy director general, and Tetsuya Yamamoto, chief of the NISA inspection unit, were traveling with Ikeda. NISA had initially considered sending a senior management team to the Tohoku Electric Power Company's Onagawa nuclear station, which seemed to have been hit the hardest, but as the situation in Fukushima escalated, they decided to set up their NERHQ at the Fukushima offsite center and sent Yamamoto there.[69]

Due to traffic congestion, they failed to link up with the patrol car that was to escort them. They were shortly caught up in the whirlpool of Tokyoites trying to get home. It took them two hours to reach Ueno. It would be impossible for them to travel to Fukushima by car.

Ikeda phoned Kazuo Matsunaga, METI permanent secretary, from the car and asked for a Self-Defense Forces helicopter to be readied.

I mean to say, it's ridiculous to expect the head of a nuclear emergency response team to reach the site by car in the first place. Why did NISA create such an unrealistic rule?

Ikeda was unable to keep his anger under control, but was forced to smile bitterly when he reconsidered: *Isn't it also the responsibility of the politicians who allowed such a rule?*

They finally got their police car escort and headed to the Ministry of Defense (MOD) and Self-Defense Forces (SDF) headquarters at Ichigaya. The only way to get to the site was to board the helicopter on the rooftop helipad and fly. It emerged, however, that this was not so easy, with the whole nuclear station area in blackout. He, therefore, flew to the Japan Air Self-Defense Force (JASDF) Ohtakineyama Sub-Base (a radar base), atop the Abukuma Mountains.

The base was covered in thick snow. Ikeda drove down the mountain. In the town at the foot of the mountains, there were cracks in the road, and some of the houses were leaning. The blackout enveloped the area, with no light to be seen anywhere.[70]

At around eleven p.m., he learned from Tokyo that the wind at the site had changed and was now blowing toward the Pacific Ocean.

If they're going to vent, now would be the time . . .

Kuroki thought as much when he heard this. Kuroki was originally a technical official in charge of examining test furnaces at the former Science and Technology Agency (STA). One of NISA's deputy director general seats was "reserved" for good old STA boys. Kuroki himself was on secondment from the Ministry of Education, Culture, Sports, Science, and Technology (MEXT).

It was the middle of the night when they reached the site. Asked by Ikeda to "check the time of arrival," Kuroki emphasized to Tokyo that they had "arrived on the night of March 11, at 12:00." This was his attempt to prevent the press from writing that they arrived the following day, but NISA's press release said, "They arrived at 00:00 on March 12."

The government officials who made it to the site during the night were the senior vice minister of economy, trade, and industry; Fukushima Prefecture vice governor Masao Uchibori; NISA inspectors from Fukushima Daiichi and Daini stations; NSA staff members; MEXT staff; and staff from Okuma Town. Ikeda was immediately briefed by Yokota about the situation at the plant. Due to instrument failure, they were unable to measure any key parameters, including the temperature, pressure, or water level inside the reactors. Additionally, of the twenty-four monitoring posts in Fukushima Prefecture, twenty-three were out of action.[71]

Ikeda was then briefed by the TEPCO unit chief. In the early hours of the morning, TEPCO vice president Sakae Muto arrived.

By March 12, staff from the SDF, the Japan Atomic Energy Agency (JAEA), the National Institute of Radiological Sciences, and the Nuclear Safety Technology Center had all assembled. However, members from the Nuclear Safety Commission and the Emergency Response Measures Committee, who were to be dispatched to the scene in line with the Basic Disaster Plan, never showed up. The Nuclear Safety Commission had contemplated dispatching a member of the commission and a few staff members, but only dispatched one staff member when told that "the helicopter is full, make it one person."[72]

Staff were also to be dispatched to the offsite center from the surrounding towns of Okuma, Futaba, Tomioka, and Namie, but only staff from Okuma made it to the center. The other towns needed all of their staff helping to evacuate their residents.

At around three a.m. on March 12, power was restored to the offsite center and everyone moved back from their temporary quarters at the Nuclear Power Center. The television was now working.

They received an alert that Minister Banri Kaieda of the METI was about to give a press conference on the implementation of venting. With things as far gone as they were, venting could not be helped. If they did vent, however, it would have a huge impact on the local residents due to the release of radioactive material. Ikeda directed the TEPCO team chief and Yokota to get as accurate data as they could as soon as possible.

4:00 A.M. They were told that Prime Minister Naoto Kan was coming to visit the site. Grouping around Ikeda, the overall coordinators discussed the matter.

"What if the prime minister suffers radiation exposure? Can that be explained externally?"

"Won't a visit at this busy time slow down the accident response efforts?"

"I expect it'll be all right since the wind's blowing out to the Pacific."[73]

Ikeda, at this stage, was opposed to a prime ministerial visit.

I understand the PM wants to see the site for himself since it's an unprecedented nuclear accident. But the quake is not just about the nuclear plants. There have been huge tidal waves and aftershocks. In a disaster like this, the first seventy-two hours, when people still have a good chance of survival, are critical. The leader should stay at the headquarters and do his utmost to save lives, as well as monitor the nuclear accident response . . . Still, if he really wants to visit the site, we can't allow anything to happen

*to our commander-in-chief (the prime minister), so he should visit the off-
site center and not Daiichi Station.*

Ikeda ordered Kuroki to convey these thoughts to Tokyo. Later, on returning to Tokyo, Ikeda learned that his directive had only gone as far as
NISA and did not reach the Kantei.[74]

The local NERHQ comprised seven teams with different areas of responsibility, including a residents' safety team and a medical team. At 10:30 a.m.
on March 12, the first general meeting with all team leaders was held. They
decided on a course of action for the offsite center, including preparing for
the distribution of stable iodine, assessing the status of resident evacuation, and implementing emergency monitoring. On the basis of this plan of
action, orders were issued to the surrounding localities.

Given this ragtag assembly of ministerial, institutional, and regional
public servants, as well as private sector workers, job descriptions were
unclear. To compound the troubles, the phones were not working, or if they
were, what was being said could not be heard.

Kuroki had been in charge of gathering information at the Science and
Technology Agency (STA) at the time of the 1986 Chernobyl accident. He
subsequently spent two years at the Japanese embassy in Moscow. During
that time, he witnessed the collapse of the Soviet Union and cooperated
with the now three separate countries of Ukraine, Belarus, and Russia in
the use and management of radioactive material. Communication between
them was poor; they did not know their counterparts' names; they could
not get through to each other on the phone; if they did, line interference
meant they could not hear each other. Kuroki was remembering how tough
it had been then.[75]

By noon on March 12, all communications, bar the satellite communication lines, were down. The emergency battery at the telecommunica-
tion company's base station had run out. The government video conference
system, the Emergency Response Support System (ERSS), the System for
Prediction of Environment Emergency Dose Information (SPEEDI), e-mail,
the Internet, phones and faxes using landlines—all of them were out. Contact between the offsite center and NISA's Emergency Response Center
(ERC) was limited to external communications via satellite phone lines.[76]

As a result, TEPCO's video conference system became a key medium.
Kuroki had "believed that NISA's ERC had the same kind of video conference system as TEPCO," but, having later learned that they did not,
thought to himself, *Damn it.*

From time to time, Ikeda would go over to the TEPCO booth and listen
to the exchange between Head Office and the Fukushima Daiichi response
team. After a while, the booth became crowded. A little after 3:30 p.m.,

someone said they had heard a loud noise from the direction of Fukushima Daiichi.

Maybe a hydrogen explosion?

Tension ran through the offsite center.

At 3:41 p.m., the videoconference linking TEPCO Head Office and the site showed everyone in the Fukushima Daiichi ERC and the offsite center jumping to their feet in the same way and staring at something. It was the moment of the explosion that was being broadcast by Fukushima Central Television.

Just before four p.m., the SDF reported an explosion at Fukushima Daiichi NPS. This was reported to NISA's ERC. After that, everyone was glued to the television screens.

THE RADIATION EMERGENCY MEDICAL ASSISTANCE TEAM

At eight a.m. on March 12, Takako Tominaga (age 33), a doctor at the National Institute of Radiological Sciences (NIRS) located in Inage, Chiba, boarded an SDF helicopter. She was accompanied by two colleagues. The surrounding area was covered in high-voltage electrical power lines. Threading its way through the power lines, the helicopter headed to Fukushima.

Tominaga was an expert in emergency medicine. She had also worked for a year at the International Atomic Energy Agency (IAEA) in Vienna. She had been working for NIRS since 2009 and was a member of its Radiation Emergency Medical Assistance Team (REMAT), made up of emergency medical experts. On her jacket was the red REMAT logo against a navy, gray, and white background. She was wearing navy pants.

They were loaded up with measuring equipment, medical supplies, five hundred stable iodine tablets and forty boxes of Prussian blue. The stable iodine acts to lower levels of radioactive iodine, and the Prussian blue reduces the effect of radioactive exposure due to cesium.

Just before ten a.m., the helicopter landed in a baseball field near the offsite center. They were met by some NISA staff, but they could not open the fence, because it was locked. They climbed over the netting to get out. She had expected someone from the government or prefectural medical team to be there, but no one came.

The medical team on the second floor of the offsite center comprised the head of the Sousou Healthcare Center (South Soma), a liaison official from TEPCO, and a member of staff from the Japan Chemical Analysis Center. Tominaga joined them.

There was an initial radiation exposure medical facility nearby, namely the Ohno Prefectural Hospital (designated by the prefecture for Okuma

Town, Futaba District). They heard that staff were still there accepting out-patients. When they checked it out, however, they found it was not func-tioning at all.

THE EVENING OF MARCH 12. An inquiry came in from Fukushima Daiichi that a worker had been exposed to "more than 100 millisieverts, what should we do?" The exact figure was 106.30 millisieverts. On further questioning, there did not seem to be an acute disorder.

"All you can do is get them to go to the emergency response center."

A little later, the worker turned up.[77] He had been to the Ohno Hospital, but since there were no doctors there, he had come here. He said he was really worried. He was examined, but did not show any acute exposure symptoms, such as vomiting. It was likely that he was completely exhausted.

"Would you like to rest here?"

"No, I'll go back to my post."

They heard later that he was resting in the Anti-Seismic Building. The radiation levels of which were on the rise when venting.[78]

The two colleagues who had flown in via helicopter with Tominaga were measurement specialists. They said dosage started to rise from four p.m. on March 12 into the night. This was a little after the Unit 1 explosion.

"The air dose rate indoors isn't rising yet, but it's climbing steadily out-side."

Contamination of the TEPCO, SDF, and police personnel traveling to Fukushima Daiichi and back was getting steadily worse. Five SDF officers came to the offsite center after they had finished pumping water, which took place before and after the explosion at Unit 1. While their levels were "normal" when measured onsite before they came, a screening test found 30,000 count per minute (cpm) before decontamination and 5,000–10,000 cpm after decontamination.[79]

A screening test involves measuring the amount of radioactive material found on clothes or the body. Everyone had to be screened and decontam-inated before entering the offsite center. The decontamination line was set at 600 cpm, but that meant everyone would be over it. Count per minute represented the amount of radiation measured in a minute. Since the type and strength of radiation cannot be measured, it was necessary to make dif-ferent calculations according to the type of instrument in order to estimate the amount of radiation a person has suffered.

Where should the decontamination line be set? The Nuclear Emergency Plan was unclear on that point also. The medical team and monitoring teams got together and decided to set 40 becquerel/cm² —or, alternatively, 6,000 cpm—as the standard, which is the equivalent of the typical dosage received by Chernobyl workers who died within a month. They confirmed this with the NSC and NISA's ERC and had a notification issued and sent to neighboring towns under the name of the local NERHQ director.

2:20 P.M., MARCH 13. Ikeda instructed the heads of Fukushima Prefecture, Okuma Town, Futaba Town, Tomioka Town, Namie Town, Naruha Town, Hirono Town, Katsurao Village, South Soma City, Kawauchi Village, and Tamura City that the screening level was to be set at 40 becquerel/cm²—or, alternatively, 6,000 cpm.

After issuing an order for residents to evacuate in a ten-kilometer radius in the early hours of March 12, people in the daycare centers and old people's facilities in Futaba evacuated to Kawamata. Some of these were said to have been exposed to radiation while evacuating. They had to be screened. That job fell to Tominaga and her team.

"Please go to Kawamata."

That was what they were told, but no one had any idea of where in Kawamata they were to go.

From the night of March 13 to the morning of March 14, Tominaga rode to Kawamata separately from her team in SDF trucks. On the way, the road was cut off by water. They were told it was too dangerous for the trucks and that they were to walk across. When they went to the police in Kawamata, no one knew who had evacuated to where. Guessing that they might learn something at the local gym, they headed there. They found the mayor of Futaba and his staff freezing in the sub-zero cold. They had fled with just the clothes on their backs. They had nothing to change into and their clothes were filthy.

They screened and decontaminated some eighty people from the town hall and daycare center. There were approximately a hundred people asleep in the adjacent building. They were all people who could not move on their own. They went there and screened them as well. Most of them were over 10,000 cpm. Their hair was up to 40,000–50,000 cpm. There were two people over 100,000 cpm.

Returning to the offsite center, they heard a thunderous noise as they were getting out of the truck. It was Unit 3 exploding. They hurried inside the building.

On the evening of March 14, the NIRS measurement experts identified cesium in their nuclide analysis of the airborne radioactive material.

"The core must be in meltdown."

The fact that cesium had been found suggested that the fuel was melting and the containment vessel had been breached. The stable iodine they had brought quickly proved to be useful. Since the SDF unit that was carrying out the water pumping operations onsite at Fukushima Daiichi had not brought any with them, the medical team gave them enough for eight people.[80]

TWO

A State of Nuclear Emergency Declared

"PRIME MINISTER KAN SUSPECTED OF ACCEPTING ILLEGAL DONATIONS"

2:46 P.M., MARCH 11, 2011. Prime Minister Naoto Kan was attending a meeting of the Upper House's audit committee. The morning edition of the *Asahi Shimbun* had run a scoop on the question of Kan's political donations.

PRIME MINISTER SUSPECTED OF ACCEPTING ILLEGAL DONATIONS
FROM SOUTH KOREAN RESIDENT; NO ANSWER FROM PM SIDE.

That was the front-page headline.

"An *Asahi Shimbun* investigation has discovered that in 2006 and 2009, Prime Minister Naoto Kan's political funding organization accepted a total of 1.04 million yen from the former director of a Japanese-based Korean financial institution. The former director's family members and several related parties have explained that the former director is a South Korean national. The Political Contributions Regulation Act forbids donations from foreign nationals."

Foreign Minister Seiji Maehara had resigned just five days earlier for receiving 250,000 yen from a Korean citizen. Politicians who violated the Political Contributions Regulation Act were subject to penalties, including a suspension of their civil rights, even if the money was returned.

For the Liberal Democratic Party (LDP) opposition, it was a unique opportunity to overthrow Kan's incumbent government, Democratic Party of Japan (DPJ). LDP Upper House member Kotaro Nogami (Toyama Prefecture) had pursued this question that day in the audit committee.

"The morning edition of today's paper has run a very serious story."

Kan went on the defensive.

"Since the name was Japanese, I thought it was a Japanese national. I had no idea that it was a foreign national, as the newspaper reports."

The LDP had no ammunition other than the newspaper story, so Kan managed to weasel his way out of it.[1]

The earthquake took place as LDP member Hiroshi Okada (Ibaraki Prefecture) was standing up to ask a question, showing to the live-coverage cameras the table he had created on a panel. Just as the government expert, Yasuyuki Takai, the bureau chief of the Equal Employment Opportunity, Children, and Families Bureau at the Ministry of Health, Labor, and Welfare (MHLW), began to answer, "The material distributed by the member . . . ," the chandeliers in the committee room began to shake violently.

Takai choked in mid-sentence and looked up at the ceiling. The chandelier screeched as the glass parts rubbed up against each other. As one, the cabinet members and Kasumigaseki central government bureaucrats all raised their voices in a groan. The stenographers hid under the table in a mad rush. Kan remained in place, grabbing the arm of his chair. He looked around in a daze.

"Please take refuge under the tables."

Audit Committee Chairman Yosuke Tsuruho (LDP, Wakayama Prefecture) said as much, but remained in his chair, clinging to the desk. After the shaking finally died down, Tsuruho declared, "We will take a temporary break," and stopped proceedings at 2:50 p.m.

Surrounded by security police (SP), Kan left the room and headed to the Diet entrance. His official vehicle took a long time to arrive. Kan could not hide his frustration. He ignored the reporters who were peppering him with questions.[2]

When Kan arrived back at the Kantei, Tetsuro Fukuyama, deputy chief cabinet secretary, was waiting for him in the basement crisis management center. At the time of the quake, Fukuyama had been watching the live coverage of the audit committee in his fifth-floor office. He could see the chandeliers shaking violently on the television. Both the prime minister and the chief cabinet secretary were looking up at the ceiling uneasily.

It was standard procedure during a crisis that the prime minister, chief cabinet secretary, and deputy chief cabinet secretary, in that order, should direct the crisis management center to respond. Fukuyama flew into the adjacent secretariat of the deputy secretary. Six staff members greeted him, still on their knees. Some were clinging to desks. Instructing an aide to "contact Ito-san [Tetsuro Ito, deputy chief cabinet secretary for crisis management] and tell him to get the emergency response team to the crisis management center," Fukuyama himself headed to the crisis management center. As the elevators were not working, he ran down the stairs.[3]

The crisis management center was a large room with a high ceiling and a round table in the middle. Minister of Economy, Trade, and Industry (METI) Minister Banri Kaieda and other members of the cabinet had all been attending the audit committee meeting. Kaieda returned to METI from the Upper House. In the car, the SP told Kaieda, "The epicenter is in the sea off Sanriku, magnitude higher than eight, more than a thousand dead."

They were listening to police reports over the small earphones they always wore.[4]

2:50 P.M. Tetsuro Ito, deputy chief secretary for crisis management, set up an earthquake response center (headed by himself) and assembled an emergency team of bureau chiefs from the related ministries. Most of them arrived within fifteen minutes.[5]

With the prime minister's chair still vacant, the round table was surrounded by the deputy chief secretary for crisis management, his aide (security and crisis management), and senior officers from the National Police Agency (NPA); the Ministry of Defense (MOD); the Fire and Disaster Management Agency; the Ministry of Land, Infrastructure, Transportation, and Tourism (MLIT); the Ministry of Internal Affairs and Communications (MICA); the Nuclear and Industrial Safety Agency (NISA); and the Nuclear Safety Commission (NSC). Their subordinates were all seated behind them.

In MOD's case, their operational planning director was always part of the emergency team, and it was standard procedure for him to head straight to the crisis management center. NPA was to send their public security director.[6]

There were ten huge screens on the walls. Yukio Edano, chief cabinet secretary, was the first cabinet member to make it to the crisis management center. He had also been at the audit committee meeting, but immediately asked Chairman Tsuruho to "please at least let me go back to the Kantei," and quickly left the Diet building with his permission.

After Edano, Kan also rushed into the center. He was followed by the minister of state for disaster management, Ryu Matsumoto. Kan joined Edano, Matsumoto, Fukuyama, and the others at the round table.[7]

There was always someone shouting something into the microphones. The police department was reporting the number of emergency calls, the fire department the number of ambulance callouts and fires. MLIT was reporting rail transportation and road conditions, and the Meteorological Agency was reporting the magnitude and seismic intensity scale of every aftershock.

Each of the officers was reporting via their own microphone. There were already more than a hundred people from every ministry crammed into the room. People were shouting everywhere. It reminded Fukuyama of the floor of the old stock exchange. He had worked as a salesman for Daiwa Securities in the heady days of the economic bubble in the late eighties, and had then run for office in Kyoto and been elected to the Upper House. Prior to his current post, he had been senior vice minister of foreign affairs.[8]

At the moment of the earthquake, Shuichi Sakurai, director general of the Defense Ministry's Bureau of Operational Policy, was watching the screen at MOD's Central Command Post. The Somalians arrested for an act of piracy in the Gulf of Oman were being transferred from a U.S. navy vessel to a maritime SDF vessel. It was just at that time that a huge tremor hit.

Sakurai tried to go back to his office to get his ID, but the MOD elevators had stopped. He could not get into the crisis management center without it. He climbed up to the twelfth floor of the ministry, then came back down. By the time he made it to the crisis management center, almost all of the other bureau chiefs had assembled. They were each reporting on the damage sustained.[9]

3:02 P.M. Yoshihiro Murai, the governor of Miyagi Prefecture, asked the district commander of the Tohoku SDF for a disaster mobilization of the SDF. The screen showed an SDF emergency helicopter. All of the television stations were broadcasting images of the tsunami. All kinds of information were being sent into the crisis management center.

"Automatic shutdown at Fukushima Units 1 and 2."

"Tohoku Expressway completely closed."

"The emperor and empress are safe."

3:14 P.M. The government set up an emergency response headquarters at the Kantei, consisting of cabinet members (headed by Prime Minister Kan), and the first emergency HQ meeting was held in the crisis management center in the basement. It was the first time in the postwar period that the government had established an emergency headquarters. Each cabinet member read out, in turn, the memos they had prepared. At the end, Edano said, "Please keep gathering information. Damage may exceed that of the Hanshin-Awaji earthquake."[10]

The results of a quake and tsunami simulation were passed to Edano. They showed "the atrocious figures of 6,000-8,000 dead."[11] As the meeting finished and the cabinet members were all getting to their feet, one of them said, "There aren't any cameras here. We'd better hold another emergency response headquarters meeting in front of the cameras."

Edano momentarily looked nonplussed, then said, "Well, then, would all of the cabinet members please gather in the fourth-floor main conference room?"

Kaieda remembered feeling a strong sense of *What on earth do you mean?* but joined the other cabinet members and climbed to the fourth floor. Holding another meeting in this new location, Edano read out the exact same memo he had just finished reading earlier. Next, the other cabinet members read out their memos and repeated the same statements. On his way back to METI in the car, Kaieda was furious.

Why did we have to hold the same meeting twice? They worry too much about the mass media![12]

At that moment, Fukushima Daiichi was being hit by a thirteen-meter-high tsunami. It was around 3:36 p.m. When a tsunami hits a thirty-meter cliff face, water splashes up as high as fifty meters.[13]

3:42 P.M. In accordance with article 10.1 of NEPA, TEPCO had reported a specific event requiring notification to METI, NISA, and the relevant local governments. In the crisis management center, an official from NISA announced over his microphone, "Fukushima Daiichi has lost all AC power!"[14]

An emergency meeting of senior officials was being held at METI. Senior Vice Minister Motohisa Ikeda and Permanent Secretary Kazuo Matsunaga, among others, were in attendance. Just as Eiji Hiraoka, NISA deputy director general, was reporting, "The control rods in each reactor at Fukushima Daiichi Station have been inserted into the fuel rods and have shut down," a junior official handed him a memo. The memo said, "We have an article 10 event."

If it was an article 10 event, they had to set up a local response headquarters and designate the vice minister as its head. They had to get Kaieda's approval as quickly as possible. When Kaieda returned to METI, information of a fire at the Keiyo Complex had just come in. This was followed by reports of blackouts everywhere.

"What'll we do if we have a mega-blackout in Tokyo?"

Entering his office, he heard from the SP that all members of the cabinet were to assemble at the Kantei. Changing into his disaster gear, he headed immediately to the Kantei.

4:13 P.M. In the fourth-floor main conference room, where the rerun of the emergency headquarters meeting had taken place, Kan was speaking on television.

"I am asking everyone to remain calm. Especially those close to the coastline, please remain alert to tsunamis and head to high ground. It is at precisely times like these that we must help one another . . ."

"KAN NEEDS COOLING DOWN"

4:45 P.M. TEPCO reported an article 15.1 event (functional loss of emergency core cooling systems) under the Act on Special Measures Concerning Nuclear Emergency Preparedness (NEPA) to METI, NISA, and the relevant local governments. This was because they could not determine the reactor water level in Units 1 and 2.[15]

4:47 P.M. NHK reported that the cooling system had ceased to function due to the loss of all AC power.[16]

4:55 P.M. Kan held an emergency press conference. He was wearing light blue disaster gear. His expression was stern.

"My fellow citizens, as you are already aware from reports on TV and on the radio, today at 2:46 p.m., an enormously powerful earthquake of 8.4 magnitude struck, with its seismic center off the Sanriku coast. This has resulted in tremendous damage across a wide area, centered on the Tohoku region. I extend my heartfelt sympathy to those who have suffered.

"As for our nuclear power facilities, a portion of them stopped their operations automatically. At present, we have no reports of any radioactive materials or otherwise affecting the surrounding areas."

It was clear, however, that things at Fukushima were serious. Kenichi Shimomura, counselor for public relations at the Cabinet Secretariat at the Kantei, thought, *We need three governments.* The three governments he had in mind were: one for normal business, one for earthquakes and tsunamis, and one for nuclear response. Just one administration was nowhere near enough.[17]

At around five p.m., Kan summoned Nobuaki Terasaka, director general of NISA; and TEPCO executives, including Ichiro Takekuro—a TEPCO liaison on assignment to the Kantei—to his office and questioned them about the reactor situation at Fukushima Daiichi.[18]

Takekuro received a general request for someone to come to the Kantei to explain about nuclear power while he was in the TEPCO Head Office Operations Center, immediately after the quake. He rushed over and remained there since. TEPCO sent three other staff members to the Kantei, in addition to Takekuro.[19]

Takekuro was a graduate of the University of Tokyo with a major in nuclear power engineering. He had been TEPCO's deputy president (and director of the Nuclear Power and Plant Siting Division) up until June 2010. In 2002, when he was site superintendent at TEPCO's Kashiwazaki-Kariwa NPS (Kashiwazaki, Niigata Prefecture), he had been penalized by a 30 percent pay cut for six months, when a cover-up was discovered.

Kan reacted fiercely to the AC blackout and the cooling system failure. He began by asking NISA's Terasaka, "Do you have a technical background? Do you understand the technology and the structure?"

For a moment, Terasaka was taken aback.

"I graduated from the School of Economics at the University of Tokyo. I work in the office, but since I am the one responsible within NISA, I have come to explain."

"If you're not an engineer, what the hell do you know?!"

After graduating from the University of Tokyo, Terasaka had joined MITI in 1976. Kan had graduated in 1970 from the Applied Physics Department of the Science School at the Tokyo Institute of Technology. He was by no means a nuclear power expert, but he prided himself on being good at technology. When the Democrats won power in 2009, he had served as the minister for Science and Technology Policy (as well as deputy prime minister) in the Hatoyama Cabinet.

Terasaka was perched upright on the edge of the sofa. To Kan, he looked completely devoid of confidence.

"Where are the emergency diesel generators located?!"

Terasaka failed to give a definite answer immediately.[20]

"Do you know how serious a power loss is?"

Kan had an animal-like instinct for uncertainty, and when he sensed it, he would move in for the kill. Kan turned to an aide and ordered, "Get me an engineer. And call everybody who needs to be called in a case like this."

Kan questioned in detail why the power had been cut. Takekuro did not have any definite information on the situation at Fukushima Daiichi Station, either.

"The battery needed to run the IC [Isolation Condenser] and RCIC [Reactor Core Isolation Cooling] systems for Units 1 to 3 will last about eight hours."

"In the meantime, we need to get power back and keep pumping water into the reactors."

Takekuro stated the general theory, but Kan wanted to know why the cooling system had stopped. When Takekuro could not respond, he said, "What? You don't know? Get me the TEPCO president!" Terasaka could not answer, either. "Then get me someone who knows!"

Kan was annoyed. His aides even called one of the NISA section heads to the phone. Goshi Hosono, special adviser to the prime minister, glanced toward Manabu Terada, another assistant. Terada winked as though he understood. Hosono stepped in.

"Prime minister, I think what we need to know now is not why the power was cut, but what needs to be done now that it has stopped."

Kan calmed down somewhat.[21]

"IT'LL BE ANOTHER CHERNOBYL"

5:40 P.M. NHK broadcast that the cooling system for two reactors at Fukushima Daiichi Station had stopped.

"This is a report on the Fukushima Daiichi Nuclear Power Station. Due to the earthquake, none of the emergency diesel generators needed to safely cool the two reactors in a shutdown can be used, and it is deemed that there is no sufficient cooling capacity."[22]

This was the first television report of the station blackout.

5:42 P.M. Kaieda came running into the prime minister's office. His face was drained of color.[23] If they had an article 15 event, the prime minister had to declare a state of nuclear emergency and set up a nuclear emergency response headquarters (headed by the prime minister). It was the job of the economy, trade, and industry minister to make such a request in order to receive the prime minister's acknowledgment. Kaieda made the request.

Kan and Edano, however, were fixated on the question of how they would know if "all power had been lost" or not.

"Why aren't the emergency diesel generators working?"

"They must have some backup power."

"They say the emergency generators have had it, but can't they draw water up by pumps and use that?"

Kan was throwing out questions to no one in particular.

"Do you all know what it means to lose power?"

"It's extremely serious. It's the same thing as Chernobyl!"

"It'll be just like Chernobyl."

He kept repeating these phrases over and over. Shimomura wrote in the margin of his memo, "It's Kan who needs cooling down."[24]

Haruki Madarame, head of the Nuclear Safety Commission (NSC), was called in. When Madarame was heading toward the prime minister's office, Eiji Hiraoka, deputy director general of NISA, offered to act as guide and walk him there. Hiraoka pleaded with Madarame.

"Please help me."

"What are you talking about?"

Madarame did not know what he meant at the time, but later speculated that it was related to the dressing-down Terasaka had received from Kan, and the fact that NISA had lost the confidence of the political members of the Kantei.[25]

Hard-pressed to fathom his reasoning, Kan gazed at Madarame and said, "You're the head of NISA, right?" It was true that among the politicians, Kan was the most knowledgeable about nuclear power, but Terada thought it strange that he could not tell the difference between the NSC and NISA.[26]

Kan questioned Kaieda and the others about the fuel meltdown, the possibility of an explosion, and even the output of each reactor. No convincing response was forthcoming. Kan got the feeling that Kaieda knew nothing about nuclear power. He became increasingly frustrated, thinking, *I can't possibly leave it up to METI. I'll have to do it myself.* NISA was a regulatory and oversight special entity of METI.

It was just after six p.m. The crucial establishment of a nuclear emergency response headquarters (NERHQ) based on an article 15 event was still undetermined. The article in question reads as follows:

"When acknowledging the occurrence of a nuclear emergency, the competent minister will immediately provide the prime minister with the necessary information concerning the event."

Furthermore, "The prime minister will immediately make public the occurrence of a nuclear emergency and the following matters (hereafter, referred to as 'a declaration of a state of nuclear emergency')."

This can be found in the Six Law Codes. However, what were the requirements for acknowledging a "state of nuclear emergency"? This was the point that Kan was stuck on.

"Article 15 events are unheard of. Does it really correspond to article 15?"

Even if all power had been lost, had the "cooling system stopped"? Was that not unconfirmed at the current juncture?

"I want to know what I can do as prime minister."

"I'm the one who has to make the judgment."

After these words, Kan, together with Katsuya Okada, secretary-general of the Democratic Party, left for a meeting with the opposition party leaders on the fourth floor of the Kantei. The request to set up a NERHQ was left up in the air for the time being. A declaration of a state of nuclear emergency could not be issued without the prime minister's approval.

Kaieda was waiting on the fifth floor during the party leaders' meeting. While he waited, the prime ministerial aides dragged out a copy of the State of Emergency Related Statutes Book from their office and were rifling through the pages with officials from NISA, looking for the provisions that would act as a legal basis. They finally found what they were looking for in the section on enforcement rules (ministerial ordinances) under the enforcement orders (government ordinances) of NEPA.

> "Inability to pump water into the reactor by all emergency cooling systems in the case of a complete loss of water supply to a boiling light-water reactor during operation" (article 21, item 1b of the Enforcement Regulations)

After the party leaders' meeting, Kan agreed to the issuance of a "declaration of a state of nuclear emergency." Kaieda was feeling very down in the dumps.

"We're heading for trouble if the prime minister is going to get hung up on these kinds of details."[27]

STATE OF NUCLEAR EMERGENCY DECLARED

7:03 P.M. The government officially announced a state of nuclear emergency at the TEPCO Fukushima Daiichi NPS. Upon doing so, the government was to establish a nuclear emergency response headquarters (NERHQ) headed by the prime minister as stipulated. The lineup was Kan Naoto as director general and Banri Kaieda as his deputy. The director general (prime minister) was empowered "when specially required" to issue the necessary directives to "the competent minister, the heads of the relevant administrative bodies, the heads of local government, and the nuclear power operator." The NERHQ secretariat, headed by the NISA director general, was to be located in the Emergency Response Center (ERC) of METI on the third floor of its annex.[28]

The first meeting of NERHQ was held on the fourth floor of the Kantei. It was made up of the relevant cabinet members. Many of those in attendance were thinking back to the "state of nuclear emergency" the autumn before.

8:30 A.M., OCTOBER 21, 2010. Kan was conducting the nuclear comprehensive disaster training drill for fiscal 2010 at the Kantei. It was being jointly carried out by the government, local municipalities, and Chubu Electric Power Company for a scenario where Unit 3 at the Hamaoka Nuclear Power Station in Shizuoka Prefecture had lost its cooling system and was leaking out radioactive material.

The large screen in the Kantei conference room was hooked up to Shizuoka Prefecture. Then METI Minister Akihiro Ohata stated, "It has been verified that cooling cannot be carried out due to the loss of all emergency cooling systems at Unit 3. I submit a draft for the declaration of a state of nuclear emergency." Receiving this, Prime Minister Naoto Kan delivered "a declaration of a state of nuclear emergency."

Everyone was reading from prepared statements. The local response team leader, the governor of Shizuoka Prefecture, and the mayor of Omaezaki read their statements in succession. Yoshihiro Katayama, minister of internal affairs and communication, listened to them, thinking angrily, *What a farce! What a pointless exercise!*

Katayama had joined the then Ministry of Home Affairs in 1974. He was well known as an expert on local government and later became governor of Tottori Prefecture. After the hour-or-so-long comprehensive drill, Katayama told Kan, "This serves no purpose," but Kan did not take any special notice.

That was a mere five months earlier. Katayama was remembering, "Come to think of it, we were in the same room then." The moment he entered the room, he had a flashback to the drill on that day. LDP Upper House member Masashi Waki questioned Kan during the budget committee meeting held on April 18, a month after the Fukushima Daiichi accident.

"On October 20 of last year . . . a very important event was held. Do you remember it, prime minister?"

After a momentary pause, Kan replied:

"I don't know what you are referring to with this sudden query."

"I am referring to the comprehensive nuclear disaster drill that took place that day . . . Do you remember the scenario used for the training?"

"Not in detail, but I think various kinds of earthquakes like this one were imagined."

One of the people watching the April 18 exchange on television was Tadahiro Matsushita, senior vice minister of METI. During the training in Shizuoka last October, he had been flown into the accident site as the head of the local response team. The training, which began by watching the movie *The China Syndrome*, lasted around four hours, including resident evacuation from a three-kilometer radius, decontamination, and lunch. In a debriefing soon after his return to Tokyo, Matsushita raised a question.

"This training assumes that power has been somehow restored, but is that appropriate? What would happen if it couldn't be restored? Shouldn't we use a scenario next time where the reactor can't be cooled and residents have to be evacuated?"

The NISA official replied:

"That would raise huge anxiety in the local area, so we can't say that."[29]

In a meeting on the night of March 11, a member of cabinet stated: "After eight hours (of using the emergency diesel generators for the reactor cooling system), there is a possibility of meltdown if the temperature starts rising in the reactor core."

"Eight hours."

Everyone noted the figure.

"Time will be up at 12:00 midnight."

Everyone in the crisis management center repeated this to each other.[30]

7:30 P.M. On the release of the "declaration of a state of nuclear emergency," Defense Minister Toshimi Kitazawa issued a command to dispatch the SDF to the nuclear disaster.[31]

Time was steadily passing. Already the establishment of the NERHQ had been delayed. According to Kaieda, it was "delayed an hour and a half."[32] The time was 5:42 p.m. when Kaieda went to the prime minister's office at the Kantei seeking approval for the "declaration of a state of nuclear emergency," based on the unfolding article 15 situation. Though Kan should have ordered the declaration's "immediate" enforcement, the action was not completed until 7:03 p.m.

7:45 P.M. Chief Cabinet Secretary Yukio Edano held a press conference.

"What I am about to say is a preventative measure, so please respond in a calm manner. It has just been verified by the Nuclear Safety Task Force that at 4:36 p.m. today an event corresponding to the provisions of article 15.1.2 of the Act on Special Measures Concerning Nuclear Emergency Preparedness occurred at the TEPCO Fukushima Daiichi Nuclear Power Station, which requires emergency measures to prevent the escalation of a nuclear disaster. In accordance with the stipulations of the article, a state of nuclear emergency has been declared. At present, no impact of radioactive material outside the facility has been confirmed.

"The reactor has been completely shut down. However, the reactor needs to be cooled. The situation is such that measures need to be taken for the power to cool the reactor down. We have issued the emergency declaration in order to prepare for every possibility and because of the extreme seriousness of the impact if the worst should happen."

From the evening into the night, the television broadcast the thousands of people trying to get home in Tokyo. No trains were running in the metropolitan area, including Japan Rail. The terminus stations at Shibuya, Shinagawa, and Yokohama were overflowing with workers and students trying to get home, prompting fears of a secondary disaster.

Responding to the images, Edano began doing the rounds. In a press conference, he asked the Tokyoites, "Please don't go home unless you are within walking distance." He asked over and over, through a bureau chief at MLIT, "When will the trains start running?" but no information was forthcoming.

He then telephoned directly Satoshi Seino, CEO of the East Japan Railway Company. They had been at school together, where Seino was Edano's mentor.

"Will the metropolitan trains resume running tonight?"

"I'm sorry. That's impossible."

"Right. Well, I'll hold a press conference to tell everyone not to go home."

"Please do so."[33]

Edano told Ito, "We have to do something about these people, don't we?"

"Leave it up to the police department. It's okay."

"How about opening up the schools?"

There were 21 million people who worked in Tokyo each day. It was estimated that the number of stranded commuters was 6.5 million. They took hours, or even dozens of hours, to get home. They were reacting to a homing instinct of wanting to make sure their families were safe, to weather the crisis out together.[34]

"How are things now?"

Edano was in over his head with the stranded commuter problem. On seeing him this way, the emergency team members started speaking up.

"The Tokyo commuters won't die if you ignore them for a night."

"In times of a crisis like this, he should be watching the affected areas, not TV."

"The problem is in Tohoku, not Tokyo."

Ito immediately told Edano to "leave the stranded commuters up to the police," but Edano was working like a beaver.[35]

In fact, the crisis was in Fukushima, not Tokyo. The situation at Fukushima Daiichi took a sudden turn for the worse. Things tensed up in the crisis management center. Someone from the emergency response team shouted out:

"When on earth are they going to get the power back?"

A NISA official replied:

"They're making adjustments now."

Hit by the tsunami, the emergency diesel generator was not working. They needed to get a new source of power in there somehow. They had to line up a large number of high-voltage power trucks, but there were not enough onsite. Takekuro was pleading, "Get us some trucks. Send them to Fukushima Daiichi Station." Everyone at the Kantei from the prime minister's office to the reception room as well as the crisis management center began searching for power trucks.

First of all, where could power trucks be found? When asked, the NISA officials were no help. NISA staff were buzzing about, going to and fro. After a while, the deputy directors and deputy director generals disappeared to be replaced by section chiefs. Someone from the emergency response team raised his voice.

"It's no use asking NISA. Let's ask TEPCO."

Ito decided to summon some TEPCO staff to the crisis management center in order to get information directly from TEPCO. The staff member TEPCO sent, however, also could not be relied on.

"I haven't heard."

"I'll check."

Every time he answered, the frustration level in the room rose.[36]

Apart from the crisis management staff, only the three top political figures (the minister, vice minister, and parliamentary secretary) were allowed in the crisis management center. Even the prime minister's aides were not allowed unconditional access. A system was set up so that calls to staff mobile phones were transferred to landlines in the center. The politicians, however, never let their mobile phones leave their sides for a moment.

The center was divided into a staff operations room and a room for cabinet meetings. Each had a large monitor to enable them to share information, including images of the disaster area. There was also a small room on the mezzanine that could house a maximum of ten people. It was on a round-the-clock status with its own generator.

The center had been built with the thought of a military threat or crisis in mind. Accordingly, its operating manual stipulated that the prime minister would stay in the center and take command. A nuclear accident, however, was not a war. It was not as if the life of the country's leader was under threat.

Koichi Kato, the prime minister's aide on national strategy and the Diet, tried to enter the crisis management center after the quake, but was blocked. The center used a heartbeat authentication system. Kato had not been registered for it. When Kan headed to the center in the evening, Kato managed to slip in behind him, entering the center for the first time. The heartbeat authentication system had been introduced during the North Korean missile crisis in 2010. It checked the pulse of the middle finger. Up until then, Kato did not even know where the crisis management center was.

Kan returned to his office on the fifth floor. As he climbed to the fifth floor, the parliamentary secretary followed his lead and went up as well. Kaieda was in place in the reception room adjacent to the prime minister's office. There were some fifty people squeezed in there. At Kaieda's suggestion, a whiteboard had been brought to the fifth floor, and secretariat staff carried it into the prime minister's office. (The whiteboard was later moved to the adjoining reception room.)

There was also a black phone set up to link the secretariat with the crisis management center. Each of the Kasumigaseki ministries was said to have "sent information to the Kantei" through their contact with the crisis management center. As to whether or not that information made it to the fifth floor, and to the prime minister's ear, was another question.[37]

"YOU MEAN TO SAY THE POWER COMPANY DOESN'T HAVE A POWER CABLE?!"

7:50 P.M. NISA received an almost panicked call from TEPCO, "Aren't the power trucks ready yet? They still haven't arrived."[38]

How were they going to get the necessary power trucks together and restore the lost AC power? Kan was constantly on his mobile phone to someone. Keisuke Sadamori, a prime ministerial executive assistant originally from METI, was also glued to his mobile phone, trying to locate power trucks. Every time he reported to Kan how many trucks there were from which locations, Kan himself jotted it down on the whiteboard.[39]

The parliamentary members and secretariat officials at the Kantei were becoming increasingly frustrated with Akio Komori, TEPCO managing director. Komori was at the Kantei, but could not access accurate data from TEPCO onsite. Kan and Edano both voiced their lack of confidence in TEPCO.

"Why isn't the company president here? What's the president up to, for goodness sake?"

TEPCO President Masataka Shimizu was in Kansai that day. Kan and Edano were informed a little while later that "it doesn't seem possible today" for Shimizu to return to Tokyo.[40]

The roads were damaged and impassable in places. There was no assurance that they could get through. So, they were asking for as many power trucks as possible. But how were they to be transported? What route should they take?

"Can't the power trucks be flown in by helicopter?"

Kan was the first to ask the question.

"Ask the SDF. If they can't do it, how about the U.S. Forces?"

AFTER 8:00 P.M. The SDF came back with a negative.

"They're too heavy to put in the helicopter slings."

The power trucks weighed 9.8 tons. The SDF helicopters could only carry a maximum of 10 tons in their slings. It was not possible to fly a long distance with that kind of payload.

The Western Division of the SDF had tried lifting power trucks by helicopter in their disaster drill with Kyushu Electric Power Company. They had even actually flown them into Amami Oshima when it was hit by torrential rains. They had never carried out any similar exercises with TEPCO, however.

The U.S. Forces response was also "they're too heavy." There was no alternative but to transport them by land. A power truck from Mito, Ibaraki Prefecture, was sent in under police escort.[41]

At 8:30 p.m., Kan descended once more to the crisis management center. More than a hundred people were working in the ruckus. Taking a microphone in hand, Kan urged them all to "keep in close, appropriate, and steady contact," then hunkered down in the small room on the mezzanine floor.

Edano, Kaieda, Fukuyama, Hosono, Terada, Madarame, Terasaka, and Takekuro were all there.[42] Hosono and Terada were discussing the division of roles in the crisis management center hallway.

"Terada, who should be doing what? There's the power trucks and the evacuation of residents."

"The secretariat aides are handling the power trucks. I've been working with them for a little while, so I'll handle that. You look after the evacuation."[43]

Tereda was 34 and Hosono was 39. Terada, a former employee of Mitsubishi Corporation, was first elected in 2003 at the age of 27. He had served three terms. His father was Sukeshiro Terada, governor of Akita Prefecture. He was from a political family. He had been appointed prime ministerial aide (for national strategy and administrative reform) when the Kan administration was launched in June 2010. Despite being a prime ministerial aide, he had received a desk in the secretariat office and worked from there. He could hear everything the secretaries said. He soon became the first of the parliamentary staff to know what appointments Kan had on any given day.[44]

After working at the Sanwa Research Institute think tank, Hosono was first elected to the Lower House in 2000, at the age of 28. He had served four terms. He was a member of Ryoun-kai, a political faction of the Democratic Party of Japan (DPJ), led by the Lower House member Seiji Maebara (DPJ, Kyoto), but had also been singled out by Ichiro "Backroom Don" Ozawa (DPJ, Iwate), working under him as the party's deputy secretary-general. He had been appointed only recently, in January of that year, as special adviser to the prime minister.

On that day, the elevators in the Kantei building stopped working. As a result, the physically fit Terada and Hosono ended up acting as the "runners" between the fifth floor and the basement.[45]

SOMETIME AFTER TEN P.M. A report came in that the power trucks sent by Tohoku Electric had arrived at Fukushima Daiichi Station.[46] On hearing the "power trucks have arrived," the female staff members in the prime minister's secretariat office broke into loud applause. Kan thought, "It's just like scoring a goal at the World Cup."[47]

A moment later, the bad news came. They learned that the first generator had gone to the offsite center, not to Fukushima Daiichi. Angry voices were raised.

"What on earth's going on with information management?!"

The power truck in question did not move. The reason given was that they did not know how far it was from the offsite center to Fukushima Daiichi. They heard from the next power truck to arrive that "we can't get in (to Unit 1)."[48]

Power trucks started arriving from all directions. However, they all immediately ran into a brick wall. They could not connect their cables. They had found a switchboard that had not been flooded, but the cable was not long enough to reach it. Laying the cable itself was also a nightmare. With the power outage, it was pitch-black. There was not a single light. The ground everywhere was cratered with gaping holes. There were no lids on the manholes.[49] The same words were being shouted on the fifth floor and in the basement.

"The cable! It's the cable!"

The power truck initiative was switched to the cable.

"Get the SDF to fly a cable in as soon as possible."

"What? You mean to say the power company doesn't have a power cable?!"

Someone spat out these words in utter disbelief. There was a wave of heartsick laughter in the room. Madarame also found himself caught up in the laughter, but then suddenly realized, *This is even worse than the diesel generators being under water.*

The metal-clad switchgear next to the diesel generator must be flooded, too.

The power center must also be under water.

If they're all under water, each motor will have to be linked up cable by cable. We'll need an endless supply of cables.[50]

If the power trucks were 6,900 kilowatts and the motors 460 kilowatts, they needed to have a transformer to drop the voltage. And they would need a transformer for each of the three different voltages of the metal-clad switchgear, the power center, and the motor control center. Without the transformers, the motors would not run. This was what had just dawned on Madarame.

It was also no good taking in any old cable. There were different types for high and low voltages. They each had to have the right dedicated terminals. It was not just a question of taking cables in and linking them up.

"Find us some cables we can link up!"[51]

Once again, angry bellows rent the air. Kan was losing his patience.

"The batteries will last eight hours. After eight hours, the water level will start to fall."

"Will it go into meltdown?"

"The reactor core will be exposed. So, getting a source of power is the most urgent concern."

"This is going to be just like Chernobyl. This is going to be just like Chernobyl."

That night, Kan repeated these words over and over.[52]

Takekuro complained in the videoconference with TEPCO Head Office, "Do you know the term 'FrusKan' [a frustrated Prime Minister Kan]? In any event, he gets mad a lot. I've been told off six or seven times. Whenever you explain anything to him, he comes back, all guns blazing, with 'What grounds do you have for that? Can you say that, no matter what happens, things will be all right?' "[53]

9:55 P.M. TEPCO announced in a press conference that "the operating status of No. 2 Reactor is unknown and we are unable to ascertain the water level in the reactor core."[54]

Left as it was, pressure would continue to mount in the reactor core. The power trucks kept arriving at the site. However, the switchboard power supply was submerged and could not be used. With a last entry of "22:37: two power trucks arrive from the SDF, but connection with Daiichi Unit 1 or 2 unconfirmed," the power trucks disappeared from the NSC office whiteboard. They had spent all evening arranging for the power trucks and cables. More than sixty power trucks had been procured. But even if they were sent to the site, the all-important switchboard was out of action.

What on earth had been the point of the power truck initiative? What had been the point of the cable maneuver? Eiji Hiraoka, NISA's deputy director general, remembers his blood running cold when he learned of this.

"The external power supply has been cut. The emergency backup diesel generator has been flooded with water. The battery room is out and there's no direct current. No wonder they can't read the instrumentation."

Fukuyama felt his whole body was sapped of power.

"Even though I got them thirty power trucks, they can't hook up the power? All thirty are useless? All thirty in vain?"[55]

MELTDOWN

10:00 P.M., MARCH 11. Teresaka brought a slip of paper to the Kantei, on which "Unit 2, meltdown at 27:30" was written. This was the recalculation NISA had made from the report TEPCO had filed with them at 9:15 p.m. on the situation in Unit 2. According to this,

Around 10:20 p.m., March 11	*Core damage initiation*
10:50 p.m., March 11	*Core exposed*
12:50 a.m., March 12	*Fuel melting*
3:20 a.m., March 12	*Highest design specification of pressure in the reactor containment vessel (527.6 KPa) reached*[56]

Nuclear power fuel came in the form of uranium oxide, which sintered at high temperature to produce pellets about the size of a cigarette filter. The fuel rods consisted of these pellets encapsulated in zirconium alloy-clad tubes. During operation, the fuel rods are cooled with water, but if they cease to be cooled, the temperature of the fuel rods rises, melting the cladding tubes and, in turn, the pellets. This amounts to core damage. Terasaka touched on the possibility of core meltdown when outlining the situation forecast as of 3:20 a.m. on March 12.

"Is it going to meltdown?!"

Kan raised his voice.

"It may not go that far straight away."

"But that's what's written here."

Kan's mistrust of Terasaka instantly grew stronger. *What is he talking about?* Kan wondered.[57]

After one p.m. on March 12, Kan, Edano, and Kaieda were briefed in a meeting in the prime minister's office by Mitsuhiro Kajimoto, deputy manager of the Nuclear Power Safety and Evaluation Division at the Japan Nuclear Energy Safety Organization (JNES). Hiraoka also attended. The topic was "What Measures Should Be Taken if the Venting at Unit 1 Failed." NISA had already conducted a simulation and started considering countermeasures.[58]

Kajimoto was an expert in emission predictions of radioactive substances in the case of severe nuclear accidents. His doctoral thesis had been "Research on the Behavior Analysis of Radioactive Material in a Core Damage Accident at a Light Water Reactor Type Nuclear Reactor Facility." He had also previously worked in the risk assessment analysis laboratory of the Japan Atomic Energy Research Institute.

At four p.m. on the previous day, March 11, he had been summoned to the Emergency Response Center and stayed there.

Sometime after nine p.m., Kajimoto was asked for his opinion concerning "the prediction of changes in the future development of the accident" during a videoconference with NISA and the NSC. He replied, "There is an extremely strong possibility of core damage in Reactors No. 1, 2, and 3.

"There is also a possibility that, if things continue as they stand, the pressure vessel will be breached in several hours.

"If no measures are taken, it is likely that the containment vessel will be damaged."

Yutaka Kukita, acting chairman of the NSC, asked him, "Do you think the fuel pool at Reactor No. 4 is all right?"

"It needs to be watched, but probably doesn't need to have immediate action taken. You have to deal with Reactors No. 1, 2, and 3 first. But measures will be needed at some stage."

Kajimoto and the engineers at JNES had predicted the radiation emission amount, if venting took place, based on the results of past venting simulation analyses.[59]

In the meeting in the prime minister's office from one p.m. on March 12, Kajimoto handed out a single piece of paper outlining the scenario if the venting operation failed.

Noble gas   100%
Iodine   10%
Cesium   1%

It was the analysis results of emission volumes some ten hours later. Kajimoto told Kan, "The time it will take the pressure in the containment vessel to reach three times its regular level is the yardstick we have used."

"What do you mean by three times of that?"

"I mean the possibility that the containment vessel will be damaged."

"Well, spit it out then, man!"

Kan's voice was raised. Just as the briefing was coming to an end, NTV News 24 started broadcasting a press conference with officials from NISA and the NSC.

"There is a possibility that meltdown is in progress. We are almost certain that meltdown is in progress."

Kan bellowed, "What's this?!"

"What on earth is this?"

"No one's told me this."

Kan questioned Hiraoka, "What's the meaning of this?"

Edano also asked, "None of what they're saying at the press conference has been through the Kantei?"

Hiraoka bowed his head in apology. "I'm sorry. I'm sorry."[60]

In a building some fifty meters high, there is a flask-shaped containment vessel, which houses the pressure vessel. Inside the pressure vessel, the reactor core with its fuel rods is submerged in water. The heat generated by the fission reaction of the fuel turns that water into vapor, which passes through tubes to turn the power turbines. The water vapor is then cooled with seawater, which turns it back into water and is fed back into the pressure vessel. If something goes wrong with this cycle and the reactor core is not cooled down, meltdown occurs.

The term "meltdown" refers to a severe accident where the fuel rods melt due to an inability to cool the core. If left unattended, there is a very strong danger that not only the pressure vessel but the building's concrete floor would melt, releasing large amounts of radioactive material.

Just before the press conference on the afternoon of March 12, Deputy Director General for Nuclear Safety Koichiro Nakamura reported to Terasaka at the Emergency Response Center at NISA.

"The monitoring value onsite at Fukushima Daiichi Station is rising. A considerable amount of time has also passed since the loss of AC power, and it is inconceivable that the emergency isolation condenser (IC) is working. The tops of the fuel rods continue to be uncovered above the water level. Since the water level is still falling, there seems to be a strong possibility of meltdown at Unit 1."

In the morning of that day, cesium was detected in the area around Fukushima Daiichi Station. Nakamura deemed it "fair to say that the fuel in the reactor core was melting," and reported this to Terasaka as well. If the radioactive material was rare noble gas and iodine, you could well say that there was a leak, but with solid particles like cesium being detected, it was necessary to assume a situation in which the containment vessel had been damaged.

If a substance that only existed in the pellets was detected outside the building, the only possibility was a meltdown. Terasaka told Nakamura, "[If that's the case,] there's nothing for it but to say so." This was why, having mentioned this point in the press conference, Nakamura used the straightforward expression "the possibility of meltdown."

That was the exchange leading up to Nakamura's appearance at the press conference. As has already been seen, he had conveyed the same information to the Kantei the night before. But his message never made it to Kan or Edano. They were both amazed to hear Nakamura's remarks. Edano was outraged about facts that had not been reported to the Kantei, which came to light for the first time at a TEPCO and NISA press conference.

"It's an unthinkable situation that the Japanese people have the information before the Kantei!"

Madarame, who was on the fifth floor of the Kantei, remembers clearly what the situation was in the Kantei at the time.

"I think it was Edano-san who was hopping mad that NISA seemed to know more than the Kantei, and the one thing I remember clearly is that he said, 'It's an affront not to tell the Kantei first!'"

One of the technical staff encamped on the fifth floor of the Kantei stated that he had come across Edano at the time, walking by at a brisk pace and issuing instructions to his aides, "Don't let NISA talk as they please" and "Make them report beforehand."[61]

Edano was not the only person dissatisfied with how NISA was passing on information. The prime ministerial secretariat and the chief cabinet secretariat were equally distrustful. Keisuke Sadamori, secretary to the prime minister, requested NISA to "submit to the Kantei in advance any NISA press announcements on the reactor meltdown." The Kantei sent the word out that "all announcements to the Japanese people were to be disseminated via chief cabinet secretary press conferences only." An internal memo from NISA, time-stamped 3:23 p.m., noted: "We've been asked to contact the Kantei before going public with any announcements on meltdowns."[62]

Nakamura was in charge of the press announcements until 5:50 p.m., after which he asked Terasaka whether he could be relieved of his position as PR official. Terasaka ordered a change in personnel. The 5:50 p.m. press conference was the last one at which Nakamura acted as NISA spokesman. He was replaced by Tetsuo Noguchi, NISA deputy director general.

In the 9:30 p.m. press conference on the same day, Noguchi stuck from start to finish with the ambiguous phrase "I don't think that the statement [regarding core meltdown] was based on a clear assessment of the situation." In a further press conference in the early hours of March 13, Deputy Director General Hisanori Nei appeared as the spokesman, saying, "I have taken over at the direction of top management."

Nei avoided the term "meltdown," using instead the statement "the possibility of fuel rod damage cannot be denied."

On the evening of March 13, Nei was replaced with Deputy Director General Hidehiko Nishiyama making his debut. Nishiyama also showed an aversion to the word "meltdown," displaying his mastery of rhetoric with "the appropriate expression is 'damage to the external cladding of the fuel rods.'" (It was only on April 18 that NISA acknowledged a meltdown.)

During this time, the Kantei did not instruct NISA not to use the term "meltdown." There is no evidence that Chief Cabinet Secretary Edano intervened directly in NISA personnel decisions. Nor is there any evidence that they applied pressure to avoid the term "meltdown." Regarding this point, Edano later revealed, "I issued a strict order that if they were to announce something in a press conference, they should at least report it simultaneously to the Kantei."

Touching on the fact that "this instruction to report simultaneously" was distorted into "press conferences require the approval of the Kantei," he wrote: "While it is regrettable that the instructions were not carried out thoroughly, I am convinced that the instructions themselves were correct."

When queried about the possibility of a meltdown in Unit 3 in a press conference from eleven a.m. on March 13, Edano responded: "There is a real possibility of that, and since we cannot confirm what is happening inside the reactor, we are, as a matter of course, taking measures on that assumption."

There is also no sign that METI Minister Banri Kaieda intervened. Permanent Secretary Kazuo Matsunaga did not make a move, either. Conversely, Matsunaga said, "Release what information you have as soon as possible." His assessment at the time of Nakamura's statement was that "it was right."

What is probably the closest to the truth is that Terasaka, guessing at the "intention" of the Kantei, had Nakamura removed. Terasaka had instructed Sakurai to pass on to Nakamura that "there were those who had expressed alarm at the nature of the statements at NISA press conferences, so be careful what you say in any press announcements." A senior official at NISA spat out: "He [Terasaka] overreacted."[63]

The removal of Koichiro Nakamura not only had NISA worried, but all of Kasumigaseki. Was the Kantei going to micromanage all the factual reporting? Was that not really the job of the officials and people in charge who were closest to the frontlines? Was not the job of the Kantei to make political judgments on what needed to be done based on the affirmed facts of the situation?

"Did you pass it on up to the Kantei?"

"Does the Kantei know about this?"

"Shouldn't you leave that with the Kantei?"

NISA, METI, MEXT, MHLW—everyone was highly sensitive to keeping the right distance with the Kantei. The submission process for information—that is, the "paperwork"—to the Kantei took a huge amount of energy. It was not permissible for "the Kantei to know, but not the permanent ministerial secretary." Almost every government ministry and agency had their rules for submitting information to the Kantei.

"It was all very time-consuming, passing papers around and sometimes waiting for the all-clear before taking it off to the Kantei," said a senior METI official.

During this time, around two p.m. on March 13, Shimizu visited the Kantei along with Komori and others. However, only Shimizu met Edano in the cabinet secretary's office. After returning to Head Office, Shimizu told a director at TEPCO that from then on, TEPCO should seek the Kantei's approval in advance for press release drafts or material they intended on sharing with the public for press announcements.[64]

TEPCO workers onsite knew that things were moving quickly toward a meltdown. As the reactor manufacturer, Toshiba had reported them as such while sending TEPCO findings as they came from its Isogo Engineering Center, TEPSYS, a subsidiary of TEPCO specializing in core damage analysis. All of the analytics predicted the development of a meltdown. No one knew this better than TEPCO Vice President Sakae Muto. Reactors were his "turf," and so knowledgeable was he that everyone clammed up if he said anything about "reactor physics."

However, both TEPCO and NISA avoided using the term "meltdown" as if it were a taboo word. In the afternoon hours of March 12, Akiyoshi Minematsu, who served as a technical adviser to TEPCO officials in the company's emergency and disaster response team, received a call from TEPCO Fellow Ichiro Takekuro at the Kantei. It was his first call from the Kantei since the nuclear crisis had begun. "Kantei is telling us not to use the word 'meltdown.'" Minematsu responded, "It isn't inaccurate to say that the reactor core is damaged, so why should we say it is?"

Minematsu later testified that "If one says 'meltdown,' people will think of the China Syndrome, so we were a bit uncomfortable with using that word."[65]

During this time, Shimizu was preoccupied with thinking of ways to "stay on the same page" as the Kantei. In the evening of March 14, during an in-house teleconference, a TEPCO employee at the Head Office's Emergency Response made the following remark to a reporter: "I would like to answer by saying that we acknowledge there is fuel damage." Shimizu interrupted and said, "Regarding that . . . be sure to, you know, with them and the Kantei beforehand." It was difficult to discern exactly what Shimizu meant, since he kept repeating "that," but everyone who heard it understood that he wanted them to report to the Kantei and seek their approval before making announcements to the press. In particular, he wanted everyone to be careful when acknowledging a "reactor core meltdown" to the outside world.[66]

From March 15 on, TEPCO always used the expression "core damage" when explaining the condition of the core at press conferences.[67] Employees at TEPCO's affiliates were aware of this "fear" of the Kantei. Cautions like the following came down the line from top management to the manufacturers in the field:

"Don't use the word 'meltdown'—it's too provocative. Don't say 'melted'; say 'melting.'"[68]

In June 2012, TEPCO announced in their Fukushima Nuclear Power Plant Accident Investigation Report the time "reactor core damage" occurred:

- Unit 1, around 6:50 p.m. on March 11

- Unit 3, around 10:40 a.m. on March 13

- Unit 2, around 7:20 p.m. on March 14

Compared with TEPCO's initial assessment that the damage for Unit 1 occurred around six a.m. on March 12, and for Unit 2 around four a.m. on March 16, the dates and times indicated in this report are roughly eleven and thirty-three hours earlier, respectively.[69]

"IT'S CRUCIAL TO START VENTING AS SOON AS POSSIBLE"

JUST BEFORE 11:50 P.M. ON MARCH 11. The security team members of Fukushima Daii-chi NPS brought a small generator that they had finally managed to get a hold of into the Central Control Room (Units 1 and 2) and hooked it up to the display terminal of the containment pressure gauge on the control panel. Lights came on on the pressure gauge display.

The operators cried out, "Six hundred kPa (kilopascals)!"

This was far higher than the design maximum of 427 kPa of operating pressure. The site superintendent, Yoshida, reported to the ERC immediately.[70]

Until then, TEPCO had believed the emergency condenser of Unit 1 to be operational. However, with the pressure in the dry well of the containment vessel so high, it was apparent that the vessel had reached a critical condition.[71] At the ERC, before a frustrated room of employees gathered around a U-shaped central desk laden with computers, Yoshida said, "The dry well pressure is six hundred kPa. This exceeds the maximum working pressure, a dangerous condition. The only way to fix this situation is to implement the containment vent. I will notify the government and seek approval for the implementation of the vent. Everyone, please make preparations for the venting urgently."[72]

According to the operations manual, the local site superintendent had the authority to vent the containment vessel at his discretion. However, taking into account the seriousness of releasing radioactive material, it was assumed that the president's confirmation and approval would be sought.

However, TEPCO President Masataka Shimizu was not in Tokyo that day, but on a sightseeing trip with his wife in the Osaka region. He returned to the Tokyo Head Office at nine a.m. the following day, March 12.

At 12:55 a.m. on March 12, Yoshida sent to NISA and TEPCO Head Office a single sheet of A4 paper signed, "Site Superintendent Masao Yoshida."

"We are currently verifying details because there is a possibility that the pressure in the Unit 1 D/W [drywell] is over 600 kPa. Abnormal rise in containment vessel pressure."[73]

Deciding that they needed government consent, TEPCO started reaching out to the Kantei via Takekuro.[74]

12:57 A.M. After speaking with President Barack Obama on the phone, Kan left his office and moved to the small room on the mezzanine floor of the crisis management center.[75]

The government had to make a decision on TEPCO's request to implement venting. Prime Minister Naoto Kan, METI Minister Banri Kaieda, Chief Cabinet Secretary Yukio Edano, Deputy Chief Cabinet Secretary Tetsuro Fukuyama, and Special Adviser to the Prime Minister Goshi Hosono were gathered in the mezzanine room.

In addition to NSC Chairman Haruki Madarame and TEPCO Fellow

Ichiro Takekuro, NISA Deputy Director General Eiji Hiraoka was also in attendance. Madarame and Takekuro voiced in unison the need to vent.[76]

Madarame told Kan, "It'll all be over if meltdown takes place. It's crucial to start venting as soon as possible."[77] Madarame became even more convinced after discussing the matter with Takekuro, who expressed the opinion that they had no other choice. Takekuro pressed TEPCO Head Office to vent.

"I want you to make an organizational decision quickly."

Takekuro appealed numerous times to Head Office. Madarame was praying that TEPCO would vent as soon as possible.[78]

Since going ahead with venting meant releasing radioactive material along with the steam, it could have a huge impact on local residents' health, as well as trigger a considerable social response. In the first place, how much radioactive material would be released? What should be done about the accompanying evacuation of residents? How should it be explained to the Japanese people? These were the issues they discussed. Takekuro also reported to the meeting, "Venting can be done in about two hours."[79]

NISA and NSC later held a discussion on the venting. There were three problems. The first was, which should be vented first, Unit 1 or Unit 2? The next was whether they should review the demarcation lines for resident evacuation. And the last was whether they should administer stable iodine to young people. If radioactive iodine entered the body, it accumulated in the thyroid, leading to the possibility of thyroid cancer. Stable iodine prevented such an accumulation.

As a result, their agreed decision was:

- Venting Unit 1 was the top priority

- The evacuation area would not be reviewed

- They were not at the stage of administering stable iodine to young people[80]

Regarding resident evacuation and the venting operation, Hiraoka explained, "Even in a regular evacuation drill, which is within a three-kilometer radius (the evacuation radius in force at that time), it is assumed that venting will take place."[81]

1:52 A.M. TBS reported, "According to TEPCO, pressure is mounting in the containment vessel of Fukushima Daiichi Unit 1, and there is a possibility of radioactive material leaking outside, a most extraordinary situation."[82]

3:12 A.M. Chief cabinet secretary press conference.

The Kantei pressroom.

"I have received a report from TEPCO regarding the Fukushima Daiichi NPS to the effect that, given the fear that pressure has risen in the reactor containment vessel, they have reached the decision that, in order to ensure the soundness of the reactor containment vessel, they need to take measures to release the internal pressure. I have consulted with the METI minister, and we believe that there is no alternative if safety is to be maintained. There is a possibility that during the course of this operation, radioactive material may be discharged, but pre-assessment shows the amount to be minute, and bearing in mind that the wind is blowing seaward, the current three-kilometer evacuation and ten-kilometer indoor sheltering measures will adequately ensure the safety of local residents, so we ask you to respond calmly."

Q&As

Reporter: At approximately what time will the release into the atmosphere take place?

Chief cabinet secretary: I think it will be at a not too distant time.

Reporter: You say there will be no problem with the wind blowing seaward, but if it did change and started blowing toward those sheltering indoors, how great an impact would it have on their health?

Chief cabinet secretary: I have received a report from the Meteorological Agency that, at present, the wind is quite stable and remains in a westerly or northwesterly direction for the time being.

Just prior to the chief cabinet secretary's press conference, METI Minister Banri Kaieda and TEPCO Managing Director Akio Komori had given a press conference from METI, regarding the venting operation. Nobuaki Terasaka also attended.

Komori was a former site superintendent at Fukushima Daiichi and a current deputy manager of the Nuclear Power Location Headquarters. Since the TEPCO chairman, president, and manager of the Nuclear Power Location Headquarters were all absent from TEPCO Head Office in Tokyo, Komori, acting on behalf of the president, was the official ultimately responsible for dealing with the nuclear accident.

The Kantei had set up Chief Cabinet Secretary Edano's press conference before this other conference. If they waited until morning for his press conference, there was a danger that the government would be unfairly accused of a cover-up.[83]

An urgent report was handed to Terasaka just before Kaieda and Komori's press conference.

"The RCIC at Unit 2 is working."

The cooling system at Unit 2 was still working. NISA decided that, if they were to vent, it should be the Unit 1 containment vessel. Up until that time, the Central Control Room at Fukushima Daiichi had been unable to confirm whether the Reactor Core Isolation Cooling System (RCIC) at Unit 2 was working. Nor could they verify whether the IC at Unit 1 was functioning. This recognition of the facts, however, was sufficiently shared between the Emergency Response Center in the Anti-Seismic Building and

Tokyo Head Office. Komori, based at the latter, was of the belief that the IC was functioning.

Just before ten p.m., TEPCO stated in a press release, regarding Unit 2, "due to a drop in the reactor's water level, there is a fear that radioactive material will be released." On the other hand, regarding Unit 1, they merely repeated their earlier press release from around one a.m. on March 12 that "the IC is cooling the vapor."[84]

The TEPCO view was that the crisis was not at Unit 1, but at Unit 2. Komori, therefore, thought that venting the containment vessel at Unit 2 was the priority—not at Unit 1. Komori had visited Kaieda prior to the press conference, at around 2:30 a.m., to request that venting be prioritized for Unit 2.[85]

TEPCO had confirmed sometime after three a.m. that the RCIC at Unit 2 was working. They realized before the press conference that there was a gap in NISA's and TEPCO's understanding. They decided, therefore, to announce the implementation of the venting but not specify which unit.[86]

At the press conference, Komori stated, "We would like to lower pressure first in Unit 2." He left things somewhat ambiguous with the phrase "first in Unit 2." The reporters wanted to know, "Why Unit 2?"—but Komori did not give them a clear answer. During the press conference, Kazuhiro Takei, general manager of TEPCO's Nuclear Fuel Cycle Department, intervened.

"This information is just in, but we have been told that it has been confirmed in the field that the RCIC equipment is providing water to Unit 2."[87]

This information had not even been conveyed to Kaieda prior to the press conference. Kaieda thought that venting at both Units 1 and 2 had to be carried out and quickly.

Yoshida was watching the press conference on television. Seeing Komori flustered when pressed by reporters about which of Units 1 and 2 would be given priority for venting, Yoshida found it beyond comprehension.

Head Office is out of step with the site. What's going on?[88]

3:59 A.M. An earthquake hit. Even the Kantei shook considerably. It was reported to the crisis management center that there had been a six-plus earthquake on the Japanese seismic scale on the Niigata-Nagano border. A new sense of tension ran through the Emergency Operations Team. Fukuyama grabbed the mike and yelled, "Is this an aftershock from the Tohoku quake or is it totally unrelated? Which is it?"

The Meteorological Agency official merely replied, "I'll ask."[89]

AROUND 4:33 A.M. Another quake hit. It was a six-minus aftershock on the Japanese seismic scale in Nagano Prefecture. The epicenter was off the coast of Niigata. Everyone felt a chill run down their spines. Fukuyama was rushed off his feet for a time, dealing with concerns raised by the after-shock, but things soon settled down.

Worried about the venting, he was dumbfounded to hear from the Kantei staff that it still had not been implemented. Kaieda had said, leaning slightly forward at the press conference, that "the venting will start after three o'clock." Now it was after four o'clock, and the venting had not been carried out. Fukuyama and Hosono popped into the chief cabinet secretary's office and told Edano.

"Still no venting."[90]

Edano was taking a nap in his office, but sat bolt upright on hearing this and shouted, "What?! Why haven't they done it?"[91]

Edano and Fukuyama headed immediately to the mezzanine office in the crisis management center. Kaieda was on his feet, annoyed. Usually self-controlled, he snapped, "I don't understand why they haven't started!"

All Takekuro could say, when they asked him, was, "The power is out, they can't vent it electrically."[92]

Why and for how long were they going to do nothing? Kaieda wondered, suspiciously, "Is TEPCO still trying to underplay the scale of the accident even at this late stage? Is that why they're hesitating?"[93]

Ichiro Takekuro and Susumu Kawamata, general manager for nuclear quality and safety management, were caught off guard.

"They're trying to, but they can't."

"Well, the radioactive dosage has risen, so I don't know if they can do it or not."

All of the TEPCO liaison officials disappeared from the mezzanine office. It was just Kaieda and Hosono now. Witnessing this, Hosono said to Kaieda, "At this stage, I don't see any alternative to sending in a suicide squad."

"We have to get TEPCO to vent no matter what. Getting them to do that is our job, the politicians. Let's gamble on that, Kaieda-san."

Kaieda replied, "My thoughts exactly. That's the only way."

"Let's do our jobs as politicians. If that doesn't work, let's stop being politicians. Let's resign from politics together."

"Yes, let's do that. Let's resign together."[94]

In the meantime, radiation levels onsite at the Fukushima Daiichi NPS were rising. One of the operators, who tried to enter the Unit 1 Reactor Building (RB) in order to measure the radiation, saw a cloud of white haze on the far side of the inner door when he opened the double doors. He quickly closed the door.

4:23 A.M. TEPCO reported in a press conference, "It's 0.59 microsieverts/hour (0.00059 millisieverts) near the Daiichi main gate." The radiation was rising. Twenty minutes later, it soared.[95]

If they did not hurry with the venting, the radiation would increase. The venting strategy was a battle against time. On the other hand, TEPCO was thinking that they had to take into consideration how far the residents had to be evacuated when they implemented the venting. In the proper order of things, the evacuation of residents was the job of the offsite center. The offsite center, however, was not functioning.[96]

With communications severed by the power outage, there were several local governments that could not be contacted. Even by the early hours of March 12, there were more than a dozen local governments that the Kantei could not reach.[97] There was no communication between local governments and the Kantei about how to handle evacuation in the light of the venting operation.

JUST BEFORE FIVE A.M., IN THE MEZZANINE OFFICE OF THE CRISIS MANAGEMENT CENTER. When Fukuyama queried Takekuro about the venting, he replied, "It's not finished."

"Why isn't it finished? They've had three hours! It was you guys who said you would do it at three o'clock. You'll make a liar out of the chief cabinet secretary before the people of Japan."

"Venting can be performed either by electricity or manually, but we can't use electricity because the power is out. It's taking time to check the procedures for a manual vent. The radiation is on the increase."

Fukuyama's blood was boiling. *Haven't you known all along that there was no power? That report that you would "vent in two hours," what were the grounds for those "two hours"?*

He went immediately with Hosono to report to Edano on the fifth floor. A little later, Kan came down to the mezzanine office with his secretary. When he was told by Fukuyama that "they still haven't vented," Kan was angry, saying, "What? Why haven't they started?"

Immediately thereafter, Kan directly asked Takekuro why they could not vent. Takekuro's response was the same excuse of "manual procedures and radiation." Kan asked Madarame, "What will happen if they can't vent? Isn't there a danger that the containment vessel will explode?"

Madarame replied, "It's possible."

There was a real fear that the three-kilometer evacuation radius, ordered the previous evening at 9:23 p.m., would not be sufficient if they could not vent and the containment vessel sustained damage.

"Venting is a wet event, and since the water is passed out via the suppression chamber (SC), I think the radioactive material released will be adequately abated."

"Three kilometers is fine for venting, but it won't be enough if the containment vessel goes up in smoke. So, how about making it ten kilometers?"

These were the suggestions made by Madarame and Hiraoka.

When Edano and Fukuyama said, "It might be best to expand the evacuation area to ten kilometers," Kan approved, saying, "Yes, let's do that."

But when was it to be extended to ten kilometers? Edano and Fukuyama suggested, "The prime minister must decide. Please decide before you leave to visit the site." Kan agreed on the spot, at 5:44 a.m.[98]

5:44 A.M. The government ordered residents within a ten-kilometer radius to evacuate. This covered 48,000 residents in the towns of Okuma, Futaba, Tomioka, and Namie. Motohisa Ikeda, METI senior vice minister and head of the local NERHQ, rang Kaieda and told him, "I think confusion will reign with a night evacuation of residents. The venting should only begin after the complete evacuation of the residents has been confirmed."

"Please make sure such arrangements are made."[99]

The success or failure of the venting, however, was a matter of life and death for the reactor, and it could have a decisive impact on the battle against radiation. Unfortunately, perceptions of the situation by the Kantei, the offsite center, and, moreover, TEPCO, were not the same and there is no evidence that anyone tried to bring them in line.

Coordinating with the local authorities about the timing of resident evacuation and the venting operation would prove problematic that morning. The onsite ERC informed Fukushima Prefecture that they were getting ready to vent at around nine a.m., but Fukushima Prefecture requested that the containment venting be carried out after evacuation had been completed. This all took time.[100]

Awareness of the venting situation within the government was also mixed, and there was not enough communication. Michihiko Kano, minister of agriculture, forestry, and fisheries (MAFF), rang Yoshikatsu Nakayama, METI vice minister, and yelled over the phone.

"Nakayama-san, they say they're going to vent, but are they going to do it without our knowledge? What on earth is going on?!"

Nakayama was a member of the Kano faction within the Democratic Party of Japan (DPJ), which made Kano his boss. The fact that they were on good terms also probably had something to do with it. He must have been concerned about the destructive impact venting would have on agricultural produce. Nakayama guessed that *Kano was putting on some sort of a show in front of the MAFF bureaucrats.*[101]

6:10 A.M. There was a report in the TEPCO videoconference.

"Iodine figures rising. Iodine is being discharged. Even if we don't vent, noble gas will continue to leak."[102]

6:25 A.M. NHK reported "eight times the normal level of radioactive material recorded in the vicinity of Fukushima Daiichi Nuclear Power Station." No matter what they were asked, Takekuro and TEPCO Head Office failed to provide convincing answers. Kaieda thought there was no choice but to ask Masao Yoshida, the site superintendent, directly. They managed to contact Yoshida once from the landline in the mezzanine office via an emergency satellite link. Yoshida said, "The operators are risking their lives to do it. Please give us a little more time."

Kaieda replied, "By all means, please go ahead. Please contact us here when the valves are open."

It was a short exchange, but they sensed that the workers in the field were working desperately to get the venting going.

Kaieda thought to himself, *Can't TEPCO Head Office decide, after all?*

Since the radiation is climbing, perhaps the manager of a single company can't order his workers to lay their lives on the line in order to get the vents operating. If that's the case, perhaps it would be better if the state gave the orders in accordance with the Act on the Regulation of Nuclear Source Material, Nuclear Fuel Material, and Reactors. It might be better if we prodded TEPCO by getting the government to take responsibility.

Kaieda told Edano, "I'll take the responsibility."

At 6:50 a.m., Kaieda switched the instruction to vent Units 1 and 2 to a formal order from the minister of economy, trade, and industry in accordance with paragraph 3, article 64 of the Act on the Regulation of Nuclear Source Material, Nuclear Fuel Material, and Reactors.

Paragraph 3 provided the minister of economy, trade, and industry with the authority to "order the necessary measures to be taken."[103]

THREE

Hydrogen Explosion

PRIME MINISTERIAL INSPECTION OF THE SITE

It was in the middle of the night of March 11 that Prime Minister Kan started considering visiting Fukushima Daiichi NPS. First, he thought of a prime ministerial visit to witness the damage wrought by the tsunami. In that case, he would fly out on an air SDF plane from Ichigaya at seven a.m. and return to the Kantei by eleven a.m. However, even though TEPCO said they were going to vent, it still had not been done.

"It is unbelievable venting hasn't started, with the mighty METI minister and chief cabinet secretary announcing that it would."

What on earth was going on? Kan was out of patience.

I want to go to the site and see what's really happening on the ground.

I'm the member of the cabinet who knows his way around nuclear matters best. If I don't do it, who can?

The words he happened to use were "knows his way around," and Kan seemed to experience a certain sense of satisfaction with this turn of the phrase.[1] Kan's intention to visit Fukushima solidified by 2:20 a.m.[2]

Voices were raised in opposition to Kan's plan to visit Fukushima. Kansei Nakano, chairman of the National Public Safety Commission, quietly expressed his objection, saying that in times of crisis, the political leader should maintain a dignified presence. The Tokyo Police Department, responsible for security, were also against the visit. Nakano passed this on.

When Motohisa Ikeda learned of the "prime ministerial inspection" sometime after four a.m. on March 12, he instinctively felt, *It's not right for the prime minister of the state to come.* He contacted NISA Deputy Director General Shinichi Kuroki, and directed him to convey his view to Tokyo.

"It's better not to come when it's dangerous . . . If he does come, he should visit the offsite center at some five kilometers distance, not the actual field site, the Fukushima Daiichi."

Ikeda's opinion, however, never reached Kan. Edano had tried to stop Kan when he first learned of the prime minister's intention.

"It's a bit early, don't you think? . . . It's a good idea in theory, yes, but politically speaking, you'll definitely be criticized for going at such a time."

Kan countered, "Which is more important now? Being possibly criticized later or being in control of the nuclear situation? I'm aware of that."

"As long as you are aware, then do what you feel is right."

This was more or less how Edano, too, threw in the towel.

Terada also advised Kan.

"I think it's better if you stay here, since you are, after all, the prime minister."

Hosono also felt disturbed about Kan going. For an instant, the thought crossed his mind: *What will happen if the prime minister is exposed to radiation?*

Would they be able to contact Kan on the helicopter if anything happened? Hosono confirmed that there was a telephone link to the helicopter.

When Takekuro learned of Kan's intention for a "prime ministerial inspection," he thought back to the 2007 Chuetsu earthquake and the visit by then Prime Minister Shinzo Abe. Takekuro had been posted at TEPCO's Kashiwazaki-Kariwa NPS as deputy site superintendent. Abe visited in the middle of the Upper House elections and was criticized for creating confusion. Takekuro, however, remained silent on this question.[3]

In fact, Kaieda was also thinking that night of visiting the site as the METI minister. On hearing this, however, Fukuyama told Kaieda, "the prime minister is thinking of going," and urged him to reconsider.

"In that case, I might go with the prime minister."

"I don't think that's a good idea. It's not good for both of you to be absent."

After an exchange along these lines, Fukuyama raced over to Edano's office.

"Chief secretary, please stop Kaieda-san."

Fukuyama filled him in on the background. Edano rang Kaieda on his mobile phone on the spot and said, "I'd like you to remain this time as the competent minister." Kaieda abandoned his visit idea.[4]

Deep down, however, Kan was not sure. When he was alone with Kenichi Shimomura, counselor for public relations at the cabinet secretariat, Kan meekly asked him, "Everyone is against it, but what do you think?"

However, he then went on to say, "A Puma is small and fast. Because it's so small, I don't think using it for transportation will create a nuisance."[5]

The Puma he was referring to was also known as the Super Puma. It was the SDF's helicopter for transporting state guests. All of the transportation helicopters were already working at full capacity. It would not do to have them diverted for a prime ministerial inspection. That is why Kan thought if he used the Super Puma, he would not be criticized for obstructing relief operations. In his own way, Kan had taken into account the risks associated with his decision. He made the final decision to visit with only minutes to spare before his six a.m. departure.[6]

The helicopter arrived at exactly six a.m. on the rooftop helipad at the Kantei. Kan was running a little late.

"Any later and the helicopter won't be able to take off."

The helicopter consumed a lot of fuel when it was idling, which would shorten its flight range. Thus urged, Kan jumped on board. He was wearing light blue disaster gear and sneakers.[7]

"JUST ANSWER MY QUESTIONS"

6:14 A.M. The Super Puma took off from the Kantei helipad. It carried Kan, Terada, Madarame, and Shimomura. Also aboard were Kenji Okamoto and Koichi Masuda, staff members of the prime minister's secretariat; Kazufumi Tsumura, a Kyodo News Agency reporter chosen to represent the Kantei press corps; a medical official; and the security police. With a maximum capacity of ten passengers, the helicopter was full to overflowing.

They were to fly to Matsushima on the Super Puma. From there, they would transfer to a CH47 Chinook, a large transporter helicopter. On the flight, Kan sat next to Madarame. Madarame had been told by a Kantei staffer only an hour before departure that he was to come along. He unintentionally queried the staffer back.

"Why? Why me?"

"The prime minister says he wishes to use the flight time to learn in more detail."

Madarame boarded the flight thinking along the lines, *So, I'm to be the prime minister's study partner.*[8]

Whenever Madarame started to explain something, Kan would cut him off.

"I understand the basics. Just answer my questions."

Kan peppered Madarame with questions.

"How do Units 1, 2, and 3 differ?"

Madarame gave various answers, including the difference in output, and added, "Unit 1 was cooled with an emergency condenser called the IC, but Units 2 and 3 were cooled by RCIC water injection."

Upon which, Kan pressed on, "Why, if Unit 1 has IC, does Unit 2 have RCIC?"

"I think it's because when the output gets larger, natural circulation like an IC doesn't sufficiently cool it, so it was changed to injecting the water via turbines."

One of Kan's questions really got Madarame's back up.

"Isn't there a professor at Tokyo Institute of Technology who knows about this?"

Madarame thought to himself, *What do school rivalries mean at a time like this?*

Kan was a graduate of the Tokyo Institute of Technology. Madarame had a degree in nuclear engineering from the University of Tokyo. Although sensing a certain discomfort, Madarame replied, "There are Professors Aritomi and Ninokata."

He was referring to Professor Masanori Aritomi, director of the Research Laboratory for Nuclear Reactors (RLNR) at the Tokyo Institute of Technology, and Professor Hisashi Ninokata of the Energy Science and Engineering department of the same institute.[9] (On March 22, Kan appointed Professor Masanori Aritomi and Professor Masaki Saito from RLNR as cabinet advisers.)

The helicopter landed in the middle of the sports ground to the west of the Anti-Seismic Building at Fukushima Daiichi NPS at 7:11 a.m. A blustery wind was caught up in the helicopter's propellers, and it was freezing cold. They were met by Motohisa Ikeda, head of the local NERHQ; Masao Uchibori, vice governor of Fukushima Prefecture; and Sakae Muto, vice president of TEPCO (and director of the Nuclear Power and Plant Siting Division), among others.

Uchibori had reached the offsite center around eleven p.m. on March 11, and Ikeda got there in the middle of the night. Muto had left the Tokyo Head Office at 3:30 a.m. on March 11 to head to Fukushima by helicopter. There was a tremendous traffic jam, however, on the way to the heliport at Shin-Kiba. Walking and hitching rides from passing cars, he finally made it there and had landed at the sports ground at Fukushima Daini NPS around six a.m.

Since the offsite center was without power and not functioning yet, that night he did the rounds, visiting the mayors of Okuma and Futaba to explain the situation. In the morning, he heard that Kan would be coming by helicopter to the Fukushima Daiichi sports ground. He had wanted to meet with Yoshida in the Anti-Seismic Building prior to that, but there was a long line of people waiting to be checked for radiation at the entrance to the building. Thinking he would not make it in time, he hurried to the sports ground and was waiting for Kan.

The party headed to the Anti-Seismic Building in a minibus. Kan sat in a window seat on the right-hand side of the bus, Muto seated beside him. Madarame sat behind Kan, and Ikeda across the aisle. All of a sudden, Kan thundered, "Why haven't you started venting?"[10]

The party arrived at the Anti-Seismic Building. The entrance had double doors. The moment they opened the outer door, someone yelled at them, "Get inside quickly!" Apparently, they had arrived at the seven a.m. shift switch. Almost everyone was in Tyvek suits. Kan was wearing his light blue disaster gear and sneakers. People in bulky disaster gear were being screened. Others were asleep in the hallway. Kan thought it looked *just like a field hospital.*

Their guide was trying to get Kan and his party to the far end of the hallway. They had to be checked for radiation by the monitoring staff. They lined up there for a time, but something did not seem right. Still, it was a narrow hallway, and there was no way you could move sideways. The survey meter was held up to Kan's body. It buzzed.

Ah, so this is the line for the workers to be checked for radiation.

Kan shouted out, "What's going on?! Why do I have to undergo this? You haven't got the time to be doing this! I've come to see the site superintendent."

The guide had the party change their shoes and forced his way through the workers heading to the second floor by the left staircase. They could hear someone nearby saying in a high-pitched voice, "Oh, the radiation level is high around here."

"Get them into the meeting room quickly!"

The party climbed the stairs with a bristling Kan in the lead.

There were people slumped in exhaustion against the walls all the way up the stairs to the second floor. Nobody was aware that the prime minister of Japan was visiting. Shimomura thought to himself, *These people are working their guts out.*

Seeing everyone in their white Tyvek suits, Madarame was quite convinced that the venting had been successful. That was why his shock was so great when he learned that they still had not vented.

Why was I thinking that they'd vented?! If they had, the site would be contaminated and I'd have to be wearing protective gear, too.

Madarame had arrived wearing the NSC work garb. He had not taken into account at all the risk of radioactive material discharge accompanying the venting, or the wind direction risk factor. Kan was the same. (His staff, however, had confirmed that the wind was blowing out to the Pacific in and around Fukushima Daiichi NPS.)[11]

KAN VERSUS YOSHIDA

As guided, they entered the meeting room adjacent to the second-floor Emergency Response Center. There was just a monitor on the wall. It was as stark and unwelcoming as a room could be. No one was there. Kan was shouting again.

"Why isn't someone here?!"

The country's prime minister was visiting, but no one greeted him ceremoniously. They did not even let people know he was there. And then, they kept him waiting.

A little later, Yoshida made an appearance. He had mixed feelings about the prime minister visiting.

"Can't Head Office take care of it? I've got to be in the field! . . . If I'm out attending to the prime minister, who's going to replace me?"

This was the kind of exchange Yoshida had with Head Office. People at the site watching via videoconference were heard saying, "He's right" and "Don't come, don't come."

Yoshida spat out at the end, "I can't put up with this!"

One of the NISA staff members who witnessed the videoconference thought to himself, *What nerve Head Office has to ask such an unreasonable thing at a time like this, and good for Yoshida-san for saying that.*

"Good for him for saying that" was imbued with a sense of awe.[12]

Across the table, Yoshida sat with Muto, while Kan was flanked by Madarame and Terada on the other side. Muto started explaining that it was taking time to organize the compressor and power supply needed to pump in the compressed air to open the vent valve. After a minute or two, Kan snapped.

"I haven't come to listen to excuses like that! Why do you think I'm here?!"

Without responding directly to this, Yoshida spread out a chart on the table and started to explain.

"We are currently readying an electric vent."

"How long will that take?"

"It will take four hours."

"We can't wait four hours anymore. TEPCO has been saying 'four hours' for hours. All they ever say is in so many hours' time."

Kan was annoyed, thinking, *Wasn't the venting to take place at three a.m.? It's already four hours after that. Is he telling me we have to wait four more hours?* Yoshida, however, did not move a muscle.

"We will vent. We are even considering a manual vent. It will be decided in one hour's time if we go ahead with a manual vent or not."

"You don't have the time. I want you to do it quickly."

"Radiation levels are extremely high. So, the operators can only go in for fifteen minutes at a time."

So Yoshida replied to Kan, but looking him directly in the eye, he added, "In the end, we will have to send people in. We'll do it with a suicide squad."

Kan nodded at the words "suicide squad." Although his aggressive tone was still in evidence, they finally seemed to be getting on the same page. Listening to the exchange, Shimomura thought, *Finally, someone who can talk to Kan without wetting himself.*

Yoshida explained the situation inside the reactor.

"I think there's a very strong possibility that vapor is leaking out of the reactor. Pressure is at seven times the normal level."

Up until this point, he had been talking about Unit 1. He then turned to Unit 2.

"This has also been flooded with seawater, and there is no power. But Unit 2 can hold out for another four hours. We'll try to hook up a power supply during that time."

The tsunami had hit the building at thirteen meters above sea level. The basement power room was flooded. Yoshida said a tsunami of five meters had been assumed.

Would the local residents be all right if they vented?

"The current ten-kilometer indoor evacuation is okay."

Yoshida reiterated that he thought the ten-kilometer evacuation radius was sufficient.

"There will be a lot of noble gas, but at present I think ten kilometers is enough."

"We can't have people up and taking iodine on their own. Some people will suffer an adverse reaction. But it's all right if a medical practitioner okays it."

"We will measure the radiation when we have the go-ahead for Unit 1. Based on that value, we will decide whether to administer iodine or not."

Yoshida also said, "There's no choice but to vent Units 2 and 3 as well . . . Radiation is low there, so we can send people in to do the venting."

Kan pressed the point.

"I want you to learn from Unit 1 and do it as quickly as possible."

Masuda, the prime ministerial secretary, told Terada, "The medical official says we shouldn't stay here too long." Terada was thinking the same thing, but could not find an opening to mention it. Kan got to his feet. The meeting had lasted some twenty minutes.

Watching Kan descend the stairs, Ikeda whispered to Terada, "Get him to calm down a bit."

Terada whispered back, "He's better than usual."

As they were about to board the minibus, a staff member of NISA asked for his autograph. Kan signed, saying, "Is here all right?"

The site Kan had visited was Fukushima Daiichi. The crux of the visit was the venting of Unit 1. He did not go on to Fukushima Daini NPS.[13]

Muto briefly explained the situation at Fukushima Daini, however, in his meeting with Yoshida.

"Units 1, 2, and 4 at Daini have power, but they can't exchange heat . . . The temperature in the suppression chamber is over 100 degrees."

In short, he was saying that the tsunami had broken the cooling system and the pumps were not working. Daini was in a precarious state as well.

Shinichi Kuroki, a deputy director general of NISA accompanying Ikeda, had been asked by the NISA ERC in Tokyo "to directly appeal to the prime minister on his inspection visit to extend the resident evacuation line to ten kilometers from Fukushima Daini NPS."

Kuroki had heard that Kan was "someone who would not approve something if he was hemmed in too much." So, he decided that his best option was to say, "I'll contact them to say we have your approval." Kuroki had the documentation on evacuation area specifications sent to the Anti-Seismic Building and sorted it out in his mind while Kan was meeting with the TEPCO side. The moment the meeting with TEPCO was over, he reported to Kan. With a sour look on his face, Kan mumbled, "Fukushima Daini, too?"—but Kuroki successfully gained his approval. The time of approval and evacuation directive was 7:45 a.m. on March 12.[14]

At 7:30 p.m. on the same day, NHK went to air with the news that a state of emergency had been declared at Fukushima Daini Station as well, due to "an inability to cool Units 1, 2, and 4."[15]

The party traveled back to the sports ground to the west of the Anti-Seismic Building and boarded the helicopter. The piercing cold air chilled them to the bone. Ikeda, Uchibori, and Kuroki lined up to see them off. The propellers refused to turn. Perhaps it was because the engines had gone cold, but the helicopter did not take off immediately. Ikeda was experiencing a deep emotion.

Political leaders need to see the big picture. Japan is not just confronted with the Fukushima nuclear accident, but with earthquakes and tsunami. Seventy-two hours will make or break us all. At a time like that, the prime minister should maintain a dignified presence and act as the commander-in-chief. Those serving as prime minister need to conduct themselves, to speak and to act with a certain air. I don't feel that about him.

Ikeda had once been a member of the Social Democrats of Japan. He did not think very highly of the politician Yasuhiro Nakasone, who served as prime minister from 1982 to 1987. Every time he met elder statesmen Etsusaburo Shiina, Shigesaburo Maeo, and Hirokichi Nadao, he was scathing about Nakasone.

"Still, it was a different Nakasone after he became prime minister. Sometimes he would do zen meditation. Not that it was important to do zen, but a prime minister needed to have some time to think quietly every day, even if only for a few minutes. You couldn't do the job if you were always running around like a headless chicken."

"In the first place, Kan was terrified that day that he would be cornered and finished off. The quake hit during the audit committee of the Upper House. He thought his response to the Fukushima nuclear accident would give him a new lease on life. He wasn't his normal self."

8:11 A.M. Circling over Fukushima Daiichi NPS, the helicopter took off. Ikeda bowed his head to Kuroki and the others, saying, "I'm ashamed to be a politician myself. I'm sorry."[16]

"Hey Terada! Something's ringing!"

Kan, on board the helicopter, was speaking. It was the dosimeter beeping. Terada pushed the button on Kan's disaster jacket and turned it off. It seemed that Kan was only aware that Ikeda had come to see him off after Terada pointed it out to him on board. Not only that, he did not appear to be aware that Ikeda had come to meet the helicopter and had sat in on the meeting with Yoshida.

Kan was hungry. He chomped on a rice ball held in his bare hands. Hands that he had not washed.[17]

The party changed helicopters at Matsushima Airport and inspected the disaster area. Kan was glued to the sight below.

"It's so different from the Hanshin-Awaji earthquake."

Kan had experience with disaster areas, being one of the first on the ground at the time of the 1995 Hanshin-Awaji earthquake. Most of the damage at that time was concentrated in Kobe. Osaka next door was safe. Here it was a different story, however. No matter how far they went, it was all flooded. You could not tell where the sea ended and the tsunami waters started.

It's the sinking of Japan.

Shimomura shared the same thought. Down below, there was something that looked like a huge sheet of corrugated iron adrift. What could something of that size be? On closer inspection, he saw that it was the roof of the Sendai Airport. It just looked like it was drifting, because everything around it was under water.[18]

The Super Puma touched down on the rooftop of the Kantei at 10:47 a.m. The inspection had lasted some four and a half hours. The moment Kan entered his office, he told Fukuyama, who was waiting for him there:

"Site Superintendent Yoshida is okay. We can trust him. We can talk with him."[19]

THE SUICIDE SQUAD

After leaving Kan, Yoshida returned to the ERC sometime after eight a.m. He gave a direction.

"We're going to aim for venting at nine o'clock."

In order to open the necessary valves for venting, someone had to go into the Unit 1 (RB), which they could not get into, because the radiation levels were already rising. Since there was no power, the remote valve operating system was offline. They could only open the containment vessel and suppression chamber valves manually.

The suppression chamber (SC) was a doughnut-shaped container at the bottom of the containment vessel connected to the dry well (DW) by vent pipes. It was filled with a huge amount of water—1,750 tons in Unit 1 and 2,980 tons in Units 2 through 4. During an accident, such as a pipe rupture or when the SR valve was opened and high-temperature steam came rushing in, the steam would be cooled by this water, returning to water itself and suppressing the rise in pressure of the entire containment vessel.

The most important valve for venting was the air-operated (AO) valve attached to the upper part of the SC in the basement of the reactor building. The AO valve consisted of a main valve called the "large valve" and a spare valve called the "small valve," which were attached parallel to the vent line.

Since neither had a handle, workers could not open them, barring one exception.

This was the "small valve" of Unit 1's AO valve. The onsite operators were aware of this from blueprints.

Yoshida called for the shift supervisor via the power-generation team at the power plant ERC.

"There's a danger of considerable exposure. But I want you to go to the site and open it manually."

The interior of the reactor building had already been placed off limits late on the night of March 11. In short, he was asking for a "suicide squad" to go in. It is not clear who first started using the phrase "suicide squad," but it is likely that it came from among those on duty at Unit 1 and 2's Central Control Room. Agreeing to work in an area that was out of bounds could be nothing other than a suicide mission. The shift supervisor acknowledged the request from the power-generation team.[20]

Five units of logistical staff, about twenty people each, were lined up with members of the Radiation Management Group dressing them, one by one, in protective gear. A woman in her twenties taped up the joints of the protective gear they had donned on her. She had volunteered to stay behind there.

The operators were as white as sheets.[21] It was not just that the exposure was high.

The shift supervisor, still in his full-face mask and protective gear, was in the Central Control Room on the side of Unit 2. They had to go into the building of Unit 1 and open the venting valves.

The "suicide squad" was divided up into three two-man teams. There was a fear that, if all three teams went to the site at the same time, they would be out of contact with the Central Control Room and unable to carry out an emergency evacuation. So, it was decided that one team at a time would go to the site, and when they had returned to the Central Control Room at the completion of their operations, the next team would go.[22]

They would still have to be prepared for considerably high levels of exposure. For that reason, young officers were relieved of their duty and each team was made up of a shift supervisor and other senior officers.[23]

To operate its nuclear power plants, TEPCO relied on the workers from its subcontractors, which were referred to as associate companies. The plant control room was the only domain in which the utility bore the sole responsibility and did not rely on subcontractors. It was a hallowed sanctum where the operators shared strong ties and a pride in their mutual professionalism.[24]

That morning, the first sign of a radiation leak had already emerged.

At 4:50 a.m., the place was in front of the main gate of Fukushima Daiichi NPS. Emission sources could not be identified immediately, but they had occurred at the same time as the almost mysterious gradual drop in pressure in the containment vessel, even though they had not vented.

By five a.m., staff members in the field and central control rooms were told to wear coveralls and full-face charcoal filter masks. Since the dose in the Central Control Room of Unit 1 had risen, staff members temporarily moved to the Unit 2 side, where the dose was lower.[25]

9:02 A.M. TEPCO verified the evacuation of surrounding residents.[26]

Two minutes later, the ERC ordered the venting. In response, the Units 1 and 2 Central Control Room Duty Manager Ikuo Izawa (age 52) issued his command.

"We've got the order from Emergency Response. Carry out the venting operation."

A directive had already come in from the ERC around midnight to "choose the staff so you can vent."

Around three a.m., Izawa told the operators in the Central Control Room, "When we get the green light from the ERC, we'll go to vent. I want to choose the members . . . I'm sorry, but I can't let young people go. On that understanding, those of you willing to go please raise your hands."

No one said a word. They all looked at Izawa. No one dropped their eyes. Everyone seemed to be looking for words. Five seconds, ten seconds . . . a silence ensued. It was the fifty-two-year-old Izawa himself who broke the silence.

"I'll go to the site first. Is there anyone who'll come with me?"

Kikuo Otomo, a fifty-five-year-old who was standing behind Izawa, volunteered then.

"I'll go to the site. Izawa, take command until the end. You have to stay here."

Otomo was head of the Power Generation Unit's Work Management Group. It was his group's job to organize the work setup and carry out safety reviews when the reactors were operating and during periodic inspections. Their office was a few tens of meters from the Central Control Room for Units 1 and 2.

The next was Katsuaki Hirano, who was also standing behind Izawa.

"That's right. You stay behind and take the helm. I'll go."

Otomo was older than Izawa by three years and had worked his way up from operator. Although he now belonged to the Power Generation Unit, he had immediately rushed over to the Central Control Room for Units 1 and 2 after the earthquake. Hirano was also older than Izawa, by four years. Hirano was originally supposed to be the on-duty shift supervisor for Units 1 and 2 that day, but had asked Izawa to switch with him because he was scheduled for some medical tests at the hospital. That afternoon after the earthquake, Hirano had returned, in despair, to Fukushima Daiichi NPS and joined Izawa's team.

The moment the two senior shift supervisors spoke up, the younger members of staff raised their voices. "I'll go." "I'll go, too."

Izawa felt on the verge of tears. And, as if to hide that fact, he turned to face the whiteboard. He began to write on it the names of some ten people, one by one, in order of their age. He then selected a total of six people— the four shift supervisors and two deputy shift supervisors—making three teams of two each.[27]

Ikuo Izawa was the eldest son of a local farmer from Futaba Town. As a boy, he had ridden his bicycle over to Fukushima Daiichi NPS and played there with his friends. It was a huge site at the top of a thirty-meter cliff. He liked gazing out at the Pacific Ocean from there. No matter when he came, the sea was always a dark color, and beyond the horizon, a sparkling white.

It was the former site of the Iwaki Army Airfield, an aviation-training base near the end of the Pacific War. Suicide flight training took place here. Young pilots would take off from here to the southern frontlines in search of death. The broad, cracked concrete of the airfield was covered in the residue from salty air.

Construction work suddenly started there when Izawa was in elementary school. Dozens of one-story houses appeared out of nowhere in the forest. So had begun the construction of Unit 1, the first nuclear reactor at TEPCO's Fukushima Nuclear Power Station.

The houses were a "village" for General Electric, which had come from the U.S. mainland to build Fukushima NPS's Unit 1. The Americans turned the old airfield's huge expanse of concrete into tennis courts. There was also a hall and a small park in the village.

Izawa's gang made friends with the American children in the village.

The radio-controlled toys they had were something new. The Japanese kids taught them Japanese marbles and card games, and the American kids taught them how to play with the radio-controlled gadgets.

After the Unit 1 containment vessel was built in June 1968, the Americans disappeared like Cinderella.

Later, after graduating from a local technical high school, Izawa was employed by TEPCO. He had many years of experience as an operator at Fukushima Daiichi Units 1 and 2. In 2009, he had become a duty manager for Units 1 and 2 at Fukushima Daiichi NPS.[28]

The previous day, Izawa had finished a night shift. That morning, he was practicing golf at a golf park with Ryuta Idogawa, who also worked as an operator at Units 1 and 2 for team D. The fortieth anniversary party of Fukushima Daiichi was to be held soon, and golf park games were one of the attractions during the party. It was supposed to be his day off, but he came to work as the duty manager for the day as a substitute for Katsuaki Hirano, the actual duty manager who was not able to come due to medical tests.

Team No. 1 was Kikuo Otomo and Tsutomu Oigawa, who was forty-seven years old. On top of their protective suits, they were clad in armor-like fireproof gear, rubber boots, masks, and yellow helmets. They carried huge air tanks on their backs. They each put an alarm pocket dosimeter (APD) into their breast pockets, set to go off at 80 millisieverts.

The two men carried flashlights in their hands. Oigawa, walking in front and carrying a box-shaped portable survey meter to measure the exposure, entered Unit 1 (RB). The temperature inside was over 40 degrees Celsius. It was pitch-dark. Steam was billowing out. The exposure was high.[29]

They had to finish their job within fifteen minutes. The two men found their way by the light of their flashlights to the containment vessel's venting valve on the second floor. Oigawa started turning the valve handle. It was some twenty centimeters long and very heavy. The opening gauge attached to the side of the valve was in 5-percent increments. Each time Oigawa turned the handle, the needle of the gauge would rise to 5 percent, 10 percent, and 15 percent. Otomo's flashlight illuminated the figures.

Perhaps a minute had passed. Oigawa asked Otomo, "Please check the opening."

Once again, Otomo checked. It definitely indicated 25 percent. Otomo shouted and Oigawa nodded decisively. "Okay!"

The two men made sure to check the onsite pressure instrument for the containment and pressure vessels. They were trying to ascertain whether the figures they were seeing in the Central Control Room with the battery connection matched the actual numerical pressure. The pressure was higher than expected.

At 9:15 a.m., the two men came back to the Central Control Room. As soon as Otomo returned, he chugged a bottle of water from the emergency supply and immediately spewed it up on the floor. He was apparently not feeling well.

Izawa was encouraged, because they had come back sooner than he thought they would.[30]

At 9:24 a.m., Team No. 2 went in to open by hand the suppression chamber's venting valve. They had to make sure they did not lower the level of oxygen consumption.

We'll have to watch our breathing as well.

That was what they were thinking in their heads as they left, but by the time they reached the Unit 1 (RB), they were moving at a trot.

In front of the double doors, they braced themselves. "Right!"

They had no idea what was waiting for them on the other side. With only their flashlights to guide them, they made it halfway to the torus room, and when they looked at the survey meter as they reached the stairs leading to the catwalk, the needle was showing 900–1,000 millisieverts/hour.

The torus room was a doughnut-shaped room that housed the suppression chamber. The catwalk was the inspection walkway above the torus room. The survey meter was going wild. Team No. 2 turned back to the Central Control Room. During this time, the two men were exposed to 89 and 95 millisieverts, respectively.

Izawa decided that further operations in the reactor building were too difficult. However, Team No. 3 was already making its way to the reactor building. Izawa dispatched someone to tell them to return immediately. It was just as the two men were about to try entering the building from the front double doors.

Izawa immediately evacuated the two men from Team No. 2 to the Anti-Seismic Building. They worked in the ERC after that, but they both became the first staff members at Fukushima Daiichi NPS exposed to more than 100 millisieverts.[31]

"THIS MIGHT BE THE LAST CHANCE"

They were forced to give up manually opening the AO "small valve."

Looking at the blueprints, the operators thought that they might be able to connect up the compressor that fed air into the narrow pipe near the big, equipment-loading entrance of Unit 1 (RB) where the AO valve was. So, they were setting out on operations for using a portable compressor to blow air remotely to the AO valve.

However, Fukushima Daiichi NPS was not equipped with an adapter for connecting the pipe to a portable compressor. The ERC asked the associate companies to locate an adapter and portable air compressor, which they had finally found.[32]

Around two p.m., they got the portable compressor working and pumped air into the pipes. As a result, pressure in the drywell at Unit 1 fell. NHK footage showed white smoke billowing out of the Unit 1 exhaust stack.

Immediately prior to this, Izawa had sent another team, put together ad hoc, to the reactor building. He had requested that the Head Office think of means to get the small valve open from the outside; however, it was impossible. There was nothing to do but try once more to open it manually. He had heard that the two operators who had just arrived to support belonged to the athletics club.

This could be the last chance. Let's bet on these two.

A third team, which had been organized beforehand, were already wearing rescue suits and were getting ready to go. They said something along the lines of "we will go, it is our job."

"Do you know how things are out there onsite?" Izawa asked. Although they shook their heads and resisted, Izawa persuaded the third team not to go. The two athletic club members went instead.

After a few minutes, Izawa's phone rang. It was the Head Office.

"White smoke is coming out of the exhaust pipe of Units 1 and 2! Any updates from the Central Control Room?"

Izawa shouted, "Stop them!"

Another team on duty immediately ran after the one that just left, to tell them to come back. They were just about to open the double doors of the nuclear reactor building when they were intercepted. The two of them, who intended to enter the building, seemed to object to being stopped. They were not even carrying a dosimeter. Izawa only found out about this act of bravado later on.[33]

APPROXIMATELY 2:30 P.M. A report came up to Kaieda that "the second valve is open."

Around 3:18 p.m., Yoshida judged that "radioactive material was being released" from the venting at Unit 1.[34]

The staff members of NISA at the offsite center reported to the cabinet headquarters visual confirmation of "vapor-like substance coming out." Madarame was relieved to hear it.

Vapor rushing out with the venting proves that the containment vessel is still alive. The containment vessel is still alive.[35]

The venting of Unit 1 had finally been successful. It was fourteen and a half hours after the decision had been made, seven and a half hours after the government's order to vent, and more than four hours since the venting operation had started.

Why did the venting take so long?

Masataka Shimizu, TEPCO president, was asked this at a later press conference.

Reporter: You say that there was a delay from the government order, but President Shimizu, do you yourself deem that it was delayed?

Shimizu: As you have already been told, the site had lost all external power and was forced to work under extremely difficult conditions, and it is a fact that it took some time before starting actual operations.

Reporter: Who was in charge on March 11? That was when pressure in the reactor's pressure vessel started to climb. At around five a.m. on March 12, radioactive material was discharged outside. Who was in charge at the time?

Shimizu: In my absence, it is, of course, the deputy head of the ERC who acts in my place, so he was in charge.

Reporter: Who's that?

Shimizu: That's Vice President Muto, sitting here.[36]

However, in this decisively critical situation, Muto had flown off to the site of the accident and was not in control at Head Office command.

There was a deep-rooted sense of mistrust between TEPCO and the Kantei. There was no proper communication between them, let alone a relationship of trust. Kan suspected TEPCO's failure to make a swift decision on the venting was because their top two managers were both out of Head Office from the evening of March 11 until noon on March 12, and they were unable to make an important management call.

Why did Takekuro turn up [at the Kantei]? First of all, the top two [in TEPCO] weren't here. They weren't even at [TEPCO's] Head Office until noon on March 12. Was TEPCO reluctant to vent for technical reasons or because the top two weren't there?

Kan continued to harbor this suspicion. He felt that TEPCO as a company, and especially its Head Office, was "more bureaucratic than the bureaucracy, with no one willing to take a risk. That's why they can't make the big decisions."

Kaieda shared the same doubts and distrust. It was only after he had repeatedly warned Takekuro and the other TEPCO representatives in the mezzanine office of the crisis management center, "If you are going to keep on hesitating and not venting, I'll make it an order. Do you hear? An order!" that he switched to an order based on the Act on the Regulation of Nuclear Source Material, Nuclear Fuel Material, and Reactors. He was afraid that, given TEPCO's corporate culture, they would never vent unless ordered to do so.

The depth of the distrust here was not merely a question of whether the top two managers were missing or not.[37] A member of the Kantei staff revealed that he suspected TEPCO of intentionally delaying the venting.

"There was a high risk that workers would suffer radiation exposure if they went ahead with venting. TEPCO didn't want to make such a momentous decision on its own. It wanted to share responsibility with the government. That's probably why they didn't step up on their own, but believed it was a better choice to do it under government orders, as in, 'We humbly await the prime minister's decision.' "[38]

Kan's visit to Fukushima Daiichi was later questioned by the opposition parties as "a fatal mistake in the initial response." His visit to the power plant was blamed for delaying the venting operation.[39]

There was significant worry that Kan's visit had taken up Yoshida's time and obstructed the onsite crisis management. Yoshida himself let slip some critical remarks about Kan's visit:

"It may sound like an excuse, but I was distracted by the prime minister's visit to F1 (Fukushima Daiichi), and wasn't able to give the order to 'vent' for about two hours. At the time, nothing moved except on my command. Since there were no commands being issued, work came to a halt."[40]

According to the daily operational reports for Unit 1 subsequently released by TEPCO, no notes were written on the whiteboard for approximately two and a half hours in the Central Control Room between 6:29 a.m., after Kan had left the Kantei by helicopter, and 9:04 a.m., after he had left the plant and headed to his next stop.[41]

Abetted by rumors that Kan's Fukushima visit was just a performance aimed at distracting national interest from the question of his illegal donations, these criticisms smoldered for a long time. It had also been observed that it was the "political initiative" of the DPJ administration that had brought about excessive meddling in the field, which, in turn, had upset the chain of command. A middle-ranking official at METI said, "It's because they interfere in everything with their 'political initiative' that the lines of authority and responsibility become blurred."[42]

Regarding this point, however, TEPCO stated in their report, "In the process of implementing the containment vessel venting, and given the gravity of releasing radioactive material, in addition to the site superintendent's judgment, we sought the confirmation and approval of the company president as well as contacted the government."[43]

So, while criticizing intervention from the Kantei on the one hand, the report recognizes that TEPCO asked for government engagement as a consequence of the "gravity" of the situation on the other.

Let us return to the "delay in venting." What was the biggest cause of the delay onsite? What was their greatest miscalculation and limitation?

The government investigation commission found that while Yoshida's sense of crisis for Unit 2 was mounting on the night of March 11 because he believed the RCIC cooling system to have failed in Unit 2, he mistakenly thought that the IC was working in Unit 1, and "did not feel an imminent necessity for the containment venting based on his misunderstanding of the operating condition of the IC of Unit 1," thereby demonstrating "the reason for the delay of the containment venting was not of their hesitation but of their misunderstanding of the plant condition at Unit 1."[44]

In other words, the investigation commission believed the decisive error was a misreading of the crux of the crisis; that the delay had been caused by pressing the wrong button.

Another factor was that the mounting levels of radiation inside Unit 1 (RB) were becoming an obstacle to operations. From four to five a.m. on March 12, there was an abnormal jump in radiation levels inside Unit 1 (RB), and it was already becoming difficult to stay on the Unit 1 side of the Central Control Room. When venting Unit 1, they had to confront a deadly environment of 300 millisieverts/hour. Even the U.S. manuals for responding to nuclear terrorism require counter-actors to abstain from taking action if the radiation level in the environment exceeds 100 millisieverts/hour.[45]

Entering the reactor building meant laying your life on the line. The continuing aftershocks also made the job more difficult. The lack of an effective and coordinated plan between onsite and offsite, which would have comprehensively linked the venting operation and resident evacuation, was another serious drawback. A disaster action plan for resident evacuation that assumed the possibility of venting couldn't have been drawn up under a nuclear safety regulatory environment that was beholden to the "safety myth."

Mari Sato later said, "It is because it is awful. By that, I mean venting. You can't just implement venting as you wish. It could become an issue of responsibility for the people at the top. So, that decision couldn't be made simply by Yoshida. I think responsibility wasn't taken."[46]

In the early hours of the morning, it was learned that the evacuation of local residents in Okuma had not been completed, and so it was decided jointly by TEPCO and Fukushima Prefecture that the venting of the reactor containment vessel should wait until the residents had been evacuated.

It was after nine a.m. when Yoshida acknowledged that the evacuation of Okuma residents had been completed. The shift team carried out preparations for implementing the containment venting after that.[47] (Hospital patients in Okuma, however, were still there. See chapter 7.)

"PLEASE! PLEASE STAY HERE!"

3:36 P.M., MARCH 12. The roof of Unit 1 blew off with a thunderous clap. The Central Control Room (Units 1 and 2) shook up and down with a crash. The ceiling shutters and fluorescent lights hung down. White dust covered the room. Right after that, even the dim light of the fluorescent lamp went out and it became pitch-black.

Ah! The containment vessel has exploded!

Is this where I'm going to die?

These were the thoughts running through all the operators' minds. At the time, Izawa was sitting in the duty manager's chair. It felt like they'd been directly hit by a bomb.

I wonder if the control room itself has been damaged.

While thinking that, he was yelling, "Masks! Get your masks on."

On hearing this, everyone checked that their masks were on. Someone instinctively took out a dosimeter and checked the number.

"That's strange. It's not rising."

"Is it all right?"

"The Central Control Room's ceiling isn't built that solidly."

"Quick! Shut the emergency doors so the outside air can't get in."

The hotline to the Anti-Seismic Building was still working.[48]

There had been a tremendous rumbling at the Anti-Seismic Building. The people sitting down slid sideways some 30 centimeters. Voices were raised.

"Is it another quake?"

Suddenly it hit Yoshida, the site superintendent of the Fukushima Daiichi NPS. "I reckon Unit 1 has exploded."

The inside door of the Anti-Seismic Building had been blown out of kilter, which put the double doors out of action. There was panic inside the building. Workers from TEPCO associate companies shouted, "Let us go home." Conversely, people trying to escape into the building started running to and fro, because they couldn't get in. The door was fixed by using a crowbar to put the door back on its rails. At that point, a white substance started floating down from above.

One of the workers outside the turbine building later said, "When I looked up, there was debris all over the sky and it was drifting down."[49]

There was widespread concern among the young operators in the control room, who were now working in complete darkness. One of them was Ryuta Idogawa. He was twenty-seven years old.

Idogawa joined TEPCO eight years prior to this. He was from Futaba-cho. He had just been promoted in July of the previous year. As a member of Team D, he was in the same group as Izawa, and came to the plant in the morning hours of March 11.

When the earthquake hit, Idogawa was at his parents' home in Futaba-cho. His father and mother were both at work. He heard the earth thunder. Sensing that it was dangerous to remain at home, he left his room and watched TV from his car navigation system. The tsunami alert was then announced.

The control room must be going through chaos. I could be of some help if I go, he thought.

He read a summary report on the challenges that workers onsite at Kashiwazaki-Kariwa nuclear power plant went through when the Chuetsu earthquake happened.

I will go no matter what. However, I need to figure out if my parents are all right.

After visiting both parents' offices to confirm that they were not hurt, he went back home.

I need to make sure nothing happens to John.

John was his beagle. Worrying that something might happen while he was gone, Idogawa unleashed him and let him go. After that, he drove to the single workers' dormitory close to Fukushima Daiichi. After stopping by his own room, as he was leaving, he saw some junior workers hanging out.

"I'm going to the office now. Do you guys want to come with me?"

"I will go," one of the workers replied.

Together they drove along the beach, following the road toward the power plant. As soon as they arrived, they were told the tsunami had hit.

"The tsunami came. I could see the bottom of the ocean from where the water had receded."

Idogawa started to become worried about John when he heard this.

Which way did he run? I hope he's doing okay.

From the evening of that day onward, Idogawa started working as the operator for Unit 2. However, one of his colleagues, who was an operator for the main reactor, sat in the operator's seat that day, while Idogawa stuck to measuring the pressure and level of the water.

In the afternoon of the following day, he promptly stood up upon hearing a loud bang from an explosion, followed by the screams of the operators. When he looked at his side, one of the senior operators was fast asleep.

This guy is a bit different, he thought.

At the same time, Idogawa was seized by fear.

I will die here if I don't do anything. I need to get away. After doing the vent, there's not much else I can do here. The reactor is definitely going to melt.

There was nothing much that could be done at that point, and everything they tried failed to work. At this point, everything was up in the air, but Idogawa managed to remain extremely calm. In reality, though, various thoughts on how he could escape were swirling in his mind.

I should let the younger staff evacuate first. First the trainees, and then perhaps we can evacuate after that.

Later, Idogawa confessed: "I was there because there was no way to escape in the first place."

"What's going on here? We're all going to die if we stay here." Idogawa's voice echoed as the impact from the blast continued to carry throughout the room.

The deputy director Mitsuru Komemasu was also there. He was ten years older than Idogawa and had experience working as an operator at the Kashiwazaki-Kariwa nuclear power plant. Idogawa said out loud what was on everyone's mind.

Idogawa-san has courage, Komemasu thought.

A veteran operator, Shizuo Takahashi realized that the younger operators were having these kinds of anxious thoughts. He had been transferred only in the past month to work as an operator for Units 1 and 2 from Units 6 and 7. Takahashi entered the Anti-Seismic Building just before noon on March 12. He later came to the control room with six other deputy managers.

The younger workers don't do anything if you leave them alone, Takahashi realized.

He made the respective roles of each operator clear, stating that younger workers without tasks should evacuate to the Anti-Seismic Building.

"Some of the people here should evacuate . . . at least temporarily. If everyone here dies and we can't do anything else, then the situation will be really hopeless," Takahashi argued.

Izawa remained silent, and so did everyone else for a moment. Then Deputy Manager Masanori Kaneyama (age 43) from the Operation Administration Work Management group stood up and called Izawa's name and directly asked him:

"Izawa-san, does it make sense for us to be here? We can't even operate, and there's nothing else we can do. What's the point in us all remaining here? Surely we can reduce the number of operators remaining?"

Kikuo Otomo raised his voice.

"Even if we leave here, there's no guarantee that we can safely get to the Anti-Seismic Building. Even though there was an explosion, things are all right in here, so we should remain. We also just vented, so the radiation dose outside will be high. There's no way it's safe to go outside now."

"We can measure the radiation dose as we run, and go through areas only with low figures," Kaneyama responded.

Kaneyama held the position of auxiliary machine instructor and was in charge of supervising the young operators who were new to the company. He realized that they had not uttered a word since the explosion and were sitting on the floor right in front of the panel. These were his fellow operators, with whom he had spent much more time than even with his own family. They usually never stopped joking. But now those cheerful operators were all shaking.

It's better to have told Izawa-san directly right here and now, Kaneyama thought, reassuring himself.

Idogawa mentally thanked Kaneyama, thinking, *Kaneyama-san, you're spot on.*

Some of the operators who had remained seated gave a slight nod. There was then a moment of silence. Izawa got up from his seat and walked toward the others.

"We . . ."

Izawa was looking for words, but nothing came out. After taking a deep breath, he could finally speak.

"If we evacuate from here, it means that we're going to abandon this whole local community. The entire world is watching us. That's why I can't leave here. I'm not going to send you anywhere dangerous. If it comes to that, I'll let you evacuate. Please, until then, stay here."

Izawa bowed deeply after saying these words. Otomo and Hirano also stood by Izawa and silently bowed. They were all in their fifties, and the three of them proceeded to bow together to the younger workers. Izawa then spoke again.

"The deputy manager and those junior to him, please move to the Anti-Seismic Building and wait there. Is that clear?"

The operators nodded.

Takahashi was moved by Izawa's words when he said, "the entire world is watching us." "I was impressed by Izawa-san, who was able to say such inspiring things. Izawa-san is calm and never panics. He acts based on what will happen in the future," Takahashi recalled.[50]

Kaneyama moved to the Anti-Seismic Building, leading nearly twenty people. He had left the Central Control Room, apologizing to one of the managers who was going to remain. It was still light outside. The Unit 1 building revealed its devastated appearance. Kaneyama instructed one of the younger operators to take a picture of it and share the information with the power generation group once he reached the Anti-Seismic Building. For ten minutes or so, everyone walked quickly up the slope as if they were racing.

"MADARAME-SAN, WHAT'S THAT?"

At the time, Prime Minister Naoto Kan was briefing the leaders of the opposition parties in the fourth-floor conference room of the Kantei. After enacting the budget and related laws for the current fiscal year by the end of March, the governing party urgently wanted to draw up a supplementary budget for the following fiscal year. In response, the opposition parties insisted that the ordinary parliamentary session be temporarily suspended and a supplementary budget drawn up for the current fiscal year.

Kan also briefed them, at the same meeting, about his visit that morning to Fukushima Daiichi NPS. Kan was extremely confident that there would be no hydrogen explosion. This was because he clearly remembered the words of Haruki Madarame, chairman of the Nuclear Safety Commission, when they had spoken during the helicopter flight to Fukushima Daiichi.

"The reactor at Unit 2 is equipped with RCIC, but Unit 1 has an IC cooling system, doesn't it? Why is that? Is it because its output is different?"

"What happens in the core when the cladding pipes and the water react?"

"That reaction creates hydrogen."

"Well, if you release hydrogen, won't that lead to a hydrogen explosion?"

"No, while hydrogen is being created in the pressure vessel, it's released first to the containment chamber. Since it's then all converted to vapor, the hydrogen doesn't explode, because there's no oxygen. If it's vented out the top of the stack, it will burn there, but there won't be a hydrogen explosion."

Madarame stated this unequivocally. When Kan got back to Tokyo, he went around all the secretaries, telling them, "There won't be a hydrogen explosion." He also displayed his "grasp" of nuclear power in front of the opposition party leaders.[51]

After four p.m., Kan was back in his office, following the meeting with the opposition leaders. As soon as he returned, Tetsuro Ito, deputy chief cabinet secretary for crisis management, came up from the crisis management center in the basement.

"There's been an explosion at Fukushima Daiichi. There's smoke coming out."

Five minutes after the explosion, a police officer, who just happened to be passing by, filed an eyewitness account, stating, "There was a boom, and then I saw white smoke coming out of Unit 1."

Kan asked Madarame, "What's the white smoke?"

"It's probably a fire. Something volatile is burning, most likely."

Ichiro Takekuro, the TEPCO fellow assigned to the Kantei, was called in and asked about it, but he merely replied, "I haven't heard anything. I'll call Head Office."

Takekuro left the office and phoned TEPCO Head Office.

"They say they haven't heard anything."

Just as he returned to make this report, Manabu Terada, special adviser to the prime minister, opened the door and came rushing into the room.

"Prime minister, there's been an explosion at the Unit 1 (RB). Please turn the television on right away."

Terada grabbed the remote control and changed the television channel. NTV was broadcasting a news bulletin.

"I am reporting from Fukushima. We have news on the nuclear power plant. What you are seeing is an image of Fukushima Daiichi Nuclear Power Station at approximately 3:36 p.m. What we believe to be water vapor is billowing out from Fukushima Daiichi. It seems to be coming from the vicinity of Unit 1."

The Unit 1 (RB) had been blown to smithereens, and white smoke was pouring out into the sky. Madarame, his head in his hands and simultaneously rubbing his forehead on the table, groaned, "Oh, no." Kan raised his voice.

"What's this? It's an explosion, isn't it?"

Takekuro responded, "Yes, it's an explosion."

Trying to remain calm, Kan said, "Madarame-san, what is that?"

Madarame was at a loss for words. His mind was spinning round and round.

"Isn't that a hydrogen explosion? Didn't you say that there wouldn't be a hydrogen explosion?"

Fukuyama muttered, "Isn't that an explosion like the one at Chernobyl? Isn't the same thing happening that happened at Chernobyl?"

Not answering Fukuyama directly, Madarame finally managed to squeeze out a response. "What I said only referred to the containment vessel."

What he was trying to say was that he had only been talking about the possibility of an explosion in the containment vessel, and had never in his wildest dreams imagined a hydrogen explosion in the building. Kan issued a strong directive to his secretary.

"The locals will have immediately realized what happened with an explosion like that. Why hasn't it been reported? Get me the information now!"

Just as Madarame, Takekuro was unable to answer. Takekuro later confessed, "All sorts of possibilities were going through my mind, like was it the hydrogen used to cool the turbines, but my hair was standing on end."

Kan then opened the door to the adjoining reception room and shouted to Kaieda.

"Unit 1 has exploded. What's going on?!"

Kaieda and the others at the time were discussing pumping in seawater and did not have the television on.[52]

Koichiro Genba, minister for national policy, just happened to be in the mezzanine office in the basement. The television was broadcasting images of the explosion. He questioned the TEPCO liaison official watching with him, but he did not know. The official called TEPCO Head Office, but they did not know, either. Stuck for an answer, he said, "I guess an aftershock has shaken loose all the dust that has collected on the roof after the quake."[53]

The only information the government had was the images broadcast by NTV. The images had been taken by their station affiliate, Fukushima Central TV (FCT).

After the JCO Tokaimura criticality nuclear accident in 1999, FCT had set up an SD camera in the mountains of Tomioka, seventeen kilometers from Fukushima Daiichi Nuclear Power Station. It had continually been filming Fukushima Daiichi and Daini plants since then, without a day's—or a single second's—break. This was the camera that had captured the moment. During this time, the images had been uploaded to Internet sites, including the BBC, and the moment of the explosion had spread widely in the blink of an eye.

But what did the image mean?

After broadcasting the first images, NTV brought Masanori Aritomi, director of the Research Laboratory for Nuclear Reactors (RLNR) at the Tokyo Institute of Technology (and Nuclear Safety Commission advisory board member), into the studio and had him comment.

> *Announcer:* You've just seen the footage of the explosion-like . . . smoke-like . . .
> *Aritomi:* They've used a blast valve . . . There was vapor escaping in that footage, wasn't there?
> *Announcer:* You're saying they have intentionally used a blast valve, right?
> *Aritomi:* Yes, I think it's intentional.[54]

Had the reactor exploded? Or was it something else? That was the point.

The only information they had was the image of the explosion on the TV. Going by that video footage, the news reported that "there was no top on the reactor building."

Apart from this, TEPCO failed to send a single item of definitive information to either NISA or the Kantei. They sent nothing on what had happened. They did, however, try fervently to convey what hadn't happened.

"At 17:34, we have a request from TEPCO to explain to the state and the people that there has not been a nuclear explosion."

That was what was written in an internal NISA memo (March 12, 2011, 5:34 p.m.).[55]

#EDANO_GET_SOME_SLEEP

It was getting on to two hours after the explosion. Kan had called Chief Cabinet Secretary Edano, Kaieda, Hosono, Fukuyama, and Ito into his office, and was discussing the evacuation area with them. Madarame and Kukita, deputy chair of the Nuclear Safety Commission, joined them. Kan fired off questions in rapid succession.

"What's going to happen next? What's going to blow next?"

"What's happening inside the reactor?"

"Is it okay to evacuate people?"

Madarame explained falteringly. Everyone was irritated. Kan pressed him.

"How large an area? What should we do?"

Chief Cabinet Secretary Edano was at his wits' end. How should he explain the explosion to the nation in his press conference? The Internet was starting to be flooded with posts about "atomic rain falling." Edano's staff had already considered saying something to the effect that "people should not be fooled by vicious rumors" in the press conference, but decided against it, as "any such announcement could possibly add to the panic."

While "atomic rain falling" was, at best, a hoax, in less than an hour after the explosion, the radiation dose at the monitoring post in front of the main gate at Fukushima Daiichi NPS recorded 1,015 microsieverts/hour (1.015 millisieverts).[56]

However, this information didn't reach Edano. The only information Edano had at hand was the TEPCO press release material that "there was a loud noise in the vicinity of Unit 1 and white smoke had risen" and "two TEPCO workers and two associate workers involved in plant safety operations had been injured," as well as a police report that "an explosion was heard and smoke had been spotted."

But the radiation level measured afterward showed no increase. Kan, Edano, and Fukuyama discussed the question. Fukuyama asked Edano, "How about postponing the press conference a bit until you have more detailed information?"

They had no information whatsoever. They were up to their necks in unknowns. Giving a press conference would be like admitting to the nation that "the government didn't know." Wouldn't that only heighten people's lack of trust in the government?

"Mmm."

After deliberating for a time, Edano categorically stated, "No, let's do it. There's been a lot of footage broadcast. If we push the conference back, people will wonder, 'What is the government doing, is it hiding something?' It'll only make people more nervous. Let's do the press conference as planned."

Kan backed Edano up, saying, "Yes, go ahead."

Edano went ahead with the press conference "empty-handed."[57]

5:47 P.M. Chief cabinet secretary press conference. Prime minister's office press room.

"As has already been reported by the media, some kind of an explosive event has been reported at Fukushima Daiichi Nuclear Power Station, but it hasn't been verified as of yet that it was the reactor itself."

"Some kind of an explosive event" was an expression that had come to Edano on the spur of the moment in desperation.

At 8:40 p.m., Edano gave a second press conference.

"It has been verified that the explosion collapsed the wall of the building, it was not an explosion in the containment vessel. The reason for the explosion was vapor arising from water in the containment vessel, which was running out, dropping down. The vapor entered the space between the containment vessel and the outer housing, and in the process turned into hydrogen, which, when mixed with oxygen, led to the explosion."

In other words, it was acknowledged that the "explosive event" was a "hydrogen explosion." Edano, however, added the following point.

"Even though the Unit 1 (RB) is no longer standing, the containment vessel is still sound. External monitors, in fact, show a drop in [radioactive] exposure, so cooling of the core is ongoing."

AROUND NINE P.M. ON MARCH 12. Keisuke Sadamori, prime ministerial secretary, was called in by Edano. Sadamori was an ex-METI man.

"Is it true that this kind of thing is circulating?"

With a fierce look on his face, Edano showed him some photos. National news was broadcasting photos of the reactor building after the explosion, which were used by the TEPCO's Fukushima office to explain the situation to Fukushima Prefecture. He hadn't known that TEPCO had taken these photos, nor had he received any reports from TEPCO. Edano told Sadamori, "Has the Kantei received any photos from TEPCO? Check the facts out."

Edano called TEPCO president, Masataka Shimizu, on the spot.

"What on earth is going on at your company?"[58]

10:05 P.M., MARCH 12. The fourth Nuclear Emergency Response Headquarters meeting. Kaieda reported.

"I have received a report from TEPCO that radiation levels of over 500 microsieverts/hour (0.5 millisieverts) have been measured by a monitoring car on the outskirts of the plant."

Genba explained the need to "assume the worst-case scenario." Not answering this directly, Kan said, "Is it possible that it will be Chernobyl-style? Will there be a meltdown, like Three Mile Island?"[59]

THE FOLLOWING DAY, MARCH 13, SUNDAY. Shimizu visited the Kantei at around two p.m. He met Edano in his office and explained the situation with the explosion at Unit 1. He asked cautiously, "May I also pay my respects to the prime minister?"

Edano took him to the prime minister's office and introduced him to Kan. Edano thought he was going to explain about the Unit 1 explosion, but Shimizu began by explaining the rolling blackouts that were to start the following day. And when he had finished, he made as if to stand up. Kan had listened to him in silence, but indicated to Shimizu to hold his horses and said, "Is that all you have to say?"

"TEPCO hasn't shown up at all since the explosion. Don't you think there's something wrong with your communication channels?"

At the sixth meeting of NERHQ, at 9:35 p.m. on March 13, Kan stated the following:

"Unfortunately, the situation at the Fukushima nuclear plants remains alarming. This earthquake, tsunami, and nuclear emergency are the greatest crisis our country has faced since World War II."[60]

With the hydrogen explosion at Unit 1, Kan's opinion of Madarame plummeted. Hardly any of the nuclear experts, however, foresaw a hydrogen explosion in the reactor building. It wasn't just Madarame who failed to see it coming.[61]

Around this time, support for Edano appeared from an unlikely quarter. Bloggers suddenly started posting: "Get some sleep, Edano!" "Hang in there, Edano!"

On March 13, three young employees of the cabinet public relations office split into three eight-hour shifts and started a round-the-clock disaster Twitter account (@Kantei_saigai = @Kantei_disaster). It consisted mainly of links to videos of the press conferences at the Kantei, messages from the prime minister and ministers, and an explanation of radioactive exposure ("What's a microsievert?") by Deputy Chief Cabinet Secretary Tetsuro Fukuyama.

The support for Edano, however, was triggered by Internet users who had seen Edano's press conferences live on TV and who had created the hashtag #edano_nero (#edano_get_some_sleep).

Edano had been giving press conferences every day, and sometimes several times a day, since March 11. He had remained cool, chosen his words well, and answered the reporters' questions articulately. Still in his mid-forties, he was young, had a good complexion, and his little round body was clad in disaster gear. His performance was popular with young people. He received messages of encouragement from women in their twenties and thirties.

The #edano_get_some_sleep call was encouragement from his supporters saying he was doing a great job, to keep it up, but to find some time to catch forty winks. Edano himself had no time to browse the Web. He just heard about it from the head of PR's secretary.[62]

A short time after #edano_get_some_sleep, someone started a #kan_okiro (#Kan_wake_up) hashtag. This severely lambasted Kan. The Kantei staffers were scared stiff about Edano—or, perish the thought, Kan—finding out.[63]

How difficult was it to communicate with the people in a time of crisis? Edano was soon to find that out the hard way.

It was the job of the chief cabinet secretary, with the exception of prime ministerial press conferences, to give two official cabinet press conferences each day, one in the morning and one in the afternoon, to the Kantei press corps. Each ministry had its own press corps and press conferences, and briefing sessions were virtually a daily occurrence there as well. The emergence of the Internet and Twitter rocked the foundations of the existing government monopoly on information and official assessments and positions.

In 2010, 78 percent of Japan's population was using the Internet. The Internet was still relatively new during the 1995 Hanshin-Awaji earthquake. It had taken off rapidly in the fall of that year, but in Japan's case, it was that large-scale earthquake that accelerated the spread of the Web. In the Great Eastern Earthquake, the Web was the main media for checking on friends' and family's safety.

The Web also played a huge role in the Fukushima nuclear emergency. Tying up with global information and assessments, and using an open information space, an infinite number of information communities emerged on the scene.

Aware that people were becoming increasingly anxious about rising levels of exposure and resident evacuation, Edano started frequently using the phrase, "There will be no immediate impact on health." And this claim was not wrong. Nevertheless, even if it was a fact that there would be no "immediate" impact, what about the long-term? How could people remain at ease if there was going to be an impact on their health at some point? He needed to cover both bases in his explanations, but only covered one. That was what made people anxious.

His remark at that time that "there will be no immediate impact on health" was criticized over and again in the National Diet. In response, Edano defended himself, saying, "In the first two weeks after March 11, I gave a total of thirty-nine press conferences, and I said there would be no immediate impact on health or life in seven of those" (House of Representatives Defense Budget Committee, November 8, 2011).

This was perceived as though he was trying to deny his statements on the accident, which reduced his popularity. One year after the appearance of #edano_get_some_sleep, tweets started expressing disappointment.

"At the time, everyone tweeted #edano_get_some_sleep out of sympathy for him trying to deal with the situation all through the night. A year later, he's pushing to reopen the Oi Nuclear Station. I feel like tweeting 'stop taking such stupid actions' and #edano_stay_asleep."[64]

FOUR

Pumping in Seawater

WE WENT DOWN ON OUR KNEES

After five p.m. on March 11, Yoshida instructed: "Look into water injection methods for the nuclear reactors using fire extinguishing lines and/or fire engines" for Units 1 and 2. The first referred to a firefighting line using a diesel-driven fire pump. The other referred to injecting water into the nuclear reactor using fire engines.

After the accident at Kashiwazaki-Kariwa in 2007, TEPCO was keenly aware of the need for alternative water injection using fire engines at times of disaster. They had, therefore, designed fire-extinguishing equipment inside the reactor, which could be used even for nuclear reactor cooling in emergencies via appropriately extended tips and deployed fire engines at every nuclear power plant, three being allocated to the Fukushima Daiichi Nuclear Power Plant.

However, due to the tsunami, the fire pumps in the turbine building could hardly be used. Consequently, there was no choice but to inject water from fire engines outside into the water inlet on the outer wall of the turbine building, to cool the nuclear reactor.

Staff checked the status of the reactor building twice, and were able to ascertain that the fire extinguishing pump in the basement pump room was working. All they had to do now was to get water in from outside.

6:30 P.M. The team of Ikuo Izawa, duty manager of Fukushima Daiichi's Central Control Room, started work on creating a line to put water from the pump into the reactor. There was a containment vessel outside the reactor and a shielding concrete wall of about two meters on the outer side of the containment vessel. Several pipes ran through it. They had to build a line connecting the fire-extinguishing pump to the piping. To that end, there were five valves that had to be opened. And they had to be opened by hand.

It was reported at around eight p.m. that the valves were open. An hour later, after nine p.m., the radiation dose at Unit 1 started rising. At 11:05 p.m., Yoshida declared Unit 1 (RB) "off limits." However, the water injection line through the fire pump had barely been secured just prior to that.[1]

Laying down a water injection line and injecting water into the reactor, however, were quite different operations. TEPCO was to learn immediately how challenging a task pumping water in was.

On the frontline at Fukushima Daiichi Nuclear Power Plant, it was the Disaster Prevention Group that was responsible for that. One of them was forty-nine-year-old Mari Sato. During the crisis, Sato would do all kinds of work, including emergency broadcasting, organizing workers' meals, refueling fuel vehicles, and so on.

Sato was born in Fukushima City. Originally, she had wanted to be a kindergarten teacher, but could not find a job and somehow ended up working at TEPCO's Hirono Thermal Power Station. It was 1981. She worked there for nearly twenty years, and later was transferred to Fukushima Daini and then Fukushima Daiichi.

She had a son and daughter in college. Her husband came back to Hirono after retiring, so they built a house there, where they lived together. The children had just been home on their spring break.

Let us rewind the clock a little.

When the earthquake occurred, Sato was on the second floor of the office building. The shaking from the earthquake sent her mobile phone flying off the gray steel desk. She tried to find it, but the tremor was so strong she was unable to get to her feet quickly. It must have slipped into a crack somewhere. She couldn't see it.

Sato was in charge of disaster prevention at the Fukushima Daiichi Nuclear Power Plant. She had to make an in-house announcement. There was no time to look for her phone. She went to the broadcasting equipment on the same second floor, in a stagger among the shaking. The broadcasting equipment had already been disconnected and was out of use. All of the ceiling panels had fallen down and were completely white with dust. The tremors were still intense and the whiteboards fell down one after another.

With a megaphone in hand, she went around the inside of the office building and called out the evacuation assembly point. Then she left the courtyard, did a roll call for the members of each team, and evacuated close to a thousand employees to the front of the office building.

Gray clouds hung low. Even at midday, the temperature didn't reach 10 degrees Celsius. Although it was finally nearing spring, it was as chilly as if it had reverted to winter.

After that, Sato went to the Emergency Response Center on the second floor of the Anti-Seismic Building. Approximately 350 personnel who were a part of the emergency setup had gathered. Everyone there was wearing different-colored bibs with the name of their section. Sato put on the Disaster Prevention Group's bib.

What were they to do with the remaining nearly seven hundred temporary workers and workers from affiliated companies? Sato asked Site Superintendent Yoshida, "What shall we do? Should I let them in?"

"Let them in."

Both the first and second floors of the Anti-Seismic Building were flooded with people.

TEPCO had two fire engines at Fukushima Daiichi and had a firefighting team organized into three groups of nine people on standby around the clock.

Takeyuki Inagaki, head of the recovery team, was in charge. Including Hiroyuki Ogawa, there were four chiefs of the firefighting teams under Inagaki. Then came Sato's boss, the group manager; then Sato. Workers from each department were concurrently registered as firefighters. However, since they all had full-time jobs, they were "kind of a voluntary force," according to Ogawa.

Despite having drilled water discharge using fire hydrants, the firefighters did not have the ability or technical knowledge to operate fire engines, start the fire pumps, and inject water by themselves—nor did they have any training. As a matter of fact, firefighting activity at the Fukushima Daiichi premises was outsourced to Nanmei Kosan, a TEPCO subcontractor, and the Japan Nuclear Security System (JNSS), who were professional firefighters.

Nanmei Kosan had an office near the main gate of the Fukushima Daiichi Nuclear Power Plant. It had two fire engines and was organized into fire brigades of three teams with nine people on a twenty-four-hour system. Nevertheless, the firefighting activities of these companies were premised on ordinary fires. It was not stipulated in their contracts that they were to conduct alternative water injection operations for the nuclear reactors in the event of a natural disaster.

The tsunami and earthquake warnings all rang constantly even after the first big shake. Each time, the fire brigade went outside and checked the situation at various sites.

"Hey, someone's up on the roof!"

They rescued workers left behind on the roof of the building.

"What's that, a fire?"

It looked like smoke was rising, but on closer inspection, a fire hydrant was broken and water was spurting out. Had a small oil tank broken down? There was a very strong smell of oil spreading on the road.

When the fire brigade came back, their boots were covered in mud. Oil was stuck to them. In the evening, the sky suddenly grew dark. Everything was enveloped in a heavy, gray cloud. Driving snow started to fall.

At two a.m. on March 12, the station ERC asked Nanmei Kosan employees, who were standing by, if they "could check the filling port on the Unit
1 turbine building and pump water in from the fire engines?" The Nanmei
Kosan people complied.

The TEPCO firefighters had made the first-floor overnight duty room
into a "firefighting zone." Workers from Nanmei Kosan were also gathered
there. But where was the water supply inlet on the Unit 1 turbine building?
Nanmei Kosan asked the question, but the ERC didn't know its location.
Someone from the power generation team took the Nanmei Kosan workers
and went to the site, but they couldn't find the water inlet. In that area,
there was a pile of rubble from the tsunami, and it couldn't be approached
easily. Therefore, they returned to the Anti-Seismic Building, once again
confirmed the position on the plans, went to the work site with workers
who knew the place, and found the water inlet.

However, the task of injecting water by fire engines was not covered by
TEPCO's outsourcing contract, as mentioned above. Consequently, asking
them to do this was equivalent to "fraudulent outsourcing."

Nanmei Kosan showed its disapproval. There was something they just
could not understand. The TEPCO firefighters, who, by rights, should have
been taking the initiative, were not going out into the field, but were holed
up in the Anti-Seismic Building and telling them to do this and that. What
was that all about?

Eventually, even when they found the filling port, the TEPCO fire brigade refused to go with them, saying they didn't know where the water inlet
was, and although, in the end, someone from the power generation team
accompanied them, he wasn't very useful. Still, Sato and the others somehow managed to persuade the reluctant Nanmei Kosan workers.

At four a.m. on March 12, employees from Nanmei Kosan started using
fire engines to inject water into the nuclear reactor. However, around 4:20
a.m., the radiation dose near the turbine building of Unit 1 spiked.

"The dose has increased so much, it's impossible."

Nanmei Kosan suspended the water injection operation, and the staff
carrying out the work returned to the Anti-Seismic Building. Nanmei
Kosan had strict dose controls in place so that employees did not exceed 20
millisieverts per year or 100 millisieverts over five years. Now, just going to
the work site once meant a dose of 10–20 millisieverts. They said repeatedly, "Headquarters has told us strictly not to go to the site several times,
so we can't go."

There was still that other thing continuing to gnaw at their hearts. Why
was it not TEPCO employees but Nanmei Kosan employees who had to go
out, risking death from a high radiation dose?

"We can't pump in water from the fire engines anymore."

But Sato and the others were desperate, too.

"No, this time our firefighters will go with you. Can't you go together with them? Please."

"We'll take over if you teach us how the fire engine's pumps uptake water and the method to adjust the pressure of the water supply."

"We're begging you. You can stay behind in the car, and we'll go outside. Can't you give us someone, just one person will do, to give instructions?"

In the end, the Nanmei Kosan side gave in. At around five a.m., a total of four people—Hiroyuki Ogawa, head of the TEPCO firefighters; two other TEPCO staff members; and one Nanmei Kosan worker—headed toward the Unit 1 Turbine Building in a fire engine.

They finally managed to get the pumping fully operational by 5:46 a.m. More than fourteen hours had passed since the loss of AC power.[2]

At 3:36 p.m. on March 12, the Unit 1 building exploded. Four TEPCO employees and two Nanmei Kosan workers involved in the water injection were injured. Hiroyuki Ogawa also broke his left hand and was forced to temporarily step aside.

By this time, every department had called back its registered firefighters, one by one, until there were almost no firefighters left. Sato's boss had been unable to gather personnel for water pumping operations. He said, almost apologetically, to Sato and one other person who happened to be there just at that time, "So, will you work with me?" Sato had no choice but to answer, "You're saying 'work with me' when there's just us three here! There's nothing else I can do but try."

The most urgent task at the time was refueling the fire engine. They had the fire engines hooked up for the water injection, but the fire engines' fuel had run out time and time again. Nanmei Kosan refused to do the job. The fact that some of their workers had been injured in the Unit 1 explosion was making people in the field nervous. Nanmei Kosan's CEO stubbornly refused to give the go-ahead.

"Nope, we can't go. Our CEO is also saying no."

Radiation levels had increased after the explosion at Unit 1. There were noticeably more people wearing Tyvek suits inside the Anti-Seismic Building as well. The doors to the Anti-Seismic Building had been warped by the Unit 1 explosion. They were double doors, normally automatic, with no handles. The automatic switch was turned off, and they were opened and closed manually by radiation management workers.

This is no good. There's a gaping crack.

After the decision to build an anti-seismic building had been made, upper management had also asked Sato, who was in charge of disaster prevention, if she had any requests for the building.

"I want you to make it bigger, more like a fortress."

That was what she wrote, but her report was treated with contempt. The official position was, "It has to be built quickly, compact, and at a low cost."

Late at night on March 13, Sato was begging the Nanmei Kosan chief firefighter and his workers for help. Unit 3 was in a critical state. The refueling work had been delayed and no progress was being made with the water injection. Even Yoshida didn't hide his anger, saying, "We decided to refuel every few hours."[3]

Sato was desperate. At that time, the disaster prevention and safety manager was also coming down from the second floor, and they came together and appealed to the chief firefighter, who was sitting on the floor. When Sato approached the chief, he told her, "Don't come near me . . . Sato-san, I'm sorry, but please don't come here again."

She knew many of the Nanmei Kosan workers there. However, there were also a few she had never met before. They looked like a kind of backup squad. They surrounded Sato. Their eyes were bloodshot. In the blink of an eye, Sato fell to her knees. On seeing that, the disaster prevention and safety manager also went down on his knees.

Sato was already wearing a Tyvek suit covered in packing tape, as well as a full-face mask. From inside her mask, Sato pleaded.

"Things have reached this state because of our lack of competence. I'm so sorry for making trouble for Nanmei Kosan. I have one favor to ask. Please go with me. I'll remember how to refuel, so please show me how."

Sato repeated this, but the chief turned away, saying, "No, we can't go."

They were enveloped by silence. Did they stay on their knees for about ten minutes? Nanmei Kosan's deputy chief firefighter mumbled, "Boss, I'll go and show them how to do it."

It was a man Sato had worked with many times before.

Sato took stable iodine, which suddenly made her stomach hurt, and she had to rest for a while. The Tyvek was sticky, and it was hard to move.

After doing refueling work like this for about three hours at several places, Sato and the deputy chief returned to the Anti-Seismic Building. If the refueling wasn't carried out continuously, water injection operations would be interrupted. They learned it the hard way.

It was the firefighting team that was responsible for water injection, but the water pumping couldn't be kept up unless refueling took place. Refueling may have been the job of a different team, but now wasn't the time to say such a thing. Something had to be done quickly . . .

When she came back to the station, Sato made that appeal to her team manager. His reply was unexpected.

"Sticking your nose in . . ."

He said it was "sticking your nose in." It's a hellish scene, and we have no one. No one would go, even when we begged on our knees. There was only myself to go. How dare he say "sticking your nose in"!

Sato felt like crying, but fought back the tears.[4]

"IS THERE NO POSSIBILITY OF RECRITICALITY?"

Pumping water into the nuclear reactors is only a feasible strategy if there is an abundant water supply. However, their source of fresh water started to run dry before their eyes. Since they had no alternative source of water, there was nothing to do but pump in seawater.

Around noon on March 12, Yoshida decided on injecting seawater into Unit 1, and instructed the station ERC and the in-house firefighting team to look into a seawater injection line.

Just before three p.m., the water in the fire protection tank dried up completely.[5]

After three p.m., TEPCO reported to NISA their plan to "inject seawater."

Although they spoke of seawater injection, they did not mean direct intake from the sea. The water source they would use was from the tsunami, which had flowed into the backwash valve pit that acts as the fire protection water tank in the powerplant.

They may have had a plan, but they were slow to implement it. METI Minister Kaieda started hinting at "orders" again.

"This company doesn't do anything unless it's ordered to, just like with the vent."

Kaieda told his secretary, "Both the government and TEPCO have to be responsible for injecting seawater. If they drag their heels, I'll order them to do it."[6]

3:20 P.M. TEPCO sent a fax to NISA, reporting their plan to "inject seawater," and started preparing at 3:30 p.m. It was immediately after this that the explosion in Unit 1 took place. The walls on the fifth floor of the reactor building were completely blown away, baring the steel frame.

Three TEPCO employees and two Nanmei Kosan employees working at the site were injured. The TEPCO employees in charge of the relief operation had to hurry to help and transport the injured. Those remaining fled to the Anti-Seismic Building.[7]

There was radioactive debris scattered all over, including the building's steel cladding, and onsite radiation was mounting. The operational environment took an immediate turn for the worse.

4:27 P.M. Yoshida reported to the government an article 15.1 event (an abnormal increase in radiation near the station perimeters) under the Act on Special Measures Concerning Nuclear Emergency Preparedness.

The firefighting hoses on the fire engines they had readied for injecting seawater into Unit 1 were damaged. After cleaning away the debris, they were forced to lay a new hose over hundreds of meters from the backwash valve pit in front of Unit 3 (RB) to the filling port of Unit 1 (RB). Once again, it was the Nanmei Kosan employees who were drafted for the job.

At 5:55 p.m., Kaieda issued the command to inject seawater in accordance with paragraph 3, article 64 of the Act on the Regulation of Nuclear Source Material, Nuclear Fuel Material, and Reactors. After turning to Takekuro and telling him, "The act requires the minister to convey the command to the company president, but I order him via you," Kaieda instructed Hiraoka to "draft up the necessary papers." (NISA released the papers after eight p.m.)[8]

AROUND SIX P.M. The prime minister's office at the Kantei.

Kan was holding a meeting on injecting seawater. Kaieda, Hosono, Madarame, and Takekuro were in attendance.

Kaieda was thinking of reporting that he had just issued the command to inject seawater according to the act, but Kan started talking before he could do so. He made two points.

One was, "There's been a hydrogen explosion. You have to ascertain whether the pipes are still working or not."

The other was, "Is there no possibility of recriticality? If there is, what countermeasures need to be taken?"

Criticality is the state where uranium or plutonium triggers a chain reaction. If these materials over and above a certain amount are placed in a single location, there is an extreme danger that they will suddenly trigger a chain reaction of nuclear fission and start emitting radiation and heat.

Japan had experienced criticality with the JOC Tokaimura accident in 1999. At the time, this was ranked as level 4 (accident with local consequences) on the international nuclear events scale. The JOC accident was still fresh in people's minds. It wasn't just Kan who was worried about criticality. Reports of "no neutrons" were being filed almost daily from the field to TEPCO Head Office via videoconference.

Takekuro's response to the question about the pipes was, "They have confirmed that the pump is still working. But they haven't confirmed the pipes yet."

Regarding the danger of criticality, Hiraoka replied, "The danger of criticality will not increase."

Takekuro was of the same opinion, commenting, "Reaching criticality is a difficult trick, artistically. Criticality takes place in the most delicate circumstances, and there is no way that could happen if you pump in seawater with all its impurities."

Kan glanced in Madarame's direction. Madarame was less emphatic.
"If you say so, then NISA . . ."
"Use your own judgment! There's no way it can happen, right?"
"No, it may happen."
"Which is it?!"
"I don't think it likely, but I can't say impossible."
Madarame's voice was almost a whisper.
Hosono was taken aback by the words "can't say impossible."
So, there's a possibility of recriticality.
Kan was frustrated by Madarame's vagueness.
"Wasn't it you who said there wouldn't be a hydrogen explosion?"
Some of the people in the room got the feeling that "Kan's not going to listen to Madarame anymore." Even so, Madarame pleaded, close to tears, "In any event, we have to get water in there now."
"Let's flood the reactor with seawater."
Madarame insisted on injecting seawater.[9]
The question was, however, that even if pumping in seawater was inevitable, were people on the ground at Fukushima Daiichi able to make the necessary preparations?
Takekuro stated that it was likely the firefighting hoses had been damaged by the hydrogen blast and that it would probably take one to two hours to replace them.
The reason why Kan was so fixated on the question of recriticality was because it related to the other item on the agenda—namely, expanding the evacuation zone. If recriticality was to take place, there was the problem that a ten-kilometer evacuation radius would no longer be sufficient, and they would have to order the evacuation of local residents from a twenty-kilometer radius. No objections were raised.
Kan also asked, "Won't the salt have an adverse impact if you pump in seawater?" adding, "Check out the technical aspects thoroughly." The meeting closed, to reconvene in two hours to make a decision.
During the meeting, Takekuro had borrowed the prime minister's secretary's landline in the waiting room to phone TEPCO Head Office.
"Muto, please decide on the company's course of action."
"Please hurry with an organizational decision."
Apparently, it was TEPCO Vice President Sakae Muto on the other end of the line. Takekuro badgered him over and over again. There was a growing distrust of TEPCO. Even staff members at the Nuclear Safety Commission were entertaining doubts about TEPCO's seemingly endless inability to decide whether they were going to inject seawater or not.
"Is TEPCO hesitating about pumping in seawater? If that's the case, it's probably because they're worried they won't be able to use the reactor again."

"A single reactor costs between 300 and 400 billion yen. Is that what's holding them back?"

"Even if the Unit 1 explosion was unavoidable, are they trying to avoid having to pump seawater into Units 2 and 3?"[10]

"WE'LL STOP IT TEMPORARILY!"

After the discussion in the prime minister's office was temporarily halted, Tadao Yanase, head of the General Affairs Division at METI, decided he would sort out the "topics that interested the prime minister" and set about doing so in the prime minister's reception room, separating them into issues associated with TEPCO, NISA, and NSC. The issues were:

- Did they have the pumps to inject the seawater?

- Were there any fractures in the filling pipes?

- What was to be made of the salt damage that would occur with seawater injection?

- Could they still control the nuclear reactor after seawater had been pumped in? (Would recriticality occur or not?)

Yanase drew up a memo sorting out the issues, returned to the waiting room on the fifth floor, and handed it to the NISA and NSC officials, as well as the TEPCO liaison, who were standing by. He did the rounds, warning them, "When the meeting reconvenes, please state your thoughts clearly. We can't postpone our decision again."

When he spoke with Madarame, Madarame said, "The prime minister doesn't trust anything I say, so it would just be counterproductive. Get Kukita-san to speak."

Since NISA said Kan would go on the attack if they sent Terasaka, they hurriedly requested both Hiraoka and Hisanori Nei, deputy director general, to attend. Hiraoka noted down in the margin of the memo Yanase had handed to him the points NISA needed to make.

It was a setup of "who should say what" when the meeting reconvened. Hiraoka thought to himself, "A rehearsal, huh?"[11]

Around seven p.m., Takekuro returned to the mezzanine office in the crisis management center and placed a direct call via mobile phone to Yoshida. Yoshida answered the landline phone next to his desk when it rang.

Takekuro jumped right in.

"Hey, what's happening with the seawater?"

"We're doing it."

Takekuro was flabbergasted.

"What? Are you already doing it? Stop it!"

"Why?"

Yoshida had already ordered the seawater injection. He couldn't very well put the water they'd already pumped out back into the hose. Takekuro was mad when Yoshida insisted that they couldn't stop it now.

"Shut up and listen. The Kantei's vacillating!"

"What on earth are you saying?"

Yoshida hung up, thinking it was pointless to listen anymore. He had no illusions. "The chain of command is a total mess. It's hopeless. I'll just have to follow my own judgment."

He felt what Takekuro was saying was inexplicable. Here they were, having worked so hard after the hydrogen explosion to get ready to pump water in, and if they stopped now, the situation inside the reactor would rapidly deteriorate.

Yoshida had been appealing in the videoconferences for the need to inject seawater as soon as possible. He had conveyed that to TEPCO Vice President Sakae Muto, who was at the offsite center. Head Office and Muto, however, were both cautious.

"As long as we don't have the prime minister's permission, we have no choice but to cease for the moment."

Head Office kept repeating that. As for Takekuro, he was struck with anxiety after he had called Yoshida.

"There's nothing to do but to get the president to directly persuade Yoshida."

Takekuro called Shimizu.

"We still don't have the prime minister's formal go-ahead. I think we should stop. Please speak to Site Superintendent Yoshida and make him stop."

Takekuro was worried that "the onsite team going ahead when an explanation to the prime minister was still in progress would create future obstacles." Shimizu rang Yoshida and requested he halt the pumping operation. Yoshida countered.

"We've already started, you know. Didn't I send a fax at four o'clock?"

Shimizu replied, "You can't do it yet. We don't have government approval. You'll just have to stop until we get it. Since it's the wish of the Kantei, please put a stop to the seawater injection. I know there are lots of different opinions, but this is an order from the president."

Yoshida was being asked directly by his company's president. He responded obediently, "I understand." He prepared himself for the worst.

"I guess we'll have to put on some kind of performance . . ."

It wouldn't do to suspend the pumping process mid-flow if they were to maintain stability in the reactor. But the prime minister hadn't given the go-ahead, and he had to help TEPCO's CEO save face.

However, they were already pouring water in. How should he explain that? Yoshida placed a call to TEPCO Fellow Akio Takahashi, who started at the company a few years earlier than Yoshida in the technology field, to seek advice. Takahashi suggested, "All you have to do is say it's a test run." The idea was it was just a test, and to say it was the full-scale water injection as soon as the Kantei gave the go-ahead.[12]

In the images of the TEPCO videoconference from 7:23 p.m. on March 12, Yoshida could be seen leaving his seat, walking around the ERC, and talking about something with the manager in charge of the pumping operation.

The manager sat with his back to the Head Office side. Still on his feet, Yoshida could be seen whispering something in his ear.

"I'm going to tell everyone to halt pumping operations, but that's just for show. Don't stop pumping, whatever you do. . . . You got that?"

It was after that that Yoshida reported in a deliberate manner to Head Office, "We've had stern instructions from the Kantei regarding the seawater injection. We'll stop it temporarily!"[13]

7:40 P.M., MARCH 12. Another meeting was being held in the prime minister's office. The only difference from the previous meeting was that Kukita had replaced Madarame, and Nei had also joined. Saying, "I have something to report," Hosono showed a table of figures. It was the monitoring numbers for the radiation in front of the main gate at Fukushima Daiichi NPS.

The hydrogen explosion at Unit 1 had taken place at 3:36 p.m. While the figures initially dropped, by 3:46 p.m. they had increased to 860 millisieverts. However, at 4:15 p.m. (108 millisieverts) and then at 5:54 p.m. (84 millisieverts), the numbers kept falling. Hosono said, "Based on these readings, I don't think the containment vessel has exploded."

Kan was somewhat relieved.

"It's not a nuclear explosion. It's a hydrogen one. It doesn't seem like a worst-case scenario."

Hosono also stated that it had been confirmed the pumps were working and the pipes had suffered no damage.

"Is that so?"

Kan nodded his apparent conviction. Kukita drove the point home, "I think we need to pump in seawater. Let's put in some boric acid as well, just to be on the safe side."

"Yes, it looks like it can be packed in properly. Well, then, let's get some water in."

Kan had approved. It was at this point that it was decided to pump in boric acid simultaneously with the seawater.

Boric acid has the effect of preventing criticality. To be precise, under article 64 of the Act on the Regulation of Nuclear Source Material, Nuclear Fuel Material, and Reactors, injecting seawater had already been directed by Kaieda, who had grown increasingly frustrated with TEPCO Head Office's indecisive attitude. As has already been noted, Kaieda issued that command at 5:55 p.m. While he intended to "report" his seawater injection command in the meeting held immediately afterward in the prime minister's office, he failed to do so clearly.

Whether thwarted by Kan's sudden question on recriticality, or overwhelmed by Kan's momentum, or because of "Kaieda-san's gentle nature" (Goshi Hosono), he did not report immediately to Kan.

To Hiraoka, it looked like Kaieda "had missed his chance or that the atmosphere prevented him from speaking up." Takekuro rang TEPCO Head Office to inform them, "They've decided on injecting seawater. They want us to start pumping seawater." His gist was conveyed to the ERC at the plant via videoconference.

Yoshida once again gave the order to recommence pumping from the ERC at 8:20 p.m., reporting the fact to both Head Office and NISA.[14]

Yoshida revealed the truth about the seawater pumping at the end of May, just before the International Atomic Energy Agency (IAEA) delegation arrived. It was he himself who exposed the fact that he had engaged in a "Kabuki play."

It also later emerged that Takekuro had overreacted in his reading of the "mood" of the parliamentary secretariat at the Kantei. The Government Investigation Commission was critical of this point, writing, "There were, however, a number of instances when measures, which TEPCO Head Office and Yoshida thought necessary, conflicted with the advice they were receiving, but in those cases, they went along with the advice nevertheless, taking it seriously as instructions from the prime minister's office. So, in those cases, the advice did influence decisions regarding specific measures for the accident site."[15]

When Charles Casto, leader of the U.S. Nuclear Regulatory Commission (NRC) Japanese support team, later asked Yoshida about covertly defying orders from the prime minister's office, the latter revealed that he would have been replaced by another operator had he openly flouted the order, putting the whole of Japan at risk.[16]

OPEN BLOWOUT PANEL OPERATION

When Unit 1 exploded, the cooling of the Unit 3 reactor was continuing. This was because of the high-pressure coolant injection (HPCI) system, which turns on automatically at the time of an accident. HPCI is the trump card of nuclear reactor cooling in the case of AC power failure.

However, it should not be relied on indefinitely. After lowering the reactor pressure so that it would be easier to put water in, it was necessary, at some point, to switch to alternative pumping, which uses firefighting trucks.

On the night of March 12, the duty head of Units 3 and 4 consulted with the head of the ERC in the Anti-Seismic Building concerning his wish to stop the HPCI and switch over to the next method of water injection. The head of the ERC replied, "Stopping it is unavoidable."

At 2:24 a.m. on March 13, the operator stopped the HPCI manually. But the valve to lower the pressure of the nuclear reactor wouldn't open. DC power supply was needed to start up the HPCI. The green light was on, showing that there was such a battery . . .

Ten minutes later, the operation was tried again, but it did not start up. In a flash, the reactor pressure shot up.

3:52 A.M., MARCH 13. Videoconference.

> *Yoshida:* "Well, I am getting in touch because something has changed, it is Unit 3."
> *Head Office:* "Yes, Unit 3."
> *Yoshida:* "It is the HPCI, it was stopped momentarily at 02:44. After the HPCI was stopped, the reactor pressure has . . . increased fivefold."

After close to twenty minutes had passed, the Head Office made an inquiry.

> *Head Office:* "Erm, about Unit 3's HPCI, did it automatically trip? Or was it stopped manually? Did you manually stop it?"

A few moments passed.

> *Fukushima Daiichi NPS:* "The tripping of Unit 3 was an automatic trip due to the decline in rotational frequency of the turbines, as reactor pressure dropped and the driving force disappeared."

That was not the case. In actual fact, the operator had stopped it.[17] Yet this information had not reached the ERC at this point. After this, pumping was put on hold until just past nine a.m.

4:13 A.M. The head of Fukushima Daiichi NPS communicated to the Head Office that the outlook was not good for the recovery of the high-pressure pumping equipment. The only option was to proceed with pumping water into the reactor using firefighting trucks. However, pumping water in with firefighting trucks differs from high-pressure water devices in that it is pushed back by the pressure inside the reactor, because its water-spouting pressure is weak.

The head of Fukushima Daiichi announced, "If there is a battery, I think it can work."

Yoshida asked, as if taken by surprise, "Is a battery being arranged at the moment?"

Someone at the Head Office jeered:

"That is impossible, impossible. How many impossible things will you try to pursue, you idiot, that is a waste of effort!"

Among the engineers who joined in the videoconference, there were also those who expressed their anger and shame at the sense of helplessness they felt about the situation.[18]

Yoshida told Head Office, "We know we must open the SR valve, and we were just talking about going with an 'old fogeys' suicide squad.'"[19]

Yoshida said, "We know we must open the SR valve," but the control panel that opened and closed the safety relief (SR) valve ran on batteries. Accordingly, batteries were needed, but they had not been prepared.[20]

At the local NERHQ, they attempted to gather up batteries to open up the SR valve from the workers' cars, but the radiation dose onsite had risen and their protective masks were insufficient.

They needed 120 volts to open the SR valve. If they could get ten 12v batteries lined up, they could, of course, solve the problem. But on that day (March 13), they didn't even have ten of those batteries at their disposal. So, they removed twenty batteries from the workers' personal vehicles, brought them into the Central Control Room for Units 3 and 2, and hooked them up to the terminals behind the control panels for each of the SR valves.

In the meantime, staff had been scouring retail stores fifty kilometers away, where Fukushima Prefecture bordered Ibaraki Prefecture, but they were only able to buy eight.

On the morning of March 12, Head Office ordered 1,000 12v batteries, but since the trucks carrying them were not allowed to use the freeway, it was taking time for them to reach the site. Toshiba delivered 1,200 batteries to TEPCO's Onahama Coal Center. They had trouble securing trucks and drivers to travel from there to Fukushima Daiichi NPS. It was close to nine p.m. on March 14 when 320 batteries were delivered to Fukushima Daiichi.[21]

Around 9:41 a.m. on March 13, Yoshida appealed to the Head Office via videoconference.

"We don't know for sure if hydrogen was responsible for yesterday [March 12], but it's crucial that we don't have another explosion like Unit 1. We need to put our heads together, Head Office included."

Head Office's managing director, Akio Komori, responded to that. Komori had served as deputy manager of the Nuclear Power Location Headquarters.

"Maybe that's it. Open the blowout panels."

The blowout panels were like exhausts that were opened to prevent damage to the building or equipment in the case of a sudden rise in pressure inside the reactor. Turbine buildings were the main vapor pipes to break. They were attached to the walls of the highest floor of the reactor building.

However, at the time of the 2007 Chuetsu earthquake, Kashiwazaki-Kariwa Nuclear Power Station's blowout panels were opened, and since then they had been improved to be sturdier and not open easily. This time, they became the enemy and wouldn't open through sheer manpower. There was a strong possibility that hydrogen was accumulating on the top floor of the Unit 3 Reactor Building. Since the radiation dose was high around Unit 3, however, it would be difficult to go inside to open them.

1:34 P.M., MARCH 13. A voice rang out in the ERC, calling Yoshida, "Station manager, station manager. May I have a word?"

"I'm worried about the haze on the far side of the double doors at Unit 3 (RB) and the fact that 300 millisieverts has been recorded. It's just like Unit 1 yesterday."

A white haze had appeared about an hour before the explosion at Unit 1 on the afternoon of March 12. The security team in the ERC was on the watch for this "white haze" more than anything else. They were afraid that a similar situation had emerged in Unit 3. They had to hurry with a response. A proposal was made by Fukushima Daiichi over the videoconference.

"We were talking about, at worst, the blowout panels being blown some distance from the reactor building this morning. I think we should also be thinking about things like that."

However, the Head Office recovery team objected.

"We've looked into various possibilities, but we think that would be difficult in terms of physical problems and safety issues. We believe opening the top floor of the Unit 3 Reactor [building] is difficult."[22]

Around that time, the information from onsite that the Unit 2 blowout panels were somehow open got to Yoshida. It looked like hydrogen could be released from Unit 2. On the face of it, it appeared the danger of a hydrogen explosion in Unit 2 had become remote.

We should narrow our response to Unit 3. Won't the blowout panels of Unit 3 open somehow?

Besides the blowout panels, perhaps an opening on the first corner of the building could be made.

Yoshida imagined even more "extreme things."

Maybe the SDF's jet planes or something could come and open a hole using a machine gun or something like that.

Yoshida urged the Head Office to "think of a way to break open the top of the nuclear reactor building from the outside."[23]

2:45 P.M., MARCH 13. The following exchange took place via videoconference.

Fukushima Daiichi: "If we can't get close (to the blowout panel), fly in by helicopter and pierce the roof with something."

Head Office: "We thought of that here at the Head Office, too, but we're worried that sparks might ignite and we'd end up in the same boat as an explosion . . ."

Head Office Fellow Akio Takahashi: "We need to think about the question of evacuation as well."

After a while, the following was also voiced.

Head Office: "Takahashi, it's pretty preposterous, but how about asking the Self-Defense Forces to blast the panels with firearms, from the ocean side?"

Takahashi: "There's stacks of important stuff below."

Head Office: "It's going to blow anyway."

Takahashi: "There must be a way of blowing just the top off, you know, like dropping something from above."

Head Office: "A helicopter might be blown out of the sky . . ."

There was still no conclusion.[24]

In that time, the instruction to "think of measures to open the blowout panels" came to Yoshida from NISA via the TEPCO Head Office. Yoshida felt an insuppressible feeling of sickness.

Being told to "think of measures"! All they can do is throw out these stupid orders.[25]

ICE DROP OPERATION

Sometime after eight a.m. on March 13, Yoshida raised a new problem in the videoconference.

"There's talk of the steam coming out of the Unit 1 fuel pool . . . The state of the pool's looking bad, so I want to take steps, but since there's no water source, no ideas are coming to mind."

"We can't get close to it. So, it might seem a bit extreme . . . a helicopter or something injecting from above."

A TEPCO official at the offsite center broke in.

"I think the situation's the same for the other plants as what was just said about the 1F1 (Fukushima Daiichi Unit 1) pool. You know, we're still unable to cool. Isn't there some way of getting something into the remaining plants? Don't we have to start thinking outside the box?"

Offsite center: "Toss in some ice."

"Chuck in something, ice or dry ice."

"All you can do is chuck in ice, at least for the plant inside the building."

Yoshida: "It's just that . . . the radiation is so high in Unit 3 we can't get close and carry ice to it."

Offsite center: "Is the radiation that high at Unit 3?"

Head Office: "How about putting ice in where the radiation isn't high? You have to start thinking in parallel."

Yoshida: "Okay, so that's it, we'll arrange for some ice. Ice, arrange it."

After Yoshida had agreed, Managing Director Akio Komori gave the directive. "Head Office Procurement Team. We may need to get hold of some ice. I don't know if we need one or two tons, but get as much as you can. For the moment, start making arrangements."[26]

TEPCO decided to add dropping ice into the Unit 1 fuel pool to its list of requests for the Kantei, and to have CEO Masataka Shimizu deliver the requests when he visited the Kantei that day.[27]

That morning, TEPCO made a sudden phone call to Bushu Seihyo, an ice manufacturer in Kumagaya, Saitama Prefecture, and ordered some ice. "We need ice, two tons or however much you can give us."

Makoto Shiozaki, manager of the Ice Division at Bushu Seihyo, who took the call, immediately figured it out—"They want it to cool the reactors!"—but didn't ask any unnecessary questions, and the TEPCO side didn't say anything more.

That afternoon, a truck rushed in from a company called TEPCO Logistics, and loaded 135 kilograms of ice blocks. A little while later, two trucks turned up, this time with several staff from TEPCO's Kumagaya office.

They were told they couldn't load 135 kilograms onto a helicopter. So they packed three four-kilogram blocks into crates and loaded a hundred or so into the trucks. They then took the ice to the airfield in Okegawa.

From there, pilots from Shin Nippon Helicopters, one of TEPCO's associate companies, loaded it into the bellies of two helicopters, a small one and a large one, and flew to the Fukushima nuclear plant from there.

The designated destination was the sports ground of Fukushima Daini rather than Fukushima Daiichi. The pilots whispered along the lines, "I wonder if the sports field at Daiichi is already contaminated and can't be used?"

After they landed at the sports ground, however, no one from TEPCO met them. Not seeing what else they could do, the pilot and the mechanic unloaded, one by one, the hundred-odd crates of ice.

There was already a huge chunk of thick ice on the ground. It looked to be about the same amount of ice as they had brought in. It was covered in some places, but mostly open to the elements.

The pilot thought suspiciously, *This must have been transported by land. How can they have brought in all this ice, with the gas shortage?*

The pilot flew wearing a raincoat over his jacket. He was not issued any radiation protective gear by his company. Thinking it might come in useful, he had bought some before the flight, but it had ripped on the way.

Shin Nippon Helicopters was receiving further requests from TEPCO.

"Can't you drop it from the air?"

"Won't you take some shots of the reactors from the air?"

Shin Nippon Helicopters refused both requests.

TEPCO seemed to be advancing its ice strategy in secret. It looked like they had chosen a distant airfield on purpose.

Were they afraid residents would panic if it leaked out that they were thinking of putting ice in to cool the reactors?

The pilots never found out what happened to the ice in question.

Inside TEPCO, they were considering dropping ice from the air into the spent-fuel pool of Unit 1, wondering, moreover, whether the drop could be "outsourced" to Shin Nippon Helicopters. It was to this end that they arranged to have a total of 3.5 tons of ice flown in, including the ice procured from Bushu Seihyo.

In the evening, however, doubts were voiced about the ice-drop strategy.

4:30 P.M. ON MARCH 13. Videoconference.

Head Office: "What with developments at Unit 1 and here as well as the extremely high radiation, we need to discuss carefully whether we can really do this work at night, and if not at night, when can we do it."

Yoshida: "Even if we start getting it ready right now, it's going to be pitch-black, right? So, it's going to be impossible today. But as to whether we do it tomorrow, we're worried now about the plant next door as well as the radiation issue, so we're hesitant about the optimal timing."

Fukushima Daiichi: "Bearing in mind the impact, it's really just a drop in the bucket."[28]

There was 990 tons of water in the spent-fuel pool at Unit 1. They were aware that the effect of dropping 3.5 tons of ice from helicopters would be minimal.

There was a second order from TEPCO to Bushu Seihyo on March 14. It was transported by road to Fukushima, but Shiozaki later heard that it had melted.

TEPCO had arranged for a total of fifty or sixty tons of ice that day from three ice-making plants in Saitama, Gunma, and Tochigi Prefectures. But the water drop strategy had melted away before it could be implemented.[29]

CRISIS IN UNIT 3

MARCH 13. Despite it being Sunday, Toshiba's chief engineer, Osamu Maekawa, was in Toshiba's Isogo Engineering Center (IEC) in Yokohama from the early hours of the morning. The IEC was the pride and base for research and development of world-leading nuclear reactor manufacturer: Toshiba. Toshiba had built Units 2, 3, 5, and 6 at Fukushima Daiichi NPS. Of those, Units 2 and 6 had been joint projects with America's General Electric (GE). (GE had built Unit 1 on its own, and Unit 4 had been built by Hitachi.)

Maekawa had joined Toshiba in 1981. His entire career had been in reactors, and he was currently the most senior official in Toshiba's engineering staff. He was working in his casual clothes when he received an urgent call from the Head Office in Shibaura, Tokyo. It was Norio Sasaki, the CEO.

"Can you come straight to the Head Office? I've been called to see the prime minister at eleven a.m. Won't you come with me?"

Sasaki had joined the company in 1972. The following year, as a trainee, he had been involved in planning the layout, plumbing, and air ventilation for Unit 3 at Fukushima Daiichi NPS. He later served as design director for the pressure vessel.

"The prime minister says he wants to hear from engineers actually involved in running the reactor."

They agreed to go with a team of six, including officials in charge of control, fuel, and reactor cores, so they would be able to answer any questions. Maekawa left the IEC and, upon arriving to the Head Office, changed into a business suit. He realized he was wearing sneakers. While he was not keen on visiting the Kantei in this kind of attire, it could not be helped.

ELEVEN A.M., MARCH 13. The prime minister's office. The delegation greeted Prime Minister Naoto Kan, Chief Cabinet Secretary Yukio Edano, and Deputy Chief Cabinet Secretary Tetsuro Fukuyama. Edano was wearing sneakers. Maekawa felt a little more comfortable.

The discussion immediately turned to the situation at Unit 3. Sasaki said, "If things are left as they stand, both Units 2 and 3 will explode." According to the reactor core simulation carried out by Toshiba's IEC, the containment vessel of Unit 3 was full of hydrogen and in a dangerous state.

"We're also exploring various ways of avoiding an explosion."

"Can't you open a hole in the roof or something, and let the hydrogen escape from there?"

"There's a danger that a spark could start a fire. I think it would be better to cut through it using high-pressure water."

"Is that so? If there's any way of avoiding another explosion, please do it. The government will help you in any way it can. So, we'd like you to help us as well."

What Sasaki had mentioned was an operation that was already covertly being readied at the Onahama Coal Center in Fukushima Prefecture. This was a coal storage depot located some fifty kilometers from Fukushima Daiichi NPS. Along with J-Village, the Japan national football team training location, it was acting as one of the emergency response support centers.

Toshiba had started sending batteries and pumps there on March 11, immediately after the quake. Behind the scenes, they were considering two options for Unit 3. The first was a so-called air-ventilation strategy, which involved restoring the normal air ventilation and extracting the hydrogen. The second was a roof-opening strategy, which involved opening a hole in the roof to let the hydrogen escape.

They had also considered flying in a helicopter from above, attaching a drilling rig to the roof, and running for their lives. The drilling rig was a container-like frame that would "stick to the roof like glue and punch out a hole." However, opening a hole up on the roof with something saw-like would set off sparks and might be dangerous. So, they would try using water to open a hole in a so-called water-jetting technique. Toshiba had already set up a life-size mockup.

The discussion on the morning of that day between TEPCO Head Office and the Fukushima site about ways of "using something to open the roof" was, in fact, referring to this water jet of Toshiba's.

However, there were problems. They were no longer able to have equipment delivered into the Fukushima Daiichi site. At 6:25 p.m. on March 12, the government had issued an order for local residents within a twenty-kilometer radius to evacuate. Since then, not a single piece of equipment had been delivered from Onahama Coal Center to Fukushima Daiichi. Sasaki met Kan a second time in his office around one p.m. the same day and raised this issue.

"They're stuck at the barrier at the twenty-kilometer line and can't move. Something needs to be done."

"We'll act immediately."

Sasaki also mentioned that a Toshiba team had been turned back at the main gate to Fukushima Daiichi NPS. Toshiba had put together a twenty-five-man team for restoring Units 5 and 6 at Fukushima Daiichi. He was sure that they could have the reactors back up and running in two days if they worked day and night. But, denied entrance at the main gate, they had turned back.

Fukushima Daiichi wouldn't let the Toshiba team in even after they showed their Toshiba IDs. No one was allowed in unless they had registered beforehand and received a badge. Most of the team had not registered beforehand. The Toshiba engineers were unconvinced.

Do the staff on the ground not want outsiders getting into the Anti-Seismic Building at a time of crisis? Is that why they won't let us in?

Toshiba had built an Anti-Seismic Building at its Isogo Engineering Center after TEPCO had shut down its reactors at Kashiwazaki-Kariwa following the 2007 Chuetsu earthquake. It was the first of its kind in Japan. Following their lead, TEPCO had built them at Kashiwazaki-Kariwa, Fukushima Daiichi, and Fukushima Daini.

Sasaki asked Kan, "There's no way we can help out when things are like this. Can you get some government people to speak to them?"

After leaving the prime minister's office, Sasaki pointed at Maekawa and told Fukuyama, "Fukuyama-san, I'm leaving him behind. He's our top engineer."

Maekawa was surprised, because he hadn't heard anything about that from Sasaki beforehand. Maekawa stayed at the Kantei until the morning of March 15, then moved over to TEPCO after Kan had ventured into the Head Office.[30]

At 1:12 p.m. on March 13, TEPCO started pumping seawater into Unit 3. They had also added boric acid.

At 1:52 p.m., the monitoring car inside Fukushima Daiichi Station recorded 1,600 microsieverts/hour (1.6 millisieverts). It was on the western mountain side of the site. It was the highest reading since the start of the emergency.[31]

2:12 P.M. ON MARCH 13. Videoconference.

> *Head Office safety team:* "Since it had been previously 40-50 microsieverts (0.04-0.05 millisieverts), we are now in a situation in which it is considerably higher."
>
> *Yoshida:* "Or, rather, it's an article 15 again."

If a radiation dose in excess of 500 microsieverts (0.5 millisieverts) had been observed at the site boundary, this fell under article 15 of the Nuclear Disaster Special Measures Act.

> *Head Office safety team:* "The unit we're now using is mSv (millisievert), and 30 or 50 mSv/h is a very high dose. The area around the Anti-Seismic Building, too, is 5-10 mSv. This means just a round trip from the Anti-Seismic Building to the office building and back involves exposure to a dosage of 1 mSv and the situation is that after the explosion in Unit 1, the radiation is higher."[32]

3:28 P.M., MARCH 13. Edano issued a warning at his press conference: "There is a possibility that a hydrogen explosion like the one in Unit 1 will occur in Unit 3."

3:07 A.M., MARCH 14. The onsite safety team reported the latest dose at the Fukushima Daiichi NPS near the main gate.

"At 02:20, 751. At 02:30, 4,133."

"Oh, my God!"

Yoshida couldn't help but raise his voice at such a high dose. The radiation dose had jumped to 4,133 mSv/h (4.133 millisieverts).[33]

In the videoconference at 5:50 a.m. on March 14, Yoshida made a formal statement. "Erm, so, I'll explain the situation at the power plant a little, since I believe the situation is not the best."

Although water injection was resumed at Unit 3 after an interruption, the drywell pressure had gradually increased. They had increased the amount of water being pumped in to nearly double, but the upward trend of the pressure had not abated. In addition, the water level had become volatile.

"We can't help but think that there is a strong possibility that some kind of reaction is taking place inside the reactor.

"This means there's a possibility of another hydrogen explosion, like Unit 1. Although yesterday's venting was fairly successful in lowering the pressure, it's back up to this level, so I'm saying we need to watch it."[34]

6:40 A.M. Yoshida warned the Head Office about the downscaling of the water level in the fuel pool at Unit 3.

"It's been downscaling since 6:10 a.m. The fact that there's been a sharp drop in the water level and it's downscaling means it's getting pretty dry, doesn't it?

"When this happens, you know, about operations . . . we have a lot of people working in and around the plant. We have a lot of people here, too. We may have to think first about what we're going to do with them, rather than operations."

Yoshida suggested evacuating employees from Fukushima Daiichi. He said, "We're no longer able to do anything, so is it all right to bring the field workers, our employees, back here for the moment?"

Vice President Sakae Muto at the offsite center responded:

"Of course."

6:42 A.M. Videoconference.

> *Yoshida:* "Please leave the field and evacuate here for the moment. What about the workers in the Central Control Room? We'd better evacuate them, too, right?"
>
> *Muto:* "Well, check the level of radiation, then decide."
>
> *Yoshida:* "The dose in the Central Control Room. I'll check what's happening with the radiation in the Central Control Room."

Komori: "If you evacuate the Central Control Room, you won't be able to vent, so what should be done, including that?"

Muto: "Yoshida-san, please look closely at the dose, the dose there as well."

Fukushima Daiichi safety team: "Regarding the dose in this room now, it's max 28 mSv/h (0.028 millisieverts)."

Yoshida: "In here?"

Safety team: "Yes, here."

Muto: "If it's 28 in the ERC now, I think there's no problem there . . . Yoshida-san, since things seems to have settled down a bit here, won't you think a bit again about what to do, including work in the field?"

Yoshida: "Yes, but since there's a fair possibility of it becoming like Unit 1, I think it'll be extremely difficult to put people in the yard, speaking in terms of such dangerous work."

Yoshida still asserted they had no choice but to halt field work in the "yard"—namely, the vicinity of the reactor building.[35]

8:40 A.M., MARCH 14. Regarding the fact that Fukushima Prefecture was to announce an abnormal increase in pressure in the containment vessel of Unit 3, triggering an article 15 event in a managers' meeting open to the press, starting at nine a.m., the prefecture requested TEPCO to go public with the facts up until that point.

Head Office officials explained to the staff onsite in a videoconference: "Both the Kantei and NISA have stopped releasing all information on this event, and they've asked the operators to also stop releasing information on it. This is the situation in which the prefecture is now telling us to go public."

Nevertheless, NHK had already reported: "The pressure in the containment vessel in Unit 3 of TEPCO's Fukushima Daiichi has risen dramatically and the operators have temporarily evacuated." The Kantei and NISA were pushing for the release of information about the current status of Unit 3 under the judgment that "since water has already been pumped in, we fear that not releasing information would cause public anxiety."[36]

The person in charge at the Head Office explained the position TEPCO found themselves in. "As the operator, we should convey what the prefecture is saying. We can only get the prefecture and NISA to make adjustments . . . This matter comes when the state's governance founded upon the Nuclear Disaster Special Measures Act is very strong. Of course, we can't totally ignore the prefecture."

"Well, the first thing to do is to inform the Kantei, let on to the Kantei. Tell them we're in a spot, because the prefecture is telling us this."[37]

"IT'S BLACK, ISN'T IT?"

11:00 A.M., MARCH 14. Videoconference.

Naohiro Masuda, site superintendent of Fukushima Daini NPS, spoke.

"Three tsunami alerts have just been given for Hamadori. One-F, can you hear? Three tsunami alerts have just been given for Hamadori. Please be careful."

Immediately after that, Yoshida's voice rang out in the TEPCO Head Office operations center. He was yelling.

"Head Office! Head Office!"

"Yes, Head Office here."

"Head Office! Head Office! It's bad, it's really bad! Unit 3. If that is steam, then perhaps we've just had an explosion."

"Yes, emergency contact."

"It's 11:01."

"The same as Unit 1?"

"There was a sideways shaking that was distinctly different from a quake. There haven't been any aftershocks like there are when there is an earthquake, so I think it's an explosion like the one in Unit 1."

Yoshida's voice was high-pitched. Akio Komori, at the Head Office, spoke.

"Onsite people, evacuate, evacuate!"

Yoshida directed his subordinates in a firm voice.

"Please evacuate and check people's safety. I want detailed readings and reports on exposure."[38]

Among those remaining, Yoshida called on everyone to write their name down on a whiteboard. These recorded names later came to be known as "the Fukushima 50."[39]

AFTER ELEVEN A.M. The prime minister's office.

Kan was holding a meeting with Natsuo Yamaguchi, leader of the Komeito Party, and Tetsuo Saito, the party's acting secretary-general. Manabu Terada, special adviser to the prime minister, burst into the room.

"It's an explosion. Turn on NTV. Channel 4, channel 4!"

The television was showing footage of the explosion at Unit 3. Smoke was billowing out. Kan whispered, "It's black, isn't it?"

"Judging from the way the smoke is rising, I reckon the pressure vessel had blown."

With Unit 1, the smoke had been white and went sideways, but this was black smoke rising up. There was a tremendous bang, and explosion preceded momentarily by a flash of orange. Dust and debris were spread far and wide. The dust shot up some five hundred meters in the air.[40]

Edano was in the middle of a press conference at the time. He passed a memo halfway through. He glanced at it.

"As you can see, I have just received a memo and it seems that there has either been an explosion at Unit 3 or there is a fear of explosion. We are currently checking the facts."

That was the best he could say. Both the reporters and the chief cabinet secretary were asking and answering questions relying only on the footage from NTV.

Kan ordered Terada to "call all the relevant parties." The key members of NERHQ assembled: Kaieda, Edano, Fukuyama, and Madarame.

Kan asked, "What's happening?" but no one could reply.

What had exploded in Unit 3? Where was the explosion? What was it? They had none of the crucial information.

After a short time, Maekawa received a call from Sasaki on his mobile. "It's on TV."

Sasaki was telling Maekawa that footage of the Unit 3 explosion was being broadcast. Staff from TEPCO and NISA were watching TV in a large room on the second floor of the Kantei.

Someone said in a hoarse voice, "Oh, it's all gone."

The moment Maekawa saw the footage, he thought to himself, *Uh oh, this time the containment vessel had it, too.*

A terrible thing had happened. And at the same time, he found himself regretting, *Damn! We should have done it earlier.* He was thinking about the "high-pressure water jet operation."

Toshiba had even carried out an operational rehearsal, but their turn had not come. The reactor had blown before they could make a formal proposal to TEPCO. Even if their turn had come, however, how much would they have been able to do . . . ?

Even if they had brought the jets in, someone would have had to operate it. And that meant shouldering an enormous risk. Nonetheless, Sasaki did not doubt that if it fell to Toshiba employees, they would be sure to do it.

On hearing that there was a shortage of engineers who excelled in radiation control in 1999 at the time of the JOC accident in Tokaimura, Ibaraki Prefecture, Toshiba had loaded several dozens of workers from the Fukushima stations onto a bus and sent them in as support.

Sasaki had often proudly recounted this episode. Was it possible, however, for a single company to take such a risk . . . ?

One of the Toshiba engineers, present onsite to deal with the emergency, later reflected that, even if top management at Toshiba had given the go-ahead, he was doubtful as to whether top management at TEPCO would have been able to do the same.

Takekuro also considered the work onsite to be virtually impossible when he heard Toshiba's proposal. So much so that he thought, *It has to be done remotely or not at all. Perhaps the only way to do it is to blow the roof off with a missile.*

Maekawa was seized by a deep sense of regret.

Unit 3 was also my plant, which I cared for. It didn't belong to us, but we fixed it.

At the time of the Unit 1 explosion, Hosono thought, *No way,* but at the time of Unit 3, he felt, *At last.* Voices had called out to each other to prevent a hydrogen explosion at Unit 3 at any cost. For that reason alone, it was devastating.[41]

11:30 A.M., MARCH 14. The following exchange took place on the videoconference between TEPCO Head Office and the Fukushima site. It was Takahashi who spoke. Seated next to him was CEO Masataka Shimizu.

"Well, the point is, isn't it, that we've just turned from Unit 1 to Unit 3. And I don't know if it was a hydrogen explosion or not, but NISA is saying it's a hydrogen explosion, so I guess that'll do, won't it, saying it's a hydrogen explosion? NISA was just on TV saying it was a hydrogen explosion. I think it's better if we stay in step with that."

Somebody made a noise in agreement.

"The Kantei is also already using the term 'a hydrogen explosion.' Don't you think we'd better say the same thing, too?"

Shimizu agreed.

"Yes, fine. That's okay . . . Time is of the essence."

A little later, it was reported that Yuhei Sato, governor of Fukushima Prefecture, had made a request to TEPCO's Fukushima office.

"He wants us to include in our press release the phrase 'The wind is blowing in a northwesterly direction, so there is no worry of adverse effects on health.'"

Apparently, the governor wanted to reassure the prefecture's residents that they need not worry, because the wind was northwesterly—that is, it was blowing out to the Pacific Ocean, not inland.

Deciding it was "risky to make an assertion," TEPCO refused his request.[42]

CRISIS IN UNIT 2

The explosion at Unit 3 dislodged and closed the circuit to the vent valve that had been opened in Unit 2. Water couldn't be injected into the reactor, because the reactor pressure was higher than the discharge pressure of the firefighting pumps.[43]

Yoshida felt that some change was underway in Unit 2.

2:54 A.M., MARCH 14. Videoconference.

> *Yoshida:* "Muto-san, what has us worried is why the RCIC is holding out so long."
> *Muto:* "Yes, that's worrying."
> *Komori:* "I think it's more than the normal run of things."
> *Yoshida:* "So, it wouldn't be strange for it to give up the ghost at any moment. It seems to be hanging in there."
> *Muto:* "You're quite right, which means, which means, which means . . ."

Yoshida questioned the fact that the reactor core isolation cooling system (RCIC) in Unit 2 was continuing to cool. Komori was also puzzled. The usual lifespan of a RCIC was eight to ten hours. For some reason or another, it was still working after nearly sixty hours.[44]

2:58 A.M., MARCH 14. Videoconference.

A report that preparations for venting Unit 2 were complete came in from the field at Fukushima Daiichi to the Head Office.

Vice President Sakae Muto at the offsite center asked, "Am I right in understanding that you're ready to vent if the pressure in the containment vessel rises?"

The recovery team replied, "We can if the drywell pressure goes as high as the level of bursting the rupture."

When the SR valve is open, steam is blown into the suppression chamber. This acts to raise both the temperature and the pressure in the suppression chamber, necessitating venting. Muto was trying to confirm that.

This was followed by a conversation between Yoshida and Muto.

"Then there'll only be water."

"Just water. It's a feat of strength."

"Everyone seems a little relieved thinking the supply of seawater is endless, but isn't there some way now of pumping directly from the sea without having to do the extra job of transferring it to the pit?"

"No, no. Of course, that's the natural course of actions to take and we're trying it. We've been trying since last night, but it's not working out as planned."

The stumbling block was the ten-meter difference in height between sea level and the plant. Since they couldn't get hold of a pump that was capable of sucking up water despite the height difference, they couldn't use the inexhaustible expanse of sea before their eyes.[45]

Before one p.m. on March 14, Yoshida took a call from TEPCO Head Office.

"We're thinking of opening a hole in the blowout panels using a water jet as a way to prevent a hydrogen explosion at Unit 2."

Yoshida listened.

"Urgently consider ways to make holes from the outside, including the use of a helicopter, since operations from the inside of the building would be difficult, due to the scaffold problem, and so on."

Yoshida was trying to make the point that it was already impossible at the site to put up scaffolding either inside or outside with the rising exposure dosage.

Head Office's response: "We're in the midst of planning a method of making holes by attaching a water-jet to a ladder truck, but transportation of the necessary heavy equipment is being held up because of tsunami warnings."[46]

A little later, Takahashi at the Head Office contacted Yoshida.

"We've had a call from the Kantei urging us to move quickly, not to worry about exposure, to keep working even up to 500 millisieverts."[47]

It sounded like "encouragement" to the effect that Head Office was doing its best to deal with the government by working with the Kantei—in truth, with Takekuro, TEPCO's liaison—so they wanted the onsite team to do its best despite the high radiation levels, and could they not "get a hole open" if at all possible?

In relation to this, an hour or so later, it was conveyed from Head Office: "It's been decided to raise the exposure limit for workers involved in emergency restoration from 100 millisieverts to 250 millisieverts."

It is true that it had been discussed at 1:20 p.m. on March 14 in a meeting at the Kantei whether the exposure level for TEPCO workers could be raised from 50 to 250 millisieverts. This was the result of Takekuro lobbying NISA and the NSC, but it was Madarame who stated "It's possible" during the meeting, and that was how the decision to raise the permissible level to 250 millisieverts came to be made.[48]

If they could get water in by 3:30 p.m., the water level wouldn't drop below the top of active fuel (TAF). But it didn't look like that was going to be possible.

At 3:57 p.m., the technical team at Fukushima Daiichi reported to Yoshida.

"It's about the time TAF will be reached, we said 4:30 p.m., but if we can correct the pressure, we reckon 5:30 p.m."

4:00 P.M. Yoshida heard the latest simulation results for Unit 2. They projected that the water level would reach TAF around 5:30 p.m.[49]

4:13 P.M. Yoshida spoke at the videoconference.

"Everyone, listen up! Everyone at Head Office, please listen, too. I've just had a call from Chairman Madarame at the NSC, and he says shouldn't we be giving priority to pumping in water [to lower reactor pressure] over venting the containment vessel."

On the ground, they were proceeding with preparations for the vent. Conveying this, with Madarame still on the line, Yoshida also asked one of the technical staff, "What does Safety reckon? About this assessment?"

Madarame advised from the phone, "Don't you think it's better to open the SR valve and pump in water to lower the pressure rather than trying to keep the PVC [primary containment vessel] alive? If you drop the pressure, the water will flow in. I think you should be pumping water in quickly."

The analysis official from the technical team that was called "Safety" answered.

"Water temperature in the suppression chamber has exceeded 130 degrees Celsius."

Yoshida spoke again with Madarame.

"Mr. Chairman, when I asked Safety, they said the water temperature in the suppression chamber is over 100 degrees Celsius. They're saying there's a high chance that it won't go in. I'll get Safety to speak."

The present status was that because of the high temperature in the pressure control room (S/C), there was a possibility that the steam would not condense enough to lower the pressure even if they opened the SR valve. If that happened, the pressure in the reactor wouldn't drop, and they'd be unable to inject water. That was the assessment of those in the field, and the technical officials supported it.

A technical official explained to Madarame, "We'd like to go ahead with venting as per provision policy."

The technical official explained to Madarame what that was. After hanging up, he reported, "He's satisfied."

A few minutes later, however, they received a call from the field.

"We've turned on the power, but the necessary valves for venting aren't moving. We need to check it out."

The report came back that "it's no good, even though the compressors are working."

They tried to open the vent valve with air pressure from a portable compressor in the same way as for Unit 1, but although the compressor was working, the vent valve wouldn't open.

4:21 P.M. Yoshida received a report from the restoration team working on the venting that they could not vent. Shimizu, who had been following this exchange on videoconference, suddenly butted in.

"Yoshida-san, Yoshida-san . . . Shimizu here. Please use Chairman Madarame's method."

Yoshida: "Yes, I understand."
Shimizu: "Please do so."

Shimizu spoke as if to warn Yoshida. Yoshida still wanted to get Muto's opinion and looked for him, but could not get hold of him, because Muto was in mid-flight on a helicopter heading back to Head Office.

Shimizu pressed the point.

"You're all right with that, yes?"

In the end, Yoshida decided to lower pressure by releasing the SR valve and at the same time preparing to vent.

4:34 P.M. The Central Control Room (Units 1 and 2) went to work on opening the SR valve in Unit 2. Ten 12v batteries had been brought in from cars onsite in the morning of the previous day, March 13. They tried the trick that had worked for opening the Unit 3 SR valve in Unit 2, but the SR valve refused to open. They could not vent. The SR valve would not open. There was nothing they could do.[50]

4:51 P.M. Videoconference.

> *Shimizu:* "Assuming that the SR valve doesn't open and water can't be injected, what will take place over how much time after that? But you're trying to release the pressure in the pressure vessels, right?"
>
> *Head Office recovery team:* "Yes, we're trying to release the pressure."
>
> *Shimizu:* "Via the SR valve?"
>
> *Head Office recovery team:* "That's right."
>
> *Shimizu:* "Up until now, it hasn't been done?"
>
> *Head Office recovery team:* "No, it hasn't been done yet."

5:08 P.M.

> *Fukushima Daiichi power generation team:* "We thought we would first open the SR valve A at, ah, 16:43, but it didn't work. At that point, the water level in the reactor was −300 mm . . . We tried opening a different SR valve at 16:57. However, the water level in the reactor at that point was −500 mm . . ."
>
> *TEPCO Fellow Akio Takahashi:* "That's not good at all, eh?"[51]

When it was reported via videoconference that opening the SR valve "hasn't been done yet," the more than two hundred people packed into the ERC fell quiet. Takeyuki Inagaki, head of the recovery team, was also there. Inagaki felt at that time "like lead had been poured into my stomach." And it was not just Inagaki. He recalls, "Everyone felt that it was all over if it didn't open."[52]

Yoshida went down to the corridor on the first floor of the Anti-Seismic Building from the second floor ERC. It was necessary to tell associate company workers about this state of affairs. Everybody looked exhausted.

These people shouldn't be caught up in this.

Yoshida turned to them and said, "We have tried our all, yet things are in a truly terrible state. Everyone, please go home. I would like you to go home."

Yoshida did not use the word "evacuate." The words "please go home" came out of his mouth instead. Izawa recalled that it was difficult to discern exactly what Yoshida meant by this, but either way, panicked staff began to leave as quickly as possible.[53] After that, Yoshida went to the first-floor smoking room without returning to the ERC and took out a cigarette. He was struck by a feeling of futility to the point of being unable to speak. He was in a daze.

Whether water will go in or not, it's just waiting from now. It's exactly like gambling.[54]

After a smoke, he did not return to the ERC but went into the site superintendent's office on the second floor. There, he curled up his tall frame and closed his eyes. His face was pallid with fatigue.

Perhaps it was for about ten minutes. Opening his eyes, Yoshida unfurled his heavy, tired body.[55]

5:56 P.M. Videoconference. There was a report at TEPCO Head Office.

"We're repeatedly trying to open the main steam escape valve. We've failed three times because there isn't enough power due to the low voltage."[56]

FIVE

The Day of Reckoning

"WE MAY BE FINISHED"

AFTER SIX P.M., MARCH 14. Hosono's mobile phone rang in the prime minister's office. It was Masao Yoshida, site superintendent at Fukushima Daiichi NPS.

"It's Yoshida from TEPCO. We've opened up the SR (safety relief) valve of Unit 2, but we haven't seen steam condensing because the temperature in the containment vessel is still high. We're facing a not-so-favorable situation with the water level in the reactor declining. It's an emergency."

Hosono had been in direct contact with Yoshida since the evening of March 12. On the afternoon of that day, after the building of Unit 1 had exploded, information did not arrive to the Kantei for two hours. In order to fix the poor flow of information, Hosono suggested creating a hotline between the Kantei and the site. That was how Yoshida came to have Hosono's cell phone number.[1]

Hosono was shocked. He had heard that pressure would be released if the SR valves were opened. Even though they had been opened, he could not imagine the next step in the plan once the water level had dropped down.

"I understand well that it is an emergency situation, sir. Don't give up, please keep trying . . . Is there anything we can help you with?"

Yoshida replied, "We will keep working. We can still do it. But we haven't got enough tools. Anyhow, get us some tools. It'll be all right if we can get a pump that can get water into the reactor even if the pressure's high in there."

Forty minutes later, another call from Yoshida came to Hosono. Hosono was once again in the prime minister's office at that time.

120

"Hosono-san, I'm sorry. We may be finished. We can't get water into Unit 2."

". . ."

"If we can't get water in, then the reactor core will melt down, the fuel rods will be completely exposed. It will be a China Syndrome. In that case, nothing can be done. Like Unit 1 and 3, water will disappear. Three plants are heading the same way. It is a tragic disaster."

Hosono was at a loss for words.[2]

When the core began to melt, the nuclear fuel would also melt down, the high temperature causing the walls of the reactor containment vessel and the reactor pressure vessel to melt, releasing radioactive material outside. This is what is known as a "China Syndrome."

Yoshida was reporting to Hosono his fear that if a China Syndrome took place in Unit 2, they would be unable to continue pumping water into the reactors and fuel pools at Units 1 and 3, triggering a China Syndrome in all the reactors.[3]

"Yoshida-san, thank you. Could you repeat what you just said to the prime minister directly?"

Upon quietly saying so, Hosono handed his mobile to Kan. Kan went silent and listened to what Yoshida was saying. Then, at the end, Kan said, "We will do what we can on our end, keep trying your best, Yoshida-san," and then hung up. Kan remained speechless for some time. And then Kan said helplessly, "Does this mean it's out of control?"

"It is no good . . ."

A long silence ensued.[4]

During this time, the water in the reactor pressure vessel at Unit 2 had evaporated due to the decay heat of the nuclear fuel—hence, the water level had dropped. After five p.m., the water level had reached TAF (top of active fuel).

At 5:30 p.m., it dropped to –100 mm. The nuclear fuel finally began to be exposed above the water.

At 5:35 p.m., it reached –300 mm. At 5:52 p.m., it was –500 mm. The reactor pressure was rising apace with the drop in water level.[5]

7:20 P.M. Yoshida received a report that the two fire trucks standing by near Unit 2 were both out of fuel. They had run out of fuel having run their engines on standby for a long time. The fire engines stopped if they were not refueled about once every two hours.

Yoshida shouted,

"What? The fire engines have stopped? Are you trying to kill the people around you?"[6]

They hurriedly set about getting a fuel tanker on the premises to bring over some fuel, but as it had a flat tire, the fuel had to be transferred to another tanker, which delayed the pumping operation significantly.[7]

From the afternoon of that day, to use his own words, Yoshida was commanding with "a feeling of his chest tightening second by second" in the face of the crisis at Unit 2.[8] They were just about able to lower the pressure inside the reactor. The connection of the hose was corrected, and it was in a condition in which it was able to pump water. At the point when they were going to start pumping water from the firefighting trucks, he heard the notice that the firefighting truck pumps were not working.[9]

He was in despair about the report that the firefighting trucks had run out of fuel. He was seized by the desire to punch in the face the person in charge who had neglected the refueling. Yoshida later confessed, in the Government Investigation Commission hearings, "With this, I'm a goner. It was then when I most felt it was the time to die."[10]

Approximately one hour after the "run out of fuel" report, the official in charge of the technical team in the ERC at the Anti-Seismic Building reported:

"It's about the status of Unit 2, we believe that fuel has been exposed from about 18:22."

"That means the fuel will be completely melted in about two hours, and the RPV (reactor pressure vessel) damaged in a further two hours, so I think it's likely we'll be in a very critical situation sometime after 22:00 when the RPV falls out. Over and out."[11]

However, after about thirty minutes had passed, some good news came flying in.

At 8:02 p.m., Yoshida spoke via videoconference.

"It's the water. It looks like it started to flow about five minutes ago. The staff who went there says the water and the pumps are operating."

The fire engine that had run out of fuel had been refueled, and its pump had started to operate.[12]

They were now able to get water into Unit 2.

After the total loss of power on March 11, the emergency cooling systems of the IC in Unit 1, the RCIC in Unit 2, and the HPCI system in Unit 3 had ceased to function, one after another, in the five days since the accident. Now, Units 1 through 3 were only just managing to be cooled by water pumped in from fire engines, the only thin thread keeping them hanging on. They had no choice but to keep that thread intact and keep on with life-saving measures.

8:05 P.M. Returning to his seat after an absence, TEPCO Chairman Tsunehisa Katsumata asked Takahashi,

"What's happening? Is it in?"

"The water's in. At Unit 2. Just a minute or two ago."

"It's in, but it's already too late, eh?"

AFTER 9:22 P.M. Loud voices and applause suddenly burst out in the ERC in the Anti-Seismic Building. Someone at Head Office asked, "Is it somebody's birthday?"

"We've finally got the numbers for the water level!"

That meant that the water injection into Unit 2's pressure vessel had worked, and a recovery in the water level had been confirmed. Cheers broke out at Head Office, too.

"Well done!"

"Congratulations!"

Voices were heard from the field.

"The vent valve is next."

"I'd like to wait just like this for the wet well."[13]

It was a short-lived moment of joy. Having been switched to "open," the SR valve started to work, but in order to keep it open, they had to keep the solenoid valve—which controlled the opening and closing—running in the Central Control Room. The fear emerged, however, that the battery might run dry.[14]

Later, pressure in the containment vessel at Unit 2 started rising once more. There was a fear that if it kept climbing at its current pace, the containment vessel would blow.[15]

Radiation readings at the Fukushima Daiichi main gate were rising.

"The 21:37 reading at the main gate: 3.2 millisieverts."

Yoshida checked the unit of measurement.

"Hang on. Is it millisieverts? That's terrible!"[16]

The figure was 3.2 millisieverts/hour—in other words, 3,200 microsieverts/hour.

LATE NIGHT PHONE CALL

Let us return the hand of the clock to the TEPCO videoconference a little while earlier. It was 7:30 p.m., a few minutes after the report came in of the fuel in Unit 2 being already laid bare.

> *Managing director Akio Komori:* "If we don't make a judgment at some point on whether people can continue to be in the Central Control Room of the power plant, it will get out of control. Therefore, please start looking into an evacuation standard."
> *Vice president Sakae Muto:* "Understood. Please do so."

Muto instructed the relevant person in charge at Head Office to proceed. TEPCO Fellow Akio Takahashi explained to Chairman Tsunehisa Katsumata next to him, "No way, we can't afford to evacuate." Katsumata could not muster up any words except for, "Eh?"

Head Office conveyed the conditions for evacuation to the site.

"Evacuating with the vents unopened, it will become very hard to control, please complete the venting."[17]

7:55 P.M., MARCH 14. Takahashi spoke to Muto while seated next to him in the NERHQ at TEPCO Head Office.

"Now, the evacuation, what time is the evacuation set for? Did you tell them to draw evacuation criteria up? Muto-san, what time do you think they'll all evacuate the site?"

Muto didn't respond.

8:16 P.M. Takahashi told Fukushima via videoconference, "All the people at 1F (Fukushima Daiichi) are going to evacuate to the visitors hall at 2F (Fukushima Daini), aren't they?"

No one from Daiichi answered. Naohiro Masuda, site superintendent at Daini, broke in. "I'll set up two ERCs, one for us at the four plants at 2F and one for the people from 1F, the old ERC team. There will be two separate response rooms, so Head Office, make sure you use the appropriate ones."

The ERC in the Anti-Seismic Building was the command post for dealing with the accident. Masuda was saying that it was to be moved temporarily to the Daini station.

In that time, Yoshida had started to draw up an evacuation plan for the workers onsite. It was an evacuation plan envisioning the worst-case scenario as described by Hosono. He had already commanded associate company workers to "please go home." At this point, what needed to be looked into was the evacuation plan fit for the TEPCO workers responding to the crisis at Fukushima Daiichi.

Yoshida called the head of the general affairs team into the site superintendent's office.

"Check for me how many people we have. In particular, find out how many people there are who have no relation to operations and repairs."

Leave "the minimum number of people who are necessary for operating" packed in the ERC in the Anti-Seismic Building. However, let all other workers evacuate.

"How many buses are there that we can use? I think we have two or three. Check for me. Are there drivers, is there fuel, check these, too. After confirming these, get the buses on standby at the front. Make preparations so that they can take off quickly if something happens."[18]

8:20 P.M. Shimizu reminded Yoshida in the videoconference, "Please confirm that the decision for a final evacuation hasn't been made at this point. So we're currently verifying that with the necessary authorities. We will decide on that while monitoring, well, confirming the condition of the plant. Please go ahead with that awareness at this point in time."

Yoshida: "Yes, understood."

Shimizu: "While monitoring, confirming the condition of the plant, please decide."
Yoshida: "Yes, roger that."[19]

Even Shimizu himself could not recall how many phone calls he made that night. Shimizu called Nobuaki Terasaka, NISA director general, who was at the Kantei at 6:36 p.m., but Terasaka did not pick up. He got a call back from Terasaka at around eight p.m.[20] Shimizu said, "The situation at Unit 2 is grave. If it becomes progressively worse, I'm considering the possibility of evacuation."[21]

What is he trying to say? I can't get his point.

For a moment, Terasaka didn't get Shimizu's drift, but his defensive instinct kicked in.

Is he sounding us out on our assessment? Any false move on our part could have grave implications . . .

"I'm sure you have a lot of things on your mind, but think about it yourselves."

Upon saying so, Terasaka hung up. He had inferred from Shimizu's words, however, that *it doesn't mean all the workers are going to leave now and the place will be deserted.*[22]

Shimizu also rang Hosono. Hosono didn't take the call. Hosono had heard that Shimizu had already rung Kaieda. He was then told by an aide that Shimizu had tried to ring him.

"He probably didn't want to talk to me, but wanted a message passed on to the prime minister."

Guessing this was the case, he refused to have the call put through. Hosono told Fukuyama that he'd had a call, adding that he hadn't taken it, telling Fukuyama, "It wouldn't have been something I should be listening to."[23]

Shimizu's target was Kaieda.

From around 6:40 p.m. on March 14 until 1:30 a.m. on March 15, Shimizu and his secretary placed numerous calls to Kiyoshi Sawaki, executive assistant to the minister of economy, trade, and industry.[24] Every time Shimizu left the message, "I want to speak directly with the minister."

Just before seven o'clock, Shimizu managed to speak with Kaieda. He spoke a few words to the effect that "We may have to think about evacuating." Just when more words looked like they were to come, he would clam up. Kaieda would then come back with some inconsequential interjection along the lines of "Ah, is that so?"

When Shimizu said to Kaieda, "I would very much like to have your approval," Kaieda responded with a curt "You're not serious?" and hung up.[25]

During this time, the situation, which had looked for a while to be taking a favorable turn, headed downhill. Both Ichiro Takekuro, TEPCO fellow, and Susumu Kawamata, general manager for nuclear quality and safety management, started speaking pessimistically about "not being able to carry out onsite operations if things stay this way." They were both totally dispirited.

"There's nothing more we can do."

They started talking like this. Pessimism spread throughout the Kantei.

It was around this time that Koichiro Genba, minister for national policy, popped into the reception room on the fifth floor. Kaieda quietly whispered to Genba, "TEPCO has started talking about evacuating."

Genba was taken aback. When he saw the figures of Takekuro and Kawamata looking so low that they couldn't even raise their heads, he was stunned.[26]

Hosono spoke to Takekuro.

"Takekuro-san, you're TEPCO's main man at the Kantei. This is no time to be downcast! Think of something!"

But Takekuro was limp and didn't respond.[27]

Fukuyama was struck with fear.

If they keep on with operations like this, some of the workers are going to become casualties. That's probably when TEPCO will start evacuating. But what will happen if they pull out . . . ?

Fukuyama had heard that Hosono had spoken with Yoshida on the phone. And the word was that Yoshida had said, "We can still do it." Head Office was steeped in pessimism, but Fukushima didn't seem to be. Fukuyama couldn't figure it out.

Why is TEPCO Head Office talking about evacuating when the people on the ground are saying that there must be something they can do?[28]

LATE AT NIGHT. When only a very select few, including Kaieda and Kukita, were gathered in the prime minister's reception room, Kaieda urged Kawamata to "please explain the situation at Unit 2 again." For some reason, Takekuro was no longer to be seen on the fifth floor. Kawamata started to speak haltingly.

"We've tried various things, but none of it's been successful . . . No matter what we do, we can't get the cooling water back online . . . I am really sorry."

As he spoke, his cheeks were drenched in tears.

Kukita then went to the large room on the second floor. He was vexed to hear young TEPCO workers rattling on about subjects that had nothing to do with the matter at hand. Unable to hold back, he unleashed his fury upon them.

"What are you amateurs talking about?"

Kawamata took their side.

"I'm sorry if they've upset you. They don't mean any harm."[29]

BEFORE ELEVEN P.M. ON MARCH 14. Preparations for venting to lower the pressure of the storage container were in place, but a sharp jump in the reactor pressure meant they could not inject water. Muto began to doubt if the SR valve (the main steam safety valve) was open.[30]

11:17 P.M., MARCH 14. A person in charge at Head Office made a statement over the videoconference. "If the core is damaged due to a state of high pressure, it will go into containment failure in a matter of hours."

11:27 P.M. TEPCO Adviser Yuichi Hayase (former deputy president) grabbed the mike during the videoconference and yelled, "Look for the easiest SR valve to open and hook it up quickly to a battery. In any event, you've got to get it open quickly. Look, if you can vent, Yoshida, if you can vent, do it straight away and be quick about it!"

They had to hurry with the venting. However, it looked like the small valve of the wet vent line that expelled air via the water wasn't open. There was no choice but to open the small valve of the dry vent line and expel without passing through water. That, however, meant releasing a large volume of radioactive material outside.

Still, Muto strongly insisted that there was no other option besides opening it. Akiyoshi Minematsu, another adviser from the same nuclear background as Hayase, also harried him.

"There'll be hell to pay if you bust the drywell, you know. At least open the small valve on the drywell already!"

Unable to bear it any longer, Yoshida spoke quickly.

"Stop asking me all these things. We're currently working on opening the valves to vent the containment vessel, so don't disturb us."[31]

It was getting on to midnight on March 15. Discussion between the officials in charge at Head Office was still going about dry venting.

"NISA says to contact them before we open."

"NISA says when we're ready to open, it's TEPCO's call, but to contact them when we're ready to open."

"Are you telling me to tell them?"

"Oh, no, sorry. I'll tell them directly."

"You mean they want advance notification, is that it? Do you mean we have to get the permission of the minister?"

12:01 A.M., MARCH 15. A report came in from the site.

"At 12:01 a.m., we opened Valve 208. It is a small valve on the small vent on the side of the drywell vent of the PCV [primary containment vessel] vent."

Six minutes later, there was a new report.

"It's 12:07 a.m. Nothing has changed compared to one minute earlier. The drywell pressure isn't falling."[32]

AFTER ONE A.M. ON MARCH 15. Kaieda and Terada were talking with Edano in the chief cabinet secretary's office, when one of Kaieda's executive assistants entered and said, "There's a call from TEPCO." Kaieda told the assistant, "I've had enough of that. I've already told them I don't want to hear any more of it." Then he explained to Edano:

"TEPCO's saying they're going to evacuate."

Edano merely stated, "That had reached me, too."

Terada admonished Kaieda.

"Minister, please stop ignoring calls."

"Hmm, I suppose you're right."

Kaieda left the room to place a call. When he answered the phone, Shimizu explained in a tight voice that the situation at Unit 2 was even more serious now.

"I think we'll have no choice but to evacuate the workers if there's no change . . . We currently have seven or eight hundred workers onsite at Fukushima Daiichi, and we'd like to evacuate them from Daiichi to Daini."

After a pause, Kaieda spoke.

"Shimizu-san, evacuating isn't possible. We need you to hang in there a bit more."

He did add at the end, however, "Given the serious nature of the matter, I'll speak to the prime minister."

After he hung up, Kaieda thought to himself, *It must be a heavy decision, given that it's the president making the call.* He then told his executive assistant, Kiyoshi Sawaki, "TEPCO have started broaching something truly awful. They're saying they're going to evacuate, evacuate to Fukushima Daini. It's unthinkable!"

Kaieda also informed Hosono that "TEPCO is talking about evacuating." This was the first time Hosono had heard evacuation mentioned. Although Kaieda had instinctively spoken harshly to Shimizu, he had promised to "pass it on to the prime minister." Kaieda asked Masaya Yasui, director general for the Energy Conservation and Renewable Energy Department, who was nearby, "What would happen if everyone cleared out from the site at TEPCO Fukushima Daiichi?"

"If that happened, it wouldn't only be Units 1 through 4 that went into meltdown. They'd no longer be able to cool down Units 5 and 6, which means trouble. And the pools at each reactor would be finished also."

If everyone leaves, with things like this, we'll lose all six reactors. If that happens, we may have to think about evacuating Tokyo.

Kaieda felt a chill run down his spine.[33]

Immediately prior to this, Shimizu had rung Edano as well, conveying his wish to consider evacuating from Fukushima Daiichi. Edano was exercising caution in "maintaining the correct distance" from TEPCO. It was unthinkable that he would get a direct call from TEPCO on his mobile phone. Edano's secretaries were also clear on this point.

At two p.m. on March 13, when Shimizu had visited the Kantei to discuss the Unit 1 explosion, one of Edano's secretaries had spoken with the head of the president's office on his mobile phone, but Shimizu's call had come not to the secretary's mobile phone, but to the general inquiries number of the Kantei.[34]

Edano was opposed to evacuation, but Shimizu persisted.

"No, but isn't there . . . There's no way the workers on the ground can hold out."

Conversely, Edano asked him, "Wouldn't doing that mean losing control, aggravating the situation even further, and make it impossible to stop?"

Shimizu was tongue-tied.

"It's not something I can say yes to. In any event, do everything you can."

Delivering this, Edano hung up.

It was impossible to know what was happening on the ground by just talking to Head Office. They needed to check up once more on the real intentions of the Fukushima site and TEPCO Head Office.

Edano went to the prime minister's reception room. Kaieda, Fukuyama, Hosono, and Terada were there. Edano used Hosono's mobile to call Yoshida.

"You can still do it, can't you?"

"We'll do it. We'll do our best."

Edano was furious as he hung up.

"Why are the people at Head Office talking about evacuation? They can't be communicating with the site at all!"[35]

That night, there were seven hundred people working at the Fukushima Daiichi station, approximately four hundred from TEPCO and three hundred from their associate companies.[36]

OFFSITE CENTER RELOCATED

Around this time, the top officials at METI and NISA were worried about the question of moving NISA's offsite center. After consulting with Akio Komori, TEPCO managing director; as well as Yuki Imaura, deputy commander of the Central Readiness Force (CRF); and other senior members of the onsite NERHQ, Motohisa Ikeda, METI senior vice minister, looked for a suitable building or facility just outside the twenty-kilometer radius. There was nothing handy, however. In the end, it was decided to relocate to the fifth floor of the Fukushima Prefectural Office.

The weather forecast showed rain from around noon on March 15. If rain fell, so, too, would the radioactive material scattered into the atmosphere. And if that happened, they would not be able to evacuate, so Ikeda's call was that if they were going to move, it would have to be before noon on March 15. Before doing so, they would have to confirm that all of the residents within the twenty-kilometer radius had been evacuated.

They had information come in that there were still patients at the Futaba Hospital and the special nursing facility, Deauville Futaba. The SDF said, "They're still there," but according to the police report, "the critical patients had been transferred." The information was conflicting.

Ikeda had the SDF contact the hospital again and hurriedly decided to send in a residents' safety unit and a medical unit. When he did so, he learned that there were ninety-six patients still there, including the seriously ill. Some of them "could not be moved." But there was no choice; everyone needed to be evacuated.[37]

At 8:40 p.m., Ikeda held a meeting with everyone at the offsite center. Komori reported, "Pressure at Unit 2 is 0.653 MPa." (One MPa, or megapascal, is a measure of pressure equal to 1 million pascals. The atmospheric pressure of our usual environment is approximately 0.1 MPa.)

Does that mean there's a leak somewhere?

There were those who had a vision of hell with the fuel rods melting down through the bottom of the pressure vessel.[38]

It was decided in this meeting to send an advance team to set up a beachhead, and a report was sent to Kaieda that they were "relocating to the Fukushima Prefectural Office."[39]

Around ten p.m., Ikeda sent off the advance team in the name of "preparing for the relocation to the Fukushima Prefectural Office." METI, however, commented that perhaps they should wait to relocate the offsite center after they had verified the evacuation of the local municipalities. This was in response to Kaieda's wishes.

Much of the exchange between the onsite ERC and NISA took place via landlines. With a landline, it was possible to put the call on speaker so everyone in the offsite center could hear. There was a risk that talk of "relocation" via this medium would upset people.[40]

It was not possible for NISA and the site to talk in depth.

After a short time, a dosage alert went off on the offsite center management unit's computer. Readings from the monitor on the wall of the second floor for both inside and outside started rising swiftly.

10:24 P.M., MARCH 14.

Maximum (external) 553 microsieverts/hour (0.533 millisieverts)

Minimum (internal) 12 microsieverts/hour (0.012 millisieverts)

The external reading reached a maximum of 1,000 microsieverts (1 millisievert).

Before long, an alarm started to sound. It continued to sound off and on whenever 100 microsieverts (0.1 millisieverts) was passed. Everyone took stable iodine.

Officials at the offsite center started wearing half-face masks even indoors. They could not talk with the half-face masks on, which meant that they could not do any work. Since there were no beds, when they lay down on the floor to sleep, other people's shoes kept hitting their heads. And then the radioactive material on the soles of the shoes would rub off, and the dosage would spike.[41]

The offsite center didn't even have air-cleaning filters. That turned out to be costly.

A recommendation from the Ministry of Internal Affairs and Communications, based on the result of an administrative evaluation and supervision program in 2009, had already warned NISA about the absence of radiation exposure dose mitigation measures (such as high-performance air filters). NISA had not taken the recommendation seriously, however. This came back to bite them.[42]

How should the request from Ikeda to relocate the offsite center be handled? It was Director Hiromu Katayama of the Policy Planning and Coordination Division at NISA who dealt with this. He was a career bureaucrat with METI and had been transferred there the previous summer. It was his first time working at NISA.

Fuel, water, and power were all starting to run out at the offsite center. Supplying these was the responsibility of NISA's Emergency Response Center (ERC). Even if they wanted to move staff to Fukushima City, they would have to get enough vehicles and gasoline to do so.

Katayama deemed the relocation of the offsite center to be unavoidable. He reported to both Hiraoka and Terasaka respectively, but when he was talking with Terasaka, Terasaka mentioned signs of a TEPCO "withdrawal." Katayama was shocked and had an uneasy premonition.

This is going to be a nuisance.

With Unit 2 in a critical situation, they were reaching the limit over which operations could no longer be carried out, whether onsite or offsite. There was no changing the facts. But if this got out, then there was going to be trouble.

It was also possible that staff would have to remain at NISA's offsite center even after TEPCO had "withdrawn." On the other hand, they might have to decide to permit the offsite center to relocate while telling TEPCO that they could not "withdraw."

If they were going to tell the TEPCO workers to stay until the last and do their best, should they not be telling the NISA staff at the offsite center the same thing?

Another factor was that they had to verify the evacuation of residents within the twenty-kilometer radius of Fukushima Daiichi had been completed. ERC, in its capacity as the emergency headquarters secretariat, had contacted Fukushima Prefecture, urging them to hurry with the resident evacuation, but it was taking time. Information to the effect that the patients at Futaba Hospital were still to be evacuated had come in.

In the late hours of the night, Hiraoka returned to NISA from the Kantei.

Just after two a.m., he heard the report from Katayama that "TEPCO is thinking about pulling out." Katayama asked Hiraoka, "I'm still working on what to do with the offsite center, but if TEPCO pulls out, it'll have ramifications on this, too. Deputy director general, can you check with the TEPCO side?"

What? TEPCO pulling out? Impossible!

Those were Hiraoka's thoughts, but he decided to ring his longtime friend, TEPCO Managing Director Akio Komori, and ask what the situation was. Komori was holed up in the offsite center.

Komori told him, "The situation at the offsite center is getting more dangerous."

"Komori-san, I'd just like to ask you, have you heard anything about evacuating employees from Fukushima Daiichi? What's the plan?"

"We're looking into it now. The radiation's climbing, and the situation at Unit 2 is pretty tense . . . Working outside and the like is getting extremely tough. There are dozens of workers in the Anti-Seismic Building, but no one can work outside anymore. We're looking into moving them to Fukushima Daini, at this stage."

"Right now?"

"We're running a simulation right now of the situation in the reactors and the progress with the venting at Unit 2, things like that. It won't blow immediately, I think we have a few hours up our sleeve, but I don't know what the morning will bring . . ."

So, not right now.

The offsite center is not an empty shell.

Hiraoka felt somewhat relieved. Komori continued.

"I'm thinking I'd like to evacuate before the last two or three hours when it will be too fraught."

"Komori-san, please let the offsite center know the moment TEPCO makes an organizational decision. I think we'll have to close the offsite center and relocate at such a time, so please let us know in advance if you are pulling out."

Pushing this last point one more time, Hiraoka rang off.

This could create a serious problem if the government pulls out despite TEPCO doing its utmost.

However, we can't let TEPCO just abandon it.

Hiraoka was extremely worried.

The next thing Katayama did was to get the minister's approval for the off-site center relocation. In order to do so, he had Terasaka go to the Kantei, but Kaieda didn't give him a favorable answer. He then spoke with Terasaka and decided to get Matsunaga, METI vice minister, to soften Kaieda up.[43]

Matsunaga visited the Kantei late on the night of March 14. Kaieda was nowhere to be seen. He was kept waiting for more than two hours in the prime minister's reception room. During this time, he heard from one of the parliamentary secretaries at the Kantei, an ex-METI man, that TEPCO might be "withdrawing." Matsunaga was surprised, but that wasn't why he had come to the Kantei. He had come to get Kaieda's approval for relocating NISA's offsite center to the Fukushima Prefectural Office.

As vice minister, he was not only responsible for the jobs and the mission of the NISA staff, but also their rights and safety. With the crisis at Unit 2 as deep as it was, Matsunaga believed there was nothing to do but approve the offsite center's relocation.

Matsunaga met with Kaieda and expressed his view. Kaieda, however, was cautious, telling him to "leave it with me for a bit."

On the one hand, we have TEPCO starting to talk about "withdrawing." We can't allow that. On the other hand, we can approve the "relocation" of the workers cooped up in the offsite center. How tenable is that?

Wait a minute. Perhaps TEPCO only started talking about "withdrawing" in the first place in anticipation of the offsite center being removed . . .

Hosono was also aware of the tricky implications relocating the offsite center would have.

Kaieda merely muttered to Hosono, "I suppose we'll have to start preparing to move the offsite center." There was a strong possibility that Kan would be furious if he heard about it, and would intervene with an order to wait.

I guess we'll just have to create a fait accompli without the prime minister being informed.

That was what Hosono thought, and he felt Kaieda was thinking the same thing.

The relocation of the offsite center was decided at once on the morning of March 15, when Units 2 and 4 were facing a new crisis. Kaieda stayed behind after he and Kan had descended upon TEPCO Head Office.

Before eight a.m., Matsunaga received a phone call from Kaieda.

"I'll approve the relocation, so I want you to contact Ikeda and tell him I'm waiting for a call."

Matsunaga phoned Ikeda immediately.

"It's been okayed."

But around nine a.m., Kaieda placed another call to Matsunaga.

"I told you okay, but it doesn't look like they've moved yet."

Here I am, giving them the go-ahead. Why don't they move?

There was something critical in his tone.

"It looks like the evacuation of the hospital patients in the twenty-kilometer radius isn't finished yet."

When Matsunaga told him this, Kaieda indicated he understood.

"So, the relocation's to be after everyone's been evacuated from the evacuation zone, right?"

Kaieda and Ikeda spoke directly on the phone after that, deciding that all the staff at the local NERHQ in the offsite center would relocate to the Fukushima Prefectural Office after they had seen through the evacuation of the local residents.[44]

MARCH 15. Ikeda handed over his position as head of the local NERHQ to METI Senior Vice Minister Tadahiro Matsushita and returned to Tokyo. He felt that he had been almost ignored, and his duties and work at the local NERHQ totally unappreciated by the Kantei and the METI minister.

There were those among the parliamentary members of the Kantei who felt displeased, believing it was Ikeda who had insisted, "You shouldn't vent until the evacuation of residents is complete." They were nervous about having it intimated that the venting was delayed because of the prime minister's visit, something Ikeda might well be prone to say.[45]

Ikeda's relations with Kaieda, as well as Kan, were tense. Both Kaieda and Kan had thought of relieving him of his post, but Ikeda managed— just barely—to keep his job through the intervention of Defense Minister Toshimi Kitazawa.[46]

IMPERIAL CONFERENCE

In the prime minister's reception room on the fifth floor, Kaieda lounged on the sofa, growing quieter and quieter. There was a possibility that Unit 2 would suffer a hydrogen explosion like Units 1 and 3. Radiation levels were already mounting.

"Do you think we should keep the TEPCO workers there to the very end?"

"Is evacuation the only option . . . ?"

"I expect we'll have to call in the SDF, won't we?"

"But what will happen with the evacuation of residents if we do that?"

In the end, the air started to get heavy with the thought that evacuation was their only option.[47]

Triggered by some thought or other, Kaieda said, "Just think of that! Here we've all been working desperately since March 11 and we haven't taken a single photo to commemorate it."

"Let's take a shot with everyone in it."

Since it was Kaieda's suggestion, Hosono, Terada, Ito, Kukita, and the aides all bunched up around him.

"This might be the last, so . . ."

As Kaieda said that, his face looked strained to Kukita. Ito felt dryness in his throat. He opened a bottle of oolong tea, took a swig, then joined the circle.

What on earth is he thinking? Has he got a screw loose?

This fellow, Kaieda-san, he must be a continental type—so careful and open-minded. Fancy being able to diffuse tension by pulling a trick like that at a time like this!

Does he think this is the end of the line? Is that what he's feeling?

I wonder if the Kantei is going to be evacuated, too?

Each was entertaining his own thoughts.[48]

Hosono was thinking about the phrase "honorable death."

We may all end up dying an honorable death . . .[49]

Madarame went home for the first time since the quake late on the night of March 14, but was called back to the Kantei by Yutaka Kukita, acting chair of NSC, just two hours later. He was surprised to hear from Kukita, "We've just taken a commemorative shot bidding this world farewell."

They could well be facing "defeat" if things continued this way. Edano and Fukuyama, who came into the prime minister's reception room a short while later, asked Madarame, Yasui, and the others, "To be really honest, what's going to happen? How long will it hold out?"

"It may be able to last somehow for the moment, but there's a chance we'll lose control at some point."

"It's not a matter of weeks. If that happens, we won't be able to touch it for a long time."

"Even if we keep opening the valves, pumping in water, opening the valves again, and pumping in water again, I think that at some point the valves won't open."

The experts came up with catastrophic scenarios. Withdrawing was out of the question now. But if the radiation reached levels where it was impossible for people to approach and there was an explosion, would it still be out of the question? Fukuyama asked, "It's not right for us to decide here. We should ask the prime minister his opinion."

Fukuyama was afraid that they would slip into deciding it was okay to withdraw. He was hoping he could change the flow by holding an official meeting and asking for the prime minister's "royal decree."[50]

Edano and Terada had no objection. And so, it was decided to hold a meeting that the parliamentary secretaries at the Kantei would later refer to as the "imperial conference" (extraconstitutional conferences of national importance with the emperor pre–World War II). Terada got someone to clean up all the radiation data and other papers lying around the reception room and had the tables arranged.

APPROXIMATELY THREE A.M. Kan was taking a nap in the backroom of his office, known as the "inner chamber." Executive Assistant Kenji Okamoto woke him.

"Prime minister, Minister Kaieda wishes to consult with you."

Kan started to get up, with sleepy eyes. He looked to be in an extremely bad mood. His hair was ruffled.

Kaieda, Edano, Fukuyama, Hosono, Terada, and Ito took their seats. Yasui and Madarame were called in. Kaieda and Edano were sitting on the sofa on Kan's right-hand side, facing Ito and Fukuyama on his left.

Kan, who had looked sleepy when he entered the room, seemed to have perked up slightly, possibly thanks to his nap. Compared to Kaieda and Hosono, who had barely slept that day, only Kan's face looked animated.

Kaieda commenced, "TEPCO is saying it wants to withdraw from the nuclear emergency site, but what should we do? The station is in a very serious situation."

What? They're thinking pulling out is unavoidable? So that's why they came and woke me up?

"Withdrawing? What's that? That's just not an option."

Kan sounded aggressive.

"Yes, we know that, but we can't tell the TEPCO employees to stay there until they die, either . . ."

Kaieda and Edano spoke in a somewhat daunted manner.

If we leave the workers at Fukushima Daiichi, it won't be long before they're exposed to a huge amount of radiation and die.

Hosono didn't open his mouth. Fukuyama was silent on the matter, too. The air was thick with gloom.

Ito was preparing for the worst, thinking, *What does this mean, the politicians clamming up? Is it up to me?* He looked Kan straight in the eye and said, "No, we need to have TEPCO hang in there . . . If we let them withdraw, it will mean abandoning all emergency response, and that's just impossible . . . We need them to hang on even if it takes something like a suicide squad."

Not a single person backed him up, however.

Kan broke the silence.

"What has the site got to say?"

Upon saying "Let's ask Yoshida-san," he rang Masao Yoshida at Fu-kushima Daiichi NPS from the phone on the desk. Kan was nodding at something with the receiver to his ear, but when he hung up, he said in an overwrought manner, "Yoshida says they can still do it. Hey, the site says they can still do it. No such thing as pulling out will go ahead!"

Ito was relieved. Resolving that "this is an important decision, so let's get all the parliamentary members together," Edano, Fukuyama, and Terada left Kan behind and moved to the reception room. The executive assistants contacted Ryu Matsumoto, minister of state for disaster management, who was pent up in the crisis management center.[51]

3:30 A.M. The "imperial conference" was convened in the reception room. Matsumoto joined Kan, Edano, Kaieda, Matsumoto, Fukuyama, Hosono, Terada, Terasaka, Yasui, Madarame, and Kukita a little later. With the two deputy chief cabinet secretaries—Hirohisa Fujii and Kinya Takino—there were thirteen in all. Edano presided.

"It has been reported that TEPCO president Shimizu has said, 'Since we cannot guarantee the lives of our staff, from Site Superintendent Yoshida down, we would like to pull them out.' TEPCO is saying there's nothing more they can do, and they want to withdraw. What are they thinking? Although it does seem to be a fact that the situation is beyond their capa-bility," Edano began his opening statement.

Terada found it hard to comprehend.

That's stupidly poor moderating for Edano-san.

Kan raised a loud voice.

"If they pull out, who on earth is going to handle the situation? Are we going to abandon five nuclear reactors and six pools? Do you know what will happen then?"

You could cut the tension in the room with a knife. Kan continued.

"All of Eastern Japan will disappear. It's just not an option! No matter how many people die, they're not withdrawing . . . It's unthinkable that we would just walk away from a nuclear emergency in our own country . . . I'll never allow them to pull out . . . If TEPCO pulls out from the site, what do you think will happen at Units 1, 2, and 3? What will happen at the Unit 4 fuel pool? In the worst case, they'll have to form a suicide squad. Handling it with people over sixty years old."

He then added, "If it comes to that, I'll have to be the first one."

Having delivered this shot, Kan glanced over at Madarame.

"What do you think?"

He looks as jumpy as a mouse.

One could almost feel Madarame's heart pounding.

"Withdrawal is unthinkable."

As if to supplement Madarame's words, Yasui added,

"Units 1, 2, and 3 will go down . . . And that's not all. If nothing is done about the fuel pools at Units 5 and 6, as well as the shared pool, there's a real possibility that we won't be able to do a thing with the entire plant. You've got to remember those fuel pools. If they pull out, it'll be a disaster. They can't withdraw."

Madarame continued,

"If they pull out now, if they pull out once, getting them back in will be extremely difficult. And I don't think it's likely that the SDF or the U.S. armed forces will conveniently come and help if TEPCO has pulled out. Bearing in mind the structure of the Anti-Seismic Building, they should be able to hang on longer."

Unit 1 might have exploded, but its containment vessel is still alive. They've somehow managed even after Unit 3 exploded, whose containment vessel is also still alive. There's only Unit 2 left now. Why do they want to pull out now? We're almost out of the woods!

This was how Madarame felt, but he struggled to put it into words. Yasui, however, voiced the same thoughts.

Kan told everyone to listen up.

"There cannot be any withdrawal."

Kan pointed at Terasaka, Yasui, Madarame, and Kukita, each in turn, and confirmed:

"How about it? There can't be any withdrawal, right?"

Kan had the habit of repeating the same thing three times.[52]

What?! He's forcing the technical advisers to make a political decision! And using such high-pressure tactics is almost like forcing an answer.

Before the morning audience, when discussing with Edano, Fukuyama, and the others, Yasui said, "The decision to withdraw or not, to approve or not, is a political decision, not something for us to decide." It had made a strong impression on Terada.

Terada interjected now, asking the four technical advisers, "Please speak in terms of objective technical theory." But Kan persisted with the questions, "What do you think about withdrawing? What do you think of that?"

If the earlier meeting in the prime minister's office with just the parliamentary members had been the venue for "making a decision," the morning audience was akin to a venue for "verifying the decision."

The meeting was coming to a close, but Terada raised an issue.

"If we don't approve a withdrawal, how are we going to prevent people who want to flee from doing just that? How can that be done, in legal terms?"

Edano took over.

"In legal terms? The law has nothing to do with it right now."

Terada considered saying, *What are you saying? Isn't it your job to think exactly about that?* but thought better of it.

Kan spoke, "We're not getting any information from the frontlines. We've got to do something about that. I'm going to set up an integrated headquarters at TEPCO with the government."

An integrated headquarters at TEPCO?

He caught everyone off balance. It was an idea that had never been discussed by the parliamentary team at the Kantei.

The idea had crossed Kan's mind the day before. It had just popped out.

They then moved to the prime minister's office to discuss the matter just among the politicians. They would get TEPCO President Shimizu to come to the Kantei. Kan called him on the spot, asking him to come, and Shimizu agreed. Kan was still pumped up.

What do they think will happen if they run away from something like this?

We'll be invaded from overseas if we do something like this!

Kan closed in on each of them, one by one, just like before. "I'm going to TEPCO. Are you coming? Are you coming? Are you coming?"

Fukuyama, Hosono, and Terada all nodded mutely. They had to think of how to deal with Shimizu when he came. Kan asked them, "Do you think I should set foot in TEPCO or not?"

Terada said, "Since the government is going to enter a private firm, we probably need some legal grounds." But Edano maintained his hardline approach that "the law has nothing to do with it."

Terada refused to let go.

"Nevertheless, since it's the country's prime minister who's going to set foot in TEPCO, we need to be sure of the legalities."

Terada whispered in the ear of Takino, who was sitting next to him, "Think about the legalities and theoretical matters in your deputy secretary section."

Although the debate between Terada and Edano concerned legal aspects, that wasn't the only issue. If the prime minister was to set foot on the TEPCO premises, it would be the second time, including his visit to Fukushima Daiichi NPS on March 12. It had to be set up so he wasn't subjected to the same criticism. They had to weigh the practical, legal, and political implications.

Edano had opposed the helicopter visit on March 12, but didn't put a stop to the TEPCO Head Office visit that morning.

Kan was also concerned about the unpopularity of his visit to the site at the time. The reason he had closed in on Fukuyama, Hosono, and Terada individually with his "Are you coming?" was because he wanted to create a firm consensus.

Edano ordered that the aides, who had been sent home late on March 14, be immediately called back in.

"It's been decided that an integrated headquarters for the government and TEPCO will be set up at TEPCO Head Office. Get back to the Kantei."[53]

"WE'RE NOT WITHDRAWING"

4:17 A.M. Shimizu arrived at the Kantei.

He was accompanied by TEPCO's Diet affairs official and public relations officer. They took the elevator from the lobby to the fifth floor and waited in the prime minister's reception room. When Terada asked Shimizu in front of the prime minister's office if all three were going in or just Shimizu, Shimizu said he would go alone, so he had the other two wait in the waiting room.

Shimizu entered the prime minister's office alone and sat on the sofa to Kan's right. Kaieda, Edano, and Fukuyama were seated on the sofa to Kan's left, and Ito and Yasui sat across from Kan.

Kan said quietly, "Now, Shimizu-san, withdrawing is just not possible."

Shimizu answered in an almost inaudible voice, "Yes."

"That's not going to happen, is it? There's not going to be any withdrawal."

"Of course not."

"There's no other course of action."

"You're right."

Kan found it almost anticlimactic that Shimizu said yes so soon.

Kaieda said in a disconcerted tone, "That's quite different from what you said on the phone." He was even worried.

This time he's going to say they'll stay. That means the possibility of acute exposure. To what extent is he thinking about such a weighty decision?

Yasui also thought, *What's going on? How strange!*

When Shimizu entered the room, Ito thought there was going to be a full confrontation between Kan and Shimizu over TEPCO's total withdrawal. That is what made it seem so incomprehensible.

What's this? Hadn't he been saying we don't care what happens to Japan, just let our workers go? Wasn't he putting his life on the line as president with that decision? Was he really talking so lightly about such a weighty matter?

Kan was also relieved deep down, but felt it necessary to shift matters at once.

Shimizu's word is not enough. We have to coordinate the government's decisions and TEPCO's decisions. Things will get serious if there's any discrepancy.

"To date, we've had separate response headquarters at the Kantei and TEPCO, but this is problematic from the point of view of sharing and quickly grasping information. This is why I would like us to join forces. We're going to set up an integrated headquarters for the government and TEPCO. We'd like to have it at TEPCO's Head Office. That's all right, isn't it?"

"We'd like to go with Chairman Katsumata—or yourself—and Minister Kaieda as the deputy chiefs, and Executive Assistant Hosono as the head of secretariat."

Although Shimizu looked surprised at Kan's words, he replied, "That's fine."

Kan also told him that he himself intended to go to TEPCO.

"How long will it take to get ready?"

"When should we be ready by? In how many hours' time? One hour? Two?"

"We don't have that much time. I'll be there in thirty minutes. All we need are some desks."

Kan turned to Hosono and said, "I'm letting you take Hosono now, all right? Shimizu-san, let's work together. Hosono, you go with Shimizu-san."

Shimizu was silent. Kan spoke to him in encouragement.

"Right, well, thank you very much."

Kan and Hosono had already decided, prior to Shimizu's visit, that Hosono was to be sent to TEPCO. Terada gave a cautionary word to Shimizu as he was getting to his feet.

"TEPCO has agreed to an integrated headquarters, correct?"

Shimizu nodded.

"Yes, it's agreed."

Hosono and Shimizu left the room.[54]

5:26 A.M. ON MARCH 15. The government established the Government-TEPCO Integrated Response Office for the Fukushima Daiichi Nuclear Power Plant Emergency. This meant putting in place a joint command tower at TEPCO Head Office to respond to the nuclear crisis.

During this time, Shiro Yamazaki (with the Ministry of Health, Welfare, and Labor since 1978), Keisuke Sadamori (with METI since 1979), and Koichi Masuda (with the National Police Agency since 1983)—all of them Kan's executive assistants—were up to their ears in statute books in the adjacent secretary's office, looking for the requisite legal grounds for setting foot in TEPCO and for establishing the integrated response office. Terada instructed Takino to do the same thing simultaneously. They were urged to hurry.

Terada was popular with the parliamentary assistants at the Kantei. He acted as the natural balancer, pulling Kan back strongly when they didn't know which way he would jump. Terada was always the first to realize when the aides had trouble telling Kan something directly, and would often go to bat for them.

The aides all felt, *Terada-san is a lifesaver to have around.*

It was decided to use article 20, paragraph 2, of the Act on Special Measures Concerning Nuclear Emergency Preparedness (NEPA) as legal grounds. This stated: "The director general can issue necessary instructions to related government institutions, the heads of local government bodies, and nuclear power operators."

This was interpreted as meaning the director general—namely, the prime minister—could issue "instructions" to the "nuclear power operators" (TEPCO).[55]

Hosono's car followed Shimizu's out of the Kantei. He and two assistants headed into TEPCO as the advance team and without any forewarning. It felt "almost like a raid" to Hosono.

After arriving at TEPCO, he headed straight for the ERC on the second floor. There were close to two hundred TEPCO employees, including the chairman and the president, wearing mesh vests in a variety of colors—green, yellow, and red—over their white shirts.

The TEPCO workers, in their blue work uniforms, were divided into nine teams, with the names of their teams—government contact, technology and restoration, security, information, and so on—printed on their backs. It was standard TEPCO procedure that, in an emergency, 233 people from nine teams would be deployed to the ERC.

At the front, there was a huge multi-screen divided into six screens. The top row of screens showed Kashiwazaki-Kariwa Anti-Seismic Technical Support C, Fukushima Daini Anti-Seismic Building 3F ERC D, and Fukushima Daiichi Anti-Seismic Building ERC, while the lower half showed Head Office ERC, Fukushima offsite center, and a blank screen on the far right.

The Fukushima Daiichi Anti-Seismic Building ERC screen showed the inside of the ERC. Desks were set up in a rectangle and men in blue work uniforms sat facing the screen. Both the images and sound were linked up in real time.

Look at that! They've got all the real-time information from the site right here!

What a difference from the Kantei, where the line between the crisis management center and the offsite center had been cut by the earthquake!

Taking in the scene, Hosono felt a wave of resentment. What's more, even though he was there, no one paid him any mind. But more important, why was the atmosphere in here so listless?

It's full of people, but you don't get the feeling that they're doing anything. They just seem to be hanging around.

Hosono shouted, "The prime minister is about to arrive. Please make way for him."

After a short while, TEPCO Chairman Tsunehisa Katsumata, Vice President Sakae Muto, and General Manager for Nuclear Quality and Safety Management Susumu Kawamata entered the room. Goshi Hosono had a mike brought over and, with the mike in his hand, once again declared, "The prime minister is about to arrive. We are going to set up an integrated response office here, between the government and TEPCO."

He had them immediately secure a place for the prime minister and his team, as well as set aside a reception room across the hallway.

At the Kantei, preparations were underway for going to TEPCO. The prime minister's regular driver wasn't immediately available. They urgently found another driver to take Kan, and he rode not in the usual Lexus but in a Toyota Century. This delayed the departure slightly.

Kan told Okamoto in a serious manner, "In the end, I'll have to go to the site."

He meant he would go once more to Fukushima Daiichi.

"Run a simulation for when the Super Puma helicopter can come to the residence."

Leaving behind these words, he headed downstairs.[56]

STORMING INTO TEPCO

At 5:35 a.m. on March 15, the delegation left the Kantei in a cavalcade of cars. It was still dark outside. They had no police escort.

The lead car was the security police. Kan's car followed behind it. Terada was sitting in the back seat to Kan's right. Next came the executive assistants' car (Yamazaki, Sadamori, and Maeda). The cars carrying Kaieda and Fukuyama followed theirs.

Madarame had also been ordered to TEPCO, but the driver of the NSC chairman's car couldn't be found. Madarame set off on foot for TEPCO Head Office with Michihiko Iwahashi, head of NSC's administrative affairs.

Kan was in such high spirits after the meeting with Shimizu that Terada was worried.

I need to stay close by and calm him down.

"Prime minister, do you mind if I ride with you?"

"That's fine."

This was how he had hitched the ride.

In terms of age, he could have been Kan's son. Kan liked the amiable personality of the tall, straight-backed Terada.

There was something else Terada was worried about. It was the "resolution" Kan had mentioned to Okamoto before leaving. That resolution was to revisit Fukushima Daiichi.

"If TEPCO pulls out, in the last instance, I'll go back to the site again."

He wasn't sure if Kan was trying to dissuade TEPCO from "withdrawing," or showing the government's determination to lead from the front. Okamoto had confessed to him in a whisper, "The prime minister revealed this to me. I don't know if I should get the Super Puma helicopter ready again or not . . ."

Terada remembered well the fear of Okamoto, Masuda, and the security police who had accompanied Kan on his visit to the site on the morning of March 12. This was because he shared their fear.

They can't speak up to him. I'll have to do it.

Terada told Kan, "Prime minister, I know better than anyone else you're putting your life on the line to deal with this. I've heard that you are also thinking about making a second visit to the site. I heard about the arrangements for the helicopter. Compared to that, I feel a sense of shame deep down that here I am, safe and warm . . . I think I'm frightened of radiation exposure. I'm married. Okamoto, Masuda, and me, we're all still young and we want to have kids. The security police are the same. Prime minister, if you are going to go by helicopter to the site, I'm sorry, prime minister, but in the end, you may have to go alone."

Kan said, almost to himself, "That's how it is, eh?"

They arrived at TEPCO before they knew it. Information was slow to come in. Verification was also slow. And yet, they were physically so close.

It would've been faster to have runners carrying messages.

The length of the distance between TEPCO's head office and the plant up until then seemed hard to believe.[57]

There was a large crowd of reporters waiting for Kan's cavalcade in front of TEPCO Head Office. Cameras flashed in the dark. The delegation was shown into the ERC on the second floor. Chairs had been set out, the large screen behind them, and Kan's place prepared in the middle. The security police stood behind Kan on the right with an air of importance.

There had been an in-house PA announcement at TEPCO that all managerial staff were to gather there. One of the technology and restoration team asked someone on the government contact team, "Has something happened?"

He was told, "Prime Minister Kan is coming to cheer us on."[58]

On returning from the Kantei, Shimizu had believed that Kan had been convinced and satisfied when he had answered no, there was to be no withdrawal. The proposal for an integrated response had also been easily "agreed" upon. Shimizu's optimistic outlook seemed to have given birth to the expectation that Kan was coming to "cheer them on."[59]

In front were the seats for the TEPCO executives, and Katsumata and Muto were already seated. Hosono set the scene, saying, "Well then, prime minister, if you will take a seat . . . ," but Kan remained standing, glaring at Muto sitting right in front of him, and shouted, "Do you have any idea of what's going on? Why on earth do you have all these people here? How do you expect us to decide anything in a room full of people like this? What on earth are you doing?"[60]

Kan had never imagined he was going to be shown into a room of more than two hundred people.

"Who's going to explain this to me?"

Just as Shimizu said, "I'll . . . ," Kan asked, "Are you an engineer? How about it?"

When Muto, seated next to him, said, "I'm in charge of the technology," Kan said, "Are you working in a barn like this?"[61]

As if to muffle Kan's angry voice, Hosono took the mike and declared, "We will now have an address from the director general of the nuclear emergency response headquarters, prime minister Kan."

Kan gestured to hand over the mike quickly and grabbed it from Hosono's hand. With the mike in his right hand and his left hand on his hip, he started speaking, still on his feet.

"What on earth is going on?! The explosion at Unit 1 was broadcast on television on March 12, but you didn't contact the Kantei for an hour, did you? . . . I'm not just talking about Unit 2. If you abandon Unit 2, what will happen at Unit 1, Unit 3, Units 4 through 6, as well as the site at Fukushima Daini? . . . If you withdraw from Fukushima Daiichi now, all the reactors will explode, Units 1 through 4 as well as Units 5 and 6. It won't just be Fukushima Daiichi that blows, but Fukushima Daini as well . . . If you abandon them, all of the reactors and the spent-fuel pools will collapse in a few months from now, releasing radioactivity. More than two or three times what they had at Chernobyl will be compounded at ten, twenty plants . . . Half of Japan's landmass will be lost. Japan will no longer be viable as a nation. This situation has to be contained at any cost, including risk to life . . . I can't just stand by and watch you withdraw. Do you think other countries, America, Russia, will just sit by and watch if Japan can't deal with its own nuclear emergency? Will they just leave it be for dozens of days or hundreds of days? They may well start saying that they'll do it themselves. That means Japan being occupied . . . You are the ones who have to do it. Put your lives on the line. Even if TEPCO turns and runs, you won't be able to run far enough. It doesn't matter how much money it takes. There's no way you can pull out when Japan may be going under. If you do, TEPCO will crash 100 percent . . . Chairman and president, brace yourselves. I want you to go at it with the resolution that it doesn't matter if all the executives over the age of sixty go to the site and die. I'm going to go. It's up to us to get it done . . . I'll say it one more time. There will be no withdrawal. If you withdraw, there will be no TEPCO left."[62]

Kan spoke for close to ten minutes, gesturing wildly with his left arm every now and then. His form looked frightful. His face was pale and full of fatigue.

The TEPCO executives had all sat up and looked stunned when he said, "It doesn't matter if all the executives over the age of sixty go to the site and die." Terada glanced over at the screen. The workers in their protective gear at Fukushima Daiichi had their eyes glued to the screen, not moving an inch.

They're all listening to the speech. That's no good. They're not moving.
His blood ran cold.
What's more, we can't decide anything in a place like this.
Terada handed a memo to Fukuyama sitting beside him.
"Let's get out of here."
Fukuyama looked stern.
His phrasing is way too intense.
Ikuo Izawa, the duty manager for the Central Control Room (Units 1 and 2), was one of the people in the Anti-Seismic Building "listening to the speech, not moving." He was appalled when he heard Kan's words.
He's telling us to die.
We've worked so hard to make it this far. Why do we have to listen to that?
He was overcome by an unspeakable sense of weariness.
The scene in the Anti-Seismic Building froze.[63]

Kan sat down for a moment, but, thinking goodness knows what, stood up again and started speaking. Halfway through, Hosono tried to hand him the mike, but he waved it off and kept talking.

"I mean to say, why on earth have you got so many people in here? It only takes five or six people to make important decisions. You've got to be kidding me. Get us a small room! Who at TEPCO is the most knowledgeable about this? I want to hear from that person. Those who understand the technology, stay here!"

Several people, mainly from the technological side, sat down. It was decided that they should introduce themselves, so they gave their names, one by one. It was Yasui's turn.

Yasui, suddenly asked by Terasaka, had recently arrived to help out NISA on March 13, still in the position of director general for the Department of Energy Conservation and Renewable Energy. He had not received an official letter of appointment to NISA and didn't even know what his title was, exactly. So, for a moment, he was puzzled as to how he should introduce himself.

When he tried to get off with a simple, "Er, Yasui's the name," Kan shouted at him, "Give your proper affiliation!"

Everyone fell silent at his angry voice.

After a short time, they had prepared a room, and they crossed the hallway to a meeting room. Katsumata, Muto, and engineers from Toshiba and Hitachi crammed in.[64]

TEPCO's top management and the government side faced each other across a long table. The government consisted of the parliamentarians Kan, Kaieda, Fukuyama, Hosono, and Terada, as well as Madarame. There were also senior officials from METI and NISA. On the TEPCO side were Katsumata, Shimizu, Muto, and others. Staff members were seated along the wall. They totaled almost thirty.

The TEPCO side presented a simulated forecast of what would happen in Unit 2. It was a chart showing the scenario of 20 percent damage to the reactor core at Unit 2 and the immediate release of radioactive material.[65]

Shimizu explained, "There is a chance that radioactive material will spread, but according to this, it will be confined to twenty kilometers (the evacuation radius for Daiichi)."

Kan asked, "That's only for an explosion event and radiation release from one reactor in operation, right? Wouldn't it be quite different if several reactors—Units 1, 2, and 3—were to go? And don't forget, there's the Unit 4 spent-fuel pool and the fuel storage pools. Are you really sure it'll be all right?"

This prompted Shimizu to say, "Yes, well, let's increase the margin to, say, about thirty kilometers."

His comments sound almost cavalier, Fukuyama thought.

Many of the people there, including Fukuyama, felt frustration as well as anger. Kan, however, said, "It'll have to be considered if the need arises."

(In reality, the government extended the evacuation area from twenty to thirty kilometers at eleven o'clock on the same day.)

Kan returned to his cross-examination.

"What will happen if all six reactors fail?"

No one replied.

Kan turned to Katsumata with a "What do you think?" but no words were forthcoming, just a "Hmm."[66]

A STRANGE NOISE

After a certain time, Kan started to nod off. Terada whispered to him, "Prime minister, steady now." Terada did not want to have the prime minister of Japan exposed so vulnerably in front of a crowd like this. However, the number of people in the room started to dwindle. Kan put his face close to Katsumata and said in a biting tone, "You, do it like your life depends on it!"

Katsumata replied, "I know. It's all right. I'll get a subsidiary to do it."

Terada was astonished by these words. "A subsidiary!!??"

The conference room was also hooked up to the site by videoconference. If someone spoke into the mikes on the table, they would be heard there, and, conversely, they could hear the voice of Site Superintendent Yoshida clearly.

After 6:10 a.m., Yoshida said, "What a noise."

Ensconced in the far-left seat, with a look of contempt on his face, Yoshida turned around with a start. He then donned his helmet and started rushing about. There was an announcement from Yoshida.

"This isn't something ordinary; unrelated staff are to evacuate!"

The implication was that something terrible might have happened.

"Sound of an explosion in the vicinity of Unit 2."

"The sound was near the suppression chamber."

"There's been an explosion somewhere there."

The readings from Unit 2 were: "Reactor pressure 0.612 MPa, reactor water −2700 mm."

Information started pouring in. Apparently, there had been an explosion in the reactor building. But was it Unit 2 or Unit 4? Someone said they had seen a smoke-like substance rising from the pool at Unit 4. Information was garbled. Kan did not seem to have comprehended yet what was happening on the other side of the screen. He was still talking. Yoshida cut him off, saying, "Prime minister, I'm sorry. We have an emergency situation here. May I leave for a moment?"

Kan still did not seem to understand. Yoshida reiterated.

"I'm truly sorry. I have to issue various orders. Please excuse me."

And then he added, "May I ask for a temporary evacuation?"

"I'll keep a skeleton team here and evacuate the rest."

Information was flooding in from the three control rooms to the ERC.[67]

Is it an explosion at Unit 2? What'll happen if Unit 2 has blown?

For a brief moment, the thought crossed Kan's mind, *I guess we won't be able to use my mom's house in Mitaka anymore.*

Kan rang Edano.

"There's been a very critical event. It's an abnormal situation."

The sky was lightening as day broke.

6:25 A.M.

Reports continued to come in from the site.

"The pressure in the pressure control room is zero. We'll keep doing our best to pump in water, but I'm withdrawing the rest of the staff."

"The entire building is in the dark and we're working with flashlights."
"We tried to get in, but the entrance is broken."
"When we tried to turn the switch on using temporary power, and to pump in the boric acid, there was an aftershock and everything was broken."
"Unit 2 needs five thousand tons of water."
There was even this comment:
"I've forgotten the camera. I'll go fetch it right away."
It was part of Unit 4 (RB) that had been blasted away. They were, apparently, filming it. Shortly after, the scene came up on the screen.[68]

Back in the ERC, TEPCO's top management had put up a document on the screen and was in the process of approving the wording for a "temporary evacuation." Shimizu was checking with the head of every unit if "this wording is okay" for the temporary evacuation. Shimizu then took it across the hallway to Kan.

6:37 A.M. An abnormal situation transmission (No. 71) arrived at Head Office from Yoshida.
"There was a large reverberation at Unit 2 approximately between six a.m. and 6:10 a.m. The necessary staff will be left behind, but when preparations have been made, some of the staff will be temporarily evacuated."
Yoshida then went to the large room in the Anti-Seismic Building and announced, "Everyone go to 2F, please."
This was the order to evacuate.

The Anti-Seismic Building was in an uproar as soon as Yoshida made the announcement. Over six hundred people converged on the only exit. They descended, running hurriedly down the narrow corridor and bumping into the stairs. People grabbing masks, people searching for masks, people hiding masks. People were pushing in as if they were trying to break through the manual double doors. Women were screaming and running. Employees who saw the scene going down the stairs from the Emergency Response Center on the second floor remembered it "like the scenes of panic in the movies *Towering Inferno* or *The Titanic*."[69]

AROUND SEVEN A.M. Leaving behind the seventy or so people necessary for plant monitoring and restoration work, 650 people went by bus or their own cars to the gymnasium at Fukushima Daini Power Station, some twelve kilometers to the south.

Going against the tide, Mari Sato, who led disaster prevention, went up to the Emergency Response Center on the second floor. It was already quiet around there. People trying to leave were lined up in an orderly fashion without saying a word. She needed to speak to her boss about how the firefighters should respond to the evacuation order being implemented. The fire chief told her, "I can't leave," and instructed Sato, along with two young firefighters, to temporarily evacuate. Sato said to the two youths, "There's no coming back from a hero's death. There's nothing to do but evacuate now and stay ready."

Almost everyone had already left and the place was deserted. Everyone who remained wore Tyvek suits.

They look just like burial outfits.

Is this a suicide squad?

Sato thought, "None of them will survive." She gave a lift to her colleagues to Daini in her own car. At the main gate, the bus that had left earlier had been refused entry and brought to a standstill. She talked to a guard she knew and finally made it to the gymnasium.[70]

Ikuo Izawa, the duty manager for the Central Control Room of Units 1 and 2, remained in the Emergency Response Center. After a while, Yoshida said, "Everyone should eat something." It already felt like the group had their minds made up.

There were people who appeared to be writing last letters to their families. Izawa headed for a computer. He had three sons between nineteen and twenty-six years old. His wife's rheumatism had been getting worse, and she had been forced to use a wheelchair for the past five years. When Izawa was working, she went to a nursing home. His eighty-five-year-old father also lived with them. Izawa wrote his sons an e-mail from the ERC for the first time since the accident.

"Your father has to stay until the last, so I'm asking you to look after your old grandfather and your nagging mother right up until the end."

He tried to hit the ENTER key, but couldn't bring himself to press it. He looked at the videoconference screen for a while. He took a breath and hit the key.

Something, a lump somewhere, melted away. There was an instant reply from his eldest son.

"What are you talking about, Dad? I'll never forgive you if you die!"

The youngest son also replied.

"No way! I want to have a drink with my old man!"[71]

6:45 A.M. The second-floor TEPCO ERC.

Shimizu held out a paper on "transferring headquarter functions." On it, was written: "TEPCO employees will evacuate, leaving behind essential operations staff."

On seeing that, Kan requested a change. He wanted "operations" changed to "pumping operations," clarifying that they were leaving behind only the pumping staff.

Shimizu replied, "Yes, fine."

Shimizu worked like a secretary without much to do on the second floor of TEPCO that day. One of the parliamentary team whispered to Kan:

"I've finally got a grip on how things work at TEPCO. It's Katsumata who's running the show. Shimizu's just hanging around like a sleepwalker."

Information kept pouring in from the site to Head Office.

"Looks like the bottom has fallen out of the containment vessel."

"There's a chance of meltdown."

The government team that had descended on TEPCO was peppering the TEPCO side with questions in the second-floor ERC. Tetsuya Nishi-kawa, assistant to the deputy chief cabinet secretary, turned to Katsumata and said, "Don't for a moment start thinking you're safe because you're in here."

"No."

Ito, returning from the Imperial Conference on the fifth floor to the crisis management center in the basement, had hurriedly pressed Nishi-kawa: "I can't possibly accompany the prime minister to TEPCO, I have to stay here. Nishikawa, would you go in my place?"

After seven a.m., when the TEPCO side asked for approval, saying, "conditions are pretty awful, we'd like to evacuate," once again Kan in-sisted: "You absolutely have to keep pumping water."

Terada was impressed by this ability of Kan's.

Even though he was floundering there a little while back, at times like these he knows how to put his foot down.

After 7:45 a.m., there was an exchange between Kan and Katsumata.

"Stop doing things one at a time, I want you to set up at least two sys-tems to work in tandem."

"Yes, thank you."

"I don't want to hear 'thank you.' Can't you just do it? Stop waiting for approval before doing something. I want you to assume the worst and act ahead."

"Yes . . ."

Hosono interrupted.

"If they pull out now, will Units 1, 2, and 3 melt down?"

"Well, I don't know how bad things are . . ."

From start to finish, Katsumata failed to get to the point.

Hosono said, "Look at the situation we're in. Please be frank!"

One of the officials brought over a map of the presumed fallout area. The scale was not at all clear. Even when he was asked what the scale was, he could not answer.

Katsumata said, in a small voice, "I'm shocked that it's spilt over to Unit 4."[72]

Kan's secretaries were thinking it was about time Kan returned to the
Kantei. March 15 was a Tuesday. It was the day for the cabinet meeting.
They said something along the lines of "Let's tell the prime minister he's
got a cabinet meeting, and get him to come back soon."

Kan left TEPCO at around 8:40 a.m. and arrived back at the Kantei at
8:46 a.m. Kaieda, Fukuyama, Hosono, and Terada stayed in the conference
room, but Fukuyama decided he should return as well. As he was leaving,
he told Hosono, "Don't let 'em take you in, Hosono!" He meant "Don't let
TEPCO take you in."

Terada: "Well, we've been left behind."

Hosono: "It's up to us then."

Kaieda: "Yes, well, that's about the sum of it."

Kaieda had wondered for a moment whether he should leave as well,
but had made up his mind that his most important job now was to stay at
TEPCO and direct operations.

After a short while, there was a call from Kan to Terada's mobile phone.

"What the hell do you think you're doing there? Get back here!"

Terada jumped into a taxi and returned to the Kantei.

The women in the secretariat room next door to the prime minister's
office on the fifth floor were all wearing masks. That was something new.
The security police also looked very worried. The security police never
spoke of anything except matters related to security. But they looked like
they were bursting with questions.

SOMETIME AFTER NINE A.M. A gloomy-sounding report came in from the measurement team at Fukushima Daiichi NPS.

"At nine a.m., 11930 microsieverts/hour (11.93 millisieverts) at the main
gate."

"What? 11930!?"

Groans escaped from the second-floor TEPCO ERC.

- 6:00 a.m. 73 microsieverts (0.073 millisieverts)
- 8:50 a.m. 2200 microsieverts (2.2 millisieverts)
- 8:55 a.m. 3500 microsieverts (3.5 millisieverts)
- 9:00 a.m. 11930 microsieverts (11.03 millisieverts)
- 9:35 a.m. 7241 microsieverts (7.241 millisieverts)
- 10:15 a.m. 8837 microsieverts (8.837 millisieverts)

Readings were conveyed to the Integrated Response Office approximately
once every ten minutes. The dam meant to "contain" radiation had burst.

MARCH 15, 2011. This became the "day of reckoning."[73]

Around noon, Terada's mobile rang. It was Hosono.

"Radiation in Shibuya is a hundred times the normal level."

Terada had goose bumps.

Something terrible is happening right in the heart of Tokyo.

He was worried about the direction of the wind. Were people's windows shut? He looked outside the window, as if to see.[74]

SIX

Integrated Response Office

BANRI KAIEDA

In the Government-TEPCO Integrated Response Office (headed by the prime minister), Banri Kaieda, head of Ministry of Economy, Trade, and Industry (METI), represented the government and acted as its deputy head. Goshi Hosono, special adviser to the prime minister, headed the secretariat. TEPCO President Masataka Shimizu acted as the deputy head for the TEPCO side. Since Shimizu had fallen ill, however, TEPCO Chairman Tsunehisa Katsumata would replace him from April 1, 2011. They were joined by a steady stream of liaison officials from the government.

From around March 17, when water was released into the fuel pool at Unit 3, liaison officials from the police, the SDF, and the Fire and Disaster Management Agency had increased.

The Integrated Response Office operated around the clock. As a consequence, each of the ministries sent at least two liaison officials. At times, there were more than a hundred people from Kasumigaseki (the government ministry district).

Kaieda was dressed in METI's dark blue fatigues and Hosono in the cabinet's light blue ones. The SDF were in their camouflage gear. Kaieda was usually in a leisurely pose at the back of the ERC, closely watching the exchange between Fukushima and Head Office via the videoconference. As he put out one cigarette and lit another, the room was always shrouded in smoke. Hosono was always off meeting with someone and was hardly ever to be seen there.

Ichiro Takekuro, a TEPCO fellow, served as coordinator. Facing the screen, Kaieda sat in the very middle, with Hosono on his immediate left and then representatives of METI's Nuclear and Industrial Safety Authority (NISA), Nuclear Safety Commission (NSC), the Ministry of Foreign

Affairs (MOFA), and the Ministry of Defense (MOD). On his immediate right was Takekuro, followed by Shimizu, Katsumata, and Muto. Hosono's seat had originally been directly behind them, but after a few days, it was moved next to Kaieda.

Also encamped on the TEPCO side were Managing Director Toshio Nishizawa, TEPCO Fellow Akio Takahashi, and Susumu Kawamata, general manager for Nuclear Quality and Safety Management, who had acted as a Kantei liaison under Takekuro up until then. Takahashi assisted Muto, while Kawamata assisted Takekuro. Top managers from general affairs and planning sat near Shimizu and Katsumata as a matter of course. Takekuro presided over the plenary sessions.[1]

Kaieda was sixty-two years old. An economic analyst from Tokyo, he had been elected five times. First, he was elected as a member of the Japan New Party in 1993. His constituency was Tokyo District No. 1. He was a "people's politician" to the bone. In the Kan administration (first cabinet reshuffle) that took office in September 2010, he was appointed minister of state for economic and fiscal policy, science and technology policy, and space policy. In another cabinet reshuffle, on January 14, 2011, he was moved to the METI minister post.

On the afternoon of March 11, when the first disaster meeting was held at the Kantei, he attended wearing disaster fatigues.

"Take a look at him! He's already in his gear!"

A member of the cabinet was impressed.

Kaieda had ordered two sets of disaster fatigues made when he was appointed METI minister; he kept one at his office, the other at home. He had had them made, thinking, "It'd be terrible if there's a nuclear emergency while I'm minister," but never dreamed that this worry would become a reality.

He spent the night of March 11 working in a small office in the basement crisis management center and had napped in the reception room next door to the prime minister's office on the night of March 12. When Kiyoshi Sawaki, his executive assistant, had indicated, "Minister, the sofa," Kaieda had replied, "No, I prefer the floor," and had rested his large frame down there.

It was too cold, however, to sleep well, and he spread a newspaper over himself like a thin blanket. Sawaki had someone hurry some blankets over from the METI ministerial office and handed them to Kaieda.[2]

On the afternoon of March 11, after Fukushima Daiichi had lost all power, he had not been able to get Kan to promptly issue a state of nuclear emergency declaration based on an article 15 event. He felt bitter toward Kan and regretted that, as a result, the declaration had been "delayed an hour and a half."

Also, on the question of venting at Fukushima Daiichi in the early morning of March 12, people around them noticed that Kan and Kaieda were a little out of sync. Kaieda had held a press conference on the venting in the early hours of March 12. But on the afternoon of the same day, the Kantei had decided all public announcements were to be made by Yukio Edano, chief cabinet secretary. From that time on, Kaieda generally no longer made media appearances.

Kaieda was also opposed to Kan visiting the site, and, in fact, had been planning to go himself. It was from around this time that senior officials at METI started saying, "Things aren't going well between the PM and our minister."

On the evening of that day, Kaieda had issued a formal order to pump in seawater, based on article 64 of the Act on Special Measures Concerning Nuclear Emergency Preparedness (NEPA), but his ministerial order ended up in limbo, due partly to Kan bringing up the question of "recriticality" in the meeting that followed. (See chapter 4.)

A little later, when they were discussing in the prime minister's office the question of pumping water, and Kaieda tried to tell Kan about the reactor situation, Kan stopped him by holding up his right hand and saying, "No, I know. It's okay. It's okay."

Kazuo Matsunaga, METI permanent secretary, who was also in the meeting, was taken aback, and when he tried to press the point, saying, "No, prime minister, this is . . ." Kan said, "No, it's not necessary. I know what's happening."

Edano had taken over, saying, "Now, now, this matter will be decided by the relevant minister."[3]

From the outset, Kan thought Kaieda "wasn't suited for the battlefield," and he was not subtle about showing it. Kaieda, for his part, thought Kan was "unsuited for leadership."

They were both from the same Tokyo electorate, both politicians for the people, and both belonged to the same generation. And yet, their temperaments were different, and they weren't on the same wavelength. If they had one point in common, it was their strong mistrust of TEPCO. Kaieda didn't touch a single prepackaged meal he was provided by TEPCO while holed up at the Integrated Response Office.[4]

Since he was a cabinet member, Kaieda was required to attend the cabinet meetings held twice a week. After a while, he started flitting back and forth between METI and the Integrated Response Office. In substance, it was Hosono who ran things in the Integrated Response Office.

The Kasumigaseki bureaucrats spent two-week shifts at the Integrated Response Office. One of them was there the entire time until Kan's resignation on September 2, 2011. That was Hiroshi Ikukawa, a bureaucrat from the Ministry of Education, Culture, Sports, Science, and Technology (MEXT), who had served as Kan's executive assistant back when Kan was minister of state for science and technology (and also deputy prime minister).

Ikukawa had subsequently been appointed as managing director for promotion of research at RIKEN, located in Tsurumi Ward, Yokohama. RIKEN was Japan's leading institute for foundational science research. At two p.m. on March 15, Kan called Ikukawa to the Kantei. Kan told him, "This time, we've set up an Integrated Response Office. Would you mind keeping an eye on what's happening there along with Saito and Aritomi?"

Masanori Aritomi and Masaki Saito were the two professors from the Research Laboratory for Nuclear Reactors (RLNR) at Kan's alma mater, the Tokyo Institute of Technology. Kan said, "I want you to bear in mind the following two points. First of all, there isn't a smooth flow of information from the site. I want you to send me straight away any information that you think is correct. Second, I don't know how correct is what the experts are saying. Is it right or not? When I asked Madarame (chairman of NISA) about the possibility of a hydrogen explosion, he said 'absolutely impossible,' but it happened. I'm worried about how far I can trust the advice of the experts. I want you to see if what they say checks out. I want you to help me on this."

The first e-mail Ikukawa sent was time-stamped 3:42 p.m., March 17.

"The riot police crowd-control trucks have arrived at Daiichi."

It was advance notice that the police were about to start pumping water. Every day, at seven a.m., Ikukawa texted Kan's mobile with his first report of the day. There were times when they discussed the situation in Units 1, 2, 3, and 4, calling them "eldest girl," "second girl," "third girl," and "fourth girl." Ikukawa made daily reports of the situation in the reactors along the lines of "Today, the girls are in excellent spirits."

Ikukawa wrote and sent off his reports unilaterally. Every day, he busied himself and continued to send e-mails. The number of e-mails he sent until Kan resigned on September 2, 2011, totaled one thousand.

6:48 P.M., SEPTEMBER 1, 2011. Ikukawa sent his last e-mail.

"Water pumping from the core spray system in Unit 3 has commenced. The Areva equipment has sprung a leak; they've found a hole in the casing."

The core spray system was a way of pumping water in—not from the bottom but from the top. The casing referred to was the casing around the pipes.

Kan replied to him for the first and last time.

"Cheers for the hard work! Thanks."[5]

"I'M NOT GOING BACK TO THE KANTEI"

The story has gotten ahead of itself. Let us return to March 15.

On the evening of March 15, Hosono was called back to the Kantei by Kan to "report on conditions today." When he returned to TEPCO's ERC some two hours or so later, there was a change in the atmosphere.

What, that fellow's come back?!
That was what it felt like.
All the cabinet members have left, so I guess they didn't dream a politician would come back and settle in.
Let's make my position clear.
Hosono took the mike and announced, "The government has declared a state of emergency. The authority to issue instructions lies with the prime minister. I'm not going back to the Kantei. I'm staying here."[6]

The position of the Integrated Response Office was somewhat dubious. The government and the Kantei had entered a private corporation and commenced to work with its management to handle the crisis as well as to keep an eye on them. It was an extrajudicial measure made possible by the broad-sweeping powers given to the prime minister by NEPA.

Kan had come up with the idea of an Integrated Response Office the day before, March 14. As long as information from TEPCO failed to reach the Kantei, they could not respond to the crisis. Just when Kan was feeling this sense of alarm, the issue of TEPCO's possible withdrawal and the government's storming into TEPCO was raised from the evening of March 14 to the early hours of March 15. In this process, Kan decided this was the government's only choice.[7]

Edano and Fukuyama felt "we should have done this earlier." One of the parliamentary secretaries at the Kantei confessed, "Why didn't we come up with the idea? It was a case that clearly demonstrated the dearth of ideas and lack of creativity on the part of the bureaucrats."

Setting up the Integrated Response Office meant that finally they had a command post to deal with the crisis. The first task this command post dealt with was the water pumping operations for the fuel pools.[8]

It was painfully obvious that, at first, the TEPCO side was not favorably disposed toward the Integrated Response Office. When Motohiko Oka, who was made Hosono's assistant on March 20, received his letter of appointment, he went to pay his respects to Hosono at the Integrated Response Office. His first impression was, *Can't this company, TEPCO, even pretend to be toeing the line?!*

It was only when Hosono's leadership initiative became clearer, after he got the U.S.-Japan dialogue up and running (see chapter 12), and also set up the project team, that, in Oka's words, "They started to recognize his authority."[9]

Two videoconference plenary sessions between Head Office and the site were held every day in the ERC—once in the morning (at nine a.m. or ten a.m.), and once in the evening (at six p.m.). After some time, it became a practice to hold a meeting with key members at ten p.m. This meeting was attended by Kaieda, Hosono, Katsumata, and Muto. Yasui also often participated.

After Kaieda was encamped in the Integrated Response Office, one of the first orders he gave to TEPCO was to set up some cameras inside Fukushima Daiichi NPS. Whenever the commercial stations ran some event on TV and asked the onsite team for an update, they would invariably reply, "We'll go outside right away and see."

The cameras were installed onsite two or three days later.

Do they want to prevent people from seeing what's going on onsite except inside the ERC, on videoconference?

That was Kaieda's impression. A member of the Kantei staff said he got the feeling that, at first, TEPCO did not even want to show the onsite ERC. Later, he put it the following way:

"TEPCO didn't seem to want anyone to see the exchanges between Head Office and the site. They probably felt uncomfortable about the Kantei getting live information directly from the site and learning of their decisions in real time without going via Head Office. That company only provides the bare minimum of information. They don't hand over raw data. Their first instinct is to keep things covered up. But it got harder to hide things after the Integrated Response Office was set up."[10]

However, from the point of view of the manufacturers working with the Integrated Response Office, the government officials who had descended upon TEPCO were just bureaucrats, and so were the TEPCO staff, who had been overrun; both looked to be the same "world of bureaucrats" to them. The manufacturers said, "In short, it's a world of ritual."

The TEPCO head office would recap the day's events in the all-staff evening videoconference. The head of each department would report on developments in their respective sections. When Kaieda was in his seat, Takekuro would wrap up the recaps by saying, "Now then, minister, could we have a word from you?"

Kaieda would take the mike and say, in his oily baritone, "This is Banri Kaieda."

"What? Why's he giving his full name? Does he think it's an election broadcast?"

You could hear these kinds of comments from the back row, where the manufacturers were seated.[11]

"LIKE A DEER STUNNED IN THE HEADLIGHTS"

It was stipulated that with the establishment of a Nuclear Emergency Response Headquarters (NERHQ), the director general of NISA would act as the head of secretariat. The secretariat was located in the Emergency Response Center (ERC) in the NISA building. Most of the secretariat staff were from NISA, but they were joined by officials from the various ministries.

On the evening of March 11, Kan called Nobuaki Terasaka, NISA's director general, to his office (see chapter 2). This meeting had tragic consequences. After being screamed at by Kan, Terasaka became thoroughly traumatized. In the words of a METI official, "He was like a deer stunned in the headlights."[12]

Just after seven p.m. on March 11, the first Nuclear Emergency Response Headquarters (NERHQ) meeting was held on the fourth floor of the Kantei, but Terasaka was not present.

With an accident on this scale, technical knowledge will be extremely critical. Mightn't it be better if someone with the technical expertise stayed at the Kantei rather than me?

Thinking so, Terasaka had spoken with Eiji Hiraoka, deputy director general of NISA, at the Kantei. They divided their roles into Hiraoka staying and Terasaka going back to the ERC to fulfill his job as head of the secretariat. Terasaka went back to NISA. He told his subordinates that he had come back "on his own initiative."[13]

Terasaka was an administrative official who had graduated from the Law Faculty of Tokyo University, while Hiraoka was a technical official. He had graduated from the Department of Electrical Engineering at Tokyo University. Hiraoka had joined the ministry in 1979, the year of the accident at Three Mile Island. While he hadn't majored in nuclear power, he had been involved in regulating nuclear safety for the previous thirteen years.[14]

Word had already gotten around that Terasaka had disappeared after being upbraided by Kan.

"That's like being told by the PM that you needn't come back."

This was the conjecture that ran through NISA. The news also reached the NSC in short time. Although a state of nuclear emergency had been declared, NERHQ had yet to decide what practical measures needed to be taken based on that declaration. Haruki Madarame, NSC chairman, thought to himself, *The response was so sloppy because the top man at NISA had disappeared from the Kantei.*[15]

In the afternoon of the following day, Koichiro Nakamura, NISA's deputy director general for nuclear safety, touched on the "possibility of a meltdown" in a press conference. Suddenly informed of this evaluation, Kan and Edano were furious. This also resulted in increasing the Kantei's lack of confidence in NISA.

Just as Madarame recollected—"It was because the Kantei bashed NISA over Nakamura's statement that NISA ended up being shut down"—this incident was a major turning point in the relations between the Kantei and NISA.[16]

An ex-METI man, well versed in nuclear power administration, had this to say about the situation at the time:

"After that, the Kantei, who should have been making political decisions, started controlling the narrative. This meant expending more energy getting information to the Kantei. In order to avoid scolding, a lot of behind-the-scenes tweaking had to be done before information was passed up. So, it took extra time. And then you were scolded for being late. And if you did it, you got ripped to shreds. And if you didn't do it, you were yelled at. So, NISA took on the attitude that it was the Kantei that was going to make decisions, in its wisdom, and that it wasn't their responsibility."[17]

The final blow was NISA's pitiful response after the explosion at Unit 1 on the afternoon of March 12. Both the first and second reports of the explosion were conveyed by policemen from the Fukushima Prefectural Police. This was then passed on to the Kantei by the National Policy Agency. NISA was unable to verify the information.[18]

Edano was forced to give a press conference "empty-handed"; that is, without any information from NISA. (See chapter 4.)

Kenichi Shimomura, counselor for public relations at the cabinet secretariat in the Kantei, recorded in a memo that the top officials from NISA acted "like school kids with their eyes downcast, hoping fervently that the teacher wouldn't call them out" in front of Kan and Edano.[19]

The top echelons of NISA started to find the thought of going to the Kantei disagreeable. They would come back from the Kantei, saying, "Today's fallout was 30 millisieverts," or the like. The emergency task force at the crisis management center in the basement of the Kantei was full of dissatisfaction with the NISA staff.

The NISA staff would be in and out all the time, never settling down. And even when they were there, they had no information and could not answer anything. Voices started to be heard within the taskforce, "There's no point asking NISA, let's ask TEPCO."

From the point of view of the National Policy Agency; Fire and Disaster Management Agency; and Ministry of Land, Infrastructure, Transport, and Tourism—which were all part of the former Department of the Interior—NISA staff looked like "they couldn't even give a proper greeting." But it was the staff from METI that annoyed them even more than the NISA staff.

"They sat as far away as possible from the put-upon NISA, with a look on their faces as if to say the nuclear emergency had nothing to do with them."

There was no choice but to have workers from TEPCO in constant attendance at the crisis management center. TEPCO was a private company, but you couldn't worry about things like that at a time like this.

THE NIGHT OF MARCH 13. At the strong request of the Kantei, TEPCO set up a direct phone line to the Fukushima Daiichi NPS from the Kantei.

From around March 14, the Kantei began bypassing NISA and calling

TEPCO directly. Tomoho Yamada, nuclear power safety review manager at NISA, who had been hurriedly added to the emergency task force, found himself playing the role of "bullied child."

After the nuclear emergency, Yamada had been the NISA public relations officer. His job was to go to the ERC, be fed information, then spit it out at a press conference. It was a job, as it were, of "swallowing, then regurgitating, like a cormorant." This time, his job became sitting on a bed of nails without moving.

Not that the TEPCO employees brought in were much better. It was on March 16 that Ito, coming down from the fifth floor, yelled at Yamada, "Get TEPCO!" They wanted some TEPCO executives there. And they had to be real executives; otherwise, there was no point having them sit at the round table. Ito had just received Chief Cabinet Secretary Edano's permission on this matter.

On the same day, Ito rang Katsumata and made a direct appeal. He had just met with Katsumata the day before at TEPCO Head Office, to talk about the ground water discharge.

"Can't you send us someone who can speak directly to you, someone who can directly convey your intentions? It doesn't matter what their title is."

"Yes, sir."

Katsumata had sent over Akio Takahashi, a TEPCO fellow.[20]

It was not just the crisis management center that was perplexed by NISA's inability to get information from TEPCO. The U.S. Nuclear Regulatory Commission (NRC) in Washington had the same doubts. Staff from the NRC, who had been sent to Japan, reported by phone to headquarters.

"We do not have an information path directly from the operators, very different than what we would experience in the United States."[21]

The Nuclear and Industrial Safety Agency (NISA) started operations in 2001, accompanying the reorganization of government ministries and agencies, and incorporated part of the Nuclear Safety Bureau at the Science and Technology Agency. It was a "special institution" under METI's Agency for Natural Resources and Energy. Of its some eight hundred staff members, over three hundred were engaged in nuclear regulation. It had inspection offices at each of the twenty-one nuclear power plants and nuclear facilities throughout the country, each with between one and nine nuclear inspectors and nuclear emergency deputies. In the event of a nuclear emergency, their role was to deploy staff to the site, to gather information at the ERC within METI, and report to the government.

NISA also had a technical support organization under METI's jurisdiction, the incorporated administrative agency Japan Nuclear Energy Safety Organization (JNES). The Seismic Safety Division of JNES had conducted an impact assessment on the Kashiwazaki-Kariwa NPS in Niigata Prefecture after the Chuetsu earthquake in July 2007. This impact assessment was highly regarded internationally for its use of the IAEA seismic hazard evaluation guide.[22]

However, JNES's emergency response was just as perfunctory as that of NISA and the NSC.

Its home page claims it "supervises and maintains the various equipment at offsite centers to ensure smooth operations in times of an emergency," but all of the equipment at the offsite center failed to work.[23]

What was the relationship between NISA and TEPCO?

In formal terms, they were "the regulating side" and "the regulated side," but the reality was very different. TEPCO outstripped NISA and even METI in terms of information, expertise, experience, length of service, and even political power. And that fact was not a state secret, by any means.

An ex-METI staff member at the Kantei later said, "The Energy Agency (NISA) looked like it was regulating TEPCO, but they were just being used as a tool." In the crisis, the power relationship between NISA and TEPCO was crystal clear.[24]

No matter what you asked the senior officials at NISA, the only reply you ever got was "We'll ask TEPCO." Not only did they have no way of obtaining their own information, their ability to make independent evaluations was paltry.

It was on March 12 that Hideaki Tsuzuki, director of the NSC's Environment Supervision Division, made a copy of the only blueprint the NSC had of Fukushima Daiichi NPS, and handed it to Deputy Chairman Kukita at the Kantei. He also ran into Hiraoka. When he reported the fact to Hiraoka, Hiraoka said, "You've come at just the right time. We don't have a single blueprint at NISA. Can you lend it to me?" and walked off with a copy. The blueprint itself had been submitted for the construction permit. It was, so to speak, only a conceptual diagram.

NISA doesn't even have that?!

Tsuzuki felt a chill run up his spine.[25]

In the midst of the crisis, NISA had three to five TEPCO staff sent into the ERC to act as liaisons. They sat at the same desk as the plant unit at the ERC and handled the NISA queries to TEPCO. A member of the plant unit would ask the TEPCO liaison a question, and the TEPCO liaison, who kept a continuous open mobile phone connection, would convey that to the Head Office ERC, and the official in charge at Head Office would respond.

The unit members would also put their ears close to the phone and listen in.[26]

In the first place, NISA had a fundamental weakness. They did not have their own "crisis response team."

About the time the police, the SDF, and the firefighters were squabbling over priorities and procedures for the draining operations at Unit 3's fuel pool, Hiraoka was being glared at by Tatsuya Kabutan, deputy director of the Fire and Disaster Management Agency, across the emergency response team's round table in the crisis management center. Kabutan asked him why NISA had not removed the debris when the Hyper Rescue Squad was draining the water. Hiraoka had no choice but to reply, "It's not as if NISA has its own squads. Our officials are merely administrators and inspectors."[27]

There was no team in Japan that could directly respond at the time of a severe accident.[28]

Nuclear accidents were not to be a "crisis." It was not permissible to foresee such a "lurid" risk. The tyranny of this "safety myth" dominated nuclear safety regulation in Japan.

When confronted by a severe nuclear accident that might well have a critical impact on the health and safety of the Japanese people, this failure of NISA was clearly shown by the NISA inspectors, who were the first to cut and run. Led on by the nuclear power industry, NISA had eliminated the possibility of a serious nuclear accident as "unthinkable." As a result, they failed to groom crisis management professionals who could respond onsite at the time of a serious nuclear accident.

It was this point that was severely criticized by the Government Investigation Commission: "There is great doubt about the correctness of the decision to allow the safety inspectors to leave the site and evacuate at such a critical moment when there was a particularly great need for onsite observation."[29]

TEPCO's survey report also mentioned this.

"From March 12 to when they returned on March 22, the government's safety inspectors were largely absent from Fukushima Daiichi NPS, limiting the information to METI from the frontlines of Fukushima Daiichi NPS to that which was provided by TEPCO."[30]

This can be read as intimating that the evacuation of the inspectors made it more difficult for METI—in other words, the government—to learn what was happening onsite, which made the government even more reliant on TEPCO and unable to fulfill its proper role.

From the point of view of those workers who dealt with the crisis at the risk of their own lives at the Fukushima Daiichi site, the inspectors who ran at the most crucial juncture, and the top officials at NISA who were aware of this and did nothing, were already disqualified as regulators. An officer with the SDF chemical special forces contemptuously spat out, "In our terms, they deserted under enemy fire. But NISA doesn't have any penalty for deserters."[31]

And, in fact, those officials were never punished.

In 2006, when NISA held a town meeting called Offsite Center Dialogue

Gathering with local residents on the offsite center at the Tomari Nuclear Power Plant run by Hokkaido Electric Power Company, they were asked, "Are four inspectors enough to maintain safety?" and NISA responded, "The inspection office acts as our eyes and ears, conveying information to our headquarters in Tokyo." With the desertion of its inspectors, NISA had surrendered its "eyes and ears."[32]

However, even if the inspectors had stayed onsite, doubts still remain as to how effective they would have been as "eyes" and "ears." This is because NISA provided the onsite inspectors with no clear mission or specific instruction on what they were to do or what was expected of them.[33]

The fact that Yokota, when asked for permission to withdraw from onsite, could not answer yes or no is a clear indication of this. Would NISA have been able to answer if Yokota had passed on that request? The "desertion under enemy fire" of the four inspectors was certainly reprehensible. They were lacking a sense of mission and professional ethics.

However, not all of the inspectors took the same course of action. There were inspectors like Akio Miyashita, who stayed in the ERC at Fukushima Daini NPS from March 11 throughout the crisis, doing his utmost to deal with the accident. Miyashita had also joined NISA from a manufacturing background.

"SO HELPFUL THAT THE REGULATORS WERE STUPID"

The executive in charge of nuclear energy at a manufacturer of nuclear equipment described the reality of NISA's regulation of TEPCO as "regulation by bucket relay."

"First of all, the manufacturer puts the paperwork together and explains it to the power company. The power company then uses that as a basis for their explanation to NISA. NISA then signs off on it. In short, it's just like a bucket relay, where a bucket of water is passed on from one person to the next. That's why we call it 'regulation by bucket relay.'"[34]

It was in the summer of 2012 that an ex-senior manager from Kansai Electric Power made the following comment at a meeting of organizations from the nuclear energy industry:

"And it was so helpful that the regulators were stupid."

An e-mail giving the details of this comment eventually found its way to an engineer at JNES. When he attached it to an e-mail he sent to an acquaintance, he wrote, "It's certain that TEPCO (and KEPCO) were carrying out the nuclear regulation . . . Even in debates at academic conferences, members from the manufacturers and general contractors merely followed the lead of the speakers from the power companies.

"This comment from the ex-senior manager at Kansai Electric Power rings true."[35]

Inspections by NISA were not technical inspections, but legal and regulatory inspections. It proved deadly that the top administrators at NISA were devoid of expertise and knowledge about nuclear energy regulation.

The very first question Kan asked Terasaka in his office, when Tersaka was called to the Kantei, was, "Are you an engineer?" Leaving aside the appropriateness of the question, it was absolutely fatal for managing the emergency that the top administrators at NISA were lacking in knowledge and expertise. A senior administrator at NISA, who had an engineering background, made the following comment:

"NISA had always put a guy at the top who was up on the legal interpretations. Why? Because he was the head of a government organization responsible for laws and regulations. The field of nuclear safety regulations is a world of enforcing regulations. The whole game was about whether something was legally permissible or not."

Director-General Terasaka could be said to be a typical example of this.[36] Here was a long shadow cast by the organizational culture of Kasumigaseki that deemed generalists to be "superior" to specialists. The Kasumigaseki philosophy of "[senior] public servants shall not stay in the same position" was another part of this culture. This practice, which was purportedly to avoid corruption, was, in reality, an organizational defense to protect individual officials from having to take responsibility. Professionals could not be developed under this kind of practice.[37]

Another issue was one of governance, concerning the balance between administrative and technical officers and treatment of personnel. Top appointments at NISA had pursued a balance of power between administrators and engineers. In METI's Agency for Natural Resources and Energy, the head of NISA was "on the promotion path to come back as either deputy director or permanent secretary" (as a member of the NSC).

The great importance attached to NISA (which is indicative of the stance to promote nuclear energy) and to the engineering officials tells its own story. For even those who didn't make it to deputy director, it was handy to have such prestigious posts. Even so, NISA was not directly under METI, but under its affiliated organization, the Agency for Natural Resources and Energy.

Why was that?

A senior official at METI revealed: "It was probably to protect the minister or vice minister from having to take responsibility if there was an accident or something, and to have the buck stop with the head of the Energy Agency.[38] The whole organization will go down if there's a big accident!"

This oversensitive reaction was deeply related to the annexation of the Science and Technology Agency into the then Ministry of Education, as well as the subsequent formation of NISA in the wake of the JCO accident and the ministerial reshuffle it triggered. Due to its responsibility for the

JCO accident, the Science and Technology Agency was "vanquished" and its only option was to be integrated into either the Ministry of Education or Ministry of International Trade and Industry (MITI). In the end, it joined the Ministry of Education.

It was rumored at the time that the determining factor was that the Ministry of Education had agreed that the permanent secretary role would be taken, in turn, by the ex–top man at the old agency and the ex–top man at the old ministry—a condition MITI refused to accept.

Behind this refusal lay the opposition of the technical officers in MITI, and the consideration of treatment of the technical officers by the new METI's administrators, who were afraid of a backlash from its technical officers.

The post of vice minister at MITI (the current METI) was always reserved for an administrator, not a technical officer. Consequently, there was no way for a technical officer from the old Science and Technology Agency to become METI's vice minister. This was the thinking.

The highest post a technical officer could achieve at MITI was director of the Agency of Industrial Science and Technology. With the birth of NISA, however, the Agency of Industrial Science and Technology was to be disbanded. No ministry was allowed to have two "agencies." They placated the technical officers by appointing a technical officer as NISA's director.

If NISA was going to be created, there had initially been a willingness to make it a solid organization. Kazuo Matsunaga, METI vice minister, who had been closely involved in NISA's establishment, recollects, "We aimed at creating a nuclear brand. Just as salmon and trout return to their place of birth, we wanted people appointed to NISA to always return there and to train up a group of professionals. We believed this was the only way to strengthen safety regulation."[39]

But with the exception of a rare few, they failed to raise a group of hardcore regulation professionals.

After its inauguration, there was a series of nuclear accidents and NISA was flat out doing its best to respond to them.

Almost every year there was some incident or accident, including TEPCO's falsifying of voluntary inspection reports in 2002, the system pipe rupture at Unit 3 of KEPCO's Mihama plant (five dead) in 2004, the reactor trip at the three reactors at the Onagawa NPS following an offshore quake in 2005, a seismic back-check scandal in 2006, and the fire at TEPCO's Kashiwazaki-Kariwa NPS triggered by the Chuetsu earthquake in 2007.[40]

A senior official at NISA snorted that, in the final analysis, NISA ended up being "a resuming operations shop" for plants that had their operations suspended by accidents. How were they to get the nuclear plants up and running again after an accident? Staff had to placate the local residents, and those who excelled at this came to be highly valued. Then they fell into their own trap. "By persuading the locals that it was safe, they became bound by their assurances, and this led to the birth of the safety myth."[41]

The Fukushima Daiichi accident developed into a crisis that could change the fate of METI. There were fears that, just as the Science and Technology Agency had been disbanded after the JCO accident, the Natural Resources and Energy Agency or the ministry itself might be abolished. METI may well have been trying to avoid that very thing by staying ahead of the game and disbanding NISA.

It was certainly true that NISA had been spineless. Its abolition was probably unavoidable. But was there not an element of cutting off the tail (NISA) to save the rest (METI) in the relentless bashing NISA received at the hands of METI? Blamed for everything, the NISA officials felt victimized.[42]

WAVING THE BANNER

When he had attended the first meeting of NERHQ sometime after seven p.m. on March 11, Haruki Madarame, chairman of the NSC, could not immediately find his seat. The NSC chairman was not a member of NERHQ. He took a seat at the back and only remembers *staring at the backside of the director general of the Japan Meteorological Agency lolling in his seat.*[43]

Eiji Hiraoka, NISA's deputy director general, was also in the meeting, and found it strange that Madarame was not sitting at the main table.

I'm pretty sure the NSC chairman was sitting at the main table during the disaster training exercises . . .

By rights, it wouldn't be out of place for the NSC chairman to be seated next to the prime minister.

Wasn't the commission supposed to have "the right of recommendation to the relevant agencies through the prime minister?"

Is it a sign that the politicians and the bureaucrats don't respect the scientists' and technical officers' knowledge?

Hiraoka was baffled.[44]

Madarame was called to the Kantei at nine p.m. of the same day and rushed over there. He went to the crisis management center in the basement of the Kantei accompanied by Akihiko Iwahashi, secretary general of the NSC, but Iwahashi was turned back by the security police and unable to enter at the time. The reason was that although Iwahashi's title was secretary general, his position was in the deputy director general class.

Madarame thought his role would probably be to answer various queries from NISA, since it was their job to respond directly to a nuclear disaster. The NSC's role was only an advisory one: the backline forces. That was his understanding.

It didn't appear that way, however. He had a premonition that he was going to be made to assume the role of staff officer for crisis response strategy. Of the politicians lined up there, he didn't know a single one. Madarame was struck by anxiety when he looked at their faces.

How am I going to convey my sense of crisis to these people who don't know the first thing about atomic energy?[45]

Apart from the Nuclear and Industrial Safety Agency (NISA), there was also the Nuclear Safety Commission (NSC), whose job was to oversee safety regulation. The commission was established as an independent body from the Japan Atomic Energy Commission in 1978, when the antinuclear movement was growing stronger in the wake of the nuclear-powered ship *Mutsu*'s radiation accident.

The research vessel *Mutsu* was launched at the end of the 1960s, later being loaded with nuclear fuel and managing to reach the level of conducting a test output run in the Pacific Ocean in 1974. It was the fourth civilian nuclear ship in the world, after the Soviet Union (the icebreaker *Lenin*), the United States (the passenger and cargo ship *Savannah*), and West Germany (the ore carrier *Otto Hahn*).

There was a radiation leak, however, as soon as it started its trials. Following the accident, it tried to return to its home port of Ominato in Aomori Prefecture, but local protests prevented that, forcing *Mutsu* to stay at sea. Demonstrations against relocating *Mutsu*'s home port also took place in Sasebo, Saga Prefecture, and *Mutsu* spent the next sixteen years sailing from port to port all around Japan.

During this time, various modifications were made at sea, and after four trial runs, it returned to its purpose-built new home port of Sekinehama, in Mutsu City, in 1990. In 1993, the reactor section of the vessel was removed and denuclearized. The *Mutsu* radiation leak was the first nuclear disaster to take place in Japan.

The safety regulation of atomic energy was directly carried out by administrative organizations such as METI and MEXT. The role of the Nuclear Safety Commission was to check the safety policies of these ministries. It possessed strong authority, including recommendations to the relevant administrative bodies through the prime minister. It was placed under the cabinet to guard its "neutrality."

The commission consisted of five committee members appointed by the prime minister with the Diet's approval, expert evaluators from specialized fields, expert advisers, and a hundred administrators. It was stipulated that, in the case of an article 15 event, the NSC was to set up an emergency advisory body, including researchers, to advise the prime minister.

In the afternoon of March 11, the secretariat put out an emergency call to twenty people from their experts list via a group e-mail system for mobile phones. No one received the group e-mail. All that Madarame, who was on top of the list, received was the subject heading. Only four people managed to make it to the commission that day.[46]

When they were suddenly called into the prime minister's office, both Madarame and Kukita, who was also at the Kantei, were expected to "just answer his questions," despite having received no information or documentation from their secretariat. Since both the commission's chairman and deputy chairman were stuck at the Kantei, this undermined the NSC's functions.

Top officials from NISA say every time they watched the videoconferences between the ERC and the NSC, they wondered what the commission was doing. The videoconference system was always on.

"Whenever you looked, you could only see Kusumi-san [Commissioner Shizuyo Kusumi]. The chairman and acting chairman were never there."[47]

While proclaiming the double-checking of safety regulation, NISA and the NSC were in a collusive relationship of a sort. Hosono pointed out, as follows, that this numbed the requisite sense of tension that was indispensable for regulating nuclear safety.

"NISA would wave the 'banner' of something being the suggestion of the NSC. The setup was one where NISA and NSC scratched each other's backs, and both had a diluted sense of responsibility for the safety of atomic energy."[48]

The greatest miscalculation of the NSC was that NISA, which was to act as the secretariat for NERHQ, ceased to function from the very day of the start of the emergency. This was also one of the reasons the Kantei began to count on the NSC not merely for advice but for proposals and coordination. And when it discovered that the NSC was not up to this in terms of intent or ability, they attacked them with marked irritation.

The top members of the commission felt that METI was plotting to make the "NSC's failures" stand out even more in order to take the focus off "NISA's failures." When, at the end of March, the Kantei sent in Kenkichi Hirose, a former chairman of NISA, to the NSC to act as "a conduit to the PM's office," they almost instinctively suspected a METI plot was behind it. (See chapter 15.)[49]

Madarame had graduated from the Department of Mechanical Engineering at the Tokyo Institute of Technology in 1970. He had worked for a time as an engineer at Tokyo Shibaura Electric (now Toshiba). He had then lectured on the regulation of atomic energy safety for many years at the Graduate School of Tokyo University. He was appointed chairman of the NSC in April 2010.

Madarame's misfortune was that Kan's evaluation of him plummeted with the hydrogen explosion at Unit 1.

"You said there wouldn't be a hydrogen explosion, but there was, wasn't there?"

Kan interrogated him thus, and then ignored him. Kaieda later noted in his book, "It was in the wake of this that Kan locked himself up in his office and started calling outside experts, especially atomic experts from his alma mater, the Tokyo Institute of Technology, to ask them their opinions."[50]

Whenever Madarame tried to voice an opinion, Kan would throw a fit.

"I know the basics. Just answer my questions."

"Just answer my question" was becoming Kan's favorite phrase. He said it not only to Madarame.[51]

Madarame later testified, however, that after that, "I was no longer able to engage in questions and answers."[52]

On one occasion, Madarame received a call from Kan on his mobile. Since it came just during a committee meeting, he left the room and went to the secretary's reception counter to listen.

"Hey, did you know that there was water in the fuel pool at Unit 4?"

"Yes."

"So you knew, did you?! Why didn't you report it to me?!"

Kan exploded like a firecracker.

"You're the one in charge!!"

"The responsibility is NISA's. The commission's role is merely an advisory one."

"That's not so!!!"

Kan's outburst was so deafening that Madarame was worried his eardrum might burst. Madarame plopped the mobile phone on the counter and left it there for some time. The secretarial staff were all ears as Kan's irate voice vibrated like it was coming through a loudspeaker.[53]

It was on April 14, more than a month after the accident, that an NSC commissioner was dispatched to the onsite ERC. Kenichi Shimomura, counselor for public relations at the cabinet secretariat, jotted down his impression of the meeting where Kan was briefed by Madarame and the atomic energy experts around the time as follows:

"Bite their tongues and hang their heads without moving a muscle, even when criticized."

"Engineers, scientists, managers, who can't come up with a single solution or preventative measure."

"I'm convinced that as a society we shouldn't have nuclear power—not because of the technology, but because of our human limitations."[54]

BORON YASUI

They had no advisers who understood the technology. Both NISA and the NSC could not be counted on. It was Masaya Yasui, director general for the Energy Conservation and Renewable Energy Department at METI's Agency for Natural Resources and Energy, who Kan and Hosono turned to.[55]

Yasui had joined METI in 1982 when it was still called MITI. He was a technical officer, who had majored in nuclear engineering at the Graduate School of Kyoto University. During his time at graduate school, he had passed the national qualification for nuclear chief engineer (reactor chief). If you asked Yasui, he would say, "It was only a paper test, so it was like a provisional license," but be that as it may, his knowledge of reactors was encyclopedic.

After joining the ministry, his first post was inspecting and examining in the Nuclear Safety Licensing Division. After that, however, he followed the same career path as the administrative officers.[56] He quickly cut a figure as a technical officer, but one "who could draft better legislation than the administrative officers."[57]

On the night of March 11, he was one of the millions of Tokyoites trying to get home. He finally made it home on the first morning train on March 12. After he had slept for a little, he got a call from Takayuki Ueda, deputy vice minister of economy, trade, and industry.

"We need your help."

Yasui returned to the ministry in the afternoon.[58]

It was Matsunaga who decided to bring in Yasui. Initially, he had wanted to give Hiraoka, who had not had a wink of sleep for two days, a bit of a break.[59]

Yasui took up residence at the Kantei straight away before noon on March 13. That morning he was immediately called upon to give a briefing on each reactor in the prime minister's office. He passed that test. Kan could not stand a bumbling briefing. Yasui's was nice and snappy.

Kan's biggest concern at the time was the possibility of a hydrogen explosion in Unit 3, but Yasui was crystal-clear: "Please expect what happened at Unit 1 to also happen at Unit 3." Kan's mind was a whirlpool of concerns, but he felt a soothing sensation at the same time. He was not alone.

Both Edano and Kaieda had a high opinion of Yasui. They viewed him as the "best of the nuclear bunch," and although they did not always agree on ideas or policy direction, Fukuyama acknowledged that "it was only after Yasui came, that we began to see how things stood."[60]

Kan's aides took to calling him Boron (as in boric acid) Yasui, because of his peculiar ability to calm Kan down when he was about to reach "criticality." This, of course, referred to the injection of boric acid to prevent the occurrence of recriticality.[61]

LATE ON THE NIGHT OF MARCH 13. Fukuyama and others were querying Yasui in the prime minister's office on the fifth floor of the Kantei.

"Will the fuel rods in Unit 3 melt down to the cave of the containment vessel or not?"

Yasui felt that Unit 3 was in danger if nothing was done. But he believed that even if the fuel rods did melt and fall below the pressure vessel, things would not progress as far as a core concrete reaction that would breach the bottom of the containment vessel. He replied, "I don't think so, given its current state."

However, the possibility of a steam explosion in the interim stages could not be denied.

"A steam explosion won't take place if the pressure in the core isn't high. At the current juncture, water is pouring out from the core. The pressure isn't so high. After all, water is falling. It's not at high pressure now. So, I don't think there'll be a steam explosion."

This was almost the same opinion as Madarame and Kukita.

From March 15, Yasui took up residence at the Integrated Response Office at TEPCO, where he performed the role, more or less, of "technical adviser." It was not unusual that when Yasui would take up the mike at TEPCO's request, to explain a technical matter in the ERC on the second floor, the buzzing room would suddenly fall quiet.

What should they make of the situation in the spent-fuel pool after the explosion at Unit 4? Was there any water in the fuel pool? If there was, then what had exploded?[62] Or, as the Americans said, was there no water? Was it on the way to boiling dry?

Katsumata turned to Yasui and asked, "Yasui-san, how do you see it?"

Yasui took the mike and did not beat around the bush.

"If my eyes are not mistaken, this event can't possibly lead to an explosion . . . The explosion may have been caused by hydrogen leaking out from Unit 3 . . . We need to concentrate our efforts back on Unit 1, not Unit 4."

He was warning them to be wary of an explosion in the containment vessel at Unit 1. Yoshida also listened carefully whenever Yasui made a comment. That was apparent from the videoconference screen.[63]

Starting with the U.S. Nuclear Regulatory Commission (NRC), a steady stream of technicians arrived from the United States and exchanged ideas with Yasui. Yasui often clashed with the technical staff from the NRC.[64]

Nevertheless, Yasui welcomed the challenge of engaging in "tough discussions as an engineer." He had long thought, *In Japan, discussion only starts after everyone has nodded their heads and said, "uh huh, uh huh." But with people from overseas, it was important for both parties to state their position and clarify where the differences lay.*

Yasui was extremely impressed by the expertise and ability of the NRC. He knew only too well from experience how good the American experts were at explaining things systemically. Having no illusions that "this is a technical battle, so it doesn't matter at all if we don't agree," he took up the tough discussions without hesitation.[65] The clashing of swords over whether the spent-fuel pool at Unit 4 was boiled dry or not was a prime example. (The lead up to this is outlined in chapter 10.)

The NRC side wanted to know how Yasui saw it. One of the senior members recollects the following:

"It was intense with Yasui. He's a very opinionated man. And he had burning pride. I don't know if it was, you know, personal pride, pride of an engineer, pride of country. He was a cluster of pride."

They were in conflict over the assessment of the situation in the fuel pools at Units 3 and 4.

"He insisted that water had entered. We challenged him on the water temperature in the spent-fuel pools. The debate over the water temperature was blistering. I eventually assumed that he just has more information than we did. He just needed to share it with us. But, you know, he didn't look to share the information with us.

"We were not just outsiders, we were an unwelcome presence. But I later really wished we had talked with him more frankly and approached him in a way that resonated with him. I think not doing that was our mistake."[66]

When the accident occurred at Fukushima Daiichi NPS, the most useful technical personnel were the fellows and advisers who were the first-generation engineers and had become the "old boys" quite a while back. Compared with these personnel, the engineers who emerged later, including TEPCO's fellows and advisers, were less helpful. Yasui was painfully aware of this.

"There was no manual for this fight. The game was to create hypotheses and come up with ideas. At a time like that, they used every bit of their knowledge and had the most flexible approach."

When he was majoring in nuclear engineering at graduate school, Yasui eyed atomic energy as Japan's technological flagship. However, after the first generation of engineers that Yasui looked up to retired, and they reached the second and third generations, things changed. Although each may have excelled in their own area, the number of people who could see the overall picture dwindled. Takaya Imai, a friend and contemporary of Yasui's at METI, remembers talking about this.

"In the 1980s and 1990s, when the whole world was making progress in the technical aspects of nuclear safety regulation, Japan didn't adapt to the evolution of technology. Sticking to precedents and style was rampant.

"Japan is probably the best in the world at building things according to the blueprints. But if you don't have the technology to change the system design, you'll never be a top runner on the world stage."[67]

The first thing Yasui felt when the Fukushima Daiichi accident occurred was, "This is the defeat of the Japanese technological team. There's no chief engineer in Japan to look at the priorities and balance of technology policy as a whole and to show the exact directions and decisions."[68]

In the response to the Fukushima Daiichi emergency, it was Yasui himself who came to act as the chief engineering officer at the Integrated Response Office. Yasui hardly went home from March 15 until the end of the Golden Week May holidays. Apart from the occasional night at a hotel, he slept at TEPCO. His wife brought him clean clothes. For the rest of March, he kept his eye on the reactors around the clock, with just a nap here and there. When he received a call from Imai, Yasui said, "My head feels like it's on fire."[69]

Yasui had been a key member during the establishment of NISA. He was never appointed to the agency, however. The only time he was involved in nuclear energy administration was his first two years at the ministry, spending the next twenty-eight years away from the field.

NISA subsequently failed to become the body of nuclear safety regulation professionals that Yasui had visualized, and it meekly accepted becoming the captive of TEPCO and the Federation of Electric Power Companies of Japan. Moreover, after the accident at Fukushima Daiichi, NISA fell into a state of utter dysfunction that Madarame described as "well, it just disappeared."

Looking at Yasui working his fingers to the bone, Hosono thought, *Does he feel "original sin" with NISA? Is that why he's working so hard?*[70]

LITTLE LEAGUE SOCCER

It was Tetsuro Ito, deputy chief cabinet secretary for crisis management, who took control of the crisis response at the crisis management center in the basement of the Kantei. Ito had joined the National Police Agency (NPA) in 1972 and had mainly been involved in security and external affairs.

He had broken down the opposing forces in the struggle over Narita Airport when he was head of security at Chiba Prefecture. He had succeeded using "drag-'em-out-and-hit-'em" tactics for the last remaining insurgents.

At the time of the 1995 Hanshin-Awaji earthquake, he had a bitter experience as the NPA's traffic control section chief. After he had put traffic controls in place, there were many spots where the fire engines and the SDF could not get into the disaster area. Sometime later, the roads became impassable as they were filled with people coming to find out if their families were safe.

After working his way up to commissioner, he was appointed deputy chief cabinet secretary for crisis management in the Yasuo Fukuda cabinet in 2008. He had since served five terms in that position under both LDP and DPJ administrations.

One of the duties of the deputy chief cabinet secretary for crisis management was to brief all members of the cabinet on crisis management basics when they were first appointed. When the DPJ Hatoyama cabinet was formed, he also briefed Kan, who was deputy prime minister. When

Hatoyama was about to make his first official trip overseas as prime minister, he was called in by Kan. Kan would have to serve as the acting prime minister during the prime minister's trip.

"I'd like to hear about that crisis management stuff one more time."

He asked, "As acting prime minister, what should I do in the case of an emergency? From what moment do I assume the prime minister's responsibilities? When the prime minister leaves the Kantei? When his plane takes off from Haneda? And when am I relieved of those responsibilities? When he touches down at Haneda?"

One of the Kantei staff seated there was surprised.

Wow, he's pretty finicky about the details!

Ito replied, "The moment of [the aircraft] spotting out and spotting in," but thought to himself, *He's feeling tense. Even though it's only acting, when it comes to the prime minister's post . . .*

This was Ito's first impression of Kan.[71] It then turned out that Ito would support Kan during the emergency at Fukushima Daiichi NPS.

The deputy chief cabinet secretary for crisis management's mission was to aid the chief cabinet secretary and his deputy to respond to emergencies that had, or were feared to have, a severe impact on the lives, bodies, and property of the people—and, if possible, to prevent the occurrence of such circumstances.

Examples of such emergencies included large-scale natural disasters (lower 6, or upper 5 in Tokyo, on the Japanese seismic intensity scale), serious accidents (including plane disasters or crashes involving more than fifty passengers and nuclear-related accidents), as well as serious incidents (mass-casualty terrorism, reactor-facility terrorism, the intrusion of territorial waters by suspicious boats or submarines). "Lower 6" refers to situations where it is difficult to stand, or building infrastructure becomes damaged to the extent that doors may not open or windows shatter, whereas "upper 5" refers to when heavy furniture or objects move and fall.

The crisis management center was born in the wake of the Hanshin-Awaji earthquake of January 1995. Its functions were subsequently strengthened in response to each crisis that followed: the sarin gas attack on the Tokyo subway system (1995), the hostage incident at the Japanese ambassador's residence in Peru (1996), the Russian tanker accident and oil spill (1997), and so on.[72]

In the event of an emergency, the emergency operation team is required to rally immediately. If appointed a member of the team, one was to keep business trips to a minimum. One was not to eat anywhere more than fifteen minutes away by car. Since being appointed deputy chief cabinet secretary for crisis management, Ito had been careful not to go to the higher floors of skyscrapers or to ride the subway.

Twenty people were gathered at the round table in the middle of the room, with some sixty people on the outside.

The important thing was the initial response. The first seventy-two hours were said to be critical for saving lives.[73]

Leaving aside the earthquake and tsunami, the prime minister's assistants and secretaries were extremely dissatisfied that they were not receiving any information from the crisis management center regarding the Fukushima Daiichi accident.

"I mean to say, the information we were getting from the TV in the office was much faster that what was coming up from below."

Frustrated, they hurriedly moved a TV into the prime minister's reception room. They left the channel on NTV, which had been the first to broadcast the explosion in Unit 1 on the afternoon of March 12. NTV's network affiliate, Fukushima Central TV, was covering the Fukushima plant live from a fixed camera.[74]

There was probably a lot of information going into the crisis management center, but it seemed to come to a halt there. Gathering information was all very fine, but why was it taking so long to evaluate the information and, based on that, get the relevant government institutions moving?

The people around Kan, especially the secretaries, became increasingly frustrated that the crisis management center wasn't functioning adequately. Criticism was voiced within the cabinet as well about the sluggish response of the crisis management center. Koichi Genba, minister for national policy, was one who felt that way. He later testified, "The crisis management center focused all the information, no matter what, on the deputy chief cabinet secretary for crisis management, and because, for formality's sake, they had to get his blessing, even for the most urgent matters, like supplying gasoline to evacuate residents in Fukushima, it took forever to get a decision, and we couldn't send in the gas trucks. Consequently, I had to make a move and arrange this."[75]

Genba's electorate was in Fukushima. After the nuclear emergency took place, he was running all over the place trying to respond to the Fukushima disaster and provide support to the residents.

To use Genba's words, he was moving about "in order to break down the walls of rigid administrative." As a consequence, he found himself colliding with Ito and the emergency operation team. Hence, this led to criticism that "he was giving his electorate preferential treatment at a time of national crisis," and he was treated by the Kantei parliamentarians as a "guerilla." Genba, however, didn't care in the least.[76]

In the eighth meeting of NERHQ, held at one p.m. on March 15, Yoshihiro Katayama, minister for internal affairs and communication, spoke out.

"Regarding the response toward TEPCO and the requests for cooperation being sent to all the ministries—and I myself have had several such requests—too many of them are unclear in their purpose. The request for firefighting also strikes me as being fragmentary and childish. Is anyone really in charge of practical operations? Who's the central person? Is it correct to assume that the basement [of the Kantei] is the center or not?"

Kan replied, "We are working out of the room next to my office. Ninety percent of the raw data from TEPCO comes there. The METI minister and special adviser Hosono are there all the time. But the fact of the matter is that not all of the wheels are turning smoothly yet."[77]

The "practical operations" mentioned by Katayama were being run out of the reception room adjacent to the prime minister's office. Kan did not have a very strong concept of using the crisis management center and his deputy chief cabinet secretary for crisis management to the full.

Kan had spoken of the concrete image he had of "running the practical operations." It was at the NERHQ meeting held just before the fifth nuclear disaster response meeting on the morning of March 13. He had clearly stated, "We're getting information directly to Edano, Fukuyama, Hosono, and Terada, and working from that."

Kaieda's name was missing from this list. Nor did he mention Ito, deputy chief cabinet secretary for crisis management, or the crisis management center. Defense Minister Kitazawa, who was later to play a crucial role in the water pumping operations, was not on his mind, either.[78]

This was as far as Kan's image of a command post went at the time. He hadn't thought through how a command post should operate during a time of crisis, and everyone had their own different images.

The gap between perceptions of how to approach a crisis held by the key members of the emergency operation team and non-key members was also pronounced.

The five ministries and agencies of the police; the SDF; the firefighters; Ministry of Health, Labor, and Welfare (MHLW); and Ministry of Land, Infrastructure, Transport, and Tourism (MILT) were used to managing crises. Every time there was an earthquake, they rallied around, exchanged information, and coordinated their movements. They also had a good understanding of their mutual roles.

In the Fukushima Daiichi accident, however, NISA, which was the regulatory authority, and the Ministry of Education, Culture, Sports, Science, and Technology (MEXT) had to play a significant role. Accurate and timely information from these two organizations was vitally important. But NISA and MEXT failed to become real members of the team. MEXT changed its members every day in eight-hour shifts. One of the regulars later looked back and observed, "They were introspective and lacking in confidence, and were terrified of taking a risk."

Whether because seeing the crisis management center for the first time was a curiosity, one of the young MEXT officials was actually taking photos on his mobile phone and had to be cautioned to stop.[79]

The most important job for the emergency operation team was to decide things on the spot. Consequently, it consisted of senior officials in the director class. As for NISA, however, although Terasaka first put in an appearance, he disappeared straight away, and then Hiraoka, who had come to replace him, also disappeared after a while.

When Ito asked NISA to send in a replacement, NISA sent over some junior section chiefs. They could not make any decisions and did not have access to all-important information.

In the first place, NISA was laid down as the agency in charge of running the secretariat (ERC) for NERHQ. Crisis response was impossible if the secretariat did not move itself.

On the night of March 11, when a response to the Fukushima nuclear accident was needed, Ito asked senior NISA officials to get cracking setting up the emergency headquarters, but all they said was "We'll get on it," and time just slipped away. Even when they did manage to set something up, it was a lifeless thing. This failure of the emergency headquarters to function remained an obstacle to the very end.[80]

However, the inability of the crisis management center to function adequately was not just because NISA scattered and MEXT ran from place to place hiding. The real hurdle lay in the silo mentality of the Kasumigaseki bureaucracy and a culture determined to avoid risk. One of the director-class members of the emergency operation team put it the following way:

"Stabilizing the reactor cooling, containing the radiation, evacuating the residents. No matter who you were, these were the three objectives of crisis management for Fukushima Daiichi. But MEXT was laid low by SPEEDI. All of the government offices were frightened of evacuating residents in the area and didn't make a move. Nobody wanted to shoulder any additional risk. But if the government ministries and agencies didn't move, it wasn't easy for the crisis management center to do anything."[81]

SPEEDI was a simulation system for predicting the diffusion of radioactive material. It had been developed by the Science and Technology Agency and later the MEXT in order to encourage the safe evacuation of residents during a nuclear accident (see chapter 14).

One of the parliamentary secretaries, an ex-bureaucrat himself, sums up the problem as nothing but a breakdown of the bureaucracy.

"They put it down to a failure of political leadership, but more than half was due to bureaucratic decay. This was especially revealed by the Kantei's crisis management. The bureaucracy (administration) was completely dead. There was not a single one of them who brought us any information. Things wouldn't have run smoothly no matter who was prime minister."[82]

Even the post of deputy chief cabinet secretary for crisis management, who was in charge of the crisis management center, was one of "cabinet secretariat" crisis management—not crisis management for the "cabinet" itself, according to the interpretation of the Cabinet Legislation Bureau. In short, the post was nothing more than one of "the right to coordinate" within the framework of the chief cabinet secretary and his deputy's "right to coordinate." The Cabinet Legislation Bureau was nothing less than the "guardian of the law," dominated by bureaucrats, and a vehicle for forcing its legal interpretations aimed at maintaining the balance of various powers within the bureaucracy onto the cabinet.[83]

The directors holed up in the emergency operation team had their doubts whether—even if they did send information up—the aides were passing it on to the parliamentarians in a timely fashion; weren't they especially lax in giving the prime minister information? In general, the secretaries were quite scathing in their appraisal of Ito, but there was one who viewed him favorably.

"Ito-san knew how to stay in step with the prime minister. He knew what buttons to press in a presentation. And when the prime minister was in a bad mood, he would cut it short. And no matter how often the prime minister asked him, he would clearly say, 'What can't be done can't be done.' His job wasn't just managing the nuclear crisis. He had the earthquake and tsunami disasters to handle as well. The prime minister was only focused on the nuclear crisis. So, someone else had to keep an eye on other things. It was Ito-san who did that. It was like Little League soccer on the fifth floor, with all the kids chasing after the nuclear ball. I think he had a more balanced approach."[84]

Looking back at the crisis management in the Kantei at the time, Fukuyama also said, "To use soccer as a metaphor, there may have been a tendency to focus on the ball too much." He sounded remorseful about the "Little League" approach. He was speaking about the "groupthink" that afflicted the Kantei, with everyone like-minded and looking in the same direction.[85]

Amid all this, it was the SDF that responded professionally. The SDF had the ability, will, and expertise to fully carry out its own crisis response operations. Defense Minister Toshimi Kitazawa acted as a buffer against the frustration and panic coming from the Kantei, and under the command of Chief of Staff Ryoichi Oriki, he aimed at using the SDF strategically—not for political ends, but for overcoming the national crisis.

As the role played by the SDF in responding to the Fukushima Daiichi emergency became more decisive, a high-ranking SDF officer was added to the emergency operation team for the first time.

This was foreshadowed when, at ten a.m. on March 15, Oriki dispatched Lieutenant General Koichi Isobe to the Kantei to report an increase in radiation at the U.S. aircraft carrier *George Washington*, anchored at the Commander Fleet Activities Yokosuka U.S. naval base.

Isobe was the first deputy commander of the Central Readiness Force (CRF) when it was launched. As Ground Self-Defense Forces staff office defense manager, he had been responsible for the National Defense Program Guidelines, and it was at this time that he envisioned the establishment of a Central Readiness Force and incorporated it into the plan. He was the leading light of the Ground Self-Defense Forces.

This gave some of the parliamentarians at the Kantei the idea that they should have a high-ranking officer from the SDF either in the Kantei or the crisis management center. Kitazawa spoke with Oriki and hurriedly decided to add Sadamasa Oue, dean of defense education at the National Defense Academy, to the emergency operation team. Kitazawa got Kan's approval.

On the night of March 23, Isobe and Nobushige Takamizawa, director general of the Defense Ministry's Bureau of Defense Policy, visited Ito to explain the addition of Isobe to the emergency operation team. Both a "suit" (from the ministry) and a "uniform" (from the SDF) came to greet Ito. There was no way he could refuse.[86]

There was no chair for Oue at the round table. He sat back behind Shuichi Sakurai, director general of the Ministry of Defense Bureau of Operational Policy.[87]

SEVEN

Resident Evacuation

"AT THE VERY LEAST, LET'S REDUCE THE RISK WITH THE EVACUATION RADIUS"

At 7:03 p.m. on March 11, after the state of nuclear emergency had been declared and Chief Cabinet Secretary Yukio Edano's press conference was over, Prime Minister Naoto Kan held a meeting in the mezzanine office of the Kantei's crisis management center with METI Minister Banri Kaieda, NSC Chairman Haruki Madarame, NISA Deputy Director General Eiji Hiraoka, and TEPCO Fellow Ichiro Takekuro to discuss the evacuation of residents.

No matter what happened, residents had to be protected from radiation exposure. In order to do that, depending on the circumstances, they would have to be evacuated. Apart from the acute disorders that occur above a certain exposure dose, late-onset disorders also can develop from low doses of radiation. In the latter's case, there is a possibility that late-onset disorders, such as genetic disorders or leukemia and other cancers will materialize within a few years to decades later.[1] These disorders had to be prevented.

But even if they were to evacuate local residents, what criteria were to be used and where were they to be evacuated to?

In the disaster response guidelines of the Nuclear Safety Commission, the "emergency preparedness zone" (EPZ) was stipulated as "within an eight-to-ten-kilometer radius from the nuclear reactor." On the other hand, International Atomic Energy Agency (IAEA) documentation set the preventive action zone (PAZ) at a radius of three to five kilometers (in the case of 100-megawatt output or more). Which should they choose?

Hiraoka proposed implementing three kilometers, using the IAEA zone as a reference. Kan asked belligerently, "On what basis? Can you say it's all right even if something happens?"[2]

Hiraoka replied:

"Regular evacuation drills also operate under the assumption of a venting operation, and even in those cases they use a three-kilometer radius. I think three kilometers will be fine even supposing that, in the future, we'll have to vent. Moreover, if we make the evacuation radius too big from the start, there'll be traffic jams, meaning there's a fear that residents in the three-kilometer radius won't be able to evacuate."

A proposal for five kilometers was also put forward, but both Madarame and Hiraoka voiced the opinion that "three kilometers is enough." Takekuro reiterated his point of view that "we should be able to maintain the water in each reactor somehow for at least the first eight hours." As a consequence, they settled on the idea of "the order to evacuate within a three-kilometer zone is just a precaution."

9:23 P.M. The government issued an order to evacuate within a three-kilometer radius and to stay indoors within a three-to-ten-kilometer radius. The number of residents covered by the evacuation was about 1,100 in the towns of Okuma and Futaba.

The order was to be made in the name of the prime minister and director general of NERHQ, and be conveyed to the municipalities by telephone from the offsite center. However, NISA's emergency response center (ERC), which was the secretariat for NERHQ, could not reach the offsite center. They tried to contact Okuma and Futaba directly, but they could not reach Okuma by phone. As a result, they conveyed the order from the National Policy Agency via the Fukushima Prefectural Police.

In fact, thirty minutes earlier, Fukushima Prefecture already ordered a resident evacuation in a two-kilometer radius from Fukushima Daiichi Station. Fukushima Prefecture, however, had not informed the government of this.

Without knowing the evacuation instructions of Fukushima Prefecture, the government had issued an evacuation order to residents within a three-kilometer radius. Resident evacuation was completed three hours after the order, at 12:30 a.m. on March 12.[3]

In the late hours of the night, pressure in the Unit 1's containment vessel showed an abnormal increase, and venting had to be carried out. If they could vent, an evacuation radius of three kilometers would be sufficient. However, if they could not vent, it was possible that they could not control the reactor pressure. In that case, it was feared, three kilometers would not be enough.

Based on these considerations, the evacuation area was expanded to ten kilometers (see chapter 3). The government decision to expand the evacuation zone to ten kilometers was made at 5:44 a.m., and the order was issued. The order covered 48,272 residents in the towns of Futaba, Okuma, Namie, and Tomioka.

The Kantei was shocked by the explosion at Unit 1 in the afternoon. No one had foreseen a hydrogen explosion in the reactor building. After learning of the hydrogen explosion at Unit 1, Kan feared that the same thing would happen at Units 2 and 3. There was a need to prepare for "the risk of simultaneous explosions in several reactors." Was it still all right to maintain the evacuation area at ten kilometers?

In the cabinet, at the fourth meeting of NERHQ, in the morning of March 12, Minister for National Policy Koichiro Genba was the first to raise the question: "There's a risk of meltdown. Is an evacuation area of ten kilometers enough?"[4]

Genba's electorate was in Fukushima Prefecture. His father-in-law was Eisaku Sato, a former governor of Fukushima Prefecture. Because of his critical stance toward TEPCO, NISA, and the government, regarding safety regulation and nuclear fuel cycles, he had made enemies within the government.

However, in 2006, his political career was brought to an end with his arrest on a bribery charge over a dam construction contract. Sato cited this as a miscarriage of justice in his book *Governor Assassinated—The Fabricated Fukushima Prefecture Corruption Scandal*. For Genba, Fukushima, TEPCO, and the nuclear stations were tinted with family feelings—or, rather, the pathos of flesh and blood.

Another factor for further delaying a decision was that this point in time—just after six p.m. on March 12—when the matter of evacuation was being discussed, coincided with Madarame's ambiguous response to Kan's question about the possibility of recriticality in the context of whether to pump water into Unit 2.

"If recriticality occurs, a ten-kilometer evacuation zone won't be enough. Won't we have to issue an evacuation order for a twenty-kilometer radius?"

This had been Kan's question. Fukuyama believed that "evacuation should be on a larger scale," and Kan thought likewise. In other words, it was better to be on the safe side, "just in case," and make the evacuation a little broader.

The problem was that they weren't getting the all-important information on radiation levels. The only information that had come in was the peripheral radiation monitoring readings for the site, which at that time were not so high. In light of these numbers, Edano's assessment was that it seemed unlikely they "had to head for the hills."

Was it to be left at ten kilometers? Or set at twenty kilometers? Or should it immediately be made thirty kilometers?

Madarame expressed caution over expanding it to twenty kilometers.

"It's set at ten kilometers in the emergency preparedness plan. Even five kilometers is more than adequate. I think, at most, ten kilometers will be fine."

"It was thirty kilometers at Chernobyl."

"At the very least, let's reduce the risk with the evacuation radius."

If the evacuation area was set at ten kilometers, that was backed up by the emergency preparedness plan, but there was nothing in the guidelines about twenty kilometers. Setting a twenty-kilometer radius would need some sort of grounds, so it was decided to use the guidelines of the International Commission on Radiation Protection (ICRP) and the International Atomic Energy Agency (IAEA).

In a recommendation from 2007 (Publication 103), the ICRP had set the annual dose limit for members of the public at

- 20–100 millisieverts in times of emergency

- 1–20 millisieverts during recovery following an accident

- 1 millisievert at all other times

Using this as a reference, NISA put forward the following guidelines:

1. Stay indoors within 20–30 kilometers to prevent a 10-millisievert dose

2. Evacuation from a 20-kilometer radius to prevent a 50-millisievert dose

These, however, only referred to immediately after an accident, so there was a need to make different arrangements if the accident was prolonged.[5]

At 5:30 p.m. on March 12, Edano instructed NISA's ERC to immediately research the towns and population within the twenty-kilometer radius and to carry out a simulation for the evacuation of residents.

At the crisis management center, Tetsuro Ito, deputy chief cabinet secretary for crisis management, ran a simulation of "how to respond" if the evacuation area was expanded to twenty kilometers. It was predicted it would take approximately three days to evacuate all the residents within twenty kilometers.

The simulation results showed it was not something that could not be done. There was a danger, however, that the evacuees and the support staff would be exposed to radiation if another explosion took place during the three days it would take to evacuate.

Somehow, while the simulation was being run, it seemed that information had been leaked.

"Evacuation has started in certain areas."

Such a report came in to the Kantei. Apparently, the locals were making a move on the assumption that an expansion of the evacuation area was inevitable. They could not delay the decision any longer.

Resident evacuation, seawater injection, and the risk at Fukushima Daini NPS—as will be later explained, this was also unstable—they were confronted simultaneously with three issues that required immediate attention. Of the three, Edano said, "We have to start with resident evacuation," and gave the go-ahead for the expansion to twenty kilometers, with Kan making the final decision.

Referring to this decision later, Kan said, "Even if something extremely abnormal took place at the reactors, there should be a period of time before radioactive fallout started reaching them, so I deemed it to be safe."[6]

An information leak in the simulation stage also took place over Fukushima Daini NPS. When Edano issued his directive to NISA for a simulation of expanding the evacuation area to twenty kilometers for Daiichi, he also confidentially instructed them to look into the necessity for a twenty-kilometer evacuation of local residents for Fukushima Daini NPS.

While the instruction for Daini was never anything more than a "consideration," the ERC jumped the gun thinking the Kantei had decided on a twenty-kilometer evacuation for Fukushima Daini as well. At the time, Hiraoka was on the fifth floor of the Kantei, and he was surprised to hear that information. He called the officer in charge at NISA.

"We're not thinking of evacuating residents within twenty kilometers of Daini. It's twenty kilometers from Daiichi, but ten kilometers for Daini. Don't get it wrong."

Ito was also amazed when he heard the information. He went to the chief cabinet secretary's office immediately and told Edano.

"Mr. Secretary, evacuating means uprooting the residents and disrupting their lives. Please remember that. It's fine if the reactors are really in a dangerous state, but are the reactors at Daini really in danger?"

Edano replied, "The actual reactors are still okay."

"Well, I'd like you to stop the evacuation for Daini then."

Edano decided to leave the Daini evacuation area at the ten-kilometer radius.[7]

The four towns covered by the ten-kilometer evacuation radius had their own evacuation plans about where and along what routes residents were to evacuate. But the towns and villages in a twenty-kilometer radius did not have any emergency preparedness plans. The chaos was immense, with the confusion reigning from the ten-kilometer-radius evacuation in the first place clashing with residents evacuating from the twenty-kilometer radius.

Government contact with the local municipalities and local residents was insufficient. They were unable to obtain the means to evacuate or places to evacuate to. Assuming they were even able to evacuate the residents, no practical measures were in place, including radiation exposure screening and life support. The government had not received beforehand the necessary information for evacuation from the relevant ministries, agencies, and local governments.[8]

What areas were inside the twenty-kilometer radius? What were their respective populations? This kind of essential information was uncertain. The offsite center in Okuma didn't even have a map of the twenty-kilometer area.

"Get them!"

They managed to get maps from somewhere, but the administrative boundaries were still unclear.[9]

6:25 P.M., MARCH 12. The government issued the order to evacuate for residents within a twenty-kilometer radius. This covered two cities, five towns, one village, and a total population of 177,503.

The ERC started preparing to send in stable iodine and drawing up a list of the officers in charge of the local health centers. First for inside three kilometers, then ten kilometers, and then twenty kilometers. In the space of one short day, the government had issued evacuation orders three times in rapid succession.

Where were people to flee from and to where? From where and to where were they to be ordered? These crucial points were vague.

There were a lot of people who fled upon hearing from the manager of a convenience store, "We've been told from up high to leave." Information started circulating that the TEPCO staff quarters around the stations were the first to empty out. It was rumored that government workers from Fukushima Prefecture had started fleeing.[10]

Almost all of the local governments learned of the twenty-kilometer evacuation order from Edano's press conference that night at 8:40 p.m.[11]

8:40 P.M. Chief cabinet secretary press conference. Kantei pressroom.

"Radioactive material is not leaking out in large amounts . . . These measures do not mean that there is a concrete danger for people between ten and twenty kilometers. They are precautionary measures . . . And to be completely sure, we have expanded to twenty kilometers."

"MR. SECRETARY, THIRTY KILOMETERS IS JUST NOT POSSIBLE"

On March 13, there was an increasing fear that even twenty kilometers was not enough. This was because Unit 3, following Unit 1, was in a perilous situation.

On the morning of this day, sometime after nine a.m., the minister's secretariat at METI asked NISA: How much time until meltdown in Unit 3? And was there a need to change the twenty-kilometer radius?

5:40 P.M., THE SAME DAY. Edano and Kaieda instructed NISA to urgently ideate a worst-case scenario if the twenty-kilometer evacuation area was adequate. This was just a "precautionary measure" in case meltdown occurred.[12]

There was no way all of the evacuees could be situated within Fukushima Prefecture alone. There were not enough places for thirteen thousand to fifteen thousand people. The government approached the neighboring prefectures of Ibaraki and Tochigi about accepting evacuees.[13]

On the afternoon of March 13, both prefectures agreed, but only on the condition that personnel and supplies for evacuation shelters would be provided, and that the evacuees were decontaminated in Fukushima Prefecture.

Since an evacuation order within a radius of twenty kilometers had been issued, it was no longer possible to carry out rescue operations for the casualties of the earthquake and tsunami within this area.

Before six p.m. on March 13, Kan had called into his office Madarame, Kukita, acting chairman of the Nuclear Safety Commission, and Toshimitsu Homma, deputy director of the Nuclear Safety Research Center at the Japan Atomic Energy Agency (JAEA), to ask them their opinion. Kan asked Madarame if there was a chance of a hydrogen explosion, and if that occurred, what measures should be taken. Madarame replied, "That is unlikely in the case of an ABWR (advanced boiling water reactor)." Kukita agreed, "Things aren't likely to go that far."

Next, Kan asked, "In the current circumstances, is there a need to expand the twenty-kilometer evacuation area? Will it be necessary, for example, to extend it to fifty kilometers?"

Madarame suggested Homma explain. Homma booted up his laptop.

Homma was an expert in public radiation protection. He was also an expert member of the Nuclear Safety Commission. The Nuclear Safety Commission, an advisory body by rights, had already exceeded that role and was directly involved in the disaster response led by the Kantei. This meant they needed the help of experts well versed in the field. It was Homma who had been called in. Kukita had asked Homma to accompany him to the Kantei that day as well.

Up until this point, Kan had never met Homma. Madarame did not introduce him, and Homma did not introduce himself. The laptop was taking some time to start up. From the outset, Kan had a scowl on his face, but he looked increasingly irritated. He asked roughly, "And what's your name?!"

Homma apologized for his rudeness and said, as he showed the simulation screen, "If the release rate of radioactive material is 50 percent, I don't think there'll be a situation where 100 millisieverts is exceeded within a twenty-kilometer area . . . Consequently, I don't think it will be necessary to expand the evacuation area beyond twenty kilometers."

Signaling his agreement with Homma, Madarame also remarked that a twenty-kilometer evacuation area was sufficient at the present juncture. Once again, Madarame referred to the Chernobyl case.

"It was thirty kilometers at Chernobyl. So I don't think we need thirty kilometers."

At this point, Madarame never dreamed that the Fukushima Daiichi accident would reach Chernobyl proportions. The meeting concluded that the twenty-kilometer line would stand for the present.[14]

The stance was that if exposure could be kept at 20 millisieverts, the bottom threshold of the 20–100 millisieverts/year dose limit for members of the public during an emergency, emergency evacuation—that is, an order to evacuate, in administrative terms—should not be issued.

At this stage, there was still a considerable number of people within the twenty-kilometer radius who had not evacuated. Evacuating them was the first priority. If the evacuation area was to be expanded to fifty kilometers, there was the chance that people living close to the plants would be late in getting out.

Madarame drew attention to the risk of shadow evacuation. This refers to the risk "that occurs when residents in areas that do not require evacuation overreact to evacuation orders. This may give rise to road congestion, which may, in turn, cause delays in the evacuation of residents from areas that actually require it."

If people within a fifty-kilometer radius were evacuated, what action would they take; what would happen at the time; how would it affect the current evacuation underway? His point was that you had to make an evacuation plan taking into account negative factors and keeping an eye on the "shadows."

In the event that the situation deteriorated and the evacuation area had to be extended to fifty kilometers, there was still enough time. It was Madarame's assessment that the negative factors outweighed the positive in terms of shadow evacuation.[15]

Around six a.m. on March 14, Hiraoka received a call from TEPCO managing director, Akio Komori.

"We are urgently looking into venting Unit 3. We've started looking into whether the evacuation area needs to be expanded immediately or not."[16]

9:30 A.M. The seventh meeting of NERHQ at the Kantei. Kan said, "Evacuating from within a twenty-kilometer radius is all right."

Koichiro Genba countered, "There's also a differing expert opinion."[17]

Kaieda reported, "The evacuation from within the twenty-kilometer radius was almost complete as of this morning." This was premature. The government later claimed that evacuation from within the twenty-kilometer radius was confirmed to have been completed at "two p.m. on March 15."[18]

However, this was also premature. It was at 12:30 a.m. on March 16 that the last remaining serious patients in the Okuma and Futaba hospitals were rescued by the SDF.[19]

11:01 A.M., MARCH 14. The explosion took place in the Unit 3 (RB).

At approximately 1:30 p.m., TEPCO judged that the cooling function at Unit 2 had stopped. Following on from Unit 3, Unit 2 was now in a state of crisis. Did the twenty-kilometer radius need to be reassessed yet again?

In the early morning of March 15, there was a second explosion at Fukushima Daiichi NPS. Wasn't there a need to expand to thirty kilometers?

Edano looked into adopting this course and suggested it to Kan, when the latter returned from having burst into TEPCO that morning. Information started filtering down that Kan was considering a proposal to extend the evacuation area to thirty kilometers. It was rumored that this "course" had already reached the ears of the Fukushima Prefectural Police.

Parliamentarians at the Kantei came to Ito, asking him to prepare for such an eventuality. Ito rushed up to the fifth floor of the Kantei.

"Mr. Secretary, thirty kilometers is just not possible. Please don't do this. Making it thirty kilometers will mean a total of 150,000 evacuees. It will take days. We had enough trouble evacuating residents within twenty kilometers. Evacuating the hospital patients was incredibly hard. The key point is whether we can arrange places to take in the evacuees. I can't even bear to think of the trouble we had when we extended to twenty kilometers. You have no idea what a job it'll be if you extend to thirty kilometers . . ."

How to deal with hospitals and their patients had been a blind spot when extending the evacuation area. Ito also told Edano that the Ministry of Health, Labor, and Welfare (MHLW) had confidentially expressed to him their caution about any expansion.

"Leaving now would, in fact, be more dangerous. If there was a large-scale release of radioactive matter, there might be a plume. They should stay indoors first. We need to avoid the plume, no matter what. Please put the people between twenty and thirty kilometers on indoor evacuation status. It's the only option."

"I see."

Edano reflected for a bit.

"I'll just go and have a word."

So saying, he left the room, then returned after a short while and simply said, "Right you are."[20]

"FUKUSHIMA PREFECTURE WILL BE WIPED OFF THE MAP"

11:00 A.M., MARCH 15. The government announced a "stay indoors" order for residents between a twenty- and thirty-kilometer radius.

In his press conference, Kan began by saying, "I want to inform the people of Japan about the situation regarding the Fukushima nuclear power stations." He then continued, "There is a heightened risk of even further leakage of radioactive material. Most residents have already evacuated beyond the twenty-kilometer radius of the Fukushima Daiichi Nuclear Power Station, but let me reiterate the need for everyone living within that radius to evacuate to a point outside of it. Moreover, in view of the developing situation at the reactors, those who are outside the twenty-kilometer radius but still within a thirty-kilometer radius should remain indoors in their house, office, or other buildings, and not go outside."

But how was one supposed to "remain indoors"? In his own press conference, Edano was more specific about this point.

"We would like you to close your windows to improve airtightness. Do not ventilate. Hang your washing indoors."

Between the twenty- and thirty-kilometer radius, more than 100,000 people—Ito had told Edano 150,000—would have to be evacuated. Evacuation within a twenty-kilometer radius had somehow been effected mainly by deploying the SDF, but there were limits to what even the SDF could do if this was extended to twenty-to-thirty kilometers.

Selecting, getting the approval, and matching evacuees with places willing to take them in would be far more demanding. Deciding on an evacuation area was not something that could be reached immediately on scientific grounds alone. How long would the evacuation take? Had places been found to evacuate to? What would the weather and temperature be when evacuating? Was there no fear of freezing to death from the cold outside? All these and more were risks that had to be considered.

Around that time Kan and other key members at the Kantei were, above all else, frightened of a hydrogen or steam explosion. If they evacuated people right away and there was an explosion, there was a danger they would suffer severe radiation exposure outdoors.

It was projected that an evacuation of the twenty-to-thirty-kilometer area would take anywhere from five days to a week. Bearing in mind the risk of an explosion during that time, having people stay indoors seemed safer.

And not only that. Once the local residents had been evacuated, even if the danger of radiation exposure had passed, there was the question of the red tape involved in allowing them to return. One condition of return was the restoration of the reactors to a cold state. As long as there was no prospect of restoration, people could not return. They had to keep in mind this risk of return.[21]

However, there were more and more voices calling for an expansion of the evacuation area.

At four p.m. on March 15, twelve parliamentary members of the Democratic Party of Japan with nuclear power plants in their electorates, including Makiko Tanaka (Niigata), Kenko Matsumoto (Hokkaido), and Tetsuo Kutsukake (Ishikawa), visited the Kantei. Tanaka and her colleagues had met in her office in the Diet members' building to exchange ideas. When someone said, "The administration's lost its way," no one objected.

Tanaka was the daughter of Kakuei Tanaka, former prime minister of

Japan. She had also served as the general director of the Science and Tech-nology Agency and had an interest in atomic power. She would later serve as the minister of foreign affairs in the Koizumi administration. She had a high opinion of the French approach to atomic energy, namely that "they know how to accelerate and how to apply the brakes, and, in fact, they do both at the same time." Bearing this in mind, she also said that Japan should ask for technical support from France and elsewhere.

Putting these points down on paper, the members of parliament had come that day to the Kantei to propose them to Prime Minister Kan. They could not secure an appointment time, however, because Kan was busy. Frustrated, Tanaka and her group ended up gatecrashing the Kantei.

The Kantei was deadly silent. The waiting room on the fifth floor, which always had someone waiting there, was deserted. The Integrated Response Office had just been set up that very morning at TEPCO.

Shown into the prime minister's office, they met with Kan. They handed their document to Kan. On it, was written:

The Prime Minister of Japan, Mr. Naoto Kan,
  In view of developments in the nuclear emergency from March 11 to date and the government's response thereto, we, the members of parliament with nuclear power plants in our electorates, request from the government further disclosure of accurate information as well as vigorously urge that the following efforts be made.

There were two points:

1. To effect a rapid evacuation and escorting on the assumption of a worst-case scenario as the top priority for ensuring the safety of local residents;

2. To seek as soon as possible the cooperation of nuclear experts in international organizations such as the International Atomic Energy Agency (IAEA) and from other countries.

Kan was exhausted. He sat well back on the sofa with an absentminded look on his face. Tanaka asked him, "Are you sure a twenty-kilometer evac-uation is all right? Shouldn't you set it wider, at, say, fifty kilometers, then reduce it when things have stabilized? . . . We would like you to effect a rapid evacuation and guidance based on a worst-case scenario."

Kan answered gruffly, "It's not a question of twenty or thirty kilome-ters! Nothing like that. I'm aware of that. But if we start talking about fifty or a hundred kilometers, it'll set off a panic."

Tanaka drew near. "Right now, the Americans are streaming out of Tokyo."

Kan responded, "There probably won't be a single American left in

Japan. Maybe even the Japanese will have to leave the archipelago. We've got to keep making efforts so that doesn't happen."

Tanaka was not convinced. "How about putting the people from Hamadori (the Pacific coastal stretch of Fukushima Prefecture) aboard a U.S. aircraft carrier and taking them to Okinawa?"[22]

Elsewhere, Genba was working to draw up a proposal for the evacuation of residents from a fifty-kilometer radius, with "Protect the Lives Within Fifty Kilometers" as his slogan.

He had a map drawn up at the time. It was a map of concentric circles in ten-kilometer increments up to a distance of eighty kilometers from Fukushima Daiichi NPS. On March 15, Genba made a direct appeal to Kan and Yuhei Sato, the Fukushima governor. Both, however, were negative. It was "a lone battle." Sato especially was strongly opposed. He told Genba, "Fukushima will be wiped off the map!"[23]

About that time, the Ministry of Defense (MOD) was also making preparations for an expansion of the evacuation area. If the evacuation was extended, it was the SDF who would receive the first call to be deployed.

Hideo Suzuki, MOD's deputy director general, advised Toshimi Kitazawa, the defense minister, "to be prepared" for when the evacuation area was expanded. Kitazawa hardened his resolve, but received a call from the Kantei shortly thereafter that "it's been decided at the chief cabinet secretary level that they're not going to extend the evacuation area."

On the night of March 16, the Kantei received the report from NISA and TEPCO that there was water in the fuel pool at Unit 4. Hosono recollected, "That was one of the factors in deciding we didn't need fifty kilometers."[24]

TAMOTSU BABA, MAYOR OF NAMIE TOWN

On the morning of March 11, Mayor Tamotsu Baba had visited a middle school to give the guest address at the graduation ceremony. In the afternoon, he was in the town office. His family ran a liquor store founded by his grandfather. It was a retail store, but they had recently started catering events as well.

The town of Namie was situated in the Futaba District of Fukushima Prefecture. It was part of the coastal area known as Hamadori. Its population was 21,434. It was linked to the inland by Route 114, which ran alongside the Ukedogawa River that flowed through the town. Salmon would swim up the Ukedogawa River from east to west to spawn.

That day, the tsunami came surging up the river at a terrible speed. After the tsunami receded, 660 buildings had disappeared from the town. Although the town offices had survived, they had no power. Candles were lit everywhere. The landlines were down. Mobile phones were down as well. Only one company's phone service was working, the company by the name AU. Three staff members had AU phones. Those three phones put in a stellar performance.

Phone calls were coming in all the time to check on people's safety. The tsunami kept pushing houses upstream even during the night. A report came in of seven or eight people frantically clinging to a roof, screaming for help.

The town hall staff numbered some 170 people. They were all there to respond. Sometime after three p.m. on March 12, Baba was watching TV in his office. He was half asleep. Chief Cabinet Secretary Yukio Edano was giving a press conference. He was saying, "there is a need to take measures to vent the internal pressure" in the reactor's containment vessel, or something like that.

This has become terrible.

Both Baba and the town hall's executive officers first heard of the nuclear accident via a television report. Namie received absolutely no information about the nuclear accident from either TEPCO or the offsite center.

We can't be worrying about a tsunami response now; we've got to respond to the nuclear plant.

Baba set up a nuclear response group in the meeting room on the west side of his office. Before six a.m., he used the town's disaster radio system to inform residents of the nuclear accident. The system kept announcing, "Please evacuate to outside a ten-kilometer radius."

The Namie town hall fell within the ten-kilometer radius, at a distance of 8.7 kilometers from the Fukushima Daiichi NPS. Approximately one-third of the town's surface area fell within the twenty-kilometer radius.

According to the emergency preparedness plan, three evacuation stations were designated at two primary schools and one nursing home outside the ten-kilometer radius. Residents with their own cars were to evacuate in those cars. A school bus was provided for other townspeople. Word of mouth was used to get the message out to everyone.

He was up to his ears in dealing with the resident evacuation, but he had an uneasy feeling.

What if the nuclear accident takes a turn for the worse? Ten kilometers probably won't be enough. Let's get everybody outside a twenty-kilometer radius.

It was sheer instinct. Having decided upon this, he started calling over the disaster radio for people to evacuate to Tsushima, close to thirty kilometers away. He also decided to relocate the town hall functions to the Tsushima substation.

3:00 P.M. ON MARCH 12. After seeing off all of his staff, Baba himself closed the doors to the town hall and, taking the wheel of his own car, headed to Tsushima. He was the rear guard.

The minute he reached Route 114, he was caught up in a huge traffic jam. A trip of usually thirty minutes took three and a half hours. It was after 6:30 p.m. when he reached the Tsushima outstation. The government had just issued the order to evacuate to twenty kilometers at 6:25 p.m.

But Namie received no information from the national government or the prefectural government. Eight thousand people had fled to Tsushima with a population of 1,400.

March 13 was a Sunday. As if the freezing cold of March 11 and 12 had been a figment of their imagination, it was a beautiful, sunny day. Baba visited more than twenty evacuation shelters to offer people his condolences. He felt his chest tighten at the sight of all the innocent children.

THE EVENING. A staff member, who had been to the offsite center some five kilometers away, returned.

"The offsite center itself is in a state of panic."

All he had been issued with from the offsite center was a satellite phone. Baba was forced to bitterly think:

What was all that emergency preparedness training about?

In October of the previous year, emergency preparedness training for a nuclear accident had been carried out on the sports field behind the Okuma Town Hall. The METI minister and governor of Fukushima Prefecture had participated via videoconference. The scenario had been that a pipe had been cut, or something. SDF helicopters had flown in from Tokyo. They had been told by an official from NISA to "make sure you know what's happening at the offsite center and follow their instructions."

That offsite center had fallen into a state of panic.

That day, blankets arrived from Niigata Prefecture. These were the first relief goods Namie received. The following day, they received food supplies from the Red Cross.

What unsettled everyone were the white Tyvek suits the prefectural police were wearing. Police from the Namie branch of the Futaba Police Station were encamped at the Tsushima Police Substation, but they were all wearing the protective garb. Kazuhiro Yoshida, chairman of the town council, asked the police officers, "Can't you take them off, because it's making the residents worried?"

"We can't do that. We don't know when we may have to go back to the town."

"Well, stay in the substation, please."

The white suits etched into people's minds the fear of radiation. Was the contamination so bad they had to wear them? Why was it just them being protected? What about us, left defenseless?

———

11:01 A.M., MARCH 14. The Unit 3 (RB) exploded. Watching on TV, Baba called a meeting of the emergency response group.

I reckon they'll go, one, two, three, four.

Following Unit 1, there had been a hydrogen explosion in Unit 3.

I reckon they'll all go into meltdown.

5:30 A.M., MARCH 15. A second meeting of the emergency response group was held.

"Everyone, we've had it. We have to move a bit farther away."

"How about Yamagata Prefecture? Or Kanto . . ."

All sorts of proposals were made, but it was decided to ask the city of Nihonmatsu. Nihonmatsu was situated approximately fifty kilometers from Fukushima Daiichi NPS. Namie had a connection with them through their jointly operated school bus service for high school students.

Baba knew the mayor of Nihonmatsu, Keiichi Miho. Baba called up his home and asked to meet. When he said he was holding an emergency response meeting from 7:30 a.m., he was told, "Well, please come over before that." He arrived at Nihonmatsu City Hall at 6:30 a.m. In the mayor's office, Baba told Miho, "There's a terrible nuclear accident taking place. The lives of our townspeople will be threatened if we do nothing. Would you allow us to evacuate to Nihonmatsu? . . . We just need a roof over our heads. Please."

Baba's eyes were bloodshot.

"How many people?"

"Eight thousand."

Miho swallowed on hearing that figure. Miho had served as the chairman of the prefectural assembly.

"During my time in the prefectural assembly, I thought about nuclear power. Contamination would be terrible. Let's see what we can do."

He rang the chairman and vice chairman of the city council on the spot, asking them to come right away. They turned up in the space of about ten minutes. The three of them decided then and there to accept the evacuees from Namie.

Later Baba learned that Nihonmatsu had 2,500 evacuees of its own forced to take shelter in the evacuation centers.

How thankful I am. What a debt I owe them!

He felt his heart bursting with inexpressible gratitude. Making a deep bow, he took his leave and returned to Tsushima. He decided to have residents start leaving after noon that day.

At eleven a.m. on the same day, the government issued the "stay indoors" order for residents in the twenty- to thirty-kilometer radius, but Namie Town had already decided to evacuate all its residents prior to that.

They reserved twenty buses from Niigata Prefecture, but the drivers turned back on the way. So, they arranged for another five buses and moved the residents to Nihonmatsu, the buses running back and forth nonstop.

At 3:30 p.m., Baba himself arrived in Nihonmatsu. Sleet had started to fall.

There had been an explosion somewhere inside Unit 2 that morning. A large-scale plume was blowing in a northwesterly direction. In the afternoon, it headed toward the Tsushima district of Namie Town, the Yamakiya district of Kawamata Town, and Iitate Village, among others. With the rain, it fell to earth.

The townspeople had been running around trying to escape the middle of a hot spot.[25]

KATSUNOBU SAKURAI, MAYOR OF MINAMISOMA CITY

On the night of March 11, Katsunobu Sakurai, mayor of Minamisoma City, had just happened to run into one of the city's residents as he came downstairs.

"The nuclear plant's in trouble."

He had come to city hall to tell the mayor this. He said he worked on site at Fukushima Daiichi NPS.

"Mr. Mayor, we have to get out of here as well."

After saying this, he left the building, adding, as he headed out, "I'm getting out of here now!"

Thinking, *This fellow's definitely been told to get out*, Sakurai felt uneasy, but had no sense of urgency yet.

It was during a meeting of the disaster response unit on the afternoon of March 12. There was an urgent call from the police.

"We've just received a report that there's been an explosion at Fukushima Daiichi."

Sakurai told his subordinates to check the facts and took up the disaster radio mike in his hands.

"We've been contacted by the police that there's been an explosion, so please stay indoors . . . Please remain indoors . . . Please stay where you are . . . Please avoid going outdoors as much as possible."

After thirty or forty minutes, they were contacted by the fire department to be told that "an explosion hasn't been confirmed." He went back to the disaster radio: "Disregard previous announcement."

Around 6:30 p.m., a staff member from the Disaster Prevention and Safety Division came running in breathlessly.

"An evacuation order for a twenty-kilometer radius has been issued, I just saw the news ticker on NHK."

Pandemonium broke out.

Although some of the residents voiced criticisms of the city authorities' lack of direction—"What the hell are you doing?!"—there was no way the city could get hold of information. Mobile phones were having trouble connecting to the network. The only place they could manage to contact was the prefecture on the disaster hotline. And that was just one phone line, which might connect once every thirty minutes or so.

The disaster hotline was on the ground floor. When it did make contact, Sakurai would yell out, "Hang on!" and come running down from the mayor's office on the third floor.

Minamisoma was divided into three districts—from the north: Kashima, Haramachi, and Kodaka. This division had been settled during the merging of municipalities in 2010. The district of Kodaka, which was closest to the nuclear station, was included in the twenty-kilometer zone. Damage there from the tsunami was horrendous. Part of the central district of Haramachi was also covered by the evacuation zone. Minamisoma had a population of 71,494. The number of dead and missing stood at 1,838. There were 1,165 houses totally destroyed by the tsunami.

Sakurai's own home was in the Enei area of Haramachi. At fifty-five, he was single and lived there with his parents. Although the house had been damaged, he had been notified that his parents were safe and in an evacuation shelter. Sakurai was to spend the next forty-seven days taking command and sleeping on a blanket on the floor of the city hall.

There was no notification whatsoever of the twenty-kilometer resident evacuation order from either the government or the prefecture. They considered evacuating people to elementary and secondary schools outside the twenty-kilometer line, but they were already filled with more than six thousand casualties from the tsunami. They had to look for places outside the city limits, but received no reply, although they asked the prefecture.

Before ten p.m. on March 14, a soldier from the SDF communications unit working on the fifth floor came hurtling down the stairs and yelled, "The nuclear station is going to explode. Save yourselves!"

He shouted out as he went to every floor.

"The SDF has also been ordered to withdraw from a hundred-kilometer zone!"

After the quake and tsunami, the SDF had asked if they could use the fifth floor for communications, and they had been allowed to do so. The city officials turned white. Some ran outside.

Surely the SDF wouldn't give us false information?

They had great confidence in the SDF. Some of the staff saw the SDF leave in a line. A rumor circulated that an SDF soldier "had seen a mushroom cloud rising." Panic spread among the city hall workers.

A report came in that Futaba District had evacuated everyone, including the whole municipal office. Sakurai instructed his staff to "wait until we've checked with the prefecture" in order to curb the panic. The prefecture's response was, "That is not accurate information." They continued to call for people over the disaster radio to "avoid going outdoors."

Late that night, a resident came to city hall to lodge a strong protest. "What the hell are you doing, Mr. Mayor? Evacuate the residents! The damage is going to be tremendous!!!"

Word had spread that the SDF were going around telling people to "flee at least a hundred kilometers," and residents in the evacuation shelters had all started to flee.

The explosion in Unit 1 on March 12 was to complicate operations by the SDF. At 7:30 p.m. on March 12, the SDF withdrew from operations near the site. After that, the commander on the scene issued the order that they should "temporarily draw back" during an explosion in the reactor buildings or if one was expected.[26]

At eleven a.m. on March 15, the government issued its "indoor evacuation" order for the twenty- to thirty-kilometer zone. Minamisoma found itself split into three areas, one within the twenty-kilometer zone, one in the twenty- to thirty-kilometer zone, and one outside the thirty-kilometer zone.

They had received an answer from Hidekiyo Tachiya, mayor of the neighboring Soma City to the north, that Soma City was willing to take in evacuees. But they didn't have the means to transport the residents. And there was absolutely no gasoline. Sakurai rang Norio Kanno, mayor of Iitate Village, on the phone.

Both Kanno and Sakurai were dairy farmers. They had known each other for thirty years, and both belonged to the Fukushima Prefecture Dairy Farming Association, but Kanno had been doing it longer than Sakurai.

"Could you possibly put our evacuees on your school buses and take them to Soma?"

"Today's not possible."

A short time later, Kanno called back.

"I think we'll be able to do something in the evening."

Kanno sent all seven of their school buses. They were all large buses. The drivers took the Minamisoma evacuees along the snow-covered road to Soma.

Just as Sakurai had been concerned, the impact of the twenty- to thirty-kilometer "indoor evacuation" surfaced straight away. He had a generous offer from the city of Aizuwakamatsu that "we'd like to send over twenty thousand rice balls," but "we wanted you to come and pick them up from the thirty-kilometer zone." The drivers delivering gasoline to Minamisoma from Tokyo came as far as Koriyama, but then refused to come closer.

They did not have enough chlorine to disinfect the tap water. They were short on manpower because workers from the waterworks had evacuated. People could not survive without drinking water.

Sakurai was resentful, thinking, *We're being starved out!*

The governor of Fukushima Prefecture, Yuhei Sato, sought the steady implementation of "sheltering in place." Sakurai disagreed with this course of action.

On the night of March 15, in an interview with NHK, Sakurai appealed, "Food, medications, medical supplies, and fuel are running out. And we have been made to stay indoors. People can't even go look for their missing family members; they can't go home; they are following the state's order to stay in the evacuation shelter and just endure . . . The state issues the orders, but they don't give us any information and we're in a situation where we're forced to ask for it from our side.

"Minamisoma is being treated as if it was a contaminated area and no supplies are getting through to the evacuation shelters. City workers are traveling to the thirty-kilometer limit to pick them up. We need the prefecture and the state to help us somehow in this tragic state of affairs. Neither the quake nor the tsunami nor the nuclear accident is the fault of Minamisoma. I ask for your cooperation in accepting our evacuees in other prefectures. I ask you to provide the gasoline and vehicles we need to evacuate."

Hirohiko Izumida, governor of Niigata Prefecture, placed a call to Sakurai. His throat had constricted on seeing Sakurai's desperate appeal on TV.

"Sakurai-san, we'll take in everyone from Minamisoma, so don't you worry . . . You can send them over in droves . . . During the Kanto earthquake, we took in thirty thousand people from Tokyo, so it'll be fine. We'll help."

This was the massive earthquake that had struck on September 1, 1923, with a magnitude of 7.9 and the epicenter eighty kilometers deep in the northwest section of Suruga Bay in Kanagawa Prefecture. Owing to the fires that broke out under strong wind conditions, the damage spread rapidly, with more than a hundred thousand dead.

Sakurai had never even met Izumida. He was heartened by his words. *We've had a narrow escape.*

He did not know how to thank Izumida.

Izumida had a premonition that "this is going to be horrendous," judging from the Meteorological Agency's weather forecast and projections of the radioactive fallout announced in Germany. He went so far as to state in a press conference on March 12, "We may need to be prepared to take in several hundreds of thousands to a million people."

At the time of the 2007 Chuetsu earthquake, there was trouble at TEP-CO's Kashiwazaki-Kariwa Nuclear Power Station. The lesson learned then was that Japan did not have the mechanisms to deal with compound disasters due to the silo mentality of the bureaucracy.

Izumida had argued that, if there was to be a severe accident at a nuclear power station, it was definitely going to be from an earthquake. This meant there would be a strong likelihood that it would take the shape of a compound disaster. NISA's ERC should not be left in charge of the emergency headquarters secretariat; in order to allow for an "all-government" response, it should be the "joint jurisdiction" of all the relevant ministries and agencies for natural disasters and nuclear emergencies.

Izumida had also instructed the prefectural administrative staff that nuclear emergency preparedness training should be based on the assumption of such a compound disaster. The administrators drew up a scenario for a nuclear emergency caused by an earthquake of "strong-5 to weak-6" on the Japanese seismic intensity scale and sounded out NISA.

The administrators reported back that NISA had pointed out that there was no need for such a plan since the nuclear power stations would not be damaged in a strong-5 to weak-6 quake.

"Well, then, let's do it for strong-6."

"We won't be ready for this year's exercises if we change the plan now."

It was not only the administrators who were indecisive. The same went for the municipalities. They backed away from the idea: "Don't do something as aggressive as that."

They ran the exercises not for a "realistic" quake, but "snow damage." A compromise was reached with a "compound disaster" for snow damage and a nuclear accident.

Even some of the Minamisoma city staff were starting to evacuate. Since the head of the city hospital had quickly said, "Any staff who want to evacuate are free to do so," the hospital staff evacuated. Reports came in afterward from the city hospital:

They've got things the wrong way around. They're a public hospital, after all, not a private hospital.

They come crying to us that the oxygen is running out, the kerosene is running out, as well as the heavy oil, get us some, and when we scramble to get it to them, the staff evacuate—that's just not right!

It was deplorable, but it was too late to tell them to come back. Sakurai decided to run with a policy of "no moving for the time being" for city workers. They would hang in, leaving city hall where it was.

If I allow the staff to evacuate now, Minamisoma will be destroyed.

On March 20, Sakurai delivered a "mayoral briefing" to all employees.

"In order to temporarily evacuate and protect residents from radiation exposure from the Fukushima Daiichi Nuclear Power Station accident, I am notifying residents of a recommendation to evacuate.

"As long as the state does not issue an order to evacuate, the city hall functions will be maintained at main office and the Kashima Ward office to offer our full support to those residents who stay behind.

"Workers will be dispatched to evacuation sites in an organized fashion in order to support those residents who have currently evacuated."

The city staff scowled at Sakurai. They looked ready for a fight. When the briefing was over, a female employee immediately asked a question. In the normal order of things, they never questioned the mayor:

"Why, if you're evacuating the residents, aren't you evacuating the city staff?"

She sounded like she was interrogating him.

I can't be beaten now.

Once they leave, it'll be impossible to get them back. They'll be sure to ask, "Why do we have to come back?"[27]

NORIO KANNO, MAYOR OF IITATE VILLAGE

The first thing Norio Kanno (age 64), mayor of Iitate Village, did after the nuclear accident was to support the evacuees who had fled from the towns and villages near the nuclear power stations.

Kanno was born in Iitate and had studied theriogenology at the Obihiro University of Agriculture and Veterinary Medicine in Hokkaido. His father started a dairy farm with three cows. Helping his father out as the eldest son, he himself had become a dairy farmer with a herd of sixty cows. In his youth, he had visited the United States on a field trip for large-scale farming. From his experience then, he became keenly aware that farmers had to be good business managers. He bought a cheese factory that had closed down in Kawamata, restructured it, and started selling cheese to department stores.

Kanno felt it was his job to provide his constituents with a place to sleep, to prepare food and encourage them.

By March 16, Iitate Village had opened sixteen temporary evacuation shelters in elementary schools and senior citizen facilities, and taken in 1,200 evacuees. In a village of 6,000, 1,200 evacuees had arrived like an avalanche. Kanno asked the agricultural coop to provide food. The village office would pay later. He also asked village volunteers to provide unthreshed rice. The village officers were all out in force, looking after the evacuees outside, in the rain, without umbrellas.

Hiroshi Tada, chief priest at Watatsumi Shrine (Hachiryu Daimyojin) in Kusano, was also involved in supporting the evacuees from Hamadori with members of the shrine's parishioners' association and women's association. Kusano Elementary School, just in front of the shrine, had taken in close to three hundred evacuees. The efforts of the women's association and the parish representatives were concentrated on preparing meals.

Situated in this pastoral village, Watatsumi Shrine was said to date back to the year 806. In 2006, it had celebrated the twelve-hundredth anniversary of its founding. The deities worshipped there were the god of water, without which life was not possible; the god of trees, who gave us clean air and recharged the water; the dragon god, who could freely manipulate the wind and rain; the god of child raising; and the guardian deity of the warlords.

The 1,200 households in Iitate were its parishioners, which came to more than 30 percent of the village residents. Tada was the eighth in a long line of priests from his family. He had, at one time, been the chief priest at Shirayama Hime Shrine in the foothills of Mt. Hakusan (2,702 meters altitude) in Ishikawa Prefecture, but had spent the past forty years as Watatsumi Shrine's chief priest. Tada's eldest son supported him as the shrine's senior priest.

Iitate was located in a beautiful countryside in the mountainous area of the Abukuma Mountains. The villagers had spent twenty years building up their own brand of Iitate beef. They were self-sufficient, feeding their livestock corn, straw, and grass from rice paddies that had been converted to pasture.

Most of the village lay outside the twenty-kilometer zone from Fukushima Daiichi NPS, so there was no need to evacuate.

MARCH 15. Light rain showers started to fall the evening before, changing to snow at night. At three p.m. of the same day, the radiation level started climbing. The monitor registered 3.44 microsieverts/hour (0.00344 millisieverts). Thirty minutes later, it had risen to 24.0 microsieverts/hour (0.024 millisieverts), and at 6:20 p.m., it had jumped further to 44.7 microsieverts/hour (0.0447 millisieverts).

That night, even in Fukushima City some sixty kilometers from Fukushima Daiichi Nuclear Power Station, a high dose of radiation, on the order of 23.88 microsieverts/hour (0.02388 millisieverts), was recorded.

On this day, a large part of Fukushima Prefecture, including the cities of Fukushima and Koriyama, were exposed to doses that corresponded to radiation-controlled areas (5 millisieverts/year).

At eleven a.m. on this day, the government issued its "indoor evacuation" order for residents in the twenty- to thirty-kilometer zone. A short time later, a line of hundreds of cars and buses packed the Haramachi-Kawamata prefectural road. It was a herd of evacuees. During the day, it was a string of vehicles. By night, a string of lights.

"It's not safe here, either."

On seeing this, the evacuees left Iitate Village in droves. The villagers trembled at the sight. Some of the villagers, feeling anxious, started to leave on their own initiative as well.

MARCH 17. MEXT chose Nagadoro in Iitate as one of three monitoring sites. Measurements were taken three times an hour. Numbers of 91.8, 95.1, and

78.2 microsieverts/hour (0.0912, 0.0951, and 0.0782 millisieverts) were recorded. This data was not conveyed to Iitate Village.

On March 19, Kanno decided to implement a voluntary evacuation. Those residents who wished to would be transported to Kanuma City in Tochigi Prefecture on group evacuation buses the prefecture had provided. However, only about six hundred people, including evacuees from outside the village, responded to the offer. The vast majority of the villagers stayed behind.

Many could not decide whether they should evacuate or not. Iitate was a cattle and dairy area, and it was said that the village had "six thousand people and three thousand cows." The cattle and dairy farmers could not just flee, leaving their cows. Moreover, since it lay outside the twenty-kilometer evacuation zone, businesses and shops were still operating.

The state was not telling them to evacuate. So, they did not know if they would be compensated if they evacuated in a hurry. Tada later revealed that Edano's statement was a major factor in their decision: "They were probably bearing in mind the fact that Edano had said on TV that there wouldn't be an immediate impact."

The only information the villagers were getting was through TV reports.[28]

YOSHITAKA SUZUKI, MAYOR OF MIHARU TOWN

On the morning of March 12, evacuees fleeing from the Pacific coastal area of Hamadori descended on Miharu Town in Tashiro County, Fukushima Prefecture. They were riding in covered SDF trucks, buses, and their own cars, escorted by police cars, having fled with just the clothes on their backs. Yoshitaka Suzuki, mayor of Miharu Town, had received a phone call from Fukushima Prefecture.

"How many do you think you can take?"

"Seven hundred."

His response was impulsive, but before he knew it, there were between seven hundred and fifteen hundred people rolling up.

Miharu Town bordered on the cities of Nihonmatsu and Koriyama. Its population was 17,662. It is a tourist spot famous for its more than a thousand-year-old weeping cherry blossom tree, which has been designated as a national monument.

Suzuki had just expressed, about a week earlier, his intention to run for a third term. He had first been elected in 2003 on a platform of fiscal and administrative reform. It was about the same time as the financial collapse of Yubari City in Hokkaido was being widely reported.

He put an end to the practice of "using up" any leftover budget and hiring consultants.

"Municipal government is basically a small and medium-sized enterprise (SME). The organization can't get things done with a silo mentality of 'I've done my part' . . . When we're in a pinch, let's all roll up our sleeves and not rely on consultants."

He had set up a disaster prevention volunteer group for town planning. He had raised the town's organizational capacity and resilience in terms of disaster response. That had showed its worth with the entire town's support of the evacuees.

The local Red Cross chapter and women's association had prepared meals for the evacuees in the elementary school gym and elsewhere. Hospital doctors and public health nurses in the town began to visit the evacuation shelters.

That night, the temperature dropped to three or four degrees below zero Celsius. An appeal was made to residents over the radio system.

"We need you to provide blankets."

In no time at all, a thousand blankets were collected.

Hitoshi Ishida was one of the evacuees. For many years, he had been in charge of resident evacuation measures at a time of a nuclear emergency at Okuma Town. On the afternoon of March 12, when they were preparing for the resident evacuation in the Okuma town offices, the moment he heard the low explosion at Unit 1, he thought, *We're going to be killed.*

After rushing to evacuate residents to two cities and two towns, he arranged for his mother and his wife to join his younger brother in Okayama City. After that, at around one a.m. on March 13, he had fled to Miharu with the last remaining residents. He brought with him Okuma's stocks of stable iodine.

A total of two thousand people had evacuated to Miharu; a thousand each from the towns of Okuma and Tomioka. Ishida was constantly opening up his computer and printing out the plume predictions. All of the prediction models from research institutes in Norway, Austria, and Germany indicated it would spread in the direction of Miharu.

The only information Ishida had at the time was a single chart, faxed to Okuma Town by TEPCO, predicting the spread of the plume if venting took place. It was a prediction of emissions per unit, but, according to that, it predicted a southerly flow.

The national SPEEDI estimations would surely be made public at a time like this. The monitoring data would surely be released. He searched for them desperately, but they were not there.

Ishida searched the Web for monitoring data from Iwate Prefecture, Miyagi Prefecture, and Ibaraki Prefecture. After eight a.m. on March 15, he heard the news that a measurement of 5 microsieverts/hours (0.005 millisieverts) had been recorded in Tokaimura, Ibaraki Prefecture. This was said to be approximately hundredfold the normal amount.

But the monitoring data from Iwaki, the middle point, was completely missing for the all-important time period.

This doesn't look good.

Somebody is hiding something.

Another thing that worried Ishida was the decision by Fukushima Prefecture to suddenly raise the screening level to 100,000 cpm. Normally, you had to write a "letter of apology" if the screening level exceeded 1,000 cpm. A 100,000 cpm was a level where one could well be asked, "Was this brought from inside the reactor?"

Fukushima Prefecture had started saying that, since background radiation was on the rise, they had decided to raise the screening level; at 1,000 cpm, the number of people who would have to be decontaminated exceeded their capacity; that was why they had raised the level.

Doesn't that mean, in essence, that the level of contamination is heading toward a state of crisis?

Suzuki had Ishida take up residence on the second floor of the town offices in a quasi-"staff officer" capacity, and with the cooperation of public health nurse Chika Takenouchi and other doctors and pharmacists in the town, gathered information on the effects and side effects of stable iodine. After graduating from a public health nurse training college in Tokyo, Takenouchi had been working as a public health nurse in the town office since 2006.

At 11:01 a.m. on March 14, Unit 3 (RB) exploded. Radiation levels started climbing everywhere. What was the weather forecast? Especially for the following day, March 15.

On the night of March 14, Ishida located predictions from Norway and other overseas research centers that the plume would pass over Miharu. If the plume did pass overhead on March 15, the residents would suffer exposure.

Miharu was forty-five kilometers to the west of Fukushima Daiichi Nuclear Power Station. The timing for administering stable iodine would be everything. Its effect would be weakened if it was not taken twenty-four hours before the plume arrived.

The town decided to measure the wind direction from the highest point in town, which was at an elevation of 450 meters. They would affix streamers to a pole in front of the public baths up there. There was a strong easterly wind blowing in from the direction of Utsushigatake. They would check the wind's direction by taking a photo every hour and sending it to the town offices. A forecast for rain on the afternoon of March 15 was being broadcast.

Under the Fukushima Prefectural Emergency Preparedness Plan, it was stipulated: "In the case of instruction from the state about the timing of taking stable iodine for preventative purposes, or on the judgment of the governor, the prefecture would issue an order to take stable iodine." Towns did not have the authority to order their residents to take stable iodine. All well and good if the state or prefecture did it, but they may very well do nothing. The town needed to seriously consider its options in such a case.

At noon on March 14, Chika Takenouchi, the town's public health nurse, went to the Fukushima Prefectural Office accompanied by a town official, asking to be provided with stable iodine, and received 12,500 tablets and 49 grams in granules. They subsequently realized that they would need more for babies, and went back to the prefectural office in the middle of the night for an extra 11,000 tablets.

NINE P.M. ON MARCH 14. An extraordinary managers' meeting was held in the public room adjacent to the mayor's office. All twelve managers were present, even those who had gone home and been recalled. With no instructions from either the state or the prefecture, would it be appropriate for the town to distribute and instruct residents to take the stable iodine? That was the critical point.

For about an hour, the debate was divided, but they finally agreed to "distribute and instruct to take it."

"I'd like to hear the mayor's opinion. How about it, Mr. Mayor?"

Suzuki was worried about people taking it. But when he heard the opinion of Takenouchi and the others, the side effects seemed to be minimal. Takenouchi had been to the prefectural emergency headquarters to get a supply of stable iodine. After receiving it and heading out to the car park, she suddenly thought, *Oh, I'd better check with the officer in charge about any precautions when taking it, just to be on the safe side,* and had turned back. The officer in charge was a male pharmacist.

"Are there any precautions to bear in mind when using it?"

He seemed to be caught off guard.

"No good asking me. I don't know."

"Umm, but pregnant women and children should be first, right?"

He did not answer immediately. After a brief pause, "Well, yes, I reckon that's right."

Takenouchi returned to the town office and reported what she had been told. Since both Mayor Suzuki and Kuniharu Hashimoto, general affairs manager, had received her report, they made up their minds knowing they could not rely on the prefectural emergency headquarters and the decision would have to be their responsibility. Suzuki told his managers, "I'll take responsibility if something happens, so do it."

Miharu Town decided that the stable iodine was to be taken at one p.m. on March 15. They drew up a document titled "To the Townspeople," providing instructions on how to take the medication. In order to distribute the leaflet, they had all the heads of neighborhood committees assemble at eight meeting places. It was to be distributed to all the residents under forty years of age. There were 3,303 households (7,248 people) to be covered.

From the early hours of March 15, close to thirty town staff started putting the tablets into envelopes. For children, they crushed the tablets and put the powder in. They stuck printed seals on the envelopes, with the neighborhood committee phone number and address, and the name, age, and medication data of the intended recipient. (They finished this at eleven a.m.) They also enclosed instructions on the distribution and administering in the event of radiation.

Sometime after six a.m., they heard the news broadcast of "an explosive sound in Unit 2." They set up streamers in two places to check the wind direction. At one p.m., the order was given to distribute and administer the stable iodine. They posted the following note of caution in each meeting place:

This medication is for people up to 39 years old. You do not have to take it if you are 40 years of age or older.

Regarding how to take the medication, please either consult the flyer or ask the staff at the venue where you received the medication.

In addition, once you have received the medication, please take it immediately.

They were able to distribute it to 3,134 out of the 3,303 households. Heads of the local neighborhood committees all assembled at the meeting places and helped with identification at the time of distribution.

There was a continuing number of cases where residents from the neighboring city of Koriyama came to the meeting places and asked, "Give us some too, please." Saying it was not possible to distribute it to non-townspeople, Miharu Town refused them. Since the number of inquiries from the city residents had not stopped, the Koriyama city office consulted with the medical association. The medical association had asked the prefecture what the stance was on distributing stable iodine. This was, apparently, the chain of events.

The prefectural emergency headquarters were aghast. At four p.m. on March 15, an officer from Fukushima Prefecture's Regional Medical Division, in its Health and Welfare Department, rang Hiroyuki Kudo, manager of the Health and Welfare Division in Miharu Town.

"We've heard Miharu Town has distributed stable iodine, but is this true?"

"Yes, that's correct."

"You are only supposed to do that at the instruction of the state or the prefecture's emergency headquarters. And it has to be taken in the presence of a doctor. We can't have you going off half-cocked!"

Kudo thought to himself that that was a bit much. They had done their

preparation, searching the Web thoroughly, as well as reading and reread-
ing the Stable Iodine Agent Handling Manual put out by the National
Institute of Radiological Sciences, one of the country's leading medical institutions for radiation.

"If I may be permitted, you keep mentioning the emergency headquarters, the emergency headquarters, but we couldn't even get in touch with
you, could we? And your officers aren't sufficiently capable of making a
judgment, are they? You speak of doctors, but it says 'medical staff' in
the handling manual. That includes public health nurses, pharmacists,
and other related medical people. We have acted in accordance with the
manual. There isn't a problem."

But the officer on the other end of the line persisted with, "Please recall
it."

Eventually, Kudo said, "We have to protect the safety of our residents.
We have to do that with nothing at our disposal. We don't have correct dose
measurements. And the emergency headquarters doesn't issue any instructions, that's the situation we have to work in."

The officer escalated to a threatening tone.

"Get it back anyway!"

Upon saying so, he hung up.

Kudo reported to Hashimoto immediately. Hashimoto said just one
thing.

"It's too late. What a fool he is!"

Takenouchi received only four calls from residents saying they felt sick,
or queasy, or asking whether nausea was a side effect, but nothing of a serious nature. They all also expressed their thanks.

Ishida worked at the Miharu town office until April 4, and after cleaning up around noon of that day, he made his farewells to everyone and
headed off to resume his work from April 5 at the Okuma town offices,
which had been relocated to Aizuwakamatsu.[29]

Fukushima Prefecture distributed iodine to all cities, towns, and villages
with administrative areas within a fifty-kilometer radius of Fukushima
Daiichi NPS.[30]

However, despite the prefectural governor having the authority to do so,
he did not instruct residents or local governments to distribute and take the
iodine. Two options are given in the exposure medical manual: the prefecture issues the order based on the state's decision or on its own decision.
Nevertheless, the prefecture conveniently forgot the latter option of "on its
own decision."[31]

Not only that, it also tried to bully local governments that tried to protect their residents from radiation exposure at their own discretion, such
as Miharu. The non-exercise of the governor's authority was one of the

factors behind the failure to distribute and administer iodine in many municipalities.

It was only after the end of August 2011 that the Nuclear Safety Commission learned the residents of Miharu Town had taken iodine. Kenji Matsuoka, director of the Nuclear Emergency Preparedness Division at NISA, mentioned it at a meeting of the Nuclear Facilities Emergency Preparedness Sub-Committee.

"Local governments that distributed iodine were Miharu Town and Iwaki City. Regarding Miharu Town, I have confirmed that approximately seven thousand people took it in Miharu Town."[32]

Following the meeting, Hideaki Tsuzuki, chief of the Environment Management Section, told Kiyoshi Kurihara, his assistant, "Miharu, eh? So there were some brave places . . . This is exactly what I wanted them to do."[33]

But Miharu was one of the very few exceptions. Almost all of the municipalities in the vicinity of the nuclear power stations waited for instructions. Local governments were waiting for instructions from the prefecture, but they never came. The prefecture was waiting for the state's instructions, but there were none forthcoming from the ERC. Actually, it is uncertain whether the prefecture really was waiting for instructions from the state. As a staff member of the NSC secretariat said, it may be closer to the truth that "they were preventing the state from issuing the order, so they didn't have to bother issuing it to the local governments and residents themselves."[34]

THE RUNAROUND

The fact that Hiroyuki Ogawa, TEPCO firefighting team chief, was injured when Unit 1 exploded was introduced earlier (see chapter 4). Immediately after the explosion, Ogawa felt a tremendous blast. Huge pieces of debris floated in the air and something metallic hit the window on the left side of his car, shattering the glass. Pain shot through his hands and arms. It seemed that he had broken his hand.

It happened when they were guiding the SDF, who were helping with water supply operations on site. They returned immediately with the SDF firefighting unit to the Anti-Seismic Building. In the car, the SDF personnel made a sling for Ogawa's arm.

He was told in the first-aid room at the Anti-Seismic Building it was impossible to treat him there, because it was a clear fracture. Power transmission staff complaining of strong ringing in their ears and being unable to hear anything, as well as a worker from Nanmei Kosan, who had hurt his lower back, were assembled in the first-aid room. They were also told nothing more could be done for them; they should go to the Ono Prefectural Hospital in Okuma Town.

So, three of them drove in two cars toward Ono hospital. When they got there, there was a piece of paper on the door:

"Ono Hospital has moved to the Health Care Center in Kawauchi Village."

While it was remiss of them, it had never crossed their minds that the whole town of Okuma had been evacuated. They called the main switchboard, but could not get through. They had no choice but to go to the Health Care Center in Kawauchi. The road ahead became darker and darker as they drove along; it was dark when they arrived at Kawauchi Village.

Several nurses and doctors were frantically treating patients. Ogawa was told, "Let's take an X-ray," but they only had a dental X-ray. It was confirmed that he had glass in his hand. Looking at the X-ray, the doctor said, "This needs surgery," while extracting some of the glass from his left hand on the spot. When the doctor finished, Ogawa was put in a wheelchair and into an ambulance that had come from Tomioka Town. He was separated from his two companions without a single word of farewell. He had no idea where he was being taken.

Two and a half hours later, he arrived at the Southern Tohoku General Hospital in Koriyama. Here, he had more X-rays taken. The doctor removed some more glass from his left hand and plastered the hand. However, he said he could not operate immediately. The water in Koriyama had been cut off, so there was no water.

Even in the temporary medical office of Ono Hospital at Kawauchi, they immediately measured his somatic dose using a G-M (Geiger–Müller) tube when they learned Ogawa had come from the Fukushima Daiichi Nuclear Power Station.

Having been told to rest for the time being, he was sleeping in an emergency bed on the first floor when he was suddenly woken up.

"Will you give up the bed, please? There's a whole heap of patients coming by bus from Tomioka and Namie. Could you please let us have it for the moment? Well, actually, a lot of people are coming, so we'd like you to leave."

When he asked at the reception desk, "Where should I go?" he was told, "The evacuation center, I suppose."

He was told about Kaiseizan Evacuation Center located three to four kilometers away. They said there was a baseball field and the area around that was a shelter. They were referring to Koriyama Kaiseizan Baseball Stadium. Koriyama City Hall, located in the immediate vicinity, had been damaged, and the city had set up its disaster response headquarters in the main stadium of the baseball park and turned the stadium and neighboring park facilities into an evacuation center.

"If you go there, you should manage somehow, I reckon."

He was told by the hospital staff that he could stay in the waiting room until morning, but there was a constant stream of patients. He did not want to be a bother. Besides, if it was only three to four kilometers, it would take two to three hours on foot, so he decided to walk. He reached the Kaiseizan Evacuation Center in the early hours of March 13, where he was greeted by some unexpected words at the check-in desk.

"People from Hamadori (the coastal area of Fukushima) can't be accepted here."

People started talking about radioactive contamination in hushed voices.

"Please go to the Koriyama Gymnasium."

This was some four hundred meters away, on the eastern side of Kaiseizan. When he got there, he saw that tents had been pitched for decontamination screenings. People were waiting in buses. It was warm inside the buses. During decontamination screening, they were told to wash their hair and remove their underwear as well.

"Please throw away everything that you were wearing."

He felt miserable wrapped up in a single blanket with just one piece of underwear on. His heart ached thinking how hard it must be for the women he saw trying to make themselves as small as possible likewise, with their one piece of underwear and a blanket.

Afterward, he traveled to the Fukushima Prefecture Agricultural Research Center in Hiwada in a shuttle vehicle. He heard that they studied rice there. It had also become a shelter for evacuees from Hamadori. It had rice stockpiles, so he was told they would be cooking in the morning. He was issued some underwear, a shirt, and a jacket, and was given a rice ball and a one-liter bottle of water.

The heating was working, and it was warm. He learned that the center was using electricity from solar cells.

"I really thought at the time that solar power was great," Ogawa said later.

The evacuation center that he had reached after escaping from a nuclear accident was a solar-powered oasis. He was able to make free phone calls. Ogawa called his family in Tokyo. His twenty-two-year-old daughter picked up.

"Where are you now?"

"I'm injured and in Koriyama. I am at Koriyama's Fukushima Prefecture Agricultural Research Center."

He tried next to contact his boss Takeyuki Inagaki, recovery team leader, and Site Supervisor Yoshida, but could not reach them no matter how many times he tried. (He later learned that he could have contacted them via a connection at Head Office in Tokyo, but by then it was too late.)

Of the two blankets he'd been issued, he placed one underneath him and wrapped himself in the other. He tried to get some sleep when he got a call from his daughter.

"Planes are flying out of Fukushima Airport. I got a ticket for the last flight. Can you somehow get to the airport?"

When he spoke to the person in charge of the Fukushima Prefectural Agricultural Research Center, he was told there was a staff member going in the direction of Fukushima Airport and they were willing to go out of their way to drop him off at the airport. Ogawa decided to accept the favor.

He was issued underwear, socks, a jacket, and a tracksuit when he left the evacuation center. He was told that the Koriyama branch of the apparel company Shimamura had provided clothing to assist the victims.

MARCH 14. Ogawa left the center a little after noon in a car driven by the staff member. On the way, they shared some bread, water, and juice. He was struck by the person's compassion. He returned home safely on the last flight, at eight p.m.

His daughter had already booked him into the Tokyo Denryoku (TEPCO) Hospital in Shinjuku. When, accompanied by his son, he went to the hospital on the following day, March 15, there was a person there from TEPCO's Saitama Branch, who had been to Fukushima Daiichi to help with the power transmission restoration.

Everyone was worried about internal radiation on the job. In Ogawa's case, he had been screened many times, with the GM placed right on his wound, but he was always diagnosed as okay. He told the doctor so, but the doctor said he could not treat him and urged him strongly, "Ogawa-san, go with them to the NIRS."

The NIRS was the National Institute of Radiological Sciences in Inage, Chiba Prefecture. It was a leading radiology institute in Japan.

"But my left hand is damaged and I have so much gear, can I leave it here?"

"No, please don't ask that of us. You may be hospitalized at NIRS, so go as you are please."

When his son said, "I'll go with you," the doctor stopped him, saying, "Your son shouldn't go too far with you."

Ogawa went to the NIRS with the power restoration group from the Saitama branch. He underwent screening once again there to determine the presence or absence of external exposure. After a while, he was told that he could return to the Tokyo Denryoku (TEPCO) Hospital, and so he did.

Why did Tokyo Denryoku (TEPCO) Hospital send them to the NIRS? Ogawa speculated, "*No doubt, some patients in the hospital didn't want to be in the same ward as people exposed to radiation. Upper-level management at the hospital was probably concerned that it would be a problem. So, they probably wanted a good guarantee that they were okay by sending all the Fukushima returnees to the NIRS for screening to be properly examined there.*"[35]

The contents of Site Supervisor Yoshida's testimony at the Government

Accident Inquiry were later made public. In the process of introducing the "runaround" epic of Hiroyuki Ogawa, a favorite subordinate of his, Yoshida said the following:

"When he went to Tokyo Denryoku [TEPCO] Hospital and was told to go to the NIRS, I couldn't help but think what a heartless hospital Tokyo Denryoku [TEPCO] Hospital was. He still had broken bones, you know. I didn't know anything about it at the time."[36]

EIGHT

The Last Bastion

"THAT'S RIGHT. IT'S THE ORDER OF THE MINISTER."

At the time, a regular executive meeting was in progress in the vice minister's office on the eleventh floor of the Ministry of Defense in Ichigaya, Tokyo. Heads of the related bureaus, the four chiefs of staff (ground, maritime, air, and the chief of staff of the joint staff) were all in attendance.

When they turned on the television, the screen showed: "Magnitude 8.4 off the Miyagi Prefecture coast." The meeting was immediately canceled. Yoshifumi Hibako, chief of staff of the Ground Self-Defense Forces, raced down the stairs and phoned Eiji Kimizuka, Tohoku District commander, as soon as he returned to his office on the fourth floor. Kimizuka said, "We've been hit. There's smoke coming up from where the newly built building behind joins the old building, and we've lost power. We've no television reception, either.

"Move out all Tohoku District units to their areas of responsibility on disaster relief. A tsunami warning has been issued. We'll send as many troops as we can from the rest of the country to support the Tohoku troops. Deal with the disaster. There's no need to wait for requests for aid."

He then contacted the Western, Central, Eastern, and Northern forces in turn.[1]

After the quake, a tsunami close to two meters high had hit the port of Yokosuka. Hiroshi Takashima, Yokosuka District commander of the maritime Self-Defense Forces, felt this was going to be disastrous. The maritime SDF issued an order for all hands on land to "stay with their units," and for all hands at sea to "stay on board."

At the time, Defense Minister Toshimi Kitazawa, along with Prime Minister Naoto Kan and the rest of the cabinet, were at a budget committee meeting in the Upper House. After the quake, he momentarily wondered if he should head to the Kantei or back to the Ministry in Ichigaya. There were no precise instructions from the Kantei. Kitazawa decided to go there.

When he tried to go directly to the crisis management center in the Kantei's basement, the elevators had stopped. Kitazawa took the stairs to the center. Most of the cabinet was already there, including Prime Minister Naoto Kan and Chief Cabinet Secretary Yukio Edano. They were all dressed in casual clothes.

3:14 P.M. The government set up the emergency headquarters for response to the disaster (headed by Prime Minister Naoto Kan) at the Kantei. Its first meeting was then held in the crisis management center. There were requests from all over, calling for SDF helicopters.

Deciding he needed to take charge at the Ministry of Defense, Kitazawa went back to the Ichigaya Ministry. All of the elevators, including the minister's private elevator, were out of order. Asking for his elevator to be fixed as quickly as possible, he went to the ministry's emergency response meeting that had been hurriedly set up in a reception room on the ground floor.[2]

Kitazawa instructed, "The SDF are to make the maximum effort."

Hibako reported, "Instructions to the key units have already been completed and troops are starting to be mobilized nationwide." Although he was a little apprehensive that he might be reprimanded for moving troops without the minister's consent, Kitazawa just nodded in approval.[3]

AFTER SEVEN P.M. The government issued its state of nuclear emergency declaration and held the first meeting of the nuclear emergency response headquarters (NERHQ). Kitazawa was also in attendance.

On his way back to the ministry, he was caught up in a huge traffic jam just as he was leaving the Kantei and heading toward Yotsuya. Usually the trip between the Kantei and the ministry took some ten minutes by car. That day, it took three hours.[4]

After he had attended a meeting in the large conference room on the ministry's eleventh floor and returned to his office, Kazunori Inoue, director of the Defense Operations Division in the Bureau of Operational Policy, came apprehensively into the room.

"TEPCO President Masataka Shimizu is saying he would like a ride on an SDF helicopter. It seems that he urgently needs to get back to Tokyo from Nagoya because of the nuclear accident."

The following appears to be the series of events that led up to this.

First of all, one of the private secretaries of the prime minister had received a call through a personal contact from a senior manager in the General Affairs Department at TEPCO. The request was immediately conveyed to Tetsuro Ito, deputy chief cabinet secretary for crisis management.

At the same time, Shimizu rang METI Minister Banri Kaieda from Nagoya.

"I can't get back from Nagoya. Would it be possible to use an SDF plane?"

Kaieda passed this on to Ito. He then asked Sakurai, director general of the Bureau of Operational Policy, to pass these messages on to the SDF at the Ministry of Defense. Inoue had received the request from Sakurai, who was ensconced with the emergency operation team in the crisis management center.

"TEPCO's President Shimizu is currently in Nagoya. I've been asked if he could use an SDF plane to rush back to Tokyo. I'd like you to get one ready."

Although the use of SDF aircraft was at the discretion of the minister (via an aircraft boarding instruction), an official directive from the minister was usually not sought. This time, however, was a time of crisis and the request was from TEPCO, so Inoue thought it best to place it before the minister.

Inoue had tried to get the minister's permission by phoning Takahiro Yoshida, Kitazawa's private secretary, on his mobile phone, but he could not get through. As long as he did not have the minister's approval, he could not say "get him on board" or "take off" or "don't." So, having no choice, he told them to "get ready."

Kitazawa's reaction was blunt.

"What do they mean? The C-130s are indispensable for disaster relief. We can't use such valuable aircraft for something like that. Don't use them for some president, use them for the victims! . . . Doesn't a company like TEPCO have a deputy president? Why isn't the deputy president good enough?"

The C-130 Hercules was a four-engine turboprop military transport plane developed by America's Lockheed. They are said to be the top choice for medium-range transport aircraft.

Since Inoue had heard that the helicopter with Shimizu on board would be taking off at 11:40 p.m., he thought he would have enough time to decide yes or no after hearing the minister's opinion. It was already close to 11:40 p.m. There was not much time. Inoue immediately conveyed the minister's decision to the Joint Staff Office. The Joint Staff Office officer in charge said the aircraft, which was due to take off at forty minutes past the hour, had departed at thirty minutes past.

"What?! It's already airborne? Damn. Tell them to turn back immediately."

"You mean now?"

"Yes, it's at the minister's instruction."

The "minister's instruction" was relayed from the Joint Staff Office to the air Self-Defense Forces to the ASDF's Komaki Base and then the aircraft. The plane carrying Shimizu turned back to Komaki Base.[5]

On March 11, Shimizu and his wife were on a sightseeing trip to Heijo Palace and the sacred water-drawing festival at Todaiji Temple. TEPCO had explained he was "on a business trip to meet with business leaders in the Kansai area," but that was only half of the matter. The problem was that Chairman Tsunehisa Katsumata was on a business trip to China at the time. So, the company president was off sightseeing during the chairman's absence.

After the quake hit, Shimizu headed to Nagoya on the bullet train, planning to board the TEPCO helicopter operated by a TEPCO affiliate at Nagoya Airport. Nagoya Airport, however, would not let the helicopter fly, because it was after the airport curfew of 10:00 p.m.

That was when they got the idea of an SDF aerial transport vehicle. Nagoya Airport was shared by the air SDF Komaki Base. Shimizu headed to Tokyo by helicopter on the morning of March 12.[6]

Voices of doubt were raised in the emergency operation team at the Kantei when they heard about this "minister's instruction."

"They don't seem to understand what goes on onsite. Nothing happens if the responsible officer isn't there. That's the ABC of crisis management."

"With his mind on the quake and tsunami disaster, Minister Kitazawa probably isn't fully aware of how serious the situation is at Fukushima Daiichi NPS."

"Why, in the first place, did the Defense Ministry take something like that all the way to the minister?"

Ito had also wanted to get Shimizu back to Tokyo as soon as possible, and had queried Chief Cabinet Secretary Yukio Edano about this, but after first saying, "Well, that's that then," when he heard Kitazawa had forced Shimizu to make a U-turn, Edano supported Kitazawa's decision, saying, "He's right. It's just as Kitazawa-san says."[7]

That night, Kitazawa was at the forefront in the large conference room on the eleventh floor, where the minister's office was also located. The minister's private elevator was working again by then.

"Matsushima Base possibly under water."

"Tagajo Camp has also been hit."

With all twenty-eight of its aircraft and most of its vehicles damaged, Matsushima Base could no longer function as a disaster relief base.

They were being flooded with inquiries from everywhere: the emergency operation team, ministries and local governments asking for troops, supplies, food, water, and transport. They were from all over the place. The plea from the Kantei for power trucks and cables to be sent to Fukushima Daiichi NPS was close to a scream.[8]

After that came a barrage of requests for freshwater tankers and the firefighting trucks located at SDF bases and airports. They sent a steady stream of firefighting trucks from their camps in Fukushima and Koriyama.

And then, in the middle of the night on March 11, they received a confidential call from the prime ministerial secretariat on the fifth floor of the Kantei to make preparations. The prime minister wanted to visit the disaster zone first thing in the morning of March 12.[9]

THE SELF-DEFENSE FORCES GO INTO ACTION

Of the entire Japanese government at the time of the Great Eastern Japan Earthquake, it was the Self-Defense Forces who were the first on the scene and the first to start rescuing people.

On the first day of the disaster, some 8,400 troops were deployed. In the case of an earthquake or tsunami, the first seventy-two hours are said to be critical for saving lives. The key is how fast you can get to the scene of the disaster.

SDF commanders everywhere moved quickly under the rallying cry of "Let's get 'em there." Private business operators helped actively to achieve that end. Of the Hokkaido troops sent in, 93 percent were carried on private ferries, an operation that was the first of its kind. The initial response of the maritime Self-Defense Forces to send out a large number of ships from Yokosuka was also prompt.

At 2:52 p.m., six minutes after the earthquake, the maritime SDF issued an order for "all operational ships to leave port." It was the first time in maritime SDF's history.[10] Before sunrise on March 12, the maritime SDF had twenty vessels, including the Aegis destroyer *Chokai*, in place and had launched a search and rescue of survivors as well as a survey of the damage.[11]

In the 1995 Hanshin-Awaji earthquake, the SDF had been severely criticized for its initially slow response. Having learned their lesson, they had reorganized their troops, established a training manual, and amended the Self-Defense Forces Law so that they could go to affected areas without waiting for a request to do so, and be on call twenty-four hours a day.

They also knew they were in for the long haul, given the size of the quake this time. So, they mobilized the ready SDF and the reserve SDF on a scale of thousands. This was also a first. Using the destroyer *Hyuga* as the main center of operations, carrier-based helicopters flew supplies into areas cut off by water. Facility units removed the debris from collapsed houses, and continued to search for missing persons. In flooded areas, they used river boats. The number of people rescued by the SDF was 19,300. This was equivalent to 70 percemt of all rescues.

On March 14, Kitazawa flew to Sendai on an SDF helicopter and appointed Eiji Kimizuka commander of the Joint Task Force (JTF). He spoke in front of the troops:

"I want you to work with the U.S. troops and make the maximum effort. I think this moment has brought the SDF and the people closer together than ever before. I want you to know that the people have extremely high expectations of you."[12]

The formation of a joint task force (JTF) between the ground, maritime, and air forces was also another first. In 2006, the SDF had replaced its previous Joint Staff Council with a Joint Staff Office, switching to a format in which ground, sea, and air could be managed in a unified way. At the time, ground, sea, and air were integrated to create strategy, but this time they were being integrated to implement strategy.

At first, the Ministry of Defense had reported to the Kantei, "We can deploy 20,000 troops immediately." Kan issued the order to deploy 20,000 straight away. But at three p.m., they asked Kitazawa to "send out the absolute maximum." Their assessment was that 20,000 troops would not nearly be enough.

Kitazawa proposed 50,000. In the third meeting of the emergency headquarters for response to disaster, just after noon on March 12, Kan stated, "I have just spoken with the defense minister, and we will be mobilizing troops throughout the country and sending in 50,000 troops at first."

Kan later asked Kitazawa to top the numbers up. "Can't you increase it a little? Is 60,000 or 70,000 unfeasible?" Kitazawa said to Oriki, "Let's go with more," and Oriki responded "We can do 120,000 to 130,000." Kitazawa took this up with, "well, shall we go with 100,000?" According to Kitazawa, "This was half the number of our standing troops, and double the 50,000 we had first thought. It was decided in a pretty subjective way."

Ito, however, had conveyed his wish for "troops in the order of 100,000" because "it's on scale with a direct metropolitan quake." It was laid down in the SDF's Direct Metropolitan Earthquake Response Plan that "a maximum of some 110,000 ground SDF troops are to be concentrated in the disaster area."[13]

The SDF deployed 100,000 troops into the affected areas by March 19. This figure was almost equivalent to half its 230,000 actual standing troops. However, they had to be careful not to create a "defense vacuum."

Ryoichi Oriki, chief of staff of the Joint Staff, decided that, of the Western District troops that protected Kyushu and Okinawa, he would not move the Fifteenth Brigade (Naha City command) or the Eighth Division (Kumamoto command) if it was at all possible. It was also decided not to move any of the maritime SDF vessels at Port Sasebo that patrolled the waters of Kyushu and Okinawa.[14]

China also sent a rescue team into the disaster area. However, this did not soften the increasingly acute Japanese sense of alarm toward China following the Senkaku Islands Shock of September 2010. This shock referred to the extreme tension in the Sino-Japanese relationship caused when China retaliated by refusing to export rare earth metals to Japan after the Japanese judicial authorities arrested the captain of a fishing vessel that had rammed a Coast Guard patrol boat in the Senkaku Islands. On March 14, Kitazawa received notification that the Chinese navy was willing to dispatch a hospital ship to the disaster area. The Chinese explained that, "The hospital ship has three hundred beds. This could be an opportunity to start military exchange between Japan and China. We still haven't got approval from the very top, but there's a 70 to 80 percent possibility. The hospital ship is currently in port at Shanghai. It can arrive in the waters off the affected area in twelve hours."

The Japanese side replied that, at the present time, "there are almost no medical and health needs."[15]

During the Indian Ocean earthquake of 2004, America, Japan, Singapore, Australia, and New Zealand were among the first to dispatch naval forces to Aceh and Sumatra for humanitarian rescue operations, but China was unable to dispatch its navy due to the lack of a similar humanitarian relief approach. It was due to the lesson of that time that China had prepared a hospital ship.[16]

Some of the local government offices had been swept away by the tsunami and were not functioning, and they asked the SDF to shoulder certain administrative areas. As Kan later wrote in his book, *The TEPCO Fukushima Nuclear Accident: My Thoughts as Prime Minister*, the role of the top is to decide on matters coming up from below, but the situation was one where the bottom no longer existed. So, there was no choice but to decide things in a top-down fashion; that was the situation that had been created.[17]

In many cases, the buck was passed to the SDF. An especially difficult matter was what to do with the dead. Transporting and storing bodies is not part of the SDF mission. But the SDF took on and transported 9,500 bodies, half of the number of casualties.[18] They tried to avoid having U.S. troops handle the dead. They would not allow the use of the huge number of body bags the U.S. military had brought in. A Japanese life was to be looked after to the very end by another Japanese. The U.S. military was taken aback at first, but decided to respect these wishes of the SDF.[19]

7:30 P.M. Following the issuance of the declaration of a state of nuclear emergency, Kitazawa issued a "nuclear disaster action order" to the SDF.

According to the disaster plan, the duties of the SDF in a nuclear disaster were monitoring support, grasping the extent of the damage, aiding evacuation, and the emergency transport of staff and supplies—not responding to the nuclear accident itself. However, such a thing could not be applied anymore in the current situation.

Suddenly, the SDF were forced to engage on two fronts—the earthquake/tsunami and the nuclear emergency. In the words of one of the senior officers in the Joint Staff Office, they rose to the challenge of dealing with the nuclear emergency in a state where "there was no plan, no strategy, no manpower, no equipment, and no training, either." He might just as well have added, "no information."

The SDF organized a five-hundred-strong nuclear emergency deployment unit from its Central Readiness Force (CRF), as well as troops from ground, sea, and air. The CRF had been established in 2007 to deal with crises and emergencies. The aim was to stop emergencies from escalating into crises and to respond quickly and in an organized fashion for international peace cooperation activities. It was a one-of-a-kind, flexible operative unit consisting of a helicopter team, airborne brigade, special operations team, and a central special weapons protection squad.

The unit was directly under the command of the CRF itself. It was headquartered in the Asaka Camp (Nerima, Tokyo) and boasted seven specialist units numbering some 4,200 troops. Its commanding general was Lieutenant General Toshinobu Miyajima. The CRF completed that mission through the Ground Component Command, which was established in March 2018 by the Ground Self-Defense Forces as a unified headquarters for the five units who had been tasked with swiftly mobilizing in the event of an emergency or large-scale disaster. Once CRF completes a given mission, troops are transferred back to the Ground Component Command, along with subordinate forces such as those from the Central Nuclear Biological Chemical Weapon Defense Unit.

After the declaration of a state of nuclear emergency was issued, Yuki Imaura, deputy commander of the CRF, ordered the dispatch of one platoon into the field as an advance team. It had just over twenty members. The platoon rode in chemical reconnaissance vehicles.

The platoon members were mainly liaison officers (LO) from the Central Special Weapons Protection Corps stationed in Omiya. The corps' job was to respond to attacks from nuclear, biological, and chemical (NBC) weapons. Its predecessor, the 101st Chemical Protective Corps, was dispatched following the sarin gas attack on the Tokyo subway and the Tokaimura nuclear accident in Ibaraki Prefecture. It had subsequently been incorporated into units in the CRF.

7:00 A.M. ON MARCH 14. Motohisa Ikeda, METI deputy minister and head of the local NERHQ at the offsite center, came to Iwakuma. "I can only count on the SDF. Could you supply water to Unit 3?" he asked in a low voice. He wanted them to get water from the river and the sea and pump it into the pit.

Iwakuma informed Lieutenant General Miyajima, his superior officer and the CFR's commanding general, via satellite phone. Miyajima reconfirmed, "The safety of the troops is guaranteed, right?"

"To the extent that it can be," Iwakuma responded, and headed to the site. Two water supply tank cars followed. Each water tank was capable of carrying five tons of water. Each vehicle carried two platoon members.[20]

They received full-face masks from TEPCO employees at the Anti-Seismic Building. They were all wearing Tyvek suits. Their first job was to attach hoses to the water supply pumps. They expected it would take five minutes.

They had decided that if their exposure exceeded 10 millisieverts going one way, they would suspend operations and head back. Avoiding the debris strewn about, they moved out in a line of three cars, each carrying six members.

AFTER ELEVEN A.M. They started working on the pump inlet at the back of the turbine building on the eastern side of Unit 3. It was just then that the roof of Unit 3 (RB) blew off with a thunderous clap and the debris scattered from above shattered the front windscreen of the armored car. And the minute that happened, the dosimeters they all wore started ringing in unison. It was over 20 millisieverts.

The force of the explosion pushed the car diagonally. Iwakuma in the lead vehicle shouted, "Leave the equipment!"

The platoon members forced the door of the car open and crawled out, groaning. Iwakuma issued his command.

"Withdraw! Quickly!"

Four platoon members had suffered injuries. Their Tyvek suits were torn to pieces. One had suffered a laceration to his thigh, but it was not life-threatening.

Nearby was a truck that had been abandoned still with the key in it. They jumped into it, headed toward the main gate, and hitched a ride in the back of a small truck owned by one of TEPCO's associated companies that happened to be passing by on its way to the offsite center. The offsite center had just organized its decontamination preparations. The injured soldiers became their first "clients."

Those with minor injuries were transported to Fukushima Medical University. Those who were seriously injured were rushed to the National Institute of Radiological Sciences (NIRS) in Inage, Chiba Prefecture, where they underwent eight rounds of whole-body decontamination. Iwakuma attended the following regular meeting of the offsite center in a brand new Tyvek suit and boots.

The members of his unit were angry when they had arrived to do the pumping for Unit 3, all the more so because local TEPCO staff had told them, "Unit 3 is stable. It's okay." Iwakuma was just as angry. Fighting desperately to keep that anger at bay, he said, "We're going to have trouble if you don't give us more proper information in advance . . . We may have to go in again, so I'm asking you to be exact."

It is, of course, unlikely that TEPCO was trying to deceive them. There was no way they could predict there would be a hydrogen explosion at such and such a time. However, in a videoconference early that morning, TEPCO had discussed the various possibilities of a hydrogen explosion at Unit 3. Iwakuma's side had no way of knowing that.

However, the incident in which SDF personnel were injured due to the explosion shocked the staff at the Joint Staff Office. Realizing why those under Iwakuma, who were expected to be operating offsite, were operating onsite, and that the site was in such a dangerous condition that the SDF had been asked to supply water, the staff became aware of the reality of the nuclear crisis for the first time.[21]

Elsewhere, on the afternoon of March 13, Imaura decided to lead a team of ten himself to the site. They still could not make contact with the Central Special Weapons Protection Corps.

They were split into two five-man teams, and loaded five days' food and water, sleeping gear, communications equipment, and computers into jeeps and trailers. There were two sets of everything. The following morning on March 14, these were loaded into a transport helicopter and they flew to Koriyama Camp. From there, they headed to the Fukushima Station by jeep.

SOMETIME AFTER ELEVEN A.M. ON MARCH 14. About midway to the Fukushima Station, they heard the television news in the jeep that there had been an explosion at Unit 3. In order to confirm the news, they contacted the Central Special Weapons Protection Corps and the offsite center, but could not get through at all. They saw five or six police cars from the prefectural police coming from the opposite direction at a furious speed. All of the police officers were wearing protective masks.

Are they fleeing, having heard about the explosion?

Imaura decided they had better turn back to Koriyama. He called the offsite center from Koriyama Camp and got through for the first time.

The offsite center's still alive.

The Central Special Weapons Protection Corps lieutenant he had dispatched on March 11 was still working at the offsite center.

"Please send us some personnel right away."

He said some SDF injured by the Unit 3 explosion had been carried into the offsite center.

Leading one of the five-man teams, Imaura arrived at the offsite center that afternoon. Their first job was to treat the injured SDF soldiers. They had a helicopter flown in from the CRF and transported two of the more seriously injured to the Fukushima Medical University Hospital. From the afternoon of that day, Unit 2 rapidly became unstable.

At a coordination meeting at five p.m. on March 14, he was sounded out by TEPCO and NISA officers to see whether the SDF could remove the debris that was blocking efforts to pump water into Unit 2. A number of other requests were made, such as whether they could supply some gasoline to the truck that was monitoring in and around the station which had run dry, and whether they could set up a generator in the offsite center's medical office.

Imaura passed on these requests to CRF Commanding General Toshinobu Miyajima. The requests were passed up to Chief of Staff of the Joint Staff Ryoichi Oriki and Defense Minister Toshimi Kitazawa. A reply was received from the CRF after six p.m.

They had just had the explosion in Unit 3. Was there any guarantee that Unit 2 would not explode in the same way? They could not accept the requests. This was the decision of both the minister and the chief of staff of the Joint Staff. That was more or less the gist. They did add, however, that they would do something about supplying gasoline and setting up a generator on March 15.

On March 18, Yuki Imaura handed his tasks over to the other deputy commander of the CRF, Masato Taura.

"The SDF hadn't foreseen a nuclear accident like this, either. The manuals, equipment, and, most important, the training, were all inadequate. I was made acutely aware that we needed more training."

During this time, a member of the First Special Weapons Protection Corps had fled and been arrested.[22] But for the most part, Imaura was grateful to them for doing a good job.

"The Corps' members didn't flinch even at the radiation. They all join the Self-Defense Forces swearing an oath to give up their lives. This time, not one of them panicked or turned their backs."

The oath he was referring to was the SDF's Oath of Duty, which runs as follows:

I swear with my own body to perform my duty without regard to danger.
(Self-Defense Forces Law Enforcement Regulations, article 39, general oath of military service)[23]

The Central Special Weapons Protection Corps continued its cooling operations thereafter, using ten rescue fire engines that were capable of discharging water. However, in the field, there was a growing feeling of boycotting TEPCO, because "someone upstairs has decided not to let the SDF into the power plant." This tangle of emotions between TEPCO and the SDF was of enough concern to make Tadahiro Matsushita, METI senior vice minister and newly appointed head of the local NERHQ, appeal directly to the Kantei about it.[24]

"WATER DROP ABANDONED. TRULY REGRETTABLE."

It was perhaps Kan who was shocked the most by the explosion at Unit 3. He was afraid that with the injuries sustained by the SDF, their operations might become clogged up. Madarame testified to the Independent Investigation Commission that, "Given that if we'd been unlucky, a member of the SDF might have died in the Unit 3 explosion, the prime minister lost it."

With the explosion at Unit 3, Kan "lost it"—in other words, he lost his composure.[25] Hosono shared a similar sense of alarm. He got the impression that "After that hydrogen explosion, the SDF just disappeared."[26]

Ito had already asked the SDF on March 13 to look into the possibility of firefighting from airborne helicopters. METI had also pushed strongly for discharging water from helicopters. The Ministry of Defense, on the other hand, just replied that water bombing from the sky would be difficult, because the reactor buildings had roofs. With the explosion, however, the roofs had been blown off. The question of water drops from helicopters was revisited.[27]

In the evening of March 14, Kazuo Matsunaga, METI vice minister, called Kimito Nakae, defense vice minister, many times.

"Are the helicopters still not flying?"

"It's up to what Kitazawa-san thinks. We're waiting on that now."

Matsunaga kept making the same appeal to Nakae over and over.[28] Nakae passed it on to the Joint Staff Office and pushed them to consider.

The water-pumping operation reached a huge turning point on March 15. The morning of that day, the suppression chamber in Unit 2 was damaged, there was an explosion in Unit 4, and TEPCO temporarily withdrew its staff to the gymnasium at Fukushima Daini NPS. All work ceased. The pumping operations could not be carried out adequately, either.

It was on that morning that the Joint Staff Office looked into the possibility of dropping boric acid from the air into the Unit 4 fuel pool. At the Integrated Response Office set up at TEPCO, the following exchange took place about boric acid.

> TEPCO: "We'd like to ask you to discharge boric acid as well when they do the water drop from the helicopters. You know, just in case."
> SDF: "We haven't heard about those procedures. You'll have to submit a plan to us."

Kaieda took the topic up.

"I'll fix it."

Kaieda appealed to Kitazawa about the matter.[29]

Ito was called to the prime minister's office around noon on March 15. He was introduced by Kan to two academics, Professor Masanori Aritomi, director of the Research Laboratory for Nuclear Reactors (RLNR) at the Tokyo Institute of Technology, and Professor Masaki Saito, also from the RLNR.

"These two gentlemen are experts in atomic power. We've decided to have them come in for today, so I wanted to introduce them to you as well, Ito."

After some time, they both said they were going to the Integrated Response Office at TEPCO and left. Ito was alone with Kan. He said, "Mr. Prime Minister, I have a proposal."

"What is it?"

"The SDF says it's going to water-bomb from the air, but even if they fly loaded to the gills, the most an aircraft can carry is five tons. Yet we need tens of tons of water. No matter which way you look at it, it's not enough. The water just has to come from the ground."

"Will water from the ground reach that far? Are there water trucks with that range?"

"I haven't looked into it closely, but the Tokyo Metropolitan Police Department has some that look like they'd reach. Let's get them to send them out."

"Will they do it for us?"

"I'll speak to them."

Kan's eyes started to sparkle at Ito's words.

"I'll get the police."

Hearing this strengthened Kan's resolve. He told Ito, "Go to TEPCO right now and get Kaieda's approval. I'll put in a call while you're on the way."

Ito left for TEPCO. He met with Kaieda and told him the plan.

"We'd be ever so grateful if the police did it for us."

He also asked for the approval of Katsumata, who was next to Kaieda at the time.[30]

Before four p.m. on March 15, Kitazawa visited the Kantei accompanied by Oriki and met with Kan in his office. Oriki remarked, "The mission of the SDF is to save the people's lives. If we get the order, we'll do everything in our power."

Kan nodded deeply. During their discussion, Kan's telephone rang.

"Power recovery? What are you saying? Pumping in water's more important than that! Why don't you hurry up and start pumping water?"

They debated over which was more important: getting the power back, or pumping water again? Kan called TEPCO president Shimizu on the spot. Shimizu seemed to be making a desperate appeal that getting power back was the first priority. Kan stuck to his guns, however, that injecting water should be done first.

It was at this meeting that Kan instructed Kitazawa to prepare the SDF to discharge water into the fuel pools.[31] It was not just the SDF. The police, the fire department, they were going to use every bit of capability the country had to get water into the fuel pools.

That day, after descending on TEPCO and setting up the Integrated Response Office, Kan made a second huge decision to pump water into the fuel pools. It was Ito who prompted Kan to make this decision.

Let us turn the clock back a little. The early hours of March 13.

It was confirmed that white billows of smoke were rising from Unit 1 (RB) after the explosion. The building had already exploded. What, then, was that white smoke? Was it, perhaps, that the water level in the spent-fuel pool had dropped considerably?

Since there was still some steam being emitted, it was not likely that it was completely dry. However, there was a danger that, if left as it was, the fuel in the spent-fuel pool would be exposed and explode, scattering radioactive material into the atmosphere. It is from this point that doing something about the fuel pool was deemed to be an urgent issue.[32]

The most pressing of them was Unit 4's fuel pool. Unit 4 had been in planned outage since the end of November 2010. In anticipation of the replacement of the shroud on Unit 4's pressure vessel, all fuel assemblies had been unloaded and removed to the spent-fuel pool.[33]

The spent-fuel pool was located on the topmost fifth floor of the reactor building. It was situated next to the containment vessel and was full of water for cooling. The fuel was submerged in this, the top of the fuel being seven or eight meters under water.

There were 783 spent-fuel assemblies and 548 fuel assemblies in use in Unit 4's fuel pool. This was far more than the 292 rods at Unit 1, 587 rods at Unit 2, and 514 rods at Unit 3 reactors. There were enough fuel rods in the Unit 4 fuel pool for two to three nuclear reactors of the same size. To make matters worse, their residual heat was high, because they had been in operation until just the previous November.[34]

The fuel pools were normally controlled at a water temperature of 40 degrees or below. From March 12, the water temperature at Unit 4 began to rise.

11:50 A.M., MARCH 13, 78 DEGREES CELSIUS.

4:18 A.M., MARCH 14, 85 DEGREES CELSIUS.[35]

The fuel pool was situated alongside the containment vessel in the reactor building. The only barrier separating it from the outside was the reactor building itself. If the high temperature spent fuel was exposed in the pool, this would be followed by a reaction between water and zirconium, and as a result, radioactive material would be released outside. In addition, the fuel would melt into mush, come in contact with the concrete walls, and radioactive material would escape directly outside from the resultant cracks in the roof.[36]

12:44 A.M. OF THE SAME DAY. Yoshida spoke via videoconference.

"I want to do something quickly about the spent-fuel pool. This is pretty serious, I think."[37]

2:13 P.M. OF THE SAME DAY. A report was received from the field via videoconference that "there's steam rising from the fuel pool. It's boiling at 100 degrees Celsius."[38]

Getting water into the fuel pool had become a matter of life and death.

The ERC in the Anti-Seismic Building and the Integrated Response Office at TEPCO Head Office talked intermittently about measures for the fuel pool at Unit 4 from the early hours of March 16.

During this time, flames were discovered to have gone up in the fourth floor of Unit 4 (RB), forcing them to take firefighting measures. In addition, they needed to remove the concrete debris and rubble piled up around Units 3 and 4, using a digger for power restoration operations.

What on earth should be the highest priority? The site was chaotic.

At about nine a.m. on March 16, Yoshida raised his voice in the videoconference.

"I'm sorry. We have various missions coming at the same time now, so I would like to check again, what is needed most now is getting the police fire engines quickly to the side of Unit 4 to pump water into the spent-fuel pool. That's our greatest aim, right?"

TEPCO Fellow Ichiro Takekuro at the Integrated Response Office replied, "That's right."

"It's all right to hold off on other operations temporarily if they get in the way of this, yes?"

Around this time, they had received a request from a power truck that had newly arrived at the main gate of Fukushima Daiichi NPS. If progress was being made with removing the rubble at the turbine building, the company wanted to start power-restoring operations as soon as possible. Takekuro said, "I understand how you feel. As I've just said, our number one priority is getting a supply of water to the fuel pool. However, since securing an external power supply is also important at the same time, make that your second priority as long as it doesn't interfere with your top priority."

"Roger that. So, please refer to getting water into the spent-fuel pool at Unit 4 as First Project. Calling it First Project will help promote better understanding, so please cooperate."

However, images of a white smoke-like vapor blowing intermittently out of Unit 3 were broadcast on TV. There was a possibility that the water temperature in the Unit 3 fuel pool had increased and the water level was falling. Takekuro called out to Yoshida.

"If the white smoke coming out is because of the heat being generated in the spent-fuel storage pool, we'd have to judge the situation to be dangerous, but then pumping water into Unit 3 rather than Unit 4 would take precedence, but what do you think?"

"Yes, there's a good possibility of that."

10:43 A.M. The Integrated Response Office decided to temporarily evacuate the workers. Yoshida declared a cease to First Project. However, no change was observed thereafter in the radiation dose on the plant site.

11:30 AM. Work was resumed.[39]

About noon on March 16, Takekuro confirmed the operation priorities.

"I'm reconfirming our priorities. First of all, the top priority is supplying water to the Unit 3 pool. Next is supplying water to the Unit 4 pool. The next is restoring power. I want to be clear on these three."[40]

On the afternoon of the same day, Kan spoke at the ninth meeting of NERHQ.

"We have a very worrying situation with temperature rising in the Unit 4 pool . . . There is going to be no withdrawal. If that happened, we'd be exposed to far more material than Chernobyl, in terms of volume."

Kaieda also spoke.

"The temperature's rising in both the Unit 3 and Unit 4 spent-fuel pools, and we need an urgent response. I have just issued TEPCO with an instruction of measures to be taken, namely to perform the water injection as soon as possible."[41]

Whether it was for Unit 3 or 4, the top priority was getting water into the fuel pools.

00:46 P.M. ON MARCH 16. The prime minister's office.

Kitazawa and Oriki were making another visit following that of the previous day. They were accompanied by Nakae and Koji Shimodaira, head of the Defense Intelligence Headquarters. Kitazawa explained the water bombing operations by SDF helicopters for the fuel pools:

- The First Helicopter Group, No. 104 Squadron of the Ground Self-Defense Force at Kisarazu, would carry out the mission.

- Sheets of tungsten would be laid on the seats of the CH47 Chinook large transport helicopter to prevent radiation absorption during the operation.

- A lead-plate vest would be worn on top of the protective clothing. This would prevent gamma rays from passing through the body.

- The crew would take stable iodine to prevent internal exposure.

- Pilots would also wear protective masks. It could not be helped that this would block their field of view.

- Everything that even looked like a window would be sealed.

- In order to suppress the radiation dose, water would be dropped from an altitude of three hundred feet (ninety meters) while passing over at a speed of twenty knots (about thirty-seven kilometers per hour). There would be no hovering.

- For the time being, they would bear in mind water discharge to Unit 3.

On hearing Kitazawa's explanation, Kan said happily, "You SDF guys really can do anything, can't you? . . . I don't suppose we could have the SDF out in front more, instead of the kind of behind-the-lines logistical support they've been doing so far?"

Kan approved the water bombing by the SDF helicopters.[42]

However, monitoring of the radiation had to be carried out before the water drop maneuver. They also had to settle on whether the target was to be Unit 3 or Unit 4. Kitazawa had merely stated they would "bear Unit 3 in mind." Whether they would actually do it or not was up to the radiation-monitoring results. That was another reason why they had to confirm whether there was water in the Unit 4 fuel pool or not.

2:20 P.M. They decided to have one helicopter do the monitoring and the remaining two helicopters drop the water (five tons each).

At four p.m., TEPCO employees boarded an SDF helicopter to take aerial shots of the top of Unit 4. The pilot was forty-one-year-old Koichi Kataoka from the First Helicopter Group at Kisarazu. The SDF helicopter arrived at J-Village, where two TEPCO employees boarded the helicopter. One of them was Noriichi Yamashita. At the age of forty-three, he was the group manager of Units 3 and 4 at Fukushima Daiichi. After the accident, he joined the water drop team at the Tokyo Head Office, and later the hydrogen explosion team to research how to prevent a hydrogen explosion at Units 2, 3, and 4. Since both Units 3 and 2 exploded, his role became redundant.

In the evening hours of March 15, Yamashita was suddenly told by his boss to go to J-Village, and he headed there in a limousine with other employees who worked on managing radiation. He was simply told, "Teach them about the nuclear reactor, since the SDF is planning to pour water over the reactors from a helicopter."

When they arrived at J-Village early in the morning, the Head Office gave additional instructions: "We aren't going to pour water today. Instead, we are flying a survey helicopter, so please get on board and take some video footage from the helicopter." Moments later, a Fukushima Daini employee came with a video camera in his hand. When Yamashita and his colleague hopped on board the helicopter, they found there were no seat belts. The helicopter only had iron boards spread in a 5.5 square meters' space. In the cockpit, there were two people, including Kataoka. An SDF member and Yamashita both sat on the iron board floor. All the SDF personnel wore headsets. Yamashita somehow came into possession of a piece of paper and a pencil and thought to himself, *What am I going to use this for?* but the helicopter took off anyway.

Coming in from up high, they gradually dropped altitude. Kataoka was headed toward the side of Unit 4. Unit 4's building had exploded, but they could not see in from directly overhead, because some of the roof was still in place. The building's concrete walls would block the radiation, but he had heard that "the needle on the dosimeter will shoot right up" when directly overhead.

He thought, *The pool may well be dry,* but he could see a square pool on the far side of the deck beneath the roof. The afternoon sun was pouring into the building, but he could not see any color where the water was supposed to be. But he could see an outdoor pool lit up by the sunlight, with small ripples on the surface.

"I see it. There's water there."

Kataoka reported this to the TEPCO workers via the headgear intercom. His voice was cheerful.

The helicopter was also monitoring the radiation from the air at the same time. After having taken the measurements several times, they dropped back down alongside Unit 4 for a final sweep and took a peep at the fuel pool. Their altitude was down to a hundred feet (thirty meters).

"There was water there, wasn't there?"

Looking back as he said this, Kataoka saw the two TEPCO workers in the rear seats—one of them being Yamashita—nod strongly.

He had been instructed to fly at the same altitude as the planned water discharge—that is, a hundred feet (thirty meters). The permissible accumulated amount of radiation for one mission was set at 50 millisieverts. The annual exposure limit for public servants involved in radioactive operations had just been raised to 250 millisieverts, but they might be required to make several flights. That was the reason for setting the limit for each mission at 50 millisieverts.

The flight was a "combined mission" aimed at monitoring the radiation for the water bombing operations the helicopter unit was to perform and to assess the situation in the fuel pool. The flight lasted one and a half hours.[43]

After the monitoring operation came the water drop. It was the ground SDF's No. 104 Squadron from Kisarazu that had been charged with the aerial water bombing mission. They had been instructed on March 14 to make preparations for the water bombing.

On the morning of March 16, they moved to the ground SDF's Kasuminome Base in Sendai and started practice runs. It snowed heavily that day. The strategy was to have two aircraft each drop water twice from up high toward the fuel pool. If they were unable to switch to water injection from the ground, the bombing maneuver would be repeated. The strategy would be implemented under the environmental conditions of a dosage of 100 millisieverts per hour or less. The target was the fuel pool of Unit 3. The mission crews had been told that there was "a possibility that the spent-fuel pool of Unit 3 is dry."

The monitoring strategy raised the possibility of there being water in the Unit 4 fuel pool. For that reason, the priority of the water release quickly shifted from Unit 4 to Unit 3.[44]

5:20 P.M. One of the two squadrons approached Unit 3. When they had dropped to a hundred feet, the air dose rate reached 247 millisieverts per hour.[45] The wind was also strong. As a result, they returned without having dropped any water. The operation was suspended.

In the ERC on TEPCO's second floor, members of the Integrated Response Office were waiting, with their eyes affixed to the screen, for the water to be released at any moment. They had received information that NHK had set up a telescopic camera twenty kilometers from the site and were going to broadcast the water drop live. Work at Fukushima Daiichi NPS had also stopped for the afternoon, because of the planned helicopter water bombing.

5:23 P.M. The Integrated Response Office was contacted by the SDF.

"Owing to high air dose, water discharge stopped for today."

The cavernous room was enveloped in silence like a wake.

Around 5:30 p.m., the screen at the Integrated Response Office suddenly went blank. The audio circuits were also dead. Had there just been a temporary blackout? Without knowing the cause, the screen stayed down until approximately 12:30 a.m. on the following day, March 17.

Hosono felt as if his blood was draining away. Kitazawa wrote only a single line in his diary for that day:

Water drop abandoned. Truly regrettable.[46]

WATER DROP SUCCESSFUL

It was communicated in a meeting at the Ministry of Defense, held from nine p.m. on March 16, that "there will be a telephone conference for seven to eight minutes between the prime minister and the U.S. president from 9:30 a.m. tomorrow, March 17."[47] (In actuality, the telephone conference would last for around thirty minutes.)

The fact that there was to be a meeting between the U.S. and Japanese leaders meant that the SDF's water bombing operation had to have been successful by then at any cost. Kitazawa was worried, however, right up until the last moment.

Although it was Kitazawa himself who had written in his diary, "Water drop abandoned. Truly regrettable," there was one point on his mind that he just could not shake.[48] The experts at the Defense Intelligence Headquarters had warned Kitazawa: "There's a possibility that water bombing by helicopter will trigger a steam explosion."[49]

"There was a fear that it would become a great disaster if it did cause a steam explosion and the helicopter crashed. The reactor would be out of control if that happened. The government would be out of options."

They were going to drop 7.5 tons of water all at once from the air; there was a risk that the pressure of the water at that time would damage the reactor inside and trigger a steam explosion. This remained the greatest risk factor till the very end.[50]

Kitazawa presided over a great many meetings on the SDF water bombing operation. An external expert, whom they questioned over the response at Chernobyl, said that as a last resort, a "suicide squad" had spread boric acid at Chernobyl. At the mention of a "suicide squad," the air in the room grew strained. It was at that time that Kitazawa said, "I'm just going to the toilet. I need to discharge some water, too."

This got a big laugh. Kitazawa stood and the air that had been so strained burst like a puncture. Kitazawa never lost his sense of humor throughout the crisis.[51]

On the morning of that day, March 16, Kitazawa attended a press conference. He responded to a question about the fact that water was being discharged from SDF helicopters despite the risk of high radiation exposure. "It is the SDF's duty to protect the lives of citizens to the end. While it is difficult to determine with 100 percent certainty that lives will be lost, the SDF and Ministry of Defense, for our part, have determined to carry out this duty to the limit."

Koichi Isobe, who at the time served as director of the Defense Plans and Policy Department at the Joint Staff Office, noted in a book he later wrote that "this may have been the first time since the founding of the SDF that a statement had been made at a cabinet minister press conference about the force risking threats to life in carrying out its missions."[52]

Actually, Kitazawa himself reflected, "I didn't say this myself, but it was certainly a suicide squad . . . Due to unpredictable explosions and such, we had to also assume that the troops would become casualties."[53]

Like Kitazawa, Oriki was also concerned about the risk of a steam explosion.

When SDF helicopters carried out mountain fire extinguishing operations, they did not use water to put the flames out. They used the pressure of the water dropped from above to beat the flames out. The same sort of huge water pressure would be applied to the fuel pool. Although the water dropped from helicopters looks like a fine spray on television, in actuality, there was a tremendous amount of water pressure.[54]

Oriki, however, had strengthened his inner resolve that morning that they had no choice but to do it. The previous day, the amount of exposure the crew had been exposed to when they flew overhead was within the regulated amount (30 millisieverts per annum). Their protective measures had proved effective.[55] Oriki was encouraged further by this report.

This is going to work. I can tell the crew to go in with confidence.[56]

Late at night, Oriki received a call from Miyajima. Miyajima spoke with conviction.

"We'll do it tomorrow no matter how high the air dose goes. Leave the water up to me."

"It's in your hands."

It was a short exchange, but enough to reaffirm their commitment.[57] Oriki then placed a call to Kitazawa.

"They're doing it tomorrow, no matter what."

At 1:15 a.m. on March 17, the Integrated Response Office made its final decision that the fuel pool at Unit 3 was to be the water bombing priority.[58]

At seven a.m. on March 17, a call from Washington came in on the U.S.-Japan military hotline to the chief of staff of the Joint Staff Office. It was from Michael Mullen, chairman of the U.S. Joint Chiefs of Staff. Mullen had made many calls to Oriki around this time. The message was always the same.

"When the survival of the state is on the line, in the end it comes down to the military."

This morning, Mullen started by saying, "I want to pass on, military-to-military, what we have conveyed through diplomatic channels to the Japanese ambassador to the United States, Ichiro Fujizaki . . . Shouldn't the SDF be taking a more aggressive role in controlling the situation?"

After saying so, Mullen spoke as if striking the final blow.

"The only person who can decide in Japan is the chief of staff of the Joint Staff."

When the call was over, Oriki told Hironaka, "I've been scolded by Mullen-san."

As well as giving Masayuki Hironaka, director of the Operations Department in the Joint Staff Office, the go-ahead, Oriki phoned Kitazawa, saying, "Please let us do it." Kitazawa accepted. Oriki had a look of relief on his face.[59]

Katsutoshi Kawano, vice chief of staff at the Joint Staff Office, said to Oriki, "This is exactly like the suicide squad in the movie *K-19*."

"*K-19*? What's that?"

"It's a Hollywood movie. It's a movie about how, during the Cold War, there's a crack in the reactor of a nuclear submarine developed by the Soviets, and the coolant starts leaking out. One suicide squad after another goes in to try and stop the reactor meltdown. It's based on a true story."

After explaining this, Kawano added, "Harrison Ford played the Soviet submarine commander."[60]

7:25 A.M. The SDF had finalized their preparations for the water bombing, which was set for "10:00 a.m."

7:42 A.M. Oriki gave the order to proceed.

8:56 A.M. Two CH47 Chinooks took off from Kasuminome Camp. The CH47 Chinook is a large transport helicopter with a fuselage of approximately sixteen meters and two rotor blades about eighteen meters in diameter.

On the way, they stopped to draw seawater from near the mouth of the Natori River, and then headed to Fukushima Daiichi NPS. When filled with water, the huge buckets hanging under them would act as ballast for the helicopters. If they were not filled to the brim, which would stabilize them, they could be buffeted by the wind, thereby destabilizing the helicopter's flight.

They flew south in a straight line. In order to sneak under the dose limit, they decided to increase their altitude. Today they would be able to enter upwind. They had heard that the helicopters had been forced to fly in downwind the previous day.[61]

The first thing they saw was Unit 1. The whole top of the building was missing. The copilot of the squad was thirty-two-year-old Yoshiyuki Yamaoka.

"What the hell is that?!"

There were huge pieces of debris scattered throughout the building.

It must have been an enormous explosion.

He felt a chill run up his spine. The dosimeters of Yamaoka and his crew were still at zero, even when they approached Fukushima Daiichi NPS. The moment they flew over Unit 3, however, they jumped.

Like Unit 1, the structure of Unit 3 was laid bare. Steam was rising from it. That was where they dropped the water. They could see the water going in. Steam was also rising from Unit 4. When Yamaoka's squad made their second drop, a pillar of white steam was rising swiftly from Unit 3. Yamaoka was sure that "the previous drop has made it in."

Mission accomplished.

None of the crew said a word. They were all struck dumb. Yamaoka felt a sense of accomplishment at having fulfilled his mission. He had been fiercely aware of his fear of dying.

What if there's a huge explosion after we drop? We'll all die instantly.

He was in a whirlpool of emotions. While he was sure that he could trust the dosimeters since they were SDF-issued, he was still worried.

Is it really catching the exposure?

And he could not get rid of doubts such as *Are they going to keep running these water bombing operations?*

Five hundred tons of water were needed to submerge the fuel rods in the fuel pool at Unit 3. Since the water would evaporate, they needed to keep adding fifty to seventy tons a day. Articles along these lines were running in the newspapers around that time.

Yamaoka's squad landed at the ground in J-Village. Both the aircraft and the crew had to be decontaminated. The other Chinook crew, which had also taken off from Kasuminome Camp, was standing by at J-Village. In the event that the crew involved in the water bombing operation was injured due to exposure, preparations had been made to transport them immediately to a medical facility, just in case.

Yamaoka let his family know he was safe. He had called his wife before the flight.

"You know somebody has to go."

His wife had answered bravely through her tears, "Yes, somebody has to."

They had just learned a little earlier that she was pregnant.

He called his father next. Yamaoka's father was a police officer. During the JCO Tokaimura criticality accident in 1999, he had flown a mission over the Tokaimura power plant as a pilot in the Tochigi Prefectural Police's Air Corps. His job had been "air traffic control," so to speak, sending radio warnings to clear the area to the media swarming in on their helicopters trying to get aerial shots.

His father told him that he had never been able to forget what he had read in a book that said all of the pilots who had flown water bombing operations at the time of the Chernobyl accident had all ended up with a form of cancer like leukemia.

Who'd have believed I'd end up piloting the same mission . . .

Yamaoka was struck by this twist of fate, but his father told him over the phone, "I was watching TV all the time, but I was too frightened to watch that time."[62]

In the command post on the basement floor at the Ministry of Defense in Ichigaya, Oriki, the post commander, was seated in the middle. Hironaka was camped out on his left. Kitazawa stayed on his feet behind him and was watching the screen that showed the SDF water drops. For some reason, Kitazawa was thinking of the scene at the Asama-Sanso Incident.

The Asama-Sanso Incident was a hostage crisis in a mountain lodge that took place in Gunma Prefecture in February 1972. Five members of what remained of the United Red Army barricaded themselves and their hostages into the lodge; the police, using high-pressure water hoses to attack them, freed the hostages and took all five into custody.

The nation watches at times of crisis like that. They watch, desperately, to see what the government is doing.

Not the best of phrasing, I know, but we need to make a splash. That's why we needed to get even a single drop in. Whether it's effective or not is not the point.[63]

A round of applause broke out the moment the squad dropped the water. Kitazawa reported to Kan.

"The water drop was a success."

His face was flushed.[64]

Meanwhile, Charles Casto and John Roos, U.S. ambassador to Japan, watched the water drop together, on a big-screen TV. "We could see the wind blowing the water away from the reactor building. It's likely that almost none of it dropped into the spent-fuel pool at all," Casto remembered. As the Japanese responded in an upbeat manner, the two were in low spirits.[65]

THE NATIONAL BACKBONE

Approximately thirty tons of water was dropped in four flights by the helicopters before 10:01 a.m. Their "success" saw stock prices rally.

Up until the previous day (March 16), the Tokyo Stock Exchange (TSE) had had four continuous days of low prices across the board after the earthquake. The closing price on March 15 was down 1,015 yen on the previous day's trading. On March 16, the futures market fell momentarily below the 8,000-yen benchmark for the first time in two years. On March 17, after the SDF's water bombing, futures were bought back, and on March 18, the Nikkei Average rallied to the 9,200-yen mark.[66]

Kitazawa was pleased with the SDF's "success," but Washington's reaction was more complex. The U.S. government was frustrated with the Kan administration for leaving the response up to TEPCO and failing to bring in the SDF to put an end to the Fukushima Daiichi accident despite six days having passed since the quake. Consequently, they were pleased that the water bombing operation by the SDF was an indication that Japan was finally "getting itself together" to deal with the nuclear crisis.

It was just that they were doubtful about how effective the operation itself had been, and even more doubtful about how long-lasting the effect would be. At the time, Kevin Maher, head of the Japan Earthquake Task Force at the State Department (former director of Japan Affairs), wrote that the U.S. government, which saw the scene, was largely shocked.

"The U.S. government felt a sense of despair that all a large nation such as Japan could do a week after the loss of power due to the tsunami was to drop water from one helicopter. What's more, despite the desperate actions of the SDF, the water they dropped didn't seem to have had much effect in cooling the reactor down."[67]

In fact, Michael Mullen, chairman of the Joint Chiefs of Staff, had passed these doubts on to Japan. Knowing Mullen was concerned about it being "doubtful how much of an effect the helicopter water drops had had," Ambassador Ichiro Fujisaki emphasized the following points in his diplomatic telegram:

"Although the U.S. government rated the helicopter water drops highly, this should not be taken as having lowered their fear about the Fukushima Daiichi nuclear crisis per se or having erased their concern about the Japanese government's approach."[68]

Oriki was also acutely aware of this.

They know the helicopter water drops were not that effective. But we're aware of that, too. What America really wants is for us to stabilize the overall situation. But that's what we want, too.[69]

He was painfully aware that the Joint Staff Office needed to strengthen its coordination with the U.S. military in order to deal with the nuclear emergency.

It was just around this time that the establishment of a Joint Support Force (JSF) under the U.S. Pacific Command at Yokota Air Base gradually started to take shape. It was decided then to dispatch Koichiro Bansho, director of the Defense Policy and Programs Department at the Ground Staff Office, to the Yokota JSF; Koichi Isobe, director of the Defense Plans and Policy Department at the Joint Staff Office, and Masato Nakanishi, deputy director at the Maritime Staff Office, as assistants to Masayuki Hironaka, director of the Operations Department in the Joint Staff Office, as well as Sadamasa Oue, dean of Defense Education at the National Defense Academy, to the emergency operation team at the crisis management center in the Kantei.

They were all placed under Hironaka's command and were to work to strengthen U.S.-Japan coordination.

It was the first time an SDF officer had been appointed to the U.S. Pacific Command JSF, which had been set up in Yokota, and the first time an SDF officer had been appointed to the emergency operation team at the crisis management center in the Kantei. This was the birth of Team Oriki, "mobilizing all of the SDF's best and brightest."[70]

They attended all the commanding officers' meetings held by the U.S. Pacific Command JSF (videoconferences and conference calls with Yokota, Honolulu, U.S. troops, the U.S. embassy in Tokyo, and the Joint Staff Office in Ichigaya), as well as NRC meetings.

At the same time, Brigadier General William Crowe (United States

Marine Corps) took up residence at the Joint Staff Office in Ichigaya. A
senior member of the Joint Staff Office later testified, "This was epochal for
the U.S.-Japan alliance. We made everything transparent for Crowe and he
shared all our information."[71]

There was virtually no decrease in the radiation dose despite the SDF's
aerial water drop operation on March 17. It was confirmed, however, that
since it was steam rising and not black smoke, there was no danger of an
explosion and that injecting water would be effective.[72] At the very least,
this operation provided the catalyst for uniting the Japanese government
and mobilizing a water injection maneuver from the ground.

For some reason, Kan had been thinking of the Korean War.

*This has put us on the attack. It's like the Inchon landing in the Korean
War. The United States had been pushed back to Pusan, but that reversed
their fortunes.*[73]

Hosono felt they had just managed to hang on. He felt, *The backbone
of Japan was about to break and we somehow managed to hold on. We
were right on the brink of whether Japan can survive as an independent
state or not.*

If we can't do this, America won't help Japan anymore.[74]

From the early morning of March 17, TEPCO started cleaning up the debris
on the road to Unit 3. They were laying the groundwork for injecting water
into the fuel pool at Unit 3 from the ground.

TEPCO had reported to the government and the Americans that the
radiation would drop 70 percent if they cleared away the debris.[75]

THE RIOT POLICE

1:00 P.M., MARCH 17. The Lower House was in session. It was the first plenary session since the earthquake. At the outset, they observed a moment of silence.
After the silence was over, Kan returned to the Kantei immediately. He met
with Kitazawa and others from the Ministry of Defense and the SDF and
thanked them for the water bombing operation that morning.[76]

THE EVENING OF MARCH 17. The prime minister's office at the Kantei.

Prime Minister Kan called in Kitazawa and Oriki, as well as Ito, to
discuss the next strategy after the water bombing operation that morning.
Hosono was also in attendance.

Hosono said, "The fuel pool at Unit 1 will need the same, won't it?" but
Kan expressed the opinion that Units 3 and 4 were in worse shape, saying,
"There's water in the fuel pool at Unit 1."[77]

SOMETIME AFTER SIX P.M. ON MARCH 17. The government held the tenth meeting of
NERHQ. Kan spoke.

"This morning, water was poured into Unit 3 by SDF helicopters. I would like to express my gratitude to the crew members and the SDF as a whole for performing this dangerous mission . . . At present, we are asking the riot police, that is, the Tokyo Metropolitan Police, mainly to carry out water injection from the ground, and if things go smoothly they should be starting soon."[78]

Kaieda also spoke.

"We were just able to verify from the SDF helicopter that water to a certain level can be seen in Unit 4's pool, therefore we will be prioritizing water injection into Unit 3's spent-fuel pool."

Kitazawa reported.

"Of the eleven high-power trucks we have, we'll pump in water from five. They arrived at the site at 5:37 p.m."

However, a series of dire comments followed from the other ministers. Akihiro Ohata, minister for Land, Infrastructure, and Transport:

"Foreign nationals are leaving Japan in droves."

Koichiro Genba, minister for National Policy:

"This is a war. It's win or lose. We're already losing on individual fronts. The question is how to keep the number of future defeats down. It's like having three Three Mile Islands happen all at once. We have to assume the worst and evacuate the residents. I'm in the process of drawing up evacuation plans with the help of the experts."

In fact, however, the water injection from the ground was nowhere near meeting Kan's hopes that "things go smoothly" and would be "starting soon."

For the groundwater injection, it was necessary to mobilize fire brigades from around the country as well as TEPCO's construction parties, including the riot police, the SDF's Central Readiness Forces, and the Tokyo Fire Department. Ito, a former chief commissioner of the Tokyo Metropolitan Police, had declared impressively to Kan, "I'll get the police," but it was not so easy when it came to actually moving them.[79]

Both Kan and Hosono contacted Kansei Nakano, chairman of the National Public Safety Commission, but Nakano was noncommittal. And this was understandable. The chairman of the National Public Safety Commission is not a commander. He cannot issue orders to the director general of the Tokyo Metropolitan Police. He does not have authority to manage prefectural police chiefs. Moreover, the riot police's water tanks had not been mobilized a single time since October 20, 1985, when they were used on shouting activists opposed to the construction of Narita Airport, who had barricaded themselves in a steel tower. And, of course, they had no preparation or training for injecting water into a fuel pool adjacent to a nuclear reactor in meltdown.[80]

Nevertheless, in the end, the police accepted the request to mobilize for the water injection operation. Nakano called Kitazawa on the phone, however, pleading to "please let the police go in first."[81]

The riot police water cannon force counted thirteen members: Captain Yoshitsugu Oigawa, two liaison officers from the National Police Agency, and eleven riot police. Oigawa's title was deputy chief of the Second Division (explosives), Metropolitan Police Security.

MARCH 15. They handed over the riot police water trucks to TEPCO. TEPCO was to transport them to the site.

THE EVENING OF MARCH 16. They headed to the site by helicopter from the air SDF's Hyakuri Airbase in Ibaraki Prefecture. They borrowed everything, including Tyvek suits, masks, and dosimeters from TEPCO.

When they arrived over J-Village, however, they were told they could not land, because the SDF was decontaminating its helicopters. No one had told them in advance. Having no choice, they tried to land in a nearby open space, but it was too dark to land. They got together a number of cars and had them turn their headlights on, but, in the end, they turned back.[82]

In the Integrated Response Office back at TEPCO's headquarters, someone was heard to say, "They've got no guts at all!"

After a short while, they received word from the metropolitan police that "they would travel through the night."

At 2:40 p.m. on March 17, the riot police arrived, as promised, by car. This time there were murmurs of admiration.

"That's like the police!"[83]

Oigawa met with Site Superintendent Yoshida in the Anti-Seismic Building. He only asked Yoshida one question.

"Is there any possibility of an explosion?"

This was because he had heard there was a chance of a steam explosion if water was injected. Yoshida's answer was an unequivocal "No." They then discussed in detail the water injection with the TEPCO side.

"Depending on the wind, the water may diffuse into a mist-like drizzle, but will that still be okay?"

"Yes, that's okay."

They set their alarms at 9 millisieverts. They had decided to fall back if the alarms went off.

Just after seven p.m. on March 17, the riot police sprayed forty-four tons of water with their high-pressure hoses into the spent-fuel pool at Unit 3. The TEPCO workers pointed in the direction of the spray. As they had feared, the water was turning into a drizzle. And what was more, they did not have enough elevation.

The TEPCO worker said, "It's fine. It should be reaching," but since it was dark, they could not visually confirm if it was reaching or not.

Are they worried about it splashing in? Are they worried about a steam explosion?

Oigawa was getting more nervous all the time.[84]

Back at the Integrated Response Office, watching on the screen as the water spread in the dark like a fine mist, a chatty little Kasumigaseki sparrow said snidely, "If you're going to piss on it, you need to stand closer."[85]

The high-pressure water trucks of the riot police were known as the "Manneken Pis," after the statue of a boy urinating into a fountain's basin in Brussels. Since they were used for riot control, they were better at spraying downward. At times like that, the water was sprayed with the nozzles facing down, but for the fuel pool on the fifth floor, they needed to spray upward. When they tried this, however, the water just turned into a misty drizzle.

"What should we do? Will we let them have another go?"

"If they can't spray upward, there's not much point, is there?"

These were the kind of exchanges taking place at the Integrated Response Office.[86]

After finishing the first maneuver and returning to the Anti-Seismic Building, Oigawa received the metropolitan police's order via a liaison officer standing by at J-Village, "Operation over. Return."[87]

The metropolitan police later congratulated itself on the water-spraying maneuver of the riot police: "In the difficult situation of having to carry out water discharge for a purpose quite separate from its original use in crowd control, they were successful in injecting a certain amount of water into the spent-fuel storage pool, thereby acting as the forerunner to the water discharging operations of the Tokyo Fire Department and Self-Defense Forces."

They were saying, "The police going in to discharge water made the Fire and Disaster Management Agency, who had been dithering, make up their mind."[88]

There were doubts, however, about the operational effectiveness of involving the police in the water maneuvers. Referring to the riot police water trucks as "water-fired riot cannons," the U.S. NRC saw them as one more example of Japan's lack of earnestness in dealing with the crisis.[89]

In fact, the water maneuvers by the riot police were supported to a large degree by the SDF. Nakano told Kitazawa that he wanted to put an SDF chemical reconnaissance vehicle in the lead when the riot police went in. The SDF chemical reconnaissance vehicle had the radiation monitoring equipment that the riot police vehicles did not have.

"We'd be grateful if the SDF led the riot police in when they go to discharge . . . And we'd like you to accompany them back when they leave."[90]

Kitazawa refrained from an immediate answer. Nakano made the same request to Kantei. The Kantei requested that the SDF give priority to the required monitoring for moving the riot police water trucks. As a result, the SDF recalled the Central Special Weapons Protection Corps already waiting at the site all the way back to Fukushima Daini NPS to lead the police water trucks in.

Opinion had initially been strong among the SDF troops dispatched to the site that "we can't trust the radiation monitoring by TEPCO and NISA," and they had been conducting their own radiation monitoring. The police and the firefighters did not trust the TEPCO and NISA monitoring, either.

Monitoring by the SDF could be trusted. Why? Because the SDF were involved in the same water maneuvers from the ground and were carrying them out based on the monitoring by the Central Special Weapons Protection Corps.

The SDF chemical reconnaissance vehicle was at the head when the riot police moved in, and stayed at the site until their water operation was over.[91]

After the riot police, it was the SDF's turn.

SOMETIME AFTER THREE P.M., MARCH 17. Kitazawa ordered the SDF to inject water from the ground into the fuel pool at Unit 3.

Flight squadrons were mobilized from all bases in the Kanto area (Shimofusa, Atsugi, Kisarazu, Kasuminome, Hyakuri, Iruma) to transport fire engines to J-Village. The fire engines were special models designed for dealing with aircraft fires in airports. The air SDF was at the center of this operation. Oriki's command was brief.

"Get them all together by five a.m."

They got all of them to J-Village on time, despite the fact that the fire engines had only ever been driven inside airports and had never been out on public thoroughfares.

Participants in the onsite water operations were confined to older troops. The SDF operation started at 7:35 p.m. on March 17 and was completed at 8:09 p.m. They had used five fire engines.

On the following day, March 18, at 2:42 p.m., they recommenced discharging water into the fuel pool at Unit 3. Seven fire engines were mobilized. Because TEPCO gave priority to restoring power until two p.m., the water operation was delayed until then.[92]

However, when it came to spraying water, the SDF was no match for the fire department.

Although they mobilized eleven fire engines and injected fresh water, every time their tanks became empty, they had to go back to J-Village to fill up, and then move out again. This meant they could only discharge water once or so a day. In comparison, the fire department operation was able to continually draw up seawater and pump it out.

At one point, Kaieda instructed the SDF to "discharge three hundred tons of water a day." The best they could do if they mobilized all the fire engines at the same time and pumped out water in eight-hour stretches was seventy or eighty tons. Three hundred tons a day meant pumping four times for more than twenty-four hours a day, and was impossible.

Miyajima told Commander Yuki Imaura, who had reported this to him on the phone, "Just keep quiet and ignore it. Pay no attention."[93]

The SDF carried out a total of five water discharge maneuvers up until March 21.

NINE

The Hyper Rescue Squad

"THE FATE OF JAPAN IS DEPENDING ON YOU"

THE EVENING OF MARCH 16. Prime Minister Naoto Kan rang Yoshihiro Katayama, head of Ministry of Internal Affairs and Communications (MIC).

"Can't we dispatch Tokyo Met's Hyper Rescue Squad?"

"Well, you know we can't exactly order them."

Katayama was an ex-bureaucrat from the former Ministry of Home Affairs. He had later served as the governor of Tottori Prefecture. He was a professional among the professionals in the field of local government and governance. He had also served as the head of general affairs in the Fire and Disaster Management Agency at the Ministry of Home Affairs, and was knowledgeable about fire and disaster matters.

Katayama explained the legal difficulties: even though he was minister of internal affairs and communications, he could not issue an order, since the Tokyo Hyper Rescue Squad came under the jurisdiction of the Tokyo metropolitan government. Kan made many calls to Katayama later.

"Why won't the fire department help us?"

Each time, Katayama stated the official position that "this basically isn't a firefighting job," but promised he would "look into it."

After the SDF had abandoned their helicopter water drops, Kan set his sights on the Tokyo Fire Department's Hyper Rescue Squad. The Hyper Rescue Squad had a bending water-cannon tower vehicle that could discharge 3.8 tons of water per minute from a height of twenty-two meters, using a boom extension. They could use a pump called the Super Pumper to draw seawater in and connect this to the tower car. The Super Pumper was a special pump the Netherlands had developed for drainage work when dykes collapsed.

246

At the time of the Hanshin-Awaji earthquake, a fire engine that could send water into the quake zone from a distance of two kilometers was required. Since then, the Tokyo Fire Department had acquired three sets (each consisting of a pair of two pumps).

In the crisis management center in the basement of the Kantei, Tetsuro Ito, deputy chief cabinet secretary for crisis management, asked Tatsuya Kabutan, a deputy director of MIC's Fire and Disaster Management Agency, "You could get those tall water cannon trucks you use for fires in buildings, couldn't you?" Ito knew the fire department had them.

"What are we supposed to do if a fire breaks out in a high place in Tokyo?"

"What do you mean, what are you supposed to do? It can't be helped if that happens. It's not as if it happens every day, is it?"

On March 11, after the earthquake, Kabutan was the first of the members of the emergency operation team to arrive.

"The fire department isn't the police. The fire departments belong to the local government."

"The police are part of the local government, too!"

"No, they're not. You say they're local government police, but the top echelon is made up of national public servants. But you see, the fire department are local public servants all the way from the top to the bottom."

In the case of the police, officers of the rank of senior superintendent and above, including the prefectural police chiefs, were national public servants, but the fire department commissioner and directors were local public servants. Kabutan mentioned concerns about the chain of command, saying, "The fire department is at the forefront of regional government decentralization. I also think the fire department should be sent into Fukushima. And when the time comes, their job is to give up their lives. Members do sometimes die in the line of duty. But as to whether the state can give that order or not . . ."[1]

The Hyper Rescue Squad had already been mobilized once to extinguish a fire at Fukushima Daiichi NPS at 4:30 p.m. on March 12. Eight units, comprising twenty-eight members, had gone because they had received a request from MIC's Fire and Disaster Management Agency.

"Could we get the Tokyo Fire Department's Super Pumper to cool down the reactor? We want to use the ones they have in Tokyo and Sendai."

Fire Chief Yuji Arai of the Tokyo Fire Department had heard from a subordinate that such a request had come in from MIC's Fire and Disaster Management Agency. Apparently, METI had approached MIC.

Arai agreed, but on three conditions:

1. The units were to be provided with and led by a radiation expert

2. Better radiation protective outfits than the Tokyo Fire Department had were to be prepared

3. Stable iodine tablets were to be readied

MIC accepted all of these conditions.[2]

Just as they reached the Moriya Service Area (Tochigi Prefecture) on the Joban Expressway, they received a phone call from MIC.

"The request has been canceled."[3]

An explosion had taken place at Unit 1. The Fire Department had been contacted by NISA to be informed, "There's been an explosion. We're not sure yet what has exploded, but we withdraw our request."[4]

6:00 P.M. ON MARCH 12. Arai brought the squad members back to Tokyo. He was sure there would be future requests, however. They needed to prepare so they would be ready when the next request for the Hyper Rescue Squad came in.

There was a good chance that radiation would be higher at that time. They needed to carry out training in protective outfits as well as get ready to send out the special disaster trucks. These were vehicles with special equipment, including lead plating around the water tank to protect it from neutron and gamma radiation. They had been built ten years earlier, after the lessons of the 1999 Tokaimura criticality accident, when the fire engines could not get near because of the neutron radiation and gamma rays.

10:35 A.M. ON MARCH 15. Arai took a call from Nobuyasu Kubo, commissioner of the Fire and Disaster Management Agency.

"We have a reading of 400 millisieverts per hour on the west side of Unit 3. Operations will be extremely difficult, don't you think?"

Nevertheless, Arai conducted training exercises for the Hyper Rescue Squad in the dry riverbed of the Arakawa River and drew up a plan of action. As a result, he knew they could start pumping even at 400 millisieverts/hour if they had fifteen minutes.[5]

Sure enough, on March 16, a request came in from TEPCO, "We want you to lend us a special disaster response vehicle." He told TEPCO, "We'll hand it over after we've explained how to use it."

The problem was that although the fire department drove the vehicle to the handover point in Iwaki City, nobody from the TEPCO side showed up at the appointed time.[6] When they asked MIC's Fire and Disaster Management Agency, they were told, "The place is in a state of confusion, it's hopeless."

The fire departments were slow to get moving. This was because Nobuyasu Kubo, commissioner of the Fire and Disaster Management Agency, was a stickler for "procedures and order." Kubo put forward the following logic:

Dealing with a nuclear power plant disaster was, first and foremost, the job of the operator. Saving lives and extinguishing fires during a nuclear disaster was the job of the fire departments, but pumping water into spent-fuel pools was, by rights, the operator's job. If the operators could not do it, the state should. So, the correct course was for institutions of the state, such as the SDF and the riot police of the Metropolitan Police Force, to try first. They should not be asking the Tokyo Fire Department right off. After all, municipal fire departments were paid by local taxes. They did not receive a single cent from national taxes. Firefighters were local public servants employed by their respective cities and towns.

After the Great East Japan earthquake, firefighters from forty-four prefectures (out of forty-seven in all), including Okinawa, carried out rescue operations in the Tohoku region. One out of every five of the country's 158,000 firefighters was mobilized.

In short, the logic was that, in the case of firefighting, they were mobilized to go to fires every day; even if there was no fire, their ambulances were called out close to a hundred times a day. If they failed to respond to accidents in their home prefectures by leaving that work and going to support other prefectures, then, well, "In America, the residents would take us to court."

Kubo was made vice governor of Hiroshima Prefecture at the age of forty-one and had served five and a half years in that position. He knew every nook and cranny of local government. When he became commissioner of the Fire and Disaster Management Agency, he traveled around the country, visiting all the top firefighters (commissioners, fire chiefs, directors).

Learning from their inability to quickly dispatch firefighters from other prefectures at the time of the Hanshin-Awaji earthquake in January 1995, firefighting headquarters of large cities had been registered as emergency support fire brigades, and the law had been amended to allow the Fire and Disaster Management Agency commissioner to instruct their dispatch in times of need.

But an "instruction" was not an "order." It was closer to a "request." When making mobilization requests to several regional fire departments, Kubo had asked them "to enter the thirty-kilometer zone (from Fukushima Daiichi NPS)," but almost all of them replied, "Let us talk to the mayor," and after that, he had drawn a blank.

Of the fire departments in other prefectures, some had flown in their helicopters. However, since they had been exposed to radiation, some of them started clamoring for compensation.[7]

In the evening of March 17, Katayama once again received a call from Kan to request the mobilization of the Hyper Rescue Squad. He called Kubo.

"Listen, Kubo, Kan-san's been on the phone again. After all, it's the prime minister asking if they'll go. I've said I'd pass it on."

Kubo replied, "I was just speaking with Arai-san about things getting pretty close, but we concluded that there's nothing to do but have the prime minister phone Governor Ishihara and beg."

Katayama passed this on to Kan. The only way to break the impasse was for Kan to make a direct appeal to Shintaro Ishihara, Tokyo's governor. The problem was that Ishihara and Kan were like oil and water, ideologically. It would be a calamity if Kan made a wrong move and Ishihara lost his temper.

Around seven p.m. on March 17, Kan telephoned Yukihiko Akutsu (DPJ, Tokyo), a parliamentary secretary in the Cabinet Office. Akutsu had worked as Ishihara's secretary for close to ten years when he was in the Lower House in the 1980s and 1990s. He was close to Kan, having accepted his invitation to join the New Party Sakigake and the Democratic Party of Japan.

"We need to get water into the spent-fuel pools, and we need the cutting-edge pump trucks that Tokyo Met has. Would you ask Ishihara-san for me?"

With Akutsu bringing them together, Kan asked for Ishihara's cooperation, and, at approximately eight p.m. on March 17, Ishihara agreed.[8]

During this time, the Kantei and the Integrated Response Office were growing increasingly frustrated with the "fire department that wouldn't budge an inch." Kaieda had even asked Katayama, "Doesn't the authority to appoint (the Tokyo Fire Department fire chief) lie with the Fire and Disaster Management Agency?"

On hearing that, Kubo told his subordinates, "Even if you give an order, sometimes they don't go. In the end, it's not orders that move people. If you want to move people, you have to have the authority to either arrest them or appoint them. Apart from that, there's only love. The fire departments move out of love."

But in the end, it was not love that got the fire departments moving. It was decided by Kan bowing to Ishihara, and Ishihara giving the instruction to Arai. It was the officials from the old Ministry of Home Affairs that made the politicians follow "procedures and order." Katayama (entering the Ministry of Home Affairs in 1974), Kubo (entering in 1975), and Kabutan (entering in 1978) were all that kind of Home Affairs bureaucrats.

To use the expression of a Ministry of Internal Affairs and Communications official, the reason Kabutan stuck to his hard line was to bring about a situation where "the prime minister would say 'I'll bow to him.'"[9]

Around eight p.m. on March 17, Kan requested the dispatch to Ishihara and the latter accepted. At 8:30 p.m., Commissioner Kubo received a call from Fire Chief Arai.

"It's been decided between the prime minister and Katayama to ask the Tokyo Fire Department. You may hear about it from the governor."

At nine p.m., Arai phoned Tokyo governor Ishihara. He had been contacted by Tokyo's deputy governor just prior to that, and told, "I want you to call the governor."

"The prime minister has said they want the Tokyo Fire Department to go. I don't quite understand, but he said they couldn't get your cooperation. What's going on?"

"We've sent a unit. We've taken the special disaster response vehicle to the area as well. But TEPCO hasn't come to pick it up."

"I don't really understand what the prime minister was talking about, but I want you to do whatever you can to help."

This was Ishihara's instruction to Arai to mobilize.

10:00 P.M. This time, it was Ishihara who called Arai.

"I've spoken with the prime minister. He also seemed confused about the situation. Anyway, do what you can."

Meanwhile, Kan had contacted MIC Minister Katayama.

"I've shown the proper deference and called Ishihara-san, so I'm asking you to contact him, too."

"Yes, sir."

Katayama told Kubo to "let Arai-san know" that MIC had also approved the mobilization of the Hyper Rescue Squad.

At 12:50 a.m. on March 18, Kubo requested Arai to dispatch the Hyper Rescue Squad to Fukushima Daiichi NPS. This became the official instruction to mobilize the Hyper Rescue Squad.

At 3:30 a.m. on March 18, Arai mobilized the Hyper Rescue Squad from the Arakawa training base (139 members). He addressed them before they moved out:

"The metropolitan governor has just received a request from the prime minister for us to go into action. I order you into action. The fate of Japan is depending on you."

At the same time, Arai also said he wanted them to prioritize saving their own lives.

"To save your own life and that of your colleagues is to be able to save other lives."

It was the "three-lives motto" that the fire department taught all their firefighters. If the first responder did not save his own life, he would be unable to save others.

The squad arrived at Fukushima Daiichi NPS sometime after 5:30 p.m. on March 18. They could have arrived earlier, but TEPCO had not been preparing the site for water discharge during the early part of the day; instead, they had been trying to restore power. This was one of the reasons they had to wait until the late afternoon. While they were waiting, stable iodine tablets were distributed to and taken by all members.

The site was cluttered with debris and driftwood, and it was impossible to approach the shore. In addition, there was the "No. 3 west problem" on the western side of Unit 3, where the radiation dose was high.

They looked for a path to the shore, but it was 2.6 kilometers away and the Super Pumper would not reach. They had not been able to receive aerial shots of the entire site and the location of its facilities from TEPCO beforehand. They were told for the first time by the TEPCO staff when they arrived at the site that they could not get through to where the fire-extinguishing pipes were laid on site. They had to change their course.

The onsite level of radiation was 60 millisieverts/hour. At this level, each shift of the squad members could be extended a little. But when they went to the shore, the quay had been destroyed by the tsunami. They might not have been able to use the precious Super Pumper.

Judging that operations would be difficult, the captain told the team to withdraw. Just as the Hyper Rescue Squad were leaving the main gate, they were stopped by the guards and other TEPCO employees. They pleaded in unison:

"Please don't go."

"There's an Anti-Seismic Building. It's covered in lead plating. The ventilation's working, too."

This was the first the squad had heard of the existence of the Anti-Seismic Building.

"No, we can't hang around here forever."

7:04 P.M. The Hyper Rescue Squad left Fukushima Daiichi NPS and headed to J-Village, a soccer sports complex that was situated some twenty kilometers south of Fukushima Daiichi NPS in the town of Hirono.[10]

"WHY ISN'T THE FIRE DEPARTMENT RELEASING WATER?"

Information arrived at the Integrated Response Office that "today's water operation has been canceled." Unlike the police and the SDF, the Hyper Rescue Squad were carrying air cylinders to prevent internal exposure. The first report said, "They've fallen back to J-Village because they've run out of air in their cylinders."

Kaieda grew red in the face and was angry.

"Why isn't the fire department releasing water? . . . The Tokyo Fire Department are pros at releasing water! What's going to happen if the pros run? . . . If they don't have enough cylinders, why don't they leave those members behind and get other members in? The others are working with just masks, who do they think they are?"

In front of the videoconference screen, Kaieda said, "Anyway, make sure we have this long-awaited Hyper Rescue Squad pump in water today."

9:43 P.M. ON MARCH 18. Kaieda took the mike in his hand during the videoconference and started talking to Masao Yoshida, Fukushima Daiichi's site superintendent.

> *Kaieda:* "This is also an order from the prime minister, we have to have them pump in water tonight. This is really the request of the prime minister, and if they don't, you've already sent back the SDF, so we want you to urge the fire department to take responsibility for getting it done today."
>
> *Yoshida:* "We're thinking of several things here, but we have no way of contacting the fire department."
>
> *Kaieda:* "We've heard from rescue command that they've reached the site. They're having trouble with the hose extension. They don't seem to be able to hook up the hose and the fire engine properly. They're not releasing water, but they're at the site."
>
> *Yoshida:* "I don't think that's right."
>
> *Kaieda:* "Can you check just to be safe?"
>
> *Yoshida:* "Is the fire department in the plant? Now?"
>
> *Plant staff:* "They said they were going back to J-Village."

Yoshida had first learned from the five a.m. news on NHK that day that the Hyper Rescue Squad was on its way. He had appealed to Hosono that morning that it would be difficult to coordinate if they just turned up suddenly without any prior contact.

Hosono had replied to Yoshida, "There seems to have been some kind of misunderstanding, but Prime Minister Kan told Governor Ishihara that the government would like to ask for their help by all means. We didn't realize they would get there so fast . . ."

Kaieda's frustration was almost at a boiling point.

The fire department has tried to turn back many times. That's the limitation of local fire departments.

Kaieda sent a message to the site that if the fire department would not do it, they would have to be replaced by the SDF. The SDF liaison at the Integrated Response Office conveyed Kaieda's instruction to Masato Taura, head of the local coordination office, who was holed up in the local NERHQ in the Fukushima Prefectural Office. Taura reported it to Miyajima. Miyajima was calm.

"Even if the SDF replaces them now, it will take three or four hours. Don't you think it's better to get the Hyper Rescue Squad to do the job even if it takes a little more time?"

After so saying, he ordered Taura, "Give the Hyper Rescue Squad some encouragement!"

"Yes, sir!"

Taura shouted over the phone to the SDF liaison back at the Integrated

Response Office so everyone in the room could hear, "Are you listening? Tell the minister this. It'll take us two hours to remove the fire department's equipment and replace it, and another hour for the SDF to mobilize, so that's a total of three hours. If the fire department would do the job during that time, that would mean a hundred tons per hour. The SDF can't shift that kind of volume. Tell him that and explain it logically. And then tell him we absolutely can't do the same job as those whose principal occupation is water-spraying."

After Taura hung up, the captain of the fire department shook his hand and said, "Thank you."[11]

Both Kan and Kaieda were horrified at the information that "today's water operation has been canceled." Arai had informed Kaieda of it directly over the phone. All Kaieda could do was badger him to "do it anyway." After that, he received a call from Kan as well.

"No matter what, do it quickly."

Arai replied, "It's in the hands of the field staff . . . the field's thinking about it."

By "field" he meant the Hyper Rescue Squad's frontline-base at J-Village. Kan's voice grew gruff.

"Do it tonight!"

A little later, Arai received a call from Ishihara.

"The prime minister's complaining about something, has something happened?"

Kan felt annoyed by Arai's response. Kan had phoned Ishihara, letting slip his grievances.

"I have also had the prime minister complaining. What can be done?"

Arai reported developments to him. Ishihara was Arai's boss. Not Kan. Immediately after this, Arai received a message from the frontline base at J-Village: "Reentry."

11:11 P.M., MARCH 18. The Hyper Rescue Squad reentered the site. There was some faint moonlight. The TEPCO staff giving road directions were all dressed in white protective suits. Steam was rising from Unit 3. The radiation was around 100 millisieverts in the vicinity of the debris. They had all been issued with oxygen respirators.

They parked the command vehicle in front of the Anti-Seismic Building. It was two kilometers to the shore. Since there was wreckage everywhere, they could not extend the pipe as it was. They decided to split it into seven segments, carry them, then reattach them.

"Manhole, this side."

"Just left of center."

With four of them extending by hand the seven segments of hose, each being 350 meters long and weighing a hundred kilograms, they carried it to the shore. In the words of the squad members, they "laid it by hand."

They checked with each other. "60 millisieverts."

"Currently, 60 millisieverts."

A shift of one meter made the radiation spike.

Narumi Suzuki, the maneuver commander, was watching the operation at a distance of some five meters from Unit 3. Suzuki was the commander of the Fire Rescue Task Force Maneuver Unit at No. 3 Headquarters (Tokyo Fire Department's third fire district headquarters) in Hatagaya, Shibuya, Tokyo.

Unit 3 looked like a terrible mountain. He had heard there was a chance that it would explode again. The wind was blowing in from the mountains toward the sea. Every now and again it would change direction and blow in from the sea. There was something eerie about the rustling of the nearby trees. He felt a chill go down the back of his spine. Unit 2 loomed in the background.[12]

At last, the hose was connected. The twenty-two-meter high, refracted water discharger was ready.

At 12:30 a.m. on March 19, water started gushing out of the nozzle aimed at the pool. Steam poured up from the middle. They discharged sixty tons of water in approximately twenty minutes.

Yoshida had been watching the video footage of the activities of the Hyper Rescue Squad that were being shown in the ERC of the Anti-Seismic Building, and clapped his hands loudly when the water came gushing out. Oohs and aahs were heard in the ERC. Takeyuki Inagaki, head of the recovery team, thought, "They'll be fine with that angle."

He had been thoroughly dispirited by the water pistol–like injection up until then by the Self-Defense Forces. However, things were different now. He felt a sense of relief that "it's in, we're saved."

Following this, the Hyper Rescue Squad pumped in 2,430 tons of water from 2:05 p.m. until 3:40 p.m. on March 19. This saw a swift drop in the temperature and a rapid reduction in the radiation dose.[13]

On the advice of radiology experts, the Hyper Rescue Squad paid close attention to radiation protection. Shingo Akashi, head of the Radiation Emergency Medicine Research Center at the National Institute of Radiological Sciences (NIRS), dispatched radiation management personnel and supplied the squad members with stable iodine, instructing, "Please take it just before departing from J-Village." Yoshihiro Yamaguchi, professor of emergency medicine at Kyorin University's School of Medicine and a radiology expert, was on standby around the clock during the water discharge operations. He was a special disaster adviser to the Tokyo Fire Department.

On March 18, he visited the site with the squad members. He gave them all iodine. He also measured their exposure and instructed them on safety management. (Yamaguchi was subsequently to look after the onsite radiation management of the squad a total of five times.)

The whole time he was on standby at the frontline base in J-Village, Yamaguchi wore the same protective gear as the Hyper Rescue Squad. More than anything else, he feared the reactor and fuel pool exploding. There was no emergency hospital nearby that could treat the squad members if they had been exposed to a high dose of radiation from an explosion.

In many cases, radiation medical hospitals were located in municipalities that had nuclear power plants. Government allocations for training were only available to municipalities where such hospitals were located. With the twenty-kilometer resident evacuation order, however, all of these hospitals were closed. Many members of the squad headed to the site battling the fear that they might not be coming back alive.

Yamaguchi, who accompanied them, felt the same way. He had been in his university lab when he was suddenly told, "Jump in, professor," and taken directly to Fukushima in a fire department vehicle. In the vehicle, he sent a text message from his mobile phone to one of his senior colleagues, whom he respected a great deal.

"I find myself suddenly on the way to Fukushima. I don't know if I'll come home safely because it's a nuclear response. I'm sorry to ask you this, but would you watch over Sakiko until she's grown? Please."

Sakiko was his six-year-old daughter.[14]

On the night of March 19, the Hyper Rescue Squad returned to Tokyo, where they held a press conference. When Troop Leader Toyohiko Tomioka was asked, "It must have been tough?" he replied, "It was different from our usual training, but I was sure with these members we would accomplish the mission. It was hardest on the squad members."

And then he choked up. After some silence, tears overflowed from Tomioka's big eyes. Top members of the SDF's Joint Staff Office were watching this "tearful interview" with mixed emotions. One of them revealed around the time, "It would have been great if you could have said 'mission accomplished,' like the end title of a movie, and closed the curtain, but that wasn't the case for us, because the crisis was only just beginning. At the SDF, we all told each other we weren't going to have any flashy PR."[15]

THE SDF MOVES CENTER STAGE

Hosono had an extremely overpowering sense of crisis around this time, feeling that "If the fuel pool runs dry, Japan will perish." They had to keep pumping water no matter what. *Now, Japan is in an emergency.* At the site, however, the police and the SDF were squabbling over who would go in first for the water maneuver.

The police and fire department would be placed under the command of the SDF for the water discharge operation. This would allow for a more agile and efficient rollout of the maneuver. This was how Hosono assessed it.

On the morning of March 18, Hosono issued "Basic Policy for the Water Discharge Operation on March 18" on behalf of Goshi Hosono, special adviser to the prime minister. It ran:

"Basic Policy for Water Discharge Operations Today and Henceforth" is the following:

1. Aiming for a time slot of 2:00 p.m. to 3:00 p.m. today, the SDF fire-fighting unit will discharge water to Unit 3, and this will be followed by a discharge from the U.S. military high-pressure water cannons.

2. After withdrawing from the discharge activity outlined above in Item 1 (approximately 3:30 p.m.), the Rescue Task Force of the Tokyo Fire Department (the Hyper Rescue Squad) will discharge water to Unit 3.

3. Future water discharge and decontamination activities, including those outlined above, will be under the overall command of the SDF.

As a special adviser to the prime minister, Hosono was sending out directives about the water discharge operations almost every day around this period. Water discharge from the U.S. military high-pressure water cannons did not mean that the U.S. military were actually doing the pumping, but that TEPCO staff were using high-pressure water cannons the U.S. military had lent them.

However, Hosono was thinking that, rather than sending off daily instructions like "ripping pages from a calendar," they had to find some way of instilling SDF command more systematically.

Is not putting the beach—as well as the water discharge and J-Village— under the control of the SDF the only practical way to go?

"The beach" was the entire surrounding area of the Fukushima Daiichi NPS on the Pacific Ocean coast, which was referred to as Hamadori (Beach Road).

Hosono asked Ito to draw up a draft text for the coordination of the water discharge operation under SDF command and the regulation thereof. Ito had already privately approached Tatsuya Kabutan, member of the emergency operation team and deputy director of the Fire and Disaster Management Agency; Yasuhiko Nishimura, security director for the National Police Agency; and Shuichi Sakurai, director general of the Bureau of Operational Policy at the Ministry of Defense, and together they were already working on "overall coordination."

Regarding the water discharge, only the SDF were keeping the same unit in place. Ito deemed it appropriate for the SDF to act as coordinator here.

SDF officials were also confused by this "instruction." Chief of staff of the Ground Self-Defense Force, Yoshifumi Hibako, suspected that politicians did not understand the weight that "the right to command" carries. "When we use the phrase 'the right to command,' it indicates our right to determine whether the force members could live or die. Are they asking the onsite SDF commanders to order the firefighters and police squads to discharge the water even though they might end up dying? We cannot do that even if the sun were to rise in the west."

Sakurai replied, "That's fine if the police and the fire department agree. But I'll need the minister to sign off . . . I'll take it back with me and then give you our answer."

Kabutan emphasized the point that "the Fire and Disaster Management Agency has no authority to issue instructions to municipal fire departments." He persisted in saying, "That's not written anywhere in the Fire Services Act."

What he was saying was that the Fire and Disaster Management Agency did not have the authority to instruct the Tokyo Fire Department's Hyper Rescue Squad to place itself under the command of the SDF.

Nishimura pointed out the difficulty of having the National Police Agency direct municipal police departments.[16]

On March 18, Hosono placed a call to Akihisa Nagashima, a member of the Lower House (DPJ, Tokyo). On the previous day, March 17, after Kan had recalled Yoshito Sengoku—who had resigned from the post of chief cabinet secretary in the aftermath of a motion of censure—as his deputy chief cabinet secretary, Nagashima joined Sengoku's team. Nagashima was the top DPJ expert on defense issues. He had served as vice minister of defense in the Hatoyama administration. Hosono was counting on Nagashima's network at the ministry, and especially with the SDF.

The only way to get on top of the Fukushima Daiichi nuclear accident was to have the SDF play a leading role. And that required recognizing the command authority of the SDF with respect to response activities in the field.

Hosono conveyed his thoughts to Kan. Kan agreed and asked Hosono to speak on the quiet with Satoshi Maeda, an executive assistant to the prime minister, originally from the Ministry of Defense.

Kan told Maeda, "I want you to go to TEPCO. We may need new contingency legislation to specify the role of general coordination by the SDF. I want you to help Hosono look into it."

Nagashima returned to the Integrated Response Office at TEPCO in the evening.

SOMETIME AFTER EIGHT P.M. ON THE SAME DAY. The second-floor conference room at TEPCO.

When Maeda arrived at TEPCO, Hosono, Nagashima, and Yasunari Umezu—a secretary to Michihiko Kano, the minister of agriculture, forestry, and fisheries—whom Nagashima had called upon as his younger classmate at Keio University, were there. Umezu had previously worked for the Ministry of Defense.

Maeda felt a little ill at ease.

It's like I've been taken hostage or something.

Hosono asked, was it not possible to have the SDF play a decisive role under current legislation? What should they make of that? Umezu was the first to answer. He had the statute book in one hand.

"I don't think you'd need new emergency legislation to define the command authority of the SDF. I think we should be able to do quite a lot if we take a good look at the Act on Special Measures Concerning Nuclear Emergency Preparedness."

Maeda commented,

"I think you're right. We can find the roots in NEPA. And if we do, then there's no need to revise the Self-Defense Forces Law."

Maeda also held a copy of the statute book in his hand.

However, when it came to issues related to private rights, such as eviction orders or disposing of abandoned cars, no matter how you read the Self-Defense Forces Law, it could not be done legally. There is no martial law in Japan.

Hosono wanted to sit down together with the TEPCO side to discuss the specifics of putting Fukushima Daiichi NPS under the control of the SDF, and dealing with the nuclear accident efficiently.

"By the way, we had Hironaka-san here today, but he left extremely worried. Would you talk to him, Nagashima-san, and ask him if he could come again?"

The Hironaka he was speaking of was Masayuki Hironaka, director of the Operations Department at the Joint Staff Office. His job involved the mobilization of troops, and he was responsible for operations. In short, he was the head of strategy. Hironaka had a calm and reassuring disposition. He was an excellent strategic thinker. He was the air SDF's leading light.

Hironaka had been to TEPCO once that night, at Hosono's request. Before going, he had asked Chief of Staff of the Joint Staff Ryoichi Oriki's permission, who told him to stop by. When he met with Hosono and Nagashima, he had been asked his opinion on raising the radiation dose for operatives dealing with the accident to 500 millisieverts.

"That doesn't matter. We're the SDF. If we're told to go, we go."

Hosono said, "No one else is willing to place their lives on the line. There's only the SDF left, who are prepared to move."

There was still not enough coordination over discharging water between the SDF, the police, and the fire department. Hosono's face was showing fatigue. Hironaka was not sure what Hosono was asking of the SDF. All kinds of orders, such as removing debris and so on, were coming into the SDF. Saying, "Please make your requirements clear," Hironaka headed back to the ministry.[17]

"WE'RE NOT A JACK-OF-ALL-TRADES"

After about thirty minutes, however, Hironaka received another call from Nagashima. "Can you come back?"

He had shuttled back to TEPCO, accompanied by a section chief. It was after eleven p.m. This time, Katsumata, Muto, and the head of TEPCO's engineers were sitting across from them. The members on this side were Hosono, Nagashima, Umezu, as well as Hironaka and his section chief, plus Hosono's aide, Noriaki Ozawa (an ex-METI man). They took the elevator upstairs to a larger room. The discussion began. Hosono was the first to speak. His tone was one of polite appeal.

"I've been working with the police and the fire department all week long. I've been asking for someone else to do it for me. I've spent all week asking, but I've gotten nowhere. The only people who can save the nation from this crisis are the SDF. The SDF are the only ones we can ask."

Hosono felt the situation was such that they had no choice other than to have the SDF manage a fairly wide area around TEPCO's nuclear power plant site.

"But if we want the SDF to do the water discharging and clean up the rubble and everything else, we may well have to ask the SDF to take over management of the whole plant. How can we resolve this problem? I'd like us to come up with a solution. That's why I've asked you all to assemble here now."

Hironaka could not believe his ears when he heard Hosono say, "Ask the SDF to take over management of the whole plant." Katsumata also looked shocked.[18]

At Hosono's urging, Katsumata was the first to respond.

"At a time like this, we'd hope we could have their support . . . their cooperation as much as possible. I'd like to renew our request."

Hironaka replied. His demeanor was cool.

"What's happening at the nuclear plant now? What about the radiation levels? As long as you're not forthcoming with detailed data, we can't cooperate even if we'd like to. I'd like you to provide more information. And to go through the proper channels."

Katsumata told Hironaka, "At any rate, couldn't you remove the debris now? If you're good enough to get rid of the debris, we can get the cooling equipment back up and running at Unit 2."

The words "remove the debris" had apparently got under Hironaka's skin.

"No, no, we do what other people can't do. What only the SDF can do. We're not a jack-of-all-trades. We'll do the water discharging, but removing debris is not our job. You people at TEPCO, you're the operator, surely you should get rid of the rubble."

Katsumata did not seem to be aware of what was seething inside Hironaka when he said "We're not a jack-of-all-trades."

"Couldn't you stop discharging water while we're carrying out repairs (on the cooling equipment)? We can fix the suppression chamber if we have three days. So, we'd like you to suspend discharging water for three days. The onsite superintendent says they'll risk their lives doing it. The request is a sincere one from the site."

One of the people in the meeting let out an involuntary groan.

It might be better if they could get the power back. But Prime Minister Kan's got his life staked on pumping in the water. I don't know whether he's aware of this or not, but he keeps rattling on about the power, not the water. I don't know whether he's just insensitive or selfish . . .

Distrust of TEPCO by the SDF and the Ministry of Defense had been mounting. Even when TEPCO had sent out a virtual SOS begging the SDF to get water into Unit 3 on the morning of March 14, they gave them absolutely no information about the reactors. And on March 15, despite the fact that getting water into the fuel pools was at a critical stage, TEPCO still insisted on restoring power.

On March 16, the Joint Staff Office even had engineers from TEPCO come to Ichigaya to hold a meeting about the water maneuver, but the TEPCO participants could not give them a proper answer on whether they should add boric acid or if just seawater would be fine, and had to keep calling Head Office.

It was only at 12:00 a.m. on March 17 that a detailed analysis of the conditions at all the reactors from Unit 1 to Unit 6, as well as the fuel pools, was delivered to the SDF. This was the first time TEPCO had handed over any decent information to the SDF. Hironaka countered Katsumata.

"What I have just heard is completely different from our understanding of the situation. You can't hold on without pumping in water. The only option is to keep getting water in. Discharging water mustn't be stopped. The U.S. military is also extremely concerned about this."

Katsumata turned to Hosono and said, "We're also working with the U.S. experts. They say it'll be all right to stop the water. We're going to talk with them again tomorrow."

Hosono responded.

"We're working with the U.S. as well. And we'll be comparing notes tomorrow, too."

Hironaka inquired of Katsumata, "Just supposing we did stop discharging water for three days, and you were going to try to restore power, how exactly would you go about it? What sort of plan do you have?"

"We have a plan drawn up. I'll put it forward to you. I'll make sure we can do that by tomorrow afternoon, say."

Hironaka nipped him in the bud here. There was no way they could stop discharging water. He probably felt he had to make this absolutely clear again. As if to make doubly sure, he said, "We've ignored our own airport safety by yanking out our fire engines and bringing them to you. I don't know what'll happen if there's an accident at an airfield, but now is not the time for me to say such a thing."

He was emphasizing the fact that they had assembled a huge number of fire engines from SDF air bases to Fukushima Daiichi, and all were ready for the water discharge.

The discussion ranged as far as who was to be in charge of the water maneuvers at the power plant. The issue was, in extreme terms, "The SDF should take control of the reactors." Hironaka's position, however, was clear.

"We're a military organization. We aren't capable of controlling and running a nuclear power plant."

Katsumata's reply was equally clear.

"No, we'll handle that. It has to be us or it can't be managed. That's quite right."

Katsumata's words might well have been implying, *As you can see, we've been at the mercy of panic-stricken politicians from the Kantei. What a relief to finally speak to someone sensible!*

In fact, the SDF had made preparations for shifting the rubble, bringing in two tanks as far as J-Village. It was at 6:10 a.m. on March 21 that a trailer, which had departed from the Eastern District Forces' Camp Komakado in Shizuoka Prefecture, loaded with one renovated tank and two Type-74 tanks, arrived at J-Village.

They were equipped with blades for pushing the wreckage. They also had high neutron-protective capabilities.

MARCH 19. The prime minister's office at the Kantei. Hosono, along with Nagashima, was meeting with Kan. Hosono reported on the previous day's meeting and strongly recommended that the SDF be given the authority to command and carry out the water operation.

Kan said, "I've instructed that. But the prime minister doesn't have the authority to command the Fire and Disaster Management Agency or the chairman of the National Public Safety Commission . . ."

Edano intervened from the side.

"Wouldn't it be okay if we issued instructions in writing?"

Kan nodded, "Yeah, let's write something."

When Nagashima left the prime minister's office, he called Umezu and told him to come to the Kantei.

"The prime minister has agreed to issue instructions giving the SDF authority to command. We're going to draw up some instructions for the sake of the country. I'd like you to write a draft straight away."

Drafting the instructions proved difficult. In contrast to the draft Ito, deputy chief cabinet secretary for crisis management, had drawn up on the quiet, this was to be a weighty document issued in the name of the director general (the prime minister) of the Nuclear Emergency Response Headquarters.

It was not just the National Police Agency and the Fire and Disaster Management Agency who shook their heads. The attitude of the Ministry of Defense was vague. Kitazawa was reluctant, if anything. Oriki, however, advocated a positive position. Oriki told Kitazawa in no uncertain terms:

"It's no good everyone doing their own thing. I think it'll be difficult for any institution that doesn't do things organizationally. I think it should be left up to the SDF."

Kitazawa was also aware that they had no choice but to give the SDF a significant role in order to overcome the crisis. Kitazawa clearly remembered how the SDF had maintained regional stability and residents' peace of mind when they had been called in for decontamination operations and resident evacuation in 2010, at the time of the swine flu scare in Miyazaki Prefecture, while the local governments had proved incapable of managing the crisis.

He acknowledged that when local governments no longer functioned, the SDF had to go in their place. Kitazawa was also thinking that he wanted the Ministry of Defense and the SDF to field and coordinate the requests for support that were flooding in incoherently from the Kantei, government ministries and agencies, as well as local municipalities. And yet, he still felt a psychological barrier to a development that would have other ministries and agencies placed "under the command" of the SDF.

Prompted by Oriki's words, he finally decided to give his support.

Kabutan, at the basement crisis management center, was not happy with the draft of the prime minister's instructions. He thought the draft Ito had quietly drawn up on March 18 was far better. This was because he felt it expressed well the fact that the SDF could only carry out overall coordination on the general agreement of all ministries and agencies, and, so, was not "subject to interpretation."

Compared to that, he thought the parliamentary initiated draft had the feel of placing the other ministries under the command of the SDF at their beck and call.

This does not correspond to my instructions from the ministry. I can't possibly accept it.

He got to his feet and started to leave the room. Ito stood and called him back.

"Where do you think you're going in the midst of the discussion?"

"I'm going back to the ministry to consult with the minister. I'll send the director general or someone to replace me."

From the perspective of Hosono and the other parliamentary members at the Kantei, however, yes, they had had Ito draw something up, but what came back (in the words of one of Hosono's aides) was a draft "where you couldn't tell who was in charge of what because everyone had to be treated equally in keeping with the traditional relationship between the bureaucracy." The draft had been sent back and they had been told to revise it.

"It's a time of emergency, it won't work unless you make the SDF leading position clearer. Fix it."

Kansei Nakano, chairman of the National Public Safety Commission, still resisted.

"The fate of Japan lies in the balance. Please."

It was the Fire and Disaster Management Agency that resisted to the very last. However, Katayama, who had initially seemed reluctant, supported it, saying, "That's right."

Katayama told Kan, "However, I do have a condition."

"I don't want the fire departments to be shamed. I want a stop put to the abuse the firefighters are experiencing on site."

Kan replied contritely, "Yes."

Yuji Arai, fire chief at the Tokyo Fire Department, received another call from Kan. He was asked by Kan to "fall in under the command of the SDF."

Katayama also told Hosono what he had told Kan. When Hosono passed the two points—that "there is to be no shaming and no abuse"—on to the Ministry of Defense liaison at the Integrated Response Office, Colonel Shunji Yoshino, the latter stated clearly, "Yes sir, I will pass on the message to exercise caution. But I think that concern is unnecessary, since we are all cooperating in performing our duties at the site."

The draft instructions were rewritten many times. The term "under the command" of the SDF in the initial version was struck out and replaced by "overall coordination."

There was still a sense of doubt among some members of the emergency operation team at the crisis management center. All well and good for the bureaucrats to create a consensus among parliamentarians who could not agree, but it looked to some of them as if the parliamentarians were pre-empting the fruits of a consensus built up by the bureaucrats, and presenting it as their own political initiative.[19]

On March 20, Kan called Kitazawa, Nakano, and Katayama, among others, into the prime minister's office and discussed coordination between the various ministries and agencies over the water operation at Fukushima Daiichi NPS. When he asked Kitazawa to approve that the SDF would take charge of overall coordination, Katayama responded, "That's fine, fine. Please do it. I'm asking you."

Before that, Oriki had phoned Kubo, and when he said, "I hope I have your understanding that we're going to assume overall coordination," Kubo had answered, "Of course, I understand. Please do it." Oriki and Kubo were on speaking terms.

The "instructions" addressed to the commissioner of the National Police Agency, the commissioner of the Fire and Disaster Management Agency, the minister of defense, the governor of Fukushima Prefecture, and the president of Tokyo Electric Power Company, in the name of the director general (the cabinet prime minister) of the Nuclear Emergency Response Headquarters, were later issued:

1. Regarding the specific implementation guidelines for onsite operations in the facilities of the Fukushima Daiichi NPS, including water discharge, observation, and other necessary tasks, these are to be decided by the Self-Defense Forces, who are to play a central role in the local coordination office, and to coordinate with the Tokyo Electric Power Company and the relevant administrative agencies.

2. Regarding the implementation of tasks in accordance with these guidelines, this is to be managed centrally in the local coordination office by the Self-Defense Forces dispatched to the site.

To use Kitazawa's words, "This was the first attempt of its kind in the history of the Self-Defense Forces that they were to perform a mission with the relevant agencies, such as fire departments and the police, placed under their command."

When Hosono and Nagashima called Hironaka in, they had called the Joint Staff Office directly without getting Kitazawa's stamp of approval, and had gone ahead with drafting the prime minister's "instructions." A sharp-eyed Ministry of Defense desk-working "suit," holed up in the In-tegrated Response Office as a liaison officer, had spotted Hironaka going into TEPCO.

The information reached Kitazawa's ears immediately. A senior member of the Joint Staff Office was meeting with TEPCO and the Kantei without reporting to the minister. Kitazawa was not happy. "He's off, doing as he pleases."

He called Oriki into his office immediately and cautioned him. Oriki bowed his head, saying, "Yes, sir. It won't happen again."

The next day, he called Hironaka in and told him, "You've been caught out!"[20]

RAISING THE DOSE LIMIT

On March 14, the government decided to raise the permissible radiation exposure in times of emergency operations from 100 millisieverts to 250 millisieverts per annum. The dose limit was set at 50 millisieverts/year in law by the government. However, this meant that no operations could be carried out. Would it not be possible to amend the law in line with international standards?

The TEPCO liaison at the Kantei had approached NISA with this idea.[21] Haruki Madarame, chairman of the Nuclear Safety Commission, was quick to catch on.

In the 1990 recommendations of the International Commission on Radiological Protection (ICRP), in times of emergency such as when a serious accident had occurred, exposure from 500 to 1,000 millisieverts/year was to be permitted, and if response was not possible even then, there were some countries that applied the rule of no upper limit in the case of volunteers.

Madarame explained this and proposed that the limit be raised to 500 millisieverts. The TEPCO side, however, shied away from this, saying that raising it to that level would, on the contrary, intimidate the onsite workers and no work would get done. It was decided to split the difference and set it at 250 millisieverts.

However, the Nuclear Safety Commission (NSC) secretariat admonished Madarame that raising the dose limit was not the job of the NSC.[22]

Finally, as a result of the Ministry of Health, Welfare, and Labor having the Labor Standards Bureau look into the matter, they received the answer that it was "all right," and the change was implemented.[23]

This change increased the number of hours any given worker could work at the site. However, after the explosion in Unit 2 on the morning of March 15, radiation had grown even higher. If the limit was to stay at 250 millisieverts/year, the areas where they could not work would quickly expand.

On March 16, Toshiso Kosako, a professor at the Graduate School of Tokyo University, who had been appointed as special adviser to the cabinet secretariat, suggested to Hosono that it be raised to 500 millisieverts/year using the ICRP standard as a point of reference. With Kan's approval,

Hosono began to lay the groundwork for raising the limit to 500 millisieverts/year.

On March 17, Hosono asked Nagashima to act as his lobbyist. Nagashima made the rounds to Takeshi Erikawa, president of the National Personnel Authority; Yoko Komiya, vice minister of health, welfare, and labor; and Motohisa Ikeda, senior vice minister at METI, sounding them out. There was no opposition. He had received their approval using the phrase "It's the wish of the Kantei."[24]

6:30 P.M. OF THE SAME DAY. Kan gathered in his office Ritsuo Hosokawa, minister of health, welfare, and labor; Banri Kaieda, METI minister; Toshimi Kitazawa, minister of defense; and Kansei Nakano, chairman of the National Public Safety Commission, to hear their opinions about raising the limit again. Kitazawa and Nakano were cautious at this meeting. Kitazawa informed Kan of his opposition later that night.[25]

Had they not only just raised the limit from 100 to 250 millisieverts/year a mere one day before? What had changed so much in the space of that day? Why did it have to be raised again? None of this had been explained. He had his doubts that this might just be the start of a very slippery slope. Another fact that made Kitazawa wary was that if the limit was raised to 500 millisieverts/year, it might well interfere with the SDF's rightful mission of saving lives by dragging them deeper into nuclear reactor–related operations.[26]

Oriki was also opposed to raising the limit to 500 millisieverts/year. An "Opinion Inquiry" was distributed at the Joint Staff Office. Oriki showed it to the three chiefs of staff, but they were all negative. The Joint Staff Office believed it was still possible to accomplish their mission at 250 millisieverts/year.[27]

How to interpret the "dose range" and how to measure it, these were difficult questions.

In the nuclear accident at Fukushima Daiichi NPS, TEPCO employees suffered exposure and were taken to the National Institute of Radiological Science (NIRS) in Inage, Chiba.

The Japan Atomic Energy Agency (JAEA) had measured the exposure using a portable whole-body counter (WBC). The results showed between six hundred and seven hundred millisieverts. The employees had been transferred to NIRS because "they might still have iodine inside them."

When TEPCO was informed of this, they were extremely dissatisfied, saying, "Give us pinpoint figures."

Shingo Akashi, head of the Radiation Emergency Medicine Research Center, told them, "Of course, it's better to have nice numbers. It's just that you usually don't get pinpoint figures. You get a range."

The TEPCO radiation management officer still insisted, "Give me a single figure, please."

In particular, there was resistance to releasing a figure over 500 millisieverts. Akashi went to TEPCO Head Office from Chiba and spoke with the radiation management officer in the evening of that day. Akashi said in an easy to understand manner, "From a medical standpoint, overestimation is permissible, but underestimation isn't. It's not to the person's advantage for us to underestimate. That isn't permissible."

However, the TEPCO officer would not back down. If it does not exceed 500 millisieverts per year, it would remain within the range recommended by the ICRP. But as the government and experts were starting to consider raising the limit to 500 millisieverts, he was concerned that TEPCO would be criticized for violating the rules if figures were to exceed 500 millisieverts. Even after Akashi went home, the dialogue continued with the radiation manager. In the heat of the debate, they cursed at each other over the phone until 2:30 a.m.[28]

After consulting Kan, Hosono had been quietly looking into introducing a standard of over 500 millisieverts. It was an "unlimited" limit.

When Kosako had mentioned to Hosono the ICRP's 500 millisieverts standard, Kosako handed him the ICRP's Publication 103 (2007) that touched on this matter. Reading that document, an "unlimited" system for informed volunteers was described.

"Reference levels: No dose restrictions if benefit to others outweighs rescuer's risk."[29]

(ICRP, Annals of the ICRP, ICRP Publication 103, the 2007 Recommendations of the International Commission on Radiological Protection, volume 37, nos. 2–4, 2007)

It was written that rescue activities were possible even in environments that exceeded the limit if they were on a voluntary basis. This was a rule, however, for "cases of rescuing life," while the case this time of flying in close by helicopter to conduct water drops was different.[30]

Still, Hosono was looking for some way to apply this. Kitazawa, however, was vehemently opposed.[31] The "unlimited" volunteer system was one that, by rights, only applied to rescuing lives. What was being asked of the SDF at the moment, however, was part of an operation to stabilize the fuel pools and reactors.

What could be done even if they did volunteer and jump in? The Ministry of Defense's secretariat was also negative, while the Ministry of Defense's top cadres opposed it head-on.

"If we did introduce a volunteer system and no one volunteered, we'd be criticized as an organization full of wimps. And if we honored volunteers with medals, it'd create an atmosphere of social pressure similar to suicide pilots. We'd be in real trouble if anyone like the Three Brave Soldiers turned up (a 1932 attack by three soldiers in Shanghai that was glorified in the press and ostensibly paved the way for other desperate suicide attacks). And it would mean calling for volunteers who know nothing about radiation exposure."[32]

DORAEMON

10:00 A.M., MARCH 20. The graduation ceremony of the National Defense Academy in Yokosuka. Kitazawa arrived at the academy in an SDF helicopter. Usually all four chiefs of staff—Joint, Ground, Maritime, and Air—were in attendance. The SDF was in the middle of its water discharging operations at Fukushima Daiichi NPS. Accordingly, they stayed behind in the ministry, and it was the deputy chiefs of staff, including Vice Chief of Staff of the Joint Staff Katsutoshi Kawano, who were there.

Kitazawa was chatting with Kawano in the waiting room.

"Whenever Oriki shows up, that hothead Kan always gets in a confoundedly good mood."

He was saying that whenever he went to the prime minister's office in the company of Oriki, Kan always suddenly brightened up. While they passed the time chatting about this and other topics, Kan arrived in the Super Puma.

Kimito Nakae, vice minister of defense, was one of the senior officials at the Ministry of Defense, who thought, "At this time of crisis, it's highly unlikely the prime minister will be able to come to Yokosuka," but Kan had turned up.[33] Kan gave the prime minister's address during the ceremony.

"In the face of this catastrophe, the whole of the Self-Defense Forces are carrying out relief and support activities on a scale never seen in the past. I am not only proud of everyone in the Self-Defense Forces who are doing everything in their power to rescue stranded people, carry relief supplies, and conduct the water discharge at the risk of life at the nuclear power plant. I would also like to pay tribute from the bottom of my heart to everyone in their families supporting them."

The words came from his heart. When his address was over, it was greeted by loud applause. On his way back in the helicopter, Kan let his emotions run somewhat.

A week has passed since then, it was this very Super Puma that I was in.

He was thinking of when he had visited Fukushima Daiichi on March 12.

We've managed to hold out for this week thanks to the actions of the 100,000 SDF troops in the disaster area. You can count on them.

More than anything else, it was the water drop activities on that morning of March 17. That was the first turnaround. That maneuver completely changed the Japanese government's approach. It was after the Self-Defense Forces that the police and the fire departments became involved in the water discharging.[34]

Kitazawa had given his top officials, including Nakae, a glimpse of his conversation with Kan.

"The SDF comes up with all sorts of things when you ask them. Just like Doraemon (a cartoon robotic cat with a magic pocket from which he produces a huge range of gadgets). That's what the PM said."[35]

Voices of ridicule and mockery were heard from people who had taken Kan for a left-wing activist about his sudden transformation into a fan of the SDF. Strong fears existed at the Ministry of Defense and the SDF when the Democratic administration came into being in 2009. They felt foreign policy and security to be the DPJ's Achilles' heel. When Kitazawa was appointed minister of defense, he gave the following address:

"We must never repeat the mistakes of our history. The first step on the way to taking the country to the brink of collapse was the emergence of a military that did not obey the direction of the government and an emasculated government and parliament that couldn't control the military. Based on this lesson, ensuring civilian control under the political leadership of the Hatoyama Cabinet is of the utmost importance." (September 17, 2010)

Kitazawa had been one of the students who had marched, shouting, "Down with the treaty!" in the anti-security treaty demonstrations of 1960. As head of the Foreign Relations Committee when the DPJ was in opposition, he had often shown a tough stance toward the Ministry of Defense and the SDF.

It was a fact that the SDF had greeted Kitazawa as minister a little defensively. In a sudden turn, however, politicians from the DPJ administration began singing the praises of the Self-Defense Forces in chorus. Some of the officers felt a little ill at ease that the prime minister of Japan was pouring it on a bit thick with the "Doraemon" homage.

One of the officers who led Operation Tomodachi said, "That 'please, SDF' way of asking is wrong. If you want to use the Self-Defense Forces, you give an order, you don't ask."[36]

Article 7 of the Self-Defense Forces Law runs, "The cabinet prime minister, representing the cabinet, holds the rights of supreme command and director of the Self-Defense Forces." He should not have been asking. He was the supreme commander and director.

At the time of the helicopter water drop, Kan had asked Oriki, who had accompanied Kitazawa to the prime minister's office, what he thought. Oriki had replied, "Prime minister, could you please stop asking me what I think? Tell me, go! The SDF does what it's ordered to do. We don't like being consulted."

Kan did not utter another word.[37]

It was not as if the SDF did not have any problems of its own.

In their initial response to evacuating residents, there were overreactions, like the case in Minamisoma where the SDF went around saying,

"Get out to at least a hundred kilometers," and in the evacuation of serious patients at Futaba Hospital, coordination between the Twelfth Brigade Mixed Force and the Tohoku District Unit Medical Squadron was poor. Dispatching young female troops to areas of high radiation acted as an impediment to operations. In the immediate aftermath of the hydrogen explosion in Unit 3 on March 14, the reaction of the Self-Defense Forces may have been overly nervous.

A police officer criticized the SDF as being too conscious of the "safety zone."

"Even in Fukushima Prefecture, they didn't put a single man inside the alert zone. They were afraid of desertion en masse if they sent them into dangerous areas. Japan doesn't have court-martials, so deserters couldn't be brought before a court-martial. So, they stuck to the safety zone."[38]

It is a hard fact, however, that in the most critical situation of the Fukushima Daiichi nuclear emergency, the political leaders depended on the SDF as "the last bastion." During this period, there were two times when Hosono felt their only option was a "suicide squad." The first was during the venting of Unit 1 on March 12. That was the time when TEPCO would not vent no matter how long they waited. They said they were going to form a suicide squad, but they never did.

Hosono spoke to Ito, deputy chief cabinet secretary for crisis management, and Tetsuya Nishikawa, assistant chief cabinet secretary, about the matter.

"Nishikawa-san, can't the SDF form a suicide squad and do the venting? As things stand, TEPCO may not be able to do it. If we don't vent, the reactor will be in danger."

Nishikawa told Hosono that the SDF had quietly looked into the possibility of sending in a suicide squad at the time of the 1999 JCO nuclear accident. Hosono was thinking of instructing TEPCO to hand over all its maps and plans inside the plant to the SDF. However, under the command of Fukushima Daiichi Site Superintendent Masao Yoshida, the shift supervisor, duty officers, and operators had formed a suicide squad and implemented the venting.

The next time was March 16, when the SDF helicopters flew as far as Fukushima Daiichi NPS, but abandoned the aerial water drop and turned back. (They carried out the maneuver the following morning.) That night, Hosono had told one of his staff solemnly, "Isn't there anyone in this country prepared to lay down their life even during a war?"

When the staff member did not reply, Hosono continued:

"Even so, we just have to get the SDF to do it. They're the only ones who can risk their lives to do it."

One of Kan's secretarial aides later described it in the following way.

"The water discharging by the local fire departments and the police was more of a performance. At a time of national crisis, in the end, it was only the Self-Defense Forces who came to our aid. At the time, I was utterly convinced that we should have had the SDF in charge of overall coordination from the outset."³⁹

Just like the onsite SDF, the firefighters and police officers who took part in the water discharging operation did so at the risk to their own lives. To simply put that down as "a performance" was unduly harsh. However, it is an undeniable fact that in the most taxing times of the national crisis, this was the way the center of the administration felt.

In the midst of the crisis, Kitazawa went to see the prime minister with just Oriki. Sometimes they were joined by Vice Minister Kimito Nakae, but more often than not, Kitazawa took with him not the "suit," but just Oriki, the "uniform." As a senior official at the Joint Staff Office put it, "It was becoming quite routine for the chief of staff of the Joint Staff to go to the Kantei."⁴⁰

Deep down, the "suits" were not happy with this turn of events. Traditionally, the chief of staff of the Joint Staff only went to the Kantei when there was a transfer between old and new, or to report the success of a peacekeeping operation. That was about it.

Oriki was a ground SDF man. He may have seemed indifferent, but he was particular about information. He was especially hungry for "raw data, he wanted the provisional stuff."⁴¹

It was Hironaka who supported Oriki. Oriki relied on Hironaka: "He knows how to negotiate and make decisions."

Apart from Hironaka, Team Oriki—comprising Koichi Isobe and Koichiro Bansho from the ground SDF, Katsutoshi Kawano from the maritime SDF, and Sadamasa Oue from the air SDF—was the biggest collection of brains the SDF had.

A senior member of the Joint Staff Office said that out of "all our politicians who don't know much about how to use the SDF," Kitazawa was unusual in "knowing the essential points in using the uniforms." This was only possible because of the trust that existed between Kitazawa and Oriki.⁴²

At one stage, Kan had considered having senior officers from the SDF take up residence on "the fifth floor of the Kantei," so they could report to him. The "suits" came out in opposition. As a compromise, Oue was sent into the management crisis center. He was placed not under the control of "the fifth floor of the Kantei," but under the chief cabinet secretary and the deputy chief cabinet secretary.

4:00 P.M. ON MARCH 15. Oriki went to the prime minister's office accompanied by Colonel Shunji Yoshino (head of the ground SDF Chemical Laboratory), because Kan wanted to ask their opinion about dropping boric acid into the reactors.

Yoshino was an expert in chemical weapons who had served as Japan's military officer in the Netherlands at The Hague. He was a regular at meetings of the Chemical Weapons Convention at The Hague. When Kan asked him about dropping boric acid, Yoshida gave him a clear answer.

"Boric acid is effective, but rather than arguing about the boric acid drop, pumping water in should be implemented as soon as possible."

"That's what I think, too."

Smiling at Yoshino, Kan said, "I want you to stay here from today."

When the Integrated Response Office was set up on March 15, Yoshino suddenly found himself the SDF liaison there.[43]

THE GIRAFFE

It was the middle of the night on March 17 when Kiyohiko Toyama, Komeito Party member of the Lower House (Proportional Kyushu Block), received a call from one of his supporters.

"Toyama-san, I'm sorry to call you so late. Do you know the truck mounted concrete pumps manufactured by a German company called Putzmeister?"

"No, I don't."

"Well, this special truck might be useful for cooling the spent-fuel pool at the Fukushima Daiichi NPS."

"Are you sure?"

"Yes. Putzmeister's concrete boom pumps seem to have played an active role in building the sarcophagus at the Chernobyl nuclear power plant after the accident. They have a boom fifty-eight meters long. You could inject water instead of ready-mixed concrete pinpoint from the tip of the boom. I've heard there's one at the Port of Yokohama."

"Thank you for this extremely useful piece of information. I'll pass it on to the prime minister."

Toyama was first elected in 2010. He had a PhD in Peace Studies from Bradford University in the United Kingdom.

On the morning of March 17, he had watched the scenes of the SDF helicopter water drop to the spent-fuel pools on television. He had been worried that water drops like this would not be nearly enough. And then there was an unexpected call. Toyama rang his old friend, Tetsuro Fukuyama, deputy chief cabinet secretary. It was a time of national crisis. Who cared about opposition and ruling parties?

Fukuyama was somewhat cautious saying they had received many calls like this and that it was hard to know which was the most appropriate, but he asked Toyama to "check three points."

1. Did the vehicle have to be transported or could it move under its own steam?

2. Given that it was built for ready-mixed concrete, would it break down if the concrete was replaced with water?

3. Could they provide the staff to teach them how to operate the vehicle properly or not?

Toyama rang off, saying, "I'll check. Just give me a little time."[44]

The Hyper Rescue Squad had not come onto the scene yet. It was clear, however, that they needed to discharge water from the ground, just as it was clear that they needed a long-necked vehicle that, once it was set up, would pump automatically and continuously.

Takaya Imai, assistant vice minister at METI, remembered getting the firefighting equipment at the time of the Tokaimura JCO criticality accident in 1999.

That long-necked thing we used that time. That's got to be somewhere.

There were various bending water cannon trucks with long necks, and various parties had circulated photos of them at the Integrated Response Office and the crisis management center. There was even a photo of the German Putzmeister concrete boom pump. The company had sold three of the pumps in Japan. All of them had "necks"—the booms that were fifty-eight meters long.

Toyama had his supporter introduce him to Hiroshi Suzuki, CEO of Putzmeister Japan, and called Fukuyama after he had checked the three points. He told Fukuyama, "The boom is fifty-eight meters in length."

It was just after two a.m. on March 18.[45]

Later on March 18, Suzuki visited the Kantei and explained to Fukuyama about his company's concrete boom pump. They had two used concrete pumps, which they were under contract to export to Vietnam, unloaded in the Port of Yokohama from a car carrier and sitting at Pier C-2. Suzuki had hurriedly contacted the Head Office to see if they could let the Japanese have them. The Head Office had given its immediate approval.

Suzuki was originally a trading man who had been the Paris representative of Mitsui & Co., but had been recruited away by Putzmeister. The ascetic culture of a company that only did pumps suited him, and he had been posted all over Europe, later being promoted to CEO of the Japanese subsidiary.[46]

Suzuki took several models of the pump trucks to TEPCO. Susumu Kawamata, general manager for nuclear quality and safety management, and Hosono were looking at the models together in the Kantei liaison office at the Integrated Response Office.

"With a pump like this, we'd be able to squeeze a lot of water in from above, eh?"

"Yes, it's obvious even to an amateur like me!"

After listening to the explanation, Kawamata said, with a sparkle in his eye, "Things may work out with this."[47]

The concrete boom pump was, by rights, a piece of operative machinery for pumping concrete. However, if you used water instead of concrete and released it above the fuel pool, it would be possible to inject water much more accurately than from fire engines.[48]

Since the boom could be extended up to fifty-eight meters, it could reach the fuel pools situated forty meters above ground. In fact, since the fuel pools were located some four meters back, fifty-eight meters was just enough for getting the water in pinpoint.

But who was to drive and operate it? Putzmeister's drivers were not coming to Fukushima Daiichi NPS. They were to be on standby in the Onahama Coal Center. There was nothing to do but ask the Tokyo Fire Department's Hyper Rescue Squad. That meant groveling before the Fire and Disaster Management Agency at the Ministry of Internal Affairs and Communications.

MARCH 18. Hosono asked Atsushi Oshima—member of the Lower House (DPJ, Saitama Prefecture), who had come to the Integrated Response Office—to help out, and had him petition Yoshihiro Katayama, minister of internal affairs and communications.

He had Yojiro Hatakeyama—secretarial aide to the deputy chief cabinet secretary—among others, accompany Oshima. Apart from Katayama, the full array of Nobuyasu Kubo, commissioner of the Fire and Disaster Management Agency, and all the executive officers were in the minister's office. After Oshima had explained the overall situation, he asked, "Could we possibly have the fire department to operate the machinery?" and said, "Please cooperate on this one."

Commissioner Kubo intervened as if to cut him off.

"Mr. Representative, I hate to refute you, but this is quite difficult. We're being told to use machinery we've never used before, we won't be able to use it properly."

Oshima thought to himself, *What is he talking about when the country's survival is in the balance?* but Katayama also said bluntly, "It's difficult."

"Firefighters aren't machine operators. They fight fires with the equipment they practice with regularly, it's just not as easy as asking them to operate this thing. How about asking someone from civil engineering?"

"No, it's dangerous. Civil engineers can't do it."

"Well, how about you people?"

Goodness knows what he was thinking, but after saying this, Katayama suddenly turned to Hatakeyama and raised his voice.

"Hey you! You're from TEPCO, right? Do it yourselves!"

When Hatakeyama held his tongue, Katayama spat out another question.

"You're from METI originally, aren't you?"

"Yes, I'm originally from METI."

"Damn Matsunaga and Ueda! How on earth do they intend to take responsibility for this?"

Matsunaga was Kazuo Matsunaga, METI vice minister, and Ueda was Takayuki Ueda, METI deputy vice minister. Oshima and his group had no choice but to return with their tails between their legs. Hatakeyama's heart sank, as he thought, "Has METI created such a grudge in Kasumigaseki?"[49]

It was decided that workers from one of TEPCO's associates, Toden Kogyo, would operate the machinery.

At 2:30 p.m. on March 19, an employee of Putzmeister Japan set off from Yokohama to Fukushima Prefecture in the concrete pumping truck. A support team, including CEO Suzuki, split up into four cars and went with him. Just as they left Tokyo, black smoke began rising from around the gearbox on the pump truck. It was broken. A repairman from a plant that was able to service Mercedes vehicles came, and they were somehow able to fix it. Eighteen hours later, at six a.m. on March 20, they arrived at TEPCO's Onahama Coal Center. They had been escorted front and back in patrol cars from prefectural police in Kanagawa, Tokyo, Saitama, and Fukushima.[50]

At the hotel where they were staying in Koriyama, Suzuki and his team were briefed by the TEPCO side on the radiation map inside the premises of the Fukushima Daiichi NPS.

"The radiation has stopped rising. The work time is less than ten minutes. It's safe."

On the afternoon of March 20 and the morning of March 21, engineers from Putzmeister Japan, including Suzuki, taught the TEPCO and Toden Kogyo workers how to operate the machinery.

The machine had four collapsible "arm joints" that expanded, and when standing upright, it rose fifty-eight meters in height. The arm had to be raised slowly. Keeping it vertical was easy enough; the difficult task was to fold and lower the machine. In the middle of its descent, the safety device would kick in, grinding the arm to a halt.

If the long boom crashed into the roof and broke it, it would have all been for nothing. It was a nerve-wracking business.

On March 21, Kyoichi Asano, an engineer who had rushed over from the TEPCO Research Institute, installed a video camera and thermography at the tip of a concrete pump truck nicknamed the Giraffe. This was so they could operate it while watching the camera's footage.

Haruaki Yasui, at the age of fifty-two, was in charge of operating the Giraffe onsite. Yasui was the manager of the nuclear administration division's facility planning group and specialized in nuclear engineering. After the accident, he worked in the emergency response room for NISA, where he liaised with TEPCO's Head Office. However, as the story about the concrete pump trickled down from the Kantei to NISA and on to TEPCO Head Office, it was not long before the Head Office gave the go-ahead for Yasui to lead the water discharge operation. Yasui immediately pulled together a team of workers from various institutions. In addition to young TEPCO employees from the Head Office, working on nuclear energy, he invited six workers from TEPCO Industries—a subcontractor that deals with heavy machinery—including two workers with licenses for heavy vehicles from the TEPCO Matsumoto Plant and three workers from Taisei Corporation, in case they needed to discharge boric acid from a mixer truck. At two a.m. on March 19, they booked a taxi with a full tank of gas and arrived at the Onahama call center early the next morning.

In the eleventh meeting of the NERHQ, on March 21, METI Minister Banri Kaieda stated, "Today we will be putting a concrete pump truck into the field, to try cooling the spent-fuel pool at Unit 4."[51]

Kaieda had said, "nicknamed the Giraffe," but it was none other than Kaieda himself who had come up with the name for the concrete pump truck with the long boom, or neck, of fifty-eight meters. Despite Kaieda's introduction, the Giraffe did not go into operation that day. They had been unable to organize the water supply for it. If the concrete pump truck was to pump water, somebody had to supply it with a constant flow of water. When they asked the Hyper Rescue Squad to do it, their request was denied.

TEPCO eventually had to do it themselves. If Unit 4's spent-fuel pool were to run out of water, East Japan would be gone. Discharging water from an SDF helicopter would be of no use, but they needed to somehow discharge a steady flow of water into the spent-fuel pool. Yasui painfully felt the weight of his mission.

On March 22, the Giraffe came onto the scene. Yasui was in charge and was now decked out in a yellow protective suit with a mask. Asano turned on the thermographic video camera, and they watched the red crane of the Giraffe cautiously extend upward into the sky until it stood up straight, like a cedar tree.

Although the water initially dribbled out slowly from the Giraffe's mouth, at 5:17 p.m. it picked up the pace and started flowing swiftly into the spent-fuel pool with a thundering noise. The water discharge took three hours and fifteen minutes, and stopped at 8:32 p.m.[52]

"March 22 (Tuesday). The day of the Giraffe."

Kaieda had jotted that down on a memo earlier, and, as predicted, the Giraffe made its debut that day.[53]

From March 22 until March 27, seawater was injected into Unit 4's spent-fuel pool by the Giraffe. Following the introduction of the Giraffe, they were able to maintain regular and stable water discharge operations.

TEPCO continued pumping water into the spent-fuel pool using concrete pumps until they installed a water discharging line from the inside, on June 16. TEPCO went on a shopping spree for concrete pumps from around the globe. Ones with fifty-two-meter-long booms were dubbed "Zebras"; those with fifty-eight meters, "Giraffes"; those longer than that, "Elephants"; and the largest of them all, at sixty-eight meters, was the Chinese-manufactured "Mammoth," which eventually went unused. It was Kaieda who named them all.[54]

On March 26, Thomas Keil from Putzmeister's head office in Stuttgart, Germany, turned up. He was a service expert from the company, and was a skilled technician with the title of *meister*. He provided detailed explanations on the structure of the parts and instructions on how to repair them if they broke down. During breaks, he told Suzuki and the others about his experiences at the time of the Chernobyl accident.

Immediately after the accident, the Soviet government had dropped approximately five thousand tons of sand, earth, and lead from helicopters to release heat and alleviate the radiation. On top of that, they had to cover the reactor in concrete. This was the so-called sarcophagus operation.

It was here that ten of Putzmeister's concrete pump trucks had come onto the scene. They had covered the driver's cabins with a lead hood weighing four tons to keep the radiation out, and had also covered the windows and video cameras with lead. They had attached video cameras so they could operate the trucks remotely.

Several dozen people were sent to Stuttgart from the Soviet Union in order to train for the operation. The people sent were all prisoners with death sentences. They had been promised a release if they took part in the operation. It was all done in the utmost secrecy.

They had terrific appetites, drinking beer from the bottles and scarfing down sausages. Keil was one of their trainers. The sarcophagus operation, which took close to three months, was a success. Keil was relieved, but a long time later heard a story that set his hair on end. They had all died from the exposure within the space of three years.[55]

Masao Yoshida was delighted more than anyone else at the appearance of the Giraffes. Up until then, Yoshida was thankful for the water pumping efforts of the police, SDF, and firefighters, but a thought was nagging him. He still felt something amiss that the fire brigade, which had returned to Tokyo soon after water pumping operations had begun, held a press conference, which was reported in the media as a hero's triumphant return. Later on, in the Government Investigation Commission's hearings, Yoshida gave harsh evaluations of each of the water pumping operations.

"To start with, the riot police were the first to arrive but they weren't very useful. They made one attempt and then were withdrawn. Even then, they kicked up a lot of fuss before coming, then came and withdrew, to cut a long story short, they were ineffective." When asked what was meant by "ineffective," Yoshida replied, "Water didn't go in."

What about the SDF, who were dispatched next? "To tell you the truth, all of it was meaningless. The total amount of water that could be pumped, in terms of volume, was in the region of ten to twenty tons. So, when you think of the fuel pool's surface area, even if all the water was put in, then it would still be meaningless."

How about the Fire and Disaster Management Agency? "At first it was working, but gradually the nozzle of the hose was falling down. Even when it had fallen down, they didn't go to fix it."

" 'They' meaning the Fire and Disaster Management?"

"Yes, the Fire and Disaster Management Agency. Let me say that clearly. The heroic Fire and Disaster Management Agency.

"I think that the helicopters were ineffective. I apologize to the SDF for saying so, but they were ineffective in terms of volume, the Fire and Disaster Management Agency were ineffective, and from the outset the riot police were not in the least bit effective." All of them were "haphazard strategies."[56]

A week after the advent of the Giraffe, Yoshida expressed his gratitude to the Head Office during a teleconference with them, which was quite unusual. "The Giraffe and the Zebra are functioning very smoothly. I believe that it was largely because of Yasui-san from the Head Office and Asano-san from the Research Institute, who both came over to help and planned this operation with us."[57]

Yasui was sitting in the "Giraffe's seat" during the roundtable being held in the emergency response room on the second floor of the Anti-Seismic Building. He was pleased to hear Yoshida's words. Delighted, even.

Yasui worked under Yoshida when he was the nuclear administration manager at the Head Office. Yoshida installed a refrigerator right next to his desk and filled it with beer. At 5:40 p.m., he would wink to Yasui and say, "Let's have a drink," and start opening beers. When he went to say hi to Yoshida in the Anti-Seismic Building after bringing over the Giraffe from the Onahama Call Center to Fukushima Daiichi, Yoshida welcomed him with a big smile on his face, saying, "Oh, I'm glad, I'm glad you came."

Nothing went right after the accident, but now I've done a good job, Yasui reflected.

Deep down, he felt a calm sense of pride from having successfully completed his mission.[58]

TEN

Operation Tomodachi (Friends)

WASHINGTON/THE WHITE HOUSE

On March 11, at 1:45 a.m. U.S. Eastern Standard Time (EST), or 2:45 p.m. on March 11 Japan Time, Jeffrey Bader, senior director for Asian affairs on the National Security Council (NSC) at the White House, was awakened by a phone call from the White House Situation Room.

"There's been an 8.9 earthquake on the Richter scale in northeastern Japan . . . A tsunami alert has been issued." (It was subsequently raised to 9.0.)

Rubbing his sleepy eyes, Bader got dressed. He had to get ready for a conference call with the emergency response team.

He had also been awakened by calls from the Situation Room at the time of the North Korean nuclear tests in 2009, but he never thought he would be contacted in the middle of the night about an incident or accident in Japan.[1]

Daniel Russel, the NSC's director for Japan, South Korea, and North Korea; Richard Reed, deputy assistant to the president for homeland security; as well as higher-ranking Thomas Donilon, national security adviser; Denis McDonough, deputy national security adviser; William Daly, White House chief of staff; and James Steinberg, deputy secretary of state, were all awakened by calls from the Situation Room.[2]

The Situation Room monitors crises throughout the world around-the-clock. Whatever happens, it never closes. That night, there were five staff members on duty.

Bader was an expert on China issues. He had been involved in WTO negotiations on China's membership as part of the Commerce Department's delegation under the Bush administration. He had subsequently researched U.S. strategy toward China and East Asia at the Brookings Institution.

Russel was one of America's most seasoned diplomats specializing in Japan, having served as the U.S. consul general in Osaka-Kobe and as the director of the State Department Office of Japanese Affairs before joining the White House. When he was young, he also served as the assistant to the U.S. ambassador to Japan, Mike Mansfield, in the 1980s.

Reed was an ex-army man. After working at the Federal Emergency Management Agency (FEMA) among others, he had become deputy assistant to the president for homeland security. He had dealt with the H1N1 pandemic in 2009, the Haiti earthquake, the BP oil spill, and so on. It was his mission to ensure "continuity and resilience" of the government functions at times of crisis.

Crisis management had emerged again as a key issue for the administration in the wake of the 9/11 terrorist attacks. However, the Bush administration drew harsh public criticism for its bungled response to Hurricane Katrina. This was partly why the Obama administration had made "crisis management and resilience" a priority policy issue.[3]

Reed lived only some eight minutes from the White House. He drove over and was in his office by 2:30 a.m.

3:30 A.M. Bader, Russel, Reed, and John Brennan, assistant to the president for homeland security, held their first meeting on the Great East Japan earthquake. All calls were classified.[4]

To respond to the Fukushima Daiichi NPS accident, they created a crisis response team at the White House, adding John Holdren, assistant to the president for science and technology, to the core group, and they were to hold daily talks throughout the month of March.[5]

James Steinberg, the U.S. deputy secretary of state, learned of this from state's operations center. The first thing Steinberg did was to contact Kurt Campbell, assistant secretary of state for East Asian and Pacific affairs. Campbell was visiting Mongolia at the time.

"We have to be seen as, and be the first among, the responders. This is what the alliance is all about."

They both agreed on this point. Campbell had only just arrived in Mongolia, but he returned to Washington immediately.

Joseph Donovan, acting assistant secretary of state, learned of the quake when he received a call from the State Department's Operations Center at three a.m. He immediately called James Zumwalt, deputy chief of mission at the U.S. embassy in Tokyo, on his mobile phone. At the time, Zumwalt was standing in the parking lot with Ayako Kimura, a political specialist on security issues at the U.S. embassy.

When the earthquake had occurred, Zumwalt was sandwiched at a table, facing officials from the Ministry of Foreign Affairs (MOFA) at their Iikura Annex guest house, and they were staring at copies of telegrams piled up in heaps. They were copies of telegrams leaked on WikiLeaks that detailed private discussions between American and Japanese officials regarding such issues as North Korea and that had been sent to MOFA from the Japanese embassy in the United States. *Asahi Shimbun* had obtained and was going to report on them. They had sent an inquiry letter for confirmation. It said, "We will report it tomorrow."

How should they respond? In a hurry, a meeting was held between the U.S. embassy and MOFA to make arrangements. Out of all of them, what made the Japanese side the most nervous was the handling of the reported remark by Akitaka Saiki, director general of Asian and Oceanian Affairs Bureau, to Kurt Campbell that he believed "the DPRK had killed some of the missing abductees."[6]

The quake attacked as they sat, arms folded, with no promising wisdom forthcoming. Everyone dived under the table. As soon as the shaking settled down, they broke off in a rush.[7]

When Zumwalt got back to the embassy, he received a call from Donovan. He replied to Donovan, saying that all of the embassy staff had been evacuated from the building and told to return to the residential quarters. Voices could be heard shouting over the line.

"What's that? I can hear something."

"It's protesters chanting, 'We won't forgive Kevin Maher's comments on Okinawa!'"

Kevin Maher, former director of Japanese Affairs at the State Department, had allegedly called the people of Okinawa "lazy" and "masters of extortion." Despite the fact that there had been an earthquake, the protesters were still chanting outside the embassy gates.[8]

An article by *Kyodo News* on the comments made by Maher on March 6 had sparked an outrage. The article reported that the comments were made in a lecture to college students at the State Department at the end of the previous year. A group from the Socialist Democratic Party and Okinawa had come to the embassy to hand over a letter of protest on Maher's comments to Ambassador John Roos, but they were not allowed inside.

Maher denied this, but it immediately became a political issue and he was forced to resign from his post as director of Japanese Affairs at the State Department. Although Maher himself had made the decision to resign, the State Department decided to appoint him as a coordinator for the Fukushima unit of the Japan Earthquake Task Force, which was headed by Donovan. Maher postponed his resignation.

He put on a brave face and decided to help respond at the State Department, telling himself, *This is a time for all hands on deck, not for personal feelings or self-interest. This is my last chance to serve my beloved Japan.*[9]

The Department of Defense had also put in place an emergency response system.

Michael Schiffer, deputy assistant secretary of defense, was at Narita Airport at the time. He was on his way back to the States after a visit to Okinawa. Upon the news of the earthquake breaking out, he found himself having to wait several hours at the airport, but his U.S. flight took off that night.

Returning home late on the night of March 11, he took a quick shower and raced to his office at the Department of Defense. The Department of Defense decided to support Japan primarily through the U.S. Pacific Command (PACOM). The problem was that their humanitarian aid budget was at rock bottom. They had no choice but to siphon off some of the budget for Afghanistan and Pakistan. That was a job for the defense secretary.

They set up a task force with members from the Office of the Secretary of Defense (OSD), the Joint Chiefs of Staff, the U.S. Navy, Naval Reactors, PACOM, and forces stationed in Japan. Schiffer was the head.[10]

9:00 A.M. Reed briefed President Obama on the disaster. Obama instructed him to "do everything we can to support Japan."[11]

After that, Denis McDonough held a deputies committee meeting on the Japanese earthquake, in the Situation Room at the White House.

The Japanese government had already issued its declaration of a state of nuclear emergency. It was reported that it was a compound disaster with not only a quake and a tsunami, but the Fukushima nuclear accident.

What do we know?

What do we not know?

What should the U.S. government do?

This was what was discussed.

9:30 A.M. ON MARCH 11. The first videoconference was held between Donovan at the Department of State and Zumwalt at the embassy in Tokyo, as well as other interagency working-level personnel. The Department of Defense, the Nuclear Regulatory Commission (NRC), the Centers for Disease Control and Prevention (CDC), and the U.S. Agency for International Development (USAID) were all represented at the working level.[12]

3:22 P.M., MARCH 13, JAPAN TIME (2:22 a.m. on the same day U.S. EST). A USAID team of 144 arrived at the U.S. Misawa Air Base. (This team arrived in Ofunato, which is closer to Fukushima, at seven p.m. on March 14.)

Gregory Jaczko, chairman of the U.S. Nuclear Regulatory Commission (NRC), decided to send two boiling-water reactor experts to Japan, and one of them, Tony Ulses, flew in as part of the USAID team. The NRC had already set up a round-the-clock operations center.[13]

This was the first NRC team of experts dispatched to Japan, which would grow to a maximum of twenty-four at one time and an aggregate of one hundred people. "We had prepared multiple accident scenarios in the Emergency Response Center, but we had never rehearsed reacting to a disaster at the plant of a political ally ten thousand miles away," Jaczko recollected.[14]

Separate from this, the Department of Defense sent the U.S. Armed Forces as part of their support for Japan. Defense Secretary Robert Gates decided to leave all strategy in the first seventy-two hours with PACOM.[15]

The U.S. Armed Forces moved swiftly and decisively. The command ship of the Seventh Fleet, USS *Blue Ridge*, was in Singapore and gave orders for all crew to return to ship. Later that evening, the *Blue Ridge* set sail for Japan.[16]

The aircraft carrier, USS *George Washington*, was at the Yokosuka naval base at the time, for routine maintenance, so it could not go into operation immediately. Therefore, the aircraft carrier USS *Ronald Reagan*, which was heading to the western Pacific for joint U.S.-Korean military exercises, was hurriedly dispatched to the sea off Sanriku, in northeastern Japan.

7:00 P.M., MARCH 11, JAPAN TIME (six a.m. U.S. EST). The U.S. government sent the Japanese government the message that "The *Ronald Reagan* is being dispatched to Japan."

On the morning of March 13, the *Ronald Reagan* arrived in the waters off Sanriku. Three SDF liaison officers boarded the *Ronald Reagan*. In the same fashion, three U.S. liaison officers boarded the escort ship *Hyuga*.

The *Ronald Reagan* became a refueling base for the helicopters of the Japan Coast Guard and Self-Defense Forces, as well as the platform for aerial operations. These were both firsts. The flag officers of the *Ronald Reagan* made it clear that the ship had a duty to the U.S.-Japan alliance: to protect Japan from threats.

In order to support humanitarian aid and disaster relief activities of the SDF in eastern Japan, the U.S. Navy mobilized 22 vessels, 132 aircraft, and more than 15,000 troops. It carried out maritime searches for survivors over 3,200 square kilometers with more than 160 reconnaissance flights.[17]

Both governments set up a joint command post (U.S.-Japan Integrated Coordination Office) and proceeded with their first fully-fledged joint operation, Operation Tomodachi (Friends). The U.S. dispatched Pacific Fleet Commander Patrick Walsh to Japan. Suddenly, there was a four-star admiral heading the U.S. command in Japan. Walsh led Operation Tomodachi from the headquarters of the U.S. forces in Yokota Air Base, Tokyo.

What awaited the U.S. fleet was an invisible enemy, radiation. The first radioactivity alarm to go off was on the *Ronald Reagan*.[18]

On the morning of March 13, Japan Time, Admiral Kirkland Donald, director of Naval Reactors, asked for a conference call with Daniel Poneman, deputy secretary of energy, and Gregory Jaczko, chairman of the NRC.

"We have detected some activity out at sea, on the USS *Ronald Reagan*, that we think you need to be aware of . . . One of the helicopters had landed on the Japanese command ship and people—the people who stepped on the decks of that command ship—came back with some elevated counts on their feet and clothing."

The *Ronald Reagan* was a hundred miles from Fukushima Daiichi NPS; the Japanese flagship was fifty miles away.

"Last night, we had given the ship some guidance, as far as positioning was concerned, to stay clear of the area of the potential plume, basically told her to stay outside a fifty-mile radius of the plant and then to keep a hundred miles from the trail of the plume."

Donald said they had detected some activity about two and a half times above normal airborne activity using on-board sensors on the aircraft carriers. It was about thirty times what you would detect just on a normal air sample out at sea. Donald added, "But this is due to the venting, not damage to the containment vessel like a crack or something."[19]

The United States had already started monitoring radiation and the temperature in the reactor and spent-fuel rod pools. They flew a state-of-the-art unmanned surveillance aircraft, the Global Hawk, from their base in Guam, over Fukushima.

The Global Hawk was capable of flying at an altitude of 18,000 meters and could detect up to 560 kilometers ahead. It could focus in on a target under adverse weather conditions and at night. The captured image could be seen back at headquarters on the ground almost simultaneously.

They also sent out the atmospheric collection aircraft, the WC135 Constant Phoenix, which was capable of measuring radioactive material, to collect their own information and analyze it. The aircraft was mobilized from Nebraska. (The U.S. forces provided Japan, free of charge, the more than 4,400 images taken in the two months up to May 11, 2011.)[20]

The White House started to be alarmed after the explosion in Unit 1 on the afternoon of March 12 (the early hours of the same day, U.S. EST). Brennan was to brief the president on this matter.

The science and technology officer brought a chart of the reactor for the briefing, but Reed thought it was a little too detailed, so he got the staff to redraw it as a simple sketch. Brennan looked at both of them and said, "Even I can understand this one. The president will understand it, too," and headed to the Oval Office armed with the sketch.

However, neither Brennan nor Reed had any idea of the scale of the accident at Fukushima. Reed asked Holdren's staff, "Is this a Three Mile Island or a Chernobyl?" but was just looked on with reproach as "a guy who didn't know the first thing about science."

"You can't make a simple comparison like that. Fukushima is different from them both."

Even so, you needed to know the "extent," to have some kind of "yardstick" when making a specific response, and if that was not clear, you had to prepare for a worst-case scenario. That was the golden rule of crisis management.

Although things had not progressed so far that they had to start thinking in Churchill's terms—"Is this the end of the beginning, or the beginning of the end?"—Reed and his colleagues decided to assume the worst.

At the time, they believed that although something had exploded at Unit 1, "the containment vessel is all right." Bader and the others still thought, "It'll be all right."[21]

TOKYO/AMBASSADOR ROOS

After the declaration of a state of nuclear emergency was issued at 7:03 p.m. on March 11, a request for assistance in responding to the Fukushima Daiichi NPS accident at the North American Affairs Bureau of the Ministry for Foreign Affairs (MOFA) landed on the desk of a worker at the U.S. embassy in Akasaka, Tokyo.

"We want you to send us water pump trucks and generator trucks urgently!"

The tone of the message was close to a cry for help.

A reminder from the Kantei came in like a flash to ask the U.S. forces for help. The MOFA section handling this was the Status of U.S. Forces Agreement Division in the North American Affairs Bureau. Division Director Hiroyuki Namazu became the go-between for the U.S. forces in Japan and the Kantei.

By rights, this was something that should have been handled military-to-military, but the atmosphere was not one where he could dismiss it with an "Ask the Joint Staff Office."

That night, U.S. ambassador to Japan, John Roos, placed a call to Foreign Minister Takeaki Matsumoto from the ambassador's residence. A reception had been planned for the evening of that day at the residence in commemoration of the fiftieth anniversary of the signing of the U.S.-Japan Peace Treaty. The food and drinks were ready and waiting.

The first thing Roos asked was, "Is the nuclear reactor all right?"

"The nuclear reactor is under control. I've heard everything is all right."

"Really?"

"It's under control."

"Non-government researchers are saying it's starting to melt down, but what's really happening?"

"No, that's not the government's position."

Roos was skeptical.[22]

Roos had only met Matsumoto for the first time the day before, when he had paid him a courtesy call with Campbell, who had stopped over on his way to Mongolia.

Matsumoto had told Roos, "My door is always open. You can knock on it anytime."

Matsumoto had been appointed foreign minister after Seiji Maehara, his predecessor, resigned over political donations from a South Korean permanent resident in Japan. His appointment took place a mere two days before the earthquake.

Appealing to the need for fire engines and generator trucks, he requested, "We'd be grateful for help from the U.S. forces in Japan." The story was that when he had asked Prime Minister Naoto Kan, "Is there no need to ask for support from the United States?," he had been told to "Please do that." This was one of the factors behind his request to Roos.[23]

Roos told him that a support team was on its way from the U.S. mainland and promised that America would help.[24]

Late that night, Kenichiro Sasae, vice minister for foreign affairs, received calls from Steinberg and Poneman. The Americans were on a conference call. Sasae had Hidehiko Nishiyama, deputy director general at NISA, and some staff from the Ministry of Foreign Affairs sit in, with Nishiyama answering the technical matters.

The U.S. side stressed, "We view this as a national emergency. We are ready to offer any kind of support."[25]

At 12:15 a.m. Japan Time, a conference call between President Obama and Prime Minister Kan took place. Obama reiterated that the United States was prepared to support any efforts and offered experts, a blank check, and U.S. AID for the first thirty days, even though U.S. AID was traditionally reserved for second- and third-world countries.[26]

Roos had learned quite a bit about foreign affairs and security between the United States and Japan since his appointment in 2009, as well as underwent baptism by fire with the "Futenma Shock" and "Senkaku Shock."

The "Futenma Shock" was the chaos that erupted in 2009, when the then Prime Minister Yukio Hatoyama, of the Democratic Party, suddenly began talking about relocating the U.S. marine base of Futenma outside Okinawa Prefecture. The "Senkaku Shock" was the highly elevated tension in Japan-China relations, triggered by the captain of a Chinese fishing boat ramming into two Japan Coast Guard patrol boats in the waters around the Senkaku Islands and getting arrested by the Japanese, followed by the Chinese government's retaliatory ban on exports to Japan of rare earth metals.

This time, however, things were very different. The high-ranking officials whom he usually dealt with at MOFA and the Ministry of Defense could offer him no immediate help. He did not have such a close relationship with METI or NISA. He also experienced trouble in contacting Japanese government officials. Even if he did manage to make contact, the information he received was not definite.

A team of nuclear power experts from the NRC and elsewhere were coming from Washington. Who should he put them in touch with to make sure they got accurate information from the Japanese side?

They would need to talk directly to engineers, not policy authorities. The question was highly technical, and he had absolutely no idea of where to find experts, whether they be government or private, or who was advising the prime minister.

Roos needed to build up a network of information exchange before the team arrived. Thinking that information was being concentrated in J-Village, the U.S. embassy looked into sending the experts dispatched from the United States there. However, they had trouble finding an interpreter. Even when they found one, they flinched on hearing they were to go to J-Village, the soccer complex near Fukushima Daiichi turned into an operations base.[27]

After a time, they received the information that this administration was being led by the Kantei, and that the parliamentary members of the Kantei from Kan down were directly involved in responding to the accident. They had to create a solid information line to the Kantei. The U.S. embassy did not know what the Japanese game plan was or how the Japanese side was going to respond to the list of support actions the United States had shown them.

THE MORNING OF MARCH 12. Katsuhiro Sogabe, president of the Japan Nuclear Energy Safety Organization (JNES), sent an e-mail to NRC Chairman Gregory Jaczko, in which he politely thanked the NRC for their offer of support but refused it for the time being.[28]

"Are the Japanese spurning support from the U.S. government?"

The American side started to wonder.[29]

THE SAME DAY. In an internal conference call within the U.S. government, a staff member from the NRC spoke up.

"I was saying that we already asked the Japanese regulatory authority if they need anything, to let us know, and up to now, they did not answer that."[30]

It seems that Kan's statement in a meeting at the Kantei—"Before we go asking America, we should first do what can be done in Japan"—had been conveyed as a "negative stance."[31]

Why was Japan negative about accepting U.S. support?

Irritation at Japan's response started to surface in the U.S. government.

"Is this due to the way Kan and the DPJ perceive America? Just as the case was with Hatoyama, the DPJ is basically following a policy of distancing itself from the United States."

"Kan seems to be worried about being questioned 'what's the DPJ administration doing?' if the U.S. forces get too far out in front."

"No, it's more a sense of pride and reverse humiliation. He wants to show they can do it themselves."

"No, Japan doesn't have the power. They're probably still hung up on the myth that they're an economic and technical superpower."

"They're underestimating the United States. The economic bureaucrats don't realize the power of U.S. military assets."

"I mean to say, why's the chief cabinet secretary always on TV? Do they think that's how a government manages a crisis?"[32]

Voices were also raised in Japan's defense.

"Even the Japanese government can't grasp the situation, they're not trying to be secretive."

"They're up to their ears trying to respond to the emergency right now, we should refrain from pushing support onto them, and we need to be careful that they don't think we're only interested in obtaining information."

This remark was also heard:

"You can't just blame Japan. Didn't the United States refuse Japan's offer of support at the time of Hurricane Katrina?"[33]

There were some Japan experts at the Defense Department who remembered the outpouring of goodwill from the people of Japan at the time of Hurricane Katrina.

An elderly gentleman had suddenly turned up at the U.S. embassy in Tokyo, and, signing a check on the spot for US$1 million, handed it over to the embassy staff, saying, "Please use this for the victims. When I was a young man, I was able to go to the United States to study, and the people in the United States were very, very kind to me, and I would like to do something. I am where I am today thanks to America."

And with those words, he left.[34]

There were also a great many Japanese who wanted to go directly to New Orleans to help. The U.S. government refused all such offers of humanitarian aid, however. This was because in times of disaster, the first lesson of crisis management is to concentrate people who know the area well into the disaster response.

Most likely, Japan was in the same situation now. It was understandable that the Japanese side wanted to concentrate on the response on their own. People defended Japan in this way in the internal meetings.

On the morning of March 13, the Japanese government held a cabinet meeting on the nuclear emergency at the Kantei. Just as the meeting was about to begin, a senior official at the Ministry of Defense received a call from someone at the U.S. embassy.

"Deputy Secretary of Energy Poneman says he can't reach anyone on the Japanese side. Could you please put him in touch with the appropriate person?"

Having heard this, Minister of Defense Toshimi Kitazawa told the meeting, "While this doesn't come under my jurisdiction, the Deputy Secretary of Energy says he wants to talk to the appropriate person, but can't. Something should be done about it."

No one in the room responded to Kitazawa's advice. The cold opinion was also voiced: "America just wants information."

After the meeting, Kitazawa stayed behind with Matsumoto and METI Minister Banri Kaieda to discuss the matter. Although the idea that "Madarame [chairman of the NSC] would be the best" was put forward, there was a return call a short while later, from the U.S. embassy, that "we've made contact." Apparently, Poneman had been able to talk with Shunsuke Kondo, chairman of the Japan Atomic Energy Commission.[35]

Roos received an instruction fired off from Washington to "give me Kondo's phone number," and he had instructed the embassy staff to contact Kondo, but they could not find his number straight away. In the end, they Googled the Japan Atomic Energy Commission's phone number and contacted him.

Matsumoto was busy handling something else that morning. He was fighting a rearguard action against the Ministry of Internal Affairs and Communications, the National Police Agency, and the Fire and Disaster Management Agency, all of which were being cautious about the fully-fledged acceptance of overseas rescue teams. Edano, however, had come out in favor of letting them in, saying, "In any event, we're going to accept them."

MOFA brought about the full-scale acceptance by showing its willingness to attach a large number of its young officers to each overseas rescue force.[36]

In the meantime, Roos received his greatest shock from a call on the morning of March 12 from Hisanori Nei, deputy director general of NISA. Nei was the first NISA official to contact Roos directly. Nei told him abruptly, "Unit 1 has started to melt down."

"Melt down! Did he say melt down?"

Roos checked with his interpreter.

"Yes, that's correct."

But what really floored Roos were Nei's next words.

"I'm sorry, but I'm terribly busy. We're preparing to withdraw."[37]

Withdraw? Who? Where? On what grounds? Roos wanted to question Nei in more detail, but Nei hung up, saying, "I'm sorry, but I'm busy."

Casto had later remarked on the United States' struggle to get timely information from NISA. In particular, Nei, their single point of contact within NISA, appeared to be limiting the amount of information they received.[38]

Roos told his staff, "Get me Edano. I've got to ask Edano directly."

However, they were not able to catch up with Chief Cabinet Secretary Yukio Edano that day.[39]

At 11:30 a.m. on March 13, Roos called Edano on the phone.

"I'm concerned about U.S. citizens in Japan. I would like to have accurate information."

"The SDF is coordinating well with the U.S. forces. We're doing our utmost to ensure the safety of the nuclear power plants."[40]

"The Japanese government has instructed residents within a twenty-kilometer radius to evacuate, but is it safe outside the twenty-kilometer zone?"

"It's all right."[41]

Roos felt Edano's reply was "by the book." He was, however, able to talk with Kitazawa later on the phone. Kitazawa's take on the situation was much more serious than Edano's.

At two a.m. on March 14, at the embassy, Roos met, for the first time, Tony Ulses, one of the NRC staff, who had come to Japan as part of the U.S. government's support team. They needed to be put in touch with the experts on the Japanese side straight away, to get the appropriate information and to provide appropriate advice.

The situation was becoming more precarious. The problem was that, as its status was ever-changing, information from the Japanese government ministries and agencies was conflicting. It was hard to know where to get the most reliable information.

Why is Kitazawa's information much more critical than the rest?

Where on earth is the Japanese government reviewing information, evaluating, analyzing it?

It was hard to know. However, Kitazawa's sense of threat at that time may have been more acute than that of the Ministry of Defense per se, or even the SDF. There was not yet an adequate shared understanding about how to respond to the nuclear power plant accident between the U.S. forces and the SDF.

Around this time, Burton Field, commander of the U.S. forces in Japan, placed a call to Chief of Staff of the Joint Staff Ryoichi Oriki, asking, "We've had a request from the Ministry of Foreign Affairs to urgently send our fire engines, but I'd like you to tell me what's happening with the nuclear reactor." The Joint Staff Office was unable to provide a satisfactory answer.

At the time, Field said, "U.S. navy helicopters have measured the radiation. We're very concerned. I've ordered all U.S. ships not to get too close, and those that are already close to move away."

Field was talking about the exposure on the *Ronald Reagan*. Oriki was shocked, because he had no idea things were so critical.[42]

TOKYO/"A QUESTION OF NATIONAL SOVEREIGNTY"

On the morning of March 14, Unit 3 (RB) exploded.

Information started coming in to Roos that the situation was becoming more and more serious. Steinberg in Washington also kept tossing out questions about the nuclear accident. He had to be able to answer them.

Up until that point, Roos had repeatedly requested information from the Japanese side, and he asked them for not second- or third-hand information, but "the best, the most accurate information."

There was no time to lose.

I need to talk directly to the heads of government, no matter what.

"I'd like you to call Chief Cabinet Secretary Edano."

That was his instruction to his staff many times that night. But they could not get ahold of Edano.

"His office says he's giving a press conference and he doesn't have any time."

"A press conference? Who gives a damn about that? Ask him to call me back as soon as possible."

It was at eleven p.m. on March 14 that Edano phoned him back.

"Could you please send me immediately the figures for the radioactive fallout at Fukushima Daiichi NPS?" Roos asked. "I don't have them here."

"I'd like you to get the documentation right away, please."

"They're in the basement [crisis management center]."

"Would it be possible to go to the basement and get them straight away?" Roos asked.

Edano's staff and staff from the MOFA, who were packed into his office, frowned.

Goodness, he doesn't have to put it that way. He's speaking to the chief cabinet secretary.

The people in the room got the impression that Roos was completely unnerved, or even panicking. The moment of greatest tension between Roos and Edano, however, was when Roos said the following:

"I'd like you to approve the placement of our experts close to the decisionmaking at the Kantei. I'd be grateful if you would allow them to be stationed there."

He wanted the experts from the NRC placed "close to the decisionmaking at the Kantei." When Edano heard the interpreter say this, his whole demeanor changed. He refused unequivocally.

"That is not possible."

Roos lost his temper.

"America is doing its utmost to support Japan. And yet . . ."

But till the last, Edano did not change his position of refusal. After the phone call with Roos was over, Edano told his staff, "Close to the decisionmaking in the Kantei means on the fifth floor, right? I can't put them on the fifth floor. He's got to be kidding."

Edano's point was that this was a question of national sovereignty.

"You're quite right. If the positions were reversed, and the Japanese government asked the U.S. government to put their experts into the White House, what would the U.S. government say to that?"

That was muttered by one of the MOFA staffers, who usually placed keeping the United States happy above everything else.

Roos was really feeling the pressure from Washington.

"Who's got the best information? I'll get someone in there."

When he asked his staff, "Where can we get the best information? The site, or J-Village, or TEPCO?" their research showed that "The emergency response is being done completely by the Kantei, that's where most of the information is."

This was why he had proposed the Kantei.[43]

Following this tense exchange with Edano, Roos phoned his old friend, Chikao Kawai, assistant chief cabinet secretary.

"Why have the sieverts started rising again?"

"Mr. Ambassador, that's a matter for the experts."

So saying, Kawai hung up, but he was worried. *He's talking on the assumption that the Japanese government is hiding something.* Kawai appealed to Tetsuro Fukuyama, deputy chief cabinet secretary, "Can't you speak to Roos just once?"

THE MORNING OF MARCH 16. Fukuyama phoned Roos. Roos let fly determinedly, "Here we are worrying about all kinds of things in an attempt to help, but what about Japan?"

Fukuyama countered him.

"The NRC experts don't give us any assessment when we ask them . . . We're not hiding anything. I find it most regrettable to be told we're hiding something."

Roos did not respond to this, but brought up again the request he had made to Edano.

"We'd like to have some experts close to the decisionmaking at the Kantei."

"When you say 'close to the decisionmaking at the Kantei,' do you mean inside the prime minister's office? If so, that's impossible. But if you mean somewhere close by, then that may be possible. I think we could prepare a place in the Kantei's liaison office."

The liaison office was a room hurriedly put together next to the crisis management center in the basement of the Kantei for staff from METI, NISA, and TEPCO to share their information.[44]

On the morning of March 15, Kan, Edano, and Fukuyama spoke about the dispatch of U.S. experts to the Kantei, and acceptance of their residency in the prime minister's office was decided. Fukuyama conveyed that.

Roos met Edano two or three days later at the Kantei. Although neither of them said "I was in the wrong," they tried to patch it up by hinting they had both "gone a little too far."[45]

The Roos-Edano phone call resulted in further deepening suspicions at the State Department about the Japanese government's response. They suspected that the Japanese side did not have that high an opinion of the nuclear emergency response capabilities of the U.S. side.[46]

Casto guessed that the impetus for this phone call had been the banter among the NRC engineers hanging out at the ambassador's office. "While there, they held casual conversations and engaged in a lot of speculation in front of the ambassador, who wasn't trained to understand and deal with that information. To be blunt, they were whipsawing the ambassador," Casto recalled.[47]

At one point, an NRC engineer told Roos that "if this gets much worse or if that containment breaches, then I'm leaving. I'm going to leave the country."[48] It was exactly this kind of fear that provoked Roos and sowed suspicion against the Japanese government on the U.S. side.

At 7:50 p.m. on March 16, Matsumoto phoned Roos. Roos told Matsumoto,

"If they don't get water in today, we will be forced to consider that Japan has failed in responding to its nuclear emergency."

This sounded like an ultimatum.

When Matsumoto tried to explain, Roos told him, "I have some things to attend to. Sorry, goodbye," and rang off.

Sasae and several other senior members of the MOFA were assembled in Matsumoto's office. Matsumoto was astonished. The room was filled with an air of "He was the one who made the call in the first place. What a rude guy!"[49]

WASHINGTON/"WE MAY LOSE ALL OF EASTERN JAPAN"

Campbell phoned Steinberg to report after the explosion at Unit 3 (RB).

"Things are going very badly at Fukushima."

"We may lose all of Eastern Japan."

Steinberg knew Campbell had the habit of putting things dramatically, but judging by the tone of Campbell's voice, the situation was alarming.

"We are about to have the worst catastrophe in history, and Japan is not even beginning to tackle it."

"They can't control the reactors."

Steinberg had worked consistently as a foreign and security policy professional in every Democratic administration since President Carter in the 1970s. Even for him, who had been through many tough experiences, "This was the most horrifying call I have gotten through my whole time with the government."

The two of them agreed. "The risk was so great that we just could not rely on the Japanese government to be in a much more active and direct role."[50]

Campbell's warning was based on the core analysis of the U.S. Naval Reactors. In a simulation based on that analysis, there was a strong possibility of an explosion inside the containment vessel at Unit 1 at Fukushima Daiichi NPS. If that happened, nothing could be done about Units 2 and 3. In fact, there was a chance that they would also lose Units 5 and 6.[51]

The NRC, however, had carried out a slightly different core analysis to that of the Naval Reactors. In an internal U.S. government conference call on March 14, NRC staff exchanged opinions.

"We were asked for technical support regarding cooling Units 1, 2, and 3 at five o'clock this morning. There's been no cooling for a period of eighteen hours."

"There's a possibility that the core is in meltdown, but our conclusion is that they haven't failed to shut down."

Jaczko interjected.

"If that's the case, there won't be a large-scale release of radioactive material, will there?"

The NRC was equally nervous about the possibility of the spent-fuel pools boiling dry. They had already heard back from the NRC engineers they had dispatched to Tokyo that "there's a chance that the spent-fuel pools are boiling."[52]

The American sense of crisis reached its peak with the damage to the containment vessel in Unit 2 and the explosion and fire in Unit 4 (RB) in the early hours of March 15.

A senior official at the State Department looked back, "Even at Chernobyl, contamination by fire in the air was serious. After that, it was decided to create a worst-case scenario. We couldn't get any information. At times like that, the first thing you do is to create a worst-case scenario."

From the results of the video analysis taken from the Global Hawk, an unmanned aircraft, the measurements of the temperature in the fuel pools, as well as the radiation dose measured by air monitoring, the U.S. side deemed that the possibility of the fuel pools being empty was high.

Steinberg and Campbell discussed, "A catastrophic event is taking place, where with one false move thousands of people may die from radioactive contamination. It's more than just Japan's problem."

Campbell voiced his fear that "With things as they are, Japan may lose the eastern part . . . There's a risk that Eastern Japan will become a nuclear wasteland."

Campbell's fears were telegrammed to the Ministry of Foreign Affairs from the U.S. embassy in Tokyo.[53]

Sasae contacted the Japanese ambassador to the United States, Ichiro Fujisaki, directly. He told him, "It's a serious affair for the state. There may come the time when we really must get the United States to help."

"I'd like you to convey to us Washington's fears live from the spot."

Fujisaki carried this out faithfully. Looking back, a senior Ministry of Foreign Affairs official laughed bitterly, "The Fujisaki telegrams were almost 'from the horse's mouth,' regarding what the senior members of the U.S. government were saying."

"It was March 16, but when the information was passed on to the American side (the U.S. embassy in Tokyo) that the Ministry of Defense's helicopter had run a surveillance flight over Unit 4 and it looked like there was water, they replied they would convey that to Washington, but then a diplomatic telegram arrived from the ambassador (Fujisaki) to the effect that 'America is saying there's no water in Unit 4's fuel pool and that the fuel rods have been boiled dry.' So even though the State Department was supposed to have our information, he would convey their messages to us unadulterated. Fujisaki-san was absolutely thorough about that at the time."

Fujisaki continued to send pinpoint diplomatic telegrams that would catch the eye not only of the foreign minister, but the prime minister, the chief cabinet secretary, and the defense minister.[54]

In the early hours of March 16, U.S. EST (the afternoon of the same day Japan Time), the Obama administration held a huge conference call with sixty officers from the related government agencies. It was an unprecedented attempt to discuss what the U.S. government should do regarding the crisis situation at the Fukushima power plant.

It was decided then to send Japan a tough message. The U.S. government still suspected Japan was hiding something, even at this stage. Did the Japanese government not know that things were really much more serious? Were they not being clear in order to avoid a panic taking place?

The fact that a five-minute-long video message from the emperor was broadcast on March 16 at 2:30 a.m. U.S. Eastern time (4:30 p.m. Japan Time) only reinforced these doubts.

"My other grave concern now is the serious and unpredictable condition of the affected nuclear power plant. I earnestly hope that through all-out efforts of all those concerned, further deterioration of the situation will be averted."[55]

This was the first time the emperor's voice had been broadcast live to the nation at large in sixty years; the last time being Emperor Hirohito's radio broadcast on the day of defeat in 1945 (August 15) and in the wake of food riots in May the following year.

Were the emperor's words trying to convey a catastrophic crisis in Japan that none of the Japanese political leaders could give voice to? The Japan experts at the Department of State pored over the emperor's words, looking for hidden truths.[56]

On the afternoon of March 11, the emperor and empress were at the Lotus Pond in the Imperial Palace, where they met with volunteers from three provincial organizations to thank them for their work that day. Then they both went to the stables to see the sacred horse that was soon to be offered to the Ise Shrine.

When the earthquake struck, the emperor was in his office. The first thing he did was turn on the television. The framed photos of heads of state and their spouses arranged on a shelf in the room began to fall.

The empress, who had returned to the Imperial Palace, opened slightly the sliding door of heavy glass across the corridor that faced onto a large front garden, to secure an exit to the outside. She was concerned that after a strong quake the doors might not open due to warping of the doorframes. This was what her mother had taught her a long time ago.

Along with the empress, the emperor went out into the middle of the front garden. The ground was buckling. The emperor firmly supported the empress by the arm.

Some of the volunteer laborers working there that day were unable to go home and ended up spending the night at the Imperial Palace.

On March 14, there was an explosion in Unit 3, accelerating the sense of crisis.

According to Yutaka Kawashima, grand chamberlain, "While being forced to contemplate the worst, including a possible meltdown at the nuclear power station, an extraordinary amount of time has started to lapse" at the Imperial Palace. That night, the emperor dined with seven senior members of the Imperial Household Agency, including the grand steward and the grand chamberlain.

On the morning of March 15, the emperor invited Shunichi Tanaka, a former acting chairman of the Atomic Energy Commission Agency, to the Imperial Palace, to hear about the Fukushima nuclear accident. In the afternoon, he was also briefed by Takaharu Ando, commissioner general of the National Police Agency, on the extent of the damage.

Tanaka was an engineer specializing in radiation physics. He had also served as director of the Tokai Research and Development Center at the Nuclear Science Research Institute (later to become the Japan Atomic Energy Agency). At the time, he was working as the head of a foundation in its headquarters at Tokaimura, Ibaraki Prefecture, mainly on the use of nuclear power–related computer use.

During the imperial briefing, Tanaka conveyed his assessment that the reactor core was melting, using the term "meltdown" at the time.

The emperor asked a series of technical questions. Tanaka replied cautiously to each one. It was his first meeting with the emperor. Forgetting at some stage the ritual formality of an "imperial briefing," Tanaka found himself speaking to the emperor as one scientist to another.

"The scale of the accident is far beyond that of Three Mile Island."

Tanaka was acutely aware of the seriousness of the situation. The emperor followed closely, without moving a muscle. When it was over, the scheduled hourlong imperial briefing had run more than an hour and a half.

After the imperial briefing, Tanaka drove back to Tokaimura in his own car, passing car after car with local number plates going at full speed in the opposite direction. He was to learn later that morning that there had been a hydrogen explosion in Unit 4 and large amounts of radioactive material were leaking from the containment vessel of Unit 2.

Recognizing "the unprecedented nature" of events, the emperor decided to make a video-recorded broadcast. Having discussed it with the empress, he created a draft document.

At three p.m. on March 16, the video recording started. The emperor's appearance went on the air at 4:30 p.m. on all television stations simultaneously.

The emperor's awareness of the situation, as expressed by the words "My other grave concern now is the serious and unpredictable condition of the affected nuclear power plant," was based mainly on Tanaka's briefing.

In his statement—"I wish to express my appreciation to the members of the Self-Defense Forces, the police, the fire department, the Japan Coast Guard, and other central and local governments and related institutions"—he consciously cited the SDF first among the first responders. According to a palace insider, the order was based on an "order of impact." That SDF personnel were injured in the explosion at Unit 3 (RB) that day was probably a factor in determining the "order of impact."

(On April 27, 2011, the emperor visited the Tohoku disaster area and had lunch in Sendai with Eiji Kimizuka, commander of the Joint Task Force (JTF). Kimizuka was in uniform. It was the first time an emperor of Japan shared a meal with a commander in uniform since World War II.)

The Japanese people were encouraged by the emperor's words, but there was also the following reaction:

"I heard a rumor that His Majesty was frightened of radiation exposure and was secretly making preparations to flee Tokyo, so I was relieved to hear that he was well and at the Imperial Palace."[57]

The emperor was amazed to learn this.

Kawashima wrote, in response, "It is unthinkable that His Majesty would abandon the people of Tokyo and leave, and he was disappointed by the irresponsible nature of false rumors in such a situation."[58]

9:00 A.M. ON MARCH 16, U.S. EST (TEN P.M. JAPAN TIME). The U.S. government called Fujisaki to Campbell's office on the sixth floor of the State Department. Fujisaki had just returned to Washington from Paris after attending a meeting between Japan's Foreign Minister Takeaki Matsumoto and U.S. Secretary of State Hillary Clinton. Fujisaki and three others, including Military Attaché Mitsuru Nodomi, entered from the C Street entrance. Two officers on the ground floor met them, but they were not smiling as usual.

While riding the elevator to the sixth floor, Fujisaki whispered, "Things are a little different today." They went to the Office for East Asian and Pacific affairs, but were kept waiting at the reception. Fujisaki took out his mobile phone and called the MOFA in Tokyo.

"Things don't seem quite right. Can you tell me what you know now?"

After ten minutes of wait, they were shown in. Campbell looked exhausted. There was no smile. The eyes of his staff were bloodshot. Campbell said, "Ambassador Fujisaki. Let me be frank. Japan is not doing what it should. The United States intends to help, but the government of Japan isn't pulling together. You need to work together to deal with this . . . If TEPCO isn't capable of dealing with the nuclear accident, the Japanese government will have to . . . It looks like the SDF and the police are running away. You need heroic sacrifice at a time like this."

Information that TEPCO had given up on responding to the nuclear emergency at Fukushima Daiichi NPS had reached the U.S. government. They had just heard that morning that the SDF had abandoned their helicopter water drop at Unit 3 and turned back.

Fujisaki's aide thought, *I guess he's referring to the canceled helicopter operation.*[59]

After fifteen minutes or so, Campbell received a phone call. He went next door to take it and was away for some time, but when he came back, he told Fujisaki, "That was the White House. They are right in the middle of discussing this very issue at the White House. But there have been no new instructions . . . The aircraft carrier *Ronald Reagan* is not to enter within fifty miles of Fukushima . . . We're going to announce within the next several hours an authorized voluntary departure."

Campbell then added, "But if we do not see a Japanese government response, we're pulling everybody out, including the military, the U.S. forces in Japan."

Campbell summoned Fujisaki to the State Department a total of four times that day.

On the second occasion, Fujisaki expressed his concern that if U.S. government personnel, especially the U.S. forces, were withdrawn from Japan, it would send neighboring countries the wrong message that relations between the United States and Japan were critical. Campbell responded with a stern look.

"Ambassador Fujisaki. This is not about politics. This is not a time for talking about politics. I want you to think seriously."

And then, striking a bigger blow, he added, "The only thing to do is to have the Japanese military lay their lives on the line."[60]

At the time, Campbell had seen the results of the worst-case scenarios devised independently by the U.S. Navy, the Department of Energy (DOE), and the NRC. The U.S. Navy simulation indicated there was a possibility of the plume reaching Tokyo, depending on the wind.

Campbell pointed out to Fujisaki that the temperature of the spent-fuel pool of Unit 4 had risen to a dangerous level, by informing him of a picture taken from the Global Hawk that showed as much. The picture was exclusive to "Five Eyes," an intelligence alliance comprising Australia, Canada, New Zealand, the United Kingdom, and the United States. Campbell refused to show it to Fujisaki then and there, claiming that "Japan is not a member of the Five Eyes. We need special permission to show this to the Japanese side." Despite Japan, as well as the U.S.-Japan alliance, facing its most critical crisis since World War II, based on this reason alone, Japan was required to ask for permission every time they sought access to Five Eyes–acquired information. This was another reality of the U.S.-Japan alliance. A staffer at the Japanese embassy in Washington later reflected, "I thought to myself: is this the reality of the U.S.-Japan alliance? I will not forget the shock I felt at that time for the rest of my life."[61]

On the morning of March 16 (U.S. EST), NRC Chairman Gregory Jaczko expressed his sense of crisis by stating clearly that the "cooling water that normally covers spent fuel was nearly or had totally gone from an uncovered concrete pool above reactor Unit 4" at a hearing scheduled to discuss the Department of Energy's and the NRC's annual fiscal budgets, which ended up focusing on the events at Fukushima.[62]

That day, the NRC released a statement that "Under the guidelines for public safety that would be used in the United States under similar circumstances, the NRC believes it is appropriate for U.S. residents within fifty miles of the Fukushima reactors to evacuate."[63]

To use Jaczko's phrase, "The tune had changed."

Up until then, Jaczko considered "the Japanese should know best what's going on," and had faced the crisis from a position of respecting the policy of the Japanese government. The more information he received, however, the more he doubted this belief.

Even in the early stages of the accident, when Denis McDonough asked him over the phone, "What on earth should we do?" he answered, "Listen closely to what Japan says." Even when the U.S. forces pushed him, "Why aren't we helping?" "Those guys don't know what they're doing," "It'll be hell if it's not fixed," he had given the same answer.

However, "the tune had changed."

Concerns about the response of the Japanese side had been reported from the NRC staff dispatched to Tokyo as well.[64]

WASHINGTON/THE FUJISAKI TELEGRAMS

There was mounting distrust about the Kan administration's approach in the U.S. government.

"We need to give Kan a shock."

Did they mean "shock therapy" for the Japanese government? The State Department flooded the Japanese side with "tough messages."

In the conference call between Steinberg and Edano after noon on March 16 (early dawn on March 17, Japan Time), America sent the same message. This conference call was set up to precede the scheduled heads-of-state conference call between Obama and Kan.

Steinberg asked for a quick briefing. Edano replied, "We're doing our utmost. I'll set up a meeting between the experts immediately." They also laid the groundwork for the summit meeting.

Edano had only taken over from Yoshito Sengoku as chief cabinet secretary in January. He was not used to dealing with overseas. Steinberg felt the Japanese government's response to be "horrifying." He was growing increasingly distrustful.

They're totally unprepared, and their crisis management is nonexistent.

Steinberg was known for being outspoken. In an internal State Department discussion, he asserted, "We have to send an even clearer message to the Japanese side . . . It's hard to understand why the Japanese government is leaving the nuclear emergency response up to TEPCO . . . Who on earth in the Japanese government is dealing with this responsibly? . . . You need a czar in charge at a time like this. I want you to know who that is . . . I want the Japanese government to deal with this emergency as their own responsibility."[65]

The Department of Defense and Joint Chiefs of Staff also started sending the same message. Michael Mullen, chairman of the Joint Chief of Staff, did so during a courtesy call by Fujisaki. The visit had been made at Fujisaki's initiation.

Mullen was a navy admiral. Fujisaki had asked for the meeting because it was necessary to keep in touch with the top brass, including U.S. Pacific Command Commander Willard and Admiral Donald, who was director of Naval Reactors. However, the usually blunt Mullen was even blunter that day.[66]

"Why has the Japanese government left an emergency of this seriousness up to Tokyo Electric? . . . There's a limit to what operators can achieve, as well as to what the police and fire departments can do. Don't they have armies for times like this? Why isn't the Japanese government using the SDF? I just can't understand it . . . If this state of affairs continues, we may have to think about bringing the U.S. forces home."

The implications of Mullen's message were clear. He referred to specific problems in the Japanese government's approach:

1. There was not enough information-sharing between Japan and the United States.
2. The Japanese government did not appear to be using all its resources.
3. He did not think their approach was strategic or long-term.

The final blow was Mullen's phone call (see chapter 8) to chief of staff of the Joint Staff, Ryoichi Oriki, at six p.m. on March 16 (seven a.m. on March 17, Japan Time).[67]

There were those among key members of the Kantei, the SDF, and Ministry of Defense who found Mullen's remarks offensive.

"We don't need Mullen to tell us that we'll have to use the SDF in the end!"

"And what's more, Mullen's information about how we're dealing with the nuclear emergency is old. We know now that there's water in the fuel pool at Unit 4, but he doesn't seem to have that information. Isn't there something wrong with the U.S. information channels?"

There was also the issue of time difference. Old information would be conveyed, as it was a day later, and it was toward the outdated information that the U.S. backlash would be directed. There was growing disgruntlement to the effect of "what's the U.S. government doing; no, it's MOFA's fault for not sending out enough information," and so on.

Oriki felt, *There's a pretty big difference in how heated the White House, the Pentagon, PACOM, and Yokota are.*

The U.S. military leaders were beginning to suggest the SDF was trying to escape from responding to the Fukushima Daiichi accident. The Japanese ambassador to the United States sent a telegram, repeating this verbatim. There must be something behind it. Perhaps MOFA was lobbying the U.S. government to apply external pressure to have the SDF deployed . . .

Whenever Kitazawa's staff passed on one of these telegrams, it came with the following memo attached:

"Minister, we've got another unpleasant one . . ."[68]

CHARLES CASTO

It was Charles Casto who was leading the U.S. Nuclear Regulatory Commission (NRC) Japanese support team in Japan.

Back in the day, Casto had been an operator at Browns Ferry, Tennessee. This was the same type of reactor as the boiling water reactor (BWR) at Fukushima Daiichi. After that, he had served as security inspector for the Brunswick nuclear power plant in North Carolina. He had also been an operator examiner at NRC headquarters. He had an academic side, as well, having spent many years on his doctoral thesis titled "Leadership in Extreme Crisis," but he had worked his way up from an operator.[69]

NRC Chairman Gregory Jaczko had ordered Casto to fly to Japan on March 13. Casto had boarded a commercial flight from his home in Atlanta, but there were no direct flights to Japan. He changed flights at Dallas–Fort Worth Airport in Texas. It did not look like he would make the flight. Having left in a hurry, he forgot to go by his office and pick up his KI (stable iodine). He thought to himself, *Darn*, but it was too late. Luckily, later that evening, another NRC staffer managed to bring the KI pills to Casto's hotel room in a small cooler. "It felt like an illicit drug deal," Casto reflected.[70]

While he was waiting for his flight in Dallas, he received a call on his mobile phone. It was Jaczko.

"Hey, I just wanted to give you a sendoff before you get ready to get on a plane. I can't tell you how important what you're about to do is . . . You're going to be coordinating a lot of activity for the ambassador in Japan in what is a very, very difficult situation."

"Oh, thank you, sir . . . I am reassured with NRC behind me."

"I want you to give thorough support to the ambassador . . . So, if you need anything, you call me directly. Take care."[71]

Jaczko had spent about three months in the summer of 1997 in Japan, writing his doctoral thesis at a physics research institute in Toyama Prefecture. It was part of a U.S.-Japan science exchange program. He had an affinity for Japan.

Jaczko sent Casto off "like a coach telling the pinch hitter, 'Go out, get a hit.'"[72]

What was more, he communicated Casto's marching orders, instructing his team to "work as closely as possible with the Japanese government authorities rather than just the people of TEPCO."[73]

In hindsight, Casto felt, "this order seriously constrained our efforts."[74]

In the afternoon of March 15, Casto touched down at Narita Airport. He was carrying just one suitcase with him.

Casto had spent his whole career in atomic safety regulation at the NRC. After becoming a noncommissioned officer in the Air Force at the age of seventeen, he worked in nuclear arms control at the Air Force Base in South Dakota. He later received training as a nuclear power plant operator in Alabama. At the time of the Three Mile Island accident, he was still learning to be an operator. After this disaster, it was said that another reactor would never be built at a nuclear power plant.

Casto thought, *My career didn't look too good at that point. I've made a really bad career decision.*

Meanwhile, he graduated college, going to school at night, and received a master's degree in public administration. He had also worked as nuclear safety adviser to Senator Harry Reid (D-NV). That was where he had developed his political acumen.[75]

There was no time to check in at his accommodation, the Hotel Okura, and he rushed straight to the U.S. embassy.

Two NRC engineers, Jim Trapp and Tony Ulses, had turned up in Japan on March 13.

On the night of the same day, a meeting was held at the Ministry of Foreign Affairs between them and key officers from NISA. The meeting ran on well into the middle of the night, but both parties left feeling frustrated that they had gotten nowhere. On the night of March 14, Tetsuro Fukuyama, deputy chief cabinet secretary, briefed them on the nuclear emergency situation at the Kantei. Fukuyama had called in Haruki Madarame, chairman of the Nuclear Safety Commission, and Hisanori Nei, deputy director general of NISA.

Casto did not attend any of these meetings, but he felt the NRC engineers were overreacting somewhat.

I get the feeling that they're trying to sell their scenario to Ambassador Roos based on uncertain and unfiltered information.

After claiming "It'll be dangerous unless we evacuate from Tokyo," they would then argue, "Wait, the situation is not as bad as we thought." The engineers were being reckless and confusing Roos in the process, Casto thought. So, the first thing Casto did was stop them from advising Roos. They were professionals when it came to doing reactor safety risk analysis, but, ultimately, they were math guys. When it came to assessing thermal images provided by the U.S. intelligence agency, they did not have a clue. What became apparent in the midst of disaster was the need for a technical interpreter or communicator, not a specialist. Engineers should not be doing the job of a technical interpreter.[76]

Casto told them, "Don't serve up the raw information. Make sure you cook it first." The situation, however, was in a state of constant and rapid change. That was undeniable.

Roos said to Casto, who had just arrived, "I have only slept twenty minutes each night since the accident." Casto parried with, "Yeah, you can sleep thirty minutes tonight."

There was a mountain of information in front of Casto, and all of it only half-baked. Casto had to start "cooking." Engrossed in his reading, he forgot to check in at the hotel. He napped on one of the embassy sofas for about thirty minutes. He worked for the next two days without a change of clothes.

Casto was able to meet Roos once a week, or anytime he wanted to see him. His access to Roos was rock-solid.[77] The problem was access to the Japanese side.

The NRC staff had reported to Casto that everyone was cold to them, TEPCO, METI, NISA, all of them. He tried to get in touch with the crisis management center at the Kantei to get some information, but was not successful. He listened to people at TEPCO and NISA, but they were incredibly busy and did not have much time for him . . .

When Jaczko had worked as a staffer for Senator Harry Reid (D-NV), he had organized opposition to the construction of a nuclear waste disposal site in Nevada. Reid had been elected on the back of this opposition. Reid requested that Jaczko get the top job at the NRC after Obama was elected in 2008, which ensured that a Democrat now would serve as chairman of the NRC. At that point, Jaczko had already worked at the NRC for four years and was the only Democratic commissioner.[78] Initially, the Obama administration declined the request, but Jaczko later got the job as chairman. Regardless, based on his association with Reid, he continued to be seen as an antinuclear proponent and antagonistic toward the industry.

Distrust toward NISA was growing at NRC headquarters. The fact that the safety inspectors had fled the scene prematurely was decisive.

The NRC had regarded NISA as its partner in responding to the accident. Jaczko later recalled, "We have to trust NISA until the point where our trust is completely lost. But it was lost very quickly." Jaczko felt great concern that the NISA inspectors had left the site without permission, so much so that he conveyed his concern about this point when he met with Ambassador Ichiro Fujisaki.

At the time, Fujisaki asked Jaczko, "How many people should be at the site?"

Jaczko replied, "Hundreds of people. You need hundreds."

Jaczko was worried that everybody, the TEPCO workers, associates, NISA, would withdraw. Jaczko told Fujisaki something else.

"You need to be more flexible in setting the allowable radiation dose for employees."

When Fujisaki asked him, "What about in the United States?" Jaczko replied, "A much higher number. But if it's a crisis situation, emergency workers can get as high a dose as they need to perform their job."

Fujisaki conveyed this to Tokyo by telegram.[79]

More and more NRC employees were speaking badly of the Japanese side. Casto gave a warning in a conference call with NRC headquarters in Washington.

"When you've got a thousand dead bodies washing up on the shore, it is tough for them, and we're over here barking at them to do this, do that. We have to be a little patient. They're working hard, and they have a lot of challenges."

The most important resource in a crisis is time, so, in a certain sense, it was only natural that the Japanese side were reluctant to meet, because they did not have time. And the United States should not forget that it was only in an advisory capacity. That was what Casto was trying to say.

"I'm just trying to have a dialog so we can work together."

Since Casto had arrived in Japan, not even a day had passed before he had begun using kilometers and not miles. Kilometers even featured in his reports to Jaczko. As Jaczko said, "That guy, he would assimilate, and that is a temperament valuable to bridging cultural gaps."[80]

When Casto heard from somewhere that the Fukushima Daiichi site was built on an old training ground (Iwaki Army Airfield) for the Japanese army's suicide pilots in the dying stages of the Pacific War, he felt it was strange that an American like himself was fighting the nuclear emergency there alongside the Japanese. At the same time, it also made him think about the complex history of U.S.-Japan relations, and he vowed he would act decently toward Japan.

However, Casto personally did feel quizzical about the chilly response on the Japanese side toward the NRC, especially from NISA.

They seem to regard us as goblins. They seem to feel we're sniffing around for something.

It's probably because there's been hardly any contact or exchange between the NRC and NISA to date, but even so, why are they acting so coldly? Is it from awkwardness or pride?

Through a go-between, the NRC also contacted the foreign affairs department of the National Police Agency. They had regular meetings, if only at the pace of once a week. But the police officers in the foreign affairs department were not a group of nuclear experts and they only had second-hand information.[81]

The day Casto arrived in Japan was the very day the government and TEPCO's Integrated Response Office was set up at TEPCO. No matter what else, he had to talk with the top of TEPCO.

After checking in to the hotel and changing his clothes, Casto met with TEPCO chairman, Tsunehisa Katsumata, at TEPCO. It was a stealthy affair that required Roos and Casto to meet staff in an underground parking garage before being ushered up to an office in order to avoid the thousands of protesters stationed in front of the building.[82] Katsumata was dressed in a suit and had come to the elevator to welcome Casto.

After being shown into a room and exchanging courtesies, TEPCO Vice President Sakae Muto initiated the discussion by updating Casto on the conditions of the plant and the seawater injection.[83]

They did not seem to share my assessment that the worst was over, Casto thought.[84]

Katsumata then told Casto to bring NRC personnel to TEPCO in order to work directly with their emergency response manager.[85] At the end of the meeting, Katsumata looked at Casto and said conditions were grave. He then added one phrase in English:

"Help me."

Casto was moved by these straightforward words. He felt Katsumata was looking at him in a sort of "grandfatherly way." He respected Katsumata's dedication even though his sense of desperation raised doubts in his mind. With his blood pressure rising, Casto thought to himself upon leaving, *The chairman of TEPCO is telling us that they cannot handle this event.*[86]

Immediately after, Casto spoke directly with Jaczko to request more help.

"We need to save TEPCO somehow. I want large-scale mobilization of NRC engineers."

Jaczko was attuned to Casto's level of concern, but also took a realistic perspective on what was possible given the difficulty of the task and Casto's responsibilities.

"Chuck, do me a favor. Take a deep breath."

This struck Casto as demeaning, but ultimately Jaczko found his request to be beyond the NRC's mandate to provide consultation and advice. He would have to compromise.[87]

The chairman just thought that I was calling to say, "The sky's falling, and we need to bring all the NRC over here."

At the time, however, he just had to say it. It felt impossible to communicate in a single phone call how dire the situation was on the ground, including the rumors that TEPCO might abandon ship, or that both the SDF and onsite workers seemed completely paralyzed.[88]

As Casto came into contact more and more with the middle management at TEPCO, however, his initial feeling—"we have to do everything. We must amass a force to help the Japanese"—started to wear off. Not only did they ignore him, they were uncooperative.

Casto had immediately gathered people from the embassy to head over to TEPCO, but by the time they arrived, they were met with staff who declared, "We don't need your help right now. We'll call you when we need you."[89]

Casto was stunned. *How could they defy their chairman's directives?*

He could not understand why, at the time when injecting water was the most crucial, they persisted in trying to get power restored first.

Now imagine you have a fire in your house and the electricity's off, and you just go in and put the electricity back on; you wouldn't do that. First, you would turn on the water. Why don't they understand that?

He remembered the advice an acquaintance who ran an American power utility had given him before he flew to Japan.

"Talking to TEPCO is just a waste of time, Chuck."

Casto started to think there was some hidden meaning in Katsumata's "help me."

Come to think of it, Katsumata didn't say, "help us," he said, "help me." I wonder why? Was he trying to say, this TEPCO organization's not going to change overnight; trying to change it quickly would be even more difficult if we weren't in crisis; I have to lead TEPCO; please understand that. Katsumata was trying to make that appeal.[90]

YOU CAN'T SEE WHAT CAN'T BE SEEN

The U.S. government was worried even more than Japan about the fuel pool at Unit 4.

In an NRC conference call at 3:30 p.m. on March 14 (U.S. EST), NRC staff gave an overview, stating, "There are no fears concerning any of the fuel pools at Fukushima Daiichi."

A phone call from Jim Trapp and Tony Ulses in Tokyo at around five p.m. on March 14 (U.S. EST; around 6:00 a.m. on March 15, Japan Time) changed that dramatically.

Trapp said, "We heard from them that there is a fire in Unit 4 spent-fuel pool." The "them" he was referring to meant "we finally got to talk to somebody mainstream with the qualifications equivalent to ours."

"That's the bad news."

"They also don't know the water level."

"We were working through an interpreter. We went over things a couple of times, I don't think we are missing the point here."

An NRC member of staff:

"Now, I'm going to be an anal-retentive regulator. Clearly, this is no longer an INES at Level IV."

Tony Ulses:

"Yeah, I think we've gone past that one . . ."[91]

Sometime after six a.m. on March 15 Japan Time. There was a supposed hydrogen gas explosion in the Unit 4 (RB), damaging the four sides of the upper operating floor's walls.[92]

In the last conference call of the day, an NRC staff member summarized "the day's developments."

"Unit 4 previously was reported as stable. That is no longer the case."

"The spent-fuel pool is dry and there appears to be a zirconium fire in the spent-fuel pool of Unit 4."[93]

On the same day, the NRC ran a RASCAL, a code used in emergencies for making independent dose projections. As a result, they predicted that the meltdown in Unit 2 would trigger the possibility of a worst-case scenario in Unit 4.[94]

Another NRC staff member described it as "The pool structure is no longer in existence. The walls have collapsed. So, you have spent fuel sitting there in a pile."

Their view was that the Unit 4 reactor was completely dry.[95]

After eleven a.m. on March 15, Japan Time, TEPCO gave a press conference on the "abnormal situation in Unit 4":

"After a loud sound around six a.m., we confirmed damage near the roof on the fifth floor of the building . . . At 9:38 a.m., a fire outbreak was confirmed in the northwest section of the fourth floor . . . We are unable to confirm the temperature of the spent-fuel pool on the western side of the fifth floor."[96]

THE NIGHT OF THAT DAY. The following question was fired at the TEPCO press conference at TEPCO Head Office: "Which is the most dangerous of the six plants at Fukushima Daiichi?"

Mitsu Kuroda, head of the Nuclear Facility Management Section, considered for a moment. Saying, "It's quite difficult to order them," he added, "Because I think Unit 4 is in the toughest situation in terms of temperature, we are placing priority on getting water into Unit 4, but I think we'll be using the same methods to pump water into Unit 1 and Unit 3, which have lost their roofs . . . I've heard we're asking both the SDF and the U.S. military. We're considering that, because we think it will be the quickest."[97]

TEPCO's internal simulation assumed that the water level in the Unit 4 spent-fuel pool would drop to reach below the top of fuel by the end of March.[98]

THE NIGHT OF MARCH 16. The third floor of TEPCO Head Office. METI's office.

"Hey, hey!"

Osamu Maekawa was called over by Masaya Yasui. They had both been ensconced in the Integrated Response Office from the previous day. Yasui said, "Take a look at this footage" and showed the computer screen to Maekawa. He said it was an image of the Unit 4 spent-fuel pool that came from footage taken by a TEPCO employee who was on the SDF helicopter flown that afternoon. Maekawa stared at the image on the computer screen and made just one comment.

"The refueler's not broken."

He was referring to the refueling machine.

"It's showing green. It's not broken."

There were two cranes on top of the building. One was for refueling—a crane designated for the fuel rods. It was located on the western side of the fifth floor. It could be seen through the steel frame, and it looked as though it was untouched. This was the crane used in every regular inspection to change a quarter of the fuel rods.

"And that beautiful yellow PCV [primary containment vessel] is still there, too."

Was that not the yellow lid of the containment vessel that could be seen farther back, behind the refueler? Yellow and green could be faintly discerned.

Yasui said, "This white stuff. Like smoke. That looks like steam, doesn't it? If it was dry, there wouldn't be any steam coming out . . . If it was dry, it wouldn't be shielded by any water, and the radiation would be huge. But the dose doesn't show that . . . There was originally 1,400 tons or so of water in Unit 4. That would fall by 70-80 tons a day, so it's not possible that it would run out in four or five days. It should take until March 20 to reach even halfway."

Maekawa nodded at each comment and said at the end, "The water's still there."

Yasui came back with, "I think so, too."[99]

So, nothing certain could be said. Nevertheless, it looked like the pool's water was glimmering. You couldn't fool your own eyes.[100]

The Japanese side subsequently showed Charles Casto and other NRC staff the footage from the helicopter at the Kantei's crisis management center.[101] Pointing at the image, the Japanese side explained:

"Look, you can see it's shining here, can't you? You can also see a reflection of the light below it, right? That reflection is the reflection of the water."

Casto screwed up his eyes, but no matter which way he looked, he could not see a thing.

You can't see what you can't see. It's impossible with just these two images from the video tape. We need more conclusive evidence that there's water in the pool . . .

Casto conveyed his opinion that "it isn't conclusive enough." The Japanese side, however, were becoming increasingly confident.

Late at night on March 16, there was an announcement in the Integrated Response Office on the second floor of TEPCO Head Office, "We want everyone to watch the footage from the helicopter."

There was a stir in the room.[102] Yamashita, who actually shot the footage from the helicopter, was also asked to come over. He just got back to the Tokyo Head Office that evening via limousine after receiving orders to return to the Head Office immediately after he arrived at J-Village.

After taking a look at the images he took, Yamashita was disappointed that "the footage hadn't captured much . . ." The surface of the water was bright, and even though he thought the water was in sight, the footage did not reveal it clearly. Nevertheless, the reactor well was full of water, Yamashita recalled. If the spent-fuel pool is empty, water in the reactor well will automatically shove the gate open and flow into the spent-fuel pool, flooding it. Therefore, if the spent-fuel pool were empty, the amount of water in the reactor well would decrease sharply. The reactor well is a space in the upper part of the reactor building above the primary containment vessel. When refueling, the reactor well is filled with water to the same level as the spent-fuel pool, so that the process can be conducted completely under water.

An older TEPCO engineer commented on Yamashita's remarks while watching the video, "It seems like there is still water in the Unit 4 fuel pool."

"Why is there water in the Unit 4 fuel pool?"

"I think the water must have flowed in from the reactor side when the panels blew off. But it's just a hypothesis."[103]

In the early hours of March 17, Takaya Imai, assistant vice minister at METI, told NISA, "They've confirmed there's water in the Unit 4 spent-fuel pool." Imai's "confirmation" was based on the craftsman-like "confirmation" of Yasui and Maekawa.[104]

The morning of the same day, Prime Minister Naoto Kan was shown the footage in his office at the Kantei. It was reported to him, "There's still water in the Unit 4 fuel pool."[105]

If there was water in the fuel pool, however, what on earth was that "explosion" in Unit 4 at six a.m. on March 15? Unit 4 had no fuel rods inside the reactor. If it was not the fuel pool, what was it then? If it was a hydrogen explosion, where was the hydrogen coming from? Doubts remained.

Kaieda had started keeping notes from March 16, and his memo for that day was, "What was the hydrogen explosion in Unit 4?"[106]

The Atomic Energy Society of Japan (AESJ) investigation committee argues in a report released in 2014: "It was assumed that if the SFP had no water, the sky-shine radiation from fuel would increase the radiation dosage rate in the vicinity of Unit 4, but the dose was actually low enough for staff to work. Therefore, it seemed that the fuel was not exposed."[107]

In addition, when TEPCO removed the fuel assemblies from the Unit 4 spent-fuel pool in January 2012 and December 2014, there was no trace that they had melted or been damaged. Later investigations revealed that the reason behind the explosion in Unit 4 was not because of the spent-fuel pool, but rather the hydrogen gas that had come through an exhaust pipe from the reactor in Unit 3.

The Integrated Response Office decided priority for the fuel pool water injection would be given to Unit 3. Up until March 16, the main target had been Unit 4, but this changed to Unit 3 on March 17.[108] This was because water had been "confirmed" in the Unit 4 fuel pool.

However, the NRC had deemed that "there was no water," based on six sources, including monitoring figures. The only information from the Japanese side that challenged this judgment was the "shadow" in the video shot from the helicopter. The Japanese judged this to be water.[109]

The difference of opinion over the status of Unit 4's fuel pool highlights a gulf between the two countries' situational awareness of the crisis. In testimony before the U.S. Congress, Jaczko himself referred to the debate over the status of Unit 4 as a "conflict" arising between the United States and Japan. While focusing on this, a *New York Times* article on March 16, 2011, reported that there was a critical gap between the United States and Japan in the understanding of conditions.[110]

ELEVEN

Yokosuka Shock

APPLES AND ORANGES

After arriving at Narita Airport on the afternoon of March 15, when Charles Casto went straight to the U.S. embassy, the staff were in the middle of a videoconference with Washington regarding the Fukushima nuclear accident.

Close to sixty U.S. government staff were debating evacuation guidelines for U.S. citizens in Japan. Ambassador Roos was also there. Casto sat in as well. Everybody was on edge.

Admiral Kirkland Donald, director of Naval Reactors, was insisting, "We should recommend an evacuation radius of two hundred miles. We need to evacuate all of the ninety thousand U.S. citizens living in Tokyo."[1]

Several people put forward counterarguments. Kevin Maher, leader of the State Department's Japan support team and former director of the Japan Affairs Office, joined in the opposition.

"It's too early for an all-out evacuation order. It would be bad, politically. We'll have the results from the radiation computer models at the Department of Energy and Nuclear Regulatory Commission (NRC) in a few hours, so we'll know if Tokyo is in danger or not when we see them. We should wait until then before issuing an all-out evacuation order. If you issue the order now, you'll rock the U.S-Japan alliance."[2]

Naval Reactors, the NRC, the Department of Energy, and the White House Science and Technology Advisory Agency were all running simulations predicting how the accident would evolve. Casto thought, *Uh-oh.*

These guys are just talking about potential. But it hasn't happened yet. All they have is a worst-case explosion scenario, what they were calling a "popcorn scenario," so to speak.[3]

Casto also spoke.

"They haven't got any water into the reactors for the past three days. So, things may get worse. But, fortunately, things aren't as bad as that at all."[4]

The recommendation to evacuate from Tokyo was passed over in this videoconference. Many of the conference-call participants heard the name Naval Reactors, a federal agency, for the first time. The remarks of Admiral Donald in the conference call were based on Naval Reactors' own simulation forecast. They were not on behalf of the entire navy, nor the official view of the Department of Defense.[5]

However, many were shocked to see both the U.S. Navy and the Department of Defense toeing the line of this agency as far as radiation was concerned.

A high-ranking U.S. government official later recalled, "Honestly, I was stunned that only I believed the U.S. Navy to be calm and the greatest voice of reason, and honestly, I was stunned to see the navy react the most emotionally of anywhere in the federal government. And not just me, but many people were shocked."

The stance of Naval Reactors was zero risk. The same official said, "With a radiation accident, everybody wanted zero risk, and they also had to be seen asking for zero risk, but this attitude was the most pronounced in the navy."[6]

Naval Reactors had a huge influence in assessing the situation with USS *Ronald Reagan* and *George Washington*. The navy had nuclear-powered aircraft carriers and nuclear submarines. The unit in charge of the power generation system, including nuclear power, was the Navy Propulsion Unit, but it was Naval Reactors' job to watch over safety regulation in the nuclear-powered sector.

Staff at Naval Reactors took safety regulation for nuclear submarines as their standard. Even the slightest amount of radiation contamination spelled the end inside a nuclear submarine. If a nuclear power plant was on land, they had contingent evacuation plans. However, there was no evacuation plan at sea. So, their golden rule was "no release" (zero emission). They were nervous about contamination and committed themselves to cleanliness.

The director of Naval Reactors is nominated by the secretary of the navy and appointed by the president, then confirmed by Congress. Their term of service is eight years, and, as is the case with Supreme Court judges, they cannot be replaced by a political appointment even with a change of administration. Their independence is guaranteed.

Naval Reactors was the brainchild of Hyman Rickover, the father of the U.S. Navy's nuclear-powered program. He spent a total of sixty-three years in the navy, working on nuclear marine propulsion, including the launch of the world's first nuclear-powered submarine, the *Nautilus*, in 1954. Congress would not let him retire, because he was "irreplaceable."[7]

The NRC staff, who had just arrived in Japan, expounded different claims and assessments from those of Naval Reactors (NR).

"Those guys are extreme. There's no need to listen to them."

The U.S. ambassador to Japan, John Roos, found it confusing to work with the NRC and NR both dispatched to Tokyo, out of sync with each other and voicing different opinions and advice at times. Roos asked Admiral Kirkland Donald, director of Naval Reactors, and Gregory Jaczko, NRC chairman, for some "coordination." Naval Reactors in Washington got in touch with the NRC straight away.

"It's not good having the NRC and NR staff giving different views at the embassy."

When Casto was told of this NR "concern" by NRC headquarters, he said, "So, there's another player, I guess, that we have to get coordinated with."[8]

Roos also asked Donald to place someone from NR at the embassy, to which Donald agreed.

After the accident, the NRC had encouraged U.S. citizens living in Japan to follow the protective measures recommended by the Japanese government. When the Japanese government decided on a twenty-kilometer evacuation zone on the night of March 12, the NRC supported that. After the explosion of Unit 3 (RB) on March 14, it looked into a fifty-mile evacuation, but did not go so far as to issue an official recommendation.[9]

When the Japanese government also issued a twenty- or thirty-kilometer indoor evacuation order on the morning of March 15, the NRC had issued a statement on the same day (U.S. EST) that "Under the guidelines for public safety that would be used in the United States under similar circumstances, the NRC believes it is appropriate."[10]

The NRC's stance, however, changed dramatically with the damage to the suppression chamber in Unit 2 and the explosion in Unit 4 (RB). On March 14, the NRC had received a report indicating that the reactor fuel had started to melt in Unit 2, signaled by a loud bang. With these changes, the latest computer simulations were now predicting that radiation could reach well beyond ten miles from the plant.[11]

"The reactor is rapidly becoming unstable and the situation is starting to deteriorate in a chain of events."

The expression on the faces of the NRC staff suddenly became grim. Another point was that TEPCO had not sent enough staff to the site, and there was the fear that they might pull out from the scene. They had to consider the risk if that occurred.

In addition, the latest calculation results from RASCAL came in. The results of the simulation with the new data were way over the conventionally assumed ten-mile U.S. protective action guideline recommendation. According to the results, the recommended evacuation zone spread from thirty miles to forty miles to fifty miles. Jaczko was talking on the phone with the White House when Catherine Haney, a senior member of the NRC, showed him the scrap of paper outlining this. The staffer said, "Contamination is progressing considerably, it's serious."

Jaczko asked his staff in a whisper, "Should we stop at thirty or forty miles?"

The staff member said, "No, let's say fifty miles. That will cover thirty or forty as well."

After hanging up the phone, Jaczko quizzed his staff. "Isn't the emergency evacuation area ten miles in the United States?"

The staff member said, "That's right, but that's in a normal case. This is a serious accident. It's different. This exceeds expectations."[12]

At this point, Jaczko was well aware that a fifty-mile evacuation zone would signal a complete one-eighty from his announcement earlier that morning that the most reliable information would come from the Japanese experts. Now he would be telling the public the exact opposite: listen to the United States and be cautious with the Japanese government.

"I really wish we were looking at a piece of paper from the Japanese showing their dose projections," he said to the others in the meeting. Ultimately, the NRC reasoned that without accurate instrumentation, the Japanese experts were flying just as blind as the United States.

"Would we act based on the information they gave me if this incident was happening in the United States?" Jaczko asked while on call. "Yes," everyone unanimously replied.[13]

The following discussion took place in an internal NRC meeting.

> NRC staff: "Given the spent-fuel pool on Unit 4 and the possibility that it's already had a fire, would fifty miles still be the appropriate evacuation distance?"
>
> Casto: "If the fuel melts, then the time it takes for the concrete to melt is a couple of inches (approximately five to eight centimeters) an hour. With no external power, you're going to lose the containment function of the containment vessel. There's no doubt about it."
>
> Jaczko: "If this happened in the United States, we would go with a fifty-mile evacuation order."
>
> NRC staff: "The chairman testified to the House of Representatives committee, and a press release was sent out. They didn't align with the Japanese evacuation order and sent out an evacuation order for U.S. citizens within fifty miles from the Daiichi plant."

In Washington, as the NRC amended its stance to a fifty-mile evacuation zone, Naval Reactors made contact with the NRC.

In a conference call, a member of Naval Reactors staff said, "NRC also talked about fifty miles for protective actions, right? If so, then it's the same . . . they're not apples and oranges—or are they apples of different varieties?"

The NRC recommendation for fifty miles was based mainly on the predicted impact of a meltdown in Unit 2. When the NRC staff told the Naval Reactors staff this, a member of the Naval Reactor staff expressed his doubts.

"If we end up losing one of those plants, there's a high possibility that we'll lose all of the plants . . . despite that, NRC's prediction is based on losing Unit 2, just one unit. So, I worry that you may be excessively optimistic here a little bit."[14]

Donald interjected and asked Jaczko, "Limiting it to the impact on Japan, what does NRC envision as the worst-case scenario?"

Jaczko replied, "At this point, I would see a worst-case scenario probably being three reactors eventually having, for lack of a better word, a meltdown. It would be a scenario in which the containment vessel would crack and radioactive material would be released. To add to that, the state of the six spent-fuel pools could deteriorate and fires could break out. But the difficult thing is how to incorporate these into scenarios."

Donald continued: "Three reactors melting down, six spent-fuel pools go up in flames. What, then, do you think would be the impact on Tokyo, for example, if the wind kept blowing in that direction?"

"At this point," Jaczko said, "I think I would still go with the fifty-mile evacuation zone right now . . . Last night one reactor, Unit 2, had a core meltdown. Therefore, we went for fifty miles."[15]

The Navy Reactors viewed NRC's worst-case scenario as "excessively optimistic." The NRC, NR, and the Department of Energy, to name a few, were starting to create their own worst-case scenarios.

The NRC's model calculations (RASCAL) released to the press on March 16, estimated

- 33 percent core damage in one reactor

- 50 percent damage to one spent-fuel pool, and 100 percent damage to a separate spent-fuel pool

Since the reactor buildings had been destroyed, there would be an unfiltered release of radioactive material with no containment.[16]

The Navy's "very worst-case scenario" was one that estimated

- 100 percent core melt

- Containment failure in three reactors

■ Four spent-fuel pools emptied of water, all the spent fuel melted, and the release of radioactive material into the atmosphere

In a conference call, Jaczko said, "This would be the worst of the worst-case scenarios. Basically, a scenario in which human society couldn't respond . . . Is it the case that they are doing something like coming up with a kind of crazy scenario like a meteor hitting the earth at the same time an asteroid strikes? Don't they want to know more realistic information about the release of radiation at source? . . . If that could be it, then wouldn't a scenario in which someone puts the core in a bag after meltdown and carries it over the Pacific to California be the worst case? (Laughter) . . . I want a scenario made which is the worst-case but also possible."[17]

The NRC was also using RASCAL, however, to create a worst-case scenario. This forecast radiation volumes for a worst-case scenario where "three reactors and six pools might be out of control." According to that, the danger zone would have to be extended to 240–320 kilometers—in short, to Greater Tokyo.[18]

However, this was just for internal consideration. Jaczko himself was thinking that they should make a recommendation on the basis of "realistic information about the release of radiation at source."

"THIS HAS IMPLICATIONS FOR THE FUTURE OF THE U.S.-JAPAN ALLIANCE"

On March 16, one of the Naval Reactors' worst-case scenarios was leaked to the press.

"Pentagon Preparing for a Nuclear Worst-Case Scenario at Fukushima" was the headline carried in the *Stars and Stripes* (March 16, 2011).

"The Pentagon on Wednesday began laying out precautions to keep troops safe, announcing a fifty-mile no-go zone around the unstable Fukushima Daiichi nuclear complex . . . Already, troops on some bases in Japan and aboard ships offshore—including two air crew members on the USS *Ronald Reagan*, who had to take iodine tablets Tuesday (March 15)—have been exposed to radiation from the nuclear plants . . ."[19]

On March 17, Robert Willard, commander of the U.S. Pacific Command (PACOM), told a press conference, "We are drawing up plans to evacuate 87,300 Americans, including military personnel and civilian employees, if the situation deteriorates." There were newspaper reports (*Stars and Stripes*) that several hundreds of civilians had already been flown to the United States on chartered flights with another nine thousand on standby.

Jeffrey Bader, senior director for Asian affairs at the White House, immediately contacted Admiral Gary Roughead, chief of naval operations.

"Gary, no one knows better than us how important it is to protect the health of the U.S. forces. But all decisions have to have a scientific basis. It also touches on the future of U.S.-Japan relations. Any decision that may affect that has to go through a solid decision-making process."

Bader was worried that U.S. military movements could cause a panic in Japan, especially Tokyo. Conveying this concern to Roughead, he said, "We understand that strategies are made discreetly. But we don't want to see that surface. We don't want physical movement."[20]

Within the hour, Roughead instructed a press officer at the Pentagon to make it clear that the U.S. forces were not withdrawing, and appeared in front of the press corps to clarify that point.

"There was never a point where I was ready to move on a mandatory evacuation."[21]

Willard and Steinberg clashed heavily in the deputies meetings at the White House. Willard insisted that the top priority was the health and safety of the U.S. forces and their civilian employees, and so, a recommendation to evacuate should be sent out the sooner the better.

Steinberg appealed that this was a question of the very fundamentals of U.S.-Japan relations, as well as, on a deeper level, one of national security. Denis McDonough, deputy national security adviser, expressed the same concerns as Steinberg. He said, "If the U.S. military leaves Japan in the middle of this crisis, they may never be allowed back to the U.S. bases in Japan."

Willard remained intransigent, however. His top priority was drawing up evacuation plans for U.S. citizens in Tokyo. In the words of a high-ranking official in the U.S. government, "He focused just on that like a laser beam."[22]

As a high-ranking official at the State Department later put it, "While it was the U.S. forces, especially the navy, that started to prepare for an evacuation from Japan, it was the diplomats and others who said we had to stay in Japan. Quite an ironic situation."

If the Navy's two hundred–mile evacuation proposal was put into action, "relocating the U.S. embassy, evacuating all U.S. citizens from Tokyo, and withdrawing all U.S. military from Tokyo and Yokosuka would have been unavoidable."[23] It would have created panic not only among U.S. citizens, but probably all of Tokyo. No, all of Japan, perhaps. This might create more casualties than the actual radiation. The State Department made this case, but the navy was unrelenting.

The State Department struggled in the face of the navy's "zero risk" principle. A high-ranking U.S. government official looked back at this dilemma:

"The military stance was to go with safety first rather than being sorry later. Their position was to evacuate everyone as soon as possible, stay ahead of the curve. At a time of crisis, when you're at the stage where it's not possible to grasp the facts, it's terribly difficult to refute the argument of making conservative estimates and going as much as possible with safety first. You can't say things won't get any worse, so there's no need to worry like that. There was no data to counter them with and no supporting facts. That was the point we struggled with the most during the crisis."[24]

Data provided by the Japanese government was not trusted.

"That's why we were desperate to get real information quickly from Japan, but that didn't happen."[25]

There was another awkward issue. Just as the *Stars and Stripes* ran their scoop, the U.S. forces were preparing to distribute iodine tablets to its troops and civilian employees in Japan. For example, the air force had decided to distribute iodine to its troops operating within a 70-mile (110-kilometer) radius.

Willard had made clear his intention that "It's predicted that radiation will double at the Yokosuka naval base. It's to be distributed now and gotten ready for use." Bader, however, checked him, saying, "There will be panic in Tokyo when it's learned that the U.S. military is distributing iodine."

This position of the navy irritated the White House and the State Department. Criticism was voiced:

"The navy's arrogant."[26]

There was no option but to make judgments based on scientific grounds. Waving the U.S.-Japan alliance flag was only counterproductive. Informed by the Naval Reactors, neither the Joint Chiefs of Staff nor the Defense Department could play the alliance card.

There was no sign of any rapprochement whatsoever in meetings at the deputy level. Was there any other choice than going with "scientific grounds"? They needed to change their strategy.

Bader woke Denis McDonough, the NSC boss and deputy national security adviser, in the middle of the night. Bader appealed to McDonough.

"Different models were coming into the White House, and we were being asked to decide on the basis of those models, but we couldn't. That is why we have a presidential science adviser. His role is to review their independent models and appraisals in an integrated manner. If we responded separately to all of the agencies' different models, it would be a disaster."[27]

JOHN HOLDREN

McDonough phoned John Holdren, assistant to the president for science and technology and director of the White House Office of Science and Technology Policy (OSTP).[28]

Holdren's field of expertise was space technology, plasma physics. He had studied at the Massachusetts Institute of Technology and Stanford University, and after having worked at the Lawrence Livermore National Laboratory, taught at the Harvard Kennedy School of Government. He joined the Obama administration as a political appointee. Since that time, he had been deeply involved in homeland security, energy, and environmental policy.

Holdren was hurrying to create a worst-case scenario model with the Department of Energy. He had a team of experts helping, including those from the Lawrence Livermore National Laboratory.

This group recognized the risk that radiation might increase to a level where the TEPCO operators at Fukushima Daiichi NPS would suffer exposure, putting a stop to onsite operations and forcing an evacuation. If it came to an evacuation, the worst-case scenario might well immediately turn into the "worst worst-case scenario."

However, they set their sights on a worst-case scenario that was a "plausible worst-case scenario." Of all the worst-case scenarios, you could say this was the "least-worst worst-case scenario."

When he learned this, something struck Richard Reed, NSC staff, deep down. A simulation was not the result of an automatic or mechanical process from the physics of the fuel pool and reactor. Ultimately, it was the decision and judgment of the people operating the plant that affected the outcome.

It's inconceivable that the Japanese would leave the job halfway. That's not what the Japanese people do.[29]

Holdren stopped the agencies from drawing up their own scenarios. The NRC was thinking it would like to run one last simulation on the radiation dose if water was injected into the fuel pools, but given Holdren's strong interdiction, they refrained from doing so.[30]

Holdren's worst-case scenario assumed that one or more of the reactors at Fukushima Daiichi NPS would melt down, and that at least two spent-fuel pools would be completely dry. Based on this, the following developments were forecast.

- A plume exceeding the U.S. Department of the Environment's standard would not reach within 75 to 100 kilometers of Tokyo

- There would be several days' warning before such an emergency situation was reached

- The radiation dose at Yokosuka was no more than 5 percent of the navy's prediction

- Of the radioactive materials, iodine would only be between 1 and 2 percent of the navy's prediction

- Therefore, there was no need to take into consideration, for the time being, the risk of radiation contamination in Tokyo, Yokosuka, and Yokota[31]

This directly contradicted the navy's two hundred–mile fallout scenario. It provided Bader and Steinberg with just the tailwind they needed.[32]

Holdren had a special ability to explain complicated scientific matters in everyday terms that even a layman could understand. After hearing Holdren explain a technically complicated matter in a deputies meeting, Reed and Russel, both White House staff, looked at each other with a nod.

"If you want to put someone from the government on TV to explain it to the people, put on Dr. Holdren."

"Yeah, his explanations can even be understood by high school students."[33]

A high-ranking U.S. government official later recalled, "John Holdren was the absolute hero of the U.S. government . . . More than anything, he was calm. When many people were panicking, he was cool to the very last. For example, with radioactive water leaking into the ocean, people would say things like we can't allow any fish from Japan into the United States, and Holdren would say that given the data grasped at present, it's impossible for that level of radioactive contamination to have an impact on the Pacific Ocean. It is not something to be worried about."

"Without him, the development of U.S.-Japan relations surrounding the Fukushima Daiichi crisis would have been awfully different."[34]

The U.S. government spent two whole days, March 15 and March 16, discussing the evacuation recommendation issue. The meeting was spread out over several occasions. The participants included Denis McDonough, deputy national security adviser; John Holdren, presidential science and technology adviser; Jeffrey Bader, NSC senior director for Asian affairs; Daniel Russel, NSC director for Japan, South Korea, and North Korea; Richard Reed, deputy assistant to the president for homeland security; James Steinberg, deputy secretary of state; Kurt Campbell, assistant secretary of state for East Asian and Pacific affairs; Daniel Poneman, deputy secretary of energy; Gregory Jaczko, chairman of the NRC; James Cartwright, vice chairman of the Joint Chiefs of Staff; Robert Willard, PACOM commander; and John Roos, U.S. ambassador to Japan.[35] During the crisis, it was mainly the deputies who dealt with this issue around the clock.

When a meeting was held in the Situation Room at the White House about the NRC's "recommendation to evacuate fifty miles," many of the participants said they had to leave partway through to attend another meeting, due to an intensification of the civil war in Libya, and left the room.[36]

The White House held a deputies meeting late on March 15. The topic was the NRC policy of recommending an evacuation within a fifty-mile radius. The navy was countering with a proposal for "two hundred miles."

Holdren also attended the meeting. Willard insisted, "If the radiation dose at Yokosuka doubles, we'll have to think about evacuating everyone from the Yokosuka naval base." McDonough countered, "That can't be done. If the whole navy pulls out first, it will mean leaving civilians behind."

Under the U.S. No Double Standard Policy, in the case of threat or risk to life or limb, such as an act of terrorism, the government cannot be prejudicial, and has to protect all its citizens. This principle must be applied to government officials, the military, and civilians alike. The distribution of iodine also had to follow this rule. If it was distributed only to the navy's sailors and their civilian employees, and not to U.S. government officials and American citizens, this would be a clear violation of the No Double Standard Policy. Using this legal argument, McDonough stated unequivocally: "It can't be done."

In fact, if the navy's insistence had been accepted, it would lead to a triple standard, not just a double standard. In other words, there was a danger that three different standards would emerge: for the military, the government officials, and the general public. Regarding the distribution of iodine, it was not possible to distribute it only to the navy first. Willard was forced to back down.[37]

It was McDonough's "victory due to his ability to never be in conflict, but to carefully disarm the opposition," in the words of a high-ranking State Department official.[38] By way of conveying "the president's interest," McDonough asked the line of deputies, "I'd like you to think about how you would draw up evacuation plans if the Fukushima Daiichi nuclear accident had taken place in America. What would be the plan if it had happened in Philadelphia? Or Washington?"[39]

Jaczko replied, "Fifty miles."

That became the decider. The proposal for two hundred miles that the navy insisted on was rejected. A high-ranking White House official testified how difficult the fifty-mile decision was:

"I've never experienced anything as hard during my long time in government. People were becoming emotional, even hysterical. The White House had to think about the different interests of the various agencies. And at the high level of secretary or deputy secretary.

"When discussions take place at this high a level, it's difficult, because there's nowhere else to go. Their job is to make decisions, so once a decision is made, they tend to stick to it. It's incredibly hard to make them change or overturn it."[40]

Before noon on March 16, a cabinet meeting was held at the White House. It was the first meeting regarding Fukushima nuclear disaster issues that President Barack Obama attended in person. Thomas Donilon, national security adviser, got proceedings underway. The issues were:

- The instructions for a fifty-mile (eighty-kilometer) radius evacuation zone from Fukushima Daiichi NPS

- A recommendation for voluntary departure for the families of U.S. government officials

A number of people threw out their doubts—"Will we be okay with just that?"—regarding the government proposal. Voices were raised, "Isn't it dangerous to base decisions on information from the Japanese government? Their information is unreliable."

Holdren replied, "We are not using the Japanese government's data information as a given. Our model is based on the type of nuclear reactor offered by NRC and GE."

That was a crucial factor. At this point, it was decided that voluntary overseas departure evacuation advice for the families of U.S. government staff and evacuation zone instructions would be released. Neither the embassy staff from Tokyo nor the sailors from U.S. Yokosuka naval base would be withdrawn.[41]

At the end, however, President Obama stated, "Let's hold off a bit before deciding. Let's do it after I have talked to Japan's prime minister directly."

The NSC press officer became a little nervous and asked Obama, "Mr. President, does that include the evacuation zone instructions in a fifty-mile area?"

"Oh no, no, that's done; that's a no-brainer."

Obama's "let's hold off a bit" was about the voluntary overseas departure of U.S. government officials and families. France and Germany had already advised their citizens to evacuate. That was in the mind of the attendees, and they all felt that pressure. Obama said, "That's a more important issue."

Jaczko argued against Obama's demand to hold off. "Mr. President, I think we need to act now. We've been asking our Japanese counterparts for several days for better insight into their decisionmaking and analyses. They don't have a better assessment than we do. I don't think we should wait any longer."[42]

Obama did not concede the point. "No, I need to call the prime minister before we make this announcement."

However, Obama did add, "I'm going to call the prime minister in the evening our time, the morning his time."

After saying this and looking at Jaczko's face, he turned toward Donilon sitting next to him and said, "I remember Tom waking me up at one a.m. I am aware of what's been going on."[43]

He was speaking about the night of March 14 (the morning of March 15, Japan Time) when the NRC, upon receiving information of a fire in the Unit 4 fuel pool, was seeking to make a recommendation for a fifty-mile evacuation zone. Afterward, however, because the NRC staff dispatched to Tokyo—Tony Ulses and Jim Trapp—stated that "there is a need to further check conditions," the execution of the recommendation was "postponed." At that time, after submitting the recommendation, Jaczko went back to his house to get some sleep. After two or three hours, the emergency contact from Tokyo informed the NRC that they had decided to "postpone" the implementation of the recommendation, which was passed on to Jaczko the next morning.[44]

Sometime after eight p.m. on March 16 (U.S. EST; nine a.m. on March 17, Japan Time), the U.S. and Japanese leaders held a telephone conversation. Obama said, "We intend to encourage U.S. citizens living in the Tokyo area to evacuate from the same area." This was tantamount to advance notice.[45]

THE VERACITY OF "FIFTY MILES"

1:15 A.M. ON MARCH 17 (U.S. EST). The U.S. government announced that it had ordered the U.S. citizens:

- A fifty-mile evacuation zone from Fukushima Daiichi NPS

- A recommendation for voluntary departure for the families of U.S. government officials

The families of U.S. government officials could leave if they wished. The government would cover the costs of their return. However, they would not be allowed to return to Japan until the government had canceled the recommendation for voluntary departure. This meant that all U.S. government officials would remain in Japan, separated from their families.

The recommendation to evacuate from a fifty-mile radius came from the NRC. The instruction for the voluntary departure of families of U.S. government officials came from the U.S. embassy. The travel advisory for ordinary U.S. citizens came from the State Department. The fifty-mile zone included the three major cities in Fukushima Prefecture—Koriyama, Iwaki, and Fukushima City—as well as the southern section of Sendai City, and covered 2 million prefectural residents.[46]

Bader later recalled: "In a real crisis like this, you were forced to consider extreme options with serious consequences. However, a sifting process is crucial. Rather than wondering about whether options will come up or not, the key is scrutinizing whether options will be no good if chosen inappropriately."[47]

In light of this point, he was full of praise for Richard Reed and Denis McDonough, who "took into account all the facts, scientific assessments and expertise, and differing views of each government department, and made the right call."[48]

The NRC's evacuation recommendation of fifty miles (eighty kilometers) at that time was to later be subjected to strong criticism for being unnecessarily far. In his book, Kevin Maher wrote, "There was, in fact, no accurate information underlying" the U.S. government's "eighty kilometers." Maher said, "Chairman Jaczko was in the antinuclear camp, and I think that may have led to setting a somewhat larger evacuation zone."[49]

Rather than being a question of Jaczko's political stance or ideology, the bottom line was that they were not getting accurate information from Japan, so they could not make an accurate decision. A senior official at the NRC later revealed that, at the time, the commission did not have its own data, and the reality was that they had to make inferences from news articles.

"Although we did talk to a NISA representative on the morning of March 16, we didn't get much information that would tell us things were going in the right direction."[50]

In reality, this figure was decided upon by Jaczko. Neither the White House nor the State Department disputed the figure itself, believing it must be right, since the NRC had decided it. A high-ranking U.S. administration official said that it was "a judgment based purely on RASCAL analysis. Jaczko had no direct role in influencing it."[51]

Casto has testified on this point:

"According to RASCAL, the NRC's own simulation program, if you incorporated the new risk of an abnormality in the spent-fuel pool, the contamination zone would expand to thirty-eight kilometers northwest of Fukushima Daiichi NPS. Rounding that up to forty kilometers and doubling it for a safety margin meant an evacuation area of eighty kilometers. In other words, fifty miles. The recommendation was based on these kinds of simulation results."[52]

An NRC engineer later reported in a review meeting of the OECD's Nuclear Energy Agency (NEA), "The decision to set a fifty-mile radius was based on the following grounds":

- Information from Fukushima Daiichi NPS was extremely limited and often full of contradictions.

- The radiation dose at the power plant site was extremely high. The dose at Unit 3 and 4 reactors was especially high. This was deemed to support the hypothesis that the spent-fuel rods at Unit 4 were exposed.

- The International Atomic Energy Agency (IAEA) had reported a fire in the Unit 4 fuel pool on March 14.

- TEPCO was suggesting withdrawing all its employees from the damaged plant on March 15.

- The IAEA reported the "level" at Unit 5 had dropped on March 16. However, they did not indicate whether this was the reactor "level" or the spent-fuel pool "level."

- The series of hydrogen gas explosions indicated considerable damage to the fuel rods in at least three of the reactors, and that the situation was ongoing.

- When NRC staff ran a RASCAL code simulation offsite, it forecast extremely high radiation doses at a considerable distance from the nuclear power station site.[53]

The same person was critical of the upper echelons of NRC. "Wasn't it the case that they overreacted by first looking at the images of Fukushima Daiichi's hydrogen explosion and judging that it was terrible?"

MARCH 15. The following exchange took place in an internal conference call within the U.S. government.

> *NRC staff:* "I heard the news that TEPCO has abandoned the site."
> *Another staff member:* "I heard that. At first, we were concerned that, you know, they completely abandoned the site. But it appeared that it was not quite as extreme as that. Rather it seems to be the case that the high radiation levels have caused them to temporarily suspend operations."[54]

However, the State and Defense Departments took this to be an extremely serious signal. The evacuation measures they had just decided on were not going to be the last. It all depended on the Japanese government's approach from here on. If their efforts were inadequate, the U.S. government might have to embark on mandatory evacuation. If the Japanese government thought that was undesirable, they had better get serious about dealing with the accident. A State Department official later gave the following testimony:

"If the Kantei continued to leave the response up to TEPCO, and if the number of workers at Fukushima Daiichi fell below several hundred, at such a time, we would be forced to take action. Our judgment was that we would have to proceed from a travel advisory to an order to evacuate."

This would mean an all-out evacuation of American citizens from Japan, including the U.S. forces. This was one of the main reasons Kurt Campbell, assistant secretary of state for East Asian and Pacific affairs, suddenly called Ambassador Fujisaki to the State Department on the morning of March 16.[55]

Even at the NRC, Jaczko was taking a stern view of the risk of TEPCO "withdrawing." He was bearing this in mind as well when he testified before a congressional hearing in the morning of March 16. Jaczko later attested as follows:

"My statement in Congress was received as if I was worried about the fuel pool drying out, but that wasn't the case. It was a statement made after considering the possibility of TEPCO withdrawing from the site."

Jaczko took it seriously that "If it is a fact that TEPCO withdrew, then we, the U.S. side, would no longer be able to work on the premise of trust."[56]

However, there was still a large discrepancy between the American side's fifty miles (eighty kilometers) and the Japanese side's twenty kilometers. The Japanese side was afraid that the gap between the United States and Japan would create panic among its citizens. Edano let slip, "If they do that, it'll only add more harmful rumors about the affected areas."

When they received the information that the U.S. government was unilaterally going to implement the fifty-mile radius, there was a growing feeling of "Who do the United States think they are?!" around Edano. When the U.S. government went ahead with it, it also led to a "feeling of having been abandoned."

Tetsuro Ito, deputy chief cabinet secretary for crisis management, asked Chikao Kawai, assistant chief cabinet secretary and an ex-MOFA man, "Pathetic, isn't it? The NRC says Japan is making the right decision, so why would America set a different evacuation zone?" but Kawai was not in a position to answer.

Kenichiro Sasae, vice minister for foreign affairs, instructed Ambassador Ichiro Fujisaki to request the U.S. side to "keep in step with us as much as possible." On March 16, when Sasae received a call from Roos, he also requested, "I'd like you to hold off on going public with the fifty miles for a while. It's not good if the United States and Japan aren't in step," but Roos would not budge, perhaps because he had already received his instructions from Washington.

Roos himself expressed caution when the NRC suddenly set the evacuation zone at fifty miles, "Isn't it a little too soon? Wouldn't it be better to wait until we have more information from the Japanese side?" He was not opposed to the policy. His point was more of a reminder: "Are we missing anything? Does everything match up? Based on that, a decision, is that okay?" However, the NRC stood firm on fifty miles when they saw the sudden destabilization in Unit 2.

There was no coordination between the United States and Japan over the area of the recommendation to evacuate. When they made the decision to evacuate in the early hours of March 17, the U.S. government agreed that they were to refrain from any statement criticizing Japan. A note was made "to be careful not to put the Japanese government in an uncomfortable position."[57]

The reason Obama had asked via McDonough at the deputies meeting what kind of evacuation policy the NRC would have recommended if this had happened in the United States was out of consideration for sending a signal that this decision was not discriminating against Japan and the Japanese people.[58]

USS *GEORGE WASHINGTON*

The aircraft carrier USS *George Washington* was moored at the Yokosuka naval base when the Fukushima Daiichi NPS accident occurred. The *George Washington* was the sixth ship in the Nimitz class of nuclear-powered aircraft carriers that used Yokosuka as its homeport.

Yokosuka became *George Washington*'s homeport in 2008. It had sailed into Yokosuka Port in November of the previous year and was in dry dock, making routine repairs after the usual tour of duty, six to eight months. During repairs, at times, almost four hundred engineers would be brought in from the U.S. mainland. And an even larger number of Japanese employees would join the operations. There were close to five thousand Japanese employees working at Yokosuka naval base.

In the early hours of March 14, Takashi Noda saw what looked to be engineers with luggage and suitcases forming a long queue in the naval base parking lot. They were boarding large buses, apparently heading to Narita. Noda thought, *Something big must be going on,* but at the time, he did not know what it was.

Noda was the manager of the Yokosuka Maintenance Machinery and Equipment Construction Division at the naval base. He had formerly worked for a Japanese oil refinery, but had switched jobs. It was around this time Noda started hearing all kinds of rumors.

"The navy's sailors are sealing up windows and doors at their homes."

"The sailors' families have all just up and disappeared, leaving all their belongings behind."

"One class in the on-base Sullivans American Elementary School has been reduced to three students."

"The on-base vet has taken in the cats and dogs left behind by their owners, but they can't handle them all. They say the *George Washington* is going to take the rest of the pets to the United States."[59]

Takanori Nakata, owner of the bar Popeye just across the road from Yokosuka naval base, was mad that "it wasn't fair" when he heard on March 14 about the rolling power cuts. He was in an area known as Dobuzaka-dori, full of bars serving the U.S. marines. The U.S. base just across the road and the hotel were exempt from the power cuts, but the bar area was forced to close down because of them. That day, there was no work to be done. Whether thanks to the protests of Nakata and others or not, they were only subject to the rolling power cuts for one day.

From March 15, he opened the bar as usual. A few navy men showed up, had a drink moodily, then left just as moodily. Nakata had heard that the officers' families had started to leave, but the sailors did not talk about it. Perhaps they were avoiding the topic.

After graduating from high school and university in San Francisco in the 1960s during the Vietnam War, Nakata had come back to Japan, where he had worked for Ishikawajima-Harima Industrial (IHI), among others, before opening the bar there in 1978. In the past, the sailors used to fight among themselves a lot. They would get drunk and make trouble. Some sailor was always taking another one home blind-drunk. There were many unshaven faces.

Nakata belonged to the Baby Boomers. You could also say he was part of the Vietnam War generation. One generation, then a second generation had passed since then. Nowadays, the sailors were a quiet lot. Even if they did get drunk occasionally, the other sailors would go home, just leaving the drunks behind. In the first place, nowadays, it was forbidden to drink alcohol after midnight, except on the weekends.

"They used to be cheerful jerks, now they're glum jerks."

No matter whether cheerful or glum, 90 percent of Popeye's clientele were loveable "jerks."

I miss those cheerful jerks.

In the immediate wake of the 9/11 terrorist attack in 2001, the military police raided every bar in Dobuzaka-dori and yanked out every sailor. It was after that that he felt the sailors, and America as well, had changed.

After the hydrogen gas explosion in Unit 1, Nakata was convinced, as he watched TV, that Unit 3 would blow, too. In the 1970s, as an engineer with IHI, he had worked on laying the pipes for the pressure vessel in Unit 3 at Fukushima Daiichi NPS. He had lived in Namie Town for a year and a half. From his experience then, he believed, *The pressure vessel pipes erode 0.2 millimeters a year. No matter how much you contain it, there's always some leakage.* He believed, *There's no such thing as nuclear safety.*

"If there's no radiation leak, then the carrier won't budge."

"Look, whether it's a carrier or a sub, they never let the radiation in the aft of the vessels be measured directly."

This was the nature of his conversations with his customers.[60]

PAST FIVE A.M. ON MARCH 15. Jim Trapp, an NRC officer at the U.S. embassy in Akasaka, Tokyo, made an urgent report by phone to the Washington headquarters. It was just past four p.m. the previous day in Washington. He was speaking with Jaczko.

Trapp: "I heard this from a navy admiral in Yokosuka—Y-O-K-O-S-U-K-A—he is saying that upon measuring with TEDE instrumentation, 1.5 millirem per hour (0.015 millisieverts) was detected at the Yokosuka naval base."

TEDE referred to total effective dose equivalent; 1 millirem was equivalent to 10 microsieverts (0.01 millisieverts).

"The navy admiral in Yokosuka says that the hourly thyroid dose exposure has reached 10 millirem (0.1 millisieverts). It is approximately 188 miles from Fukushima Daiichi NPS to here."

Jaczko: "Have you confirmed the source of the data?"

Trapp: "They measured directly. It has been confirmed through several measurement procedures, and it is thought that the shift in wind direction has had a big impact. You know, we did have a wind shift to the south-southwest recently, and the plume (radioactive cloud) has come this way. They are saying that it looks like the wind will shift back out to sea in about ten hours, which would give you a total dose of about 10 millirem (0.1 millisieverts) per hour until then."

Jaczko: "Okay . . ."

Trapp: "The problem is that Tokyo and its suburban area is in between Fukushima Daiichi and this base."[61]

The "they" Trapp was referring to was the Nuclear Reactor sailors at the Yokosuka naval base. Immediately prior to this, a staff member had made the following statement in an internal NRC conference call:

"There's an aircraft carrier in the port just south of Tokyo (Yokosuka naval base). It's a mere ten miles from Tokyo. Over a twelve-hour period, 10 to 20 millirem (0.1-0.2 millisieverts) of effective dose was measured. The thyroid dosage value is five to ten times of that."[62]

But how far could the naval measurements be trusted? The NRC was undecided. The following discussion also took place.

"Are these exposure dose volumes consistent with what might have been released?"

"They don't seem to be consistent with the amount of radioactive material released. It is clear that it would take some time for a plume to get 180 miles away; if you think of that, then it doesn't match."

"From the start I sensed there was something odd."

"Yet we just heard from the admiral through Trapp that they used multiple systems to confirm."

"They do operate nuclear-powered aircraft carriers, so they must have a level of competence that's fairly decent."[63]

THE MORNING OF MARCH 15. A report from the U.S. forces at Yokota that radiation had risen at the Yokosuka naval base arrived at the SDF Joint Staff Office in Ichigaya. They said the radiation sensors on the *George Washington* had gone off. At the same time, the radiation sensors on the Japanese vessels moored at Yokosuka Port remained silent. The Joint Staff Office people were shocked by the Americans' alarmed tone.

After the earthquake, the *Ronald Reagan*, which had been the first to arrive off the Sanriku coast, withdrew as soon as its radiation sensors went off and never came close again. The U.S. forces, especially the navy, were incredibly sensitive about radioactivity.

The U.S. forces might possibly withdraw from the Yokosuka naval base . . .[64]

Aides at the Joint Staff Office had been hit by the "Yokosuka Shock."[65] One of them remembers his sense of fear at the time, "On the morning of that day, when we heard from the U.S. forces that radiation had reached as far as Yokosuka, we felt as if it was all over, you know? It was so bad we thought that perhaps people would no longer be able to live in Eastern Japan, from Tohoku all the way down to Kanto."[66]

Deeming it necessary to report this information reliably to the Kantei, including the nuance of "an emergency situation," Joint Chief of Staff Ryoichi Oriki sent Koichi Isobe, director of the Defense Plans and Policy Department at the Joint Staff Office, to the cabinet's crisis management center and had him report to Tetsuro Ito, deputy chief cabinet secretary for crisis management, and Chikao Kawai, assistant chief cabinet secretary.[67]

"Base panic" was sweeping through Yokosuka naval base. March 16 was the last day of classes for the on-base schools, but only a quarter of the students turned up at Kinnick High.[68] On March 17, talk that the plume had already passed on March 15 spread around Yokosuka naval base like wildfire. On March 20, the distribution of stable iodine began.[69]

"The officers' wives were the first to run away."

Such a rumor was flying about.

A high-ranking official at the U.S. Navy Yokosuka headquarters later recounted, "Because the wives of high-ranking officers had left before the instructions for voluntary departure were released, the wives of officers of lower ranks began to panic . . . Their husbands weren't involved with measures against the disaster, or rescue operations from the stricken areas of East Japan, but also they couldn't make contact. In fact, most of the wives of high-ranking officers hadn't evacuated. All of them had heard the talk about withdrawal. Because of that, it became a panic . . . A base is a small world, secrets can't be kept."

The family of a high-ranking officer had purchased direct flight tickets for a commercial airline and set off. As a family, even if it cost over US$10,000, they would be reimbursed by the U.S. government later. However, many families of lower-ranking officers and general servicemen did not have the financial leeway to purchase commercial airline tickets on such a short notice. They had to wait for a chartered plane hired by the U.S. government. This took time.[70]

The *George Washington* made ready to sail immediately. For the U.S. Navy, it was absolutely imperative to avoid radioactive contamination of a nuclear-powered aircraft carrier. It was a serious issue of responsibility for the commander if a ship became contaminated. If they were contaminated by radiation from the Fukushima Daiichi NPS accident, there was a concern that they would not be able to tell whether the contamination was coming from inside the ship or outside.[71]

Whether on board an aircraft carrier or a submarine, if it had a nuclear drive, the crew worked in an environment "side-by-side with the nuclear reactor." In the case of a submarine, they "slept as little as ten feet from the reactor." If only for that reason alone, they were extremely sensitive about radiation leakage. It becomes a serious issue of responsibility for a commander if a nuclear-powered carrier becomes radioactively contaminated.

To begin with, the aircraft carriers are the cornerstones of America's global strategy. It is vitally important that carriers can sail anywhere at any time. If they were contaminated with radioactivity, they might also be denied access to foreign ports. If that were to happen, there was a risk of seriously compromising national security.

However, from the point of view of the army, air force, and the Marine Corps, this looked like "navy radiation paranoia." One of them said, looking back, "The navy, especially the U.S. Navy in Japan, showed an emotional backlash."[72]

On March 21, after the *George Washington* left Yokosuka naval base, the U.S. side explained to the Japanese side that "They had to leave immediately, before radioactive contamination became so great that they would not be allowed to call in at other Asian countries, such as Singapore."[73]

There was no clear advance warning to the Maritime SDF from the U.S. Navy. Arrival to a port has to be reported within twenty-four hours, but there is no such arrangement for departure, just gentlemen's agreements.

The Maritime SDF and the Joint Staff Office were again shocked to not have been informed in advance.[74]

The *George Washington* subsequently headed to the East China Sea via the Izu Peninsula, the seas off Tosa Bay and Sasebo. There are countries in Southeast Asia, such as Singapore, that have stringent standards on radioactive contamination. It was reported that when the *George Washington* pulled into port in Thailand, they were alerted by the Thai government that their radiation dose was high.[75]

EMOTIONAL MELTDOWN

Around that time, all kinds of pressures from all corners broke loose. The morale had already started to drop in the embassies. The European embassies in Tokyo had already moved to Seoul and Osaka, and diplomats and their families were fleeing. The U.S. embassy staff and families were feeling anxious and restless that they would be the only ones left. In particular, the movements at Yokosuka naval base were a big shock. The American Forces Network (AFN), a U.S. forces FM station, started broadcasting, "People living in Yokosuka, please stay indoors and put your laundry inside."

"What's going on?"

Inquiries by American citizens came rushing into the U.S. embassy. Even though Yokosuka was slightly farther west of Fukushima than Tokyo, it is farther away, so why were people in Yokosuka being warned like this? Was not Tokyo contaminated even more . . . ?[76]

From March 15 onward, the U.S. Navy roused attention by ordering an "indoor shelter" notice for sailors' families inside the Yokosuka naval base. This information soon reached the embassy and then American citizens residing in Japan. The embassy staff were seized with anxiety. The navy was conspicuous as the only one to issue such instructions to sailors and employees. What about embassy staff and general U.S. citizens? Was it okay to do nothing?

The U.S. embassy staff and their families were getting a constant stream of e-mails from friends and family stateside.

"Fukushima has gone into meltdown and isn't Tokyo dangerous, too? That's what they're saying on the TV reports over here. Come home quickly!"

CNN and other U.S. television stations were reporting with a much greater sense of urgency than NHK, Japan's national broadcaster. The families of embassy staff fell into a state of panic. In the words of a top embassy official, the embassy families went into "emotional meltdown."

Roos met Sanjay Gupta, CNN's chief medical correspondent, by chance on the way to the Hotel Okura. Roos could not go without saying a few words.

"Wasn't that report a little sensationalist? On what grounds are you reporting, 'Meltdown, meltdown'?"

Nonetheless, the content of the CNN reports did not change at all.

Some of the embassy staff started becoming addicted to Arnie Gundersen's blog. Arnie Gundersen had an almost forty-year career as a nuclear engineer. He was an antinuclear activist based at the NGO Fairwinds. Almost as soon as the Fukushima Daiichi NPS accident happened, he started posting his own independent analysis and evaluation of the information, as well as response ideas, and became famous overnight. The embassy staff reading this daily, and especially their spouses, became increasingly anxious: "Is the Japanese government really telling the truth?"

Roos set up a nuclear briefing by Casto every morning at nine. Casto would explain the situation at the reactors and fuel pools, unequivocally dismissing Gundersen's views as groundless. On the weekends, he would invite embassy staff families to town hall meetings. Casto also gave briefings there.

And yet, the families were anxious. This started to affect the work of the embassy staff. Roos decided it would be difficult to keep them in Japan any longer. There was the concern, however, that allowing the families to evacuate would lead to an evacuation of the embassy staff themselves.

An evacuation plan for the embassy staff was already in place for when the time came. There was also a lot of whispering about who was where on the pecking order. If it got to the point of the U.S. forces' withdrawal, then it would inevitably have a huge impact on the future of the U.S.-Japan alliance. On the other hand, "voluntary departure" for the families of U.S. government employees would probably not have a great direct impact upon the future of the U.S.-Japan alliance. Rather, Roos thought, this should be seen as a question of "morale." In order to overcome the situation where people could not concentrate on their work because of worrying about their families, would it not be better to allow the families to "evacuate voluntarily"? That was Roos's decision.

When Casto went to the embassy to report to Roos, he found him talking to the embassy staff's families.

"We have authorized the voluntary evacuation of staff dependents. You will most probably leave Japan on a chartered flight."

The family members looked relieved. Casto heard that charter flights were leaving from U.S. bases at the rate of one every fifteen minutes.[77]

Another issue that created a headache for Roos was distribution of stable iodine. The U.S. government had decided, when it set the evacuation zone at fifty miles, that the distribution of stable iodine was not necessary at that point. However, the military had already distributed iodine to the helicopter pilots working in eastern Japan. Even after the instruction to evacuate from a fifty-mile zone, the military had allowed stable iodine to be distributed to forces before they entered the zone on duty.

In an internal meeting at the embassy, everyone was astonished to hear from the military, "We have been ordered to take stable iodine." The fact that the navy was distributing stable iodine to the forces and their civilian employees soon reached the embassy staff and their dependents. Why was it being distributed to the military and their families, but not to them? American residents in Tokyo also soon heard the news and felt the same concern. The embassy staff made a strong request for stable iodine to be distributed.

Roos was faced with another dilemma. He had to observe government policy. The situation was completely changed, however, now that the military had distributed it. In the end, he decided to distribute stable iodine to those who wanted it as a "psychological stabilizer." In such a case, would they distribute it to Japanese people working at the embassy? There was a concern that the U.S. government just handing it out to Japanese nationals could lead to legal issues. The stable iodine the U.S. government was supplying did not have the approval of the Japanese Pharmaceutical Affairs Law.

Nevertheless, the Japanese staff at the embassy were just as anxious and concerned as the others. The U.S. embassy could not discriminate against the Japanese nationals working at the embassy. So, it was decided to give it to those who asked for it. The embassy decided to "make it available" to American citizens in two places—the embassy and the New Sanno Hotel. The position was that it was not "distributed."[78]

The State Department had withdrawal scenarios for all embassies during a crisis, as well as evacuation plans for government officials and U.S. citizens. The U.S. embassy in Japan also had them. However, no one had foreseen an evacuation scenario due to a nuclear accident. There was no evacuation manual for American citizens in the face of radiation danger.

Roos demanded of Washington, "Give me your best sense of the risk to Tokyo." He checked with Holdren, Chu, and Jaczko many times. Holdren gave his endorsement, "Tokyo is okay." The embassy staff and their families, however, were in a state of panic, and the navy was pursuing its own concerns.

Whether it was partly because he was a lawyer, Roos had the habit of cross-examining people. He would not let up questioning until he was thoroughly convinced, but there was a whiff of "skeptical questions," and discussions were likely to take a heated turn. During the crisis, this habit became more pronounced. He would ask questions like, "There is a risk of radiation contamination. There are unknown risks. How can the decision to remain in Tokyo be justified in spite of this?"

In a phone call with Roos, Steinberg replied, "We all have to bear responsibility for those risks. That's what being in government means."[79]

Steinberg was logical and liked a good argument, too. There were times when their discussions did not end. Gradually, however, they converged toward the same angle.

In the light of America's long-term strategic issues, they had to build a framework for crisis response. Steinberg said in the deputies meeting, "You know, the steps we take now will have an impact on our lives in ten years or twenty years, so we have to think together. We need to try to not forget what kind of impact the decision will have upon the future of the U.S.-Japan alliance."

A high-ranking U.S. government official remembers, "Steinberg's statements at that time had a lot of weight; when he spoke, people stopped and listened."[80]

Roos's final decision was based on those strategic demands. The U.S. embassy would not withdraw from Japan. Families, however, would be allowed to evacuate the country at their will. Richard Reed recalls, "Roos made the decision at that time based on scientifically defendable grounds and information, not things like what other countries seized by fear were doing (starting to withdraw). It was the right choice. In those sorts of times, it is at times easier to withdraw. It was a much more difficult choice to stay, but he said, 'We are staying.'"[81]

The decision to allow U.S. government employees to evacuate at will gave the U.S. embassy some "breathing space." Roos's relations with the navy, however, were sometimes tense after that as well. A high-ranking U.S. administration official was surprised when such a scene unfolded all of a sudden before his own eyes. Roos told a senior U.S. Navy officer, "Look, people with the requisite expertise are handling this issue, so I'd like the military to work with them. I can't have you taking things into your own hands . . . Please remember that I'm the ambassador here. I want you to follow my orders."[82]

BENNY DECKER THEATER

On March 21, Robert Willard, PACOM commander, visited Defense Minister Toshimi Kitazawa and Joint Chief of Staff Ryoichi Oriki in Ichigaya in the company of Patrick Walsh, commander of the U.S. Pacific Fleet.

Willard had appointed Walsh, a four-star admiral, as supreme commander of Operation Tomodachi. Since Lieutenant General Burton Field, commander of the U.S. forces in Japan, was three stars, he came under Walsh. The commander of the U.S. forces in Japan does not hold authority over a Joint Task Force (JTF). In this respect, this differs from commander of the Marine Corps. In addition, the headquarters of the U.S. forces in Japan is not furnished with the structure to respond to this kind of crisis. The roles were split between Walsh taking charge of the military operation side and Field taking charge of the foreign relations side. Fortunately, they got along.

The first day Walsh came to Yokota U.S. military base, Field told him he wanted him to use the commander's office on the second floor of the headquarters. However, Walsh declined with a "We can't have that," and it was decided he would use the office of Field's chief of staff on the same floor. The office of Koichiro Banjo dispatched from the Self-Defense Forces was also on the same floor.[83]

Walsh was later to display his leadership at Yokota Air Base and call Oriki daily to exchange ideas. If Oriki went to Yokota, then Walsh would come to Ichigaya the next time.[84] However, Ichigaya did not feel quite comfortable.

Is he thinking about a doomsday scenario for Japan?

Is his hidden agenda a strategy to evacuate naval personnel and American citizens from Japan in an emergency?

A Ministry of Defense official who was in contact with Walsh recalls, "Walsh didn't want the Japanese government to know too much about the Non-combatant Evacuation Operation (NEO). He was very careful about not creating a bad impression that the Americans were busy getting ready to run while the Japanese government was trying hard."[85]

Willard had set up two command posts at Yokota Air Base. One was 519, the command post for Operation Tomodachi. It was part of the Japan Support Forces (JSF) and led by Walsh. It was responsible for joint U.S.-Japan decontamination operations.

The Maritime Self-Defense Forces had to carry out the decontamination of SDF ships exposed to radiation at Fukushima Daiichi NPS. If the vessels remained contaminated, they would not be able to call at U.S. ports. Although the ships had radiation officers on board, they had never invoked actual decontamination operations. So, the maritime SDF received practical know-how on decontamination from the U.S. Navy. The U.S. side briefed the maritime SDF maintenance staff on decontamination methods onboard an Aegis.

The other command post, in the basement at Yokota Air Base, was 505 for the Non-combatant Evacuation Operation (NEO). Here it was Lieutenant General Kenneth Glueck who took command. He was the commander of the Okinawa Marine Corps. Glueck was a trained Marine Corps pilot and had served in Japan four times. On his previous tour in Japan, from 2003 to 2005, he had participated in the humanitarian rescue operations for an earthquake in the Philippines and the Sumatra tsunami.

After the U.S. government had decided the notice for voluntary departure of government staff's families, Willard created the 505 command post, which Glueck would head.[86] Only command post 519 was devoted to the short-term disaster support and nuclear power response, because there was fear that in a crisis, missions to rescue their own citizens could be neglected. 505's headquarters were located in the basement of Yokota Air Base.

It was here, under Glueck's command, that they drew up the NEO for the evacuation of U.S. citizens in general (and citizens of other designated countries) if the emergency situation took a turn for the worst. This mandatory evacuation plan ("possible evacuation plan") was created by aides from Marine Corps headquarters in Okinawa, who had come to Yokota Air Base. The JSF worked closely with the Japanese side, but the NEO was a U.S.-only operation. Glueck was to report not to Walsh but directly to the commander of the Pacific Command in Hawaii.[87]

NEO became a large operation of five hundred people. Fifty were in Yokota. A further four hundred and fifty troops at Camp Courtney in Okinawa were in charge of logistics. Willard preached the importance of the NEO mission to Glueck, who had flown into Yokota Air Base from Camp Courtney. He emphasized this was why he had created a separate task force from JSF. And he told Glueck, "I want you to draw up a plan to evacuate everyone in five days."

That's impossible!

How are we supposed to get a hundred thousand Americans out in five days?

In a worst-case scenario like that, the 24 million residents of Tokyo would also flee at once: What's more, the U.S. side didn't control the transportation infrastructure . . .[88]

That was what everyone in the meeting thought, but no one said it.

The NEO was led by the State Department. Raymond Greene, state's consul general in Naha, joined the command post. Even though they were talking about an NEO, the strategy would vary greatly depending on how they drew up a worst-case scenario. The NEO command post examined each of the worst-case scenarios the entire U.S. government had issued, but they were all over the place and they were confused not knowing which to use as a reference or what the "bottom line" was. All of the scenarios predicted the metropolitan area would suffer major radioactive contamination.

Among the U.S. military, reactions to accident response were mixed. The Marine Corps had already jumped the gun going to Fukushima Daiichi NPS prior to the fifty-mile evacuation recommendation. Even after the evacuation recommendation of "fifty miles," the captains did not question "whether we are to withdraw as well."

On the other hand, the navy was extremely nervous. One of the U.S. administration officials from the command post said, "Navy personnel were pathologically averse to the sea being radioactively contaminated. They have calculation models for oil leaks and contamination. However, none for radioactivity. It has totally different waves. The navy is extremely concerned about marine pollution, because all of their drinking water comes out of the ocean. I think that the water supply becoming a big health hazard was their biggest concern. This point was an unknown no one had predicted beforehand."

According to this official, the U.S. Air Force took "the most sensible action." While everyone was immersed in making evacuation plans, an officer from the Air Force raised an issue.

"At this time of year, even if the wind there did blow in a southerly direction, it would only happen at most one day in a year. Why are you all so worried about radiation reaching Tokyo?"

This took everyone by surprise. When you thought about it, U.S. Air Force were definitely right.

In fact, when experts were asked to look into it, they researched the past hundred years of data of spring wind around Fukushima Daiichi NPS. It was found that it almost always blew to the northwest. "It would never happen that the wind would blow in a southerly direction for four consecutive days in the direction of Tokyo."[89]

On learning this, the command post was somewhat relieved. Glueck laughed, saying, "I thought at the time it would be best if the air force planned the war and the Marine Corps carried it out."[90]

Even so, in the case of a worst-case scenario, U.S. citizens living in Japan had to be evacuated to a safe haven, but where on earth would that be? Glueck was considering three candidates: South Korea, Okinawa, and Iwakuni. In a crunch, they could be airlifted with aircraft like CV30s. They would bring in beds, food, and water. However, this would only be a relay point. From there, they would shuttle them back to the U.S. mainland in charter and U.S. military aircraft.

However, the number of people that had to be evacuated was a hundred thousand. It would be the biggest NEO in U.S. history, even greater than the 1975 Fall of Saigon. The biggest stumbling block was not transporting out of Yokosuka, Atsugi, and Yokota. It was how to get U.S. citizens from Tokyo to the U.S. forces' bases. Perhaps the 24 million Tokyo residents would also begin evacuating from Tokyo all together at the time. The road situation would be a pandemonium. The U.S. government cannot control the domestic transport infrastructure within Japan.[91]

If they were to evacuate this many people, they would have to rely on U.S. aircraft carriers. They would have to recall the George Washington to Yokosuka Port, move the U.S. citizens to the flight deck, then take them to Sasebo or Busan. The flight deck could accommodate five thousand people.[92]

On the other hand, U.S. forces had begun preparing a tent village at Osan air force base in South Korea. They would shuttle back and forth from Yokota Air Base dozens of times. Civilian aircraft could not be used in a case like this. There was no choice but to do it all with military aircraft.

The plan was, after briefly housing the evacuees in the tent village, to fly them to the United States in civilian aircraft from South Korea.[93]

This was, however, a worst-case scenario, and the worst of the worst-case scenarios at that. According to Glueck, they later started getting reliable information, and as they formed a better understanding of the situation, they modified their response and decided people should remain indoors for four days (ninety-six hours) until the risk level decreased. In short, it was a sheltering strategy.

The nuclear accident seemed to be over the worst by the end of March. Glueck decided the NEO was no longer necessary. The NEO ended only at the planning stage and was never implemented.[94]

A U.S. Navy high-ranking officer in command of the *Ronald Reagan* aircraft carrier later attested, regarding the "panic at the base" over evacuation and withdrawal, that "I personally experienced several conflicts of heart" regarding the decisions of the navy top brass, and related the following:

"What's an alliance? It is an oath to fight together, fight until the death. An alliance is the highest form of relationship that two countries can have, right? There is no relation higher than this. So, when things get worse, it's not appropriate for us to say, 'The radiation has come, so we're out of here, guys. Good luck with that.' At this kind of time, we have to stay; we have to help, otherwise we can't call it an alliance. There are still people dying in Tohoku. Too much attention and interest was turned on, including by the leaders, saying this and that about one's own family at this time. I personally thought that this was a little bit pathetic.

"Frankly, I don't think they acted like that because Americans only love themselves. From when the Yokosuka base radiation dose was released, officers engaged in strategy couldn't help but be worried, very worried, about their families, and were distracted. So, military leaders needed to preempt that and say, 'We will take care of your families, so don't worry, do your current duty properly.' Precisely because leaders do so, officers on the front line can devote themselves to their work. I wonder if the upper levels were considering such a thing.

"From the point of view of commitment to sustaining the U.S.-Japan alliance, the *Ronald Reagan* aircraft carrier turning around and going far away as soon as the radiation dose was detected, the *George Washington* departing from the Yokosuka base due to the radiation, these could be viewed as dubious. I, too, was on the *Ronald Reagan,* but I personally felt regret on the way to Okinawa far away and when distant.

"However, aircraft carriers are something like the crown jewels of U.S. national defense. If the carrier is radioactively contaminated, then it can't go around the world. Every country will reject us. Access becomes difficult. If it comes to that, it is a huge problem from the perspective of national security. Willard was quick to be perceptive of this. This problem is not just today's problem. He was afraid that it could bring about a serious effect spreading over the next thirty to forty years."[95]

On March 22, Willard visited the Yokosuka naval base in the company of his wife, Donna. When they arrived at the base, the couple went straight to the on-base cinema, the Benny Decker Theater. This was to attend a town hall meeting with the officers and men working at Yokosuka base, and their families. Benny Decker was the name of one of the longest-serving and best-known commanders of fleet activities (Yokosuka base). He worked tirelessly to create goodwill among the local residents, and there was a statue of him in Yokosuka Central Park to honor his work in making the Yokosuka base the cornerstone of the U.S.-Japan alliance.

Willard and his wife were introduced and went up on stage, but immediately stepped down. The place was packed with over seven hundred officers and their families. There were young mothers holding babies that would not stop crying. Willard started talking as if he was speaking to guests invited to a party in his home. The Willards had lived in Yokosuka twice. Once when he was the commander of the *Kitty Hawk* group, and once when he was the commander of the Seventh Fleet.[96]

"We love Japan. My relationship with the Self-Defense Forces in Japan is a very strong one. General Oriki (chief of staff of the Joint Staff) and I know each other well.

"As Pacific commander, I'm responsible not just for the navy, as I was as Pacific fleet commander in my previous assignment, but now I'm responsible for everyone, army, air force, and Marine Corps, and special operations command . . . and we have a broader responsibility to the nation for the U.S. citizens in Japan.

"We're going to stay with the Japanese and work with them through this in a supporting role until we win . . . That's the role that I've been assigned by the secretary of defense and the president, and that's the role you're playing.

"I would offer my thanks to all of you. For those of you who are experiencing this uncertainty associated with the reactor accident and the air quality and the fear of radiation effects and so forth, for the first time in your lives . . . Number one, I appreciate it, and number two, I thank you for your patience, your courage, and your help . . . and I thank you for your leadership."

He then introduced his wife, Donna.

"She was watching the Yokosuka departure today from Yokota . . . Donna helped load an airplane today. So, she'll probably be more informative than me. And there are some personal issues with spouses and families that I think she'll help with, too. She's joining me here for the express purpose of interacting with all of our military families."

Donna then spoke at Willard's urging.

"We were here when 9/11 happened, in Yokosuka . . . In the navy, when you have a catastrophe such as this, where do the principals go, where do the servicepeople go? They go to sea. And who's left behind? The spouses, the children, to deal with all this. That's what makes us all strong, but it also adds a lot to the stress. So, I'll never forget the anxiety I felt on 9/11, when suddenly I was locked down on the base and he was gone. So, I appreciate that and I know, so we're trying to help you to get through it with informed decisions on what's best for you and your family.

"I was at Yokota this morning. I found out that 240 of our families were taken through to the passenger terminal . . . Those navy spouses, they were all exhausted . . . and the kids were totally out of control . . . I had given them Tootsie Rolls, I wasn't helping . . . We had airmen up there, carrying babies . . . But I'm here to tell you that it went smoothly."

They then answered questions. Donna remained standing beside Willard. The town hall meeting was initially scheduled for an hour, but ran for three hours, including Q&A.[97]

At the schools on Yokosuka naval base, teachers instructed students to "stay indoors," but Willard stated with confidence that "children should be allowed to play outside."[98]

The Willards' visit had a huge impact. A high-ranking U.S. Navy officer told an SDF aide at the Joint Staff Office, "Things calmed down after that. I don't think we'll have any confusion now."[99]

Willard had taken the toughest stance in internal U.S. government discussion up until then, insisting on the broadest evacuation plan, but the deputies' meeting knocked back the navy's request, and the NRC's proposal for a fifty-mile evacuation zone was adopted.

On reception of this government policy, Willard decided to convey directly to the navy, and especially the families of military personnel at the Yokosuka naval base, the policy of the U.S. Armed Forces:

- The U.S. forces would stay in Japan "until we win."

- There was no need to overreact about radiation contamination.

- However, it was only natural to worry about your families. Families would be returned to the mainland and be well protected.

This was the message the Willards imparted in their own voices that day. When he heard about this performance by the Willards, Katsutoshi Kawano, vice chief of staff at the Joint Staff Office, thought to himself, *The Americans are so good at this kind of thing.*

The commander's wife also played a key leadership role. This was considered to be a vital factor, especially in times of crisis.

"There's a Mel Gibson film on the Vietnam War called *We Were Soldiers*. There's a scene where the commander's wife goes to tell a soldier's wife that he's been killed. All she could do was cry with the soldier's wife. That tough job was her role. The wives were responsible for looking after the families of officers and men living on the same base if they were killed. Commanders fought with their wives alongside."

This was how Kawano described it.[100]

TWELVE

The Hosono Process

10:22 A.M., MARCH 17. Prime Minister Naoto Kan had a telephone meeting with U.S. President Barack Obama. The meeting lasted some thirty minutes. It was Obama who had suggested a telephone meeting. Obama reiterated, "The Fukushima nuclear power plant is the immediate issue.

"I'll send planners from the U.S. Armed Forces Nuclear Reaction Force to Japan to work with your civilian and Self-Defense Forces planners. It's my intention to send a large team promptly." After so saying, and acknowledging, "I know, Mr. Prime Minister, you are aware of the seriousness of this matter," he expressed the hope that "it is possible to avoid a catastrophic situation."

Kan responded, "The word 'withdrawal' does not apply to the Fukushima nuclear accident. We are doing everything we can to deal with the situation and will continue to do our utmost in the future." He cited "the temperature rise in the fuel pools at Units 4 and 3" as a "particular problem," and also mentioned the water injection into the pools by the SDF that morning. "In addition to this, we will be carrying out watering by high-pressure water cannons by the Self-Defense Forces and the police from the ground."

At this point, the government was not yet ready to mobilize the fire department to inject water into the pools. Kan gave only the names of the Self-Defense Forces and the police.[1] Thirty minutes earlier, the first of the ground SDF helicopters had dropped 7.5 tons of water on Unit 3 at Fukushima Daiichi NPS. Kan had watched the live coverage on NHK in his office.

"President Obama will be making a call from Air Force One on his way back from New York to Washington."

Kan did not seem to be paying attention even when being briefed by a Ministry of Foreign Affairs (MOFA) official. One of the MOFA staff was worried.

The prime minister is in a daze.

After the first pilot made a perfect hit, Kan said, smiling broadly, "Oh, he did it." However, he became depressed when the following helicopters' water drops turned into mist.[2]

The water drops were completed at 10:01 a.m. It was just in time for the conference call.[3] The call had been requested by the U.S. side, but Kan jumped at the opportunity.

Obama emphasized in the telephone conference, "We are prepared to make every assistance," and, true to his word, the U.S. government passed on to the Ministry of Defense (MOD) a support list of thirty items from the U.S. Pacific Command immediately after the helicopter water drop. This was conveyed to the Kantei.[4]

From soon after the nuclear accident occurred, Obama took a deep interest in the accident and U.S.-Japan relations. On March 12, he had made a ten-minute phone call of encouragement to Kan. The day after phoning Kan for a second time on the night of March 16 (U.S. EST), Obama stopped off at the Japanese embassy in Washington to sign the condolence book. He shook Ambassador Ichiro Fujisaki's hand and told him, "We'll do everything that we can."[5]

Daniel Russel, the White House's NSC director for Japan, South Korea, and North Korea, proposed the condolence book entry. Obama swiftly decided to make one. It was instructed, "No press, only photos." Prior to it, Russel made arrangements over the phone with Ambassador Ichiro Fujisaki. Fujisaki's reaction was "somewhat cautious reasoning."

President Jimmy Carter had visited the Japanese embassy to sign the condolence book when Prime Minister Masayoshi Ohira died on June 12, 1980. However, there was no tradition, diplomatically speaking, of a condolence book for the victims of a natural disaster. The embassy side was just following protocol that "a condolence book was associated with the state or head of government." With that in mind, Fujisaki minded his words when he said, "It would be better not to overreact."

Russel felt deflated.

A bureaucratically curt reply.

But even so, Fujisaki said he would "make an inquiry at the ministry" and hung up. After some time, a phone call came from Fujisaki, "We would be honored for the president to come early next week."

On the afternoon of March 17 (early hours of March 18 in Japan), Obama visited the condolence book room in an embassy annex. "Keep on going, Japan" cards from children all over America were stuck on one of the walls. The president prayed in silence and then made an entry.

"My heart goes out to the people of Japan during this enormous tragedy. Please know that America will always stand by one of its greatest allies during this time of need. Because of the strength and wisdom of its people, we know that Japan will recover, and indeed will emerge stronger than ever. And as it recovers, the memory of those who have been lost will remain in our hearts, and will serve only to strengthen the relationship between our two countries. May God bless the people of Japan."[6]

Without entrusting it to a speech writer, Obama had written his own words.

Afterward, Obama returned to the White House, had a press conference in the Rose Garden, and read aloud a statement. In it, he promised that America would support Japan as much as it could and that measures had already been taken for the safety of Americans living in Japan. On top of that, he emphasized that even if it became the worst-case scenario, the West Coast of the United States would not be in danger of contamination from radiation caused by Fukushima, and called for the people of America to remain calm.[7]

While it looked like the telephone meeting and the president's signing of the condolence book had brought a break in the invisible tensions in U.S.-Japan relations, Kan was concerned about the bilateral relationship during this period. After the cabinet meeting on March 15, Kan asked Kitazawa, "Can you stay?" and spoke with him in private.

"Edano has fallen out with Roos. In fact, both MOFA and the Kantei aren't getting on so well with the U.S. side, so I'd like you to help us respond, Kitazawa-san."[8]

Kan had learned late the previous night that Chief Cabinet Secretary Yukio Edano had clashed with Ambassador Roos. There was a look of serious crisis on Kan's face. Kitazawa promised Kan he would do what he could.[9]

Kitazawa asked Ayako Kimura, a political specialist on security issues at the U.S. embassy, who was at the Tohoku Ground Defense Force Headquarters in Sendai, "What should be our priority in regaining U.S. trust?"

Kimura was effectively in charge of relations between the Japanese government and Roos. Kimura replied, "I think you should provide the NRC staff in Japan with as much information as possible."

Kitazawa conveyed this to Kan and Hosono, and they invited the NRC staff to the Integrated Response Office that had just been set up that day at TEPCO Head Office to exchange information.[10]

On March 17, Kimura rang Kitazawa's private secretary, Takahiro Yoshida.

"There is something I want you to convey to the minister."

Yoshida asked her to come immediately to the ministry. The moment Kimura stepped into the minister's office, she said to Kitazawa, "The ambassador is in trouble."

Roos was being pressured on all fronts. No information was coming in from the Japanese government. The U.S. government had shown its willingness to assist by sending over NRC staff, but they were not being accepted. The U.S. government had decided to issue an evacuation order of fifty miles (eighty kilometers) to U.S. citizens in Japan, but there were still voices calling for an all-out evacuation. U.S.-Japan relations would collapse if nothing was done. This is what Kimura conveyed to Kitazawa.[11]

Kitazawa invited Robert Luke, political minister-counselor at the U.S. embassy, and Charles Casto, head of the NRC's Japan support team, who had just arrived in Japan, to the minister's office, and gave them the information MOD had. He also promised to share data and radiation measurements with them. Nobushige Takamizawa, director general of the Bureau of Defense Policy, was also at the meeting.

Worried about the head-on collision between Edano and Roos, Kan told Kitazawa he wanted MOD to play a central role and "be always present in the decisionmaking field" and to cooperate with the U.S. side, including the NRC, over the nuclear emergency response. This was the background to Casto's first place of call being the Ministry of Defense.

Roos handed over the images that the Global Hawk unmanned aerial vehicle (UAV) surveillance aircraft had taken over the Unit 4 fuel pool. The image in that area was red and swollen, to emphasize that the temperature was high. The U.S. side told them that the United States' greatest concern was still the Unit 4 fuel pool.

On the television, the scene of the SDF helicopter water drop was being aired. Yoshida handed an incoming call on the mobile phone to Kitazawa. Kitazawa walked over to his desk, smiling and nodding several times while on the phone. Casto imagined, *Kitazawa is being congratulated on the success of the water drop. It's obviously the prime minister on the other end.*

While Roos praised the success of the SDF water drop operation, he stated his opinion, "You need a sustainable supply of water." In other words, he was conveying the fear that, while they thought highly of the helicopter water drop, it was far from sustainable. Casto had warned Roos that "you can't expect a miracle from stuff like this."[12]

The action was a successful "optical solution," Casto thought.[13]

To the NRC staff, the only U.S.-Japan dialogues that seemed to be functioning were the MOD and SDF meetings at the U.S. military's Yokota Air Base, and those between the U.S. embassy in Japan and the U.S. forces. Casto had reported to NRC headquarters that, within the Japanese government, "the main important contact points are the Kantei and the MOD."[14]

Discussions between the United States and Japan continued at the MOD on March 18, 19, and 20. There they coordinated on organizing the crane trucks to take the water pumps in for discharging to the fuel pools. It was agreed to urgently transport a crane owned by U.S. Bechtel Corporation, which was in Perth, Australia, but when they checked, it was discovered that it was not the "boom model" that the Japanese wanted, but a "cannon model." They were at odds, but when the U.S. side requested, "We want you to consider it as an option," the Japanese side agreed, but it was never called for. A boom-type crane had already been unloaded in Onahama, a port near Fukushima Daiichi.

The boom had been part of a system jointly designed by the NRC team and a few TEPCO engineers in order to introduce a long-term pumping solution, while moving away from a dependency on firetrucks. The project would cost US$750,000, and several times even the State Department issued stand-down orders. They were cautious about the operation. When it did arrive at the U.S. Air Force base, local government officials hesitated to approve its transport along roads toward Daiichi, as permits were typically required. Once this was agreed upon, Japanese vehicles towed the system to Onahama port, where it remained unused.[15]

Washington subsequently criticized the NRC team for building an expensive system that was not necessary. "The best we could offer in our defense was the fact that building it had catalyzed the Japanese government to build its own system," Casto reasoned. The development of the pumping system "seemed to stir the Japanese, who were somewhat threatened by our interventions."[16]

In fact, while searching for the necessary equipment for the pumping system, the NRC team was surprised to discover that the Metropolitan Fire Department had purchased the same items and was building a duplicate system. "There was significant reluctance to allow an American-designed-and-built pumping system to be implemented at Fukushima Daiichi," Casto added.[17]

These U.S.-Japan talks, initiated by Takamizawa, were reported to Kitazawa and had started to function to a certain degree, but still maintained a strong sense of "being led by the MOD desk guys."[18]

At a later date, a debate between MOD and METI over which type of nozzle should be used for the pumping system—a spray nozzle or a hard pipe— took place. Casto noted the debate underscored that "MOD did not understand the spent-fuel pools . . . After that debate, we no longer went to MOD for our meetings, but conducted them at the offices of METI/NISA and TEPCO." It was a proxy power struggle between the two government ministries, and MOD had lost.[19]

ON THE KANTEI'S INITIATIVE

Hosono was also concerned about U.S.-Japan relations. He spoke about it with the "helper" he had brought in, Akihisa Nagashima, a former vice minister of defense and member of the Lower House (DPJ, Tokyo). He asked Nagashima to come up with a response. The two of them agreed: "The accident response is not just TEPCO's problem. Let's build a framework for a U.S.-Japan response."

On March 17, Nagashima spoke with Kitazawa about the water pumping operations at the fuel pools at Fukushima Daiichi. The conversation was focused on the squabbling that was going on between the police, the fire department, and the SDF about whose turn it was to inject water.

At the time, Nagashima also asked if they should not create a forum for U.S.-Japan discussions about the nuclear emergency response, to which Kitazawa replied, meaningfully: "Takamizawa's running some kind of shady meeting." He was speaking of the U.S.-Japan discussions that Takamizawa had started on his own initiative. The words sounded a little barbed to Nagashima.

I wonder if he had not briefed the minister properly beforehand . . .[20]

The NRC's miscalculation was the absence of a strong government agency specializing in nuclear safety regulation on the Japanese side. The Nuclear and Industrial Safety Agency was part of METI's Agency for Natural Resources and Energy, and was not an independent regulatory agency like the U.S. NRC. The Nuclear Safety Commission (NSC) was nothing more than an advisory body.

The fact that the Japanese and U.S. "Operation Tomodachi" was part of the alliance strategy also complicated U.S.-Japan cooperation in the nuclear power plant accident response. At the October 2005 meeting of the U.S.-Japan Security Consultative Committee between foreign and defense cabinet-level officials, known as the "2 plus 2," both governments strengthened their joint stance toward crises, agreeing to improve the interoperability of the U.S. forces in Japan and the Self-Defense Forces, increase joint training opportunities, and to engage in plan drafting, transport cooperation, and information sharing. Operation Tomodachi could well be said to be the culmination of that process.

However, it was hard to build a U.S.-Japan interface in the nuclear emergency situation. The all-important NISA could not build smooth relations with the NRC. The NRC grew increasingly dissatisfied with their access to NISA. NISA was not sufficiently aware of the manpower, resources, and influence Naval Reactors wielded. They had their own information and were analyzing, evaluating, and making proposals independent of the NRC. NISA was dissatisfied that, in addition to briefing the NRC, at this hectic time, they also had to brief other sections of the U.S. government.[21]

Moreover, information confidentiality related to the alliance impeded the smooth flow of information within the Japanese government. Both METI and NISA were not insensitive to the barriers of the "2 plus 2" from the Ministries of Defense and Foreign Affairs. A middle-ranking official at MOD later attested the following:

"The SDF protected, as a rule of thumb, the confidentiality of military-to-military information. So, they didn't even tell the internal bureaus at the ministry. And then there were some of the internal bureaus themselves observing the rule of confidentiality and tending not to share with other government agencies. However, a nuclear power plant disaster can't be responded to unless information is shared as soon as possible and everyone has the same level of awareness."

This applied not only to the Ministry of Defense, but to MOFA as well. They had a morbid fear of sharing information obtained in the "2 plus 2" framework with other Japanese government agencies. The images taken by the Global Hawk UAV of the Unit 4 fuel pool were not directly conveyed to METI or NISA by the Ministry of Defense or MOFA. Initially, it did not even reach Kan and Edano. When Edano found out, he was absolutely furious.[22]

Sharing information like this required written clearance from the U.S. Department of Defense. No one was going to be bothered with that at a time of crisis. This was partly why information-sharing within the Japanese government was so poor. The Integrated Response Office got its hands on the images via METI, but METI itself had received them through unofficial channels from the police.[23]

On the morning of March 18, three NRC staff members visited the Integrated Response Office at TEPCO.

"Could you deal with them?"

At Hosono's request, Nagashima went to a room on the twelfth floor and "dealt with them."

"Where should we ask for information?"

"Who's making the decisions?"

These were the two key points. They asked them relentlessly.

A week's already passed and the U.S. side is still asking stuff like this?

Nagashima told Hosono to "come up straight away," and introduced Hosono to the NRC members.

"This is the guy responding to the nuclear accident."

"Him?"

Goshi Hosono was thirty-nine years old. The NRC fellows looked blank. Hosono wanted to go downstairs as soon as possible. While he was playing "partner" to the NRC, he was distracted. His mind was full of the water pumping operations from land.[24]

Nagashima went to the Kantei later. Takeshi Niinami, CEO of the Lawson convenience stores, and Masayoshi Son, CEO of Softbank, a telecom company, had visited Yoshito Sengoku, deputy chief cabinet secretary, with some proposals for disaster recovery, and had just left.

Sengoku was the acting president of the Democratic Party of Japan

(DPJ). Sengoku had previously served in the Kan administration as chief cabinet secretary, but had been forced out by a motion of censure in November 2010. But Kan called him back into the Kantei on March 17 as the successor for Deputy Chief Cabinet Secretary Hirohisa Fujii, who had expressed his desire to resign due to his age (he was seventy-eight). Sengoku told Nagashima, "Hey, hey, hey, are things okay? Roos is in a bit of a panic, you know. They say he hung up on Foreign Minister Matsumoto, saying, 'I don't have time to talk to you.'"

Nagashima replied, "The ambassador's not getting any information. What kind of an alliance is this?"

Nagashima called an acquaintance at the U.S. embassy on the spot, and asked for a meeting with the ambassador.

At 3:30 p.m. on March 18, an unofficial meeting between Japan and the United States was held at the Yamazato restaurant in Hotel Okura in Akasaka, Tokyo. It was attended by Goshi Hosono; Akihisa Nagashima; Shunsuke Kondo, chairman of the JAEC; and on the U.S. side, John Roos, Robert Luke, Charles Casto, and some senior officers from the Department of Energy.

Roos voiced his dissatisfaction with the Japanese side's uncooperativeness in sharing information with the NRC and the navy, even though he had striven to appeal the Japanese position to Washington when the U.S. government decided on the fifty-mile evacuation instruction.

"Can't we unify the discussions between Japan and the United States?"

"I agree. I will convey the ambassador's idea to the prime minister."[25]

Both Hosono and Nagashima thought the U.S.-Japan discussions should take place "under the Kantei's leadership."

MARCH 19, 2011. When they both met Kan, Nagashima won Kan over, saying, "We need to build an interface on the Kantei's initiative by which we can unify all the Japanese information and do away with the negative effects of compartmentalization and share it with the U.S. side as soon as possible." While espousing the need to start a U.S.-Japan dialogue "on the Kantei's initiative," Hosono said at the time that he would like to help.

Kan agreed, but when they told him that MOD and MOFA were already engaged in a joint dialogue at a working level, Kan became angry, saying, "I haven't been told anything about it!" Kan called his two executive secretaries, Kanji Yamanouchi on secondment from MOFA and Satoshi Maeda on secondment from MOD, into his office and gave them a stern dressing down.

"Get me the vice ministers from MOFA and MOD on the phone."

Kenichiro Sasae, MOFA vice minister, answered the call first. Kan yelled, "What the hell are you doing? I don't know anything about it!"

Sasae had reported everything about this matter to Minister Matsumoto. The thought *Hasn't the minister spoken to the prime minister about this?* crossed his mind, but Sasae made no excuses and just put up with the roar on the other end of the line.

After he was finished, Kan called Kimito Nakae, vice minister of defense. Nakae was at home this weekend for the first time in a long while when he had suddenly received a call from Satoshi Maeda, executive assistant to the prime minister, giving him advance notice that "The prime minister would like to speak with you," his mobile phone ringing later with a call from Kan.

"The SDF are doing a great job, but you've got to report thoroughly. I want you to do things properly."

"I'm sorry for not reporting fully. I will take more care."

After apologizing, Nakae explained the gist of the U.S-Japan discussions at MOD.

When Kitazawa later heard that the "vice minister had been cautioned by the prime minister," he complained to Kan. "Why are you mad at my vice minister?"

"If the prime minister says come, the bureaucrats go straight away without worrying about what the minister will think. That's their job, but if you keep biting their heads off, you'll make enemies out of everyone who wants to work for you."

Kan made excuses, looking slightly abashed.

"Do you think so? I thought we had a good discussion."[26]

During this period, METI Minister Banri Kaieda and Deputy Chief Cabinet Secretary Tetsuro Fukuyama were feeling mounting dissatisfaction with the MOD-led discussions with the United States. Kaieda placed a call directly to Kitazawa on March 19.

"Is it so that the Ministry of Defense has received a support list from the United States? The list hasn't been shared with METI. I fail to understand why that would happen. I'd like you to include METI when you have U.S.-Japan meetings. In the first place, isn't it better to have the Kantei decide on things like this?"[27]

Fukuyama felt it was strange that the cabinet secretariat was not involved in U.S.-Japan talks when it was trying to deal responsibly with the Fukushima Daiichi NPS emergency. However, it does appear that Kan had already asked Kitazawa directly to handle it carefully. Additionally, especially when the military forces (SDF and U.S. forces) were working together closely with Operation Tomodachi, careless steps had to be avoided. However, he felt keenly that the cabinet secretariat should be making an effort to strengthen coordination between Japan and the United States.

Acting in accordance with Fukuyama's wishes, Tetsuro Ito, deputy chief cabinet secretary for crisis management, visited the MOD on March 20, and asked the intention of the MOD and SDF leaders, including Kitazawa and Oriki.

"Could we have those meetings at the Kantei?"

MELTDOWN

Oriki replied, "That'd be fine."

Only the MOD had been shown the U.S. forces' list, but this was something that could not be handled by the MOD alone. Kitazawa said, "Send out the instruction to all the ministries for me."

A meeting of the related ministries was later held at the Kantei, where it was decided to instigate a joint crisis management coordination group at the Kantei's initiative.[28] They decided to hold the meetings in a conference room on the ninth floor of the cabinet annex, just behind the Kantei. This was where the secretariat of the cabinet, secretariat cabinet security, and crisis management office were located.

COALITION

This is how the Joint Coordination Group on the Nuclear Emergency came into being. Kicked off by a preparatory meeting on the night of March 21, it officially started work on March 22. Usually running from 8:00 p.m. to 9:30 p.m., more than forty meetings in total were held in the cabinet annex. The first meeting was held at one p.m. on March 22.

The U.S. co-team leaders were James Zumwalt, deputy chief of mission at the U.S. embassy, and Charles Casto, head of the NRC Japan support team. Representatives from the NRC, the navy, Naval Reactors, the U.S. forces in Japan, the Department of Energy, and the U.S. embassy all attended. Casto played the most central role for the Americans. The leader on the Japanese side was Tetsuro Fukuyama, deputy chief cabinet secretary. Each ministry was represented at the deputy director general level. Hosono initially attended in an observer capacity, but ended up running the meetings.[29]

The U.S. side made "setting response priorities and establishing communication between Japan and the U.S." the aim of the joint meetings. They also aimed at making each meeting an "action-forcing event."[30]

Fukuyama focused on three goals for the joint meetings. The first was to share each other's knowledge on the status of Units 1 to 4. The second was to exchange ideas on what should be done to avoid the worst-case scenario. And the third was to raise requests from the Japanese side for useful equipment and apparatus, and have the U.S. side look into it.

The first task was bridging the perception gap concerning the situation at the reactors and the fuel pools.[31] At the same time, they needed to coordinate the requests for materials from the Japanese side with the support materials the United States was considering. At the start of the meeting, the U.S. side handed Hosono a twenty-page spreadsheet of Japanese requests to the United States for support. It listed all the items that the ministries and departments had requested piecemeal.[32]

Hosono was acutely aware that they needed to define their priorities and get in control of operations. On the other hand, the U.S. side had drawn up a list reflecting not what Japan needed, but rather what they wished to do. Zumwalt described this as "push assistance" and cautioned the U.S. side about this.[33]

Hosono kept in mind one thing when starting the joint meeting process. That was that he would not create a *gaiatsu* ("foreign pressure") dynamic, where the United States pushed and Japan acquiesced.

"The Japanese side will speak."

"Initial courtesies will come first from the Japanese side."

"Japan will make requests, to which the United States will respond."

The Japanese side was to take the initiative. Another point Hosono drilled into the Japanese participants was: "Give all the information you have. If you don't raise it as the opinion of the Kantei, then the Kantei will have no choice but to take a stern attitude."

Takamizawa turned to the Americans and said, "I think there will be some information that is of a military-to-military nature. I would like for us not to hold on to it, but to share it with NISA and TEPCO. Will you allow that?"

The U.S. side was quick to respond.

"We have no objection whatsoever. That's why we're holding these meetings."[34]

Sitting in the meeting on the night of March 22, Nagashima thought, "Gosh, the U.S. uniforms are all lined up in the front row, but you can't see any of the SDF commanders." Taking a good look, he saw Koichi Isobe, director of the Defense Plans and Policy Department at the Joint Staff Office, sitting in the back. After the meeting, Nagashima asked Hosono, "Where were the uniforms sitting at the first meeting at one p.m.?"

"In the back seats, why?"

"The U.S. forces were there, right?"

"The UFJ, the navy, PACOM, they were all there."

"We have to have the uniforms sit in proper seats. You definitely have to speak to them about it."

Representatives from the ministries and agencies on both sides sat around the square table in the front row. To Fukuyama and Hosono's left was the deputy chief cabinet secretary for crisis management, and on their right, the TEPCO representative. Directly opposite in the center was Casto, and next to him sat the military, Rear Admiral Thomas Rowden and Brigadier General William B. Crowe. Hosono appealed to Kitazawa for a better seating order for the uniforms. The SDF was seated in a position that corresponded to their U.S. counterparts.

Some of the MOD suits (internal bureau officials) had initially thought it would be better if there were no uniforms at the joint meetings. MOFA, however, asserted that the SDF should be there, reasoning that "The U.S. forces are very interested in having the SDF at the meetings." A senior MOFA official later recalled, "The atmosphere changed completely with the U.S. military presence. Things were decided quickly, because they were action-oriented."[35]

In the meeting on March 24, NRC staff suggested the Japanese side look into an "emergency event."

"We also need to be prepared for an emergency event. U.S. engineers are looking into how to respond if the fuel and reactor pressure vessel are damaged. We need to respond to this urgently."

Hosono replied:

"Japan is doing its utmost, but there's a limit to individual Japanese responses. I'd like to hear the U.S. advice on what we should be doing to fundamentally overcome this accident. We have a room ready at the government and TEPCO's Integrated Response Office. Would it be possible to have a U.S. party take up residence there and put their expertise to work with the Japanese side?"

NRC staff:

"We'd be pleased to participate. We can provide five people. I'd also like to include someone from the industry as well, if that's all right. What we have here is an international coalition on a nuclear problem."[36]

When this kind of positive approach and information was reported on the Japanese side, no matter how small, Casto said, "That's good. Congratulations."

This would soften the atmosphere.[37]

In the meeting that day, Fukuyama requested, "We don't have enough plastic baby bottles, could you supply some?"

William Berger, USAID's principal regional advisor for Southeast Asia, drew the Japanese side's attention.

"Don't you think bringing them in from overseas would only fan uncertainty? Japan must have lots of plastic bottles. I think bringing some over from Kyushu would settle the issue. There's no need to bring them from the States."[38]

The issue of stable iodine (potassium iodine) was also discussed.

U.S. embassy staff: "I've heard Japan is interested in potassium iodine. The United States has a strategic store of liquid potassium iodine. We can provide you with a million bottles from there. One bottle is equivalent to fifteen doses, each dose being 130 mg. For children, you just have to reduce the amount. If the Japanese side made a formal request, we can provide surplus supplies from the Department of Health. I think USAID would handle the transport."

Hosono: "NISA, how many bottles would you request?"

Hisanori Nei, deputy director general, NISA: "I thought 500,000 bottles would be enough, but if the United States has a million, we'd be grateful for them all."

U.S. embassy staff: "We'll think along those lines."

Hosono: "We'd be grateful for a million bottles from the United States. On behalf of the Kantei, I thank you from the bottom of my heart. Everyone at the ministries, okay? Ministry of Health, Labor, and Welfare, you're okay with this, right?"

The moment Hosono finished speaking, an official from MHLW rose to his feet.

"There are certain matters that have to be cleared in terms of the Pharmaceutical Affairs Law, so I'd like you to bear that in mind."

The Pharmaceutical Affairs Law was the law covering the management of pharmaceuticals, quasi-drugs, cosmetics, and medical devices within Japan. Hosono told the MHLW official, "Could you clear it immediately?"

A U.S. embassy staff member spoke up.

"We have instructions on how to use potassium iodine. We'll give them to you."

The potassium iodine supplied by the United States did not have approval under the Japanese Pharmaceutical Affairs Law. By rights, it could not be used in Japan. It was normal practice in emergencies like large-scale earthquakes, however, to allow medical supplies sent in from overseas or brought in by overseas rescue teams through customs as assistance materials. The problem was, who would be responsible in the case of side effects? The U.S. supply of potassium iodine was offered on the condition that "the recipients would bear unlimited responsibility."

The lawsuit regarding a case of AIDS contracted from a tainted blood transfusion was still vivid in the memory of the Ministry of Health, Labor, and Welfare. After more than 400 people lost their lives, the government along with four pharmaceutical companies paid the 1,800 people who contracted HIV US$450,000 each and officials were charged with professional negligence resulting in death.[39] It looked like their position was that they would take no responsibility whatsoever. A METI official hearing this statement felt a little sad.

Are they scared the state will be held liable if there are any side effects?

Is this official only thinking about his ministry, its authority, and avoiding responsibility at this time of crisis?

Isn't it the job of MHLW to have a supply of potassium iodine in the first place?

The following day, a "lodgment note" arrived at NISA from MHLW, stating that if there were any side effects from the potassium iodine supplied

by the United States, MHLW would not bear responsibility under the State
Redress Law. (In any event, at this juncture, domestic supplies of stable
iodine were almost at the required amount. Japan later reported this fact to
the U.S. side and there was no need for them to supply it. In this way, the
question of responsibility for side effects was averted.)[40]

After a while, the U.S.-Japan meetings became known as the "Hosono
Process." People found something refreshing in Hosono's youthfulness, his
candor, his leadership, his certain grip on the facts, and his skill in using
the bureaucracy.

"The Hosono meetings turned the tide in our communications with the
Japanese," Casto said.[41] "We established an efficient system by which the
Japanese could request resources from the many American agencies that
had offered help, and we could approve, track, and fulfill those requests."[42]

However, there was still a difference between Japan and the United
States over situational awareness of the accident and crisis response. One
such difference was the assessment of the situation in the spent-fuel pool
at Unit 4.

"IF THERE'S STEAM, THERE'S WATER"

The headquarters of the NRC in Washington.

On March 16 (U.S. EST), an NRC staff member was reporting in a conference call, "The explosion has blown away the walls of the Unit 4 spent-
fuel pool, water leaking out, the fuel rods are exposed, and there's probably
a large-scale release of radioactive material."

Jaczko had started looking into response measures based on this scenario. Casto was not involved in analyzing the data or preparing the assessment used at the time that Jaczko testified before the House subcommittee
that the fuel pool at Unit 4 was in a dangerous state, but was worried in
the same way about the situation in the fuel pool at Unit 4. Upon hearing
Jaczko's statement, Casto thought it was a mistake. "It was not his job to
make predictions that he didn't really understand."[43]

Jaczko reported to Congress in Washington on March 16:

"What we believe at this time is that there has been a hydrogen explosion in this unit due to an uncovering of the fuel in the fuel pool. We believe
that secondary containment has been destroyed and there is no water in
the spent-fuel pool, and we believe that radiation levels are extremely high,
which could possibly affect the ability to take corrective measures."[44]

Information that there had been a fire in Unit 4's fuel pool on March
15 also worried Casto. If cesium was released, the workers would lose all
access, placing the reactor out of control. Afterward, the Japanese side confirmed that "there is water in Unit 4." Casto was called by the Japanese

government to go to the emergency center at the prime minister's office and was shown those images, but could not consent. The video was of very poor quality and was taken during a high-speed flyby. "Just a few frames showed the debris on top of the spent-fuel pool," he recalled. He had come to think that "I am not sure there's no water," but at the same time, "I just didn't see it. Neither did two team members who accompanied me."[45]

Past eight p.m. on March 16 (around nine a.m. on March 17 Japan Time), Jaczko queried Casto in an NRC telephone conference call. Casto had just outlined to the NRC the briefing by the Japanese side on the images of Unit 4, which had been held at the Kantei's crisis management center.

> *Casto:* "TEPCO and the Kantei showed us snapshots, and it looked like the pool has lost structural integrity. They're saying, well, originally there was no outer wall in the pool, so the structure could still be intact. They flew a helicopter and filmed. Just looking at the video, you can't say conclusively that there is water."
>
> *Jaczko:* "So, am I right to think we have any change in our view on whether there is water in the Unit 4 fuel pool?"
>
> *Casto:* "I would say, with steam, there is some water in the pool."
>
> *Jaczko:* "Is there water? So, at this point, you no longer believe that the pool is dry?"
>
> *Casto:* "I would say, as of five o'clock yesterday, the pool had some water in it."
>
> *Jaczko:* "Now I've said publicly the pool is dry, and now you say that. So you're saying I was wrong. There is no mistake that you're saying it's empty?"
>
> *Casto:* "I would say it's probably a mistake to declare that it's dry. Otherwise, steam wouldn't be coming out."

Having been told unequivocally that morning that there was "no water," in the evening, the report was "there's steam, so there must be water." It was a complete about-face. Jaczko was worried that if there was water in the pool, it would become a "question of my credibility."[46] What's more, the media in the United States and around the world had begun to side with Jaczko's statement, for it played into the assumption that the Japanese government was downplaying the situation.[47]

The U.S. side was starting to change its opinion that the Unit 4 fuel pool was dry. In a joint coordination meeting between the United States and Japan on the morning of March 18, the U.S. side stated, "We initially believed that the outer walls of Unit 4 had been damaged and there was no water in the spent-fuel pool, but we understand that that was not the case."

They had deemed that it was appropriate to assume there was water in Unit 4 judging by the estimated water level. Casto concluded that the U.S.

view on the fuel pool at Unit 4 was wrong; that there was water in the pool. Nonetheless, the water level was still dangerously low, and "the Unit 4 pool contained ten times more radioactive cesium-137 than that released in the Chernobyl disaster—five thousand times more than was released by the Hiroshima bomb," Casto contended. Even Yoshida was heard mentioning to Hosono that "we'll die if that pool explodes."[48] It was perhaps the higher-risk gamble, to speculate that water remained.

On April 1, U.S. Energy Secretary Steven Chu stated, "There are temperature measurements in all the pools that indicate there must be water in there." This amounted to a public denial of Jaczko's assessment of Unit 4 before the House subcommittee on March 16.[49]

The U.S. side, however, kept requesting evidence other than the video to prove the existence of water. On April 12, at the request of the U.S. side, the Japanese side used the Giraffe pump to extract water from the fuel pool and sent a sample to the Americans. Results of the nuclide analysis showed that it did not contain a high concentration of radioactive substance. Still, the U.S. side was not fully convinced. The Japanese took a second sample and analyzed it, but once again a high concentration of radioactive substance was not found. This put an end to the question of the Unit 4 fuel pool.[50]

During this period, the U.S. side was wary that injecting seawater into the reactor would lead to salt being deposited on the fuel rods, which might then interfere with the water pumping, causing the temperature of the reactor to fall. TEPCO was trying to get water in from Sakashita Dam, but they were running into trouble.

The Americans proposed using a barge they had at the Yokosuka base, filling it with fresh water and taking it to the site; they were ready to leave immediately. On March 24, Hosono stated:

"We have discussed the barge on our side, too, but there are two problems. The first is how are you going to tow the barge to the site? The second is, can we use the power station's port? We need a quick conclusion. I'm hoping we'll have a better idea tomorrow about switching to freshwater."

U.S. military officer:

"The U.S. Navy has two barges, both capable of carrying 350,000 tons of freshwater. They are currently being filled with water at Yokosuka. However, the navy barges are originally intended to engage in the business of carrying water to ships at sea, and the U.S. Navy can't tow them to a port with a nuclear reactor. Could the Japanese side possibly hire a tugboat to tow the barges?

"We need to be careful of the radiation dose, but even if radiation is escaping from the debris, surface radiation should fall when it's immersed in water. I think we should be able to bring the barge alongside if we carry out the transportation while measuring radiation near the wharf."

Hosono: "This should be done at the Japanese side's risk."

U.S. military officer: "When can the Japanese side give us their answer about our proposal? If there's not enough water in Sakashita Dam, a delay in the barge transportation may prove fatal. The later we are the greater the risk."

Hosono: "The Japanese side has decided to use the barges. We'll think about the logistics tomorrow."

U.S. military officer: "So, it's all right for the UFJ to issue an order to move the equipment, right? The U.S. Navy in Japan will immediately start moving its tugboats. We'd like to hand them over to you somewhere."

During this exchange, when Hosono said, "We'll think about the logistics tomorrow," for towing the barges, the U.S. naval officer rose to his feet. Everyone was wondering, *What's going on?*

"You mentioned a decision tomorrow morning, but if you can decide now, we can have the barges move out from Yokosuka now. I will issue the order."

His words were replete with a sense of urgency; time was of the essence; even an hour's loss was a waste.[51] They did not just have to tow the barges and hand them over to TEPCO. Someone had to bring the barges alongside the pier right in front of Fukushima Daiichi NPS and pump the water out. Hosono asked the Japanese Coast Guard, but the JCG refused to budge, saying they did not have the ships.[52] In the end, the job fell to the maritime SDF.

The Americans often asked directly, "Who will be in charge of this on the Japanese side?" At times like that, the Japanese ministerial representatives would all look down, and then turn to Takamizawa and Isobe. The SDF staff at the meeting felt, *We really are the last bastion.*[53]

In the meeting on March 25, Sakae Muto, TEPCO's vice president, spoke up:

"We switched to freshwater pumping at Unit 1 at 3:10 p.m. Unit 3 was also switched to freshwater pumping at 6:00 p.m. We are planning to switch to freshwater at Unit 2 as well on March 26."

The atmosphere grew a little more upbeat. Hosono closed that day's meeting with the following words:

"We have discussed a great many items, and are moving forward to realizing them in a short time. I'd like to see the Americans we have at the Integrated Response Office involved in the discussions not as the guests they first were, but as colleagues."[54]

For the whole of March, the U.S. government had a total of 160 support staff sent to the U.S. embassy—including 11 staff members from the NRC and 47 from the Department of Energy.[55]

Many of them would return to the embassy after the Joint Coordination Group meetings and send e-mails and make phone calls to the relevant NRC departments, reporting the events of the day, their exchanges with the Japanese side, new issues, and developments in the U.S. support operations. After tossing the ball to Washington, they would sleep, and when they woke up, the answers would be waiting. Their day would then begin by conveying these answers to the Japanese side. Every representative from the U.S. departments and agencies followed this routine.

Both governments were dealing with the crisis around the clock, via the Hosono Process. The Japanese and American participants started telling each other, "Let's meet before eight o'clock."

Both sides carried out pre-meeting briefings with their own ministries and departments. This improved interagency communication. There was also a hidden agenda of overcoming the reluctance of MOFA and MOD to give out information on the grounds of security-related confidentiality. It was what Fukuyama had in mind when he told each ministerial representative, in one of the early Japanese pre-briefings, "I want you to put all your information on the table here. Any information given here will be treated as the official information of the Japanese government. It will become the sum total of the Japanese government's information."[56]

Similarly, this process also lowered the interagency barriers in the U.S. administration. A senior official at the Department of Defense said, "The Hosono Process also helped us to get organized because it put Ambassador Roos in the center and everything on our side had to work through him. So when the focus shifted there, we were completely uncoordinated for a while on our side, and so it was really only when the Hosono Process started that we also began to be more synchronized."[57]

THE U.S. FORCES FANTASY

Returning to an earlier point in the story, a strange rumor was spreading in Washington on March 15, 2011. TEPCO had given up. They had suggested to the Japanese government, could we not ask the U.S. forces? The Japanese government was asking for U.S. troops to be dispatched to handle the nuclear accident. That was the rumor.

Kevin Maher, in charge of the night desk at the State Department's task force, was one of those who heard it. The information, however, was unconfirmed. There was even a kind of joke, "Call in the U.S. forces to Fukushima? Would you like us to bomb the nuclear reactor, too?"

Speculation that, in the worst case, a special U.S. military force would be dispatched to deal with the nuclear accident and solve the problem was heard even in Kasumigaseki. Maher thought this came from a misunderstanding about the duties of the Marine Corps' Chemical Biological Incident Response Force (CBIRF) that was to be dispatched to Japan.

The dispatch of this force became a reality because President Obama had told Prime Minister Kan in their U.S.-Japan telephone conference on the morning of March 17 (Japan Time) that he would send "the best team" of the "U.S. Armed Forces' Nuclear Response Force." Obama said, "The same people would be dispatched in a similar domestic situation," and specifically mentioned their mission as "dealing with contamination, containment of radioactive material, medical services, evacuation, and decontamination."[58]

This unit was a specialist unit for rescuing victims from contaminated areas. They were responsible for monitoring radiation contamination in a terrorist attack, and for protecting nuclear power plant operators and local residents through medical support and decontamination. Their position was similar to the Japanese Chemical Defense Unit, except that they also had medical support capabilities. There were two units in the United States, both under the aegis of the Marine Corps. However, they were not a unit for doing something about a nuclear meltdown.[59]

The person who came up with the idea of dispatching the CBIRF to Japan was Patrick Walsh, commander of the U.S. Pacific Fleet. When he was talking to Burton Field, commander of the U.S. Forces Japan, at the Yokosuka base, he said, as an afterthought:

"Come to think of it, there is CBIRF. That's a special unit for handling nuclear power disaster in the U.S. Could we bring them over to Japan? As it is a crisis."[60]

It was ultimately Robert Gates, defense secretary, who decided to dispatch them to Japan. Gates had very little to do himself with directing the response during the Fukushima crisis. With two wars in Iraq and Afghanistan, he was not able to spare the time. The two things he decided directly were the funding for Operation Tomodachi and the dispatch of the CBIRF.[61]

It is not true that the Japanese government officially requested the U.S. government to dispatch special U.S. military forces to deal with the nuclear accident. A high-ranking U.S. government official attests, "I haven't heard of a direct request from the Japanese government for support from the U.S. military. I didn't hear it at the time, either."[62]

Initially, the resolve of both the Japanese government and TEPCO was strengthened by the U.S. easygoing attitude of "We'll cooperate fully. Tell us anything you need." At the same time, when the U.S. presented its support list, there was a backlash in some quarters to the effect that "We don't need to accept all this support. It's just like being occupied!" A parliamentary member of the Kantei recollects, "There were those in the Kantei and NISA who expressed such sentiments."[63]

However, from March 14 to March 15, when the situation changed completely, key Kantei officials began to raise their voices that America should be relied upon to give proper assistance. Maher later looked back on this change.

"In the few days after the accident, the Japanese government and TEPCO both took the stance that they didn't need help from the United States. They may have thought Japan's nuclear record over the past thirty years was better than that of the United States, and they were technologically more advanced. Perhaps there was too much confidence that it could be managed by Japan alone.

"However, this bullish stance on the Japanese side later changed completely. They knew clearly that Japan alone couldn't handle it. And their psychological swing was large, this time apparently shifting to a strong dependence on the United States."[64]

As a matter of fact, psychologies of both reliance on the United States and desire to exclude the United States simultaneously erupted among politicians involved with the crisis response at the Kantei. In the midst of the reactors finally getting out of control, just as the desire to rely totally on the United States grew, so, too, did the feeling that U.S. intervention, if that happened, would be a political burden.

In the early hours of March 15, the terrifying image that was conjured up by Kan, faced with the possibility of a TEPCO withdrawal, was the "demise of Japan," as TEPCO withdrew and all of eastern Japan was destroyed by widespread contamination and Japan occupied by foreign powers. The end result would be the loss of independence and self-reliance of Japan as a nation.

But it was not only Kan who had this fear. Hosono also experienced a similar mounting anxiety. He said, "A sign of weakness to rely on the United States is emerging. This isn't great. We are going to lose." If TEPCO withdrew, leaving everyone helpless, it would be impossible to have the U.S. forces take over. At such a time, there would only be the SDF. He sometimes told himself, *This feels just like Jiro Shirasu.*

Jiro Shirasu was remembered for showing his spirit during the occupation after Japan's defeat, in the ruins of the burned city, by saying, "What does GHQ think it's doing?!"[65]

"We have to protect our dignity as a sovereign state at all costs," Hosono said.

By saying this to his secretarial aides, Hosono was trying to inspire himself. A member of the Kantei staff remembers the words Hosono muttered around this time:

"If we can't clean up our own mess, we'll be occupied by America."

The staffer looked back to that occasion. "At the time, there were those in the Kantei who thought it didn't matter if we were occupied by America, as long as they dealt with the nuclear emergency. But Hosono-san always said that no matter what, we had to do it ourselves."[66]

At the same time, at the center of the Japanese government, a psychological reliance on the United States was emerging. The sentiment was that there was no way to make a breakthrough except asking the United States for help. In the early hours of March 15, the Kantei instructed NISA to check if TEPCO had made any requests to the U.S. forces. TEPCO had requested two large-volume fire trucks.[67]

That day, officers from MOD, NISA (METI), and TEPCO, as well as the U.S. government and U.S. forces, gathered in the Bureau of Defense Policy director general's office. The aim of the Japanese side, and especially TEPCO, was to clarify what the support was they most wanted from the U.S. forces. MOD had asked TEPCO beforehand to outline the specific kind of support they wanted to request the most.[68]

The afternoon of March 15. A single sheet of "Implementation Request Items to the U.S. Army" was sent to MOD by TEPCO. It listed the items they wished to request in order of priority.

1. A helicopter water drop, including boric acid, over the spent-fuel pool at Fukushima 1–4
2. Groundside water injection to the spent-fuel pool at Fukushima 1–4
3. A hole opened in the roof of Fukushima 1–4 Reactor Building
4. Transportation (by sea or land) of the large pumps at Onahama to Fukushima 1 (five trailers)

At the same hour, a list of "Implementation Request Items to the Ministry of Defense" was also forwarded from TEPCO. Priorities one and two were the same as those addressed to the U.S. Army, but the third request to MOD was "2,000 tons of freshwater (Fukushima 1) and 4,000 tons of freshwater (Fukushima 2)."[69] The key point at this time was the fuel pool at Unit 4.

From around March 15, some within the political division of the Cabinet Office started to argue that they should directly ask the U.S. military for assistance in controlling the nuclear power plants. "If the SDF isn't up to it, then wouldn't it be better to leave the whole nuclear response up to the U.S. forces?" These were heard as Kantei officials' "mutters," indeterminate between a sentiment and a question, to the MOD and SDF.

In fact, Kitazawa called the chief of staffs, including Oriki, the administrative vice minister of defense, and advisers Kozo Oikawa and Tetsuya Nishimoto to the minister's office and stated, "Kan-san is saying that we should ask for the U.S. military's help," and then added, "what do you all think?"

"If that means that the Self-Defense Force will be under the command of the U.S. forces, that is out of the question" Oriki replied. The other senior officials chimed in, voicing negative responses to Kitazawa's question.

Kitazawa replied, "I understand," and left.

"If it ever comes to that, I will resign. I can't resign now during this crisis, but I'll have no choice but to step down at some point," Oriki pledged.

Top officers at the Joint Staff Office warned, "That's ridiculous, this is an internal problem for Japan. Having the U.S. forces in command is unthinkable. We have to do it ourselves."

"For a start, the U.S. forces can't go into the fifty-mile (eighty-kilometer) zone. It's impossible for them to handle the Fukushima Daiichi NPS accident."

They were extremely sensitive to the atmosphere in the Kantei and MOFA of "leaving it up to the United States," as well as to the voices from Washington about "the SDF being cowards."

The U.S. forces will be seen as an occupying army if we do that. Operation Tomodachi will be destroyed.

Even if we did give the U.S. forces the right of command, they'd only use us as their subcontractors. In any event, it'll be the SDF doing the job . . .[70]

THE EVENING OF MARCH 16. Minister of Defense Toshimi Kitazawa, Vice Minister of Defense Kimito Nakae, and Chief of Staff of the Joint Staff Ryoichi Oriki visited the Kantei and met with Prime Minister Kan. Hosono was also in attendance. Kitazawa was visiting because he needed to check the prime minister's wishes regarding the support list for the Fukushima nuclear emergency that the U.S. government had tendered. The U.S. side had shown the support list to MOD and the SDF, but things like the potassium iodine weren't something MOD and the SDF could decide by themselves. It had to be dealt with by the government as a whole. A government approach had to be worked out.

There was one other point that Oriki felt he had to check. He had come to ask about the fact that Hosono, who had heard that the United States was apparently going to dispatch the CBIRF, had more or less run by the Ministry of Defense: "If that happens, how will the Self-Defense Forces cooperate with the United States, working under them? How should we think about that?"

Is that what the Kantei's really thinking?

Kan's head, however, was full of the water pumping for the fuel pools. Kan asked for the fortitude of the SDF.

"If the SDF can't do it, Japan will collapse."

Hosono interrupted, at this point, "There is information that the United

States will dispatch a nuclear response unit to Japan. If that happens, how about the SDF working under them and the United States and Japan jointly taking measures?"

Kan was nodding, as he listened to Hosono, but after glancing at Oriki, he said,

"With things like this, perhaps we'd better leave it up to America."

He sounded like he was trying to convince himself. A high-ranking official in attendance thought, *Whatever's happened? The PM sounds incredibly weak.*

But Oriki, who had remained silent up until then, looked Kan directly in the eye and stated unequivocally, "You cannot allow America to do the same thing as an occupation force. I will not abide the right of command being passed to the U.S. side. I cannot permit that.

"The respective chiefs of staff share my opinion."[71]

On March 21, Willard visited the Joint Staff Office at MOD in Ichigaya in the company of Patrick Walsh and Burton Field. Oriki told Willard at this meeting, "There may be loss of life. But if that means saving many more lives, then we have to do it."

This went without saying. Oriki was conveying that the SDF was the last bastion and that they had the necessary resolve. Oriki felt there was a slight difference in how the U.S. and Japan perceived the command functions of Operation Tomodachi. The U.S. side called it the Joint Task Force (JTF). Oriki asked Willard, "Does the JTF include the administrative organization?" Willard looked momentarily surprised, but soon caught on.

"No, it's a military organization. It's not administrative."

There was a possibility that if the force did incorporate administrative functions, it might be seen as the GHQ of an occupying army. Ground Chief of Staff Yoshifumi Hibako was concerned when he heard the United States would be giving support in a JTF arrangement.

Do they intend to get substantial rights of administration like their recovery support troops have in Iraq and Afghanistan? Wouldn't that restrict Japan's sovereignty?

The U.S. forces generally establish a JTF in times of emergency. Since this was currently an emergency, it was not strange that they should set up a JTF. But Japan was sensitive about this point. They had the name changed to Joint Support Force (JSF).[72]

Oriki and Masayuki Hironaka, director of the Operations Department in the Joint Staff Office, decided they needed to clearly communicate the SDF's firm intentions. Japan would look out for Japan. In the worst case, the SDF would be the "last bastion."

They would communicate this directly. Hironaka went to Yokota Air Base on his own. Major General Koichiro Bansho, who had been sent to the

U.S.-Japan joint command post at Yokota Air Base, was waiting for him. Hironaka spoke before eight officers of the joint command post, including commander of the U.S. forces in Japan Burton Field, and four hundred and fifty men.

"I am grateful from the bottom of my heart for the assistance of the U.S. forces. Operation Tomodachi is becoming more challenging. But I have come here today to tell you one thing. The SDF is doing what it should. Anything that threatens our dignity is not allowed, and we won't allow it.

"I, myself, was educated in the United States for a number of years. So, I think I understand how the United States does things. You may find the Japanese way of doing things frustrating. Why don't they do things top-down? Why does it take so much time? But even if we were told all of a sudden to do things like America, we couldn't. We do things differently. I want to reiterate how grateful I am for America's assistance. However, I would appreciate it now if you can help us in the way that we think is best."[73]

There were tears in Hironaka's eyes. Field was touched.

He's determined to fight until the end. He came to say, "I don't mind dying to save my country."

Although Field was a fighter pilot and Hironaka a missile man, they were both air force through and through. Field heard loud and clear what Hironaka was trying to say: *Japan is grateful for your help with the Fukushima Daiichi NPS emergency, but the final responsibility lies with the Japanese government, and the SDF is ready to fulfill its duty.*

The resolve Hironaka was trying to convey can best be expressed by the following statement:

"The last bastion is the SDF, not the U.S. forces."

After Hironaka had gone home, Field called Mullen directly. Mullen was an old friend of his.

"Although it's not the case that the SDF has expertise in managing nuclear accidents, Hironaka came here to say that they are determined to keep going until the end. I think that when the time comes, General Oriki and his team can partner with the TEPCO engineers onsite to struggle with the accident."[74]

Throughout the Fukushima accident, the U.S. government, however, had no thought of a strategy to take control of the nuclear disaster from the SDF. If TEPCO withdrew and the Japanese government was helpless, what should America do? This "hypothesis" was whispered in U.S. government circles at times. If the Japanese government became totally helpless in dealing with the Fukushima Daiichi emergency and became a kind of "bankrupt state," what would the U.S. government do? What, as Japan's ally, could it do?

The U.S. government did not draw up this kind of scenario. This was because it had decided on a clear policy of "devoting itself to a supporting role for Japan." This policy was profoundly approved inside the U.S. government. When one of the NRC experts seconded to Japan said they were "embedded" with TEPCO, another NRC staffer corrected him immediately:

"That's not the right expression. They've been talking to TEPCO but it's not the case they've entered inside."[75]

The U.S. government's approach to the Fukushima Daiichi emergency was crystal-clear. It could best be expressed by the following statement:

"The last bastion is the SDF, not the U.S. forces."

The CBIRF arrived at U.S. Yokota Air Base in early April. The Japanese side did not have a clear awareness of the purpose of dispatching this special unit, and there was insufficient coordination between the two countries regarding it. For a start, they did not know of its existence. There were even many commanders at the Yokosuka base who were hearing the name CBIRF for the first time. One of them said, "U.S. Marine Corps are treated as the greatest troops, so CBIRF were treated as second-class citizens. However, this was the first time they had been sent overseas for real. The generals looked like they wanted to be placed close to a specialized military unit for nuclear and radioactivity. Because of this, they became famous in a moment."[76]

The top of the maritime SDF read it as, "They've been sent in for a worst-case scenario."[77]

Doubts still remained, however, about how effective the CBIRF would have been even if their turn had come in an "emergency." "The CBIRF's vehicles were too heavy and were likely to contravene Japanese traffic laws. This wasn't a problem because they were never mobilized to Fukushima . . ."[78]

The only chance they got to show off their stuff was in a joint disaster rescue training exercise between the CBIRF and the SDF on April 23 at Yokota Air Base. However, the inside reality was "creating an opportunity to show that Operation Tomodachi was in fine working order here as well." A member of the U.S. embassy revealed, "Their performance was not very different from that of Japan, or rather in terms of equipment and training, I got the impression that the Japanese were better."[79]

"ALLIES WON'T SHARE THE SAME FATE"

What was the most difficult aspect of U.S.-Japan coordination in responding to the Fukushima nuclear emergency? When asked this at a later date, Casto unhesitatingly cited two factors:

"The fifty miles and Unit 4 fuel pool."[80]

The conflict between Japan and the United States over the two has already been detailed.

What was the most difficult aspect of U.S.-Japan coordination over the crisis response? Relations between Japan and the United States were perhaps at their most tense with the late-night telephone conversation between Edano and Roos on March 14. This was when Roos asked desperately to have an NRC staff member "close to the decisionmaking," which Edano refused on the grounds of "national sovereignty."

The crux of this clash lay in whether Japan was going to make an earnest request for assistance from the United States in dealing with the nuclear emergency, and whether the United States would provide assistance in earnest or not. Assistance from an ally requires protocols and determination on the part of both those asking for help and those offering help.

From the American viewpoint, when offering assistance, they had to gather information, analyze it, and then evaluate it. They could not provide assistance if they had no information. Did Japan not know the protocol for receiving assistance?

"Even if we were told 'Trust us,' we couldn't provide assistance. The essence of the clash between Roos and Edano was this issue."[81]

After saying this, a high-ranking official at the Department of State added, "The tensest time in the bilateral alliance was doubting whether we were truly being accepted into the heart of our partner. And we didn't know if the Japanese just didn't know the status of the reactors and the fuel pools or knew but weren't sharing it for some reason . . . Hence, we requested that the NRC experts close to the decisionmaking be let in the room. John Roos was not a career diplomat, so he could have used more diplomatic turns of phrase. There was a lot of pressure from Washington, so he sometimes said things a bit too strongly."[82]

The U.S. government considered sending high-level officials from Washington in the midst of the crisis. They were thinking of paying a courtesy call to Kan and placing the U.S.-Japan response to Fukushima onto a higher strategic level in one fell swoop. This was because, as Richard Reed, deputy assistant to the president for homeland security, put it, "We were missing a seat at the strategic table."[83]

However, judging there was a fear that a VIP visit could hamper the crisis response of the Japanese government, they decided against sending a special envoy. The first senior government official to arrive was Jaczko, on March 28. All of Washington's demands and orders were concentrated on Roos alone. The clash with Edano came when he was under enormous pressure.

The United States was frustrated because it could not see who was making the decisions where. Who was deciding things in Japan? Who was the interlocutor? How should they work with Japan on actual operations?

In terms of managing the alliance, the framework was "2 plus 2," with MOFA and MOD/SDF being the central players. And, in fact, both Japan and the United States tried to use this framework initially. The framework, however, was not up to dealing with a nuclear emergency and radiation threat. The stakeholders were many—METI, NISA, NSC, TEPCO—and the nuclear safety regulatory system was complicated. It was difficult to cover all of these bodies in the existing framework.

The United States also felt that the Japanese were only focusing on nuclear safety and accident response from the perspective of the safety of commercial plants, and not paying enough attention to the nuclear security aspect. They also suspected that this was what lay behind the Japanese side, especially NISA's looking somewhat down on America's nuclear power program. A high-ranking U.S. administration official had the following to say regarding this point:

"America has not built one new nuclear reactor since the Three Mile Island accident. However, from this accident, an initiative for strict accident countermeasures began in earnest, many lessons were learned from the Chernobyl accident, and there was the thought to put these to use in nuclear power accident prevention planning, manuals, and training. After 9/11, I was proud we took B.5.b response measures for when a serious accident occurs due to a nuclear terror attack. (The B.5.b response refers to the anti-terrorism measures that the United States took in the wake of September 11, 2001, to increase security and develop mitigation strategies to maintain or restore cooling, containment, and spent fuel pool cooling if large areas of the nuclear plants were lost.) Fundamentally, America is a nuclear weapons state. We have accumulated nuclear disaster prevention and emergency responses from military affairs. We have come to look over a well-prepared crisis management system."[84]

Japan was immature in terms of "national security," and it had a "blind spot" in crisis management. The United States was concerned about this point.

It was even more difficult to discern who was making the decisions and where, because of the clash between ministerial leadership and secretariat leadership under the DPJ administration. The U.S. government regarded the Kantei as the "where," but it was hard to fathom how the Kantei, the basement crisis management center, and the fifth-floor prime minister's reception room and office were connected to the various ministry liaison officers.

In short, they could not find the "command post." In a case of gargantuan science and technology striking back, such as a nuclear accident, what they could not grasp, more than anything else, was whose scientific knowledge was the basis of the Kantei's response. A high-ranking U.S. administration official later recollected:

"Usually, we would reach them through MOFA, but MOFA had no

more than a supporting role in the Fukushima nuclear crisis. The White House is powerful, and was searching for a positive counterpart, but there was no such interlocutor. I suppose that should be the role of the Kantei, but their uptake of scientific knowledge was insufficient."

He continued:

"We wanted to know who was playing the role of John Holdren in the Japanese government. But there wasn't anyone like him. Who is doing this on the Japanese side? Who is thinking about the modeling and who is figuring out? I mean there is no sign of any of this on the Japanese side. What models were they basing their measures on? We wanted to speak directly with the government officer who was running the models, but that never happened. There was no science and technology adviser performing that role at the top of the administration."

The U.S. government requested many times that the "whole of a government" be involved in the crisis process. This was because they were skeptical whether the Japanese government was fully integrating all of its national resources. They were afraid that the Japanese government lacked the ability to govern.

In the shadow of Operation Tomodachi, the Fukushima Daiichi NPS crisis highlighted potential crises in the U.S.-Japan alliance.[85]

One was that the threat of radiation exposure and a nuclear power plant meltdown would lead to withdrawal of the U.S. forces from Japan. Jeffrey Bader stated at the time, "If the U.S. forces had withdrawn from Japan, it would have been the end of the U.S.-Japan alliance."[86]

Officers at the White House and the State Department shared almost the same sense of crisis. And it was due to this sense of crisis that they fought so hard to stop the navy proposal of a two-hundred-mile evacuation zone.

"If the two-hundred-mile proposal had been adopted, relocation of the U.S. embassy, an all-out evacuation of U.S. citizens from Tokyo, and the withdrawal of U.S. forces from the U.S. Yokosuka naval base would have been inevitable."[87]

Another was the fear that radiation released from Fukushima Daiichi NPS would cross the Pacific Ocean and threaten the health of American citizens. A high-ranking U.S. government official attested, "If the pollution spread over the Pacific, I doubt whether we could have remained as calm as we were at that time. If such a thing happened, we would have been forced to withdraw all the U.S. forces."[88]

Regarding this point, however, the U.S. government released a statement on March 18 that radiation from Fukushima Daiichi NPS had not reached the U.S. West Coast. The EPA's RadNet system concluded that radiation levels of concern had not been detected. Other monitoring equipment at the DOE also made it clear that no radiation levels of concern had been detected.[89]

The Japanese people realized afresh how blessed a thing the U.S.-Japan alliance was. The United States had sent in the USS *Ronald Reagan* straight away, and ran Operation Tomodachi. With the destruction and loss of function of airports in the disaster area, the transportation capacity of the aircraft carrier offshore was impressive. The *Ronald Reagan* let the maritime Self-Defense Force helicopters land and take off from its deck.

A U.S. aircraft carrier usually does not even let aircraft from the U.S. Air Force or Army land on their decks, let alone the aircraft of foreign forces. And yet, they allowed the maritime SDF helicopters to land and take off. It was a strategy made possible only due to the relationship of trust that existed between the maritime SDF and the U.S. Navy.[90]

The U.S. military had dispatched some twenty thousand troops on humanitarian assistance. They had put in place the strongest support by sending the best of the best from the NRC to help deal with the Fukushima nuclear emergency, monitoring radiation, running simulations and analyses of the accident, looking into response measures, and providing material supplies.

When almost all the diplomats from other countries were leaving, the U.S. embassy and its staff stayed in Japan until the very last. In its greatest postwar crisis, its ally, America, fought side by side with Japan.

It was probably the Self-Defense Forces who felt that gratitude more acutely than anyone. At the same time, it was also the SDF who were probably made the most acutely aware of the potential crises in the U.S.-Japan alliance brought to light by the Fukushima Daiichi NPS crisis. Officers from the maritime SDF were made to see the fiction in their hitherto sentimental "friendship of the sea" vision of the alliance.

"America in a time of emergency wasn't like that. That was really brought home to me. When the chips were down, the United States would run away. They would flee to safety, saying they had to protect their civilian employees. That Japan could depend on the United States to the last for its safety, not even that, it was all fiction . . . America was the spear, Japan the shield, these shared roles didn't happen in reality. As long as Japan didn't become the spear, America wouldn't come to its aid."[91]

This was how one of the maritime SDF officers, who was running around in the midst of the crisis at the forefront of the response, recalled it. An officer of the ground SDF, who was involved in U.S.-Japan coordination on the front lines as well, said, as if to remind himself, "If you don't take the first risk, your ally most certainly won't. Countries that can't help themselves don't get helped."

At the time, he was pondering the words of French president Charles De Gaulle: "Allies will give you help, but they won't share the same fate." He was certain that those were the words.[92]

THIRTEEN

Worst-Case Scenario

"WHAT'S THE REAL BOTTOM LINE?"

A worst-case scenario had to be drawn up. It was the night of March 14, when Goshi Hosono, special adviser to the prime minister, started thinking about that after receiving a phone call from Masao Yoshida, site superintendent at Fukushima Daiichi NPS.

On the evening of March 14, increases in the reactor pressure at Unit 2 were interrupting water injection. The TEPCO local ERC at Fukushima Daiichi believed the possibility of a meltdown was growing stronger as the nuclear fuel in the core melted. At a loss for what to do, Yoshida had called Hosono to inform him directly of the seriousness of the situation. The stoic Yoshida was unusually upset. Hosono was shocked not only by the gravity of the situation, but also by Yoshida's agitation.[1]

What's really at the bottom of this?

That was what Hosono wanted to know.

Things were going from bad to worse. The experts thought so, too. But what was the real bottom of the crisis, what sort of situation? What would happen to Tokyo at that time? Was there a chance that the residents of Greater Tokyo would have to be evacuated?

We need to change our thinking.

Let's think about the worst-case, and then draw up our countermeasures from that.[2]

Prime Minister Naoto Kan was devastated on learning from Hosono the reason for Yoshida's call. At the time, Kan was plagued by the fear that "if things continue to deteriorate, we'll lose Eastern Japan and the country will be split in two."[3] The speech he gave in the early morning of March 15, when he had stormed into TEPCO, was an expression of that fear.

It was from around this time that key members of the cabinet started mentioning a worst-case scenario.[4] The first cabinet member to use the phrase was probably Koichiro Genba, minister of state for national strategy. Initially, every time the Kantei said, "The nuclear reactors won't explode," Genba would counter it with, "What will you do if they *do* explode?" which got on the nerves of the parliamentary members at the Kantei.

As already mentioned, Genba was a member of the Lower House from Fukushima Prefecture and the only representative from Fukushima Prefecture in the cabinet. From March 11, he had the Meteorological Agency reporting to his secretary several times a day on the wind direction forecasts. Genba's major concern was not only the reactor situation, but the safety and livelihood of the Fukushima Prefecture residents, as well as their evacuation.[5]

In the fourth meeting of NERHQ, held at 10:05 p.m. on March 12, Genba appealed, "We should be assuming a worst-case scenario." His eyes were bloodshot. Yoshihiro Katayama, minister of internal affairs and communication, agreed with Genba, "It would be better to assume the worst."[6]

This feeling of Genba's grew stronger from March 14 to March 15. Residents had to be evacuated to a safer place as soon as possible. The existing twenty-kilometer zone was not enough. Should they not be thinking about evacuating from a fifty-kilometer zone?

On the morning of March 15, when the cabinet meeting was over, he had Shunsuke Kondo, chairman of the Japan Atomic Energy Commission, come to his ministerial office to discuss worst-case scenarios. The Japan Atomic Energy Commission (JAEC) was under the jurisdiction of the cabinet, of which Genba was a minister. Genba's father-in-law, Eisaku Sato, a former governor of Fukushima Prefecture, was highly critical of the nuclear fuel cycle, and had once disagreed with Kondo over it. Whether because of that or not, Kondo appeared a little defensive to Genba.

"No one in the government has drawn up a worst-case scenario. I'm worried. It's not within my authority to do so, but I was wondering if you couldn't get some experts together to help you draw up one. I would really appreciate your support."

Kondo was cautious.

"When you say worst, no matter what worst case, you can always draw up a scenario that's even worse than that. If you come up with one, you can always think of something worse than that."

Kondo was uncomfortable even with the phrase "worst-case scenario."

"Thank you for raising this with me, but I am in charge of promoting atomic energy. I can't move openly in responding to this accident."

What Kondo was saying was, government regulation of nuclear safety and accident response was the job of NISA and the Nuclear Safety Commission (NSC). JAEC, whose job it was to promote atomic energy and security, could not move openly on this. Genba thought, *Gee, he's keeping a safe distance*, but there was nothing to do besides ask Kondo.

"It would, of course, be unofficial. I'll talk to the key government members on the quiet."

Kondo finally gave a nod. Genba made doubly sure, saying, "Kondo-san, I'm sorry to rush you, but do it quickly. Draw up a worst-case scenario and appropriate resident evacuation plans."

"I'll see what I can do."

In actuality, Kondo shared Genba's sense of crisis. With the explosion in Unit 4 (RB) in the early hours of March 15 and the damage to Unit 2's containment vessel, even central Tokyo had been contaminated. Kondo's sense of danger was mounting.[7]

In the afternoon of March 17, Genba, armed with a fifty-kilometer evacuation proposal, met with Yukio Edano, chief cabinet secretary, at the Kantei to appeal for extending the evacuation zone to fifty kilometers. He then met with Tetsuro Ito, deputy chief cabinet secretary for crisis management, to make the same case. Ito listened in silence, and did not counter him.[8]

Genba issued a warning in the NERHQ meeting held on the same day.

"This is a war. We either win or lose. We've already lost the battle. So, the fight now is how to keep our losses to a minimum . . . The accident at Fukushima Daiichi is like having three Three Mile Islands happen at once. We should be evacuating residents in line with a worst-case scenario. I've created just such a plan with the help of some experts."[9]

It was from around this time that interest in the "final solution" at the Chernobyl accident started to grow. The NSC was being asked for briefings on their survey report on Chernobyl from various quarters.[10]

The concept of a worst-case scenario differed from person to person. None other than Masao Yoshida had imagined a scenario that might be "Chernobyl times ten." He later told the journalist Ryusho Kadota the following:

"If the containment vessel exploded, radiation would be scattered and the radiation level would make it impossible to get near. Of course, this would prevent ongoing cooling of the other reactors as well. In other words, human beings would no longer be able to approach them. Since this would mean not being able to approach Fukushima Daini, either, the maximum core meltdown would be a total of ten reactors at Daiichi and Daini, which would lead to the simple figure of Chernobyl times ten."[11]

Edano shared almost the same image.

"If One (Fukushima Daiichi) fails, radiation doses will rise in the not-too-distant future and Two (Fukushima Daini) will fail as well. That means the Tokai (Tokai Daini NPS) will be finished, too. It'll be a devil's chain reaction. And if that happens, it's only common sense that Tokyo will be finished as well."[12]

From the night of March 14 to the morning of March 15, Kan and Hosono were worried about the question of TEPCO's "withdrawal." If things became worse, they did not know how long TEPCO would hold out. More critically, how long could they keep up the measures of releasing pressure from the pressure vessel, injecting water, releasing pressure again, injecting water again?[13]

In the case of Tetsuro Ito, it was his job to think about worst-case scenarios. At around two a.m. on March 15, Ito had been told on the fifth floor of the Kantei by "someone apparently from TEPCO" that in the worst case, they would have to abandon Units 1 through 4, which would mean the possibility of abandoning Units 5 and 6, as well as expect the same fate for Fukushima Daini NPS. When he heard that, Ito reflexively thought, *If that happens, Tokyo will be in danger.*[14]

Ito was thinking they had to deal with two different types of time: physical time and psychological time. It would depend on the wind, but generally speaking, it should take the plume anywhere from ten days to two weeks to reach Tokyo. So, they had some leeway in terms of physical time. But there was no leeway in terms of psychological time. There was a strong possibility that a tremendous panic would take place in Tokyo. As deputy chief cabinet secretary for crisis management, Ito bore the responsibility for "keeping the Kantei functioning." The thought crossed his mind, *There's nothing to do but flee to the Kansai Region. We'll have to rent a whole hotel and carry on there, temporarily.*

They would also have to evacuate the emperor and the empress. *It might be best if they went as far south as Kyushu.*[15]

Hosono assumed the position of head of secretariat at the Integrated Response Office set up on March 15. Using this opportunity, he decided to set up at the Kantei an advisory team of mainly experts, which could act quickly. They would not act merely as depositories of wisdom, but be a task force putting into action the ideas put forward. As was already mentioned in chapter 6, he called several young to medium-experienced DPJ parliamentarians to the Kantei for this purpose, and tried to strengthen readiness.

One of them was Seiki Soramoto (Lower House, Hiroshima Prefecture). After receiving a doctorate in nuclear engineering, he had worked on nuclear plant design at Toshiba. He was the DPJ's top nuclear man. After the nuclear accident, Soramoto visited his old acquaintance, Akihiro Ohata, minister for land, infrastructure, transport, and tourism (MLIT). Ohata was an ex-engineer from Hitachi's nuclear division. The Tokai NPS was in his backyard, in Ibaraki Prefecture. He had a strong interest in nuclear administration.

"Isn't there something I can do? My professor at Tokyo University is really worried. He says he wants to do something, too."

"Well, how about creating a team with you and that professor in it? Why don't we get a team like that at young Hosono's place?"

The professor they were referring to was Toshiso Kosako, a graduate school professor at the University of Tokyo. Kosako had been Soramoto's thesis advisor. He was an expert in radiation protection, and when he was younger, had made an impact assessment on the atomic bombs in Hiroshima and Nagasaki. After the Chernobyl accident, he had carried out repeated field surveys and was active internationally. He had served for many years on the expert committee at the Nuclear Safety Commission.

Kosako and Soramoto's relationship was one of master and apprentice. They were both from Hiroshima Prefecture. Kosako was a second-generation hibakusha (A-bomb survivor) through his mother, and Soramoto a third-generation hibakusha through his grandmother, both of whom had entered the city immediately after the bombing to help with rescue efforts. This strengthened the bond they shared.[16]

Ohata suggested to Hosono that he set up an advisory team. This was music to Hosono's ears.[17] This is how the advisory team came into being. Hosono asked Kondo to chair the advisory team, which Kondo accepted.

The Japan Atomic Energy Commission was an independent body to promote the use of atomic energy established in 1956. Commission members needed to be approved by the Diet, but it had been treated as a special body not subject to government intervention. Until the 2001 ministerial reshuffle, it had been headed by the director general of the Science and Technology Agency. The chairman served for three years.

Kondo had been appointed chairman in 2004. He was the foremost authority on probabilistic safety assessment (PSA) in Japan, and also an authority on nuclear safety regulation. There were those who called him the "nuclear village chief." He had graduated with a degree in nuclear engineering from Tokyo University in 1965 as part of the department's second graduating class. At the time, it was the toughest department in the engineering faculty to get into.[18]

Some people found him hard to approach. He had the habit of rolling a pencil around when he was in a bad mood. He was notoriously tough on students in his seminar, but would fight hard for his students' masters and doctoral theses. There were not many professors who took care of their students as well as Kondo did. His exchange students all thought of him as a father figure. He was a kindly boss.[19]

He had a broad international network. When the Fukushima Daiichi accident occurred, he was the first person that John Holdren (assistant to the president for science and technology), Steven Chu (secretary of energy), and Daniel Poneman (deputy secretary of energy) tried to contact.[20]

Although Hosono placed Kondo at the head of the advisory team, it was difficult during an accident to overtly use the head of the JAEC, whose role it was to promote atomic energy. Even when Kondo went to TEPCO Head Office, he came up straight from the basement garage and did not show his face in the Emergency Response Center on the second floor.

On the night of March 15, Kan called Soramoto on his mobile phone and told him, "Soramoto-san, I hear you know a lot about nuclear power. Won't you come over to the Kantei?"

Soramoto later went to the Kantei and was directly asked for his cooperation by Kan in the prime minister's office. On the following night, March 16, Kan phoned Kosako. "I'd like your help."

Kosako agreed immediately. He later went to the Kantei and spoke with Kan.[21]

Akira Omoto, commissioner at the Japan Atomic Energy Commission, also joined the advisory team. Omoto was an ex-TEPCO nuclear engineer. TEPCO had been involved in a shroud cover-up scandal, which forced the resignation of all the top management. While Omoto was not directly involved, being a TEPCO nuclear engineer, he found himself in an uncomfortable position. It was just at this time that the International Atomic Energy Agency was looking for a director of the Division of Nuclear Power, a job that he successfully applied for. TEPCO tried to convince him not to accept the position, but Omoto felt resolute about his "decision of a lifetime" and went to Vienna. After returning to Japan, he was appointed as an adviser to TEPCO.[22]

Soramoto served as the head of the advisory team's secretariat. The team was deemed to be not an official government body, but an unofficial group. Nevertheless, it included Yoshikatsu Nakayama, METI's parliamentary vice minister, and Masaya Yasui, director general for the Energy Conservation and Renewable Energy Department; and Hisanori Nei and Eiji Hiraoka, both NISA deputy directors general.[23]

On March 16, Kondo went to TEPCO Head Office to meet with Hosono. On the afternoon of the same day, the first meeting of the advisory team was held in the conference room there. They discussed not only TEPCO's management stance during the crisis and strengthening monitoring, but also the need to draw up a "rational worst-case scenario." By "rational," they meant that they would use conservative figures but try to avoid going too far.

From the following morning, they relocated to the JAEC's chairman's office on the seventh floor of the cabinet secretariat building and held a meeting. They agreed here that they needed to use their worst-case scenario to plan the progression of the accident and to make a forecast in order to plan dose distribution.

The first thing they had to do was to forecast a worst-case scenario where water can no longer be injected. Since there was a possibility that the water supply could not be reopened due to delays in restoring power—or even if the power was restored, in parallel with the helicopter water drops, they should set up measures for keeping up a constant supply of water by attaching weights to the end of hoses and flying unmanned helicopters to drop them into the spent-fuel pools.[24]

Next was the possibility of a criticality worst-case scenario. In addition to injecting boric acid with the water, a thin piece of boron compound should be dropped into the pool of Unit 4 by helicopter. The possibility of recriticality had already been discussed in the Kantei on the night of March 12, when injecting seawater was being mooted, but people in the field at Fukushima Daiichi were still warning that this was a serious risk. Field reports were being sent daily to TEPCO Head Office, to the effect that "neutrons (dose detection) none." An absence of neutrons meant there was no fear of recriticality.[25]

Around the time, Haruki Madarame, NSC chairman, was urging caution about using boric acid, so coordination was difficult. Nevertheless, the voices calling for injecting boric acid were in the majority.[26]

They also had to decide about the "seawater issue." Since salt is produced when you continually boil sea water, there was a fear that this would cause a malfunction. Therefore, they should switch to fresh water as soon as possible.

On March 16, Kondo sent an e-mail to Mitsumasa Hirano, technical adviser to the Japan Nuclear Energy Safety (JNES) organization.

"Since we are injecting seawater, salt has accumulated gradually. It is certain that it is building up in the bottom of the pressure vessel, and Chairman Madarame says that it will lead to a blockage of the inner flow passage. What would happen if that took place? Do you have any analysis?"

Hirano responded by e-mail.

"There will be salt from ten tons of seawater a day . . . No one knows whether it's partial or complete, but the bottom of the RPV (pressure vessel) has been penetrated, so I believe there's no point worrying about it. What happens if no water gets into the Unit 4 pool? What will happen at the other units if TEPCO withdraws? They seem to have begun considering this kind of worst-case scenario in earnest."

By "they" he meant the JNES experts. Although JNES as an organization was not drawing up a worst-case scenario, its experts were starting to think about individual worst-case scenarios.[27]

But should they change the evacuation zone or not? With the changes in Units 2 and 4 on March 15, there was a rising fear of contamination outside the twenty-kilometer limit. Residents had to be protected from exposure. However, the majority position was that even if the fuel pools were all dry and radioactive material was released, it was hard to imagine radiation at the twenty-kilometer mark being over 50 millisieverts, so there was no need to change the evacuation zone immediately.[28]

Both Kondo and Kosako spoke on the assumption that a meltdown had already taken place. Kosako said, "This is not a Three Mile Island, it's already a Chernobyl."[29]

THE NIGHT OF MARCH 19. In another meeting, they drew up a proposal to be submitted to Hosono.

- They would consider several measures to avert a worst-case scenario in the case that water release and injection operations became impossible.

- They would use an unmanned helicopter to check what the situation was in the spent-fuel pools at Units 3 and 4; what was the water level and temperature?

- Bearing in mind averting a criticality scenario, a boron compound would be dropped into the spent-fuel pool at Unit 4 along with the boric acid injection.

- Care would be provided to the exhausted emergency operators and radiation operators.

Every now and again, Nei would nod off in the meetings. Having been up night after night, it was as if this meeting was the only time he had to sleep. At one point in the middle of a meeting, there was a loud bang. Nei had fallen off his chair onto the floor. He blinked as he rose to his feet.[30]

In parallel with the advisory team, but in a completely separate way, Kondo was working secretly on a Plan B. This was the worst-case scenario he had been asked by Genba to draw up. Plan B was to consider possible new events, including possible chains of events, and decide beforehand how to avert them, as well to consider how to handle the scope of the emergency, including issues such as soil and marine contamination. Kondo said he was considering an "out-of-this-world scenario."

He decided to set up a study group separate from the advisory team, approaching Akira Omoto, commissioner at the Japan Atomic Energy Commission, and Toshimitsu Homma, deputy director of the Nuclear Safety Research Center at the Japan Atomic Energy Agency (JAEA), to work with him. Homma was the foremost expert on nuclear disaster prevention. He had known Kondo for more than twenty years. Kondo had decided, "Homma will do the calculations." Kondo, Omoto, and Homma were the three key members of the Plan B team. At the first meeting of the Plan B team, Kondo told them:

"We have to address the nuclear accident response with everything Japan has. I think now is the time."[31]

"NOW IS THE WORST"

Both Kondo and Omoto thought the greatest risk would be if the Anti-Seismic Building was destroyed. If that happened, with radiation mounting, both Units 5 and 6 would have to be abandoned.

Kondo was wondering, "Can't we build some kind of shielding equipment for Units 5 and 6 so the operators won't be too exposed?" but Omoto was of the opinion that "that isn't easy. The shielding wouldn't be enough. It's no good if you can't stop the source; injecting slurry would be the only way." Slurry was a mixture of sand and water.

In fact, Site Superintendent Masao Yoshida was also worried about the risks should the Anti-Seismic Building be lost. So much so that on the afternoon of March 15, he was secretly considering using the joint pool building as a replacement ERC in readiness for such an event.[32]

Using Omoto's opinion as a base, the Plan B team traced out a worst-case scenario:

- They would take into account, for Units 1 through 6 and the spent-fuel pools (SFP), a concrete interaction after the loss of the cooling function in the fuel pools, a steam explosion, a hydrogen explosion, pressure damage, and so on.

- They would assume a scenario where the radiation environment of the power plant worsened, forcing the evacuation of workers, and new events developing one after another.

- They would calculate exposure doses from radioactive materials released from the plant, running an analysis to pinpoint areas over 10 millisieverts and 50 millisieverts. Each would respectively require a "stay-indoors evacuation" and an "evacuation."

- They would calculate the surface contamination distribution of cesium-137 and analyze which areas would exceed the contamination density index (forced relocation during the Chernobyl accident: 1480 kBq/m²; relocation: 555 kBq/m²).

Calculating changes in the radiation environment, exposure levels, and mapping surface contamination was mainly conducted by Homma. When carrying out his analysis based on the above scenario, he predicted the following possibility, especially if the cooling function was lost at the Unit 4 fuel pool:

"The relocation zone would be 250–300 kilometers from the plant."[33]

The main points here were a sequence covering the risk of another hydrogen explosion in Unit 1; the risk of the bottom falling out of the spent-fuel pool at Unit 4, causing a reaction of the nuclear fuel with the core concrete nuclear; and the risk of this causing the cessation of operations. Omoto described this danger as "If one goes, everything goes, that's what's frightening."[34]

The explosion in Unit 4 (RB) on March 15 acted to raise the sense of crisis among key members of the Kantei about the danger not only of the reactors but of the spent-fuel pools as well. Unit 4 was storing a large number of spent-fuel rods with large decay heat that had not long been taken out. In the parallel chains of crises, this was the "weakest link." As Hosono had also instructed, NISA and JNES had started running a simulation on the impact the destruction of the fuel pools would have.[35]

At the time, Yasui's greatest fear was, "If there's a meltdown in the fuel pools, they won't be able to continue with the running repairs at Units 1, 2, and 3. That will be the greatest crisis. If that happens, there'll be nobody left."[36]

Yutaka Kukita, acting chairman of the NSC, envisioned a scenario where "the nuclear fuel would melt, a fire would break out, the bottom of the pool would fall and the nuclear fuel would drop down. That would be the worst."[37]

The Integrated Response Office, however, decided from the visual reports of the SDF helicopter on March 16 that there was water in the Unit 4 fuel pool. Steam had been seen rising after the SDF dropped water from overhead on March 17. This was taken as confirmation that there was water in the pool.[38]

Although the immediate fear of the fuel pool running dry had been removed for the moment, it still did not change the fact that it was structurally crippled. Unit 4's fuel pool was located on the equivalent of the fifth floor of a building. Debris had fallen into the pool when the roof of the reactor building had blown.

Hosono was up to his ears in directing the water injection operations from groundside by the SDF, the police, and the fire department, but he felt from around March 20 that things had calmed down somewhat.

In the eleventh NERHQ meeting, on March 21, Kan praised the Tokyo Fire Department for its brave operations in pumping in three thousand tons of water, mainly to Unit 3, up until the previous day, saying, "I think we can see some light at the end of the crisis tunnel."[39]

They could catch their breath a bit. But anything could still happen. Hosono told Kan now was the time to draw up a worst-case scenario. It was Kondo that Hosono had in mind. While working on a worst-case scenario, Kondo, however, did not think the word "worst" meant much. He told Hosono, "There's not much point in trying to foresee which will be the worst moment." It was more important to identify where lay the most danger, recognizing it accurately and responding ahead of the curve.

He was especially worried about the strength of the Unit 4 fuel pool structure. He was wary of aftershocks.

"The bottom would fall out, water would leak, and injecting water would come to a standstill, especially if there was an aftershock."[40]

Kan followed Hosono's suggestion and decided to ask Kondo to do the job. Up until that point, Kan was in the habit of saying, "I want you to look at things in parallel." If there was another hydrogen explosion at one of the reactors, work would be interrupted. Which meant that the water-pumping operations would stop as well. That was what Kan was afraid of. Kan also told Hosono that in the process of drawing up a worst-case scenario, he wanted countermeasures to be considered at the same time.[41]

Careful attention had to be paid to drawing up the worst-case scenario. Any leaks during the process could lead to panic. So, the work had to proceed in the strictest confidence.

Sometime after four p.m. on March 22, Kan invited Haruki Madarame, NSC chairman; Shunsuke Kondo, JAEC chairman; and Nobuaki Terasaka, NISA director general, to his office at the Kantei and asked their opinion about drawing up a worst-case scenario. Edano, Hosono, and Soramoto were also present.

This day was also the day when the Giraffe appeared on the scene for the water pumping operation. Kan said, "Things have settled down a bit. But we still don't know what will happen. There've been many predictions that were right, haven't there? That's why I think I'd like to draw up a worst-case scenario, but what do you think?"

Kondo thought, *It's a strange turn of phrase, to say you'll draw up a worst-case scenario because things have calmed down.*

Terasaka remained silent. Madarame could not meet Kan's eyes, but had his face turned down. Kondo opened his mouth to speak.

"If you're talking about worst-case scenarios, now is the worst . . . In short, what I mean is things will probably not get worse than they are now."

Kondo looked favorably on the impact the Giraffe would have on keeping up a steady and stable supply of water to the fuel pool. He continued, "Rather than a future worst-case scenario, we need to be urgently considering where we should be focusing our attention onsite now, what can we do to stop possible contingencies from happening."

Kan looked like he was in a hurry. However, he never mentioned a deadline. Kondo asked him.

"When would you like it by?"

Kan did not reply.

"Well, how about in three days' time?"

"Yes, please."

That was how the discussion ran. The reason why Kondo had offered three days as the deadline was because he was already in the process of drawing up Plan B. Kondo told Madarame, "You're incredibly busy right now, so shall we do it at my place?" to which Madarame agreed.

Kan said, "I want you to throw everything you have into this and work together . . . I want you to draw up a worst case that way, too."

In times of nuclear disaster, it was laid down that it was the role of the NSC chairman to advise the prime minister in his capacity as head of the NERHQ. By rights, it should have been Madarame's advice that was sought on the question of a worst-case scenario. Kan, however, never issued such an order to Madarame. Nevertheless, the government could not decide on a worst-case scenario while totally ignoring him. Terasaka and Madarame had been called to the prime minister's office to confirm their support for Kondo and to perform the requisite courtesies.[42]

"ROUGH SKETCH OF THE CONTINGENCY SITUATION SCENARIO"

From March 22 to March 25, in addition to Omoto and Homma, Kondo put together a team of experts from NISA, JNES, and JAEA to draw up a computer-analyzed worst-case scenario. Each participant was there in an individual capacity. Mitsuhiro Kajimoto, deputy manager of the Nuclear Power Safety and Evaluation Division at JNES, was one of them.

As has already been mentioned in chapter 2, Kajimoto was an expert in emission predictions of radioactive substances in the case of severe nuclear accidents. Omoto and Kondo had drafted him with the blessing of JNES President Katsuhiro Sogabe.[43]

There were also those who did not participate in the meetings, but interacted indirectly via e-mail. The work under Kondo was aimed at giving an outline to contingencies given that "the emergence of new events that might lead to contingencies couldn't be ruled out at Fukushima Daiichi NPS where the accident had occurred." The work was a rush job of three days, with experts toiling around the clock on computer analyses.

Around this time, the Integrated Response Office deemed that the critical situation at the fuel pool had been averted for the moment with the arrival of the Giraffe, their focus shifting once again to the temperature at Unit 1 and hydrogen explosion countermeasures.[44]

Kondo's work on the worst-case scenario took a two-sided approach on the reactors and the fuel pools. There would be a hydrogen explosion either in the Unit 1 pressure vessel or containment vessel, discharging radioactive material. Pumping water into Unit 1 would no longer be possible, and damage to the containment vessel would ensue. The fuel in the spent-fuel pool at Unit 4 would be exposed and melt down. Subsequently, the molten fuel would interact with the concrete, discharging radioactive material.

The work was carried out with Kajimoto doing the worst-case scenario calculations for the reactor, Homma the worst-case calculations for exposure, and Omoto combining these two and then passing it up to Kondo. When the work was in its final stages, Kondo called in Kajimoto and Homma for a final check. Homma worked through the night at the NSC. His calculations were not finished even though dawn was breaking. It was already March 25.

"It's almost time."

"Isn't it done yet?"

"Hurry up!"

He was constantly harried by the secretariat, but finally managed to hand in his results.[45] In the worst-of-the-worst case, where both the reactors and fuel pools were out of control, there was a possibility that residents would have to be forcibly relocated from a radius of 170 kilometers from the plant, and a possibility that voluntary relocation should be permitted for a radius of 250 kilometers, where the annual radiation dose would substantially exceed natural radiation levels.

Using this as a reference, Kondo himself wrote the final page. This covered the countermeasures that Kan had requested, namely:

- The current 20-kilometer evacuation zone should be allowed to stand for the time being.

- If the Unit 4 fuel pool was damaged and there was interaction with the core concrete, residents from a 50-kilometer zone should be evacuated, and those in the zone between 50–70 kilometers should "stay indoors."

- If the same thing happens at another fuel pool, we will contemplate mandatory relocation within 170 kilometers, and voluntary relocation within 250 kilometers.

- As a last resort, "shielding by a mixture of sand and water" would be the most effective (1,100 tons required per reactor).

The title was "Rough Sketch of the Contingency Situation Scenario for the Fukushima Daiichi NPS." It consisted of fifteen pages. There was no main text, just PowerPoint slides.

When Hosono received it, he looked hard at the Plan B members' faces and said, "If this gets out, I won't rest until I find out who leaked it." They were later instructed over the phone by the NSC secretariat to "destroy everything," including the documents and data they had used.[46]

On March 25, Kondo met with Hosono in his office at the Kantei and reported the results of the simulation. Kondo apologized, "We didn't have enough time, so I just made PowerPoint slides."

Flipping through the pages, Hosono said, "It's pretty packed for a PowerPoint, isn't it?"

Kondo told Hosono that "the possibility of the contingency situation described in the Rough Sketch actually happening is close to zero." He then said that in order to prevent heading toward a worst-case scenario, it was crucial to have:

- The reactor containment vessels filled with nitrogen gas.

- Remote operation of the equipment to inject water from a height.

- Reinforcement of the bottom of the spent-fuel pool at Unit 4.[47]

Looking back, the period from March 15, when the Unit 2 containment vessel was damaged and Unit 4 (RB) exploded, until March 16, when the footage shot from the helicopter showed water in the Unit 3 fuel pool—or to expand it somewhat until March 22, when the Giraffe arrived after the water injection operations for the fuel pool at Unit 3—was the phase when things might have been headed toward the worst-case scenario. Viewed in this light, just as Kondo had told Kan, "Now is the worst," around March 22, may well have been the worst. However, Kondo explained that in order to avoid the worst-case scenario, "Now is crucial."

Judging that it would be impossible to meet with Kan that day, Hosono decided to meet with Kondo by himself.

"Leave it with me. I'll speak to the prime minister in due time. I think it's better to wait for the right moment."

Hosono noticed that the usually dandy Kondo was wearing the same suit as three days ago. It was wrinkled. Kondo was roughly the same age as Hosono's father.

He's worked on this all night.

Kondo left the room. Hosono bowed his head deeply at the wrinkled back of his suit. That same day, Hosono popped into the prime minister's office to report and hand Kan the PowerPoint slides. He also briefed Edano, Fukuyama, and Terada separately. He showed them the slides of the "Rough Sketch of the Contingency Situation Scenario," but took the papers back immediately after he finished explaining.

He heard someone say, "In the worst case, we're going to have to evacuate the whole metropolitan area, aren't we?"

"It can't be done. That's why we have to think of what's to be done to prevent that!"[48]

In Hosono's case, his "secret agenda" in having a worst-case scenario drawn up was the defense of the capital if it was contaminated by radiation. Hosono told himself, "What will happen if Tokyo's hit? We're talking about defending the capital. The capital will be protected. That's the last fight."

That was one of the reasons he had ordered nine Giraffes. It was also why he pushed through the remote operation of the Giraffes.[49]

Hosono later returned from the Kantei to the Integrated Response Office at TEPCO. On the way, his view of Tokyo through the car window momentarily took on a sepia tone. He had been toing-and-froing between the Kantei and TEPCO every day since March 15. Some days, he went several times. The slope down from the Kantei through the government district of Kasumigaseki and onto Hibiya was wreathed in a pale sunset.

In short, this worst-case scenario project is a project for the defense of the capital.

Being unable to defend Tokyo means the end of Japan.

Tokyo suddenly seemed unbearably precious to him.[50]

U.S.-JAPAN DISCUSSION OF THE WORST-CASE SCENARIO

Around this time, the U.S. NRC was also drawing up a worst-case scenario that assumed a nuclear meltdown as outlined earlier. (See chapter 11.)

On March 14, the NRC ran RASCAL projections assuming 40 percent core damage for Units 1 through 3. The conclusion was: "The bottom line is that the core could, in fact, drop." They also predicted, "If the core goes into 100 percent meltdown and the containment vessel is damaged, radiation will reach as far as eighty kilometers downwind." Based on this, there was the announcement for a fifty-mile evacuation recommendation that was held, but after that, a simulation was undertaken for a situation in which matters got even worse.

"The pool structure is no longer in existence. The walls have collapsed. So, you have spent fuel sitting there in a pile. Three reactors melting down, six spent-fuel pools go up in flames. And what, then, would be the impact for Tokyo, for example, if the wind kept blowing in that direction?"[51]

Based on this assessment, the NRC prepared a scenario for evacuating U.S. citizens in Japan to 240–320 kilometers away.[52]

Kondo felt suspicious about the NRC suddenly shifting from supporting the Japanese government's evacuation zone to a recommendation of fifty miles, thinking, *They're overestimating.* Kondo and his team were reaching the conclusion that even if such a scenario took place, the twenty-kilometer zone would be sufficient for the time being.

Since Kondo and his team were considering a worst-case scenario assuming four reactors out of control, when they learned of the NRC worst-case scenario, they felt it was a lot like theirs.[53]

However, Plan B did not assume a simultaneous occurrence, but a chain of events. What should they make of the dose calculations that were the grounds for the NRC's shift? Kondo wrote to Mitsumasa Hirano, a JNES technical adviser, with a request to "please explain this."[54]

Kondo's "contingency scenario" also had alternative significance in verifying the scenarios developed by the U.S. government and the NRC.[55] Hosono felt the need to compare the contingency scenario Kondo was drawing up with the NRC's worst-case scenario. It was just that he had to proceed with extreme caution.

On March 25, before briefing Kan on the outline of the report, Hosono invited U.S. Ambassador John Roos and Charles Casto, head of the NRC Japan site support team, to his office at the Diet members' office building. He had Kondo brief them on the Japanese side's worst-case scenario. Up until then, both governments had drawn up worst-case scenarios, but had neither checked nor compared them.

Hosono wanted to boil down, for once, what the actual differences were. The Joint Coordination Group had started work on March 22, improving communication between the two countries markedly, but he wanted to let them know that Japan was taking things seriously and dealing earnestly with the situation by showing the top of the U.S. side, in strict confidentiality, the Japanese worst-case scenario.

During this meeting, Kondo explained the calculation results for the contingency situation scenario, and Casto gave the NRC simulation results. "The premise of Dr. Kondo's analysis was that a new hydrogen explosion would necessitate another site evacuation, and the resulting abandonment would lead to further meltdowns . . . It was masterfully laid out, but based solely on conjecture," Casto recalled.[56]

Casto showed them a sheet of paper with calculations assuming the wind continued to blow from Fukushima Daiichi NPS in the direction of Tokyo. Kondo commented, "They have seasonal winds there, and the wind blows every which way all day long. I don't think it would blow constantly in the direction of Tokyo."

Casto believed Kondo's scenario to be overly pessimistic and "predominantly anecdotal."

However, he refrained from saying that directly to Kondo. This was a nuclear engineering expert representing Japan. And he was resolved that "the U.S. role is only a supportive one; I shouldn't go challenging him." He asked Kondo, "Professor Kondo, what should they be doing right now to prevent your scenario from happening?"

Kondo did not reply to his question directly. He was also weighing up the situation. Casto then told Kondo with a certain amount of reserve, "I think creating a sustainable pumping system that doesn't depend on human power is important. You run that for ten days. You beat the worst-case scenario with that . . . I'd be grateful if you could hurry to automate all the water systems like the current Giraffe pumping system without human intervention."

Kondo agreed, "You're quite right."

Casto told Hosono, "Mr. Hosono, Professor Kondo just told you what you need to do."[57]

Casto then briefed the Japanese side on the interim assessment the NRC had conducted in conjunction with the Department of Energy, Naval Reactors, and GE.

While acknowledging such instabilities as:

- Active radiation releases ongoing

- Unknown ocean impacts

- Accident conditions static but fragile

- Mitigating features temporary and highly unconventional,

the situation in the reactors was acknowledged as:

- Fuel damage estimates: U-1 70 percent; U-2 30 percent; U-3 25 percent (est.)

- 1–10 to 1–100 probability of future energetic release

- Probability driven by seismic events without diversity or redundancy of injection system

- 1–100,000 probability with training and preplanning of fire equipment and diverse and redundant injection system.

Casto was emphatic.

"Tokyo is not seriously threatened. The use of Giraffes from March 22 has clearly had an impact."

At the end of the interim assessment, recommendations for next steps to prevent further events included:

- Diversity and redundancy in feeding system

- Automation of Giraffes

- Additional venting system.[58]

Several days later, Kondo also met with Gregory Jaczko, NRC chairman, who visited Japan. He had been sent to Japan suddenly, as a special envoy of the U.S. government.

March 26 was Jaczko's mother's birthday. Jaczko's parents had driven to Washington, from Baltimore where they were living, to celebrate with the whole family. As they were partway through the birthday party celebrations as a whole family, a call came in from Denis McDonough, the White House deputy national security adviser.

"I want you to go to Tokyo immediately, on the next flight. The ambassador [Roos] wants a senior government official from Washington sent in."

That night, Jaczko departed from Washington Dulles Airport and arrived, via London Heathrow Airport, in Japan the next day, on March 28. He could not see any other passengers on the plane bound for Japan.

He was worried about the U.S. reputation being bad in Japan, with America's unilateral decision of a fifty-mile evacuation area, but everywhere he went he was first given thanks for their support of Japan. On arrival at Narita Airport, he received a message that John Holdren, the president's science and technology adviser, wanted to speak with him urgently. He placed a call to Holdren while going through customs. Holdren answered the phone just as Jaczko was showing his passport to the officer. Holdren said, "I've just spoken with Kondo, and his team has drawn up a worst-case scenario that's got me worried. Please meet with Kondo while you're in Japan."

Holdren and Kondo were fellow scientists. Holdren held Kondo in high esteem and valued his opinion. Apparently, having heard a summary from Kondo, Holdren had become more worried about the outcome.

Jaczko was, in reality, only spending one day in Japan. Before returning home, he had breakfast with Kondo and spoke to him. Kondo said quietly, "Things could be devastating in Tokyo if we're not careful."[59]

"Kondo believed enough radiation could be released to cause widespread contamination in Tokyo," Jaczko remembered. "The NRC staff was not yet predicting such dire scenarios. But the situation in Japan was very different from what nuclear analysts in America were used to," he added.[60] Upon hearing Kondo's sobering prediction, Jaczko assured him that the U.S. government would be aware of his concerns. The United States had already given its recommendations to the Japanese government, so all they could do was wait and see.[61]

THE SDF'S WORST-CASE SCENARIO

Another part of the government that was secretly considering a worst-case scenario was the Ministry of Defense (MOD) and the Self-Defense Forces (SDF).

On the morning of March 15, senior officers at the Joint Staff Office "thought perhaps people won't be able to live in eastern Japan, from the Tohoku district all the way down to Tokyo," when they heard that radiation had risen at the Yokosuka navy base. It was the Yokosuka Shock that made staff at the Joint Staff Office start thinking about a worst-case scenario.[62]

The helicopter water drops on the morning of March 17 were pushed through, as a last-ditch battle, as it were, against the backdrop of recognizing the seriousness of the situation. Kitazawa's remark in his press conference after the water drop was over—"Today was the limit"—was an expression of the awareness that if they did not carry out the water drop, things would head toward a worst-case scenario.

Both MOD and the SDF were considering adding boric acid to the water drops. On the afternoon of March 15, TEPCO asked the SDF to drop boric acid onto Units 1, 3, and 4 the next day.[63]

Information was rife that Tokyo would be covered in a "deadly fallout" if recriticality occurred.[64] That was why they were saying it was imperative to have boric acid dropped. Boric acid is known to absorb neutrons, thereby preventing recriticality. It had been dropped from helicopters along with sand and lead during the Sarcophagus Operation at Chernobyl. If they had to build a sarcophagus at Fukushima Daiichi NPS as well, dropping boric acid would be unavoidable.

However, differing from the fuel pool drops, it would have to be dropped into the reactors in a pinpoint way. In the case of Fukushima Daiichi, they would need at least twenty tons of boric acid. It would have to be slowly lowered from helicopters on twenty-meter ropes, and then cut loose. They would have to do it four times with five-ton buckets, and then repeat the procedure. That meant hovering. As a matter of course, the crew would be exposed to a higher level of radiation. They would need to use two helicopters.

Miyajima, a lieutenant general in the Central Readiness Force (CRF), asked the flight captain, "You're working on rotation, but should you ask for volunteers just for this?"

"There's no need for that. We'll run the rotation. You don't need to worry."

The SDF has really become a fighting force.

Miyajima was overcome by a strong emotion when he heard these words.[65]

Yoshifumi Hibako, the ground chief of staff, also felt the need to show the extent of his resolve.

"If the worst comes to the worst, we'll have to scrap the reactors, or else half of Japan will become a graveyard. At the very least, I'll ride the helicopter. And I'll be the first to drop the boric acid. I'll go down the rope like a monkey."[66]

He told his subordinates of his intention. This was why the boric acid drop strategy became known as the Tsuruichi Operation, a reference to a legend in Hibako's home prefecture of Oita, which tells of a mother (Tsuru) and her son (Ichitaro) who drowned themselves as human sacrifices to prevent continual flooding in their village from burst dikes.[67]

It was in late March that MOD and the SDF started drawing up and preparing operations in earnest for a worst-case scenario. This was triggered by Casto suggesting that the United States was preparing a worst-case scenario, so perhaps the Japanese side needed to do so, too, when he visited Minister Kitazawa on the two days of March 17 and 18. Kitazawa had called Masaya Yasui from NISA to the Ministry of Defense again, and listened to his briefing, because he was thinking about preparing for the worst.[68]

In the evening of March 20, Kitazawa called at the prime minister's office at the Kantei with Oriki, chief of staff of the Joint Staff. It was to be decided by the cabinet members that the onsite water operations at Fukushima Daiichi NPS were to be placed under the command of the SDF, but Kitazawa met with Kan immediately prior to that with Oriki and Kimito Nakae, vice minister of defense. During the meeting, Kitazawa strongly urged that the Japanese government should be preparing for the "worst."

At the same time, Kitazawa also told Kan, "I need to be involved," adding that the Defense Ministry was ready to take the lead and carry out the operations if the Kantei were to go through with them. This was because, in the worst case, the SDF would have to be mobilized.

However, Kan's response was vague up until the last minute.

Because there was no proactive judgment demonstrated from the prime minister, the SDF decided to draw up a contingency plan and operational guidelines for a worst-case scenario in accordance with Kitazawa's instructions.[69]

This was the run-up of events that led Hosono to report to Kitazawa on the contingency situation scenario and to hand him a copy.

Like Kan and Hosono, sharply and quicker than anyone else, Kitazawa had sensed the seriousness and destructive potential of the Fukushima Daiichi crisis. Of all the cabinet members, Kitazawa was the first to inform U.S. Ambassador Roos of the gravity of the situation.

The fact that Kitazawa maintained Kan's trust and was a veteran politician of some note also added to the role he played, and raised his credibility. Not to mention that information gathered around him. A trusted senior official at MOD recalls at least three occasions when Kitazawa thought things might be heading toward a critical situation.

"The Fukushima NPS accident was Japan's greatest crisis since the war. The prime minister had perhaps the greatest sense of crisis. When the prime minister met with Minister Kitazawa alone, I remember he used the phrase 'Half of Japan will be devastated.' I think that during this time, there were three times that the minister and I thought we had had it.

"The first was when the NRC [U.S. Nuclear Regulatory Commission] warned us that all hell would break loose if we didn't inject water quickly. If only one out of seven [three reactors and four spent-fuel pools] failed, we wouldn't be able to work at the others anymore. The NRC was worried that if that happened, people would no longer be able to live in Tokyo. You see, the NRC had initially been making approaches to the Ministry of Defense.

"The next was when the MOD experts pointed out the possibility of a steam explosion with the helicopter water drops. If there was a steam explosion, you wouldn't be able to get close anymore. The government would be powerless. We would just have to sit back and wait. In the end, the decision for the helicopter water drop was made by the minister and chief of staff of the Joint Staff.

"And the last time was when the question was raised by the information HQ at the stage of internal inquiry whether sparks would cause an explosion when power was restored to Unit 2 and elsewhere. We were warned that radiation doses of 400 millisieverts/hour had been observed in the vicinity of Unit 2, and since they couldn't get close, pressure was rising in Unit 2 and there was a strong possibility of an explosion. I remember quite clearly even now. It was March 20, because the minister went to the graduation ceremony of the National Defense Academy that day."[70]

After March 20, the SDF, with the Joint Staff Office playing a central role, started creating in earnest "operational plans" and "implementation guidelines" for a "worst case." Several experts, including SDF officers who had majored in nuclear engineering, were gathered around Masayuki Hironaka, director of the operations department, in the Joint Staff Office, to start working on a plan in mind for a worst-case scenario that hypothetically assumed a meltdown in all five reactors (excluding Unit 4). The team was disbanded later, after some twenty days, when there had been no major aftershocks and the situation seemed to have stabilized somewhat.

In practice, they regarded sudden aftershocks as a major risk factor, and drew up operational plans and implementation guidelines in response to a worsening scenario divided into four phases. This they did in the space of three days.

Phase 1 was the case of an explosion in a reactor or containment vessel, or a new explosion in a reactor building at Fukushima Daiichi NPS, scattering a large volume of radiation. In this case, an evacuation order would most likely be issued to all TEPCO staff and associate workers. The strategy was, therefore, a rescue operation of TEPCO workers and their associate companies.

Phase 2 was an evacuation strategy, to be conducted by the ground, maritime, and air SDF throughout Fukushima Prefecture when radioactive materials had been dispersed.

At that time, they would transport residents unable to evacuate on their own outside a fifty-kilometer radius from the plant.

Phase 3 was security patrolling within a 250-kilometer radius of the plant if Units 1 through 4 underwent a chain meltdown and there was an extremely high probability of large-scale diffusion of radioactive material.

The total population covered in such a case would probably exceed 35 million.

They used the U.S. Department of Defense's National Security Agency and Defense Threat Reduction Agency radiation diffusion prediction models as reference to predict atmospheric diffusion of radioactive materials. This had been provided to the SDF by the U.S. forces. According to this simulation, a plume would spread throughout the metropolitan area, including Tokyo after six hours, and spread more widely after twelve hours.

Phase 4 assumed a complete loss of control if several reactors and containment vessels exploded. If this happened, they would implement a so-called concrete "sarcophagus strategy."

In conjunction with drawing up the operational plans and implementation guidelines for Phases 1 through 4, logistics covering which and how many troops would be mobilized were also specified. It was assumed that the most likely worst-case scenarios were the following two:

- Meltdown would take place with the molten fuel breaking through the concrete below, causing a steam explosion on contact with groundwater. Because buildings would be destroyed at such a time, much of the molten fuel would be dispersed into the atmosphere.

- The cooling water trapped beneath would trigger an explosion just by the molten nuclear fuel dropping down. In this case, even if the buildings remained standing, all piping would be broken and radiation would leak out from there.[71]

In whichever case, there was a strong possibility that the scale would be greater than Chernobyl, with an evacuation area set at a hundred kilometers and residents unable to live in the vicinity.[72]

Oriki and Hironaka told Toshinobu Miyajima, commander of the CRF, in the strictest confidence about MOD and the SDF's worst-case scenario response plan. Miyajima met with Oriki and Hironaka several times in Ichigaya to discuss it. When he returned to the Asaka Command Post, he spent a long time looking at the map in his office. He decided to keep it to himself, and went through simulations of expanding the evacuation zone to a hundred or two hundred kilometers on his own. When the time came for it, which troops from what areas would be mobilized, and how and where would they direct residents?

A hundred kilometers means including the Kanto Plain.

It can't be a radius; we'll have to direct the evacuation according to topographical features.

The U.S. Chemical Biological Incident Response Force (CBIRF) will definitely not enter the zone. But they may help us with decontamination.

If it's two hundred kilometers, we won't be able to maintain the capi-

*tal's functions. If that happens, Japan will be finished . . . But I won't think
about Tokyo. It's physically impossible and we should have some time
before the plume reaches Tokyo.*

"Commander, you're always looking at the map . . . Is there something
wrong?"

"You get a good understanding of the lay of the land if you look at a
map."

Sometimes he had this kind of exchange with his lieutenant. Miyajima
had already been secretly looking into a rescue operation of the nuclear
power station workers as per Phase 1.

The SDF had sent in two Type 4 tanks from the ground SDF Komakado
Camp (Gotemba, Shizuoka) to clear away the debris. The tanks had a certain amount of radiation protection and could travel at a maximum speed
of fifty-three kilometers per hour. Perhaps they could be used for evacuation purposes when the time came.

They also had eight Type 96 wheeled armored personnel carriers (WAPC)
standing by in readiness. They had been refitted with handrails and slopes.
In an emergency, the onsite workers could run up the slope, grab the handrails, and escape from the power plant. There were two hundred troops
secretly carrying out training drills in Iwaki City for this purpose.

Miyajima saw the arrival of the Giraffes as preparation for a worst-case
scenario. They were concrete-pumping machines. This time they were using
water instead of cement, but if the reactors went into total meltdown and
they had a China Syndrome situation, they would have to pour concrete in
from above and contain the reactors. Miyajima believed the Giraffes could
be used for that.

With the arrival of the Giraffes and the start of the Joint Coordination Group on March 22, the situation was showing signs of improving.
However, senior officers at the Joint Staff Office told each other, "The reactors still aren't stable. We're almost there. We've just got to get through
March."[73]

Kitazawa felt there was a need to discuss a joint response by the SDF
and the U.S. forces should the worst-case scenario become a reality. They
held a highly confidential meeting at Yokota Base, between a small number
of senior offices from both forces, with Oriki and Sadamasa Oue, director
general of the defense plans and policy department of the Joint Staff Office,
visiting. The U.S. side made communications through Lieutenant General
Kenneth Glueck, commanding general of the III Marine Expeditionary
Force (3MEF). As explained in chapter 11, Glueck was leading the 505
headquarters and had drawn up a plan for a non-combatant evacuation
operation (NEO) in times of an emergency.

They showed the Japanese a three-phase evacuation operation plan.

PHASE 1: Voluntary departure of U.S. government officials' families

PHASE 2: Evacuation of all U.S. government officials

PHASE 3: Mandatory evacuation of all U.S. citizens from Japan

It was not clear, however, what would be the grounds for implementing Phase 2 or Phase 3. A withdrawal zone based on the U.S. government's fifty miles (eighty kilometers) evacuation area from the plant was one reference. If they went way over or way under this, it might lead to unnecessary doubts. They would, therefore, use virtually this area as a yardstick for "evacuation of all residents."

Bearing in mind the SDF's capabilities and the practicality of implementation, this seemed liked a reasonable line. Any more than that, especially if it meant the evacuation of residents from Greater Tokyo, would far exceed their capabilities.[74]

Soon after the start of April, a phone call came into the office of the minister of defense, where Kitazawa, Nakae, and Oriki were having a meeting from the Kantei. It was from the prime minister's executive assistant, Satoshi Maeda, formerly a defense bureaucrat. Maeda said to Kitazawa's private secretary, who picked up the phone, "The PM is saying, 'We want it to be clear that there was no such conversation.' We want that conveyed to Minister Kitazawa."

"Such conversation" was about the evacuation plan and SDF operations for responding to the worst-case scenario conveyed by Kitazawa to Prime Minister Kan. The worst case touched upon the possibility of operations that included an evacuation plan of Tokyo. In response to Kitazawa's explanation, Kan replied by saying, "Let me think for a while," without any further reaction. In the end, Kan decided not to make the residents of the metropolitan area evacuate.[75]

DRAFTING THE PRIME MINISTER'S STATEMENT

MARCH 18. Oriza Hirata, a playwright, was called in by Kan Suzuki, the MEXT vice minister. Hirata ran the Agora Theater. That day was the first performance of his play *The Balkan Zoo*. He was finally free of commitments.

Hirata was a special adviser to the cabinet secretariat. One week had already passed since the earthquake, but when he sent an e-mail to Suzuki, asking, "Isn't there something I can do?" Suzuki immediately replied, "Please come."

When he arrived at the MEXT vice minister's office in Toranomon, Tokyo, Suzuki asked him, "Assuming a worst-case scenario, I'd like you to write a backup draft for the prime minister's statement."

He said, "At the moment, the Kantei is overwhelmed by things that need an immediate response, so I don't expect they've prepared anything."

Hirata wondered, "What's the worst-case scenario?" but Suzuki only said, "It's still an extremely grave situation, but even if we fail, I don't think it'll end up like Chernobyl," and didn't clarify any further. Suzuki said, "What can we do to prevent a panic, and a panic in Tokyo at that? I want you to write something from that perspective." Hirata was given some simple documents, the gist of which was that depending on the effect of the water operations and power restoration, there was a chance that a considerable amount of radiation would be discharged from the fuel pools at Units 3 and 4. However, the possibility of that reaching Greater Tokyo was extremely low.

Hirata saw the worst-case scenario as being "nuclear fallout reaching the outskirts of Tokyo."

He immediately got in touch with Associate Professor Ekou Yagi from Osaka University and asked for her help. Yagi was an expert in risk communication. She had conducted research over a period of many years on resident and operator perceptions at the Onagawa and Rokkasho reprocessing plants, especially risk communication. She had received her doctorate on this topic from Tohoku University. Hirata taught at Osaka University's Communication Design Center, which was how he came to know Yagi. Hirata told her, "This is not about doing something for the government. We haven't been subcontracted by the government. This is a job in our individual capacities. My stance is what can we do as citizens, how can we help?"

Although he was a special adviser to the cabinet, Hirata was saying he wanted to be involved as an "individual." This was what convinced Yagi. The next day, he received an e-mail from her.

"I will do everything in my power to help. I believe I have a duty to offer my services in this matter."

Hirata replied, "There'll be no pay, nothing, and it won't even be made public, but I thank you."

The only problem was that Yagi was pregnant and could not come to Tokyo to work with him. The work became an exercise of putting crisis communication theory into practice, with the survival of the state hanging in the balance. Yagi commented on every issue Hirata raised.

Point 1: Range of Impact

First of all, the extent of "a considerable release" and the specific range of impact (danger zone) had to be clearly indicated. What image should they apply?

Regarding the range of impact, Hirata was also unsure, "About a hundred kilometers?"

Hirata also placed emphasis on the "message to Tokyo" during the prime minister's statement. Yagi asserted that whether they could send a proper "message to Fukushima" or not would act as a "message to Tokyo." To put it another way, "preventing panic in Fukushima" would lead to "preventing panic in Tokyo."

Point 2: Very Dangerous Areas

Under the stay-indoors shelter measure for the twenty- to thirty-kilometer zone, "significantly dangerous areas" were not indicated, and so, as a result, Yagi believed that this was accelerating the trend for voluntary evacuation in the fifty- to sixty-kilometer zone.

Consequently, it was crucial to clearly indicate "which places were in significant danger." In short, they had to give a clearer indication of very dangerous areas, and paradoxical as it seemed, this would alleviate the panic of people farther out. If "preventing panic in Tokyo" was the main aim, they would probably need to clearly acknowledge the nuclear power station vicinity as a danger zone.

Point 3: Individual Judgments

Each individual person had his or her own life and future. If citizens were in a normal psychological state, judgment should be left up to the individual after providing the most accurate information possible as well as the risks.

However, it was not as if every individual could judge for themselves. The farther you went out to the regions (Fukushima), the lower the proportion of people who could judge for themselves was likely to be. These were areas where blood relations and community ties were strong, and given that they also tended to be more elderly, it was not an easy situation in which to make one's own decision. They needed to bear this fact in mind.

Point 4: Pregnant Women and Children

The "message to Tokyo" might be better targeted specifically at pregnant women (depending on their numbers) and children (depending on their age). It would be smarter if the government prepared explanations according to individual demographics when announcing an evacuation of Tokyo residents.

Point 5: Immediate Risks and Future Risks

The phrase "no immediate effect" was frequently heard, but this was being interpreted as "there will be an effect in the future." They needed to distinguish between immediate risks and future risks. Would using Chernobyl as a comparison be one way of doing this?

Point 6: Other Risks

On the other hand, care needed to be exercised when comparing the risks at hand to other risks (such as X-rays). Facile comparisons with other risks might be interpreted as trying to unnecessarily downplay dose levels. Being easy to understand was important, but they needed to examine how to use such comparisons.

Point 7: Now Is the Worst

At the stage of sending out the above messages, messages that the current dose was all right and that it would not get worse ("now is the worst") were both needed. At that time, they needed to show that there was no possibility of a "deadly fallout." As grounds for this, they needed to go public with the SPEEDI simulation as supplementary material.

Yagi wrote the initial drafts, with Hirata adding to them, and after numerous exchanges they finished the backup draft of their prime minister's statement on March 20:

> Let me apologize once again for the significant worry many people of Japan are experiencing with the large-scale accident at the Fukushima Daiichi Nuclear Power Station.
>
> At the present juncture, the possibility of adverse effects on the health of the people has emerged, which I will report to you.
>
> First, since the current radiation levels pose no immediate danger to health, I would ask you all to please remain calm and act in a composed manner.
>
> Let me repeat. The situation is not one that poses immediate danger to health. I ask you all to please listen carefully to the following explanation and to act calmly.
>
> Now is precisely the time that our wisdom, our reason, and our self-control are being put to the test.
>
> Please, please cooperate.

The statement then went on to mention that the current twenty-kilometer evacuation zone was being expanded to X kilometers; that the indoor evacuation zone was being expanded from the current thirty kilometers to X kilometers (to be decided depending upon the situation); possible health risks for residents by specific distances; considerations for pregnant women and people with babies in the comparatively safe X-kilometer zone ("Please give priority to pregnant women and people with babies boarding trains and such, for western Japan").

In addition, I would like to point out that with this nuclear power plant accident, there is no possibility of a mass diffusion of radioac-

tive material, a so-called deadly fallout, spreading through the atmosphere such as happened at the Chernobyl nuclear power plant
accident.

The government is doing everything in its power to respond to the
accident, to aid evacuation, and provide life support. Nevertheless,
the situation is such that the government's power alone is not enough
to protect everyone's life. I ask each and every one of you to please act
calmly and to maintain a spirit of consolation and support for each
other in order to get us all through this crisis.

This meant the government acknowledged that the situation was such
that its power alone was not enough to fulfill the government's single greatest responsibility, "to protect its citizens." Hirata was not confident that
this would be enough to prevent panic in Tokyo. He decided, "In the final
analysis, we may have no choice but to make an emotional appeal to the
Japanese people." Appeal to their emotions, and promote sensible actions.

Hirata also had to decide what to do about his theater company members and whether to continue running the performance of *The Balkan Zoo*.
On March 21, he sent the company members an e-mail. One of them had
gone back to Iwaki City to give birth. He immediately evacuated her and
her family to Tokyo. Apart from these individual episodes, he had to explain the situation to the company as a whole.

"First, everyone has a different view on radiation and radioactive material, because of your view of life and the world as individuals, so I'll leave
the final judgment up to you.

"I have no idea whether there will be an explosion like Chernobyl in the
future. I personally believe things will not go that far, but considering what
has happened so far, anything may happen."

What to do if, by any chance, a Chernobyl-class accident occurred?

"If there is a high probability of a Chernobyl-class accident, we may
need to just put the children of the company members into the Mitsubishi
Delica van and evacuate them as far as possible . . . At this point, I don't
think it is reasonable to cancel the performance because of the severity
of the nuclear accident, or to close the Agora Theater . . . I think making
the best choice is impossible. All we can do is gather the best information
possible, and consider what is the second-best solution, or the third-best."

The performers stayed in Tokyo. *The Balkan Zoo* continued its run.

The draft of the prime minister's statement, which had supposed a
worst-case scenario of an eighty- to hundred-kilometer evacuation zone,
sleeps on in Hirata's computer.[76]

FOURTEEN

SPEEDI

"WE CAN'T POSSIBLY GO PUBLIC WITH THIS"

Due to the total loss of all AC power resulting from the earthquake and the tsunami, all of the eight monitoring posts installed within the premises of Fukushima Daiichi NPS and the fourteen stack tower monitors connected to each reactor were out of action. As a result, from five p.m. on March 11, TEPCO used a monitoring car to measure radiation at the front gate as well as several other points inside the site, making the results available on TEPCO's and NISA's websites.[1]

Fukushima Prefecture had installed twenty-four monitoring posts in the prefecture at NISA's request. Each small reinforced concrete building housed radiation dosimeters, telemeter electrical transmission equipment to send the data to the local NERHQ, and a small emergency generator. By 4:30 p.m. on March 11, twenty-three were rendered inoperative by the impact of the earthquake and tsunami.[2]

At the time of a nuclear accident, monitoring—such as sampling dust and soil, surveying the sea, and measuring the air dose rate via aircraft—is necessary. It is the Ministry of Education, Culture, Sports, Science, and Technology (MEXT) that is in charge of monitoring environmental radiation, the implementation of which includes its national network of detectors.

On the evening of March 11, MEXT requested that seven Japan Atomic Energy Agency (JAEA) staff members be dispatched to the offsite center. They arrived at the offsite center just after 6:30 a.m. on March 12. In order to support Fukushima Prefecture's monitoring, and as part of the prefectural monitoring team, they carried out monitoring on the same day, in the vicinity of Namie Town, within the ten-kilometer radius from the plant.

On the evening of March 12, MEXT once again dispatched three monitoring vehicles from JAEA in the neighboring prefecture of Ibaraki. Both of these actions were to support the paralyzed monitoring functions in Fukushima Prefecture.[3]

Monitoring operations by the all-important MEXT itself, however, were not going smoothly. Because the instruction to dispatch monitoring vehicles was delayed, the arrival of MEXT's support personnel at the offsite center was also delayed, arriving on the scene before noon on March 13.[4] Since the vehicles were not equipped with GPS, even if they did take measurements from the cars, they frequently wondered, "Where are we now?"[5]

Niigata Prefecture also made an initial move to support monitoring in Fukushima Prefecture. This was triggered by an SOS message from Fukushima Prefecture to the effect, "Our monitoring posts are out. We want to start monitoring right away. Can you lend us some people?"

Prefectural staff with the necessary expertise drove a transport vehicle all the way to Fukushima City from Niigata to deliver some portable monitoring equipment. When they arrived at the Fukushima Prefectural Office, however, they were told, "No, we don't need it now."

When the Niigata staff asked for radiation monitoring data, they were told, noncommittally, "We've been told by the state not to give it out without permission."

"They're vacillating," the Niigata staff reported to their boss. "They seem pretty indecisive."

We were initially supposed to be giving it all we've got, but pressure seems to have been brought to bear, some kind of force is stopping the monitoring, they thought.

Hirohiko Izumida, Niigata governor, was not convinced. After the hydrogen explosion in Unit 1 in the afternoon of March 12, Izumida pulled the Niigata team back to the border of Niigata and Fukushima Prefectures, and had them continue monitoring work there.[6]

Fukushima Prefecture was already moving to withdraw from monitoring operations. It had started monitoring in the early hours of March 12, but due to rising radiation caused by the explosion in the Unit 1 (RB), they were thinking of pulling out, and by nine p.m., almost all of the monitoring staff had been relieved of their duties. (By March 15, they had withdrawn from the offsite center, leaving behind materials and equipment, such as the monitoring vehicles.)[7]

On the afternoon of March 14, Goshi Hosono, special adviser to the prime minister, called Shigeharu Kato, MEXT director general, to his office. There had been an explosion in Unit 3 (RB) just after eleven a.m. that morning. At the time, Kato was downstairs with the emergency operation team in the crisis management center in the basement.

"There'll be serious trouble if you don't monitor the radiation properly."

After Hosono told Kato this, he asked just how MEXT was carrying out the monitoring and what the results were.

Kato was unable to answer. Kato had asked MEXT's emergency operations center (EOC) for their monitoring data the minute he heard Hosono wanted to see him, but the officer in charge only replied, "We have no data." No data was being compiled at the EOC at all. Hosono stared him down and told him, "Do a better job with the monitoring."[8]

In the end, MEXT's support unit only started its monitoring from March 15.

What was more, MEXT did not take into account the extended duration of the situation, which resulted in a shortage of fuel and other supplies, forcing the team to leave behind the monitoring vehicles at the offsite center when the local NERHQ relocated to Fukushima City.[9]

Deputy Chief Cabinet Secretary Tetsuro Fukuyama and Deputy Chief Cabinet Secretary for Crisis Management Tetsuro Ito were angry that the MEXT bureaucrats "had a look on their faces as if to say the field was nothing to do with them."[10]

In the eighth meeting of NERHQ, held from one p.m. on March 15, many demands were made, mainly of MEXT. Prime Minister Naoto Kan started the ball rolling.

"Regarding the impact on water, food, and agricultural produce, I want to carry out density monitoring thoroughly. I want each ministry to consider how they are going to respond in light of this as soon as possible."

Edano continued, "Let me know five minutes prior to public release . . . I want you to use the same unit for the monitoring values."

Michihiko Kano, minister of agriculture, forestry, and fisheries: "I want you to decide the standard for radioactive food."

Toshimi Kitazawa, defense minister:

"The SDF will be monitoring, too. Let's coordinate on which monitoring posts."[11]

As a response to this dissatisfaction from the Kantei and the government, MEXT dispatched a further six monitoring vehicles that day, as well as five MEXT employees, four JAEA employees, and four Nuclear Safety Technology Center employees as a monitoring team.[12]

It was only the SDF that was carrying out monitoring within the twenty-kilometer radius for operations near Fukushima Daiichi NPS. This situation continued up until March 28, when the Integrated Response Office decided that monitoring needed to be carried out swiftly in the area, which had been designated as a Caution Zone, before allowing people temporarily back in. (On March 30 and 31, with the help of the Federation of Electrical Power Companies of Japan, TEPCO conducted monitoring at thirty-three sites within the twenty-kilometer zone.)[13]

In the end, aircraft monitoring was never carried out in a timely fashion.

The Nuclear Safety Technology Center (NSTC) advertised in a brochure that they would "conduct monitoring at the time of an accident," but this assumed that a private helicopter could be chartered.

This assumption proved very optimistic indeed. During the crisis, there was not a single private helicopter company prepared to fly over the exposed area. MEXT asked MOD to fly a helicopter for them. The SDF decided to allocate one air SDF medium-size helicopter that had up until that morning been carrying out rescue operations in tsunami-stricken areas for monitoring, and had it fly to Rokkasho Village in Aomori Prefecture, to a nuclear fuel reprocessing plant.

11:10 A.M., MARCH 12. The helicopter left Kasuminome Camp in Sendai, landing at the sports park in Rokkasho Village at one p.m.

However, the NSTC staff instructed by MEXT to deliver the monitoring equipment did not show up at that hour. The aircraft waited ten minutes, then took off. It was an hour and a half later that two staff members from the NSTC showed up at the sports park. Their instructions from MEXT were to be there at 1:30 p.m. They waited an hour, but no one came. They left, thinking, *They've probably been diverted to a rescue operation.*

After the earthquake, Rokkasho Village had undergone a twenty-eight-hour blackout, with mobile phones being out of action as well. Contact from the NSTC to the local site became a "game of telephone," the cause being attributed to "contact disorder"—namely, information was not transmitted accurately.

There are those, however, who cite other reasons for this failure to connect. The specifications of the aerial monitoring equipment the NSTC had ready were for commercial charter craft and not SDF specifications, so, apparently, they were mucking around and missed the rendezvous—this was the story that came into the Nuclear Safety Commission.

When he heard this, one of the NSC staffers thought to himself, *Why doesn't the center have its own helicopter? Even Aum* (Shinrikyo, a Japanese religious cult) *had one . . .*

MORNING, MARCH 14. Just when a MOD (SDF) helicopter was about to take off on a monitoring operation, information was received that "Unit 3 may explode," and the departure was canceled.

11:20 A.M., MARCH 15. An SDF helicopter took off for monitoring, but the operation was shortly canceled when the pilot received information of "an explosion in Unit 4."[14]

MEXT implemented aerial monitoring on March 25, with the cooperation of the Japan Aerospace Exploration Agency (JAXA). They first loaded radiation-monitoring equipment onto a small aircraft for meteorological purposes owned by JAXA.[15] In the midst of crisis, Japan's monitoring ended up being only a "ground war."[16]

8:00 P.M., MARCH 15. The minister's office at MEXT.

A discussion was held by five political officers, including Minister Yoshiaki Takagi, Vice Minister Kan Suzuki, Vice Minister Ryuzo Sasaki, and two ministerial officials.

The officer responsible showed the estimates from the system for prediction of environmental emergency dose information (SPEEDI). SPEEDI is a real-time damage-prediction system to protect residents at the time of an accident from radiation exposure.

According to the NISA homepage, SPEEDI was "a system that, in the event of an emergency, where a large amount of radioactive material was released or there was a risk of such a release from nuclear facilities, made rapid predictions from emission source information, weather conditions, and topographical data for dose exposures and the atmospheric concentration of radioactive substances in the surrounding environment."[17]

In the case of an article 10 notification, it was laid down that MEXT was to direct the Nuclear Safety Technology Center to switch the SPEEDI network system immediately to emergency mode, and to predict the radiation impact when they had received the emission source information from the Nuclear and Industrial Safety Agency or the power companies, and to then deliver the results to the MEXT terminals. Its dedicated terminals were set up at the ministry, NISA, and the Nuclear Safety Commission.

Suzuki claimed the following. If the SPEEDI results got out, it would immediately lead to reputational damage, putting a stop to transport from Tokyo to Fukushima. Truck drivers were already refusing to transport goods from Fukushima and Koriyama cities to the eastern coastal zone known as Hamadori, where the Fukushima Daiichi NPS was, bringing logistics to a standstill.

What was needed, above all, was getting gasoline and crude oil delivered to Fukushima Prefecture. Without this, not even the ambulances would be able to move.

Moreover, SPEEDI made its calculations based on the premise of a 100 percent release, namely a complete reactor collapse. How appropriate was it to make predictions on the basis of such a high release?

According to a memo by the radiation team at MEXT, the three political officers deemed, "We can't possibly go public with this." It was decided to "prepare another, more standard basis for the SPEEDI results."

Regarding this point, Madarame later attested the following:

"If you look at the calculation results published by MEXT, clouds of radioactive iodine would spread over a wide area, including the metropolitan area, if all the reactors collapsed. Results showing severe damage had come out. When this was shown to the top three political officers at MEXT, they apparently decided that they couldn't possibly release it, because they were worried about a panic."[18]

THE MONITORING TEAM

9:26 P.M., MARCH 15. MEXT's EOC received an urgent call from the monitoring team.

"A number of 330 microsieverts (0.33 millisieverts) has been recorded at Point 32."

Point 32 was Kawafusa in Namie Town.

Makio Watanabe and Takayuki Amaya, two members of the monitoring team MEXT had dispatched, were calling from a pay phone in Yamakiya, Kawamata. They were spending the night at Sugitsuma Hall, a government accommodation facility next door to the Fukushima Prefectural Office. They faxed their results from there to MEXT's EOC, but the EOC did not pass the information on to the local NERHQ or the affected municipalities.[19]

Watanabe was a specialist in extracting uranium and plutonium at the Japan Atomic Energy Research Institute and Rokkasho Nuclear Fuel Reprocessing Facility, and had set up his own business. He had been hired by MEXT as a technical expert six years before. He held the twin posts of nuclear safety inspector and nuclear disaster prevention officer. At the time, he was working at MEXT's Ibaraki Nuclear Safety Management Office.

Amaya was a specialist in radioactive waste disposal (backend) at the engineering company JGC Corporation, but had also been hired mid-career by MEXT. He was a nuclear protection inspector. For the past six years, he had been in charge of nuclear security and safety regulation for research reactors.

After the accident, MEXT sent more than ten officers into the field, including these two, as their monitoring team.

THE MORNING OF MARCH 14. Watanabe and Amaya headed to Fukushima NPS by car from the offsite center in Ibaraki Prefecture. They had been instructed by the officer in charge at MEXT's EOC to go to the offsite center in Okuma, Fukushima Prefecture.

"Just go, for goodness sake."

That was all they were told. They were not given any instructions on what they should do when they got there.

Sometime after four p.m. on the same day, they arrived at Okuma Town. When they went to the offsite center, their shoes and clothes were screened at the front door. Officers clad in Tyvek suits, half-face masks, and shoe covers were carefully checking for contamination of the workers going in and out. Watanabe and Amaya were screened, and contamination of 1600 cpm was found on the soles of their shoes. This meant they had to wear shoe covers.

Up until that point, the highest contamination they had ever registered at any of the nuclear facilities they had inspected had been 200 cpm. This brought home to them the gravity of the nuclear accident.

Putting on two pairs of shoe covers, they climbed the stairs to the Emergency Response Center (ERC). The second floor of the nuclear power center in Fukushima Prefecture was the base for the MEXT and JAEA radiation monitoring teams. Watanabe and Amaya were part of that group. The head of the Mito Nuclear Power Office was there as MEXT's commanding officer. Their only communications link seemed to be a mobile satellite phone. Everyone had their ears pricked up to catch any information coming in over this phone.

SOMETIME AFTER NINE P.M. The group meeting was over, and people were just taking a break. Someone came thumping up the stairs.

"Withdraw! Withdraw! Everyone withdraw!"

Yelling this out over and over at the top of his lungs, he ran back down the stairs. No one knew what was going on. The MEXT commanding officer ordered, "Leave everything behind and withdraw. Everyone, into the JAEA bus." He added, "Leave the keys in all the government cars." They heard the local NERHQ had decided to relocate to the Fukushima Prefectural Office.

On reaching the car park, they were issued with half-face masks and everyone put them on. The bus headed west, along Route 288, going north on Route 14 from Koriyama. It was 1:40 a.m. on March 15 when they arrived at Sugitsuma Hall. The soles of their shoes registered over 10,000 cpm and had become "radioactive waste."

They were told, when they were lying on the floor, unable to sleep, "It looks like there's been an explosion in Unit 2."

The dose at the main gates of Fukushima Daiichi NPS was reportedly "not in the order of microsieverts/hour but millisieverts per hour." This meant they had entered a thousandfold area of contamination. Watanabe and Amaya later learned that the EOC deemed their relocation to the Fukushima Prefectural Office "dereliction of duty."

"It's outrageous to abandon their jobs without permission. And to withdraw, leaving behind all their equipment and government vehicles!"

This was the nature of the EOC's "anger." At the words "dereliction of duty," Watanabe and Amaya were overwhelmed with a feeling of futility.

With radiation steadily increasing at the offsite center, staying would have just meant undergoing unnecessary exposure.

So, what would those guys have done, exactly, if they'd been at the offsite center in Okuma at the time?

Amaya remembered an English phrase he had learned somewhere: "They do not know what they do not know."

So that's how it is. The government ministry thinks equipment and cars are more important than the safety of their personnel.

Although they turned back to the offsite center in Ibaraki Prefecture, they were again instructed by the EOC on the same morning of March 15, "Go to Fukushima again."

They arrived at Sugitsuma Hall around five p.m., and just as they were catching their breath, a fax arrived from the EOC, indicating their monitoring points. The instruction was to monitor the area twenty kilometers northwest of the plant (Kawafusa and Hirusone, Namie Town).

The EOC was using the SPEEDI results as a point of reference. The map that had been faxed in also showed the twenty-kilometer boundary. There were three points, numbered 1, 2, and 3. Checking it against a roadmap he had borrowed at Sugitsuma Hall, Amaya made certain of the monitoring points. The three mountainous locations of Hirusone, Kawafusa, and Nagadoro, in Namie Town, were pinpointed.

7:00 P.M. ON MARCH 15. They entered the town of Namie. There were hardly any lights. There was a light, sleet-like rain falling outside, with fog hanging over the streams.

The dose on the survey meter kept rising steadily. By the time they had passed Yamakiya in Kawamata, the NaI survey meter for low doses was thrown out of whack, because the amount of radiation exceeded its range. When they took readings from the high-dose IC survey meter they had brought along just in case, it showed 50 millisieverts/hour.

MEXT must have known the radiation was high here, that's why they sent us to monitor. Why didn't they tell us to take the high-dose gear in the first place? It wouldn't hurt them to say, be careful, it's high.

That was how they felt.

They took a reading at the first monitoring point near the Hirusone Tunnel.

"It's over 200 microsieverts (0.2 millisieverts)!"

This was a huge number, six to seven thousand times higher than the natural radiation level, on the order of needing to use machines to pick up nuclear material on the other side of metallic glass, a kind of solid metallic material with disordered atomic-scale, glass-like structure; another world, a different dimension.

Can this really be the radiation dose in a normal environment that isn't a restricted zone or anything?

They could not allow the survey meter to get contaminated, for fear it would start giving inaccurate readings. After he took the measurement, Watanabe wrapped the meter in a paper towel and read the number, Amaya repeating it as he wrote it down.

From 8:40 p.m., they took measurements for ten minutes at the Akougi/ Teshichiro Intersection. The atmospheric radiation dose rate showed 330 microsieverts/hour (0.33 millisieverts). It was also high at Nagadoro at 78–95 microsieverts (0.078–0.095 millisieverts).

Nagadoro was located at the town limits of Namie in the southern part of Iitate Village.

The mobile phone was showing "out of range." Even the mobile satellite phone was playing up. They went back to Yamakiya and reported to the EOC from a public telephone there. When they looked at their watches, it was 9:30 p.m.

They came across several people on their way back. Amaya called out in passing, "The radiation is 330 microsieverts/hour at Akougi. Please let everyone know."[20]

On the way back, they took measurements at the places they had monitored two days earlier, meeting Yoshitomo Shigihara, chief of the Nagadoro District. Shigihara was serving his first term as district chief. He was getting ready for evacuation. His home was some 150 meters from the Nagadoro Crossing. Showing him the survey meter and the reading results, Amaya told him the dose was high in the area.

They received another message from the EOC, instructing them to go to the Hirono Medical Center. This was a round trip of two hundred kilometers. They were exhausted, but, telling each other, "There's a patient waiting," they went to J-Village and were notified that they "no longer need to go to the medical center."

It was just before nine p.m. when they returned to their accommodation in Fukushima City.

It was only later that Watanabe learned through the grapevine that Shigihara had told the following story.[21]

A WHITE STATION WAGON, WHITE PROTECTIVE GEAR

There was a white station wagon parked by the intersection near Shigihara's house. There were a couple of people inside, wearing white protective gear (Tyvek suits) and protective masks, and they were sticking a long, thin nozzle (a metal rod) out of the window. They all had integrating dosimeters. He asked them for the readings, but they refused to answer and left in a hurry.[22]

What are you so afraid of? Settle down and do it. Radiation penetrates glass and concrete, right? Those masks are just a placebo, aren't they?

That was what Shigihara felt like saying to them, but he kept quiet.[23]

It was the JAEA monitoring team that Shigihara had run into. When Watanabe heard this story later, he felt, *I can understand how Shigihara-san feels, but you have to think about the situation the monitoring team was in . . . I feel a little sorry for them.*

Many of the JAEA monitors were young. I can understand why they wore the Tyvek suits when doing their job. Everyone was working desperately. Many of them had families who had been affected by the disaster.

Besides, you can't wear a snowsuit on top of the protective clothing. At the time, it was very cold. You can't blame them for taking measurements from inside the car.

But it's an undeniable fact that the residents, including Shigihara, did feel, "Who do those guys think they are? They don't even get out of their cars!"

Watanabe and Amaya's "measurement protocol" of "not wearing Tyvek suits or half-face masks," and "showing the survey meter and telling the residents the readings" was something they had discussed and decided together in the field. Watanabe had pondered long and hard whether he should impose this "protocol" on the whole JAEA team, but avoided forcing the issue.

Watanabe had worked previously at the Japan Atomic Energy Research Institute (JAEA's predecessor) and, given his older age, he was acting as the leader of MEXT's and JAEA's monitoring team.

On the issue of "whether or not to wear protective clothing," Watanabe and Amaya asked themselves how the residents being monitored would feel, and decided not to wear them. However, they worried a lot about imposing this on others.

From the perspective of crisis management, wearing protective clothing was probably the right thing to do. The disaster prevention officers had to remain healthy to perform their role. There was a possibility that contamination would spread if members of the monitoring team became contaminated. Residents could be evacuated for a time, lowering the risk of exposure, but disaster prevention officers had to stay in the field, so their risk of exposure was increased. For that reason alone, members of the monitoring team had to exercise extreme caution in preventing contamination. In light of all this, it was not only right but also imperative that the monitoring team wore protective clothing.

Somewhat later, in mid-April, Chief Cabinet Secretary Yukio Edano visited Minamisoma, wearing protective clothing. At the time, he was shown on TV taking off the protective gear once outside the twenty-kilometer zone. The footage showed several people near him who were not wearing protective suits. He was immediately criticized on the Internet for "just trying to protect himself from radiation."

The critics were not aware that wearing protective clothing was compulsory in the twenty-kilometer evacuation area from the plant. Moreover, the original and main reason for wearing protective clothing is to stop the spread of radioactive material in the vicinity.[24]

The JAEA team had brought with them a monitoring car that cost 30 million yen. It was supposed to be able to carry out dust sampling from inside the vehicle. However, since the vehicle itself became contaminated, it could not be used. Watanabe and Amaya's light van was more than sufficient.

Watanabe thought, *The monitoring cars are probably part of the safety myth, too. We have this wonderful vehicle. We can measure properly. So, it's all right . . . When push comes to shove, all you have to prepare is a car you can dispose of.*

The EOC officer always said to them, "I'll report to the Kantei" or "It's the Kantei's instruction."

Why are they making such a point of mentioning the Kantei?

The two of them were perplexed. The members of the JAEA monitoring team also asked, "Is the monitoring an initiative of the Kantei?"

Is MEXT trying to do the monitoring in the Kantei's name because a high radiation reading will lead to an evacuation of the residents?[25]

On the day that they were forced to travel 550 kilometers, Amaya thought, as he held the steering wheel, *It's just like Kiyoshiro Imawano shouted.*

Kiyoshiro Imawano was a rock musician and protest singer for the anti-nuclear movement. Amaya had listened to him many times in his younger days. The song he liked best was "Summertime Blues," released in 1988.[26]

> *Still, the TV says,*
> *"Nuclear power plants in Japan are safe."*
> *Who knows? It's groundless,*
> *These are the last Summertime Blues.*
>
> *They take your hard-earned tax,*
> *And when you go on holiday to the countryside,*
> *Thirty-seven plants have been built,*
> *Nuclear power plants are still increasing,*
> *And before you knew it, they were leaking.*
> *What a scandal! Summertime Blues.*
>
> *They've got power to spare,*
> *We don't need it, we don't need it anymore.*
>
> *We don't need nuclear power,*
> *It's dangerous, we don't want it.*
>
> *They can't protect the safety,*
> *Impossible for those guys,*
> *Cowards can't protect you.*

"EDANO'S RULING"

The monitoring by different agencies was totally uncoordinated. Edano later described the situation as "There was no list, it was all structured as this department measured here, and that one measured there, so even if it was posted on their websites, people couldn't understand."[27]

He was saying, "No matter how advanced the technology and the absolute volume of information, it didn't function at all if it wasn't condensed, organized, and shared."[28]

Who in the entire government was responsible for the monitoring was ambiguous. The Nuclear Safety Commission (NSC) complained that the compiled data could not be collated, because the monitoring methods at MEXT were not unified. Secretary general of NSC, Akihiko Iwahashi, looked back.

"Because the measurement methods weren't unified, it wasn't easy to compare the data even for deposits. Was the data really credible or not? You get high doses when the instruments are contaminated. So, whether or not this was the case, we had to confirm, one by one, all of the data when we used it."[29]

The Kantei was becoming increasingly frustrated with MEXT, the government body with the greatest responsibility for monitoring. Fukuyama and Ito heard that a team lead by Akira Watanabe, deputy vice chancellor of Fukushima University, was carrying out monitoring, and had drawn up a contamination map, including Iitate Village. Ito called in the MEXT officer and said, "Fukushima University has managed to do this. Why can't MEXT?"

"No, we could. It's just that we don't have enough people or cars."

"Doesn't MEXT have them?"

"We'd have enough if we brought them in from all over the country, but they have to be FEPC cars."

FEPC was the Federation of Electrical Power Companies of Japan, and FEPC cars were those capable of carrying out dust sampling from inside the vehicle. He was admitting, without the slightest embarrassment, that they could not do it unless they borrowed cars from the power companies.

In other words, are the MEXT bureaucrats just letting the resources out in dribs and drabs? Or don't they think it's their responsibility?

Ito was indignant.[30]

Late on the night of March 15, on Edano's instructions, his aides called section chiefs from MEXT, NISA, MOD, the police, NSC, Japan Nuclear Energy Safety Organization, and the Nuclear Safety Technology Center to a meeting in the basement conference room at the Kantei to discuss strengthening monitoring operations. Aware that monitoring by MEXT alone would be impossible, the point of the discussion was what they could do to improve the monitoring.

"MEXT has monitoring cars, but they're just doing it in trickles. They're not using fixed observation points, and the absolute number is way too low."

"It's no good unless it's done on the same basis. For example, measuring one meter above the ground. We need to decide on the point and do it on a regular basis."

"Let's get MEXT to compile this."

Such was the discussion.

"Compilation of data by MEXT, evaluation by the NSC," this was the division of responsibilities they decided on and reported to Edano.[31]

On the other hand, MEXT Vice Minister Kan Suzuki phoned Deputy Chief Cabinet Secretary Tetsuro Fukuyama on the night of March 15 to ask that the Kantei rule on the division of responsibilities for the monitoring.

"For monitoring, you have to divide the job properly between operations staff and intelligence staff. MEXT will act as the intelligence units and staff. The NSC can be responsible for the operations staff."

This was Suzuki's logic.

At approximately eight a.m. on March 16, an emergency meeting was held in the small office to the side of the Kantei's crisis management center between Edano, Suzuki, NSC Commissioner Shizuyo Kusumi, NISA Director General Akira Fukushima, and MEXT Deputy Director General Toshifumi Tanaka.

Around the emergency operation team's round table, participants were told, "Please gather around, because the meeting is about to start." To use the phrase of an NSC staffer, the meeting began with "little fanfare."

The small office was used privately by the deputy cabinet secretary for crisis management for matters too sensitive to be discussed in the large office. Kusumi had rushed over, having been told, "Kusumi-san, they want you at the Kantei. Right away."

When she first went to the fifth floor, Suzuki was there, as if waiting for her. Edano had then emerged, and they ended up going downstairs together to the basement. They entered the small office, but there were no more seats, so they stood during the meeting. Akira Fukushima, who arrived a little later, also had to stand.

Suzuki touched on the issues involved in monitoring in the field. Both Fukushima Prefecture and the local NERHQ had lost their monitoring functions.

"You do the head work at the NSC. We'll do the stuff from the shoulders down," Suzuki said. "MEXT will keep on surveying and keep the information rolling in, whether it's good or bad data."

Edano spoke up:

"The radiation monitoring data is coming up in dribs and drabs. I want to set up a proper monitoring system."

After saying this, Edano pointed out that monitoring functions in Fukushima Prefecture were paralyzed, and that with the local NERHQ having relocated to the Fukushima prefectural office, they were unable to adequately perform their monitoring function.

"I want the monitoring activities themselves to be concentrated at MEXT."

Suzuki made doubly sure.

"So, you want us to concentrate on monitoring observations and collation, right?"

Edano nodded and said, "I'd like the NSC to do the evaluations. That's all right, isn't it?"

Kusumi spoke:

"Please record if there was any rain when you were monitoring. And if possible, we'd like to have the GPS coordinates."

She then asked, "We'll be able to get the data from MEXT in some kind of file format, won't we?"

Edano did not reply directly to this, but said he wanted to clarify once again the division of responsibilities for each institution conducting monitoring in the twenty-kilometer zone from the plant, and asked for their opinions.

As a result, an "Edano's Ruling" was handed down, to the effect that "MEXT will be responsible for implementing and compiling the monitoring and making it available to the public, NSC will be responsible for evaluating the monitoring information, and NERHQ (NISA as secretariat) will handle the responses based on that evaluation."

I suppose simulations are included in the monitoring evaluation.

Tanaka left the room with this impression.

People had rushed over from NISA and the NSC as well, and a senior official from the NSC later recollected, "The decision had already been made, so it was just a formality."

This "ruling," however, only applied to monitoring, and did not touch on making SPEEDI, or its evaluation and responses, public. Neither Edano nor anyone else made any mention of SPEEDI in the meeting. Kusumi said nothing in particular about the division of monitoring, but this was because she felt, *Rather than a meeting, it was more a handing down of a decision.* Fukushima was only included in the consultation when they were coming to a close and they were simply told the conclusion.

In fact, Edano, Fukuyama, and Suzuki had discussed the division of monitoring activities on the fifth floor of the Kantei on the morning of the same day, just on their feet, and then called in the concerned parties. Suzuki instructed Tanaka to take notes of the meeting.

Those folk at the NSC are quick to say, "we haven't heard" or "we weren't told," so let's make sure things don't get troublesome later.

That was his thinking.

At approximately eleven a.m., MEXT held an executive meeting with the three top political officers. Suzuki stated, "Since it's been decided that MEXT will not evaluate the monitoring data, I think hereafter it would be better to let NSC, who's handling the SPEEDI evaluations, operate and publicize SPEEDI matters."

The other participants all agreed.

In the afternoon of the same day, after mentioning in a press conference that "the Ministry of Education, Culture, Sports, Science, and Technology has today begun monitoring radiation levels in an area a short distance outside the twenty-kilometer evacuation area from the power station," Edano stated, "I think it is appropriate that a detailed, precise evaluation of the data should be made by specialists from the Nuclear and Industrial Safety Agency and the Nuclear Safety Commission."[32]

Around noon on March 16, the telephone of Hideki Mizuma, director of the Management and Coordination Division at the NSC, rang. It was from the lengthily named Disaster Environment Office of the Nuclear Safety Division of the Science, Technology, and Academic Policy Bureau at MEXT. Mizuma was a little hesitant receiving a phone call from a woman he did not know at all.

"Please excuse me, but who are you?"

She said she was a researcher seconded to MEXT from the Nuclear Safety Technology Center (NSTC).

Why would MEXT get a researcher on secondment to call the director of management and coordination, and not their director?

Mizuma thought it all rather odd. The woman started to talk.

"You're aware of the chief cabinet secretary's decision today, aren't you? In response to that, it's been decided to enhance and strengthen environmental monitoring measurements at MEXT.

"I would like to convey to you, therefore, the decision made by the top executives at MEXT. Please listen to what I have to say.

"Since it has been decided that MEXT will not use SPEEDI, which by rights is not able to predict radiation exposure, the operators from the NSTC, who are currently at our EOC, have nothing to do. In order to improve the usability of SPEEDI for the evaluation the NSC will be doing, we will send over these operators today, if you like, for you to use . . ."

Mizuma interrupted to ask, "Isn't the Nuclear Safety Technology Center commissioned by MEXT to maintain and run SPEEDI? Wouldn't having the operators work over here change the nature of the commission and the center's role?"

When another government body apart from MEXT wanted to use

SPEEDI, they were not allowed to ask the NSTC directly but had to go through MEXT, and the results also could not be made public without MEXT's approval. Those were the rules and the contract. The woman replied, "I don't think it will be necessary in the case of the NSC using SPEEDI to go through the ministry each time in the future, and you should just tell the operators at the center the conditions you want to have input. Oh, and the NSC wouldn't have to bear the cost of new operators or anything like that."[33]

"HE'S A BAD 'UN, THAT ONE"

A little while later, Mizuma received a call from Yasutaka Moriguchi, the deputy director general of MEXT. Mizuma was also from the former Science and Technology Agency, where he had been involved in administrating nuclear fuel cycles such as plutonium reprocessing.

The former Science and Technology Agency was one of the least political or Machiavellian bureaucracies in Kasumigaseki, and was said to be "spineless," but "the guys in the nuclear village were hard as nails," as a MEXT section chief put it. Moriguchi especially was a force to be reckoned with as a member of the "tough guys club." Moriguchi said, "The Kantei has decided you'll be in charge of running SPEEDI. So, I'll leave it up to you. Let's work things out."

Mizuma replied, "That's not how things are going to be. What's more, we come under the Cabinet Office."

The top officers at the NSC were indignant when they heard from Mizuma about Moriguchi's call. Like Mizuma, some of them were from the old Science and Technology Agency.

"What does he mean, 'let's work things out'?!"

"I mean to say, do those guys think we're a castle outpost or something in the Warring States period [when the feudal system collapsed and warlords fought for power from the fifteenth to the seventeenth century]? Are they just passing on some troublesome work only to cut us loose when it comes to the crunch?"

That day, there was also a sudden call on Madarame's mobile phone from Moriguchi.

"Now is the time when the government has to work together to use SPEEDI. I'd like you to do your best."

Madarame knew Moriguchi's name, but had never met him.

Why does someone I've never met have my mobile phone number?

Madarame was puzzled. On the spur of the moment, he was at a loss for words, but he had a rough idea of what Moriguchi was trying to say.

By stating that the Kantei has decided on the division of monitoring responsibilities, he's trying to make it sound like SPEEDI's role, by extension, has also been decided.

Is that what he's trying to make us think?
Who's going to fall for that kind of scam?

After Madarame told Mizuma he had a call from Moriguchi, he muttered, "He's a bad 'un, that one."[34]

In the afternoon of March 16, two operators from the Nuclear Safety Technology Center (NSTC) turned up at the NSC offices. Madarame was not convinced, but still, from March 16, the NSC started using the analytical results of WSPEEDI—the world version that could estimate the diffusion situation in a broader context—to run reverse estimations of the emission source information, with Deputy Chairman Yutaka Kukita playing a central role.

On the other hand, with the exception of two occasions when the Kantei's expert advisory team intervened to give instructions to JAEA, MEXT stopped accepting calculation requests for WSPEEDI.

"You can use SPEEDI any way you like." Just thinking about it should whet the engineers' appetite. Was Moriguchi also counting on that?

This was what the secretariat staff at NSC speculated. However, the NSC took the position that the work of Kukita and the others was only "estimating emission source information" and that they were not involved in "operating" the system.

MEXT thought they had "transferred" SPEEDI's operational jurisdiction to the NSC, but the NSC had received no notification of any such "transfer" from the Kantei, and they stuck to their view that "we just happened to lend the NSTC operators a room."

The following morning, a member of MEXT's EOC turned up at the NSC. It was the officer in charge of radiation surveying specialization (Type Two). He pleaded with Iwahashi, "Let me work on SPEEDI here."

Iwahashi said, "You mustn't abandon your post."

The officer went back to MEXT.[35]

In the afternoon of March 16, the following Q&A took place at the press conference given by Vice Minister Ryuzo Sasaki at MEXT:

Reporter: "How about making the SPEEDI data available?"
Sasaki: "It's up to the Nuclear Safety Commission what they do or don't do with SPEEDI."
Reporter: "Aren't you running SPEEDI at the moment?"
Sasaki: "It's being run at the NSC."
Reporter: "But isn't it JAEA who operates it? They come under the jurisdiction of MEXT, don't they?"
Sasaki: "We've provided the software, but the actual operation is taking place there."

MEXT secretariat: "It's the Nuclear Safety Technology Center."
Reporter: "But the Nuclear Safety Technology Center comes under your jurisdiction, doesn't it? So, I think the ministry could actively make the decision about going public, but you're not going to do that?"
Sasaki: "That's up to the NSC, including whether they use it or not."
Reporter: "Is that because there's a risk of the results coming out confusing things?"
Sasaki: "I am speaking for myself here, but to be frank, this is the first time I have seen SPEEDI."[36]

In other words, he was trying to say that the responsibility for going public with the SPEEDI simulation results from the start of the accident all the way through had shifted to the NSC.

When Kusumi heard that MEXT was leaving the evaluation of the monitoring up to the NSC and had also moved two operators to the NSC offices, she thought for a moment, "How generous of them."

But this was not so. In Kasumigaseki parlance, it was nothing less than a "negative turf battle." Taking advantage of the Edano Ruling, they were trying to offload the SPEEDI evaluations to the NSC.

Apart from predictions based on the unit amount released, MEXT had been running various simulations from the day after the accident on the total release of radioactive material if all of the reactors at Fukushima Daiichi NPS were destroyed, as well as if all the radioactive material from one unit was dispersed. They were running not only SPEEDI, but also WSPEEDI. Nevertheless, the original SPEEDI calculations were only half-baked data assuming the unit amount release.

They did not reflect the actual conditions of radioactive material diffusion accurately enough to be used for evacuation. This is why the results could not be made public. However, they were not completely useless. They gave an indication of the diffusion status to some extent. If they did not get rid of SPEEDI quickly, including the estimated results so far, they might be forced to go public and possibly be accused of concealing data.

There was also the fear that they could be accused of exposing people to radiation due to their not going public. On the other hand, if they did release all the data to date that was estimated using various hypothetical conditions, it could set off a panic. This was also something they wanted to avoid.

With the series of hydrogen explosions in the reactors, interest in the SPEEDI estimations was growing. This could well lead to severe criticism from local residents and the populace in general. There was nothing like backing out of all the risky operations of running SPEEDI, evaluating its results, and going public, dropping the whole lot into the NSC's lap.

MEXT must have plotted a backdoor transfer of SPEEDI's data evaluation to the NSC by linking SPEEDI to the partition of monitoring data roles, per instructions of the chief cabinet secretary. That was how Madarame saw it, describing it as "sneak tactics" by MEXT.

However, NISA was also involved in a similar "negative turf war." By rights, it was the radiation team at NERHQ who should have been conceiving plans on how to use SPEEDI, but NISA, the NERHQ secretariat, was quick to raise a white flag.

METI and NISA are in the process of creating a "myth" that "the NSC should be the command post." That's why they are so keen to have the NSC Chairman Haruki Madarame out front.

They're using the NSC as a shield so NISA doesn't have to bear the brunt.

These were the doubts entertained by Madarame and other senior members of the NSC at the time. With the Edano partition, the NSC suddenly ended up being charged with evaluating the radioactive monitoring, as well as being asked to run SPEEDI's reverse estimations.

"We were framed by MEXT and we were framed by NISA at METI."

They felt a sinister hand hiding behind the chief cabinet secretary's order.

The monitoring data set Kusumi had asked MEXT to provide the NSC with at the time of the Edano Ruling never materialized. In response to the NSC request, MEXT replied, "We'll post it on our website, so please look there."

The NSC staff ended up accessing the MEXT website and writing down every entry by hand.[37]

REVERSE ESTIMATION

Late on the night of March 18, the following readings were sent to the NSC from the coordinating team at NISA's Emergency Response Center (ERC):

March 17 Point 32 (Namie Town)   158–180 µSv/h (0.158–0.18 mSv)
               Point 33 (Iitate Village) 78.2–95.1 µSv/h (0.0782–0.0951 mSv)
March 18 Point 32 (Namie Town)   140–150 µSv/h (0.14–0.15 mSv)
               Point 33 (Iitate Village) 52 µSv/h (0.052 mSv)[38]

Monitoring results from March 17 to March 18 confirmed high radiation doses in Iitate Village and Namie Town, both located more than thirty kilometers from the Fukushima Daiichi NPS. The dose at Namie was especially high, exceeding 100 microsieverts/hour (0.1 millisieverts).

The integral dose was up from March 17 to March 18. The area subject to radiation exposure was spreading. How were they to ensure the safety of residents in those areas? Perhaps a new evacuation was required. Could SPEEDI not be used for that?

On March 18, the advisory team chaired by Shunsuke Kondo, chairman of the Japan Atomic Energy Commission (JAEC), suggested to the Kantei that they start using SPEEDI to examine whether the evacuation zone needed to be changed or not. Both Toshio Kosako, a graduate school professor at the University of Tokyo, and Seiki Soramoto, Lower House Representative (Hiroshima), were getting information from the Nuclear Safety Technology Center (NSTC). Kosako asked one of the center's engineers, with whom he was friendly, "Why aren't you running SPEEDI?"

His reply was, "We are. We were scratching around for the first two hours, when we lost power, but we've been working steadily since. But we can't show it to anyone outside the related sections. We've been told in no uncertain terms by upstairs."

So, Kosako knew that the center was running SPEEDI.[39]

In the advisory team meeting that day, pointing out that the monitoring results for Iitate Village on March 17 were "in the area of 80 microsieverts (0.08 millisieverts)," Kosako raised the question: "Why can't we use SPEEDI even though we're getting dose readings like this at Iitate?"

Iitate Village was part of Soma City, Fukushima Prefecture. It was a village blessed with natural beauty on the plateau of the northern Abukuma mountain range. It was adjacent to Minamisoma and forty kilometers northwest of the Fukushima nuclear power plants. Kosako turned to Hisanori Nei, deputy director general of NISA, and strongly urged, "Show us the SPEEDI data. Why won't you show it to me? I want you to share it."

Nei did not reply. Kondo agreed with Kosako's view.

"Just like the name, SPEEDI, do it speedily!"[40]

That day Soramoto called Moriguchi to his office in the Diet members' building and made a strong request to use SPEEDI. Kosako was also there.

In the days when Shojiro Matsuura had been chairman, the NSC had drawn up an internal manual that clearly stated SPEEDI was to be used in disaster prevention plans. This was the *Nuclear Disaster Prevention Instruction Manual (Laws, Regulations, and Guidelines)*, edited by the NSC (Nuclear Safety Technology Center, May 2010).

Pointing at the manual, Soramoto demanded, "You have to follow the manual."

Moriguchi had brought with him two manager-level staff members, one of whom replied quite calmly, "We don't have to."

Kosako countered, "You're not serious!"

"It's just a manual. This is an emergency now. We can do things differently during an emergency."

422   MELTDOWN

"No, this is an emergency manual. It says what you should do in an emergency."

But that was the end of the discussion. Kosako realized, *MEXT is not going to use SPEEDI, no matter how they've decided not to use it.*[41]

Edano called for the senior MEXT official at the crisis management center to ask if they could not use SPEEDI, but this also failed to hit home. Edano asked Madarame, "There's a monitoring post around there, can't you do a reverse estimation? Look, even a liberal arts fellow like me can think of that, so think! It's the NSC who's in command, you know."[42]

Madarame promised to take it back to the commission and look into it.

Since NISA, like the NSC, thought SPEEDI could not be used, they were totally unprepared for Edano's "estimation" remark. Kei Katayama of NISA's Planning and Coordination Division felt *touché!* when he heard it.

Of course! Use the monitoring and run a reverse estimation afterward. Yep, that's doable.[43]

MARCH 19. In the Kantei crisis management center, Naoyuki Fukuuchi, deputy director general of the Japan Meteorological Agency (JMA) and a member of the emergency operation team, grumbled to Tetsuro Ito, deputy chief cabinet secretary for crisis management.

"We're sending weather forecast data to international bodies like the World Meteorological Organization, but the German Meteorological Agency has published a forecast of radioactive material diffusion based on it. The JMA is being blamed, why didn't you announce it in our country? It's a problem for us, since we're not in charge of publishing diffusion prediction data. We don't have it, it's the NSC, MEXT, and NISA. This is by rights an issue for MEXT."

The JMA was providing results from IAEA calculations on the diffusion situation for radioactive material. The IAEA simulation used units of a hundred square kilometers, and its aim basically was to act as a reference for the international impact. However, it was very strange to provide data overseas that had not been published inside the country.

"Why don't you get the four ministries and agencies to consider what to do as soon as possible?"

"The four ministries and agencies? Right, I'll look into it immediately."

The four ministries and agencies, in this case, were NISA at METI, MEXT, the NSC, and JMA. Contact, however, was a long time coming.

On March 21, when Ito asked Fukuuchi, "How's that coming along?" an officer from the NSC answered, "I'll answer on their behalf. In short, it's no good, because the release amounts aren't clear. It's nothing more than a weather chart. If you don't know how much was released and at what time, then the weather chart is wrong."

"But we've got the monitoring results, right? Why can't you just do a reverse estimation from that?"

"Huh, reverse estimation? I hadn't thought of that."
"Do a reverse estimation and give us the results."
"Yes, sir. I'll look into it."[44]

The job of running the reverse estimations was left up to the NSC. It was Deputy Chairman Yutaka Kukita who went ahead with it.

On March 15, Kukita had gone to TEPCO, a little after Kan had stormed in, and he had the chance to speak with some TEPCO engineers. What could they do to pinpoint the direction of the radioactive diffusion? It looked to him like the TEPCO side did not have a definite approach.

"With things this far gone, I guess all we can do is run some reverse estimations with the data that's released."

Kukita said so without thinking, but the others did not show any interest.[45]

MARCH 16. The NSC hurriedly invited Masamichi Chino, deputy director of the Nuclear Science and Engineering Directorate at JAEA. Given the fact that "it was now possible for even the NSC to operate SPEEDI," "operation" amounted to directly requesting the JAEA operators to run specific calculations.

Chino was known as Mr. SPEEDI. Not only had he been involved with its development from day one, his PhD thesis at Nagoya University was titled "Building SPEEDI" and received the Atomic Energy Society Award. Chino had worked for many years at JAEA, located in Tokaimura, Ibaraki Prefecture.

On March 11, Tokaimura was also hit by the earthquake and tsunami. Fortunately, everything was okay at the nuclear power plant, but Chino stayed there all night to ensure its safety, returning home on the following day, March 12.

His house was also without power, so there was no TV. His mobile phone was out as well. There was no water. All he could rely on was the news on the radio. In the evening of March 12, he and his wife heard the news of the explosion at Fukushima Daiichi's Unit 1. That day was his fifty-sixth birthday. His wife helped him celebrate by the light of a candle and a flashlight with the cheese, bread, and wine they had in the fridge.[46]

It was 1979 when Chino joined JAERI, the forerunner of JAEA. In the spring of that year, the Three Mile Island accident took place in the United States. Chino watched events on the television in JAERI's dormitory. He was called out straight away and participated in drawing up the NSC's Five-Year Emergency Response Plan. The NSC had just been set up the year before.

Part of the Five-Year Emergency Response Plan was to develop a system for predicting the diffusion of radioactive material. At the time, the U.S.

Department of Energy was developing a diffusion prediction system called Atmospheric Release Advisory Capability (ARAC). Chino's supervisor said, "I don't expect our young fellows can do something like that" and tried to introduce ARAC from the States, but Chino and his colleagues pursued a course of self-reliance, constantly improving the system.

Efforts to develop a diffusion prediction system, which began as contract research from the Science and Technology Agency, started to take shape with the full-out support of Fujitsu. It was one of the first examples of industry-government cooperation.

Chino rushed to the NSC offices on the sixth floor of the Central Government Building No. 8 only to find them deserted. He saw a technical adviser, who by rights should have immediately rushed to the commission, sounding off on television about the nuclear accident issue. He thought, *What on earth is this?*[47]

In the evening of March 16, Chino met up with Kukita, who was temporarily back at the NSC from the Kantei. Kukita told Chino, "Chino-san, can SPEEDI be used for reverse estimations?"

"Yes, it can."

"Well, please try and do it."

Chino agreed. He was irritated that SPEEDI was not being fully utilized. If it was possible to get hold of the emission source information by "estimation," and SPEEDI calculated based on that to reproduce the diffusion situation of radioactive material up to that point, then it should be useful for future evacuation measures. Chino both believed and expected it would be so.[48]

Chino started the reverse estimations from March 17. He was given Kukita's room and, with the help of the NSTC operators who had been sent over, he started running the calculations for the reverse estimation of emission source information and reproducing the diffusion of radioactive material based on those results.

Reverse estimation was a way of calculating past radiation source terms on the basis of the ratio when comparing actual dose figures from environmental radiation monitoring for a given point and a given time with the predicted value of radiation dose from the SPEEDI release unit (1 Bq seconds) for the same point at the same time. Furthermore, based on the past emission source terms obtained by the reverse estimation, SPEEDI could also calculate that point.[49]

After the accident, monitoring vehicles had been used to survey environmental doses. However, measurement of the environmental dose amount was not enough; it was only when you entered the data on dust sampling that a fairly robust reverse estimation of emission source information could be run.

Moreover, it was necessary that a certain period of time had elapsed since the radiation diffusion had actually begun to run the reverse estimation, as well as to have a considerable number of accumulated measurements of the environmental radiation dose to compare with. As a matter of course, reverse estimations cannot be performed in advance. Ultimately, it cannot take place until contamination has arisen and been measured. Reverse estimations had been calculated during the JCO accident and Chernobyl nuclear accident. However, a protocol had not been put in place.[50]

Edano had said, "Even a liberal arts fellow like me can think of that, so think!" but there was a world of difference between thinking and actually doing a reverse estimation. It required people to go to places where radiation was spreading and take samples. You had to run SPEEDI for twenty-four hours the previous day and predict the radiation diffusion for the following day, then give instructions—"I think it's going to be like this, so I want you to do the sampling here"—and then you had to feed the actual measurements back into the system.

When you did not get the concentration, you had to use the atmospheric dose as a reference, but this meant guessing what kind of radioactive material would be contained at what ratio. In addition, in order to pinpoint internal radiation exposure, it was necessary to have thyroid dose measurements.[51]

Chino was lucky. On the morning of March 15, the previous day, he got some dust samplings from Tokaimura in Ibaraki Prefecture (from JAEA) and Chiba Prefecture (Atomic Analysis Center). The concentration was a hundred times higher than the concentration measured in Chiba (Atomic Analysis Center) earlier.

It was clear that radiation had been released from the night of March 14 to the early morning of March 15. The "first half of the estimation" had been made possible by the opportunity to use these measurements. The first half referred to the period from March 12 until the early morning of March 15.[52]

However, with rain falling from the evening of March 15, they were able to measure the atmospheric dose from radionuclides deposited on the ground surface, but they were not able to collect dust samples in Fukushima Prefecture.[53]

The wind, which had been blowing seaward from the afternoon of March 16 until March 19, started blowing landward from March 20. On the following day, March 21, JAEA and Fukushima Prefecture measured iodine concentration in the air at three locations above ground.[54]

Chino used them to proceed with the "second half of the estimation," and was convinced on the night of March 22 that "this looks okay." The second half covered March 15 through March 22.[55] Afterward, thorough radiation calculations were done once, using SPEEDI.

WHY WAS SPEEDI NOT USED?

THE UPPER HOUSE BUDGET SUBCOMMITTEE, MARCH 22. Mizuho Fukushima, leader of the Social Democratic Party, was seeking information disclosure of SPEEDI from the government, as well as asking NSC Chairman Haruki Madarame why they had not disclosed it.

Mizuho Fukushima:

"The SPEEDI results have not been made public yet. Why haven't you announced them?"

Madarame:

"The software known as SPEEDI is a prediction system for doses in specific locations when we know there has been a release from a reactor facility using the weather conditions at the time. Unfortunately, since we don't know the nature of the release from the nuclear facilities at the present time, it is not possible to use it at this stage . . . I urge you to understand that predictions are not possible."

Mizuho Fukushima:

"The public is anxious because various government data is not being made public. I ask you to announce it immediately."[56]

There were even voices raised within the government, calling for the use of SPEEDI.

After his appointment as cabinet secretariat special adviser on March 16, Toshiso Kosako, professor at the University of Tokyo Graduate School, had stressed that SPEEDI should be made public and put to good use for the evacuations, but NISA, MEXT, and the NSC did not make a move. Kosako was later scathing in his criticism of the "incompetence of the Nuclear Safety Commission and the Kantei's leadership."[57]

Voices on the operation side also wanted SPEEDI to be used to the best advantage. There was strong dissatisfaction among the officers of the Nuclear Safety Technology Center (NSTC), which was entrusted with the SPEEDI analysis by MEXT, that the government was not trying to make use of SPEEDI for resident evacuations. During this period, with the exception of the first two hours, the NSTC was continuously running SPEEDI. The staff worked around the clock.[58]

Voices were raised at the NSTC that they should appeal directly to the Kantei, but senior management was cautious. Under its contract, the NSTC was supposed to "deliver" its output to MEXT. It was then up to the ministry to decide how it would be handled. They knew how the operators felt, but they could not allow a direct appeal to the politicians. This was their rationale.

The operators continued to post from March 16, "SPEEDI is being operated" ("It's not out of action") on their website. It was the very least they could do to show their resistance.[59]

SPEEDI, however, was never used as a material in judging whether to evacuate citizens at the time of the Fukushima nuclear accident. Why was that so? Where did the problem lie?

The first factor was the absence of a game plan and a scant willingness to use SPEEDI for resident evacuation. While creating an emergency preparedness plan using SPEEDI estimates for resident evacuation, the government will to carry it through was deficient, nor did they draw up a game plan.

In the disaster plans, evacuation at the time of an emergency was to be carried out based on dose predictions. The projected dose was estimated by radiation monitoring and the results of SPEEDI's calculations.

There were three ways to run SPEEDI:

- An atmospheric diffusion simulation of radioactive material based on the emission source term

- Estimation based on emission units or assumed emission

- Estimation of the emission source term (volume, release time) based on reverse estimation from monitoring results (air dose rate, dust sampling)

If the purpose of SPEEDI was preventative measures for the safety of residents, especially the use of SPEEDI-estimated results for evacuation, estimates of projected future doses should have been a top priority.

However, this could not be done under circumstances where there was no emission source term. As a consequence, they ran an "estimation of emission source term based on reverse estimation," and using that as their cue, ran a simulation for the atmospheric diffusion of radioactive materials.

Rather than being a prediction based on actual emission sources, it was a simulation based on assumed emission sources, including emission units. SPEEDI estimations alone should not be relied on to make judgments about evacuation.

In fact, actual evacuation instructions from the night of March 11 were based on an overall decision using monitoring results and conditions such as temperature and water pressure in the reactors at the site as a reference. In this regard, Tetsuro Fukuyama, deputy cabinet secretary, testified as follows:

"I have my doubts as to whether we could have used these SPEEDI results even if we were really familiar with it and NISA, MEXT, and the NSC reported to us in advance . . . Could we have pinpointed the spot for resident evacuation instructions to ten or twenty kilometers using SPEEDI predictions that used a hypothetical unit? No, probably not. Prediction software can't provide political justification to that extent."[60]

There is no doubt that the inability to obtain emission source information increased the unreliability of the prediction. In reality, it would have been difficult to use material of heightened uncertainty in deciding the extremely politically sensitive question of an evacuation order. The data and tools that could be used in the Fukushima NPS accident were very limited. The release of radioactive material was not a one-off but ongoing situation, and moreover, the release was uneven, with a lot being released at some times and a little at other times. The job of making reverse estimations could only ever be extremely difficult.[61]

Nevertheless, or rather because of this, should not using the results to the full, to reduce as much as possible the risk of residents' exposure and for safer prevention responses, have been explored more seriously?

If "wind direction, wind speed, and wind direction forecasts" had been grasped as quickly as possible, SPEEDI would have been able to give a more accurate picture of the radiation diffusion trend. This should have been regarded as one preventative use in the early stages of a nuclear accident—in other words, as a "warning."

However, regardless of whether it was NISA, MEXT, or the NSC, there was no "concept" of using SPEEDI to help evacuation. Yasutaka Moriguchi, MEXT deputy director general, said SPEEDI was used as "reference material for internal deliberations on the scope of emergency monitoring surveys," but since the Fukushima nuclear accident took place in a commercial reactor, they thought that NISA should be the judge of how the SPEEDI forecast data was handled for evacuation instructions and so on, and so, they did not take further action.[62]

The Kantei quickly came up with the evacuation plan for concentric circles by March 12. Looking back, a senior officer at NISA thought this was what made them think it was too late, when they learned about SPEEDI. He said, "Because they had gone with the concentric circle evacuation, any notion of using SPEEDI to contribute to evacuation plan faded away." At the same time, the same senior officer testified that when NISA tried to pass the SPEEDI information to Chief Cabinet Secretary Edano, they were told, "Forget about such confusing stuff."[63] In the end, the Kantei being cautious about using SPEEDI was probably a decisive factor.

There was no definite game plan on how or for whom to publish the results of the SPEEDI calculation, including NERHQ and the Kantei. Kaieda remarked, "The thing I most regret about the accident response is that we didn't take advantage of SPEEDI for evacuations, and as a result, we were unable to evacuate residents in a timely manner from high-dose areas within twenty kilometers and then thirty kilometers and beyond."

He confessed to "feeling ashamed," saying, "Looking at the SPEEDI results afterward, the results were pretty close for many of the hot spots that are a problem now, and I think that could have acted as a reference when issuing evacuation instructions."[64]

The second factor was a lack of governance. Role descriptions for politicians and bureaucrats were ambiguous, and a chain of command and decisionmaking process for crisis management had not been established.

Initially, the radiation team in charge of drawing up resident evacuation area plans at NISA asked the Nuclear Safety Technology Center for SPEEDI estimates. When the Kantei decided on a three-kilometer evacuation and a three-to-ten-kilometer shelter-in-place at 9:23 p.m. on March 11, voices of consternation escaped at NISA's Emergency Response Center. This was because the evacuation instructions from the Kantei had used a concentric configuration for the evacuation area.

There were voices both for and against this at the ERC, however. The radiation team view was, "It would be difficult, perhaps impossible, to use SPEEDI with the wind veering about morning and afternoon," and the majority at the ERC were reluctant to incorporate SPEEDI. However, the evacuation team was preparing its evacuation plans on the assumption of the SPEEDI prediction in the emergency preparedness plan.[65]

In the six days from March 11 to March 16, NISA, MEXT, and the NSC came up with a total of eighty-four different sets of SPEEDI forecast data, but did not share this information or work together on its evaluation at all. In a parliamentary Q&A session, when Nobuaki Terasaka, NISA director general, was asked if MEXT, NISA, and the NSC knew they were each using SPEEDI forecasts, he replied, "I was not aware of it."[66]

This exposed the downside of a double or triple layer of nuclear safety regulatory authorities. The Edano Ruling of March 16 was a graphic illustration of that downside. In a crisis, despite the fact that you have to integrate the resources at your command and demonstrate your powers of integration, the Kantei was engaged in distributed factorization, parceling out monitoring surveys, their evaluation, and publication.

And at the bottom of this double or triple system swirled the murky undercurrents between bureaucrats from the former Science and Technology Agency (now part of MEXT) and the former Ministry of International Trade and Industry (MITI, now METI) at the time of the JCO criticality accident.

It was Kosako who was arguing strongly for using SPEEDI after being appointed as cabinet secretariat special adviser on March 16, but he pointed out that MEXT pulled out of SPEEDI operations because MEXT, and especially bureaucrats from the old Science and Technology Agency, bore a grudge against METI's NISA. He spoke as follows:

"They thought, 'Didn't METI give us a beating during the JCO accident, it's because of those guys that the old agency was carved up. This time, it's METI's responsibility; it's your job now. How about contracting out to the Nuclear Safety Technology Center and doing everything yourselves, because we're stepping back.' So, no one was trying to hide the SPEEDI results, they were passing the buck for who would be responsible for running

SPEEDI and just ignored it, because it was handed over to the NSC, a group that didn't know the first thing about it."[67]

At the core, the battle over the authority of both parties with regard to nuclear power goes back to well before the JCO accident. Iwahashi recollected:

"Career officers at the old Science and Technology Agency, including myself, were involved night and day in a turf battle over nuclear power with the former MITI. And we had a history of our turf being eaten away, inch by inch, by MITI. So, the feeling was strong that we needed to keep the thin edge of the wedge for nuclear power somehow. And that thin edge of the wedge was SPEEDI."[68]

The third factor was risk avoidance in the name of panic avoidance. There was no difference here between the politicians and the bureaucrats, but the bureaucrats were even more pronounced in this regard.

There would be information that cut too close to the bone in the calculation results of the SPEEDI. There would also definitely be unreliable data. How should its impact be determined at such a time? Or, conversely, would a panic occur if the estimates were not released? They were confronted with difficult decisions.

Even after the estimated results of the reverse calculation were released, the previous prediction results never made it to the parliamentary members of the Kantei. Regarding the reason for this, Goshi Hosono, special adviser to the prime minister, said, "I received an explanation that the radiation emission sources were uncertain, unreliable, and there was a concern that the public would panic if they were released."[69]

However, the Kantei was just as concerned about people panicking. Akihiko Iwahashi, secretary general of the NSC, recalls, "I got the impression that the Kantei was reluctant about going public even after they learned of SPEEDI's existence."

There was a clear shift in the stance of the Kantei on releasing the SPEEDI data toward the end of March.[70] The government, initially reluctant to go public for fear that the unadulterated data would cause panic, did a complete about-face after being criticized for this, and posted five thousand to ten thousand diagrams on the Web in one go.[71]

Every time Masamichi Chino, known as Mr. SPEEDI, heard, "SPEEDI can't be used," he felt doubts to the effect that *No one ever says, 'It must be infallible, so it can't be used for high tidal warnings.' Why are you asking for SPEEDI to be perfect this time?*[72]

It was only at a time of nuclear disaster that this perfectionism went unchallenged. Not even the slightest risk was allowed regarding nuclear safety. Japan had a pathological aversion to representing risks in terms of probability. The mantra of "SPEEDI can't be used" was probably also a reflection of the nuclear safety myth.

If a panic did break out as a consequence of going public with SPEEDI, the bureaucracy was terrified that it would be forced to take responsibility. They were afraid of the risk of residents in high radiation areas swarming to be the first to reach evacuation shelters and getting out of control; of the risk of a secondary disaster; of the risk that the estimates might prove to be wrong later on; and, above all, of the risk of demands for compensation and the resultant litigation.

They chose to take the risk of not acting rather than the risk of acting.

The fourth factor was the silo mentality and negative turf wars that were a trademark of the Kasumigaseki bureaucracy. A negative turf war was a secret-of-success tactic in Kasumigaseki: of not raising your hand, not jumping out in front, and not being conspicuous for anything that would not score you a political point; that would not be a plus for the ministry's authority; that would reduce the number of your *amakudari* ("revolving door") posts; that was tedious work; or that would get in the way of advancing the careers of top executives.

Tetsuro Fukuyama, deputy cabinet secretary, recalled that this trend toward negative turf battles was particularly strong at MEXT.

"MEXT was involved in protecting itself. At first, it was on the run. That's why they tried to impose things onto NISA in the beginning, and then the NSC. I think in the end they moved in the direction of turning tail . . . They must have been really shocked when the Kantei told them they had to do the monitoring. Even after that, they moved slowly."[73]

In the midst of the crisis, MEXT unilaterally transferred SPEEDI operations to the NSC. From that time on, MEXT stuck to its attitude of "please ask the Safety Commission about it."[74]

This incident needs to be remembered as the most atrocious example of a negative turf war in the inglorious history of Kasumigaseki.

When ex-METI man and member of the Lower House Nobuyuki Fukushima (DPJ) posed the question in a parliamentary Q&A session of "Why MEXT couldn't release the SPEEDI information sooner?" he received a phone call from ex-MEXT man and director of the Atomic Energy Agency (JAEA), "Sir, please don't make waves."

Fukushima had been in charge of nuclear safety issues at the then MITI (now METI) during the JCO accident in 1999. The JAEA director said, "MEXT will do the monitoring, but evaluating and running simulations on the numbers is not their jurisdiction, it's the safety commission's job. That's what the Kantei decided, isn't it?"

Fukushima asked in return, "Well, if that's the case, why on earth is the ministry doing research then?"

The director replied:

"Our research is on normal conditions. It's not research on times of emergency."[75]

Edano felt, in retrospect, that "the former Science and Technology

Agency was the black box of the ministry," but it was all old boys from the former Science and Technology Agency who were running safety regulation and nuclear administration at MEXT and the NSC.[76]

And there were also the interests of the "nuclear village." Iwahashi commented on the difficulty safety regulation posed for the "nuclear village," saying, "People on the promotion track had nothing to do with safety regulation. Why? Because that would place you in conflict with the interests of the 'nuclear village.' So, personnel who had a future were not posted to safety regulation."[77] In other words, nuclear safety regulation was the end of the line for the "useless mah-jongg tiles" of Kasumigaseki.

The fourth and final factor was that SPEEDI had been used both politically and administratively as "something realer than real, something beyond the bounds of reality." Commissioner Yutaka Kukita from the NSC said, "I think SPEEDI might have had an impact if it had been understood in life-size terms, or used as a reference."[78]

SPEEDI was touted as one of the tools of the "safety myth"; it was the case that it was stuck in the gap between its real effect and political effect. Under the nuclear disaster law, which was established after the JCO accident, it became so that nuclear power disaster prevention training was held by the government, but at that time, SPEEDI calculation results were seen to be data to serve as the direct grounds for protection measures, such as evacuation and shelter in place. Blueprints were placed on top of desks at the countermeasures headquarters.

Even if there was a severe accident, it was assumed that highly reliable, detailed information about the radiation at source would be obtainable. It was assumed that SPEEDI's prediction calculations could be used as a realistic prediction, so was put in place as "fundamental information" for deciding protective measures, such as evacuation.

But the people in charge of the actual evacuation plan placed it ultimately as "reference information" to be used in conjunction with other resources for judgment. When the accident did, in fact, happen, opinions and perspectives were divided on whether it should be "fundamental information" or "reference information."

Because SPEEDI predicts well, when something happens, it's possible to evacuate everyone safely. The view that SPEEDI was that sort of "magic wand" for protection measures was "fiction."[79]

As pointed out by the Independent Investigation Commission, "SPEEDI and the off-site centers were little more than shiny security baubles introduced to secure the docility of the public and obtain support for nuclear plant construction."[80]

That SPEEDI was not used is the story of the collapse of this myth.[81]

FIFTEEN

Planned Evacuation Area

"THE NUMBERS ARE SKY HIGH IN IITATE"

Sometime after seven a.m. on March 23, the calculation results that had been requested of the NSTC arrived at the NSC.

Internal exposure, organ equivalent dose
Date and time: 3/12/2011 06:00–
                    Integrated value 3/24/2011 00:00
Nuclide name: iodine total
Age: one-year-olds
Organ name: thyroid
(Evaluation)
The thyroid dose was calculated assuming the conservative condition of having stayed outdoors all day after the Fukushima Daiichi NPS accident

This one piece of paper reflected the overall simulation. According to it, a thyroid amount equivalent dose (internal exposure) in excess of 100 millisieverts was found outside a range of thirty kilometers. Depending on the exact location, it was five or ten kilometers over the line.

Anxious about the accuracy of the calculations, Chino checked them and conveyed the results to Kusumi. Battling her own anxiety that he was correct, Kusumi was at the same time grateful to Chino.

It was only because Chino-san had a number of parameters for how to run SPEEDI that he was able to do something like this in a week, otherwise it would have taken three months or more starting from scratch.[1]

"The prime minister wants to have the SPEEDI estimations as soon as possible."

433

Mizuma had been told something to that effect by Hiroshi Ikukawa, a previous aide of Prime Minister Naoto Kan at the Integrated Response Office. Everything else had to be put aside to notify the Kantei of the results.

They had to consider the immediate evacuation of residents in high dose areas. At the same time, in areas where the thyroid exposure exceeded an equivalent dose of 100 millisieverts, residents would need to take stable iodine tablets. This was what Kusumi stated to Madarame, who said, "Let's take it to the Kantei right now."

Madarame had Kusumi and Chino head straight to the Kantei as well.[2]

THE MORNING OF MARCH 23. Kusumi and Chino visited the Kantei to report to Hosono and Edano. They went to the Hosono's office first. Kusumi told Hosono, "It's serious. According to SPEEDI, the radiation dose in the direction of the northwest has reached 80 to 100 millisieverts. This is three to four times the norm. And the numbers are sky-high in Iitate and elsewhere."

Kusumi showed him the single sheet of paper with the integrated values (internal exposure, organ equivalent dose) for March 12 through March 23. This was a map estimating the integral dose any children in the surrounding area would have been exposed to due to the radioactive iodine emitted by the Fukushima Daiichi NPS accident.

Hosono was aghast at what he was shown. He hurriedly had Ito come up to the fifth floor from the basement crisis management center. When he was shown the piece of paper, Ito asked, "What's the current release amount?"

"It's constant."

"Well, that's not exactly accurate, because it is changing."

Ito pressed on, "And one more thing . . . We have to know the release amount at the source. The numbers have fallen with the monitoring results out now. In short, they're only external exposure. What we need to do is internal exposure. We won't know the internal exposure if we don't have dust monitoring."

Up until then, the monitoring surveys were on environmental radiation, using monitoring vehicles. That data was not sufficient to get a grasp on the specific status of radioactive emission sources. It was only when they had measurements of the radioactive concentration in the atmosphere, as well as the spatial dose rate, that reverse estimations could be partially made for the emission source information. The most important thing was to have measurements of the radioactive concentration (dust sampling).

"What's happened with the dust sampling? Didn't you say you couldn't do it?" Ito asked.

"We've got two samples from Fukushima Daini and Tokaimura, so we can pretty much do the estimate," Kusumi replied.

"I thought you said you couldn't do it two days ago . . . And there's not a single sample from the northwest, is there?"

"No, but we're making the estimates," Kusumi insisted.

"But since you don't have any dust monitoring numbers now, back calculation will be difficult after all."

Kusumi responded, "No, we've done the back calculation. From the monitoring data . . . Even outside the thirty-kilometer zone, the internal exposure is over 100 millisieverts accumulated per annum. That's why we've come here to ask you to issue an evacuation order immediately."

"What's more, we have data saying if a one-year-old—not naked, mind you—stands in a paddy field twenty-four hours a day, every day for a year, his exposure will be 120 millisieverts," Ito replied. "No one-year-olds are going to be outdoors in freezing cold weather like this. They're going to be indoors most of the time. Exposure indoors is about one-tenth, right? Even if they go somewhere, it's by car and not even for an hour. Using calculations for twenty-four hours is just not helpful."

"No, but we do need to take a conservative view."

Ito continued, as if pressing home his advantage.

"Well, then, you force me to ask the question: has anyone measured children's or anybody's thyroid exposure?"

"No, we haven't measured anyone," Kusumi replied.

"Don't you think it's a bit strange wanting to evacuate them then?"[3]

After a conversation along these lines, Ito went down to the basement. Everyone else headed together to Edano's office. He was just coming back from the chief cabinet secretary's eleven a.m. press conference. Hosono ran behind him like a tailwind, calling out:

"Chief Cabinet Secretary, this is very serious!"

Kusumi showed the same sheet of paper with the SPEEDI calculation results to Edano in the chief cabinet secretary's office. Hosono closed in on Edano.

"Secretary, we have to evacuate or this will become very serious."

"I think we should be evacuating residents immediately from beyond the twenty-kilometer zone, depending on the location."

Edano, however, was surprisingly calm.

"Is this true? Can we really trust this?"

Kusumi answered, "I think it is better to evacuate immediately."

"If I were to take measures, what would be necessary?"

"Supplying iodine is urgent."

Edano was cautious even here.

"Since this assumes being outdoors for twenty-four hours, wouldn't it be considerably mitigated if you stayed indoors?"

"I see these are very conservative calculations. But I don't think there's a need to evacuate," Edano said.

Kusumi suggested to Edano going public with SPEEDI.

"It's not the SPEEDI results that are so important, necessarily, but the chance that a wide range of people may have been absorbing iodine, so I'd rather take measures against that."

"Please get them to announce the SPEEDI result in order to raise awareness."

Edano had no objection to that.

"Mm-m, we should by all means publish it. Please do it at the NSC."

This was where it was decided that the Nuclear Safety Commission was to make the SPEEDI results public.[4]

"WHY DIDN'T WE HAVE THESE FIGURES BEFORE?!"

2:00 P.M., MARCH 23, 2011. Haruki Madarame, chairman of the Nuclear Safety Commission (NSC), had come to the Kantei with Commissioner Shizuyo Kusumi and Masamichi Chino, deputy director of the Nuclear Science and Engineering Directorate at the Japan Atomic Energy Agency (JAEA).

Having been asked by the Kantei to explain SPEEDI, Madarame had arranged to brief the prime minister at 2:30 p.m. Since the SPEEDI reverse estimation just happened to have been finished that morning, he decided to brief Kan on that as well.

Madarame believed that "radioactive material was still leaking from Fukushima Daiichi NPS," and was also reading the situation as "there might by chance be another event, meaning we might have to extend the evacuation zone." He, therefore, thought that, based on the reverse estimation results, they should extend the evacuation zone.[5]

Sometime after 2:30 p.m., a meeting on the redesignation of the evacuation zone was held in the prime minister's office. Madarame had spoken with Edano in his office prior to the meeting, but Edano was extremely cool, just as he had been with Kusumi and Chino that morning.

"But this is a pretty severe estimate, isn't it?"

"So? It's not so urgent, is it?"

And then, as if in a warning, Edano said, "Look, this is too rigid an estimate, so for the time being, I don't think we need to think about expanding the evacuation zone, right?"

Madarame was then taken by Edano to the prime minister's office, but while they were walking there, Edano asked Madarame, "In the first place, you have all kinds of experts at the commission. This matter is Kusumi-san's area, isn't it?

"I'm right in thinking, aren't I, that all of the commissioners have to be approved by the Diet, so in that sense, their opinions are the opinions of people even the Diet has acknowledged as experts?"

What a strange thing to say.

Madarame was not able to grasp the implications immediately.[6]

Kan, Edano, Fukuyama, and Hosono were at the meeting, as well as Madarame, Kusumi, and Chino from the NSC, MEXT Deputy Director General Yasutaka Moriguchi, and Kazuo Sakai, director of the Research Center for Radiation Protection at the National Institute of Radiological Sciences (NIRS), among others.

Madarame showed a diagram of the calculation results from SPEEDI's reverse estimations. On top of that, he stated that evacuation should be the top priority, that he would like them to consider expanding the evacuation zone, and that, in such a case, the evacuees should take stable iodine during the evacuation process.

Madarame already felt, after reporting to Edano immediately before, that expanding the evacuation area would be difficult. So he took care to say not "I would like you to expand the evacuation zone," but "I would like you to consider expanding the evacuation zone."

Kan burst out in a loud voice.

"Why didn't we have these figures before?!"

Chino then described the reverse estimate process. Kan requested, "I don't understand this very well. Explain it in simpler terms."

Madarame said, "The plume is spreading like an amoeba in the direction of Iitate Village. You should not stick to the twenty-kilometer radius. I think we have to evacuate quickly beyond the twenty-kilometer zone, depending on the location."

Kan said with a frown, "What do you expect, dropping something like this on us suddenly?"

Madarame gave a different explanation.

"Since SPEEDI assumes that you are outdoors twenty-four hours a day, and gives estimates for the integral dose, I don't think we'll see levels of 100 millisieverts as of today. However, we have learned from this round of SPEEDI estimates that even beyond the thirty-kilometer line, there's a possibility of an iodine equivalent dose of 100 millisieverts in the future.

"Indoors evacuation is like taking shelter from the rain. However, since issuing the evacuation order, radioactivity has consistently been released from Fukushima Daiichi NPS. Taking into account the possibility of future increases in the dose, you should consider evacuating residents. If you were to implement an evacuation, I think oral administration of stable iodine would be desirable."

Up until that point, Hosono had not been very impressed with the confidence-lacking Madarame, who looked "unable to put his body on the line and make an appeal," but Madarame was different this time. Hosono, however, left after a while. Work was waiting for him at the Integrated Response Office at TEPCO.[7]

Kosako and Soramoto entered the prime minister's office when they were discussing stable iodine. They had rushed over after receiving a call from Fukuyama, telling them that "the prime minister's mad, can you come?"

Since Kosako and Soramoto had come in, the aides made a space for them on the sofa opposite Kan. Soramoto immediately caught on, *Ah hah, Madarame's pushing strongly for an expansion of the evacuation zone, so Fukuyama's called us over to quash it.*

Kusumi was asserting passionately the need to distribute stable iodine. "It should be ingested at the time of the evacuation."

Kosako shook his head, as if he found that quite unacceptable.

"It's too late now. It should have been handed out between March 11 and March 15. Stable iodine is meaningless unless you take it *before* the plume passes. It's pointless doing it now that it's all over. That's why amateurs are useless."

Kusumi countered,

"Iodine is only effective for a specific time after it's been ingested. Even in the unlikely event, it should be ingested at the time of evacuation."

Kosako continued to argue,

"It's got to be done before evacuation. It's too late at the time of evacuation."

Sakai voiced an opinion here,

"The effective period of orally ingested iodine is about one day."

Sakai had been suddenly called to the Kantei on March 16, after which he was mainly engaged in providing Edano with advice in terms of radiological science.

Kusumi was getting overpowered by Kosako's aggressive tone, and her voice started to tremble. The expert opinions were all over the place and not converging at all.

Listening to Kosako's argument, Chino felt a certain discomfort, *They're talking as if the crisis is over.* He was thinking, *What will happen if a large volume of radiation is released again, like on March 15? Won't it become a serious question of responsibility at the time if iodine hasn't been distributed?* But he kept quiet.[8]

Terada came into the room. He had hurried in, having been told by a prime ministerial aide, "Things are getting rough. Can you come in?" He arrived just when Kosako and Madarame were having it out.

Kosako was insisting that all the SPEEDI data be made public. Kan asked Kosako, "Why wasn't this published until now?"

Kosako replied, "Because NISA won't release the data."

Eyeballing the room, Kan shouted, "Is there anyone here from NISA?"

Tomoho Yamada, head of the Nuclear Power Safety Inspection Section at NISA, who had been holed up as part of the emergency operation team in the crisis management center was in the background by the wall. He walked over to the table and, remaining on his feet, explained,

"Since we didn't know how much radiation has been released, we couldn't. Usually we can tell from the stack pipe emissions, but we don't know where it's coming from. We can't make any estimates, because we can't manage the monitoring."

Kan also said, "Explain why it's taken so long."

Even if they did publish the SPEEDI estimates, it was likely that they would be vilified by the opposition parties and the press to the effect of why were the numbers not published until now, why were they late?

A number of people, including Chino and Kusumi, went next door to the prime minister's reception area, to write a memo on "the reason." The fact that the wind direction was mostly seaward from March 11 and did not blow landward; that they were now able to monitor more reliably with the wind blowing landward; also that they were able finally to conduct dust sampling, which enabled them to take measurements, and so on, and so forth.

Edano asked, "I wonder if I should announce at the press conference this evening that we're going to issue a new evacuation order?"

Kosako was opposed.

"If the plume has already passed over, people who go outside will suffer more external exposure . . . It's already evening. It will soon be night. It will mean thousands of people fleeing in the dark. Shouldn't you leave it for today? . . . In the first place, can you give a reasonable explanation with dust sampling from only three locations?"[9]

It was at this point that Ito entered the room. He had been called in suddenly by one of the prime minister's aides when he was in the downstairs crisis management center. "Something strange is happening," the aide told him. "Please come to the prime minister's office. Right away."

It felt like the talking was over, and everyone looked exhausted. Kusumi was bathed in sweat as she talked about something. It sounded like they were rehashing the discussion they had had in the morning at Hosono's, about expanding the evacuation zone that Ito thought he had put an end to.

So, this time, the NSC is talking directly to the PM, eh?

He was not happy.

Madarame was still urging that they consider the evacuation of residents in areas beyond the twenty-kilometer zone. However, he had only brought along the diagram and no other explanatory material.

It had already been decided that SPEEDI results would be made public. However, if they were made public, it would immediately trigger a debate on the pros and cons of the existing indoor evacuation measure. And what should they think about the SPEEDI estimates being used for evacuation in the first place?

Ito spoke up.

"Look, SPEEDI can't be used, for a variety of reasons. First, let's do the dust sampling. If we have dust sampling data, the estimates will be neat as well."

Monitoring radiation was the responsibility of MEXT. Yasutaka Moriguchi, deputy director general, gave the excuse, "We're totally helpless without enough people."

Kan said, "If you need people to do the monitoring, we can give you lots of people. You can have them from the SDF or anywhere."

Goodness only knows what he was thinking, but Kan appealed to Kusumi, who was sitting on the sofa to his right.

"Do it, please. Please do it."

Taken by surprise, Kusumi did not understand what Kan was saying. She felt wary: *What was with his honeyed tone?*

"I'll give you the manpower," Kan continued to plead with her.

Kusumi was nonplussed, as he became more and more incoherent, but she could not afford to say the wrong thing. She kept her silence.

(Kusumi later reached the conclusion that Kan was trying to get the NSC to do the offsite monitoring. Did he mean the SDF when he said "manpower" . . . ? It looked like Kan thought MEXT was running away from the monitoring, and was making a direct appeal to the NSC. She thought it suspicious: the commission was only an advisory agency, didn't the prime minister know that? At the same time, however, she was struck by the serious thought of how helpless the prime minister of Japan was.)

Ito also advised caution about the distribution and ingestion of stable iodine. He asked Kusumi, "In short, it's a prediction, isn't it? Or do you have empirical data on the thyroid exposure dose for children?"

"No, we don't."

Ito queried Sakai.

"Sakai-san, I'm sorry, but you can find out the thyroid exposure dose for children, can't you?"

"Yes, I can do that."

"Please start estimating now."

"Of course. I'll start right away."

Kosako said they should immediately release the SPEEDI data rather than decide on the "redesignation of the evacuation zone," criticizing the government for not having already done so.

Kan raised his voice.

"This stuff is absolutely hopeless! You're asking me to decide on this basis?!"

Madarame still repeated his claim that they "should keep in mind an evacuation beyond the thirty-kilometer line as well," but Kosako refused to budge, saying, "I'm opposed to any reckless kind of evacuation without policy," and the debate just fizzled out.[10]

"YOU EXPERTS, WORK IT OUT AMONG YOURSELVES"

At this point, Hiroyuki Fukano, director general for commerce and distribution policy at METI, came into the room. He had been sitting at the emergency operation team table in the basement only a few moments earlier.

After serving as the planning and coordination manager, who formulated safety policies on nuclear power since NISA's founding in January 2001, Fukano had experience working as NISA's deputy director general in 2008. (In August 2011, after the Fukushima nuclear accident, he was appointed as the agency's director general).

From March 11 on, he was run off his feet trying to keep up a steady flow of goods to the disaster areas, Fukushima Prefecture in particular, arranging every day for gasoline, coffins, and dry ice. He was also appointed later to the new position of supervisor of nuclear disaster special measures. This was part of METI permanent secretary Kazuo Matsunaga's reinforcement of disaster accident response measures. This was how Fukano came to be pent up with the emergency operation team when he suddenly received the message to come as soon as possible to the prime minister's office.

Just as he was about to enter the prime minister's office, his mobile phone rang. It was Matsunaga.

"They're holding a meeting there now about reviewing the evacuation order, but they're still not laying the groundwork with the municipalities at all, just doing it on the Kantei's initiative, so it won't go down well at all, and I want you to speak in light of that."

Before attending the meeting, he had been handed something like a thick statute book by the NISA staff. It was titled *Nuclear Disaster Prevention Instruction Manual (Laws, Regulations, and Guidelines)*, edited by the NSC.

After entering the prime minister's office, Fukano was flipping through the book, when he exclaimed, "What?"

"100–500 millisieverts: Indoor shelter at home."

This was what was written on page 225.

Ito, sitting on the sofa in front of Fukano, had just finished remarking, "It's no good having an evacuation like that."

Fukano whispered in Ito's ear.

"Doesn't it say in the NSC's disaster prevention plan that staying indoors should be applied to internal exposure of 100–500 millisieverts?"

Ito had never met Fukano up until then, but he told him, "You, please read it out loud."

"May I have everyone's attention?"

Upon saying as much, Fukano rose to his feet.

"You have been repeatedly mentioning an evacuation for areas with over 100 millisieverts, but according to the NSC's disaster guidelines, only sheltering indoors is mentioned for 100 to 500 millisieverts, right? How do you explain that?"

Everyone in the room turned to Madarame. Madarame, however, was not saying anything. Fukano thought Madarame was going to refute him, but since he did not respond, it felt anticlimactic.

"What the hell are you doing?!"

Kan threw harsh words in Madarame's direction. Kosako gained momentum.

"I've worked on public radiation exposure all my life. I've worked on it all the time even at the ICRP (International Commission on Radiological Protection).[11] I'm an expert in this field."

Saying this, he turned to face Madarame.

"The NSC should discuss things more properly."

His words had a critical undertone, as if admonishing Kan for using people like Madarame as advisers. Whether he felt compelled to make some excuse, Kan said, "Well, the prime minister is continually required to take advice from the Nuclear Safety Commission . . ."

Kan had been listening to Kosako and Madarame quarrel, with his head in his hands and a deep frown on his face, but said, as if he had had enough, "That's enough. You, experts, work it out among yourselves."

After making this remark, Kan stood up, went over to his desk, and dropped down into the "prime minister's seat."

According to Fukuyama's recollection, "The experts were repeatedly arguing in an almost emotional way in front of the prime minister about whether it was better to evacuate people even if that meant taking them outside when the radiation dose was high, or keeping them indoors."

It was the appearance of Kosako, whom Fukuyama had called in because he was worried that the "prime minister is angry," that led to the raging debate "scratching about, scratching about, and making a complete mess of things," to use Madarame's words.

The meeting collapsed in disarray. Kosako turned toward Ito, as if in appeal. He raised his voice, perhaps so that Kan, who had gone over to sit in his chair, could hear.

"We are making various proposals to the government and the Nuclear Safety Commission. We've made more than thirty proposals. But these recommendations haven't gotten across. Nobody listens to what we say. Nothing is carried out."

"What do you mean?"

"I have our recommendations here, so please read them. Here it is. Recommendations 32, 33, 34, and 35, are all about the distribution of stable iodine."

Saying this, Kosako handed the manual to Ito. Terada was standing talking to Soramoto in the corner of the room.

"The prime minister has told the experts to work it out among themselves, so let's call it a day."

"Yeah, let the experts work it out on their own."

Terada picked this up and declared that the meeting was over.

"We'll have a second go in another room."[12]

Madarame and Kusumi returned to the NSC by car. Madarame said, "I wonder if Kosako-san thought the iodine had an indefinite effect once you took it."

Kusumi looked surprised. She was thinking the same thing. However, neither of them had refuted Kosako on the spot. Both Madarame and Kusumi were afraid of thyroid exposure for children. It was the thyroid equivalent dose—namely, internal exposure—that they had had in mind when they had gone to the Kantei.

If that was the case, then "shelter in place" should certainly be applied for "100–500 millisieverts," as Fukano had pointed out, and according to the disaster prevention plan, the need to expand the thirty-kilometer evacuation zone no longer held.

However, if you took the position that the disaster prevention plan itself was no longer effective under these circumstances, it was a different story.[13]

An experts' meeting was later held in the conference room on the eleventh floor of the Central Government Building No. 4 from five p.m. Eiji Hiraoka, NISA vice director general, and Yoshinari Akeno, chief of MEXT's Nuclear Safety Division in the Science and Technology Policy Bureau, among others, were also called in. Soramoto moderated the meeting.

Kosako criticized Madarame for suddenly "rushing headlong" into insisting on "evacuating residents from the thirty-kilometer zone" in the meeting that afternoon in the prime minister's office.

"The NSC needs to think more calmly."

Fukuyama appeared after a while, as well as Madarame. When Kosako criticized Madarame's proposal, Madarame responded by saying, "I don't remember having ever once said to immediately run away."

Soramoto yelled, "Please, don't lie."

After a time, Madarame left hastily, saying, "I have to prepare for a press conference on the SPEEDI results."[14]

Madarame was an expert on reactors, but not on radiation contamination. Still, feeling a sense of crisis with the SPEEDI results, he not only called the prime minister's secretary himself, but had an appointment with the prime minister squeezed in that day. However, he avoided explaining directly to the prime minister about the radiation contamination, entrusting that role to Kusumi.

From Kan and his secretary's perspective, they were dissatisfied that although they had taken the effort to make time for Madarame, he was not able to explain anything clearly. That Madarame had come only armed with a diagram of the SPEEDI estimates and no explanatory material also gave the impression of "sloppiness."

What? Has he come with just a slip of paper to tell us to evacuate?

Both Kan and Fukuyama had this impression.

In fact, there was no discussion on this issue at the Nuclear Safety Commission. Based on the position of the NSC, Kusumi and Madarame had not gone to the Kantei in their NSC capacities.

The following exchange also took place between Kan and Madarame.

"Has the NSC decided on this matter?"

"No, that is not the case. The commission hasn't made a decision yet."

Another exchange took place between Ito and Madarame.

"Look, you're the safety commission, right? Why are you bringing this story?"

"No, I don't understand radiological science, so I've left it all to Kusumi-san . . ."

"You're an administrative organization, too, so please bring the results after the commission has considered them."

Ito was astonished that when officials at the safety commission had suggested the "reverse estimation," Madarame had said, "That's the first time I've heard of that. Let me think about it," with a blank look on his face, and now here he was, the minute the reverse estimations were in, screaming that they were right.

Is this what scientists are like . . . ?

The NSC secretariat staff were later to regret that the "chairman had gone off half-cocked." Ito had made a very biting comment to Akihiko Iwahashi, secretary general of the NSC, about Madarame's performance at the time. When Iwahashi answered, "the king is mad," Ito told him, "It's your job to keep him under control."[15]

AFTER FIVE P.M., MARCH 23. Chief Cabinet Secretary Edano gave a press conference at the Kantei.

"At around noon today, I received a report from the Nuclear Safety Commission on estimation of radiation exposure with the SPEEDI system. The details will be released later today by the Nuclear Safety Commission, so please refer to them for more information.

"The results of the simulations carried out based on the data show areas where the thyroid gland exposure dose may have been 100 mSv or higher, assuming that a person spends the whole day outdoors. The simulation suggests that even in some areas beyond the thirty-kilometer radius of the Fukushima Daiichi Nuclear Power Station, it is possible that radiation exposure doses may have reached levels of 100 mSv or more. However, the analysis does not suggest that it is necessary for people to evacuate or remain indoors at the moment."

Back at the Integrated Response Office at TEPCO, Hosono was appalled to hear the results of the meeting on the redesignation of the evacuation zone that took place at the Kantei that afternoon.

The crisis isn't over yet, so is it all right to be saying you can't do this or that?

They're dragging their heels with lengthy debates.

It was around this time that he had the feeling that meetings at the Kantei were starting to get longer. He was also worried that Kan was a little low in spirits that day.

Kan-san, what's wrong? Are you leaving behind your sense of emergency as things return to normal?[16]

At a press conference on the night of March 23, Madarame released a map of the SPEEDI estimations. The next day, many of the newspapers ran headlines such as "SPEEDI Information Finally Released by NSC Twelve Days After the Accident."

"Having suddenly been made the leadoff hitter, we were completely demonized."

Madarame was later to refer to events in this manner.[17]

PLANNED EVACUATION AREA

On March 26, Edano called Madarame and Iwahashi to the Kantei.

"These must be tough times for you, too, chairman."

After saying so, Edano told them he had decided to send Kenkichi Hirose, a professor at the International Student Education Center at Tokai University and a former director general of NISA, to the NSC.

"I think we'll let him liaise with the Kantei."

That was it.[18]

Inside the Kantei, the perception had spread that the "chairman is unreliable and the secretary general doesn't make a move." While replacing Madarame had been considered at one stage, to shore up the NSC with Edano playing a central role, it was decided against, since Diet approval was needed for personnel changes and they could not afford to have a ruckus about dismissing him during an emergency.

Replacing Iwahashi was also suggested, but this was tossed out by sending Shigeharu Kato, deputy director general at MEXT, in as "special support." Kato had been NISA's deputy director general prior to that.

Iwahashi had been called in by Fukuyama on the question of strengthening the environmental radiation monitoring. Fukuyama told Iwahashi, "You need to strengthen the monitoring system. The Kantei will give you all the manpower you want."

Iwahashi replied, "Deputy secretary, it's not a question of reinforcing numbers. Increasing them in one place only opens a hole somewhere else."[19]

Iwahashi's reasoning was probably sound, but he only ended up damaging his reputation more as a "tight-ass pedant."

After the nuclear power plant accident, Hirose was serving as an adviser to Kazuo Matsunaga, METI's permanent secretary, but Edano suddenly decided to use him and issued his official appointment as special adviser to the Cabinet Office as of March 28. The first job he tackled was drawing up a new evacuation plan to replace the "voluntary evacuation" decided on March 25.

There were places like Iitate within the twenty- to thirty-kilometer indoor evacuation zone as well as outside the thirty-kilometer line, where the plume had passed and significantly higher radiation doses had been detected. Iitate Village was becoming a symbol both inside and outside Japan.

Hirose consulted Ito and Fukano. First, was it possible to evacuate even at this late a date? Next, what level (radiation dose) should be used for setting a new evacuation area? Then, how much time would have to be allocated to complete the evacuation? And, finally, how was the evacuation area to be established in practical terms?[20]

The key to this was establishing the grounds and radiation level for the evacuation area. Staring at a map, they discussed the pros and cons for five respective numbers—1, 5, 10, 20, and 100. They examined how to go about establishing an evacuation area using these five levels of radiation exposure—namely, 1 millisievert, 5 millisieverts, 10 millisieverts, 20 millisieverts, and 100 millisieverts per annum.

At 10 millisieverts/year, all of Fukushima Prefecture would, in fact, have to be evacuated. That would mean no recovery, reconstruction, or responding to the nuclear accident in Fukushima. The exposure of 10 millisieverts would be very hard to accept.

Going by the claim of Professor Shunichi Yamashita of Nagasaki University, an authority on radiology, that "100 millisieverts was safe," Fukushima Prefecture had embarked on its own measures.

The Fukushima Prefectural Board of Education had already started moving in the direction of reopening schools on the assumption that "100 millisieverts was safe." So, the moment it was decided that "100 millisieverts wasn't safe," it would become an issue of liability for Fukushima Prefecture and its governor. This also had to be avoided.[21]

Ito was thinking, *100 millisieverts looks all right to me.*

This would mean Iitate Village did not have to evacuate. However, the doubt was growing, day by day, whether it was really okay not to evacuate Iitate. At one stage, he thought, *Let's go for 50 millisieverts*, but there were no real grounds for that. In the end, 20 millisieverts was settled on. Ito thought, *This means all six thousand people in Iitate will have to evacuate. The poor things.* Hirose felt the same way, but it could not be helped.[22]

However, no matter which option they chose, they had to provide a basis for it. Regarding determining mandatory evacuation areas, the disaster prevention guidelines provided the following criteria for projected doses:

> Projected dose is 50 millisieverts for external exposure effective dose, or over 500 millisieverts thyroid equivalent dose.

At this point in time, none of the areas with comparatively high radiation within the twenty- to thirty-kilometer zone, or beyond the thirty-kilometer line, was over this level. There was no need, therefore, for mandatory evacuation of these residents.

On the other hand, the reference levels for emergency intervention recommended by the International Commission on Radiological Protection (ICRP) on March 21 was "20–100 millisieverts effective dose."

This was based on the ICRP's 2007 recommendations. If this was taken as the standard, an instruction for mandatory evacuation was necessary.[23] The point here was that the current juncture still had to be recognized as "a time of emergency."

By the end of March, it looked like the worst reactor situation was going to be avoided, but they were still not stable. Acknowledging it was still "a time of emergency" had to be the starting point.

Therefore, it was decided to use 20 millisieverts as the basis for creating a new evacuation plan, a figure that was the minimum value for the ICRP's reference level of "20 to 100 millisieverts in times of emergency" and the maximum value for its "1–20 millisieverts after accident convergence."[24] From that point of view, the 20-millisievert standard was a welcome figure.

Taking the 20 millisieverts as the "bottom of the emergency range" would make it possible to give the impression that health and safety were being taken into consideration. Taking the 20 millisieverts "upper limit during recovery" would make it possible to send a message both inside and outside the country, and especially to the international community, that the nuclear accident was gradually coming to an end. This was the manner in which it was decided to set a new evacuation zone only "in areas that may have a cumulative dose of 20 millisieverts/year." The ICRP reference figures turned out to be a lifesaver.

If it was 20 millisieverts, Iitate Village and Kawamata Town would be included, but not Fukushima City.[25] Fukushima Prefecture stood in the way of expanding the evacuation zone and setting a new evacuation zone.

"The locals are dead set against it. Fukushima Prefecture, too."

Fukuyama was dealing with Fukushima Prefecture extremely carefully.[26]

It was not only the local governments. There was no change in the fact that the government wanted to minimize the decontamination zone and evacuation zone, if possible.

What should they call the area covered by the new evacuation order?

Hirose was initially thinking about naming it the "planned evacuation advised zone." At the time, he was looking at two proposals for beyond the thirty-kilometer line.

However, the opinion was voiced that including "advised" was "somehow weak," because if you continued living in areas with a high integral dose, there was a fear that the integral dose would also be higher, so they finally settled on the name "planned evacuation area."

According to Fukano, the term "planned" was used based on the "idea to have people prepare properly and in an orderly manner, shutting up what needed to be shut up, and leaving in an orderly way."[27]

However, there was "some trouble" over whether to set up an "emergency evacuation preparation area" for "shelter in place areas" not included in the planned evacuation zone. This area would be requested to prepare for staying indoors and immediate evacuation in times of an emergency. It was initially proposed in tandem with the setting of a new planned evacuation area, and to abolish the voluntary evacuation zone of twenty to thirty kilometers.

It was Tadahiro Matsushita, head of the local NERHQ, who objected. He was the vice minister of METI. He called Madarame to request that the "voluntary evacuation area not be abolished out of the blue." He said:

"The government asked people to evacuate voluntarily. And yet, the people who stayed indoors and didn't evacuate will tell themselves, well, that's over and done without us having to do anything, what fools the people who ran around in a tizzy and evacuated voluntarily are. This would be bad."

Madarame passed Matsushita's opinion on to Hirose. This was where the concept of an "emergency evacuation preparation area" appeared. It was to be an area where people would be required to "evacuate on a voluntary basis," preparing for evacuation or indoor evacuation at a moment's notice.[28]

However, setting up such a zone was only tenable based on recognizing there was still a crisis. Believing that there was no longer any such risk, NISA was thinking about doing away with the voluntary evacuation zone.

If they were going to set up an emergency evacuation preparation area, however, they would have to prepare a situational development scenario of "Things are settling down somewhat, but caution is still required." To do this would require evaluating once more the reactor risk at Fukushima Daiichi NPS.

NISA sought the advice of the safety commission about this. On March 31, the NSC, with Acting Chairman Yutaka Kukita playing a central role, looked into a scenario where the molten fuel was in contact with the concrete and gas, which would include releasing a large amount of radioactive material.[29]

As a result, they handed down the assessment that "the impact is small on the area outside twenty kilometers." This also meant there was no need for a thirty-kilometer evacuation zone.

Besides the reactors, the NSC also ran an analysis that showed there was still an undeniable possibility of the fuel rods in the fuel pool melting, and in the light of this evaluation, Hirose submitted his draft to the Kantei for an "emergency evacuation preparation area."[30]

"CAN YOU BREATHE DEEPLY HERE NOW?"

On April 7, the mayor of Iitate Village, Norio Kanno, visited Tokyo and handed a five-point proposal to Deputy Chief Cabinet Secretary Tetsuro Fukuyama at the Kantei. The contents of this were as follows:

> The fact that survey information from various agencies, including the state, was unilaterally made public without any prior reporting to or consultation with the village, and the fact that only "the numbers are high" was reported and emphasized, has created immeasurable fear and anxiety among the village residents, who, in complete contrast to their lives before, have become part of a "world-famous Iitate Village," the village being most concerned about the huge reputational damage now and in the future.[31]

Fukuyama gently hinted to Kanno at the need to evacuate Iitate Village.

"The dose is pretty tough in Iitate, so couldn't you possibly evacuate somehow for a set amount of time?"

"I don't think so."

Kanno resisted strongly.

"Even if we did evacuate, no place is going to accept residents from a municipality evacuating this late in the game."

"There's a place in Nagano Prefecture that says it's willing to accept five hundred people."

Fukuyama read off a list of places and the numbers they were willing to accept.

Kanno said, "Thank you for having looked into it. I'm grateful, but I decline."

When he returned from Tokyo, Kanno instructed the village officials, "I don't care where, but look for a place about an hour from here."

Even if they were to evacuate, he wanted to evacuate to a place where it was still possible for people to commute to work and school. That was how he would protect the livelihoods of the villagers. Evacuating to Nagano or other prefectures was out of the question. All he had in mind was "protecting the village."

On April 10, the Nuclear Safety Commission held a special meeting. The NSC decided in this meeting to advise the government to amend the "voluntary evacuation" and to establish a "planned evacuation area."

On this day, Kanno received a phone call from Fukuyama: "I'd like to meet in Fukushima City."

Kanno replied, "Let's meet at the official residence of the Fukushima governor, so the media doesn't get wind of it."

In the evening, Kanno went to the governor's residence with the deputy mayor and the head of the village council, and met with Fukuyama, Matsushita, and Hosono in the presence of Governor Yuhei Sato. Matsushita was head of the local NERHQ.

Fukuyama handed out a map and a sheet of paper with the words "planned evacuation area." Fukuyama said in a matter-of-fact tone, "Accumulation of radioactive material released from the Fukushima Daiichi NPS is occurring locally, and we have identified areas where the integral dose is high. If people continue to live in these areas, there is a possibility that the integral dose will become even higher."

Evacuation measures were now required not for one-off radiation exposure, but to avoid cumulative radiation exposure. The whole village of Iitate had been designated as an area of high radiation dose. Unfortunately, it had to be regarded as a planned evacuation area. He conveyed that the "whole village has to be evacuated."

Kanno had been prepared for part of the village being specified in the evacuation area, but had never dreamed of the entire village having to be evacuated. He appealed to Fukuyama for two things.

The first was that Iitate would "absolutely not be made into a ghost town." The second was, if the government was going to use the word "planned," then the government would also have to "plan" on the logistics of the evacuation, not just the timeframe.

"How can we balance the risk of radiation and the risk of changing our lives? Of course, the risk of radiation is much greater. Much greater, but how can we balance it out?" Kanno said, asking the government to provide support to prevent any increase in the risk of changing lives.

Next, Kanno tackled Fukuyama, asking, "Why have you reduced it to 20 millisieverts despite many scholars saying it's safe at 100 millisieverts?"

On the following day, April 11, Edano announced his "concepts" on the establishment of a planned evacuation area:

- The area within a twenty-kilometer radius of Fukushima Daiichi NPS was designated a restricted area

- Outside that area, all or part of five municipalities throughout Fukushima Prefecture with possible integral doses of up to 20 millisieverts/year were designated planned evacuation areas

- Areas outside the twenty- to thirty-kilometer radius from the plant, and not designated as planned evacuation areas, were to be designated emergency evacuation preparation areas.

The restricted area was an off-limit zone. It was legally binding, and violators would be fined. In the planned evacuation area, it was a requirement to "plan an evacuation to another location" within "about one month." It was an area where the residents were urged to "evacuate by all means." In the emergency evacuation preparation areas, it was required to "make the necessary preparations to be always ready to evacuate or shelter indoors in the event of an emergency," with "voluntary evacuation" being requested. It was an area where the residents were urged to "evacuate if possible."[32]

All of the villages of Katsurao, Namie, and Iitate, and part of the town of Kawamata and the city of Minamisoma, were included in the planned evacuation area. The number of places with high radiation doses was spreading beyond the thirty-kilometer zone, making a radial evacuation plan no longer sustainable.

But what was to be done about the places under 20 millisieverts? There were two districts in the Kawamata area that were under 20 millisieverts. There was a place in the southern section of Katsurao Village that was also low. How should these districts be handled? Should they be included or exempted from the planned evacuation area? Hirose, Ito, and Fukano stewed over these issues.[33]

And it was Matsushita who was charged with explaining the "concepts" to the relevant municipalities and persuading them. His family business was dairy farming, and he was the proud owner of Hirashigekatsu cows, which were Satsuma black-haired cattle of the highest grade.

Matsushita belonged to the People's New Party (PNP), which had formed a coalition with the Democratic Party. He had been elected from Kagoshima Prefecture, and as Matsushita himself was fond of saying, "The Sendai Nuclear Power Station is right on my doorstep." The parliamentary officers at the Kantei strove to keep Matsushita away from sensitive issues.

They were wary of information being leaked to party leader Shizuka Kamei (PNP, Hiroshima). They did, however, think very highly of Matsushita's practical skills. Matsushita was good at "pulling the emotional heart-strings," which was the weak point of the Democratic Party eggheads.[34]

After Motohisa Ikeda handed him the baton as head of the local NERHQ, Matsushita had diligently gone around all of the municipalities related to the nuclear disaster.

On March 26, he went to Minamisoma and met with Mayor Katsunobu Sakurai. The government had just announced the "voluntary evacuation" instructions for residents within the twenty- to thirty-kilometer zone the day before.

Sakurai asked him, "I'd like you to explain what on earth is happening at the reactors. I can understand residents within twenty kilometers being ordered to evacuate, but not this voluntary evacuation for the twenty- to thirty-kilometer zone. Are things so bad, so inevitable that evacuation is a must?"

Matsushita replied, "To be honest, I don't know the state of the reactors. They're in the process of cooling them now. But we just don't know what may happen. What would you do if there was an explosion and we didn't have the twenty- to thirty-kilometers evacuation plan in place?"

But Sakurai could not assent.

"We've got 78,000 residents here. We're not like other places. The numbers are bigger. And we've got the whole lot, some within twenty kilometers, some in the twenty- to thirty-kilometer zone, and some beyond the thirty-kilometer line. If we carry out the voluntary evacuation, as we're told, we'll lose four-fifths of our population. The town will collapse if we do something like that."

Matsushita did not back down.

"Look, I'm begging you. I'd like you to make an evacuation plan. I'd like you to find a place you can escape to, just in case. The government will help, we'll send you the manpower, too."

Sakurai had been listening hard; he spread out the map and diagrams on the table.

Has he finally opened his heart?

Matsushita wept.

I've never seen anyone so passionate.

Sakurai's eyes welled up as well when he saw Matsushita's tears. They wept together thinking of the town's misfortune. Matsushita was firmly convinced:

If Minamisoma toes the line, so will all of Fukushima.[35]

Prior to the chief cabinet secretary's press conference on April 11, Matsushita spent four days—April 7, 8, 10, and 11—making the rounds to all of the municipalities that had been designated either as planned evacuation areas or emergency evacuation preparation areas. He would leave his accommodation at six in the morning, returning at eleven at night. He went around in rubber boots.[36]

As well as visiting the municipalities that were to evacuate, he also went around all the municipalities that had taken in evacuees, asking for their understanding.

A senior official at METI, who had helped Matsushita, recalled, "Fukushima Prefecture was running every which way to avoid having to explain the planned evacuation area to residents. Matsushita-san shouldered it all and went to every municipality, one by one. As for the prefecture, their attitude was, we don't care as long as the municipalities are convinced. You know, I thought at the time, why do we need prefectures? The basic unit of local government is more than enough."[37]

APRIL 13. Kanno explained about the evacuation to residents in the junior high school gymnasium in the Nagadoro District, which had the highest radiation dose in Iitate. He had to persuade the residents to evacuate.

Just at that time, Kanno's mobile phone rang. It was one of his political supporters.

"It seems like Kan said something about not being able to come back for about twenty years. He shouldn't be allowed to get away with that. Mr. Mayor, you have to get angry."

Kanno told the residents at Nagadoro the information, tears falling from his eyes just as he said, "I don't know if this information's correct or not. But if he did say it, I don't think it's something that the top leader of Japan, the person who is responsible for all the people in the country, should say at this particular time. It breaks my heart."[38]

On April 16, Fukuyama and his group went to Iitate again to attend a residents' briefing. At the outset, one of the residents challenged Fukuyama.

"Can you breathe deeply here now?"

His words sounded to Fukuyama like a *cri de coeur*.[39]

On April 22, the government officially decided on and announced the planned evacuation area. The planned evacuation area covered ten thousand people, and the emergency evacuation preparation area sixty thousand people.[40]

Even after everyone had evacuated, Hiroshi Tada, chief priest at the Watatsumi Shrine in Iitate, remained at the shrine. Although the thought did cross his mind, *I wonder if I'm breaking the law?* he resolved to deal with that when the time came.

He decided to take his ninety-year-old mother to his married brother, who lived in Yaizu, Shizuoka Prefecture, where they could take care of her. His wife and younger son evacuated to Fukushima City, and his elder son to Soma. After all of these arrangements had been made, Tada vowed to himself that he would remain at the shrine. He thought this was his duty to his 1,200 parishioner households. The entire village had evacuated, but villagers would come back to work with dosimeters hanging around their necks, or to tend their homes and graves.

Sometimes he would receive unexpected requests, such as, "I need to have a tree felled. Could you do the blessing?"

There was even a parishioner who came all the way from his place of evacuation in Hamamatsu City with his seven-year-old daughter to pay their respects for the rites of passage Seven-Five-Three Festival, when three- and seven-year-old girls and five-year-old boys on November 15 mark the milestone of their growth by dressing in kimono and visiting shrines.

Conversations began with, "And where have you evacuated to?" Villagers who had come back would drop by the shrine and say, "What a relief you're still here."[41]

"DON'T WAKE A SLEEPING CHILD"

Hirose was appointed cabinet office adviser on March 28. Madarame held a regular meeting of the Nuclear Safety Commission every Monday. He mentioned there that Hirose had been appointed "to liaise between the NSC and the Kantei."

"He will be in charge of all communication with the Kantei."

The commissioners all remained silent.

That day, Hirose bounded into the NSC on the sixth floor of the cabinet office with an aide in tow, dressed in METI's disaster fatigues. His position was that of adviser to NISA.

When he entered the secretary general's room, he opened up his computer and began to work silently.

Hirose was a graduate of Kyushu University. He had joined the Science and Technology Agency as a technical officer in 1974, obtaining a doctorate in nuclear engineering from Kyoto University during his time there. His 1998 thesis was titled "The Current Status and Challenges of Nuclear Insurance Programs Around the World."

He had been the nuclear safety section chief at the Science and Technology Agency during the 1999 JCO criticality accident in Tokaimura, Ibaraki Prefecture. Blamed for the way it was handled, he left the agency. He later served as secretary general of the NSC and director general of NISA.

In his first meeting with the commissioners in the chairman's office, Hirose sat at the table without an invitation. The meeting was attended by the five commissioners, four managers, and the secretary general. Secretary General Akihiko Iwahashi was sitting in a reserved manner on a small chair in the lowliest position by the door. It was one of those folding pipe chairs that you see in high school gyms.

When the meeting commenced, Hirose declared, "I'm running the commission from now on. I'll serve as the conduit to the Kantei. I'd like you to consider what I say as the opinion of the Kantei."

One of the commissioners thought disagreeably, *He didn't have to say he was running the show.*

Since April 11, members of the advisory team, such as Toshimitsu Homma, deputy director of the Nuclear Safety Research Center at JAEA, who had been working at the round table in front of the chairman's office, were told by staff from the secretariat, "I'm sorry, but could you clear this space?" and had been shunted over to the large office. The explanation they were given was that Hirose and his staff would be using that space.

After the meeting, Hirose immediately began giving instructions to the secretariat. In the evening, he said, "Well, I'm off to METI now," changed back into his METI disaster fatigues, and headed off.

"Where the hell did he come from? Who does he think he's representing?"

Disgruntlement and anxiety were swirling all around. At one point, Hirose phoned Commissioner Shizuyo Kusumi about the planned evacuation area. Kusumi, who could not stand Hirose's longwinded pedantry, yelled at him, "Just tell me what do you want to do?!"

Hirose was despised by everyone. After he started "running the show," the commission became just a "rubber stamp" for whatever the Kantei decided.

In setting the planned evacuation area, NSC staff holed up in the Integrated Response Office at TEPCO started faxing the gist of Hosono's and Hirose's comments to the secretariat with a request "to draw up advice on this."

"We've become nothing more than a rubber stamp, haven't we?"

Sighs escaped from the secretariat staff.

However, it is also true that Hirose's entrance smoothed the relationship between the Kantei and the NSC. He exercised almost excruciating care with the parliamentary members of the Kantei, especially Fukuyama and Edano.

A member of the NSC staff accompanied Hirose on a visit to Edano in the chief cabinet secretary's office. Learning that Edano was not there, Hirose sat on the floor in traditional Japanese style, then lay facedown and wrote a letter to Edano.

After he finished writing, he handed the letter and some reference material to the secretary in the chief cabinet secretary's office.

"Well, then, let's go home."

With those words, Hirose left the room.

Fukuyama, Edano, and Hosono all trusted Hirose. Fukuyama said, "Up until then, the safety commission was in a bind with problems from ministries like MEXT, MAFF, and MHLW, and nothing being decided," but after Hirose got there, "they understood what we wanted, what was expected of the commission, and did the job to match."[42]

The commissioners and executive officers at the NSC had not forgotten "a certain incident" that had taken place between them and METI's NISA some five years earlier. They were still carrying around the bitter thought that they had been badly let down by the NISA director general at the time. That NISA director general was Hirose.

In March 2006, the commission had started looking into reviewing the existing EPZ (emergency planning zones requiring priority measures) in response to the IAEA's proposal, made in November of the preceding year, that they were going to introduce new guidelines for nuclear emergency measures.

The new IAEA guidelines were to carry out immediate evacuation in the event of radioactive contamination and expand the evacuation area. The commission's disaster management guidelines stipulated the EPZ as "a radius of eight to ten kilometers from the reactor." If the new IAEA guidelines were introduced, Japan's EPZ would be insufficient.

As it was necessary to bring Japanese nuclear disaster prevention plans to global standards and guidelines, the commission began considering a modification. Kusumi was especially passionate in advocating the need to keep Japanese safety regulations close to international standards. She proposed "immediate evacuation" in the case of an emergency, and expanding the evacuation zone to thirty kilometers.

There is a reason why Japanese disaster guidelines stipulate resident evacuation at "eight to ten kilometers." In the first place, if an accident happens, any iodine or noble gas that was released from the reactor into the containment vessel would only be discharged externally through a leakage mechanism, and no consideration was given to the situation of damage to the containment vessel or venting. A Level 5 (Three Mile Island–level) event was assumed. The reactor construction permit guidelines also used the same assumption.

In short, the discharge rate was calculated assuming that the containment vessel was sound, that there would be no damage to the containment vessel, and the evacuation plans and training programs used this as their basis. Any enlargement would challenge this assumption.

NISA counterattacked the commission with a vengeance.

In April of the same year, NISA filed a "proposition [memorandum]" with the commission:

"Since considering new nuclear disaster prevention guidelines using IAEA concepts . . . will trigger social confusion, increasing public anxiety about nuclear safety, in turn, we would like you to cease all consideration of this matter."

For the EPZ to meet the new IAEA guidelines, local residents and areas with nuclear facilities would have had to be convinced about relocating off-site centers and immediate evacuation. To do so was akin to professing that the current EPZ framework of disaster prevention measures was inadequate, which was impermissible. That was the point NISA was trying to make.

In fact, the Japanese government had lobbied behind the scenes to have the "five kilometers" added to the new IAEA guidelines of "five to thirty kilometers." If they could get "five kilometers" added, they would not have to change the Japanese EPZs and they could claim that the Japanese EPZ met international standards.[43]

Why was the safety commission starting to "consider" such a thing anyway?

"We are forced to say that the failure to thoroughly confirm the opinion and approach of this agency [NISA] and to unilaterally begin considering the amendment of disaster guidelines amounts to a highly regrettable oversight on the part of the honorable division."

The "honorable division" referred to here was the commission's Management Environment Division. By using this phrase, NISA had thrown down the gauntlet.

In May 2006, NISA approached the commission about exchanging views over lunch. The commission accepted. The lunch was arranged for May 24 of the same year. Immediately prior to it, NISA held an executive meeting at the agency. Besides Hirose, Deputy Director General Nobuaki Terasaka, and both deputy directors, Shin Aoyama and Kiyoharu Abe, were also in attendance. Abe was the deputy director at NISA for international affairs.

The day before, Abe had received an e-mail from Hidehiko Nishiyama from NISA's Planning and Coordination Division. The gist of it was, "I'd appreciate a brief list of possible topics on the disaster prevention guidelines" for the lunch.

On the morning of May 24, Abe responded to Nishiyama's e-mail, writing that he, Abe, had made the following report to the NSC about the emergency response safety guide approved at the November meeting of the IAEA the previous year.

"It is expected in the future that Japanese emergency response will conform to international standards using this guide as a reference."

Abe wrote in his e-mail to Nishiyama, "Given these circumstances, I think this revision is highly desirable."

At the executive meeting, Abe reiterated this point, but drew a strong rebuttal of "we don't necessarily have to comply [with international standards]." By way of supporting this objection, Hirose stated, "Disaster prevention guidelines are of a highly social nature and should take into account factors in each country," then handed down his decision that "the current system should be kept as is for at least ten years."

Given that "in the first place, the NSC's relationship with local government is poor and it's an advisory body," Hirose instructed his executives that NISA should take the initiative in breaking this impasse.

If only because Abe had just the day before asserted a "review from the stance of egging the commission on," he was both surprised and puzzled by Hirose's quick decision to "deny the review."

During the lunch, Kusumi stuck to her position of reviewing disaster prevention guidelines in line with international standards. In response, Hirose stressed that local government disaster prevention systems had been put in place following the JCO criticality accident. He countered Kusumi forcefully:

"Now that the public is finally reassured, don't wake a sleeping child."

Since the lunch meeting took place at "the dining table," no minutes were taken. Kusumi was later convinced that *They only invited us to lunch from the outset so there would be no minutes*, but at the time it did not occur to her that this was their intention. To use Kusumi's expression, the "let's have lunch" was nothing less than a NISA "raid."

In a meeting between the commission and NISA the next month, the NISA officers requested of the commission's Management Environment Division that "Since the reaction and response of the honorable division, which can only be interpreted as misplaced anger, is a waste of time and effort, we'd like to avoid that in the future," and urged them to "make efforts that are sufficiently convincing to us."

Why did NISA intimidate the commission to such an extent? It has been interpreted as being out of concern that the "plutonium-thermal project would not go ahead" if the EPZ was expanded.

This was a plan scheduled to start in 1999, but had been delayed significantly by a data tampering scandal at British Nuclear Fuels Limited (BNFL) and a cover-up at TEPCO. Things had finally quieted down, and from September 2005 to March 2006, plutonium-thermal project power generation had just been permitted at Unit 3 of the Kyushu Electric Genkai NPS and Unit 3 of the Shikoku Electric Power Ikata NPS.

If the EPZ was extended at such a time, it would create a sense of insecurity among residents that the nuclear power plants were dangerous, after all. Furthermore, NISA was alarmed that the plutonium-thermal project might be stopped. Because Japan had fallen behind in completing the nuclear fuel cycle through the late 1990s to the 2000s, plutonium, which was recovered from spent-fuel pools, had accumulated. This drove Japan to be in conflict as a non–nuclear weapons state with the international pledge of "do not hold surplus plutonium." For that reason, the government has been in a situation in which it has been trying to change its policy direction toward "pluthermal" light water reactors, which burn mixed oxide (MOX) fuel—namely, plutonium blended with uranium.[44]

After the Fukushima Daiichi NPS accident, the NSC commissioners and staff members ruefully acknowledged that "We should have expanded the EPZ then." In late April, Hirose told Hosono that he wanted to resign as cabinet office adviser.

"I think the situation has settled down. It's about time I got back to my original job . . . I seem to have also lost the trust of all the commissioners . . . there's nowhere for me there, I don't even have a desk."

Hosono accepted.

The NSC secretariat had not set up an office for Hirose. As a consequence, METI provided him with an office, and Hirose commuted to the Kantei and the NSC from there.[45]

SIXTEEN

Castle Lost in a Day

"It is just like the Battle of Guadalcanal."

In times of crisis, one missing screw or piece of the puzzle, no matter how small, can be fatal. In the case of the Fukushima Daiichi nuclear accident, it was the batteries, which can usually be found all over the place, that were in short supply.

SOMETIME AFTER SEVEN A.M., MARCH 13. The Fukushima Daiichi ERC. A member of the procurement group of TEPCO made a "request" to employees who commuted to the plant by car:

"Excuse me. Those car batteries I just talked about borrowing, I think we'll need them to ensure a power supply to Unit 2."

In order to get the water indicator and other instrumentation back online, they needed to restore power via batteries or small generators, but Fukushima Daiichi's NPS had nothing like this prepared at all.

A shout of "Ten! Ten!" was heard from behind. "We need ten batteries for the time being."

After a short time, an urgent voice broke in.

"Sorry, four more. We need four more batteries for Unit 2's SR valve. Can someone lend us their battery? Oh, but you'll have to remove it yourself . . ."

However, even if the batteries from the workers' cars were gathered together, it would be nothing more than a temporary measure.

"This is the procurement group. Sorry. We're leaving now to buy some batteries. We don't have enough cash. Can any of you who have some cash to spare, please lend it to us? Excuse me. Sorry, but if you have some cash, would you lend it to us?"

There was cash in the safe in the main office building. However, the ceiling there had collapsed during the earthquake, and entry and exit had been banned at the time.

Akio Komori, managing director at Tokyo's Head Office, who heard this exchange via videoconference, called out, "Is there anyone flying to Fukushima by helicopter today?"[1]

If there was a helicopter flying that day, shouldn't they be giving the visitors batteries, not cash?

Didn't they have any staff there capable of looking at the big picture and putting together a game plan?

Later, many people watching this videoconference were wondering exactly that. However, at that time, no one at the Head Office posed this question.

Yoshida was frequently at loggerheads with the Head Office. Much of it was about responding to the accident, supplying and replenishing manpower and supplies, and managing the radiation exposure of the workers as well as doing something to improve their living conditions.

Among these issues was a decisive shortage of manpower. Moreover, there was hardly any supplementation. On March 11, 256 people had hurried to their assistance, but no one came after them.[2] Some of the onsite staff had been rushed off their feet without a moment's sleep for thirty-six hours after the accident; there were even some sitting on chairs on the verge of losing consciousness.[3] But no support troops arrived.

On the afternoon of March 14, forty-nine staff from Kashiwazaki-Kariwa NPS, eight from the Engineering Department, and five from the Head Office arrived, sixty-two in total. The Engineering Department was in charge of maintenance for transmission lines, and so on, and did not deal with nuclear power itself.[4]

This amounted to a "sequential input of troops." Except they were not really troops. This was because, as one of the executives of an associate company said, "They had no troops. There was a decisive shortage of nuclear plant 'techies,' operators who actually did the work onsite. They had no troops. The nuclear plant [sector] folk at the Head Office would have only been in the way, even if they had gone. There was a gaping hole at the bottom of the pyramid. Even if they went from the Head Office, it wouldn't fill up the gaps at the bottom, only make it top-heavy, ending up with an inverted triangle."[5]

The fact that Fukushima Daiichi NPS itself was inside the evacuation zone complicated logistics. In the early hours of March 13, when the situation at Unit 3 was becoming critical, there was a running exchange on the videoconference connecting the Head Office and the ERC in the Anti-Seismic Building over who and how they would deliver the necessary material. Trucks could not enter the evacuation zone, they could not find any drivers, they needed to be trained before they came on site or there would be trouble, and nothing was being decided.

Yoshida said, "If the people bringing the stuff are saying they don't want to come on site, we'll just have to create a rule for a delivery pickup outside. Decide the place, and the site will be responsible for bringing it in.

"Nothing can be done, nothing, nothing. It's already set. Saying you will do it is the most important thing. Because thoroughly abiding by the rules is the most important . . . I asked yesterday, I need a favor, we don't have enough gasoline. Or water. We will take all the gas, water, and light oil we can get. Could you supply us with gasoline as a matter of urgency?"[6]

Faced with the managers at the Head Office repeatedly replying to his requests by making excuses that they "could not" or "that is difficult," Yoshida yelled more than a few times.

"Give me a break, Head Office. We're putting our lives on the line over here.

"You tell the field to do this and to do that, but we only have limited staff and we can't do everything. Send us some people from the Head Office."[7]

On listening to the exchanges, Makio Miyagawa, director general of the Disarmament, Non-Proliferation, and Science Department in the Ministry for Foreign Affairs, who was holed up at the Integrated Response Office, thought, *It's just like Guadalcanal.*[8]

The Battle of Guadalcanal in the Solomon Islands of the Western Pacific was one of the hardest-fought battles of the Pacific War. As a result of the desperate struggle waged from August 1942 until February of the following year, Japanese troops were defeated, and along with the Battle of Midway, it became a turning point in the Pacific War. It was considered a classic example of battle by attrition and the logistical blunder of "sequential input of troops."

Hosono had also made a tearful appeal to the TEPCO executives lined up in a row at the Integrated Response Office after watching one such exchange on the videoconference.

"What are you, guys? What kind of response is this? They're your buddies working desperately over there! You know their faces, don't you?"[9]

Another serious issue was the increase in the dose employees were exposed to. In the morning of March 14, Unit 3 (RB) exploded. Around 1:30 in the afternoon of the same day, as the radiation dose continued to rise, Yoshida told the Head Office, "The two explosions, Units 1 and 3, have made the exposure skyrocket, so I ask for your consideration."

TEPCO President Masataka Shimizu merely replied, "Do your best to hold out."[10]

Around 10:20 p.m. on March 14, a report was made to Yoshida in Fukushima Daiichi's Emergency Response Center (ERC), in a monotonous, businesslike tone:

"The measurement results at the front gate at 21:37, 3.2 millisieverts per hour of gamma rays."

Yoshida raised his voice.

"Wait, wait a minute. That's 3.2 millisieverts? If that's milli, then it is 3,000 when converted to micro?"

TEPCO Vice President Sakae Muto, who was watching the videoconference at the Head Office, whispered, "That's awful."[11]

The lack of personnel and radiation protection equipment was a serious hindrance, especially in the early stages of the accident response. The majority of protective equipment and personal alarm dosimeters (APD) had been washed away by the tsunami. Fukushima Daiichi NPS had enough support for the minimum emergency response organization, which was approximately fifty people, and more than five hundred people were involved in the initial response.[12]

Before the accident, the maximum allowed dose was 100 millisievert/year for all workers. At the request of TEPCO, the government raised this to 250 millisievert/year. Before then, the operators could not access the containment vessel vent valve due to this provision, and even after it was raised, it was not well communicated to the workers.[13]

From March 13, there was stable iodine in the Anti-Seismic Building, which was distributed to workers at Fukushima Daiichi. In one day, one or two doses were handed over, and there were those who took it every day. The worker who took the most had had eighty-seven doses of stable iodine.[14]

On March 18, as they were going ahead with restoring power for the cooling of the fuel pool, Yoshida had it out with the Head Office over personnel.

"All of my staff have been working around the clock for eight days. And they're going all over the site. They're pumping in water, running checks, putting out fires, and checking the oil regularly. With all this, I can't let them undergo any more exposure.

"I only have staff members whose exposure is already close to 200 millisieverts, or over 200. I can't tell them to go out into the field and lay wire in such high-dose areas."

Muto replied, "We're currently soliciting a wide range of people, including OBs, and we'll know by tomorrow morning how many people we can send you."[15]

Yoshida warned the Head Office more than once about the risk of worker exposure to large amounts of radiation. It was Yoshihiro Yamaguchi of the School of Emergency, Faculty of Medicine at Kyorin University, who accompanied the Hyper Rescue squad and became aware of this.

The medical team leader at Daiichi told Yamaguchi, "We don't need any manuals or leaders. All we want is a doctor who can tell us, when a staff member falls over, whether we can just put them on a drip here or if they have to be removed immediately from the site."

Yamaguchi fully realized that they were engaged in a real sword fight out in the field. With the exception of one person, all of the industrial physicians active at Daiichi NPS were like a Foreign Legion mobilized from Japan Nuclear Fuel, Mitsubishi Heavy Industries, and Kansai Electric Power. Without a space of their own, or a place even to lie down and rest, they had spent several days inside.

They repeatedly asked the TEPCO Head Office for more people, but the industrial physicians under contract to TEPCO and the doctors working at TEPCO's hospital maintained that their job was "the medical care [health management] of TEPCO employees during non-emergency times" and did not respond to the request.

Yamaguchi complained about this by e-mail to senior doctors at the Japanese Association for Acute Medicine.[16]

Yoshida visited TEPCO's Head Office for the first time after the accident on Sunday, March 27, 2011. He had a private meeting with Kaieda. Kaieda drew Yoshida out by saying, "I want you to speak frankly about what you want to say, even if it is about the government or TEPCO."

Yoshida replied frankly.

"The Anti-Seismic Building could resist the earthquake, but it was totally inadequate to resist radiation. Please get work done to heighten the shielding and sealing of the Anti-Seismic Buildings immediately. I also want them to have the ability to eliminate iodine."[17]

On March 30, he urged, "Out of the workers, nineteen people were exposed to over 100 millisieverts. There were many reserves. Decisions need to be made about handling required personnel in the future."[18]

Similar exchanges took place throughout 2011. The radiation exposure of nine workers who went into Unit 3 (RB) to investigate climbed above the 5 millisieverts originally expected.

Yoshida said, "The radiation dose was high, so we took care not to go over 5 millisieverts, but we went over. Overall, the Head Office were sloppy in managing the radiation dosages, I want it to be done properly."

The Head Office replied, "The plan was too naïve, management was loose, hence we plan to do it thoroughly" (June 10, 2011).

The Japanese robot Quince investigated the amount of radiation inside Unit 2 (RB). Participants at a meeting came out strongly against a report that suggested workers could probably carry out operations in some places that had registered 11 millisieverts per hour.

"It's no good at all thinking that 11 millisieverts is low. Sending workers out into the field from the Anti-Seismic Building is like sending out kamikaze pilots. We don't have too many Zero Fighters [legendary Japanese pilots who engaged in aerial dogfights with the United States during the Pacific War] left. We can't use kamikaze pilots forever. I'd like you once again to take a firm hold of the facts."

Quince's communications failed halfway through, and it ended up being left behind at Unit 3 (RB).[19]

It was the U.S. government that took this problem seriously from the start. It was the first thing the manager of NRC's Japan Site Support, Charles Casto, pointed out to headquarters after arriving in Japan. On March 16, the NRC's staff in Tokyo warned Washington headquarters via conference call:

"There aren't enough people. Doing something about it is the priority."

"One operator was looking over this: four reactors and six fuel pools. It exceeded their capability. It totally surpassed TEPCO's capability."[20]

> *NRC Staff:* "TEPCO is overwhelmed. People had left the site earlier, but they have been supplemented with additional people now. Our understanding is they had about fifty before and maybe up to about a hundred now."[21]

At one stage, Yoshida appeared in the videoconference wearing sunglasses, saying, "I'm having trouble with my eyesight."

Yoshida was pleading desperately for pump trucks needed to inject water into Unit 2, but no one from the Head Office was responding. Yoshida exploded.

It was at times like these that he wore sunglasses and camouflage fatigues. When the people in the Tokyo ERC saw them, they knew he was on the warpath. Around this time, whenever someone wondered about the camouflage gear on Yoshida's chair, Yoshida would say, "Well, I'll probably have to go into combat mode."[22]

At the Head Office, the whisper went around that Yoshida was a dangerous person intent on opposing the Head Office. One of Hosono's staff pent up at the Integrated Response Office at TEPCO attests that "there were even people at the Head Office who said Yoshida had been exposed to radiation and lost his sanity."[23]

The fact that the Head Office was having trouble dealing with the Kantei also complicated the crisis response at the site. The chain of command between the Kantei, the site, and the Head Office was in a tangle. The clash between the Head Office and the "Kantei" (actually, TEPCO Fellow Ichiro Takekuro at the Kantei as TEPCO liaison) over the water injection into Unit 1 on the night of March 12 was a typical example.

In this case, while pretending to put an end to water injection, Yoshida, guessing the intentions of the Kantei, made a "Kabuki play," so to speak, and actually continued to pump seawater in (see chapter 4).

The exchange between the site and the Head Office over the fire trucks after three a.m. on March 14 also shows vividly the lack of crisis response at the Head Office.

> TEPCO *Fellow Akio Takahashi:* "We transported four fire trucks arranged by the Kantei to 1F, but you're not using them yet. Could you tell us why you're not using them? We have to give the reason to the Kantei."
>
> *Fukushima Daiichi:* "We received two of them yesterday."
>
> *Takahashi:* "And the remaining two vehicles? I am very sorry to have to talk about all these trifling things, but it's to satisfy the Kantei. We want you to bring the two fire trucks at the offsite center to the site and put them to some use."
>
> *Yoshida:* "Basically, we don't have enough manpower. Even if we get these things, we don't have personnel to handle them. People from Nanmei are not around. On top of that, there are the radiation worries."[24]

What this depicts is the Head Office trying to force the site to toe the line on what Takekuro had sniffed out as "the feeling upstairs [a.k.a., the Kantei]."

Later, in the Diet Investigation Commission hearings, Yoshida confessed about the serious dilemma he had at the site over pumping seawater into Unit 1, when the executive "chain of command was a real mess":

"The chain of command is, for example, like this. If the Head Office tells us to stop, then we can discuss it, but when you actually get someone telephoning from the Kantei, who has nothing to do with the command, you think, *What on earth is going on?* You can't sufficiently discuss things, because you're on the telephone. You're told to halt operations and not to argue about it.

"I told the staff that I wouldn't halt operations, and someone said that if it came from the Kantei, there was nothing we could do about it. But to cut a long story short, I thought this was ultimately my judgment at a time when everything was so dispersed and nobody knew what the chain of command actually was."[25]

Leaving the "chain of command in a real mess" in this way, the TEPCO Head Office kept putting the ball into the site's court. The result was that Yoshida was forced not only to deal with emergency response at the site, but to also take into consideration the political and management implications.[26]

Takeyuki Inagaki, who worked under Yoshida as the recovery team leader, recalls: "If it hadn't been him, anyone else would have been completely overloaded, enough to make them go crazy."[27]

KAIWO MARU

Somehow the living and working environment of workers at Fukushima Daiichi NPS had to be improved. Hosono consulted Kan sometime after entering the Integrated Response Office.

"Prime Minister, I'd like to ask a favor."

"What is it?"

"If we don't do something about the work environment for the TEPCO workers at Fukushima Daiichi NPS, they won't be able to keep working for long. But we can't use any of the inns or hotels in the area, because they're closed. So, I was thinking about sending in a ship."

Kan gave an immediate yes.[28]

Hosono phoned Yoshida to tell him they were sending a ship for them to use as living quarters for the workers. Yoshida thanked Hosono for the offer, but turned him down.

"There are many people who've evacuated because of the nuclear accident. You can't improve treatment at the site when they've been evacuated. Improving treatment of the evacuees should come first."

Hosono felt a bit caught off guard, but Yoshida was adamant. Yoshida also mentioned another concern.

"If Prime Minister Kan boarded the ship, it'd be on TV, wouldn't it? I'd like you to make sure that never happens. If it's going to get out, we, any of the workers, won't go on board."[29]

It seemed this statement was in consideration of the fact that Kan's visit to the site in relation to Unit 1 venting on the morning of March 12 had become a political issue. Hosono promised Yoshida "that won't happen."

On March 19, Hosono got in touch with Shiro Yamazaki, Kan's secretary, to look for a ship. As a result, it was decided to send the *Kaiwo Maru*, a tall-ship training vessel for merchant marine cadets, owned by the National Institute for Sea Training under the jurisdiction of the Ministry of Land, Infrastructure, and Transport, to the port of Onahama as soon as possible, as support for both evacuees and TEPCO staff.[30]

Onahama Port was situated sixty kilometers from Fukushima Daiichi NPS. Around nine a.m. on March 21, the *Kaiwo Maru* arrived at Ohtsurugi Pier in Onahama Port. There were fifty-one crew on board, including Captain Shigetoshi Kai. Its tonnage was 2,500 tons.

The strategy was twofold: providing accommodation for the Fukushima Daiichi NPS workers and acting as a soup kitchen and bath facility for evacuees at elementary and junior high schools in Onahama City. It was nerve-wracking, if only because it was providing support to both evacuees and TEPCO employees. This felt like "assisting both the victims and the perpetrators in the same place at the same time," said Captain Kai.

They devised a schedule to avoid the two parties coming into contact.[31]

The TEPCO workers were exhausted. Some were so debilitated they were unable to climb the ramp to board the ship. Some were even "working with a drip"—managing their tasks while being sustained by an intravenous drip. They had their first real meal in ten days. They ate salad and fruit, sighing, "I'm so grateful" and "It's delicious."

It was especially after a bath that everyone perked up. They were given kits, each containing shampoo, toothpaste, a razor, and a towel. Charging mobile phones and dropping a line to families on postcards of the *Kaiwo Maru* were popular activities.

The *Kaiwo Maru* could accommodate a hundred people. Six to eight people to a room slept in bunk beds. Most would arrive before eight in the evening, spend the night, and head out at six the next morning. On their way back to Fukushima Daiichi NPS in the early morning, the crew would send them off with a round of applause as they disembarked.

After disembarking, they would turn back, gaze at the white sails of the tall ship, then get in their cars. Looking back later, Kai said, "I think the sails of the tall ship lightened their hearts a bit."

The workers would arrive in groups of six or seven to a van, undergoing decontamination at J-Village and then again at Onahama Coal Center before arriving at the wharf. Everyone had their dose measured before boarding. There was only one person who was not allowed to board due to the severe contamination of his hair.[32]

The *Kaiwo Maru* sailed out of Onahama Port on March 28, heading for Tokyo Bay. During its time in port, 180 TEPCO employees had stayed on board.

The *Kaiwo Maru* was due to set sail on a long voyage to Hawaii, in April, with cadets on board. There was talk that the U.S. port authorities were extremely nervous about port calls by ships from Japan. After drawing up alongside the Ariake Pier in Tokyo Bay, they immediately asked radiation protection officers from TEPCO to sweep for the radiation dose everywhere, starting with the cabins. They also had them issue a certificate in English stating "zero radioactive contamination."

However, there was a concern that a "certificate" issued by TEPCO would not be trusted by the U.S. port authorities. So they also requested that the Nippon Kaiji Kentei Kyokai (Japanese Marine Survey Association) measure the radiation dose and issue the results as a "survey report." During Japan's May holidays, the *Kaiwo Maru* arrived in Hawaii. The screening was thorough, and all the crew was able to disembark.[33]

Sometime later, a weekly magazine ran a critical article with a photo of the Fukushima Daiichi NPS onsite workers "sleeping on the floor," which may have added to the U.S. government's attention to this problem.

Casto contacted Hosono to tell him of his "grave concerns."

"You really need to address the dormitory issue. I can't understand why nothing's being done. There's nowhere near enough consideration for those onsite . . . If this was America, we would be taking more care of onsite."

They were going to have to mobilize thousands of people for a long time. It was a drawn-out battle. Did the Japanese side not have such a long-term perspective? That was how Casto felt.[34]

When Casto met Yoshida, his first question was, "Are the workers sleeping properly?" Yoshida did not explain to him why they were not paying more heed to the workers' needs, although he did explain it to Hosono. Hosono thought Casto was right to be concerned, but told him directly Yoshida's words:

"There are people who have been forced to evacuate because of the nuclear power plant accident. When I think of them living hand-to-mouth, how can we eat our fill? You can't just improve treatment of the onsite workers. Improving treatment of the evacuees should come first."

After taking a deep breath, Hosono said, "That's what Yoshida-san told me."

On hearing this, Casto was at a loss for words. After a short silence, he muttered, "I guess it's a cultural difference . . ."[35]

At a meeting of the Joint Coordination Group, which had been launched on March 22, several times the U.S. side asked the Japanese side about "working conditions" at Fukushima Daiichi NPS.

When one of the Japanese said, "Given the feelings of the evacuees, we can't let the TEPCO workers get too comfortable," the U.S. side preached the importance of " 'a nuclear safety culture' in the nuclear power business as a lesson from Three Mile Island, and that the safety of the workers at the plant, too, was an important requirement."[36]

In mid-April, Hosono once again phoned Yoshida. "I'd like you to improve conditions for the workers. Please."

Yoshida was also convinced. He tried to improve conditions by bringing in beds and opening up J-Village. At a press conference on April 25, Hosono mentioned for the first time, "The local TEPCO workers are making great efforts."

Up until then, it was not the atmosphere in which such a statement could be made.[37]

CONTAMINATED WATER RELEASED INTO THE SEA

On March 24, three workers from TEPCO's associate firms, who had been working to install a power cable in the basement of the turbine building for Unit 3, suffered radiation exposure after standing in a puddle of water.

Water that had come in contact with the molten fuel from the containment vessels and pressure vessels of Units 1, 2, and 3 must have leaked into the turbine building by some route or other. A considerable amount of contaminated water must have accumulated there. Treating this contaminated water became a major problem.[38]

Pumping water into the reactor from the pipes started from March 12. Although there were some people at the NSC and NISA who wondered where on earth the water being pumped in and drained out had gone, no one questioned TEPCO on this point. The safety regulatory authorities did not know what was going on with the contaminated water.

On March 27, a report came in from the Fukushima Daiichi NPS site. They said they had found out that the contaminated water had a high concentration of 1,000 millisieverts/hour.[39]

As if unable to hold back, Yoshida broached this subject via videoconference on March 30.

"We're just standing by. It's as if we're just waiting to die."

Saying it was "the biggest cause of my heart- and stomachache," Yoshida criticized the lackluster efforts of the Head Office.

"There's no sense of urgency in the efforts of the recovery team at the Head Office. I've been telling them all week that the water is the biggest problem. Aren't they going to do something about it?"

The site was carrying out patrols on the assumption that there was a possibility that contaminated water from Unit 2 would overflow via the underground tunnel and drains, but someone at the Head Office said over the videoconference, "We thought the place of the leak wasn't connected to the Unit 2 turbine building, and so we weren't thinking about that."[40]

Hosono hurriedly launched a contaminated water collection and treatment project team at the Integrated Response Office. Susumu Kawamata, general manager for nuclear quality and safety management, and Ichiro Takekuro, a TEPCO fellow, joined as members from TEPCO, and so did people from the NSC and NISA.

Around this time, Cabinet Secretariat Special Adviser Toshiso Kosako was consulted by Akira Omoto from the Japan Atomic Energy Commission, in the morning meeting of Hosono's advisory team, to the effect that "the contaminated water process is stalled. Can't you do something?"

Omoto believed that "in order to avoid a big risk, there was no choice but to take small risks," and had stated as much to the advisory team, but the politicians in Hosono's advisory team were not prepared to listen, saying, "No way," and so they were deadlocked.[41]

Omoto wanted a favor from Kosako here. From the outset, Kosako had thought there was no choice but to discharge the contaminated water into the ocean, but at the time TEPCO was negative, saying, "Upstairs says it's a no-go." When he asked, "Who is 'upstairs'?" he was told it was Takekuro. They said the only reason Takekuro was opposed was because "Kan would be mad if we did that."[42]

On April 1, the Integrated Response Office discussed the issue at its regular morning meeting. Busy with other matters, Hosono was quite late in attending the meeting. When he entered the room, the meeting was almost coming to an end. Lower House member Toshiro Ishii (Democratic Party, Hyogo) was sitting in the next seat. Ishii had been kept up in the Integration Response Office after Hosono asked him in as a helper.

Ishii said to Hosono, in a low voice, "They're saying they're going to release the water into the ocean, but do you think that's okay?"

"You say release the water from the storage space into the ocean?"

"Uh-huh."

That's what's been decided in my absence?

Hosono spoke in a forceful tone.

"An emergency release of the seawater in the underground storage space into the ocean is absolutely inconceivable."

The contaminated water collection and disposal project team had proposed in the meeting that the contaminated water in the underground storage space in the basement of the Radioactive Waste Building (Central RW) be released into the ocean, and the highly contaminated water that had accumulated in Units 1 through 3 be moved to the storage space.

TEPCO people had also decided among themselves to accept the proposal. However, with these words from Hosono, the ocean release plan was shelved.[43] Kan had conveyed to Hosono his wish, "Don't let any radioactive material out whatsoever."

Hosono cautioned the meeting.

"No intentional external release is permissible."[44]

VIDEOCONFERENCE, ELEVEN A.M., APRIL 2. "I have an urgent report."

Yoshida cleared his throat to speak.

"We currently have the worst situation of a leakage of highly contaminated seawater from the reactor."

His voice was high-pitched. The ERC at the TEPCO Head Office was abuzz.

On receiving a report the previous evening, which stated that there was a pit where the radiation dose was high, they had measured the radiation of the water in the pit near the Unit 2 intake, but the dose was low. During the 9:30 a.m. patrol on April 2, they found that it was more than 1,000 millisieverts per hour.

They said there was a twenty-centimeter crack in the concrete on the side of the pit, and highly contaminated water was leaking into the ocean from there. This report was immediately conveyed to Prime Minister Naoto Kan, who was visiting J-Village.[45]

In the afternoon, they poured ready-mix concrete into the pit. In the plenary session the same night, Yoshida spoke.

"It's no good putting in concrete, because there's debris in the bottom of the pit. How about pouring concrete into the trench in front of the pit?"

"Can't we switch the concrete to one that has a better water-plugging effect?"

The TEPCO Head Office suggested using a high molecular polymer, for example.[46]

Around the same time, Kosako put together a proposal titled "In Order to Avoid Large-Scale Marine Contamination" and sent it to Kan, Edano, Fukuyama, and Hosono.

"It is extremely important that measures are taken according to the level of the radioactive waste [high, medium, low], and I believe the most appropriate approach at this stage is to quickly store comparatively high-level radioactive waste in the shared Radioactive Waste Building [Central RW] and to release into the ocean the comparatively low-level radioactive waste stored in the Central RW."

The Central RW was a processing facility for radioactive waste on the south side of Unit 4. Kosako claimed there were "only five or six plastic bottles" full of high-level concentration contaminated water. At the end of his proposal, Kosako wrote, "I propose that the Nuclear and Industrial Safety Agency provide emergency guidance to the operator on processing radioactive waste, and that the operator implements rapid countermeasures."

He was advising the application of article 64 of the Nuclear Reactor Regulation Act (Emergency Measures).[47] That night, Hosono read Kosako's recommendations several times.

The writing style's professional.

He was impressed as he read, and sharpened his resolve: *I guess this is our only option.*[48]

On April 3, once again the Integrated Response Office discussed the question of highly contaminated water. Hosono said, "In light of the highly contaminated water leak yesterday, we may be forced to release low-level contaminated water into the ocean as an emergency measure to prevent the high-level contaminated water leak."

On this day, Yoshida said in a teleconference, "The water plugging strategy at Unit 2 is the most important thing today. I thought of various names for the strategy, but would like to use Operation Beaver."

Apparently, they were going to stuff in this and that, like a beaver building a nest.

"Operations named after animals are mostly successful," Yoshida remarked.

Since the Giraffes had been successful with the water-pumping operation at the fuel pool, they were hoping to capitalize on this luck with another animal name. Yoshida blurted out, "I don't care whether it's socks lying around, stuff in whatever you can for the time being."[49]

Placing their hopes in Beaver, TEPCO stuffed in polymer, sawdust, even newspapers to block the outflow of contaminated water, but the leak did not stop.

Sometime after seven a.m. on April 4, they injected tracer solution, but it still continued to leak into the sea from crevices around the pit. The scene of the ongoing leak was screened at the ERC on the second floor of TEPCO's Head Office. Hosono was stunned by the sight.

Is this the kind of thing that Japan, the technology superpower, does?

In the videoconference that morning, with water also beginning to accumulate in the building basements of Unit 5 and 6 (RBs), Yoshida complained that "we won't be able to keep up by building water tanks."

"I need you to make some kind of decision. Dealing with the water is the most important issue. If something isn't done about it, you can tell us to hang in there all you like, but we won't be able to."[50]

At 9:30 a.m. on April 4, Hosono made a change in policy direction clear at the meeting at the Head Office. The question was how to convince Kan. Kan was a person who "wasn't swayed by logic alone."

Hosono called Kan and tried to persuade him, but Kan refused to give the nod. At one p.m., after putting together a draft press release with TEPCO Chairman Tsunehisa Katsumata, among others, Hosono went to the Kantei to meet with Kan.

"It's our only option."

Hosono repeatedly explained that there was no other choice. Kan indicated midway that he understood. He flashbacked again to his early morning visit to Fukushima Daiichi NPS on March 12.

This is just the same as the vent. If we discharge it, radioactive material will be released, but if we don't, it will mean much greater contamination in the long run. It can't be helped.

At three p.m., Hosono received Kan's consent.[51]

Because the leakage was not "unintended"—meaning, out of control— but a controlled discharge that would "only release so much," NISA decided, on the basis of section 1, article 64 of the Reactor Regulation Act, that the ocean release was "reasonable."[52]

However, prior to its decision, NISA asked the "advice" of Hideaki Tsuzuki, chief of the NSC's Environment Management Section.

Just their usual camouflage tactic, so NISA doesn't have to bear the risk alone.

He was not very enthusiastic, but Chairman Haruki Madarame also made a prompt decision that it was "unavoidable."[53]

4:02 P.M. Chief cabinet secretary press conference. Kantei press room.

"Both measures will be taken out of compelling necessity for the sake of safety, and will be conducted by the Nuclear and Industrial Safety Agency as emergency measures pursuant to the Act on Special Measures Concerning Nuclear Emergency Preparedness, based on the report from TEPCO and upon receiving advice from the Nuclear Safety Commission."

Suddenly informed of the release of contaminated water into the ocean at a press conference by the chief cabinet secretary, the fishing cooperatives throughout the east Japan region were furious.

In the cabinet meeting on the morning of April 5, citing "a lack of prior notification," Michihiko Kano, minister of agriculture, forestry, and fisheries, rebuked Kaieda and asked that he be "placed under close supervision."[54] The neighboring countries of China and South Korea strongly criticized the actions of the Japanese government. The Japanese government had not given advance notification.

At 3:17 p.m. on April 5, TEPCO began injecting water glass. They would dig a hole and pour a solidifying agent into the outflow path. This time it was named the Operation Mole.[55]

"Water glass" was sodium silicate. It was a transparent liquid tack that had a property of solidifying when mixed with soil-hardener. It was used in civil engineering for constructing sewers and tunnels.[56]

However, even after the water glass was injected, it failed to solidify, and night came on. Since TEPCO Vice President Sakae Muto was showing signs of closing up shop, saying, "Well, it's night now, so we'll do it tomorrow," Hosono told Muto, "Please absolutely stop the flow by today," and he had TEPCO do a rush job throughout the night.

"I'm not going home today. I'll be watching this all the time. Please see it out," Hosono said.

Accordingly, he spent the night glued to the screen at the Integrated Response Office on TEPCO's second floor. Images from the digital camera that workers had taken to the site were being sent there via the videoconference link from Fukushima Daiichi NPS.

When the water glass was injected, it would momentarily start to solidify, stemming the flow of water a little, but after a while the water would come streaming out. Still, it looked like the water had been finally stopped. At 5:38 a.m. on April 6, TEPCO confirmed that the outflow of highly contaminated water had stopped.

Hosono was relieved, but his relief came with a sudden onset of a ferocious hunger. Accompanied by an aide, he walked over to a noodle stand in front of Shimbashi Station and swallowed a bowl of noodles. Hosono was plagued by nightmares of a water leak for some time after that.[57]

ROBOTS

The robots appeared onsite at Fukushima Daiichi NPS at the end of March. They were from the U.S. company iRobot (Boston). They were there to measure radiation, do surveillance, and carry out situation assessments.

In the early hours of March 11, 2011 (EST), Gerald Rondoe, senior international sales manager of iRobot's military division, received a text message from the Singapore office while on his way to the airport from his home in Boston.

"I know you are leaving for Singapore today. But there has been a large earthquake in Japan. You had better call the airlines to see if you can still transfer in Narita Airport. Most of the flights from the U.S. to Singapore go via Tokyo or Hong Kong."

Rondoe flew to Singapore via Hong Kong.

On Monday March 14, Rondoe rang Ichiro Yamaguchi, program director of Sojitz Aerospace, a trading company, which was iRobot's representative in Japan. Yamaguchi had gone into the Akasaka Head Office that day, but no one was there. He was the only person in the deserted office.

Yamaguchi said in a quiet voice, "Things look pretty bad at Fukushima Daiichi." He then asked Rondoe, "Wouldn't iRobot's robots be useful?"

Rondoe responded, "I'll ask Boston. Give me a little time."

When Rondoe passed this on to the Head Office, he immediately received a call from the iRobot CEO, Colin Angle.

"If our robots can be of any assistance, use whatever you want."

The iRobot Corporation was established in 1990, when Colin Angle and Helen Greiner were still students at MIT, where Angle received a doctorate in robotics. They partnered with their supervising professor, Rodney Brooks.

The company included providing humanitarian aid at times of disaster as part of their Corporate Social Responsibility program. At the time of the 9/11 terrorist attacks in 2001, they were the first to send in robots to the World Trade Center to help search for survivors. During the 2008 BP oil spill in the Gulf of Mexico, they sent marine environment monitoring robots under water. These were able to send back real-time images to the base station from the seafloor.

The greatest strength of iRobot's robots was that they were all field-proven military-grade. They also included some models that were highly resistant to radiation. The PakBot had been used in Afghanistan and Iraq for the surveillance of caves housing enemy forces and to remove explosives. iRobot had provided the U.S. military with 3,500 PakBot units.

The company called for volunteers for a team that would be dispatched to Japan. Six, including Rondoe, volunteered. They would send two Pak-Bots and two Warrior Robots to Japan. The robots worked in pairs.

The PakBot weighed 25 kilograms and came equipped with a camera and manipulators. This time they were also equipped with radiation dose sensors. The Warrior Robots weighed 150 kilograms. Their arms were two meters long and could lift 4.5 kilograms. They could be used for cleaning up the debris.

On March 14, Rondoe placed another call.

"We'll do anything. Tell us what you want."

There was no senior manager Yamaguchi could consult. First of all, could they be exported to Japan from the United States? And even if they were a gift, whom were they to be given to? All day that day, he used his connections to make contact with TEPCO and NISA.

TEPCO said, "We don't know who would be in charge of that."

NISA told him, "Speak to public relations."

The day ended in futility.

MARCH 15. When he was watching television, he heard a university professor say, "What we most need now is to know what the situation is in the reactor buildings. They should use robots for that. Japan is a robot superpower, so I would like to see them using robots to look inside and see what's going on."

He found out that the person on TV was Ken Nakajima, a professor at Kyoto University, who specialized in neutron source engineering. Yamaguchi sent him an e-mail straight away.[58]

Nakajima replied, saying, "I've forwarded it to a unit at TEPCO."

Nakajima was on the technical committee for nuclear safety at Niigata Prefecture, home to TEPCO's Kashiwazaki NPS. This was how he knew a TEPCO engineer.[59]

On the afternoon of March 19, a TEPCO officer from the Nuclear Power Location Headquarters rang Yamaguchi to say, "I'll handle it."

He asked, "How long will the training take? Where will you do it? Can Sojitz offer any support?"

There were no preliminary courtesies, just straight into details.

MARCH 20. A freight plane from Boston arrived at Narita with the iRobot products. Since they had prepared diverse options for the PakBots and Warrior Robots, it was carrying sixty accessories. There were ten boxes of freight. On the same day, the iRobot employees also arrived. Rondoe had made it there, too, from Singapore.

In the Joint Coordination Group meeting on March 22, Goshi Hosono, special adviser to the prime minister, asked the U.S. side to provide robots.

"Could you provide us, if possible, with something using robot technology? For example, please let us know if there is a robot that can monitor or remove debris removal and such, that can go into buildings and carry out measures that by rights should be performed by personnel. METI has already started looking into robots."

The U.S. response was positive:

"We are already asking the U.S. forces and the related government agencies about the possibility of robot support. Tomorrow, March 23," the representative said, "I can make a proposal about the necessary robots if you can show me the photos the Japanese side has taken."[60]

On March 24, iRobot handed over its robots to TEPCO in Tsuchiura, Ibaraki Prefecture. The six iRobot staff members spent some three hours showing eight TEPCO staff how to use the robots. According to Rondoe, "They got used to them using Sony PlayStation–style game controllers."

When they were just about done, whether because it was fun operating them or not, the TEPCO staff started to laugh. However, when they started to use the robots for real, one issue after another emerged.

On March 27 and April 1, they conducted a second training session at Onahama, which was located about sixty-eight kilometers from Fukushima Daiichi NPS. For U.S. citizens, this meant being inside the designated evacuation zone. The six iRobot staff members had all taken stable iodine the day before. They left Tokyo early in the morning and returned late at night. Yamaguchi constantly checked the wind direction and speed on the AMeDAS (Automated Meteorological Data Acquisition System). The wind was not too bad.

When they were at Onahama, even during the training, they walked and worked close together in order to keep their exposure to a minimum. Thanks to the training, the distance covered by the PakBots was gradually expanding.

TEPCO wanted the robots to measure the radiation, carry out surveillance, and assess the situation.

Their aim was to measure the amount of radiation around the containment vessel, and to gather enough material to ascertain where work could be done in the reactor building. As a consequence, they mainly equipped the robots with manipulator arms, cameras, and radiation dose–monitoring functions.[61]

There were many problems at the site before the robots could be introduced. When they tried to climb the stairs in Unit 2 (RB), the width of the staircase turned out to be narrower than had been reported, and they could not get through. When they brought in a new cable for the water gauge, they could not feed the cable in, because it was coated with wax.[62]

A more fundamental issue was communication problems with the radio controls. Since the radiation was high, the radio control had to be operated at 100–200 meters' distance. It would have been fine, had they been able to use fiber-optic cable, but TEPCO was reluctant to do so, because they feared that if the fiber got caught on the wreckage and became exposed, a fire might break out.

Besides, the Japanese government was extremely fastidious about frequency regulations. They did not allow the use of strong frequencies. This was a major stumbling block.

Another issue was finding out how strong the robots' radiation resistance was, because they would be exposed to a large amount of radiation. Would the equipment be able to withstand it? If a highly contaminated robot broke down, it would be even harder to handle than the radioactive debris. They could not be washed over and over, so it would be big trouble if they were contaminated at high concentrations.[63]

To use Rondoe's phrase, "it was a complete world of maybe" for iRobot as well. The robots had never been used in this kind of high-radiation environment. And, in fact, the robots ended up being exposed to extremely high doses of radiation during operations at the Fukushima Daiichi site.

APRIL 17. The first day of battle for the two PakBots arrived. It would be fine if they could be remotely operated from the Anti-Seismic Building, but that would be more than one kilometer over a hill to the reactor buildings. Wireless communication could be received at a distance of two kilometers with a clear view, but not when there was a hill in the way.

So, they selected a spot near the reactor buildings where the radiation was low, and operated them from there. They had no choice but to operate them in their Tyvek suits, covered by additional protective suits and protective masks.

All around them was a mountain of debris. They had to operate the robots while avoiding it. Although the PakBots got near to the reactor building, they were stumped by the double-door entry.

At first, it was difficult to use the robots. There was no choice but for someone to open the door. But who was to be sent in first? Things came to a standstill here once again. In the end, one of the operators went over to the entrance, opened the external door, then opened the internal door a fraction, letting the robots do the rest.[64]

However, it was initially more effective for a worker to monitor the radiation using a hotspot monitor attached to a five-meter-long pole and observe the readings. But the workers gradually became used to operating the robots, and after that, they became indispensable.

What would happen to the PakBots and Warrior Robots that had gone into battle at Fukushima Daiichi NPS? Rondoe said, "The robots that work here die here. That's their fate. They were exposed to such a large amount of radiation that they can't be taken out again. We can't take them back to the United States, either. We have no choice but to dismantle them, then bury them."[65]

Were Japanese-made robots not supposed to be the best in the world? Why did Japanese nuclear disaster–relief robots not lead the vanguard?

After the Fukushima Daiichi NPS accident, the Japanese people were perplexed to read reports of U.S. and French offers of nuclear disaster–relief robots. Some people remembered that President Clinton had offered to lend robots at the time of the Tokaimura JCO criticality accident in 1999. Professor Shigeo Hirose, a robot researcher at the Tokyo Institute of Technology, was one of them.

After the JCO accident, the Japan Atomic Energy Agency (JAEA) launched a development project for remotely operated disaster response robots, allocating 3 billion yen from the supplementary budget in 2000. Their standard-bearer became building "nuclear disaster prevention support systems."

Six prototypes were built by Mitsubishi Heavy Industries, Toshiba, Hitachi, as well as a foreign nuclear power–related firm. However, the project was terminated after a year, having built only these six prototypes, because TEPCO decided they were "not suitable for immediate deployment."

A senior official at MOD said, "I heard that TEPCO had them built for a billion yen (per annum), but in the field trials, they couldn't go up or down the stairs, so they were dropped." Yet Hirose attests, "They were said to be unnecessary, since a situation where nuclear disaster–relief robots would be required would never happen in Japan."

A senior MEXT official, who was in charge of the Science and Technology Agency's response to the JCO accident at the time, and who was also later involved in robot development, remembered the words of a TEPCO general manager.

"We can't introduce nuclear disaster–relief robots. The locals wouldn't stand for it. Accidents don't happen. The likelihood of an accident occurring is 1 in 108. We only think of a single event. We don't assume that everything will go down."

The budget allocation for developing nuclear disaster–relief robots ended up being a one-shot deal. The reason for this was that "maintenance alone is costly." The government also followed the nuclear power companies' line, and held on to the safety myth.[66]

The six prototypes built at the time all had miserable fates. One was donated to a university research lab, another to a science museum, one was abandoned in a warehouse, another missing, and another was waiting to be discarded as soon as its depreciation was over, because the cost of warehousing it was a loss . . .

There had been a growing interest in robots even before the JCO accident. Following the 1979 Three Mile Island disaster, robot development was launched in 1983. This was ostensibly a robot project for hazardous inspection operations. Up until 1990, 20 billion yen was allocated, but then discontinued. Following the Chernobyl accident, the Nuclear Safety Technology Center built two robots, but this did not last, either.

Professor Toshiso Kosako from the Graduate School at the University of Tokyo states that the reason for this was that TEPCO was against it.

"They were having some success, but they were never adopted, just left at Rokkasho Village. The reason was that TEPCO wanted to avoid having outsiders, especially people from the private sector, coming into the plant and taking nuclear power–related data."[67]

CASTLE FALLS IN A DAY

MARCH 26, 2011. This day was the fortieth anniversary of operations for the first unit of TEPCO's first nuclear power plant. When asked about this in a press conference, Vice President Sakae Muto apologized, "It is most regrettable that this is the situation in our fortieth year, and I am extremely sorry."[68]

On March 29, TEPCO President Masataka Shimizu was hospitalized. A few days earlier, Katsumata had approached Banri Kaieda, METI minister, saying, "It's all over. This is the limit. The deputy head is not doing his job. Please replace him."

"Well, then, suggest a secretary general," Kaieda said.

"We don't have the right person."

"Act responsibly, please."

TEPCO later submitted to Kaieda a list of candidates for secretary general. At first glance, Kaieda thought, *This is no good.*

He called Katsumata and told him, "Give us someone who can take over from Shimizu-san. The person who's going to lead TEPCO into the future has to deal with this mess."

Katsumata named Toshio Nishizawa, managing director for planning.[69]

Katsumata was the don at TEPCO. A graduate from the Faculty of Economics at Tokyo University, he had joined TEPCO in 1963. He had worked in the planning field, which was TEPCO's elite course. In 2002, when it was discovered that TEPCO had been tampering with its nuclear power plant data and covering it up for many years, the then president of TEPCO, Naoya Minami, was forced to take responsibility by resigning.

It was Katsumata who took over as president. The first thing he did was to reform TEPCO's management culture. Under the policy of "a mechanism that stops people from doing the wrong thing and a culture of not doing the wrong thing," he carried out an awareness-raising campaign. It was about a year after taking office that Katsumata said the following:

"Nothing good comes out of just 'mopping up,' not even mentally. This may be a dream of mine, but I want to move TEPCO forward."[70]

In 2008, he handed over the post of president to Shimizu and became chairman. Up until then, TEPCO's top manager had always come from either the General Affairs Department or the Planning Department. Maintaining a good relationship with Nagatacho (the Diet) and Kasumigaseki (the bureaucracy) was a prerequisite for the top.

Shimizu was a rarity as a TEPCO president in that he came from the Procurement Department. Its role was that of contracting public works projects with huge budgets. Every year it handled purchases from traders, they dealt with hundreds of billions of yen. This alone meant that temptations were great.

Shimizu often preached "Procurement Department ethics and business ethics" to his subordinates. He was fond of saying, "Don't cross to the other side of the train tracks." From TEPCO's Head Office in Uchisaiwaicho, the bars of Ginza spread out on the far side of the JR Keihin Tohoku Line. Even if they were using their own money, the world would not see it that way.

Another favorite was, "Avoid the appearance of evil." TEPCO's Procurement Department was still weighed down with bitter memories of its coal delivery diversion scandal after the war. It also had a special section for rejecting bribes. When an executive from the Procurement Department was given a U.S.-made mechanical pencil by a supplier as a souvenir from his trip to the United States, he broke it in half on the spot.

"You know, I can't afford to make any exceptions."

The Procurement Department had told this story with pride. The number of companies it traded with exceeded ten thousand. An internal rule was "a total ban on golf, meals, and drinking" with suppliers. The HR department was also set on "changing personnel where there was smoke."[71]

If times had been normal, Shimizu would have risen up from manager without incident. However, he was a totally unsuitable manager when the nation's survival hung in the balance. When all of the key political members of the Kantei, from Prime Minister Naoto Kan down, stormed TEPCO's Head Office, one of the Kantei staff on the scene described his impression of Shimizu at the time as follows:

"There was a person flitting back and forth between the conference room across the hallway and the operations room. He looked almost idle. At the time, I thought it must be the PR officer or something like that, but I later learned that it was TEPCO President Shimizu."[72]

To add to this, Shimizu did not express himself clearly. Before eight p.m. on March 14, Shimizu spoke on the phone with Nobuaki Terasaka, NISA's director general. According to Terasaka, "I felt that I couldn't make out what he wanted to say." Shimizu had also telephoned Edano and Kaieda over TEPCO's "withdrawal" in the early hours of March 15, but they both testified to his poor powers of expression, saying they "couldn't make out what he wanted to say."[73]

"Folk from TEPCO's Procurement Division were people who spent their whole lives in the guest-of-honor's seat. Even if their words were obscure, suppliers would bend over backwards to understand them."

This was how one senior official at NISA, who knew Shimizu, put it.[74]

However, when crisis struck, it was not Shimizu who was running TEPCO, but Katsumata.

On March 30, Katsumata gave his first press conference since the accident. This was because Shimizu had been hospitalized the previous day. The following exchange took place in the press conference:

"This accident and its situational convergence have been prolonged, and it has been pointed out that the situation has an aspect of man-made disaster due to poor operations, first, and poor support, second, including the faults of the government and TEPCO, but how would you respond to such a point of view?" Katsumata was asked.

"I have not seen anything 'poor.' But in the onsite situation, where there is no electricity and communications are very bad, a variety of tasks takes longer than expected. Up until now, all you had to do was press a button, as it were, but now everything needs to be done by hand, in the field. So I think this has led to unintentional delays."[75]

He was as cold, tough, and firm as graphite. He would grimly defend the organization's interests. Just like Shimizu, Katsumata was cocooned in TEPCO's rock-solid silo mentality and corporate culture of risk aversion.

TEPCO's castle consisted of various villages: nuclear power, thermal power, systems operations, planning, administration, procurement, and so on. A senior METI official could not forget his surprise when he was pent up in the Integrated Response Office. He had been given a seat behind Kaieda, Hosono, Katsumata, Takekuro, and Muto in the front row. The TEPCO managers were seated even farther back.

Exchanges with the site could be heard via the videoconference link with Fukushima Daiichi.

"What's happening with the hoses?"

"We're checking that now."

"Just passing the gate. Please confirm."

The managers all sat there with their arms folded, just staring at the screen as they listened to the conversation. At a time like that, section chiefs from the Thermal Department and the Procurement Department were busy exchanging business cards.

Is this what TEPCO is really like?[76]

Shimizu had a meeting with Yuhei Sato, governor of Fukushima Prefecture, for the first time after the nuclear accident on April 22, 2011.

"I deeply apologize for the massive damage that has been caused."

He added, "That I've worked 'ten years to build a castle to lose it in one day' is engraved on my heart, and I am full of regret."[77]

The TEPCO castle had fallen.

FUKUSHIMA 50[78]

Political members of the Kantei, from Kan down, as well as Tetsuro Ito, deputy chief cabinet secretary for crisis management, took the reports and intimations from TEPCO, including President Masataka Shimizu, from late on the night of March 14 until the early hours of March 15, to mean a "full withdrawal."

In contrast, TEPCO asserted they "wanted to consider it because with the situation at the plant being so serious, we would have to think about withdrawing staff not directly engaged in operations sooner or later," and regarding "full withdrawal," "that's not what we're thinking."[79]

TEPCO has consistently maintained this stance, creating a controversy with Prime Minister Kan, the other political members of the Kantei, and crisis manager Ito's perception of a "full withdrawal."

What does the videoconference between the site and TEPCO's Head Office tell us? Although it has already been described in chapter 5, let us once again look at the exchanges on the night of March 14.

The first time President Masataka Shimizu spoke the words "worst-case scenario" in front of everyone was before five p.m. on March 14. Shimizu deemed they needed to consider countermeasures for "the worst situation of not being able to get water into" Unit 2, and asked for a "timeframe scenario" to be drawn up. The response that came back from the Head Office recovery team was that the "time in hand" was about two hours. Shimizu said, "Well, we have to get to work on it immediately."

There was not much time.[80]

About 7:25 p.m. on April 14, TEPCO Managing Director Akio Komori, at the offsite center, made the following request to the Head Office:

"Somebody needs to consider stuff like evacuation criteria . . . A decision has to be made somewhere whether or not people from the plant can still stay in the Central Control Room. Please move ahead with looking into withdrawal criteria."

This was the first remark mentioning withdrawal from the Central Control Room, where the on-duty officers were watching the reactor around the clock.

Close to eight p.m. the same day, TEPCO Fellow Akio Takahashi at the Head Office asked Vice President Sakae Muto, also at the Head Office, "Muto-san, this evacuating everyone from the site, what time do you think that's going to happen?"

About twenty minutes later, Takahashi reminded Muto:

"It's now, isn't it, that they're going to evacuate everyone from Daiichi to the visitor hall at Daini?"

Takahashi was questioning what kind of plans they were thinking of at the site, with an eye on the "evacuation of all the staff," everyone at Fukushima Daiichi, to Fukushima Daini. However, there was no answer from Daiichi. It was from Daini's Site Superintendent Naohiro Masuda that a response came.

"We'll set up two Emergency Response Centers, ours at Daini at Plant 4, and the old ERC for people coming from Daiichi, so please make sure at the Head Office that you use the right ERC."

The Emergency Response Center was the command tower itself, where the site supervisor was in charge of the accident response. Masuda was talking about an emergency evacuation situation of shifting Daiichi's ERC to Daini if the one in the Anti-Seismic Building at Daichi could no longer be used.

Once they withdrew from the ERC, it could well change operations altogether. The situation was also one where the Head Office had no plans regarding such a serious problem, and left it up to the site. In addition, it appears that communication between the Head Office and Daiichi on this issue was not going well. Also, it seems that Masuda-san, unable to ignore the situation, came to the rescue.[81]

In fact, Yoshida had begun to consider evacuation procedures for all personnel except those necessary for monitoring and restoration of the plant. In order to avoid any panic from the workers, he instructed a very small number of executives from the General Affairs Team to arrange a bus for evacuation, and was preparing to evacuate quickly, depending on the situation. However, he avoided, as much as possible, mentioning the evacuation plan in the videoconference in order to keep worker panic at bay.[82]

Yoshida testified about this in the Government Investigation Commission hearings:

"It's not the China syndrome, but it could be heading that way. If it does, the water pumping into Units 1 and 3 will have to be stopped . . . if that happens, then in the end, we will have to evacuate from here . . . If I was talking about it in the Anti-Seismic Building, it would have scared everyone. I think I said on the phone to Muto . . . 'this kind of situation is truly dangerous. Leave behind the minimum number of people for operating and recovery.' . . . I have a memory of a conversation that it would be better to withdraw . . . I have a memory of going outside and doing that. To tell the truth, this is the thing I want to remember the least."[83]

However, a few minutes later, Shimizu said via videoconference,

"Please confirm that we have not yet decided on a final evacuation at the moment. We are currently checking with the powers that be."[84]

Shimizu was warning that they were not yet at the stage to decide on a "final withdrawal." Any unnecessary anxiety should be avoided. And such a crucial decision was to be decided by "checking with the powers that be," making subtly sure that it was not a matter for the site to decide unilaterally.

Depending on the way it is taken, this can be read as if Shimizu was restraining Yoshida from issuing instructions on his own for a "final withdrawal." It is obvious that the "powers that be" that Shimizu was referring to was the Nuclear and Industrial Safety Agency, the Ministry of Economy, Trade, and Industry, and the Kantei.

Indeed, it was at this time that Shimizu first mentioned the necessity of contingency planning for a "final withdrawal." However, the government, the Diet, and independent investigations were unable to fully clarify the response of TEPCO's top management, including Tsunehisa Katsumata and Shimizu, to this "final withdrawal." However, a member of TEPCO's management team, who criticized President Shimizu's "incomprehensible behavior" chasing after the political staff at the Kantei at the time, said, "The evacuation criteria for a final withdrawal were determined by an extremely small number of people." (He also added, "I was not one of them.")[85]

Shimizu probably tried to contact political officers at the Kantei all the while envisioning a "final withdrawal" scenario. And his ambiguous expression as to whether it was a half-baked approach with scenario formulation or an emergency response gave the political staff at the Kantei the impression that TEPCO was considering "a complete withdrawal."

Shimizu did not offer any refutation when the political members of the Kantei, afraid of a TEPCO withdrawal, summoned him to the Kantei after the early morning meeting, and Prime Minister Kan and others told him they "would not approve a withdrawal." Due to his response, Kan later testified that he judged that "they were thinking of a full withdrawal."[86]

There is a strong possibility that these actions of Shimizu caused doubts not only at the Kantei but also on site at Fukushima Daiichi. During the government investigation, Yoshida said the following, concerning the "TEPCO withdrawal nonsense" that night:

"I wanted to say, what are you talking about, we're still here, aren't we? I didn't know what kind of silly debates were going on at the Head Office or the Kantei, but had the onsite workers cut and run? No, we were still there. I want to state this clearly."

This shows Yoshida's strong distrust of the fact that the Head Office and the Kantei were having "silly debates" about withdrawal unbeknown to him. In his testimony, he also said, "I heard that, at the time . . . President Shimizu asked Kan to let them withdraw. I don't know how what I told someone at the Head Office, which was conveyed to Shimizu, is connected to what I told Hosono, but there was some kind of a miscommunication."[87]

There is no doubt that Yoshida consulted with the Head Office about a "temporary withdrawal" by means other than the videoconference.[88]

How was that conveyed to Shimizu and how was it conveyed as a signal for "withdrawal" to the Kantei? And how is it connected with Yoshida's telling Hosono about his "resolve"? Yoshida replied that he reported to Hosono that night as follows:

"The plant's in a tremendously dangerous situation. It's going to be close. It's a gamble whether we can get the water in or not, but we'll do it. It's just I think we need to evacuate the people who aren't involved, I'm preparing for that now."[89]

Yoshida was resolved to stay onsite until the end and continue to respond to the accident. During his testimony to the government investigation, Yoshida occasionally showed loathing for Prime Minister Kan. He even called him, "This joke of a country's joke of a politician."[90]

It was painfully awkward when Kan flew into Fukushima Daiichi by helicopter without a thought for what was happening in the field in the early hours of March 12, shouting his way through, and when he stormed into TEPCO's Head Office on the early morning of March 15 and "behaved quite badly, ranting like mad."[91]

Another person Yoshida made no effort to conceal his contempt for was TEPCO President Shimizu. Many times he spoke of him without any honorific title. Shimizu was clearly in a state of panic and was not in a frame of mind to judge calmly. Yoshida did not bother with him, and consulted exclusively with Vice President Sakae Muto about an evacuation scenario, on Muto's mobile phone instead of the videoconference.

When Muto instructed his subordinates to draw up a withdrawal plan on the evening of March 14, he apparently tossed the plan-making back to the site, saying, "This is something for the site to decide." However, Yoshida tossed the ball back to the Head Office, saying that the Head Office should think about a worst-case scenario plan, because "We're busy responding. We don't have any time to be working on plans."[92]

However, the Head Office had neither the ability to determine how to conduct emergency planning, including a withdrawal plan, nor the resolve. The Head Office had no other countermeasures than to rely on the superhuman and dedicated efforts of everyone at the site, from Yoshida down.

Unlike Nobuaki Terasaka, director general of the Nuclear and Industrial Safety Agency, who interpreted the content of Shimizu's telephone call as a "temporary withdrawal," both METI Minister Banri Kaieda and Chief Cabinet Secretary Yukio Edano regarded it as "a step toward full withdrawal."

Although Kaieda initially took Shimizu's remarks to mean a "temporary withdrawal from Daiichi to Daini," he trembled at the thought of the "full withdrawal" scenario that was likely to follow a "temporary" one, and conveyed that feeling to Kan. Edano, as well, considered Shimizu's call to be asking for consent for not only a temporary but also a full-scale withdrawal, and reported to that effect to Kan.

Perhaps the Kantei political officers were overreacting. There are several signs described in chapter 5, which intimate that Kaieda and other political officers had fallen into a psychological state close to elite panic that evening. There were probably many other ways of checking on whether TEPCO was considering a "full withdrawal," besides calling Yoshida, but they do not seem to have tried very hard.

Why was the information on withdrawal not carefully examined by Edano and his staff? If Shimizu's remarks were ambiguous, why did they not confirm them with Katsumata? Madarame said of Kaeda's and Edano's response that they "completely misunderstood it as a full withdrawal," taking the critical view that they overreacted. (Madarame, however, did not receive a direct telephone call from Shimizu.)[93]

However, if it was only a "temporary withdrawal," why did the TEPCO president have to call the Kantei politicians so many times late at night? Edano is on record, in his hearing with the Government Investigation Commission, saying, "It was definitely a matter of withdrawing completely, I am confident about this . . . Because there was no need to talk about unnecessary personnel fleeing on up to the cabinet secretary. A misunderstanding just wasn't possible."[94]

Moreover, it is understandable, as a crisis management approach, that between midnight on March 14 and the early hours of March 15, political officers at the Kantei directly confronted the risk of a "full withdrawal" by TEPCO, and responded "conservatively," erring on the side of safety, by attempting to preempt a worst-case scenario in risk management terms of a "full withdrawal."

In fact, early in the morning of March 15, after the "withdrawal nonsense," when the Unit 2 containment vessel was damaged and there was an explosion in Unit 4 (RB), workers were evacuated, but sixty-nine remained behind at the time.

The Fukushima 50 was by no means an exaggeration.[95]

In terms of the site, this number was woefully inadequate for struggling with five reactors and six fuel pools, and was on a scale where they would be either forced to completely withdraw or die trying to keep things under control.

A fear of death struck workers in the field with each explosion at Unit 1, Unit 3, Unit 2, and so on. Yoshida himself said that he was ready to die many times during the crisis. When Unit 3 exploded, "I thought to myself that there were around ten people with whom I had been working for many years that might be willing to die with me."[96]

Thinking of the possible deaths of the staff members left behind at the nuclear power plant, Yoshida listed the names of his colleagues on the whiteboard in the place of a "tomb inscription." He wanted to "leave behind something that said these were the people who fought right up until the end." He also confessed, "I could feel, even in such a hellish state, the image of the Bodhisattva rising from the Lotus Sutra."[97]

Yoshida's presence was deeply engraved on the hearts of those who fought during the crisis, and gave them their resolve. Mari Sato of the Disaster Prevention Group spoke of the psychological frame of mind in the following way:

"It's not as if you could run away from it even if you tried. You just had to step up to the plate. Nobody was coming; nothing was coming. And besides, everyone instinctively knew that Yoshida-san wasn't going to run. You can tell by instinct who's a runner. I also thought that he would die with me. We all felt that we couldn't let him down."

Yoshida ordered the evacuation to Fukushima Daini, leaving behind the "necessary minimum." However, he did not specify who was included in "the necessary minimum." This was because they had not drawn up an emergency response plan. In the end, it was left up to the resolve of the individual.

This was no longer contingency planning. It was in the realm of spirituality.

TEPCO's Head Office had no emergency planning for major accidents, nor did the government have countermeasures or resident safeguards in the case of a nuclear reactor out of control. There was no rapid response force standing by. As a result, the TEPCO leaders became helpless, and all the government could say was "withdrawal is unthinkable." As a result of these omissions on both sides, the workers at Fukushima Daiichi NPS were forced into a situation of "laying their lives on the line." An engineer from Toshiba, who spent the duration of the crisis at Fukushima Daiichi NPS, recalled it this way:

"I think the Japanese still have the mentality that if you go to war, you don't come back. They would back us into a corner and wait for us to loyally die a hero's death."

He then added, "They didn't know if it would be fifty or seventy or a hundred, but the United States sensed that someone was going to die a hero's death at Fukushima Daiichi."[98]

In fact, State Department officials regarded TEPCO's site response at the time, especially the worker numbers, as being on a "scale that was laughably low," and worried seriously that TEPCO's withdrawal would be inevitable with numbers like this. One official from the same department later said, "We'd have thousands of people dealing with a nuclear accident on this scale. You have to go in with something like a war plan."[99]

Gregory Jaczko, chairman of the U.S. NRC, was also shocked at the marked lack of manpower at the TEPCO site, so much so that, in addition to directing this concern of the U.S. side to be conveyed to the Japanese side, he also cautioned Ichiro Fujisaki, Japan's ambassador to the United States, directly about it.[100]

At the end of the day, it appears that, without drawing up any emergency plans for a worst-case scenario, the Head Office invited the intervention of the government in the form of setting up an Integrated Response Office by hinting at a "full withdrawal."

Shiro Yamazaki, secretary to the prime minister, remembers another Kantei staffer on secondment from METI sadly muttering when information of TEPCO's "withdrawal" seeped into the Kantei late at night, "I reckon TEPCO's given up the ghost and is trying to lure the government into stepping in."[101]

Getting "the government to step in" was an option that meant the Head Office's management would not have to take responsibility. Is there not something strange about Shimizu—who responded to the crisis by taking all the government instructions as presidential orders, from the Unit 1 venting to seawater injecting, and said, "Please follow Mr. Madarame's method" for the opening of the SR valves at Unit 2—thinking that the ultimate judgment on "withdrawal" was "following" government instructions?

If they decided to withdraw all staff, then the TEPCO management team would be held responsible for the consequences. In order to avoid a complete withdrawal, even if Yoshida and his "suicide squad" were to die as heroes, the TEPCO management team would be held responsible for the result. Out of these two courses, did TEPCO management not opt for "a complete withdrawal, or a de facto abandonment of control"?

An executive from one of the associate companies, who worked with TEPCO on crisis management throughout this period, said, "After all, it was just President Shimizu-san going through the motions of saying, 'I'm not going to be held responsible for the lives of TEPCO employees in this matter,' and for a salaryman at TEPCO who had survived, it was probably the ultimate form of avoiding responsibility."[102]

EPILOGUE

"The Mercy of the Gods"

A CHANGE OF CLOTHES

APRIL 1, 2011. Prime Minister Naoto Kan had taken off the disaster fatigues he had worn ever since reaching the Kantei after the earthquake at 2:46 p.m. on March 11, and changed into his usual clothes. For almost three weeks, he had not returned to his official residence but slept in his office always clad in disaster fatigues.

By the end of March, however, the Kantei staff began exploring whether there was a need to switch from "emergency mode" to a "day-to-day mode" with the start of the new fiscal year.

Even before that, there had been pros and cons to the prime minister sporting the disaster gear. When he was visiting Fukushima by helicopter, the outfit was appropriate, but would it not appear odd to the world to turn up at a press conference at the Kantei in disaster gear? There was a risk that it would be interpreted as "the Prime Minister's wearing that gear for a press conference at the Kantei. Does that mean Tokyo and Japan are in danger? Wearing disaster fatigues could be considered as a message that we're in an emergency here; it's dangerous here."

But, in fact, Japan was in an emergency situation from March 11, and the risk of radiation emissions was ongoing. The fact that the prime minister, the chief executive responsible for crisis management, appeared in disaster gear was not a mistake, in terms of showing the government and the people were united in facing the crisis, and it was also stipulated in the emergency preparedness plan. It was accepted as such by most people. Nonetheless, he could not wear it forever, but what was the best time for taking it off?

Manabu Terada, special adviser to the prime minister, was in charge of looking into it. If the prime minister continued wearing the disaster garb forever, it would prolong the feelings of self-restraint and malaise among the public, thereby risking a negative impact on the economy.

On the other hand, victims in the earthquake- and tsunami-affected areas were still suffering, and more than a hundred thousand people from Fukushima Prefecture were living as evacuees. The disaster outfit was also a symbol of solidarity with them. There was a risk of being accused of quickly forgetting the disaster areas if he changed out of them.

After a discussion of these issues, the decision was made to change clothes. This act could convey the message that thanks to the crisis management and desperate accident measures of the government during this period, the reactors had been somehow stabilized and were out of danger at last, and therefore things were getting back to normal.

Marking the start of the new fiscal and school year, April 1 was the perfect day for changing clothes. They would also raise the Japanese flag at the Kantei, which had been at half-mast since the earthquake.[1] This was the decision Terada and his colleagues made.

In an interview with Lionel Barber, executive editor of the British *Financial Times* newspaper, Chief Cabinet Secretary Yukio Edano said, "I'm thinking of changing into a regular sort of business suit." The title of this article was, "Japanese Ready for Return to Normalcy."[2]

To use the words of Haruki Madarame, Nuclear Safety Commission chairman, of all the parliamentary members at the Kantei, Kan "lost it" the most during the crisis. In "emergency mode," Kan "lost it" when he visited Fukushima Daiichi NPS on March 12, when he stormed into TEPCO and established the Integrated Response Office on March 15, and during the fuel pool water pumping operations on March 16 and 17.

In late March, the situation had changed. More than anything, many people began to feel a sense of relief that the worst aspects regarding the onsite situation were over. By late March, the Giraffes were engaged in supplying water to the fuel pools in a steady, accurate manner.

Likewise, the launch of the Joint Coordination Group had made sharing information and discussing responses between Japan and the United States, as well as their various ministries and departments, much smoother. The Integrated Response Office set up in TEPCO's Head Office was also starting to function properly, and by the end of the month the videoconference connecting the site and TEPCO Head Office was hooked up in real time to NISA.

Wanting to get Kan away from the pressure, if only for a short time, Edano suggested he return to the official residence to rest. Edano himself was sleeping at the Kantei.

"I'm going to go home, too. Who should go first?"

Kan became bad-tempered, saying, "I'm not going back." Kan had only returned to the prime minister's residence a week after the earthquake, on March 18.[3]

It also seemed that Kan still wanted to cling to the "emergency mode." Hosono, however, felt that the tenacity and urgency of Kan's political instincts and political reflexes were starting to fall away. Meetings at the Kantei started to become more drawn out. Hosono was often left in the middle. Furthermore, information from the bureaucrats was no longer coming up to him as before. Conveying these points to Kan, Hosono had his title changed from "special adviser to the prime minister [social security]" to "special adviser to the prime minister [nuclear accident]."

The key members of the Kan administration involved directly with the nuclear crisis response twenty-four hours a day at the Kantei were a relatively young group, consisting of Kan, Edano, Fukuyama, Hosono, Terada, and a little later Mabuchi. All were in their prime and strong both physically and emotionally. They were all in a state of military readiness, wearing their disaster outfits, catching fleeting naps when they could, and heading off immediately to the next meeting. Looking back, Kan said, "I had no idea what day of the week it was in the first few days after March 11. I had no sense of today or yesterday. There was just a constant flow of time running on."[4]

Fukuyama might have been the toughest among them, in terms of fatigue not showing on his face. Still, his trademark immaculately combed hair was starting to get disheveled. It was the youngest team member, Terada, who never lost his smile or sense of humor even during the crisis.

In comparison, round-the-clock response was tough on the older members. The only time Tetsuro Ito, deputy chief cabinet secretary for crisis management, slept in the first three days was a mere two hours when he went back home. When he got home, he had lost so much weight that his wife jokingly said, "I think we'd better take a commemorative photo," and caught him on camera. As he became short on sleep, he had trouble enunciating and wanted to sit down immediately.[5]

In the case of Haruki Madarame, chairman of the Nuclear Safety Commission, in the evening of March 16, five days after the accident, he suddenly lost consciousness and collapsed. He was on the fifth floor of the Kantei at the time, but was immediately seen by a medical officer in the room adjacent to the crisis management center in the basement and put on an IV. He returned to the fifth floor after lying down for about an hour.[6] Looking back, Madarame had only about ten hours of sleep in total until March 17.

"Whenever I tried to get some sleep, I was always woken up. This went on all the time. It was an overrun experiment for making you realize that you really needed sleep, for your short-term memory to be transferred into long-term memory."[7]

NAOTO KAN

Heading into April, subtle changes emerged, although no one actually spoke about them. It was not just the feeling that they had emerged from the bottom, that they had risen from the depths; it was rather a deep feeling that "we were lucky."

Of course, neither the government officials nor Kantei politicians could officially say as much. An area of 1,800 square kilometers in Fukushima Prefecture alone had become a 5mSv/year zone. There were still more than a hundred thousand people who had lost their homes and were living as evacuees.

So, there was no way they could say "we were lucky." And the outlook was still not bright enough that they could use the past tense. Improving the sustainability of the water injection, shielding from radiation and contaminated water, and even, in a pinch, getting ready to pour in slurry, they needed to move quickly on medium- and long-term restructuring measures, and more than anything else, there was the fear of aftershocks.

Nevertheless, looking back on the aftermath of March 11, there was an unmistakably deep feeling that "We've been saved. Luck was on our side."

Depending on your outlook, you could also say the Fukushima Daiichi NPS accident was "bad luck":

- It turned out to be a complex, chain disaster of earthquake, tsunami, and nuclear power plant.

- The power supply board was submerged by the tsunami, and put out of action.

- Four reactors underwent a simultaneous full loss of power.

- The fact that the reactors were lined up in the same direction with very little space between them led to a parallel chain of meltdown crises.

- When the nuclear accident occurred, TEPCO's two top executives were away on trips and not at the Head Office.

- On March 15, there was a north-northwesterly wind at Fukushima Daiichi NPS, followed by rain and snow. This caused the radiation released to fall and stick to the ground.

There are probably many more such factors.

However, apart from the complex disaster and the wind direction, they all could have been avoided. They were not things that can be put down to "bad luck." On the other hand, they felt "lucky" about the following points:

- The earthquake happened during the day. If it had been at night, initial relief efforts would have been far more difficult.

- It was not the weekend, but a weekday, Friday. This meant there was a large number of employees working in the plant.

- The wind continued to blow toward the Pacific Ocean from March 11 to March 14. If, during this time, the wind had blown inland, radiation contamination would have been much more serious.

- At the time of the hydrogen explosion at Unit 3 on March 14, although TEPCO workers and the Self-Defense Forces sustained injuries, miraculously, nobody was killed. Fatalities would have made strategy far more difficult. Fukushima Daiichi Site Superintendent Masao Yoshida later told Takeyuki Inagaki, recovery team leader, "It was a miracle, really, that time. If someone had died, I thought it would go to ruin."

- Something added momentum to the flow of water into the fuel pool at Unit 4, allowing the quantity of water to be maintained.[8]

- At the same time as the explosion in Unit 4, pressure in the pressure vessel of Unit 2 underwent a rapid drop. There was a hole somewhere, with a large amount of radioactive material being released. That, in itself, was unlucky, but it prevented an explosion in the containment vessel proper. If Unit 2 had exploded, nobody would have been able to go near.

- The stock market closed thirty minutes after the earthquake. This allowed time for emergency response, making the emergency measures taken by the government and the Bank of Japan on Monday, March 14, effective.

- The radiation risk did not extend to the Americas. If it had, Operation Tomodachi would have become a completely different operation.

- In the period of disaster response, there were aftershocks onsite, but it was exempt from any big earthquakes. If that was not the case, then "it would've been surrender" said Gregory Jaczko, chairman of the U.S. Nuclear Regulatory Commission (NRC), which reflected the real feelings of people working desperately onsite to respond.

- They were able to respond to the accident from the Anti-Seismic Building, which had its own independent power supply because it was completed in the fall of the preceding year.

- As J-Village, which became the logistical hub for the central government to respond to the disaster, was just outside of the twenty-kilometer range from the site, it was available (within twenty kilometers, it would have been classified as "evacuation zone" and would have been unavailable).[9]

Kan himself said, "It was nothing less than the mercy of the gods," citing, as an example, "The Unit 4 reactor was full of water, and some shock or something made the water flow into the nuclear fuel pool," and "If the pool had boiled dry, a worst-case scenario would have been inevitable."[10]

It was not just the politicians. There were examples of similar deep feelings among practitioners and engineers. For example, Kiyoharu Abe of JNES, one of the first experts to say the water gauge was off, looked back and observed, "The gods were controlling that accident from some-where."[11] In the four days after March 11, when the wind kept blowing seaward, there was even talk of a *kamikaze* ("divine wind").

But what should we think of the "luck" the political leader Naoto Kan had? Was it good luck or bad luck?

In the sixth meeting of NERHQ on March 13, Kan said, "The perfect storm of this earthquake, tsunami, and nuclear power plant is the greatest crisis Japan has faced since the war."[12]

Regarding the Fukushima Daiichi NPS accident, Charles Casto, head of the U.S. Nuclear Regulatory Commission's Japan site support team, had the following to say:

"In the history of mankind, Fukushima was a battlefield where a fight was fought against physics and nature. Just one step short of war, but in a certain sense it was a harsher ordeal than war. In war, you have the choice of surrendering. But such a luxury wasn't allowed at Fukushima. They had to fight nature and physics to the bitter end. Fukushima experienced in just seven days seventy years' worth of ordeals, from the Great 1906 San Francisco earthquake to Three Mile Island and Chernobyl."[13]

Kan spearheaded the efforts to overcome this huge crisis at the Kantei. His crisis management style, however, was erratic. The Government Investigation Commission, the Diet Investigation Commission, and the Independent Investigation Commission all point out this issue.

Government Investigation Commission: "Intervening in the site of the disaster as a commander may create confusion on site, and lead to a loss in the opportunity of making important decisions or lead to making wrong judgment. As such, such an action should be viewed more as a possible cause of a greater harm than that of good."[14]

Diet Investigation Commission: ". . . because Prime Minister Kan's attention was drawn toward details, such as the state of the nuclear reactor, he did not give sufficient consideration to the emergency response issues required of the government."[15]

Independent Investigation Commission: "It is certainly undeniable that

Prime Minister Kan, by immersing himself in individual tasks of accident management, failed to direct sufficient attention to overall crisis management."[16]

Kan could not see the forest for the trees. He lacked perspective. He was too inclined to micromanage. He did not use the bureaucracy well. After a report from the bureaucracy, Kan often asked Shiro Yamazaki, his secretary, "Hey, is that all right?" This was rooted in his distrust of the bureaucracy.

Additionally, his words were gruff and he tested people's patience. He was rude and angry, and bullied people. Thus, information did not come up from the bottom and flow around smoothly. And up until the very last moment, there was never a time during the crisis when he'd found words that resonated in the hearts of the people.

The reality of the crisis response, whether it was "Kantei-led" or "Kan-led," was one where they themselves panicked while telling the people not to panic. The dismissal of Koichiro Nakamura over the use of the word "meltdown" was perhaps the first sign of this. An ex-METI official familiar with nuclear administration recalled the following:

"After that, the Kantei, which should have been making political decisions, started announcing facts. That meant that the bureaucrats had to expend even more energy in getting information to the Kantei. I think all the organizations started to shy away after that."[17]

In terms of leadership style, Kan gets a failing grade. It cannot be helped. Nevertheless, if Kan had not been there, there would probably not have been the drastic switch from "day-to-day mode" to "emergency mode." Regarding evacuation measures, a bureaucratic member of the Kantei staff said the following:

"I don't think an LDP administration [opposition party at the time] could have pulled off as tough a measure as evacuating all residents, because they would be thinking about who would take responsibility later. The Democratic Party was awfully logical about that. But how were you going to bring people back? I wondered if they had really thought about the seriousness of this policy. Did they do it with a firm resolve or without really thinking about it? However, since the reactors were in meltdown, as a result, it was the right decision. Kan and Edano were both decisive."[18]

It should be noted that even when dealing with a crisis, Kasumigaseki was still engaged in "negative power struggles." At the time of the evacuation, cooperation between NERHQ, the crisis management center, the Self-Defense Forces, the police, the fire departments, and the prefectures was highly inadequate.

The commotion over SPEEDI "roles" was an extreme avoidance of responsibility and the ultimate negative power struggle. The clash over "turns, procedures, and face" between the SDF, the Fire and Disaster Management Agency, the National Police Agency, and the Self-Defense Forces at the time of water injection also inhibited an integrated strategy.

Confronted by the hurdle of a structural silo mentality and risk aversion, Kan at once switched from "day-to-day mode" to "emergency mode." He quickly sensed the nature and scale of the crisis, and shifted to emergency response. Even sensing this, switching from "day-to-day mode" to "emergency mode" is not a simple matter.

To take an example, how enforceable were orders issued under article 64 of METI's Act on the Regulation of Nuclear Source Material, Nuclear Fuel Material, and Reactors? How coercive was Kan's "appeal" to the workers fighting inside TEPCO's Fukushima Daiichi NPS plant, to stay at their posts until the last? In a hearing before the Diet Investigation Commission, the following exchange took place between Banri Kaieda and Shuya Nomura, a lawyer.

> *Shuya Nomura:* "There is one point I would like to confirm, and that is the authority of orders that the government issues based on the Reactors Regulation Act. Even if it hypothetically led to the death of civilians, is it correct to interpret it as having the authority to order something to be done?"
>
> *Banri Kaieda:* "Well, this was a very grave decision, so . . . At the time, there appeared to be a need for some kind of support, but it wasn't saying it was all right to die, or anything like that."
>
> *Shuya Nomura:* "No, of course not, but is it correct to interpret the Reactors Regulation Act as including powers in that sense?"
>
> *Banri Kaieda:* "I don't think they are included in the Reactors Regulation Act."
>
> *Shuya Nomura:* "Well, turning to the question of evacuation, assuming that a request was made that everyone wanted to evacuate, does the government have the authority to issue an order to not evacuate?"
>
> *Banri Kaieda:* "I don't think it could order that. Not an order. It would be a request. Can't you hang in there? I believe that that is the kind of statement I always made."[19]

The government had neither the authority nor the power to force the employees of TEPCO to stay at their posts and put their lives on the line. According to Hosono, the essence of the discussion by political officers on the fifth floor of the Kantei in the early morning of March 15 was about "whether we could tell the workers to die or not." Hosono has testified that the political officers of the Kantei—Kaieda, Edano, Fukuyama, and himself—concluded they could not.

"Simply, if there was a possibility that the TEPCO workers were going to die, we couldn't tell them to die, after all. On this point, Kan had the guts to go so far as to say that. Albeit indirectly, Kan said, 'Die, TEPCO workers, it's okay for them to die.' I think he said, 'Even if they did die, the importance of the state was greater than the life of one person.' They were not his exact words, but I couldn't compare the lives of the workers to the importance of the state. I had the weakness of thinking about their individual lives and their families. Naoto Kan was by no means a humanist. He was a realist. There was no middle ground with him. It was micro or macro. So, he worried about the smallest details, but there was no middle ground, just the state."[20]

Hosono said he thought, "What a fierce life force, a survival instinct Naoto Kan has as a politician.

"Determining what needs to be done in order for the country to survive, I think he was a man of tremendous instinct. Withdrawing was impossible, and he charged into TEPCO . . . I believe even now, his judgment that there was no other choice saved Japan."[21]

No doubt, there is a touch of tribalism in the evaluation of Kan by the Kantei politicians. However, even bureaucrats who were critical of Kan and the people who worked directly on crisis response give a similar evaluation as far as this point is concerned.

Sometime after 5:30 a.m. on March 15, in his ten-minute-long prime minister's address, when he stormed TEPCO, Kan expressed vividly his sense of crisis if TEPCO withdrew from responding to the accident at Fukushima Daiichi NPS accident response, saying Japan could well be "occupied" by foreign powers like Russia or the United States. Japan would become a failed state unable to protect itself and the safety and lives of its people. Kan was fighting the terrifying scenario of "there being more than a good chance that international forces would have to come and respond."[22]

Kan looked back at his sense of fear at the time as follows:

"If it had been the Soviet Union, they could only use their Soviet forces. If it was Japan, we could only use the Self-Defense Forces in any event. If we didn't do that, someone would force their way in from somewhere. If that happened, the meaning of Japan as a country would cease to exist."[23]

The battle of Naoto Kan was a battle for the very existence of a country called Japan. His sense of crisis was on target. On the night of March 14, when it became impossible to pump water into the Unit 2 reactor, none other than Masao Yoshida feared the China syndrome and envisioned "the destruction of East Japan."[24] The Fukushima Daiichi NPS accident was nothing less than Japan's greatest postwar crisis. The vitally important core of leadership in such a crisis was a "life force, a survival instinct." And Kan had more than his fair share of both of these.

What lessons did Kan learn from Fukushima? He later testified the following during a hearing with the Diet Investigation Commission:

"Gorbachev, who was once the president of the Soviet Union, highlighted in his memoir that the Chernobyl accident illuminated the dysfunction of the entire system of his country. I think the same could be said about the Fukushima nuclear plant accident. I consider that, in a word, it illuminated the source of the dysfunction of the entire country.

"In the prewar era, the military had control over politics in Japan. From my perspective, that process appeared to coincide with what we call the 'nuclear village,' which consists of TEPCO and the Federation of Electric Power Companies (FEPC) of Japan. In other words, TEPCO and FEPC gradually strengthened their grip on nuclear policy in the past forty years. Experts, politicians, and bureaucrats who were critical of them were marginalized due to the rules of the 'village,' and were driven to the periphery. As a result, many of the people idly observed this to protect themselves by staying away from trouble. I am stating this as a way to reflect on my own regrets."[25]

THE NINETEENTH MEETING OF NERHQ, AUGUST 26, 2011. This meeting at the Kantei was Kan's last meeting as prime minister. (He resigned on September 2, 2011.) Kan spoke, "When I visited an evacuation shelter in Fukushima, I was told by one of the evacuees that his hometown was now farther away than America; that it was more difficult to go home than to go to America. Even now, these words remain clear in my mind. It is in such a context that basic emergency implementation guidelines for decontamination have been decided. This is an important first step for allowing residents to return to their hometowns."[26]

MASAO YOSHIDA

It was Site Superintendent Masao Yoshida who led at the Fukushima Daiichi NPS. He had been posted to Fukushima Daiichi NPS four times. He knew almost every employee's name there. He had remembered the names of the subcontractor company employees, too. Yoshida saw this as one of his own "strong points."[27]

Yoshida married his wife, Yoko, in 1980, the year after he joined TEPCO. It was here that Yoshida spent his life as a newlywed and raised three children. An engineer and friend of Yoshida's for nearly thirty years shared his memories:

"When Yoshida-san was working at Fukushima NPS, we used to drink a lot together. After drinking way too much, I think it was two o'clock in the morning when we both got back to his house and his wife wouldn't let us in. After a while, she came out and gave him a tongue-lashing, 'You, staying out all hours drinking!' We both apologized, saying, 'It's our fault. We're sorry.' Another time we stayed out late, drinking again, coming back to his house absolutely plastered. After keeping us waiting in the same way, his wife ripped into us, 'You two, how late have you been out drinking!' Now it had become 'you two.' At the time, Yoshida-san had three small children."

He never let his colleagues down. He kept his word. He never told his subordinates to give a report. That was why they always reported to him without him having to ask.[28]

"Charismatic." "Like a big brother." "Larger than life." A great many people used these epithets to describe Yoshida's personality and job performance. They all unanimously said that if Yoshida had not been the site superintendent, it would have been almost impossible to get anything done at Fukushima Daiichi amid the crisis.

However, there was a problem in Yoshida's accident response. In the case of Unit 1, Yoshida was not aware that the isolation condenser (IC) had stopped. He only remembered a report of "open" and judged thereafter that the IC was "open," and the core cooling was being carried out smoothly.[29]

The problem was probably more structural than a question of individual misjudgment by the operators, shift supervisors, or Yoshida. The site ERC did not independently review and provide feedback prior to the decisions by the control room staff to stop both Unit OL1's isolation condensers and the Unit 3 high-pressure water injection system (HPCI) pump. In addition, while the Head Office ERC helped develop plans and strategies, gave advice, and assisted in obtaining needed equipment and support, this group did not view its role as providing independent oversight of site decisions or actions.[30]

In the first place, operators had only limited experience actually operating the IC system. A twenty-five-year-veteran shift supervisor later stated, "I had never seen the IC system in operation and I don't think it had ever been operated during my career."[31]

In the case of Unit 2, it may well have been saved if they had switched to low-pressure injection while the RCIC was in operation, and pumped in water from fire engines. In the case of Unit 3, putting an end to water injection early on the morning of March 13 was probably a costly mistake.

2:42 A.M. ON MARCH 13. Thinking they would be able to inject water using the diesel-powered fire pumps, an operator stopped the HPCI. As a result, the pressure in the reactor soared, making it no longer possible to inject water through the diesel-powered fire pumps. Although they made a flustered attempt to restart the HPCI, it failed to operate, because they had lost the DC power supply and with it all means of water injection. Yoshida did not know this for nearly an hour. Eventually, water pumping recommenced at 9:20 a.m. During that time, nearly six hours and forty minutes, it led to the reactor being heated up with no water in.

Another factor was the overreaction to the comment "Isn't it too soon to be using seawater?" from a TEPCO officer at the Kantei. The seawater injection that was under preparation was halted, forcing them to start all over with preparations to pump in freshwater. This wasted valuable time and effort.[32]

In this case, TEPCO Vice President Sakae Muto, who was at the offsite center, questioned, "Shouldn't we be thinking about seawater? Shouldn't we be consulting with the Kantei?" In response to this, Yoshida stuck with injecting freshwater, saying, "We've added a little boric acid, I'm thinking we'd like to do without seawater."[33] It is hard to believe that the Yoshida so particular about freshwater at this time was the same man who had pretended to halt seawater injection operations at the request of Head Office and Takekuro while daring to continue seawater pumping operations on the night of March 12.[34]

Based on TEPCO's later assessment of the reactors, it was estimated that the distance between the steel plate of the reactor containment vessel and the area eroded by the molten fuel was only 37 centimeters for Unit 1. Tsuneo Futami, professor of nuclear engineering at Tokyo Institute of Technology, believes that if they had stopped injecting seawater in the evening of March 12, the molten fuel would have flowed down and exacerbated the "core concrete reaction," which causes the concrete to melt. Futami was a year older than Yoshida when they attended graduate school together at Tokyo Institute of Technology and later was his superior at TEPCO. Nevertheless, he noted that not only Yoshida, but all those on site shared the concern that "under these severe working conditions, there is no guarantee that they can inject water again once it stops." Futami later reflected that he "can only respect the selfless effort and courageous decisions made by the workers on site."[35]

The root of the problem was the misjudgment of TEPCO Head Office and the excessive intervention of the Kantei sticking its nose into individual accident responses, but Yoshida also bore a large responsibility.[36]

Likewise, there were flaws in Yoshida's response regarding radiation protection and measures for a serious accident, as well as accident response training before the accident. Had the government and TEPCO taken earthquake and tsunami countermeasures more seriously, they could have prevented the total power outage and would never have had to evacuate people by hundreds of thousands. The employees would also have not been placed in such a situation.

Yoshida had been responsible for the development of disaster response as nuclear power facilities management director at the Head Office. It was in 2008, and despite being told by a tsunami expert group of the need for taking serious countermeasures against tsunamis, he shared responsibility with Takekuro and Muto for ignoring this advice.

Their claims were based on calculating that the height of a tsunami hitting Fukushima Daiichi NPS would be 15.7 meters if a great earthquake happened along the trench off Fukushima Prefecture, on the same scale as the 8.2-magnitude Meiji Sanriku earthquake, which hit the Tohoku region in 1896.

MARCH 11, 2011. A tsunami of just that height came rushing in.[37]

In the Government Investigation Commission hearings, the most convoluted and defensive logic was Yoshida's response to questions about the lack of preparedness for a tsunami:

"This time, 23,000 people died. Who killed them? They died because a magnitude-9 quake came. If you're going to say that to me, why weren't measures taken then, so those people didn't die?

"If you're talking about basic things to protect Japanese lives and property, that's something that has to be taken up in the Central Disaster Management Council and measures put in place by local governments as well. That's where the state is not performing. All it does is talk about nuclear plant design."

What does this mean?

It sounds as if he bore a grudge, a sense of being victimized, implying that since there were no seawalls in the vicinity of the general public's homes, "23,000 people" (actually, the number of dead or missing was 19,610) became casualties of the tsunami. Although it was the same for the nuclear plants, he seems to grouse, why was only the lack of seawalls around the plants criticized—and that despite the fact that there were no direct casualties from the nuclear accident?[38]

Is it not the case that Yoshida should have been ashamed when TEPCO's tsunami countermeasures were compared with those at Tohoku Electric Power's Onagawa nuclear power station?

Despite being located on the same Pacific coast, as well as being the closest nuclear power station to the epicenter of the earthquake, Tohoku Electric Power's Onagawa NPS escaped the tyranny of relentless tsunami waves. It was good fortune that it had embankments that could withstand 17-meter-high tsunamis and its levees were raised a further 3.5 meters.

Thirty minutes after the tsunami waves swept in, the local residents near Onagawa nuclear power station had evacuated there. That was because it was built on a hill and was the only place with electricity running, televisions that could be turned on, and potable water. The site superintendent, on his own judgment, opened up a gym and office for them. Onagawa nuclear power station became an isolated island, but a designated communication line showed its power when a helicopter from the Sendai headquarters arrived on the morning of March 12, loaded with water, food, blankets, and other necessities. The nuclear power plant became the residents' shelter. The numbers reached 360 people at one point. They lived there for three months after the earthquake disaster.

In its report, the Government Investigative Commission points out that "there is no evidence that such issues [preparing for a tsunami] were considered essential in the whole of TEPCO."[39] That is true.

Here, Yoshida bears a heavy weight of responsibility.

The accident did happen. However, after it happened, Yoshida, in extremis, gave his all to respond to the crisis. Looking back, Yoshida himself said his top crisis management priority was "to throw in water for cooling."

"For my men, it was like being blindfolded in the cockpit of an airplane that has lost everything, even its hydraulic pressure. How could we land the plane in such a situation? You know, we had no idea what the state of the valve was when the 'power outed.' The only certain thing was throwing in water for cooling. As we explored ways of restoring power, that was the single thing we tried constantly to do."[40]

Masaya Yasui comments as follows:

"When a plane is in trouble and is forced to make an emergency landing, the first thing the pilot must do is to make a safe landing and safely disembark his passengers no matter what. Instead of asking why such a plane was built in the first place, the top priority is to make a safe emergency landing. The battle was in a world without manuals. Hypotheses had to be made and ideas put forward, those would be the game changers."

In this, most extreme of conditions, his evaluation of Yoshida was that the latter had done as much as possible.[41] As an organizational leader in crisis, Yoshida was a strong presence.

In the early morning of March 12, this was Kan's first impression when he met Yoshida at Fukushima Daiichi NPS for the first time. After returning from this visit, Kan told everyone Yoshida met his expectations.

Toshimi Kitazawa, minister of defense, remembers Kan saying immediately after his visit, "I thought everyone at TEPCO was useless, but there was a really solid guy when I went to the site."[42]

Kan had the feeling, when he met Yoshida, that "Finally I could talk with someone who didn't speak anonymously." This was because up until then, "I had no idea even when I asked who was calling the shots, who was responsible. Everything was being done in anonymity" at TEPCO.[43]

Looking back, Charles Casto also had a strong impression of Yoshida.

"I don't know that I'd call him a charismatic leader, but he puts so much confidence in his people; they'd put their lives on the line for him. I felt that he had some knack to make those under him admire and be devoted to him."[44]

Yoshida told him, "We spent our days wondering whether to drink the water in the bottle or use it to cook some rice, one or the other," and smiled. Casto saw him as a "Spartan samurai."[45]

There was a time when that samurai shed tears. It was on April 21, when Masato Taura, deputy commander of the Central Readiness Forces (CRF) and site coordinator, visited Yoshida in the Anti-Seismic Building.

On April 11, a month to the day after the earthquake, another earthquake hit. Taura was at the helm at J-Village, but they also had a power outage. Even after an hour, there was no contact from Fukushima Daiichi

NPS. This was no good. What on earth was TEPCO thinking? Taura asked to see Yoshida, and a meeting was set for April 21.

He met with Yoshida in the Anti-Seismic Building. After first greeting the workers in the ERC and offering words of encouragement, they moved to a small room to talk. Yoshida was a little defensive. The very first thing he said was, "I'm really sorry about that time."

"What do you mean?"

He mentioned having requested the SDF to inject water just before the explosion in Unit 3 (RB) on the morning of March 14.

"The figures (radiation dose in the vicinity of Unit 3) had been climbing, but it had leveled off a bit, so I asked the SDF to come. I'm so sorry I didn't say, 'It's dangerous, don't come.' "

"No, I haven't come about that today. We were lucky things didn't turn out worse and the morale of the troops is still high."

Taura then told Yoshida, "We are thinking of rescue strategies for everyone working here, starting with the TEPCO workers, should something happen. We can fly helicopters and rush tanks to the scene; we have eight specially equipped armored vehicles at the ready, and we are currently using every drop of knowledge we have to plot the fastest routes to escape. However, there is only one thing I would like to ask you. Please give us the information first. That's all I ask."

A big tear dropped from Yoshida's eye, as he listened in silence. He clasped Taura's hand firmly and said, "I had no idea that the Self-Defense Forces were making such evacuation plans for us. I really had no idea."

Taura changed the topic.

"By the way, Yoshida-san, what makes you the angriest, the maddest these days?"

Yoshida was a little taken aback by such an unusual question.

"Well, every day many ideas are put forward on the daytime talk shows. All those professors saying, do this with the reactor, do that with the water, on and on. When those shows are over, our fax machine starts ringing. It's always queries coming from Head Office along the lines of, 'How about trying something like this?' "

"That would make anyone hopping mad!"[46]

In the ERC on the second floor of the Anti-Seismic Building, Yoshida sat at his usual seat at the round table. He did not look directly at the screen, and did not face directly forward either. He was always looking not at the Head Office, but at his colleagues working at the site. The people who knew Yoshida well felt this typified his attitude and perspective.[47]

Every day, at five p.m., a twenty-minute meeting was held in the ERC on the second floor of the Anti-Seismic Building, chaired in rotation by each group leader of Fukushima Daiichi NPS. The leader of the power generation team, the recovery team, the construction team, the civil engineering team, and the security team would report briefly on their recovery work and accident response for the day, as well as projected future developments. More than a hundred people attended, including the heads of the associate companies' respective Fukushima Daiichi offices.

When he heard some positive news of something being restored or a system hooked up, Yoshida always took the lead in applauding. That was how they kept each other's spirits up. At the end, the unit chief would thank everyone for their hard work that day. And then Yoshida would say, "Thank you very much. Let's finish up with *ippon-jime* (traditional applause to celebrate the conclusion of something) then."

"Ready?"

And when the ritual was over, he would say, "Take care." Yoshida spent most of the crisis in the Anti-Seismic Building. Once in a while, he went for a smoke or a nap in the site superintendent's office behind the duty room on the first floor. A rotation had been organized for staff, but there was no rotation for Yoshida.

On only one occasion was he carried off to the medical room. It was before eleven a.m. on March 20; on that morning, he was often repeating and slurring his words. He left the ERC supported by several people, saying, "I can't think, change the leadership."[48]

When Yoshida resigned as site superintendent, he recalled, "My life was saved by the staff at the associate companies."[49] Yoshida's affection and respect for the people from the associate companies were most likely founded on the terrible truth that they were working in the most dangerous places. Yoshida's conviction was that "If you didn't protect the people working at the most dangerous jobs, you couldn't protect the residents."

"It's the staff from the associate companies working in the most dangerous places in the reactor, and if I can't protect their lives, there is no way I can tell the residents, 'It's safe,' and how can anyone who holds those lives in disregard be able to protect the lives of residents?" Yoshida told his men repeatedly.

Yoshida retired as site superintendent of the Fukushima Daiichi NPS on December 1, 2011. His robust body had been afflicted by cancer.[50]

He had a surgery in February 2012, but was struck by an intracerebral hemorrhage in July that year. He passed away on July 9, 2013, at the age of fifty-eight. Upon Yoshida's passing, the emperor sent his condolences to Yoko, his widow.

DECEMBER 9, 2011. Yoshida visited Fukushima Daiichi NPS and gave a resignation speech. In front of hundreds of people wearing Tyvek suits in the Anti-Seismic Building ERC, he picked up the microphone.

"I have been diagnosed with stage three esophageal cancer. From now, I will have treatment and surgery for cancer.

"We have all worked here together. It's a great pity to have to leave here in this way. Everyone, please take care of yourselves. Those of you who smoke, don't smoke too much."[51]

NAOHIRO MASUDA

It was Masuda's third time stationed at Fukushima Daini. He had first worked here as an apprentice after graduating from college. For the first two years, he had been in charge of the "instrumentation" for measuring and controlling the water level and the temperature of the reactor. After that, he was entrusted with electrical operations for a year. The next time he served as unit chief from 2005 to 2008. At the time, Yoshida was also unit chief of Fukushima Daiichi.

Then, in June 2010, he was appointed site superintendent at Daini. In the same way, Yoshida also took up the position of site superintendent at Fukushima Daiichi. Masuda was three years younger than Yoshida, but he had served at Fukushima three times, his terms coinciding with Yoshida's.[52]

On March 10, the day before the earthquake, he had a meal with Yoshida at a TEPCO staff facility in Tomioka. They exchanged views on their respective plans as superintendents in the 2011 financial year. It was their first meeting since they had been appointed to Fukushima. They had much to talk about, and it was the middle of the night before they finished.[53]

When the earthquake and tsunami struck, all Fukushima Daini Units—1, 2, 3, and 4—were in operation. There were fifty people in the Central Control Room (Units 1 and 2), and fifty more in the other Control Room (Units 3 and 4). This made for a total operational staff of a hundred people in all.[54]

After the tsunami hit, both the Anti-Seismic Building and the office building lost power and everything went black. Masuda took command in the ERC of the Anti-Seismic Building, but on the afternoon of March 11, there were so many tsunami warnings issued and so many aftershocks that there was nothing they could do.

He was dying to know what the situation was onsite and to send in a recovery team as soon as possible, but could not send personnel out of the Anti-Seismic Building under these conditions. The entire plant was in a dangerous state for two hours after the first tsunami. After about four hours, Masuda made up his mind.

"We can go now, please go."

"Give me a walk-down."

A walk-down was a site status survey via accessing the site, listening in, and so on. The tsunami had put the seawater pump for cooling the reactor near the coast out of action.

For six hours, they were unable to access some damaged areas of the plant.[55] Walk-down reports kept coming in one after another. Nearly a hundred hydrogen cylinders in the hydrogen cylinder building by the sea had toppled over. This hydrogen was used to cool down the heat of the generator. They had to be stood up. But what if they exploded . . .

While writing down procedural instructions, Masuda felt his chest pounding. After he finished writing, he ordered the power generation team, "You, do it." He visualized the faces of every member of the power generation team.[56]

Sometime after ten on the morning of March 12, they actually set up a vent line. The work was completed in thirty minutes for each of the Units 2, 3, and 4. However, Unit 1 took eight hours.[57]

At 3:36 p.m. on March 12, the Anti-Seismic Building shook with a rumble. A few minutes later, news at the local television station ran footage of the instant of the explosion.

"What? Why now? What is this?"

They did not know what had exploded. The Anti-Seismic Building has no windows, so a sense of direction and time gradually fades. Both TEPCO Head Office and Fukushima Daiichi were in a state of confusion, with people all over shouting simultaneously on the videoconference. The chain of command was unclear. In addition, neither the ERC at Fukushima Daiichi was issuing appropriate instructions to the site, nor the Head Office to Fukushima Daiichi. Staff at Fukushima Daini told each other, "Let's make sure we don't end up like that."[58]

To use the words of Izawa, who had deep respect for Yoshida, during the crisis, Yoshida's was precisely "a lone struggle." Or, to reverse the statement, Fukushima Daiichi did not work well as a team. Masuda made every effort to work as a team.

Immediately after the accident, Masuda devoted his time to clarifying the division of duties while overseeing the entire chain of command. He asked the operations administration manager to take charge of cooling down the reactors and the preservation manager to focus on recovering the power supply. In doing so, the preservation team managed to reconnect the cables from the remaining outlets and recover power supply to the reactors. At the same time, the cooling-down team was able to maintain the cooling function by injecting water into the reactors using a low pressure system called Make-Up Water Condensate (MUWC) until the seawater pipe damaged by the tsunami was repaired.

There was another thing Masuda was careful about. He had to make sure that the hydrogen explosion at Unit 1 of Fukushima Daiichi did not demoralize staff members at Daini. Masuda later reminisced about the time:

"I'm sorry to say there was no time to worry about Daiichi. Everyone's minds go completely blank at times like that. You know, everyone's homes have been swept away by the tsunami, so they're wondering if their families are all right. So, even if I issued instructions, a lot of staff just couldn't process them. At times like that, I shouted out in a booming voice, 'Damn you! You there, repeat what I just said!' and had them repeat . . ."[59]

After the explosion, the first thing he did was create a separate entrance and set up a shelter for personnel evacuating from Daiichi. These were measures to protect Daini from contamination. Everyone had to undergo a thorough decontamination before they were allowed into the shelter. That was practical and clear. Even if it was thought to be cold and heartless, he ordered them to do it.[60]

Masuda did not participate much in the videoconference, but when he raised his voice, he was insistent, and he stuck to his guns when making demands of the Head Office. In the videoconferences between the Head Office and Fukushima Daini, it was decided that Masuda would be the single spokesperson for Daini. Masuda noticed, on hearing Daiichi's interactions with Head Office from the side, that the important matters were insufficiently wrapped up, as there were many interruptions to the conversation, because only the things from each person's post, respectively, were reported. Therefore, he took all responsibility to respond himself.[61]

One of his strongest demands was for water to be arranged. They had a water tank for the showers and toilets. He wanted to get water in there. Sometime after ten p.m. on March 14, Masuda made a direct appeal to the Head Office.

> *Site Superintendent Masuda:* "We don't have any water . . . We had a contract for four thousand tons with the SDF scheduled to bring it in, but when they saw the reactor building explosion at 1F, they went back. 2F will be at risk if you don't get us water somehow."
>
> *TEPCO Fellow Akio Takahashi at Head Office:* "How many tons do you need at minimum? A thousand, two thousand?"
>
> *Site Superintendent Masuda:* "I want four thousand tons. Four thousand tons."

After a while, Masuda once again complained to the Head Office, "Water for living is at zero now."

On hearing this, a voice piped up from Daiichi NPS, "We're in trouble, too."

Unable to keep quiet, Daiichi Site Superintendent Yoshida had butted in, "That's right. Any water we have is being chucked into the reactors."[62]

Masuda also broke in, as if he could not bear to stay silent. "People have been coming over since the explosion at 1F, but we don't have the water to decontaminate them."[63]

They had no choice but to do everything themselves. Masuda declared his decision to the staff: "We are going to be independent from the Head Office."

This later became known at the Head Office as "Masuda's Declaration of Independence."[64]

The two hundred workers laying nine kilometers of cable was nothing less than an autonomous operation from the Head Office. The Head Office Transmission Group (less than a hundred people) initially went to Fukushima Daiichi, but Unit 1 had a hydrogen explosion. So, it was decided that they should stand by at Fukushima Daini. They did an outstanding job in laying the cable at Fukushima Daini. They insisted, "We're not going to rely on the associate companies. We're not managers. We'll do it on our own."

Fukushima Daiichi went into meltdown, but Fukushima Daini escaped that fate. What set Daiichi and Daini apart was whether they controlled the pressure smartly and kept up water injection or not. At Fukushima Daini, from the start, they reduced the reactor pressure by the SR valve without hesitation, and while the high pressure water injection was still working, they were able to inject water into the reactor and stabilize it using MUWC.

In dealing with accidents in Units 1 and 2 at Fukushima Daini NPS, they were able to conduct the decompression operation with agility, and maintain the means of injecting water, but this was where Fukushima Daiichi stumbled. This was what the Government Investigation Commission criticized in its final report when it conducted a detailed comparison with Fukushima Daini's response.[65]

Just as at Fukushima Daiichi, there were no power trucks at Fukushima Daini. The first thing Masuda did after the accident was to scrape together some power trucks. He thought only of electricity, and got twenty.

He received a borderline screaming request from Fukushima Daiichi NPS to "send some over," but Masuda refused. He stuck to that unsentimentally. He resolved that he would only help others after he had carried out his responsibility—namely, restoring power to Fukushima Daini NPS.

In fact, Fukushima Daini had also lost its seawater pump near the coast for cooling the reactors, and at one stage, three out of four reactors were in a precarious state. Masuda later stated at a press conference that "we were only a hairbreadth away from the same situation as Fukushima Daiichi NPS."[66]

At 7:47 a.m. on March 12, Fukushima Daini was also pushed to an article 15 emergency declaration. Before eight a.m. on the same morning, a report—"A force is being put together from 2F to work on opening the vents"—arrived at the Nuclear Safety Commission. Much like Fukushima

Daiichi, Fukushima Daini were preparing a "venting suicide squad" to release the pressure inside the storage container.[67]

It was only from the night of March 15 that Fukushima Daini sent power trucks over to Fukushima Daiichi. Before six p.m. on the same day, they sent twenty out of the fifty-three power trucks to Fukushima Daiichi for restoration work at Units 5 and 6. Toshiba had pointed out that "Units 5 and 6 were in danger," and, as a result, the Head Office had taken action to send power trucks from Daini to Daiichi.[68]

After the earthquake, Yoshida told the workers from associate companies, who were not directly involved in stabilizing the reactor, to go home. Masuda, however, immediately closed the gate, ensuring employees could not leave without permission. The TEPCO executive who related this episode described them as "Yoshida a leader from the heart, Masuda a leader from the head."[69]

It was just before the accident that a Toshiba engineer met Masuda for the first time in a long while. When Masuda asked him, "Which job are you on now?" he answered, "1F."

Masuda said, half-jokingly, "It's dirty over there. Don't come over here."

Masuda was a Fukushima Daini man through and through.[70] In contrast, Yoshida was a Fukushima Daiichi man through and through. To borrow Masaya Yasui's turn of phrase, "At Fukushima Daiichi and Daini, there was the leader Yoshida and the Masuda team. In terms of accident response, the Masuda team is the best model. Rather than being a capable engineer, Masuda was an outstanding risk manager."[71]

A Toshiba engineer, who had a long-standing relationship with both Yoshida and Masuda, put it this way:

"Fukushima Daiichi would not have escaped if it hadn't been for Yoshida. Fukushima Daini would not have ended to the degree it did if it hadn't been for Masuda."[72]

In terms of crisis management and handling an actual accident, Charles Casto, head of the U.S. NRC's Japan support site, praised Naohiro Masuda as a "real hero." "There was a lot of talk about the Fukushima 50, but the Daini 200 were heroes, too." In fact, Fukushima Daini was in a dangerous state, as well. Saving it was Masuda's achievement.[73]

For two hours after the tsunami, the plant was in a dangerous state with operating personnel unable to access it. For six hours, they were unable to access some damaged areas of the plant.[74]

As the technicians say, with nuclear power, "you live by electricity and die by it." Masuda was an electrician. The electrician's world was one where "you couldn't afford to have a single connector diagram missing." You turned on the switch and things either lit up or they did not. Yoshida was a machinist. Machinists tend to be more lackadaisical. If something went wrong, they would tap or hit it first. From the electrician's perspective, this looks unscientific and barbaric, but to the machinist it is in the realm of craftsmanship.

The relationship between the Daiichi plant, led by Yoshida, and the Daini plant, led by Masuda, was sometimes delicate. Some of the people stuck in Daiichi's Anti-Seismic Building resented the fact that even if they asked Daini for some logistical support, the answer was always no. Some of those temporarily evacuated from Daiichi to Daini felt humiliated by the persistent decontamination screening. However, Daini was the only available place for temporary evacuation when Daiichi entered a crisis situation.

On the morning of March 15, when they heard a "strange noise" in the Anti-Seismic Building, and the pressure in the suppression chamber fell to zero, Yoshida decided to "temporarily evacuate." This was because there was a possibility of a sharp increase in radioactivity. Yoshida arranged for a bus and contacted Daini's Masuda.[75]

Yoshida initially thought of a two-stage evacuation, first to somewhere else at Daiichi and then withdrawing to Daini if that proved untenable, but there was no longer anywhere to evacuate on the Daiichi site. Yoshida and Masuda had talked it over that morning and decided on a strategy for a large-scale evacuation of more than six hundred people to Daini.[76]

It was on March 23 that Masuda gave permission for the virtually incarcerated workers from the associated companies at Daini to go home. It was on that day that a three-stage backup system was completed to cool the decay heat from the fuel rods with seawater. He watched them go, everyone clapping each other on the back. Daini had succeeded impressively in bringing the decay heat under control.

In the spring of 2013, Masuda was to return to the Head Office. Someone had the idea of taking a group photo of all the Fukushima Daini staff before he left his post. It was March 11, 2013, the second anniversary.

All the staff members gathered in front of the office building. Where should it be taken? And from which angle? Usually a lot of people had their heads down when you took a photo. A staff member and keen photographer waited for Masuda's instructions. Masuda said, "Hey, take the photo from the roof of the office building."

If you took it from the rooftop, everyone would be looking up. And looking up, your eyes seem to absorb only the brightness of the world. You get the feeling that your heart is being lifted up into the sky. They got the staff members to stand in front of the main entrance of the office building, all with a smile, and look up at the camera lens on the roof. The people in the front row were holding a banner.

"Let's do our best with one heart."[77]

HEROES

Charles Casto had a deep respect for both Yoshida and Masuda, describing both men as heroes. Even in the midst of the crisis, he recalled the friendly conversations he was able to have with them.

Casto said, "The people doing the low-profile jobs without uttering a word in the field were the true heroes." Yoshida, Masuda, Sato, and Izawa were all heroes in that sense. He went on, with a caveat:

"I used the word 'heroes,' but what is more important in the unique nuclear industry is to need no more heroes. Even if Yoshida, Masuda, and the duty managers were heroes, they need to be the last heroes."[78]

There were many hard workers on site who silently performed tedious tasks. However, they are often forgotten. They were even perhaps forgotten individuals to begin with. To sing the praises of TEPCO employees after the accident was taboo, after all. But many heroes remain whose songs have been unsung, from the likes of Mari Sato and Ikuo Izawa to Ryuta Idogawa.

Mari Sato, the officer in charge of disaster prevention at TEPCO, evacuated from Daiichi to Daini at this time, but she returned to Daiichi on March 17. Two people responsible for Fukushima Daiichi from Kajima Corporation came to Daini to help. In the midst of everyone running all over the place, there were people who came to help at the risk to their own life. Sato felt a lump in her throat. The ERC was suffering an overwhelming shortage of manpower. She could maybe do something to help. If she let them down, she would regret it for the rest of her life. She decided to go back.

However, since there was smoke coming out of Unit 4 on March 23, she was told that women should leave, and so she left the site. At Iwaki City, there was an NTT DoCoMo store with a poster saying, "We've reopened." She went straight into the store and bought a mobile phone. The first shock from the earthquake had sent her mobile phone flying off her desk, and, having lost sight of it, she had been without a cell phone all this time. When Sato called her parents, she heard that they were staying with relatives in Tokyo. She saw her husband, son, and daughter again on March 28.

On April 1, she went to the Safety and Disaster Prevention Division at the Head Office in Tokyo. When she went to check out the Emergency Response Room, she was stopped when she got off the elevator at the second floor, being asked, "Excuse me, are you with the press?"

Sato told an officer from the Disaster Prevention and Safety Division at the Head Office, "I don't think there's much choice but to set up a support team and tough it out," but he replied in a few words, "There's nothing more we can do. It's all been organized.

"Sato-san, if you want to work at the Head Office, I'll find something for you."

It was probably the best he could do. And while she was grateful, she was also aware of her mind distancing itself as she thought,

The site is still a battleground. They are battling to the death. Despite that, the Head Office itself is business as usual, just like another world.[79]

Ikuo Izawa left the Fukushima Daiichi site on March 25. Until then, he had remained in the emergency response room in the Anti-Seismic Building as one of the "Fukushima 50." His wife had evacuated to the apartment her niece shared with her husband in Iwaki City. He met up with her there. His beard had grown out and his hair was flattened. When they met, he was told, "You don't look like my uncle at all!" He was worried about whether his wife's rheumatism had been aggravated by the disaster, but was relieved to find that it did not seem to have been too much.

This day was the first time since the day of the disaster that he had a bath. As he sunk into the bath, his whole body started shaking uncontrollably.

"Oh, I'm alive, I'm alive now."

That is what he found himself saying. Tears came welling up and he began to sob. He put his face under water so the women would not hear him.[80]

Even when Izawa bumped into childhood friends in his hometown, he would keep on apologizing, "I'm sorry, I'm so sorry." As time passed, he started to feel as though the people's hostile views of TEPCO workers were gradually easing. However, the tough truth that TEPCO destroyed their lives will remain forever. What is more, Izawa's heart felt as heavy as lead. He could not escape feeling as though he had failed in the initial response to the IC as shift manager of Units 1 and 2, toppling the first piece of the domino. He could not get away from this thought. There was no end to his regret.[81]

In the morning hours of March 15, the main reactor operator, Ryuta Idogawa, also "temporarily evacuated" to Fukushima Daini. When he arrived, he was shocked to find out that he was not even allowed to enter the school gym. He was "treated as a *hibakusha* [a survivor of a nuclear bomb who often experienced discrimination], or a thing." Later on, however, Idogawa started to think that the protocol had been "right" under those circumstances.

At the end of March, Idogawa visited the Tokyo Head Office. Even though they were all TEPCO employees, he was startled by the difference between the Fukushima site and the Tokyo Head Office. "They could go home on time, but we had to stay on site twenty-four hours. No supplies came to Daiichi. We were forced to keep fighting on the front lines of a battlefield without weapons."

We were simply disposable pawns, he thought.

It was when the exposure dose limit was raised that Idogawa started to think like that. "During a crisis, the government can raise the exposure limit as much as they want without any limitations. I will be killed by my company and country." It was at this point that Idogawa considered quitting his job.

In summer 2011, a groundbreaking ceremony was held in Futaba-cho. On the beach by the Pacific Ocean, while gazing out at the coast, everyone prayed for those who had died. Idogawa's father was the mayor and organizer of the ceremony. John, Idogawa's pet beagle, was there, too. His father said that he had seen John's face, for sure.

Those narrow and clever eyes. That must be John, he thought.

However, the mayor could not simply run to get his pet dog in the middle of a ceremony. But once the ceremony had finished, John had disappeared again. Six months later, Idogawa's cousin told him that a picture of a dog resembling John was on the town's website in a section where pictures of found pets were uploaded. John had a hairless patch around his eyebrows. "It is John. It's definitely John."

Idogawa's mother went to the facility where the missing dogs were kept. It was John, for sure, and he happily shook his tail at the sight of her. Unfortunately, though, John passed away shortly afterward.

In November 2011, Idogawa was transferred to become the operator of Unit 6. The reason was "overexposure to radiation." In December 2011, the government announced that the Fukushima Nuclear Plant accident was now under control. *Under control? How?* Idogawa was far from convinced. He had lost all his motivation and energy, and quit TEPCO soon after that.[82]

Notes

Acknowledgments

1. http://rebuildjpn.org/en/project/Fukushima/report/.
2. *Rashomon* refers to the award-winning film by Akira Kurosawa that recounts a crime from four mutually contradicting perspectives. The term "Rashomon effect" has since been often used to refer to contradictory interpretations of the same event by different people.
3. http://www.tepco.co.jp/en/press/corp-com/release/betu13_e/images/130329e0801.pdf.
4. https://www8.cao.go.jp/genshiryoku_bousai/fu_koukai/fu_koukai_2.html (Japanese only).
5. http://rebuildjpn.org/en/project/Fukushima/yoshidachosho/.
6. English versions of Government Investigation's Interim Report http://www.cas.go.jp/jp/seisaku/icanps/eng/interim-report.html; National Diet's Official Report https://www.nirs.org/wp-content/uploads/Fukushima/naiic_report.pdf; Government Investigation's Final Report http://www.cas.go.jp/jp/seisaku/icanps/eng/final-report.html.

Introduction

1. English versions of Government Investigation's Interim Report http://www.cas.go.jp/jp/seisaku/icanps/eng/interim-report.html; National Diet's Official Report https://www.nirs.org/wp-content/uploads/Fukushima/naiic_report.pdf; Government Investigation's Final Report http://www.cas.go.jp/jp/seisaku/icanps/eng/final-report.html.
2. Japan Electric Power Information Center, Inc.,"The Electric Power Industry in Japan 2020," March 2020, 3.
3. James M. Acton, "Wagging the Plutonium Dog," Carnegie Endowment for International Peace, June 2015.

Chapter 1

1. Charles Casto, *Station Blackout: Inside the Fukushima Nuclear Disaster and Recovery* (New York: Radius Book Group, 2018), 33.
2. "TEPCO Staff Survey—Situation in the Immediate Aftermath of the Accident,"

Asahi Shimbun, December 23, 2011; Government Investigation Commission on the Accident at the Fukushima Nuclear Power Stations of Tokyo Electric Power Company, "Interim Report," December 26, 2011, 95–100; interview with a Toshiba engineer, December 9, 2011; Ryusho Kadota, *The Man Who Went to the Brink of Death—Masao Yoshida and his 500 Days at the Fukushima Daiichi Nuclear Station* (Kyoto: PHP, 2012), 31, 49–50; Ikuo Izawa, interview, August 8, 2013; Ikuo Izawa's lecture at Japan Nuclear Safety Institute's Duty Manager Training, February 12, 2014.

3. NHK Special Meltdown Report Crew, *Meltdown: The Truth About the Chain Reaction* (Tokyo: Kodansha, 2013), 39; Ikuo Izawa's lecture at Japan Nuclear Safety Institute's Duty Manager Training, February 12, 2014.

4. Regarding the time of the second tsunami, the Government Investigation Commission on the Accident at the Fukushima Nuclear Power Stations of Tokyo Electric Power Company (Interim Report) places it at 3:35 p.m. and the National Diet of Japan Fukushima Nuclear Accident Independent Investigation Commission at 3:37 p.m. Bearing in mind that the first horizontal impact of the tsunami on the breakwater sent up a vertical column some 30 meters high, tsunami experts later calculated the energy volume of the tsunami at this time as a tremendously destructive force equivalent to a medium-sized passenger jet crashing in at 600 kilometers per hour. See, Yanagida Kunio, "My Final Report on the Nuclear Plant Accident 2, Reactor Meltdown, Superintendent Yoshida's Failure," *Bungeishunju* (October 2012), 355.

5. Ikuo Izawa, interview, August 8, 2013; Kadota, *The Man Who Went to the Brink of Death*, 31, 61; Ikuo Izawa's lecture at Japan Nuclear Safety Institute's Duty Manager Training, February 12, 2014.

6. Charles Casto, *Station Blackout: Inside the Fukushima Nuclear Disaster and Recovery* (New York: Radius Book Group, 2018), 38.

7. Kadota, *The Man Who Went to the Brink of Death*, 31, 37.

8. Rebuild Japan Initiative Foundation (RJIF), *Independent Investigation Commission on the Fukushima Nuclear Accident* (Abingdon: Routledge, 2014), Prologue, xlv; TEPCO, "Fukushima Nuclear Accident Report," June 20, 2012, 142–44; Government Investigation Commission on the Accident at the Fukushima Nuclear Power Stations of Tokyo Electric Power Company, "Final Report," July 23, 2012, 98–99; Banri Kaieda, *The Kaieda Notes—A Record of the 176-Day Nuclear Struggle* (Tokyo: Kodansha, 2012), 117.

9. Kunio Yanagida, "My Final Report on the Nuclear Plant Accident 2, Reactor Meltdown, Superintendent Yoshida's Failure," *Bungeishunju* (October, 2012).

10. Government Investigation Commission, "Interim Report" (Japanese version), 91; Government Investigation Commission, "J-Village, July 22, 2011," *Masao Yoshida, Hearing Results Report*, August 16, 2011, 20–21, 28; Government Investigation Commission, "J-Village, November 6, 2011," *Masao Yoshida, Hearing Results Report*, August 16, 2011, 51–52.

11. Ibid., 92–93.

12. Interview with a Toshiba engineer, December 9, 2011.

13. Charles Casto, *Station Blackout: Inside the Fukushima Nuclear Disaster and Recovery* (New York: Radius Book Group, 2018), 39.

14. Government Investigation Commission, "Interim Report," 109.

15. Charles Casto, *Station Blackout: Inside the Fukushima Nuclear Disaster and Recovery* (New York: Radius Book Group, 2018), 39.

16. Ibid., 42.

17. NHK Special Meltdown Report Crew, *Meltdown*, 31–32.

18. Yanagida, "My Final Report on the Nuclear Plant Accident 2," 358; NHK Special Meltdown Report Crew, *Meltdown*, 46.

19. Charles Casto, *Station Blackout: Inside the Fukushima Nuclear Disaster and Recovery* (New York: Radius Book Group, 2018), 46–47.

20. Ibid., 49.

21. Takeyuki Inagaki, interview, December 10, 2013.
22. NHK Special Meltdown Report Crew, *Meltdown*, 58.
23. Ikuo Izawa, interview, August 8, 2013; NHK Special Meltdown Report Crew, *Meltdown*, 65; Yanagida, "My Final Report on the Nuclear Plant Accident 2," 359; NHK Special Meltdown Report Crew, *Meltdown*, 65; "88 Hours of the Nuclear Meltdown Crisis," *NHK Special*, March 13, 2016; "Meltdown file 6: Nuclear Reactor Cooling, The Overlooked Crisis 12 days In," *NHK Special*, March 12, 2017.
24. "88 Hours of the Nuclear Meltdown Crisis," *NHK Special*, March 13, 2016; "Meltdown file 6: Nuclear Reactor Cooling, The Overlooked Crisis 12 days In," *NHK Special*, March 12, 2017.
25. Government Investigation Commission, "J-Village, July 22, 2011," Masao Yoshida, Hearing Results Report, August 16, 2011, 31.
26. Government Investigation Commission Secretariat, Report on Investigation of Masao Yoshida, August 16, 2011, Hearing conducted at J-Village on July 22, 2011, 31.
27. "Meltdown File 6: Nuclear Reactor Cooling, the Overlooked Crisis 12 Days In," *NHK Special*, March 12, 2017.
28. RJIF, *Independent Investigation Commission on the Fukushima Nuclear Accident*, Prologue, xlvi; Government Investigation Commission, "Interim Report," 96–97; interview with a Toshiba engineer, September 20, 2012; Toshihiro Okuyama, "A Reporter's Independent Examination of the TEPCO Nuclear Accident Announcement and Reporting, Part 1," *Journalism*, June 20, 2012.
29. Charles Casto, *Station Blackout: Inside the Fukushima Nuclear Disaster and Recovery* (New York: Radius Book Group, 2018), 53.
30. The Government Investigation Commission on the Accident at the Fukushima Nuclear Power Stations' Interim Report states that the "white haze" at the double doors of Unit 1 Reactor Building was found later at around 4 a.m. on the 12th, and that regarding the place of its discovery, "the possibility that the steam leaked into the dry wall (D/W) arising from the damaged portions associated with the reactor pressure vessel, pipes or penetrations cannot be ruled out." In Government Investigation Commission, "Interim Report," 166–67, footnote.
31. RJIF, *Independent Investigation Commission on the Fukushima Nuclear Accident*, Prologue, xlvii.
32. Government Investigation Commission, "Interim Report," 109.
33. "Fukushima Daiichi Nuclear Station: The TEPCO Videoconference Tapes," *Asahi Shimbun*, September 5, 2012; RJIF, *Independent Investigation Commission on the Fukushima Nuclear Accident*, Prologue.
34. Government Investigation Commission, "Interim Report," 137, 164; TEPCO videoconference participant memo shown to the author, September 12, 2012.
35. Takeyuki Inagaki, interview, December 10, 2013.
36. TEPCO videoconference participant memo shown to the author, September 21, 2012.
37. Ibid.
38. On May 11, 2011, TEPCO released its amended measurement of the water level in Unit 1. According to this, the actual water level was so low as to be unreadable and the figures they had read up until then were more than three meters too high. Moreover, when they examined the IC condensate tank onsite on October 18, 2011, they learned that a large part of the cooling water remained without having been used. In the final analysis, it would appear that the figures reported at 9:19 p.m. on March 11th after the water instrumentation had been temporarily restored were way above the actual level. It is surmised that the water level fell during the 11th, exposing the fuel rods, it fell down below a large portion of the fuel, and the pressure vessel ruptured in the early hours of the 12th with molten fuel leaking down into the containment vessel. See, Okuyama, "A Reporter's Independent Examination of the TEPCO Nuclear Accident Announcement and Reporting, Part 1."

39. Takeyuki Inagaki, interview, December 10, 2013; NHK Special Meltdown Report Crew, *Meltdown*, 58.

40. Government Investigation Commission, "J-Village, July 22, 2011," *Masao Yoshida, Hearing Results Report*, August 16, 2011, 34–36.

41. Charles Casto, *Station Blackout: Inside the Fukushima Nuclear Disaster and Recovery* (New York: Radius Book Group, 2018), 53.

42. Tsuneo Futami, interview, November 22, 2012.

43. Charles Casto, interview, August 24, 2011.

44. Interview with a Kashima Corporation engineer, October 5, 2011.

45. TEPCO, "Fukushima Nuclear Accident Report," 74–76, 405.

46. Interview with a senior Nuclear and Industrial Safety Agency official, September 29, 2011.

47. Ibid., October 19, 2011.

48. TEPCO, "Fukushima Nuclear Accident Report," 405; Shingo Akashi, interview, August 10, 2011.

49. "Investigation: The TEPCO Videoconferences," *Asahi Shimbun*, 2012, 195.

50. TEPCO, "Fukushima Nuclear Accident Report," 420.

51. RJIF, *Independent Investigation Commission on the Fukushima Nuclear Accident*, Prologue, xlvi.

52. TEPCO, "Fukushima Nuclear Accident Report," 57.

53. Hideo Suzuki, interview, September 22, 2011.

54. Kazuma Yokota, interview, September 3, 2011.

55. Ibid.

56. Government Investigation Commission, "Interim Report," 57–58.

57. Ibid., 60–61.

58. Ibid., 77.

59. Kenji Matsuoka, "Minutes of the Working Group to Review the Regulatory Guide for Emergency Preparedness for Nuclear Facilities," Nuclear Safety Commission, August 12, 2011.

60. Government Investigation Commission, "Interim Report," 78.

61. NISA internal memo, 11.

62. Banri Kaieda, interview, July 10, 2012; Eiji Hiraoka, interviews, June 1, 2012; August 9, 2012; interview with a senior METI official, August 17, 2011.

63. Interview with a senior Nuclear and Industrial Safety Agency official, July 5, 2012.

64. Fukushima Nuclear Accident Record Team, Tomomi Miyazaki and Hideaki Kimura (eds.), *49 Hours of the Fukushima Nuclear Accident TEPCO Videoconference Records* (Tokyo: Iwanami Shoten, 2013), 39.

65. Government Investigation Commission, "Interim Report," 78, 549.

66. Interview with a senior Nuclear and Industrial Safety Agency official, July 5, 2012.

67. Ibid., September 3, 2012; interview with NISA inspector in charge of the inspection, January 18, 2012.

68. Interview with a senior Nuclear and Industrial Safety Agency official, July 5, 2012.

69. Ibid., January 13, 2012.

70. Motohisa Ikeda, "The Fukushima Nuclear Station Accident: March 11–15, 2011 (Memorandum)," December 19, 2011.

71. Interview with a senior Nuclear and Industrial Safety Agency official, July 5, 2012.

72. Haruki Madarame, interview, December 17, 2011.

73. Interview with a senior Nuclear and Industrial Safety Agency official, January 13, 2012.

74. Ikeda, "The Fukushima Nuclear Station Accident."

75. Shinichi Kuroki, interview, January 13, 2012.

76. Rebuild Japan Initiative Foundation (RJIF), *Independent Investigation Commission on the Fukushima Nuclear Accident* (Tokyo: Discover Twenty One, 2012), 155. (Only included in the Japanese version.)

77. NRC staff whiteboard, Appendix 1–16/38.

78. NSC, "Changes in screening levels," Document No. 6, 12, September 13, 2012 (http://www.nsr.go.jp/archive/nsc/info/20110829_dis.pdf).

79. Ibid.

80. Takako Tominaga, interview, December 20, 2011; Shingo Akashi, interview, November 5, 2012.

Chapter 2

1. Kan later wrote of this illegal donation question in his book, "Having had this pointed out to me, I appointed a lawyer to confirm the situation, and when it was found that he was a Korean citizen born in Japan but with Korean nationality, I returned the funds. The matter was taken to the Tokyo Office of the Prosecutor, but was dismissed. It was further raised in the Prosecution Council, but was also dismissed here as not prosecutable, bringing the legal process to a complete end." In Kan, *The TEPCO Fukushima Nuclear Accident*, 45.

2. Political Bureau, Yomiuri Shimbun, *Chancellor of the Lost Kingdom: The 180 days of the Kantei's Function Loss* (Tokyo: Shinchosha, 2011), 17.

3. Tetsuro Fukuyama, interview, June 9, 2012.

4. Banri Kaieda, *The Kaieda Notes—A Record of the 176-Day Nuclear Struggle* (Tokyo: Kodansha 2012), 13.

5. Tetsuro Ito, interview, April 9, 2012.

6. Interview with a senior Ministry of Defense official, December 2, 2011.

7. Manabu Terada, interview, July 26, 2012.

8. Tetsuro Fukuyama, testimony before the Independent Investigation Commission, October 29, 2011.

9. Shuichi Sakurai, interview, December 2, 2011.

10. Genba Koichiro, interview, July 24, 2012.

11. Interview with a senior Kantei official, September 15, 2011.

12. Kaieda, *The Kaieda Notes*, 16.

13. "Inside the Meltdown," *BBC*, February 23, 2012.

14. Tetsuro Fukuyama, *The Nuclear Crisis: Testimony from the Kantei* (Tokyo: Chikuma Shinsho, 2012), 25.

15. Government Investigation Commission on the Accident at the Fukushima Nuclear Power Stations of Tokyo Electric Power Company, "Interim Report," December 26, 2011, 96.

16. Mamoru Ito, *TV Coverage of the Nuclear Accident* (Tokyo: Heibonsha Shinsho, 2012), 36.

17. Kenichi Shimomura, interview, November 25, 2011.

18. Government Investigation Commission, "Interim Report," 65.

19. TEPCO, "Fukushima Nuclear Accident Report," June 20, 2012, 71.

20. Government Investigation Commission on the Accident at the Fukushima Nuclear Power Stations of Tokyo Electric Power Company, "Final Report," July 23, 2012, 216.

21. Interview with a Kantei staff member, October 12, 2011; Manabu Terada, interviews, November 30, 2011; July 26, 2012; interview with a senior Nuclear and Industrial Safety Agency official, February 27, 2012; interview with a Kantei parliamentary secretary, February 27, 2012; Naoto Kan, *The TEPCO Fukushima Nuclear Accident: My Thoughts As Prime Minister* (Tokyo: Gentosha Shinsho, 2012), 63.

22. Ito, *TV Coverage of the Nuclear Accident*, 52.

23. Fukuyama, *The Nuclear Crisis*, 26.

24. Kenichi Shimomura, interview, November 25, 2011; Banri Kaieda, testimony before the Government Investigation Commission, Minutes No. 14, May 17, 2012.

25. Koji Okamoto, *Testimony: Haruki Madarame—Where NISA Went Wrong* (Tokyo: Shinchosha, 2012), 39.

26. Manabu Terada, interview, November 30, 2011.

27. Interviews with a senior METI official, November 7, 2011; March 5, 2012; Kenichi Shimomura, interview, December 1, 2011; Manabu Terada, interview, July 26, 2012; Kaieda, *The Kaieda Notes*, 20.

28. Government Investigation Commission, "Interim Report," 59.

29. Upper House Budget Committee, "Minutes," April 18, 2011; "Why has PM forgotten the training that supposed a nuclear accident? Kan 'doesn't recollect in detail'," *Asahi Shimbun*, April 19, 2011; Tadahiro Matsushita, interview, September 12, 2011; Yoshihiro Katayama, interview, July 18, 2012; interview with a senior official, Ministry of Health, Labour and Welfare, October 15, 2012.

30. "The Fukushima Daiichi Nuclear Accident: An Outline of the Response HQ Minutes," *Nihon Keizai Shimbun*, March 10, 2012; interview with a Kantei staff member, June 28, 2011.

31. Toshimi Kitazawa, *Why Japan Needs the SDF* (Tokyo: Kadokawa Shoten, 2012), 70.

32. Banri Kaieda, interview, June 5, 2011.

33. Yukio Edano, testimony before the Independent Investigation Commission, December 10, 2011; Yukio Edano, *What Has to be Said Even If Not Popular: 'De-modernization' and 'Negative Redistribution'* (Tokyo: Toyo Keizai Shinposha, 2012), 18-19.

34. Tetsuro Fukuyama, interview, June 9, 2012.

35. Tetsuro Ito, interview, April 9, 2012.

36. Fukuyama, *The Nuclear Crisis*, 33; Tetsuro Ito, interview, May 19, 2012.

37. Koichi Kato, interview, September 22, 2011; senior METI official, interview, August 17, 2011; interview with a senior Ministry of Defense official, October 7, 2011; Manabu Terada, interview, July 26, 2012; interview with a high ranking Kantei official, October 31, 2012.

38. NISA internal memo, 2.

39. Naoto Kan, interview, September 14, 2011; Kenichi Shimomura, interview, November 25, 2011.

40. Interview with a Kantei staff member, February 23, 2012.

41. Naoto Kan, interview, March 23, 2012; interview with a senior Ministry of Defense official, November 9, 2011; Yoshifumi Hibako, interview, November 25, 2011; Interview with a high ranking Kantei official, October 31, 2012; NISA internal memo, 2.

42. Fukuyama, *The Nuclear Crisis*, 41.

43. Goshi Hosono, interview, May 30, 2012; Manabu Terada, interview, July 26, 2012.

44. Manabu Terada, interview, July 26, 2012.

45. Goshi Hosono, interview, September 5, 2012.

46. TEPCO, "Fukushima Nuclear Accident Report," June 20, 2012, 119; NISA internal memo, 3.

47. Kenichi Shimomura, interview, November 25, 2011; Kan, *The TEPCO Fukushima Nuclear Accident*, 67.

48. Interview with a secretarial staff member at the Kantei, February 27, 2012; "The Mortal Sins of TEPCO," *Shukan Bunshun Special Edition*, July 27, 2011, 24–25.

49. Interview with a Toshiba engineer, September 4, 2012; Toshihiro Okuyama, *Report: A Month of TEPCO's Nuclear Accident* (Asahi Shinsho, 2011), 45; interview with a high-ranking official at the Kantei, September 15, 2011.

50. Haruki Madarame, testimony before the Independent Investigation Commission, December 17, 2011.

51. TEPCO videoconference participant memo shown to the author, September 21, 2012.

52. "The Accident Investigation Commission: Detailed Report on the Statement of Former METI Minister Kaieda," *Mainichi Shimbun*, May 18, 2012; Kan Naoto, interview, November 14, 2012.

53. "Detailed Report on the Videoconference Footage Released by TEPCO," *Yomiuri Shimbun*, August 7, 2012.

54. Ito, *TV Coverage of the Nuclear Accident*, 67.

55. Government Investigation Commission, " Interim Report," 158; Nuclear Safety Commission, Whiteboard memo, Appendix 1–4/38; Edano, *What Has to be Said Even If Not Popular*, 23; Tetsuro Fukuyama, interview, May 19, 2011; Tetsuro Fukuyama, *NHK Special*, rebroadcast on June 19, 2011.

56. Kaieda, *The Kaieda Notes*, 22–23, 29.

57. Interview with a senior METI official, October 12, 2011.

58. Nuclear Safety Commission, Whiteboard memo, Appendix 1–13/38.

59. Mitsuhiro Kajimoto, interview, September 3, 2012.

60. Ibid.; interview with a secretarial staff member at the Kantei, October 10, 2012; interview with a senior Nuclear and Industrial Safety Agency official, June 1, 2012.

61. Interview with a technical staff member, June 17, 2013.

62. NISA internal memo, 6.

63. Government Investigation Commission, "Final Report," 324–27; interview with a senior METI official, November 7, 2011; "Lessons Learned from the Nuclear Power Plant Disaster," *Nihon Keizai Shimbun*, November 27, 2011; Haruki Madarame, testimony before the Independent Investigation Commission, December 17, 2011; interview with a senior Nuclear and Industrial Safety Agency official, February 27, 2012; Edano, *What Has to be Said Even If Not Popular*, 39; Kazuo Hizumi and Ryuichi Kino, *The Fukushima Nuclear Accident Press Conferences: What did TEPCO and the Government Hide?* (Tokyo: Iwanami Shoten, 2012), 15.

64. Report by a third-party investigation committee on the Fukushima Daiichi Nuclear Power Plant Accident, June 16, 2016, 30.

65. Akiyoshi Minematsu, interview, April 19, 2017; Akiyoshi Minematsu, interview, May 25, 2017.

66. Report by a third-party investigation committee on the Fukushima Daiichi Nuclear Power Plant Accident, June 16, 2016, 31.

67. Government Investigation Commission, "Interim Report," 414.

68. Interview with a TEPCO affiliate engineer, August 30, 2012.

69. The Government Investigation Final Report is demanding a "reassessment" criticizing that this assessment result is "insufficient." Government Investigation Commission, "Final Report," July 23, 2012, 475–76. The latest analysis from TEPCO revealed that reactor core damage for Unit 3 started around 5:10 a.m. on the 13th. According to TEPCO, "Results of investigation concerning the examination of unconfirmed matters on specific development mechanisms after the Fukushima nuclear accident (5th Progress Report)," December 25, 2017.

70. Kunio Yanagida, "My Final Report on the Nuclear Plant Accident 3, Plant Suicide Squad Fights Despair," *Bungeishunju* (November issue, 2012), 210.

71. The National Diet of Japan Fukushima Nuclear Accident Independent Investigation Commission, "The Official Report," July 5, 2012, Ch. 3, 7.

72. Yanagida, *My Final Report on the Nuclear Plant Accident 3*, 210.

73. Nuclear Safety Commission Secretariat, http://www.nsr.go.jp/archive/nsc/jikeiretsu_kanri/index.html.

74. Government Investigation Commission, "Interim Report," 167.

75. Fukuyama, *The Nuclear Crisis*, 47.

76. "Examining the Great Disaster: Testimony from Former PM Kan," *Mainichi Shimbun*, September 7, 2011.

77. NHK Special, "The Nuclear Crisis Episode 1: Why Did the Accident Become So Serious?" June 5, 2011.

78. Haruki Madarame, interview, December 17, 2011.

79. Fukuyama, *The Nuclear Crisis*, 48.

80. NISA internal memo, 4.

81. Government Investigation Commission, "Final Report," 264.

82. Ito, *TV Coverage of the Nuclear Accident*, 68.

83. Tetsuro Fukuyama, interview, May 19, 2011.

84. Toshihiro Okuyama, "A Reporter's Independent Examination of the TEPCO Nuclear Accident Announcement and Reporting, Part 1," *Journalism* (June 2012).

85. TEPCO, "Fukushima Nuclear Accident Report," June 20, 2012, 72.

86. Government Investigation Commission, "Interim Report," 147; Haruki Madarame, interview, December 14, 2011.

87. Okuyama, *Report*, 55; interview with a senior TEPCO officer, May 10, 2012.

88. Kaieda, *The Kaieda Notes*, 32; Yanagida, *My Final Report on the Nuclear Plant Accident 3*, 211.

89. Fukuyama, *The Nuclear Crisis*, 53.

90. Interview with a Kantei staff member, June 28, 2011.

91. Tetsuro Fukuyama, interview, May 19, 2011.

92. Interview with a Kantei staff member, August 17, 2011; Yukio Edano, testimony before the Independent Investigation Commission, December 10, 2011; Rebuild Japan Initiative Foundation (RJIF), *Independent Investigation Commission on the Fukushima Nuclear Accident* (Abingdon: Routledge, 2014), 15.

93. Banri Kaieda, testimony before the Diet Investigation Commission, Minutes No. 14, May 17, 2012.

94. Goshi Hosono, interview, February 13, 2012.

95. TEPCO videoconference participant memo shown to the author, September 21, 2012; Government Investigation Commission, "Interim Report," 171.

96. Interview with a senior TEPCO officer, May 10, 2012.

97. Edano, *What Has to be Said Even If Not Popular*, 18.

98. Interview with a Kantei staff member, August 17, 2011; Manabu Terada, interview, November 30, 2011; Banri Kaieda, testimony before the Diet Investigation Commission, Minutes No. 14, May 17, 2012; Eiji Hiraokoa, interview, May 28, 2012; Kan, *The TEPCO Fukushima Nuclear Accident*, 72–73; Fukuyama, *The Nuclear Crisis*, 56; Tetsuro Fukuyama, interviews, November 3, 2012; November 15, 2012.

99. Interview with a Kantei staff member, August 17, 2011; Manabu Terada, interview, November 30, 2011; Banri Kaieda, Testimony before the Diet Investigation Commission, Minutes No. 14, May 17, 2012; Eiji Hiraokoa, interview, May 28, 2012; Kan, *The TEPCO Fukushima Nuclear Accident*, 72-73; Fukuyama, *The Nuclear Crisis*, 56; Tetsuro Fukuyama, interviews, November 3, 2012; November 15, 2012.

100. Government Investigation Commission, Interim Report, December 26, 2011, 175; NISA internal memo, 9.

101. Toshikatsu Nakayama, interview, May 16, 2012.

102. TEPCO videoconference participant memo shown to the author, September 21, 2012.

103. Okuyama, *Report: A Month of TEPCO's Nuclear Accident* (Tokyo, Asahi Shinsho, 2011); Yukio Edano, testimony before the Independent Investigation

Commission, December 10, 2011; Banri Kaieda, interview, August 18, 2011; Banri Kaieda, testimony before the Diet Investigation Commission, Minutes No. 14, May 17, 2012; Kaieda, *The Kaieda Notes*, 34.

Chapter 3

1. Manabu Terada, interview, July 26, 2012; Tetsuro Fukuyama, interview, January 21, 2012; Government Investigation Commission on the Accident at the Fukushima Nuclear Power Stations of Tokyo Electric Power Company, Final Report, July 23, 2012, 437.

2. Tetsuro Fukuyama, *The Nuclear Crisis: Testimony from the Kantei* (Tokyo: Chikuma Shinsho, 2012), 66.

3. Interview with a senior TEPCO officer, August 27, 2011; Motohisa Ikeda, interview, September 1, 2011; interview with a high-ranking Kantei official, November 22, 2011; Yukio Edano, testimony before the Independent Investigation Commission, December 10, 2011; Manabu Terada, interview, July 26, 2012; Goshi Hosono, interview, February 13, 2012; interview with a Kantei secretary, October 10, 2012.

4. Tetsuro Fukuyama, interview, January 21, 2012; interview with a senior official of the Ministry of Economy, Trade, and Industry, March 5, 2012.

5. Kenichi Shimomura, interview, November 25, 2011; Sakae Muto, testimony before the Diet Investigation Commission, Minutes No. 6, March 14, 2012.

6. Manabu Terada, interview, July 26, 2012.

7. Interview with a senior official of the Ministry of Defense, December 2, 2011.

8. Koji Okamoto, *Testimony: Madarame Haruki—Where NISA Went Wrong* (Tokyo: Shinchosha, 2012), 15.

9. Kenichi Shimomura, interview, December 1, 2011; Haruki Madarame, testimony before the Independent Investigation Commission, December 17, 2011; Haruki Madarame, interview, October 4, 2012; Okamoto, *Testimony*, 68; Ryusho Kadota, *The Man Who Went to the Brink of Death—Masao Yoshida and His 500 Days at the Fukushima Daiichi Nuclear Station* (Kyoto: PHP, 2012), 141.

10. Sakae Muto, testimony before the Diet Investigation Commission, Minutes No. 6, March 14, 2012; Manabu Terada, interview, July 26, 2012.

11. Interview with a Kantei staff member, June 28, 2011; Kenichi Shimomura, interview, December 1, 2011; Haruki Madarame, testimony before the Independent Investigation Commission, December 17, 2011; Okamoto, *Testimony*, 18; Manabu Terada, interview, July 26, 2012; Naoto Kan, interview, November 14, 2012; TEPCO, "Fukushima Nuclear Accident Report," June 20, 2012, Appendix 56; Naoto Kan, *The TEPCO Fukushima Nuclear Accident: My Thoughts as Prime Minister* (Tokyo: Gentosha Shinsho, 2012), 75.

12. Interview with a Nuclear and Industrial Safety Agency staff member, February 3, 2012; Sakae Muto, testimony before the Diet Investigation Commission, Minutes No. 6, March 14, 2012.

13. Kenichi Shimomura, interview, December 1, 2011; Haruki Madarame, testimony before the Independent Investigation Commission, December 17, 2011; Okamoto, *Testimony*, 24; Manabu Terada, interview, July 26, 2012.

14. Kenichi Shimomura, interview, December 1, 2011; Haruki Madarame, interview, December 14, 2011; Haruki Madarame, testimony before the Independent Investigation Commission, December 17, 2011; interview with a senior official of the Nuclear and Industrial Safety Agency, January 13, 2012; Nuclear Safety Commission, whiteboard memo, Appendix 1–10/38.

15. Mamoru Ito, *TV Coverage of the Nuclear Accident* (Tokyo: Heibonsha Shinsho, 2012), 78.

16. Motohisa Ikeda, interview, September 1, 2011; Motohisa Ikeda, memorandum on the Fukushima Nuclear Power Station Accident March 11–15, 2011 (December 19, 2011).

17. Naoto Kan, interview, September 14, 2011; Manabu Terada, interviews, November 30, 2011 and July 26, 2012.

18. Kenichi Shimomura, interview, November 25, 2011.

19. Kan, *The TEPCO Fukushima Nuclear Accident*, 79.

20. Government Investigation Commission on the Accident at the Fukushima Nuclear Power Stations of Tokyo Electric Power Company, Interim Report, December 26, 2011, 174; National Diet of Japan Fukushima Accident Independent Investigation Commission, Official Report, July 5, 2012, ch. 2, 20; Takeyuki Inagaki, interview, December 12, 2013.

21. Rebuild Japan Initiative Foundation (RJIF), *Independent Investigation Commission on the Fukushima Nuclear Accident* (Abingdon: Routledge, 2014), prologue, xlviii.

22. TEPCO, Fukushima Nuclear Accident Report, July 5, 2012, 145.

23. Government Investigation Commission, Interim Report, 174–76.

24. National Diet Commission, Official Report, ch. 2, 54.

25. Institute of Nuclear Power Operations, Special Report on the Nuclear Accident at the Fukushima Daiichi Nuclear Power Station, November 2011, 17.

26. Banri Kaieda, *The Kaieda Notes—A Record of the 176-Day Nuclear Struggle* (Tokyo: Kodansha 2012), 37.

27. Charles Casto, interview, July 26, 2013; Ikuo Izawa, interview, August 8, 2013; Kadota, *The Man Who Went to the Brink of Death*, 124–27; Ikuo Izawa's lecture at Japan Nuclear Safety Institute's Duty Manager Training, February 12, 2014.

28. Ikuo Izawa, interview, August 8, 2013; Kadota, *The Man Who Went to the Brink of Death*, 9–20; Ryuta Idogawa, interview, August 10, 2018.

29. "Inside the Meltdown," *BBC*, February 23, 2012.

30. Ikuo Izawa, interview, August 8, 2013; Kadota, *The Man Who Went to the Brink of Death*, 173–77; Mitsuru Komematsu, interview, June 21, 2017.

31. Government Investigation Commission, Interim Report, 176; TEPCO, Fukushima Nuclear Accident Report, June 20, 2012, 146; Ikuo Izawa, interview, August 8, 2013; Kadota, *The Man Who Went to the Brink of Death*, 31, 171, 183–86.

32. NHK Special Meltdown Report Crew, *Meltdown: The Truth About the Chain Reaction* (Tokyo: Kodansha, 2013), 274.

33. Takeyuki Inagaki, interview, December 10, 2013; Ikuo Izawa's lecture at Japan Nuclear Safety Institute's Duty Manager Training, February 12, 2014.

34. Government Investigation Commission, Interim Report, 180; National Diet Commission, Official Report, ch. 3, 8; Kaieda, *The Kaieda Notes*, 39.

35. Haruki Madarame, testimony before the Independent Investigation Commission, December 17, 2011.

36. Toshihiro Okuyama, *Report: A Month of TEPCO's Nuclear Accident* (Tokyo: Asahi Shinsho, 2011), 208.

37. Tetsuro Fukuyama, interview, May 19, 2011; Naoto Kan, interview, September 14, 2011; Manabu Terada, interview, November 30, 2011; Fukuyama, *The Nuclear Crisis*, 60; Kaieda, *The Kaieda Notes*, 34.

38. Interview with a Kantei staff member, August 18, 2011.

39. Political Bureau, Yomiuri Shimbun, *Chancellor of the Lost Kingdom: The 180 Days of the Kantei's Function Loss* (Tokyo: Shinchosha, 2011), 38; "Station Manager Masao Yoshida Directs Staff to Prepare for Venting in an Hour's Time," TEPCO document 6/18 = Kan's visit during the missing 73 minutes [6:50 a.m. to 8:03 a.m.].

40. "New Timetable Bogus: A Senior Officer at Fukushima Daiichi Speaks Out—The Truth About Fukushima, Sequel," *Asahi Weekly*, July 29, 2011, 28.

41. "Fukushima Daiichi Power Plant: The Truth About Fukushima from a Senior Officer," *Asahi Weekly*, July 29, 2011.

42. Interview with an official of the Ministry of Economy, Trade, and Industry, August 17, 2011.

43. TEPCO, Fukushima Nuclear Accident Report, June 20, 2012, 56.

44. Government Investigation Commission, Interim Report, 181–82.

45. National Diet Commission, Official Report, ch. 2, 54.

46. Mari Sato, interview, January 15, 2016.

47. Government Investigation Commission, Interim Report, 183.

48. TEPCO, Fukushima Nuclear Accident Report, June 20, 2012, 200–02; Ikuo Izawa, interview, August 8, 2013; Ikuo Izawa's lecture at Japan Nuclear Safety Institute's Duty Manager Training, February 12, 2014.

49. "TEPCO Staff Survey—Situation in the Immediate Aftermath of the Accident," *Asahi Shimbun*, December 23, 2011; TEPCO, Fukushima Nuclear Accident Report, June 20, 2012, 149; "Inside the Meltdown," *BBC*, February 23, 2012.

50. TEPCO official, interview, December 12, 2012; Kadota Takamsa, *The Man Who Saw the Edge of Death: Masao Yoshida and 500 Days at Fukushima Daiichi* (Tokyo: PHP, 2012), 204–09; "TEPCO Investigates Operators on Situation Immediately after the Accident," *Asahi Shimbun*, December 23, 2011; NHK Special, Meltdown Investigation Team, Truth of the *Meltdown Chain* (Tokyo: Kodansha, 2013); Ikuo Izawa, interview, August 8, 2013; Ikuo Izawa, remarks at the JANSI Lessons from Accident Manager Seminar, December 12, 2014; Mitsuru Komemasu, interview, June 21, 2017; Shizuo Takahashi, interview, March 29, 2018; Ryuta Idogawa, interview, August 10, 2018; Masanori Kaneyama, interview, May 19, 2020.

51. Haruki Madarame, testimony before the Independent Investigation Commission, December 17, 2011; Kenichi Shimomura, interview, December 1, 2011.

52. Tetsuro Fukuyama, interview, September 27, 2011; Haruki Madarame, interview, December 14, 2011; NTV, "2011 Reporting Footage that Should Be Kept for a Millennium," Friday Super-Prime, December 23, 2011; Ichiro Takekuro, interview, January 11, 2012; interview with a Kantei parliamentary secretary, May 23, 2012; Kaoru Endo, *How the Media Reported the Disaster and Nuclear Emergency* (Tokyo Denki University Press, 2012); Fukuyama, *The Nuclear Crisis*, 75; Kan, *The TEPCO Fukushima Nuclear Accident*, 80; Kaieda, *The Kaieda Notes*, 42.

53. Koichiro Genba, "Minister Genba: The First Seven Days" (memo on the movements of Minister Genba in the immediate aftermath of the Great East Japan earthquake).

54. Ito, *TV Coverage of the Nuclear Accident*, 89–90.

55. NISA internal memo, 7; Ikuo Izawa, interview, August 8, 2013.

56. Institute of Nuclear Power Operations, Special Report on the Nuclear Accident at the Fukushima Daiichi Nuclear Power Station, November 2011, 21.

57. Tadahiro Matsushita, interview, November 8, 2011; Kenichi Shimomura, interview, November 25, 2011; Yukio Edano, testimony before the Independent Investigation Commission, December 10, 2011; Yukio Edano, *What Has to Be Said Even If Not Popular: "De-modernization" and "Negative Redistribution"* (Tokyo: Toyo Keizai Shinposha, 2012), 24; Fukuyama, *The Nuclear Crisis*, 79; NISA internal memo, 6.

58. TEPCO, Fukushima Nuclear Accident Report, June 20, 2012, 87–88; interview with a Kantei parliamentary secretary, February 27, 2012.

59. Fourth Nuclear Emergency Response Headquarters Meeting, minutes summary.

60. Interview with a Kantei parliamentary secretary, February 27, 2012; "An Outline of the Nuclear Emergency Response Headquarters Minutes," *Yomiuri Shimbun*, March 10, 2012; "The Fukushima Daiichi Nuclear Accident: An Outline of the Response HQ Minutes," *Nihon Keizai Shimbun*, March 10, 2012.

61. Tatsujiro Suzuki, interview, June 22, 2011.

62. Rebuild Japan Initiative Foundation (RJIF), *Independent Investigation Commission on the Fukushima Nuclear Accident* (Tokyo: Discover Twenty-One, 2012), 139. (Only included in the Japanese version.)

63. Manabu Terada, interview, July 26, 2012.
64. @G_D_Greenberg, Twitter, April 4, 2012.

Chapter 4

1. Ryusho Kadota, *The Man Who Went to the Brink of Death—Masao Yoshida and His 500 Days at the Fukushima Daiichi Nuclear Station* (Kyoto: PHP, 2012), 76–77, 81–82; Ikuo Izawa, interview, August 8, 2013; Takeyuki Inagaki, interview, December 10, 2013.

2. Government Investigation Commission on the Accident at the Fukushima Nuclear Power Stations of Tokyo Electric Power Company, Interim Report, December 26, 2011, 142–62, 529; Asahi Shimbun, *Investigation: The TEPCO Videoconferences* (Tokyo: Asahi Shimbun Press, 2012), 67–68; Inagaki Takeyuki, interview, December 10, 2013; Hiroyuki Ogawa, interview, December 7, 2015; Mari Sato, interviews, January 16, 2016 and April 21, 2017.

3. Masatoshi Fukura, interview, December 2, 2014.

4. Mari Sato, interviews, January 16, 2016, and April 21, 2017.

5. Government Investigation Commission, Interim Report, 123, 133–35.

6. Interview with a Kantei parliamentary secretary, February 27, 2012; Eiji Hiraoka, interview, June 1, 2012; NISA, Provisional Report on the Time Series from the Eruption of the Earthquake, June 30, 2011.

7. Government Investigation Commission, Interim Report, 156.

8. Banri Kaieda, interview, July 10, 2012.

9. Akihiko Iwahashi, interview, December 5, 2011; Ichiro Takekuro, interview, January 11, 2012; TEPCO videoconference participant memo, released September 21, 2012; Goshi Hosono and Shuntaro Torigoe, *Testimony: Shuntaro Torigoe Closes In on the Truth about "The 500 Days of Nuclear Crisis"* (Tokyo: Kodansha, 2012), 73; Eiji Hiraoka, interview, June 1, 2012.

10. Akihiko Iwahashi, interview, November 11, 2011; Haruki Madarame, interview, December 17, 2011; Government Investigation Commission, Interim Report, 194; Ichiro Takekuro, testimony before the Diet Investigation Commission, Minutes No. 8, March 28, 2012; Banri Kaieda, testimony before the Diet Investigation Commission, Minutes No. 14, May 17, 2012; Naoto Kan, *The TEPCO Fukushima Nuclear Accident: My Thoughts as Prime Minister* (Tokyo: Gentosha Shinsho, 2012), 85.

11. Eiji Hiraoka, interviews, August 10, 2011 and June 1, 2012; interview with a senior METI official, March 5, 2012.

12. Sakae Muto, testimony before the Diet Investigation Commission, Minutes No. 6, March 14, 2012; Kunio Yanagida, "My Final Report on the Nuclear Plant Accident 3, Plant Suicide Squad Fights Despair," *Bungeishunju*, November 2012, 218; Government Investigation Commission, "J-Village, July 29, 2011," *Masao Yoshida, Hearing Results Report*, August 16, 2011, 9.

13. "Seawater Injection Suspension Restart: Government Gets No Information," *Asahi Shimbun*, May 22, 2011; Nippon TV, "2011 Reporting Footage that Should Be Kept for a Millennium," *Friday Super-Prime*, December 23, 2011; National Diet of Japan Fukushima Nuclear Accident Independent Investigation Commission, Official Report, July 5, 2012, ch. 3, 66; Sakae Muto, testimony before the Diet Investigation Commission, Minutes No. 6, March 14, 2012; Ichiro Takekuro, testimony before the Diet Investigation Commission, Minutes No. 8, March 28, 2012; Kadota, *The Man Who Went to the Brink of Death*, 221; Yanagida, "My Final Report on the Nuclear Plant Accident 3, Plant Suicide Squad Fights Despair," 218; Government Investigation Commission, "J-Village, July 29, 2011," *Masao Yoshida, Hearing Results Report*, August 16, 2011, 9; Takeyuki Inagaki, interview, December 10, 2013.

14. Goshi Hosono, interview, October 6, 2011; Government Investigation Com-

mission, Interim Report, 197; Tetsuro Fukuyama, interview, January 21, 2012; interview with a Kantei parliamentary secretary, May 31, 2012; Takeyuki Inagaki, interview, December 10, 2013; Eiji Hiraoka, interview, June 1, 2012; Tetsuro Fukuyama, *The Nuclear Crisis: Testimony from the Kantei* (Tokyo: Chikuma Shinsho, 2012), 86–87; Kan, *The TEPCO Fukushima Nuclear Accident*, 85.

15. Government Investigation Commission, Interim Report, 73.

16. Charles Casto, *Station Blackout: Inside the Fukushima Nuclear Disaster and Recovery* (New York: Radius Book Group, 2018), 63.

17. At the time, Tadayuki Yokomura, site superintendent of Kashiwazaki-Kariwa power station, who attended the videoconference from there, spoke in the following manner about the mistake of stopping the HPCI: "Even if up until then the ability to put water into the HPCI reactor had been overused, stopping was premature. In actuality, by consuming steam, it was relieving the pressure. Therefore, at the moment it stopped, the reactor pressure reverted. It was thought that the diesel-driven fire pump (DDFP) was operating, so the HPCI was stopped. That should never be done. From then, when trying to open the SR valves, the lamp was on, thus it was thought that the SR valves would open, but without testing whether the SR valves would open, the HPCI was stopped. That, too, was a mistake. That, too, took place without consulting Head Office. I guess that the head on duty went on thinking about it alone with his utmost efforts. If, at that time, they were asked, I think that they would have said that it is definitely unacceptable to turn off the HPCI and to keep turning it over, as it is even okay for it to break. It was somehow stopped. It became a casual conversation of 'Oh really, is that so?'" In Tadayuki Yokomura, interview, September 19, 2014.

18. "Five Years after the Nuclear Accident: The Crisis Started from Unit 1," *Asahi Shimbun*, March 2, 2016; Fukushima Nuclear Accident Record Team, *49 Hours of the Fukushima Nuclear Accident TEPCO Videoconference Records,* edited by Tomomi Miyazaki and Hideaki Kimura (Tokyo: Iwanami Shoten, 2013), 13, 16–17; during the Fukushima nuclear accident, Units 1, 2, and 3 all lost their cooling function, so the firefighting trucks provided water as a substitute. A firefighting truck was connected to the fire extinguishing system, and an attempt was made to inject water from the fire extinguishing system through the condensate makeup water system, the core spray system for Unit 1, and the residual heat removal system for Units 2 and 3. However, a bypass flow emerged during the water injection process. The water cannot be injected if the pressure of the nuclear reactor rises. How much water had actually reached the containment vessel? According to a report released by TEPCO in 2013, before the hydrogen explosion (3:36 p.m. on March 12), about 20 percent of the discharged flow of water from the fire truck reached the containment vessel. The report also analyzes that the rate had risen to nearly 50 percent after the hydrogen explosion at Unit 1 ("Study on Unit 1 Water Injection Amount by Fire Engine," in TEPCO, Report of Investigation Results Concerning Unresolved Matters in the Fukushima Nuclear Accident: 1st Progress Report, 2013, 11–14). As for Unit 2, the 2017 TEPCO report estimates that the achieved flow rate was less than half ("Estimation of Reactor Water Level in Unit 2 at the time of Core Damage and Meltdown," in TEPCO, Report of Investigation Results Concerning Unresolved Matters in the Progression Mechanisms of the Fukushima Nuclear Accident: 5th Progress Report, 2017, 20). In addition, the 2014 TEPCO report states that it is unlikely that all of the fire engine water was injected into the Unit 3 reactor ("Study on the Injection of Water into the Nuclear Reactor" in TEPCO, Report of Investigation Results Concerning Unresolved Matters in the Fukushima Nuclear Accident: 2nd Progress Report, 2014, 23). Afterward, Yoshida recalled to the Government Investigation Commission hearing about the alternative water pumping plan, which made use of firefighting trucks, was "the last throw of the dice" and the following: "We didn't know until the very end whether water would go in or not using a firefighting pump line. Wasn't depressurization needed and wasn't it

necessary to reduce the reactor pressure to a level at which water from the firefighting pump could enter? In turn, this meant that the water level would drop. Then, at that point, pumping water in using firefighting pumps. However, if the firefighting pump line is cut off somewhere by an earthquake, however much water is put into the reactor, it won't go in . . . to the end, it was a gamble, whether the firefighting pump line would be intact or not. But that was the only option, so we used it to pump water in." In Government Investigation Commission, "J-Village, November 6, 2011," *Masao Yoshida, Hearing Results Report*, November 30, 2011, 56–57.

19. "The Fukushima Daiichi Nuclear Power Station: TEPCO Videoconference Exchanges," *Asahi Shimbun*, September 5, 2012.

20. NHK Special Meltdown Report Crew, *Meltdown: The Truth About the Chain Reaction* (Tokyo: Kodansha, 2013), 144.

21. "TEPCO Videos—Emergency Response—Always Behind," *Yomiuri Shimbun*, August 7, 2012; "The Fukushima Daiichi Nuclear Power Station: TEPCO Videoconference Exchanges," *Asahi Shimbun*, September 5, 2012; Nuclear Safety Commission, whiteboard memo, Appendix 1–20/38; TEPCO videoconference participant memo, shown to the author September 21, 2012; TEPCO, "Fukushima Nuclear Accident Report," June 20, 2012, 242–47; Government Investigation Commission on the Accident at the Fukushima Nuclear Power Stations of Tokyo Electric Power Company, Final Report, July 23, 2012, 42, fn. 73; Government Investigation Commission, Interim Report, 220, fn. 64.

22. Fukushima Nuclear Accident Report Team and others, edited by Tomomi Miyazaki and Hideaki Kimura, *49 Hours of TEPCO's Fukushima Nuclear Accident Videoconference Records* (Tokyo, Iwanami Shoten, 2013).

23. Government Investigation Commission, "J-Village, July 29, 2011," *Masao Yoshida, Hearing Results Report*, August 16, 2011, 14.

24. Fukushima Nuclear Accident Record Team and others, *49 Hours of the Fukushima Nuclear Accident TEPCO Video Conference Records*, 113–14.

25. Government Investigation Commission, "J-Village, July 29, 2011," *Masao Yoshida, Hearing Results Report*, August 9, 2011, 8, 9, 19.

26. Fukushima Nuclear Accident Record Team and others, *49 Hours of the Fukushima Nuclear Accident TEPCO Videoconference Records*, 54.

27. Ibid., 82.

28. Ibid., 127.

29. Ibid., 130; Makoto Shiozaki, interview, December 10, 2012; interview with a Shin Nippon Helicopters–related party, July 31, 2012; August 2, 2012; Government Investigation Commission, Interim Report, 249.

30. Takaya Imai, interview, June 30, 2011; Norio Sasaki, interview, August 3, 2012; Osamu Maekawa, interviews, January 5, 2012 and August 5, 2012; Toshiba engineer, interview, August 30, 2012; TEPCO videoconference participant memo, shown to the author September 21, 2012; Kan, *The TEPCO Fukushima Nuclear Accident*, 85, 94.

31. Fukushima Nuclear Accident Record Team and others, *49 Hours of the Fukushima Nuclear Accident TEPCO Videoconference Records*, 107; TEPCO videoconference participant memo, shown to the author on September 21, 2012.

32. Fukushima Nuclear Accident Record Team and others, *49 Hours of the Fukushima Nuclear Accident TEPCO Videoconference Records*, 107.

33. Ibid., 190.

34. Ibid., 213.

35. Ibid., 221–23; National Diet Commission, Official Report, ch. 3, 12–14.

36. Government Investigation Commission, "J-Village, August 9, 2011," *Masao Yoshida, Hearing Results Report*, August 16, 2011, 37–39.

37. Fukushima Nuclear Accident Record Team and others, *49 Hours of the Fukushima Nuclear Accident TEPCO Videoconference Records*, 240.

38. National Diet Commission, Official Report, ch. 2, 31; "TEPCO Videoconference Footage Released: Fear and Tension in the Midst of Chaos," *Mainichi Shimbun,* August 7, 2012; "Detailed Coverage of the Videoconference Footage Released by TEPCO," *Yomiuri Shimbun,* August 7, 2012; Fukushima Nuclear Accident Record Team and others, *49 Hours of the Fukushima Nuclear Accident TEPCO Videoconference Records,* 264.

39. Charles Casto, *Station Blackout: Inside the Fukushima Nuclear Disaster and Recovery* (New York: Radius Book Group, 2018), 69.

40. "The orange flash of light observed immediately before the explosion can be explained as an imperfect combustion of the carbon monoxide contained in the explosive gas." In National Diet Commission, Official Report, July 5, 2012, ch. 2, 31.

41. Interview with a Toshiba engineer, October 14, 2011; Manabu Terada, interview, November 30, 2011; Nippon TV, "2011 Reporting Footage that Should Be Kept for a Millennium," *Friday Super-Prime,* December 23, 2011; Osamu Maekawa, interview, January 5, 2012; Ichiro Takekuro, interview, January 11, 2012; Norio Sasaki, interview, August 3, 2012; interview with a Toshiba engineer, August 30, 2012; Hosono and Torigoe, *Testimony,* 77, 79; Kan, *The TEPCO Fukushima Nuclear Accident,* 93–94.

42. "TEPCO—PR without Confirming 'Hydrogen Explosion' Uncovered by Nuclear Emergency Meeting Footage," *Asahi Shimbun,* August 8, 2012; "Uncovered by TEPCO Meeting Footage: Immediately After the Nuclear Emergency, Request for Cooling Water—Prefecture Considers—Government Directly Asked," *Yomiuri Shimbun (regional edition),* August 11, 2012; Fukushima Prefecture later denied that it was Governor Yuhei Sato who made this request. See, "Correction of TEPCO TV Conference Recording Statement: Not Fukushima Prefectural Governor, Prefectural Staff," *Mainichi Shimbun,* August 24, 2012.

43. Government Investigation Commission, Interim Report, 256.

44. Fukushima Nuclear Accident Record Team and others, *49 Hours of the Fukushima Nuclear Accident TEPCO Videoconference Records,* 186.

45. Ibid., 187.

46. National Diet Commission, Official Report, ch. 3, 14.

47. Fukushima Nuclear Accident Record Team and others, *49 Hours of the Fukushima Nuclear Accident TEPCO Videoconference Records,* 290.

48. NISA internal memo, 13.

49. TEPCO, "Fukushima Nuclear Accident Report," 102.

50. National Diet Commission, Official Report, ch. 2, 22; "Detailed Coverage of the Videoconference Footage Released by TEPCO," *Yomiuri Shimbun,* August 7, 2012; NHK Special Meltdown Report Crew, *Meltdown,* 187–90; Fukushima Nuclear Accident Record Team and others, *49 Hours of the Fukushima Nuclear Accident TEPCO Videoconference Records,* 322.

51. Fukushima Nuclear Accident Record Team and others, *49 Hours of the Fukushima Nuclear Accident TEPCO Videoconference Records,* 328.

52. Takeyuki Inagaki, interview, December 10, 2013.

53. Charles Casto, *Station Blackout: Inside the Fukushima Nuclear Disaster and Recovery* (New York: Radius Book Group, 2018), 72.

54. Government Investigation Commission, "J-Village, November 6, 2011," *Masao Yoshida, Hearing Results Report,* November 30, 2011, 57.

55. NHK Special Meltdown Report Crew, *Meltdown,* 191–92.

56. *Asahi Shimbun, Investigation,* 97.

Chapter 5

1. Government Investigation Commission, "J-Village, August 9, 2011," *Masao Yoshida, Hearing Results Report,* August 16, 2011, 6–8.

2. Government Investigation Commission, "J-Village, August 8, 2011," *Masao*

Yoshida, Hearing Results Report, August 16, 2011, 55; Goshi Hosono, interview, October 17, 2014; Fukushima Nuclear Accident Record Team, *49 Hours of the Fukushima Nuclear Accident TEPCO Videoconference Records,* edited by Tomomi Miyazaki and Hideaki Kimura (Tokyo: Iwanami Shoten, 2013), 342.

3. Government Investigation Commission on the Accident at the Fukushima Nuclear Power Stations of Tokyo Electric Power Company, Interim Report, July 23, 2011, 257.

4. National Diet of Japan Fukushima Nuclear Accident Independent Investigation Commission, Official Report, July 5, 2012, ch. 3, 20; Manabu Terada, interview, July 26, 2012; Goshi Hosono, interviews, September 5, 2012, and October 17, 2014; Naoto Kan, interview, September 20, 2012; Naoto Kan, *The TEPCO Fukushima Nuclear Accident: My Thoughts as Prime Minister* (Tokyo: Gentosha Shinsho, 2012), 95.

5. Fukushima Nuclear Accident Record Team, *49 Hours of the Fukushima Nuclear Accident TEPCO Videoconference Records,* 329, 331, 333.

6. Takeyuki Inagaki, interview, December 10, 2013.

7. Fukushima Nuclear Accident Record Team, *49 Hours of the Fukushima Nuclear Accident TEPCO Videoconference Records,* 347.

8. Government Investigation Commission, "J-Village, November 6, 2011," *Masao Yoshida, Hearing Results Report,* November 25, 2011.

9. Kunio Yanagida, " 'The Yoshida testimony': Unwritten Important Evidence," *Bungeishunju* (November 2014).

10. Government Investigation Commission, "J-Village, August 8, 2011," *Masao Yoshida, Hearing Results Report,* August 16, 2011, 51.

11. Fukushima Nuclear Accident Record Team, *49 Hours of the Fukushima Nuclear Accident TEPCO Videoconference Records,* 347.

12. Ibid., 354.

13. Ibid., 366.

14. Ibid., 372.

15. "The Fukushima Daiichi Nuclear Power Station: TEPCO Videoconference Exchanges," *Asahi Shimbun,* September 5, 2012; Goshi Hosono, interview, September 5, 2012; Ikuo Izawa, interview, August 8, 2013.

16. National Diet Commission, Official Report, ch. 3, 20–21; "Tense Videos: Full of Modifications," *Yomiuri Shimbun,* August 7, 2012.

17. "The Fukushima Daiichi Nuclear Power Station: TEPCO Videoconference Exchanges," *Asahi Shimbun,* September 5, 2012.

18. Government Investigation Commission, "J-Village, August 9, 2011," *Masao Yoshida, Hearing Results Report,* August 16, 2011, 52.

19. National Diet Commission, Official Report, ch. 3, 24; "The Fukushima Daiichi Nuclear Power Station: TEPCO Videoconference Exchanges," *Asahi Shimbun,* September 5, 2012; Fukushima Nuclear Accident Record Team, *49 Hours of the Fukushima Nuclear Accident TEPCO Videoconference Records,* 358.

20. Fukushima Nuclear Accident Record Team, *49 Hours of the Fukushima Nuclear Accident TEPCO Videoconference Records,* 328.

21. Government Investigation Commission, Interim Report, 83.

22. Nobuaki Terasaka, interview, February 9, 2012.

23. Tetsuro Fukuyama, interview, January 21, 2012; Goshi Hosono, testimony before the Government Investigation Commission, November 19, 2011; Tetsuro Fukuyama, *The Nuclear Crisis: Testimony from the Kantei* (Tokyo: Chikuma Shinsho, 2012), 103.

24. It is noted in the Report of the Diet Investigation Commission, "According to TEPCO's telephone records, President Shimizu, either personally or through his secretary, placed a total of eleven phone calls to the secretary of METI Minister Kaieda between 18:00 on March 14 and 03:00 on March 15. Since the duration

of most of the calls were just several seconds long, only three calls are deemed to be ones in which actual conversations took place: (1) 133 seconds from 18:41 on March 14; (2) 50 seconds from 20:02 on March 14, and (3) 276 seconds from 01:31 on March 15." In, National Diet Commission, Official Report, ch. 3, 25; Regarding calls between Shimizu and Edano, however, the Diet Investigation Commission said, "TEPCO President Shimizu stated he does not recall placing the call to Chief Cabinet Secretary Edano," ibid., ch. 3, 26.

25. "President Shimizu Intent to Withdraw," *Asahi Shimbun*, May 16, 2012; TEPCO, "Fukushima Nuclear Accident Report," June 20, 2012, 76; National Diet Commission, Official Report, ch. 3, 25; Banri Kaieda, interview, July 10, 2012.

26. Koichiro Genba, interview, July 16, 2012.

27. Goshi Hosono, interview, February 13, 2012.

28. Tetsuro Fukuyama, interview, January 21, 2012.

29. Yutaka Kukita, interview, November 27, 2012.

30. Fukushima Nuclear Accident Record Team, *49 Hours of the Fukushima Nuclear Accident TEPCO Videoconference Records*, 385.

31. Ibid., 390–92; "TEPCO Advisors Urge 'Do the Vent Quickly'—Footage of Nuclear Emergency Meetings Modified and Released," *Asahi Shimbun*, August 7, 2012; "Investigation of the Nuclear Emergency Six Months after 'TEPCO Withdraws, Government Stops Functioning,'" *Yomiuri Shimbun*, September 14, 2011.

32. Fukushima Nuclear Accident Record Team, *49 Hours of the Fukushima Nuclear Accident TEPCO Videoconference Records*, 396–97.

33. Banri Kaieda, testimony before the Independent Investigation Commission, October 1, 2011; Kiyoshi Sawaki, interview, November 7, 2011; Manabu Terada, interview, November 30, 2011; Goshi Hosono, interview, February 13, 2012; Banri Kaieda, testimony before the Diet Investigation Commission, May 17, 2012; "Fukushima Nuclear Station—Government Investigation Commission—State of Emergency Declared—PM's Decision Takes Time—interview with Former METI Minister Kaieda," *Nihon Keizai Shimbun*, May 18, 2012; Banri Kaieda, interview, July 10, 2012; Banri Kaieda, *The Kaieda Notes—A Record of the 176-Day Nuclear Struggle* (Tokyo: Kodansha, 2012), 59.

34. In reference to this point, both Edano and an aide testified that they had definitely received a call from Shimizu. They stated that it was not to a mobile phone, but came in via the general switchboard at the Kantei. See, Yukio Edano, testimony before the Independent Investigation Commission, December 12, 2011; interview with a Kantei parliamentary secretary, October 10, 2012.

35. Yukio Edano, testimony before the Independent Investigation Commission, December 10, 2011; Yukio Edano, testimony before the Diet Investigation Commission, Minutes No. 15, May 27, 2012.

36. Kaieda, *The Kaieda Notes*, 60.

37. Interview with a senior official of the Nuclear and Industrial Safety Agency, January 13, 2012; "The Fukushima Nuclear Station Accident: March 11–15, 2011 (Memorandum)," December 19, 2011.

38. TEPCO videoconference participant memo shown to the author, September 21, 2012.

39. Japan Nuclear Energy Safety Organization, "Initial Activities of the Local Response Headquarters," May 2011, 42.

40. Interview with a senior official of the Nuclear and Industrial Safety Agency, June 20, 2012.

41. Ibid., January 13, 2012.

42. Government Investigation Commission, Interim Report, 552.

43. Eiji Hiraoka, interview, June 1, 2012; interview with a senior METI official, January 4, 2012; Hiromu Katayama, interviews, June 20, 2012 and October 25, 2012.

44. Interview with a Kantei parliamentary secretary, February 27, 2012; Goshi Hosono, interview, March 15, 2012; Banri Kaieda, interview, July 10, 2012; Kazuo Matsunaga, interview, October 25, 2012; Naoto Kan, interview, April 9, 2012; Government Investigation Commission on the Accident at the Fukushima Nuclear Power Stations of Tokyo Electric Power Company, Final Report, July 23, 2012, 239.

45. Interview with a senior METI official, January 4, 2012.

46. Ibid.; Naoto Kan, interview, December 21, 2011; Toshimi Kitazawa, interview, February 29, 2012.

47. Yutaka Kukita, interview, January 20, 2012; Manabu Terada, interview, July 26, 2012.

48. Ibid.; Haruki Madarame, interview, July 26, 2012.

49. Goshi Hosono, interview, March 15, 2012.

50. Manabu Terada, interview, July 26, 2012; Tetsuro Fukuyama, interview, January 21, 2012; Haruki Madarame, interview, October 4, 2012.

51. Goshi Hosono, interview, March 15, 2012; Tetsuro Ito, interview, April 9, 2012; Yoshikatsu Nakayama, interview, May 16, 2012; Naoto Kan, testimony before the Diet Investigation Commission, May 28, 2012; Manabu Terada, interview, July 26, 2012; Kaieda, *The Kaieda Notes*, 59.

52. Goshi Hosono and Shuntaro Torigoe, *Testimony: Shuntaro Torigoe Closes in on the Truth About 'The 500 Days of Nuclear Crisis'* (Tokyo: Kodansha, 2012), 92.

53. Interview with a senior Ministry of Defense official, November 18, 2011; interview with a Kantei staff member, June 28, 2011; Haruki Madarame, testimony before the Independent Investigation Commission, December 17, 2011; Masaya Yasui, interviews, February 9, 2012 and June 20, 2012; Goshi Hosono, interview, March 15, 2012; interview with a Kantei parliamentary secretary, May 23, 2012; Manabu Terada, interview, July 26, 2012; interview with a Kantei parliamentary secretary, October 10, 2012; Kan, *The TEPCO Fukushima Nuclear Accident*, 111.

54. "Investigation of the Fukushima Daiichi Station: Reactors 1–5, All Without Power!" *Asahi Shimbun*, April 10, 2011; Manabu Terada, interview, July 26, 2012; Masaya Yasui, interview, February 9, 2012; Tetsuro Ito, interview, April 9, 2012; Tsunehisa Katsumata, testimony before the Diet Investigation Commission, Minutes No. 12, May 14, 2012; "Detailed Report—Ex-METI Minister Kaieda Testimony— Government Investigation Commission," *Mainichi Shimbun*, May 18, 2012; Naoto Kan, testimony before the Diet Investigation Commission, Minutes No. 16, May 28, 2012; Tetsuro Fukuyama, testimony before the Independent Investigation Commission, October 29, 2011; Goshi Hosono, interview, March 15, 2012; Kan, *The TEPCO Fukushima Nuclear Accident*, 113.

55. Manabu Terada, interview, November 30, 2011; interview with a Kantei parliamentary secretary, February 27, 2012.

56. Goshi Hosono, interview, May 30, 2012; TEPCO, Fukushima Nuclear Accident Report, June 20, 2012, 73; Manabu Terada, interview, July 26, 2012; Toshiyama Okuyama, "'Hothead Kan Is Always Mad'—Ex-Deputy President of TEPCO, Nuclear Emergency Videoconference," *Asahi Judiciary*, September 6, 2012; interview with a Kantei parliamentary secretary, October 28, 2012.

57. Manabu Terada, interview, July 26, 2012; Kan, *The TEPCO Fukushima Nuclear Accident*, 114.

58. Interview with a senior TEPCO officer, May 10, 2012.

59. Masataka Shimizu, testimony before the Diet Investigation Commission, June 8, 2012.

60. "TEPCO's Mortal Sin," *Shukan Bunshun Extraordinary Supplement*, July 27, 2011, 37; Ikuo Izawa, interview, August 8, 2013.

61. Interview with a senior Kantei official, February 22, 2012.

62. "Investigation of the Fukushima Daiichi Station: Reactors 1–5, All Without Power!" *Asahi Shimbun*, April 10, 2011; "Investigation into the Great Quake: Tes-

timony from Ex-PM Kan," *Mainichi Shimbun*, September 7, 2011; "Investigation of the Nuclear Emergency Six Months after 'TEPCO Withdraws, Government Stops Functioning,'" *Yomiuri Shimbun*, September 14, 2011; Goshi Hosono, interview, January 13; March 15, 2012; Naoto Kan, interview, December 21, 2011; Kaieda, *The Kaieda Notes*, 62.

63. Ikuo Izawa, interview, August 8, 2013.

64. Interview with a Kantei staff member, August 17, 2011; interview with a senior JNES official, October 28, 2011; interview with a senior METI official, November 7, 2011; Manabu Terada, interview, July 26, 2011; Masaya Yasui, interview, June 20, 2012; "Detailed Report on the Videoconference Footage Released by TEPCO," *Yomiuri Shimbun*, August 7, 2012.

65. The estimation of damage in the reactors that TEPCO later (April 17) conveyed to the Americans was 70 percent in Unit 1, 30 percent in Unit 2, and 25 percent in Unit 3. See, Nuclear Regulatory Commission (NRC), final slides, April 17, 2011.

66. Kenichi Shimomura, interview, November 25, 2011; interview with a Kantei parliamentary secretary, February 27, 2012; Fukuyama, *The Nuclear Crisis*, 113; Rebuild Japan Initiative Foundation (RJIF), *Independent Investigation Commission on the Fukushima Nuclear Accident* (Abingdon: Routledge, 2014), 31–32.

67. Osamu Maekawa, interviews, December 9, 2011 and January 5, 2012; Manabu Terada, interview, July 26, 2012; Mitsuhiko Tanaka and Sakae Muto, testimony before the Diet Investigation Commission, Minutes No. 6, March 14, 2012; Masaya Yasui, interview, June 20, 2012; TEPCO videoconference participant memo shown to the author, September 21, 2012; Fukuyama, *The Nuclear Crisis*, 114; Kaieda, *The Kaieda Notes*, 65.

68. Mitsuhiro Kajimoto, interview, September 3, 2012.

69. Ikuo Izawa, interview, August 8, 2013; Ikuo Izawa's lecture at Japan Nuclear Safety Institute's Duty Manager Training, February 12, 2014.

70. Mari Sato, interviews, January 16, 2016 and April 4, 2017.

71. Ryusho Kadota, *The Man Who Went to the Brink of Death—Masao Yoshida and His 500 Days at the Fukushima Daiichi Nuclear Station* (Kyoto: PHP, 2012), 274, 317; Ikuo Izawa, interview, August 8, 2013.

72. "Investigation of the Nuclear Emergency Six Months after 'TEPCO Withdraws, Government Stops Functioning,'" *Yomiuri Shimbun*, September 14, 2011; Kenichi Shimomura, interview, November 30, 2011; Tetsuya Nishikawa, interview, February 22, 2012; Goshi Hosono, interview, March 15, 2012; Manabu Terada, interview, July 26, 2012.

73. Osamu Maekawa, interview, January 5, 2012; Goshi Hosono, interview, March 15, 2012; Banri Kaieda, interview, July 10, 2012.

74. Manabu Terada, interview, November 30, 2011.

Chapter 6

1. Osamu Maekawa, interview, January 5, 2012; Goshi Hosono, interview, March 15, 2012; Banri Kaieda, *The Kaieda Notes—A Record of the 176-Day Nuclear Struggle* (Tokyo: Kodansha 2012), 69; interview with a TEPCO executive, March 6, 2012.

2. Banri Kaieda, testimony before the Independent Investigation Commission, October 1, 2011; Kiyoshi Sawaki, interview, November 7, 2011.

3. Interview with a senior METI official, September 22, 2011.

4. Banri Kaieda, testimony before the Diet Investigation Commission, Minutes No. 14, May 17, 2012.

5. Hiroshi Ikukawa, interviews, October 25, 2011, October 27, 2012, and November 15, 2012; interview with a Kantei parliamentary secretary, February 27, 2012.

6. Goshi Hosono and Shuntaro Torigoe, *Testimony: Shuntaro Torigoe Closes in*

on the Truth About "The 500 Days of Nuclear Crisis" (Tokyo: Kodansha, 2012), 105; Goshi Hosono, interview, May 30, 2012.

7. Naoto Kan, interview, November 14, 2012.

8. Interview with a Kantei parliamentary secretary, May 31, 2012.

9. Ibid., September 28, 2012.

10. Interview with a Kantei staff member, June 28, 2011.

11. Interview with a Toshiba engineer, September 4, 2012.

12. Interview with a senior METI official, August 17, 2011.

13. Nobuaki Terasaka, testimony before the Diet Investigation Commission, Minutes No. 4, February 15, 2012; Koji Okamoto, *Testimony: Haruki Madarame— Where NISA Went Wrong* (Tokyo: Shinchosha, 2012), 42.

14. Eiji Hiraoka, interview, May 28, 2012.

15. Okamoto, *Testimony*, 42.

16. Haruki Madarame, testimony before the Independent Investigation Commission, December 17, 2011.

17. Interview with an ex-METI official, May 7, 2012.

18. National Diet of Japan Fukushima Nuclear Accident Independent Investigation Commission, Official Report, July 5, 2012, ch. 3, 40; interview with a senior METI official, November 7, 2011.

19. Kenichi Shimomura, interview, December 1, 2011.

20. Interview with a senior official of the Ministry of Internal Affairs and Communication, October 3, 2012; Tetsuro Ito, interview, April 9, 2012; Tomoho Yamada, interview, July 31, 2012.

21. Nuclear Regulatory Commission, Official Transcript of Proceedings: Japan's Fukushima Daiichi ET Audio File, March 17, 2011, 417.

22. NHK Special Meltdown Report Crew, *Meltdown: The Truth About the Chain Reaction* (Tokyo: Kodansha, 2013), 276.

23. Japan Nuclear Energy Safety Organization, "Annual Report for Fiscal 2004," Japanese Home Page.

24. Rebuild Japan Initiative Foundation (RJIF), *Independent Investigation Commission on the Fukushima Nuclear Accident* (Abingdon: Routledge, 2014), 101.

25. Hideaki Tsuzuki, interview, July 4, 2012.

26. TEPCO, "Fukushima Nuclear Accident Report," June 20, 2012, 78.

27. Eiji Hiraoka, interview, August 10, 2012.

28. Hideo Suzuki, interview, September 22, 2011.

29. Government Investigation Commission on the Accident at the Fukushima Nuclear Power Stations of Tokyo Electric Power Company, Interim Report, December 26, 2011, 549.

30. TEPCO, "Fukushima Nuclear Accident Report," June 20, 2012, 81.

31. Interview with a senior officer of the SDF Chemical Special Forces, October 18, 2011.

32. Notification from NISA, March 17, 2006.

33. Eiji Hiraoka, interview, August 9, 2012.

34. Interview with a Toshiba engineer, December 9, 2011.

35. JNES engineer email, September 19, 2012.

36. Hideaki Tsuzuki, interview, July 4, 2012.

37. The Basic Policy of Employment and Promotion, which is based on Article 54 of the National Public Service Act (approved by the cabinet in 2009) says, "With regard to a personnel transfer, efforts must be made to give the staff a variety of job opportunities, while it shall be implemented in consideration of the following points: development of an administrative processing system, which is able to respond appropriately to various administrative issues and changing work load; prevention of negative effects resulting from the situation in which a specific staff member is assigned

to the same official post for a long period of time." In Government Investigation Commission, Final Report, July 23, 2012, 416.

38. Interview with a senior METI official, September 6, 2011.

39. Kazuo Matsunaga, interview, October 26, 2011.

40. Government Investigation Commission on the Accident at the Fukushima Nuclear Power Stations of Tokyo Electric Power Company, Final Report, July 23, 2012, 414–15.

41. Interview with a senior official of the Nuclear and Industrial Safety Agency, October 25, 2012.

42. The Nuclear and Industrial Safety Agency was officially abolished in September 2012.

43. Haruki Madarame, testimony before the Independent Investigation Commission, December 17, 2011.

44. Eiji Hiraoka, interview, May 28, 2012.

45. Haruki Madarame, testimony before the Independent Investigation Commission, December 17, 2011; Norihiko Iwahashi, interview, August 2, 2012.

46. Lower House Budget Committee Meeting, Minutes No. 13, May 1, 2011; Haruki Madarame, testimony before the Diet Investigation Commission, Minutes No. 4, February 15, 2012; Okamoto, *Testimony*, 32; RJIF, *Independent Investigation Commission on the Fukushima Nuclear Accident*, 65–68; National Diet Commission, Official Report, ch. 3, 41; Government Investigation Commission, Final Report, 419.

47. Interview with a senior official of the Nuclear and Industrial Safety Agency, February 27, 2012.

48. Hosono and Torigoe, *Testimony*, 231–32.

49. Haruki Madarame, interview, October 4, 2012.

50. Banri Kaieda, *The Kaieda Notes—A Record of the 176-Day Nuclear Struggle* (Tokyo: Kodansha, 2012), 43.

51. Interview with a Kantei parliamentary secretary, December 16, 2011.

52. Haruki Madarame, testimony before the Independent Investigation Commission, December 17, 2011.

53. Haruki Madarame, interview, October 4, 2012.

54. Kenichi Shimomura, interview, November 25, 2011.

55. Interview with a Kantei staff member, August 18, 2011.

56. Masaya Yasui, interview, June 20, 2012.

57. Interview with a Toshiba engineer, August 25, 2011.

58. Masaya Yasui, interview, June 20, 2012.

59. Kazuo Matsunaga, interview, February 2, 2012.

60. Tetsuro Fukuyama, interview, September 26, 2012.

61. Interview with a Kantei parliamentary secretary, January 6, 2012.

62. Hiroshi Ikukawa, interview, July 12, 2012.

63. Takaya Imai, interview, September 6, 2011.

64. Masaya Yasui, interview, June 20–21, 2012; Fukuyama Tetsuro, interview, September 6, 2011.

65. Masaya Yasui, interview, June 20, 2012.

66. Interview with a senior NRC official, August 24, 2011.

67. Takaya Imai, interview, September 30, 2011.

68. Masaya Yasui, interview, February 9, 2012.

69. Takaya Imai, interview, September 6, 2011.

70. Goshi Hosono, interview, March 15, 2012; Masaya Yasui, interview, February 9, 2012.

71. Tetsuro Ito, interview, April 9, 2012; interview with a Kantei staff member, July 4, 2012.

72. National Diet Commission, Official Report, ch. 3, 39.

73. Tetsuro Ito, interview, September 25, 2012.

74. Manabu Terada, interview, July 26, 2012; interview with a Kantei parliamentary secretary, November 7, 2011.

75. Koichiro Genba, interview, July 16, 2012.

76. Ibid.

77. "Outline of the Nuclear Emergency Response Headquarters," *Yomiuri Shimbun*, March 10, 2012.

78. Kenichi Shimomura, interview, November 25, 2011.

79. Interview with an Emergency Operation Team member, October 31, 2012.

80. Ito Tetsuro, interview, April 9, 2012.

81. Interview with a senior government official, July 28, 2011.

82. Interview with a Kantei parliamentary secretary, January 6, 2012.

83. Interview with an ex-deputy chief cabinet secretary for crisis management, October 26, 2012.

84. Interview with a Kantei parliamentary secretary, December 16, 2011.

85. Tetsuro Fukuyama, testimony before the Independent Investigation Commission, October 29, 2011.

86. Interview with a high-ranking member of the Joint Staff, June 17, 2012.

87. Interview with an emergency taskforce staff member, October 31, 2012.

Chapter 7

1. National Diet of Japan Fukushima Nuclear Accident Independent Investigation Commission, Official Report, July 5, 2012, ch. 4, 71–72.

2. Fukushima Nuclear Accident Record Team, edited by Miyazaki Tomomi and Kimura Hideaki, *49 Hours of the Fukushima Nuclear Accident TEPCO Videoconference Records* (Tokyo: Iwanami Shoten, 2013), 2.

3. "SDF Officer Came to Say, 'The Reactor Is Going to Explode. Evacuate 100 Kilometers,'" *Asahi Shimbun*, September 11, 2011; Government Investigation Commission on the Accident at the Fukushima Nuclear Power Stations of Tokyo Electric Power Company, Interim Report, December 26, 2011, 307; Ichiro Takekuro, testimony before the Diet Investigation Commission, Minutes No. 8, March 28, 2012; Tetsuro Ito, interview, April 9, 2012; Eiji Hiraoka, interview, May 28, 2012; National Diet Commission, Official Report, ch. 3, 77–78; Government Investigation Commission on the Accident at the Fukushima Nuclear Power Stations of Tokyo Electric Power Company, Final Report, July 23, 2012, 264; Kenji Matsuoka, "Minutes of the Second Meeting of the Working Group to Review the Regulatory Guide for Emergency Preparedness for Nuclear Facilities," Nuclear Safety Commission, August 12, 2011; Kenji Matsuoka, "Minutes of the Tenth Meeting of the Working Group to Review the Regulatory Guide for Emergency Preparedness for Nuclear Facilities," Nuclear Safety Commission, December 27, 2011; Banri Kaieda, *The Kaieda Notes—A Record of the 176-Day Nuclear Struggle* (Tokyo: Kodansha, 2012), 25.

4. Koichiro Genba, interview, July 17, 2012.

5. Tetsuro Fukuyama, testimony before the Independent Investigation Commission, October 29, 2011; Yukio Edano, testimony before the Independent Investigation Commission, December 10, 2011; Government Investigation Commission, Interim Report, 313; Eiji Hiraoka, interview, June 1, 2012.

6. NISA internal memo, 7; "Investigation of the Great Disaster: Ex-PM Kan's Testimony," *Mainichi Shimbun*, September 7, 2011; Tetsuro Fukuyama, interview, November 29, 2011; Tetsuro Fukuyama, *The Nuclear Crisis: Testimony from the Prime Minister's Office* (Tokyo: Chikuma Shinsho, 2012), 191; Yukio Edano, testimony before the Independent Investigation Commission, December 10, 2011; interview with a Kantei parliamentary secretary, May 23, 2012; Eiji Hiraoka, interviews, May 28, 2012 and June 1, 2012.

7. Tetsuro Ito, interview, April 9, 2012; Eiji Hiraoka, interview, June 1, 2012.

8. Government Investigation Commission, Interim Report, 195.

9. Interview with a senior official of the Nuclear and Industrial Safety Agency, January 13, 2012.

10. As a result of an inquiry from locals on this matter, TEPCO replied as follows (July 31, 2012) after investigating employees (eighty-one households) living in company housing in the three neighboring towns of Fukushima Daiichi NPS (Okuma, Futaba, Namie): "The majority of residents began evacuating around 15:00 on March 11 and later around 13:00 on March 12. Depending on the company housing, there were examples where the majority of residents evacuated to the same place in accordance with local government directions, but there was no situation where they all evacuated as a group in buses provided by the company."

11. NISA internal memo, 7; Tatsuo Hirano, interview, May 21, 2012; Nuclear Emergency Investigation Working Group, All Japan Council of Local Governments with Atomic Power Stations, "Survey Results of the Local Governments Affected by the Fukushima Daiichi Nuclear Power Station Accident," March 2012, 59.

12. NISA internal memo, 9, 10; Yukio Edano, testimony before the Independent Investigation Commission, December 10, 2011.

13. Nuclear Safety Commission, whiteboard memo, Appendix 1–23/38.

14. Haruki Madarame, testimony before the Independent Investigation Commission, December 17, 2011; Yutaka Kukita, testimony before the Independent Investigation Commission, January 20, 2012; Toshimitsu Homma, interview, June 1, 2012; Nuclear Safety Commission staff, July 18, 2012.

15. National Diet Commission, Official Report, ch. 4, 17; Nuclear Safety Commission staff, July 18, 2012.

16. NISA internal memo, 11.

17. Koichiro Genba, "Minister Genba: The First Seven Days" (memo on the movements of Minister Genba in the immediate aftermath of the Great East Japan earthquake).

18. Matsuoka, "Minutes of the Second Meeting of the Working Group," 29–30.

19. Nuclear Emergency Investigation Working Group, "Survey Results of the Local Governments," 61.

20. Tetsuro Ito, interview, April 9, 2012; Government Investigation Commission, Final Report, 266.

21. Tetsuro Fukuyama, testimony before the Independent Investigation Commission, October 29, 2011; interview with a Kantei parliamentary secretary, October 12, 2011; Haruki Madarame, testimony before the Independent Investigation Commission, December 17, 2011.

22. "Democrats—Slow to Respond to Disaster," *Asahi Shimbun*, March 17, 2011; Sunday Frontline, Asahi TV, May 29, 2011; Makiko Tanaka, interview, May 9, 2012; interview with a senior official of the Ministry of Education, Culture, Sports, Science, and Technology, October 27, 2012.

23. Koichiro Genba, interview, July 16, 2012.

24. Hideo Suzuki, interview, September 22, 2011; Goshi Hosono, interview, November 1, 2012.

25. "SDF Officer Came to Say, 'The Reactor Is Going to Explode. Evacuate 100 Kilometers,'" *Asahi Shimbun*, September 11, 2011; Tamotsu Baba, interview, November 20, 2011; Tamotsu Baba and Kazuhiro Yoshida, testimony before the Diet Investigation Commission, Minutes No. 10, April 21, 2012; Nuclear Emergency Investigation Working Group, "Survey Results of the Local Governments," 29–32.

26. TEPCO videoconference participant memo shown to the author, September 21, 2012.

27. Katsunobu Sakurai, interview, May 28, 2012; Reconstruction Planning Department, Minamisoma City, "The Great East Japan Earthquake: The Situation in

Minamisoma City, Fukushima Prefecture," May 24, 2012; Nuclear Emergency Investigation Working Group, "Survey Results of the Local Governments," 24–27; Hirohiko Izumida, interview, May 7, 2012.

28. Norio Kanno, *Radiation Fell on a Beautiful Village: Iitate Mayor's 120 Days
of Decision and Resolve* (Tokyo: Wani Books PLUS Shinsho, 2011), 20; Hiroshi
Ozawa, *Iitate Village: 6,000 People Forced Out of Their Beautiful Village* (Tokyo:
Nanatsumori Shokan, 2012), 23; "Prometheus Trap: Kingfisher Diary 4," *Asahi
Shimbun*, August 19, 2012; Norio Kanno, interview, September 4, 2012; Hiroshi
Tada, interview, September 27, 2012.

29. Government Investigation Commission, Interim Report, December 26, 2011,
361; Matsuoka, "Minutes of the Second Meeting of the Working Group," 33; Yoshitaka Suzuki, interview, October 23, 2012; Kuniharu Hashimoto, interview, October 23 and 29, 2012; Hiroyuki Kudo, interview, October 23 and 29, 2012; Chika
Takenouchi, interview, October 29, 2012; "Prometheus Trap: Part 14, The Town of
Streamers 'Distribute the Iodine,'" *Asahi Shimbun WEB Shinsho*, July 7–27, 2012.

30. Matsuoka, "Minutes of the Second Meeting of the Working Group," 32.

31. Interview with a senior officer of the Nuclear Safety Commission, September
26, 2012.

32. Kenji Matsuoka, "Minutes of the Fourth Meeting of the Working Group to
Review the Regulatory Guide for Emergency Preparedness for Nuclear Facilities,"
Nuclear Safety Commission, September 14, 2011, 8.

33. Hideaki Tsuzuki, interview, July 4, 2012.

34. Interview with an NSC secretariat staff member, October 9, 2012.

35. Hiroyuki Ogawa, interview, December 7, 2015; May 9, 2017.

36. Government Nuclear Investigation Committee, "J-Village, August 9, 2011,"
Masao Yoshida, Hearing Results Report, August 16, 2011, 66–67.

Chapter 8

1. Yoshifumi Hibako, "The Realities and Challenges of the Ground Self-Defense
Force Disaster Relief," National Defense Academy, Japan Society of Defense Studies
2011 Research Conference symposium, November 25, 2011; interview with a senior
officer of the Joint Staff Office, June 17, 2012.

2. Toshimi Kitazawa, interview, February 29, 2012.

3. Hibako, "The Realities and Challenges of the Ground Self-Defense Force Disaster Relief."

4. Ministry of Defense, "Lessons Learned from the Response to the Great East
Japan Earthquake (Interim Findings)," August 2011.

5. Interview with a Joint Staff Office senior officer, July 20, 2011; interview with
a senior official of the Ministry of Defense, October 7, 2011; interview with a senior
official of the Ministry of Defense, November 18, 2011; interview with a Kantei parliamentary secretary, December 16, 2011; Kaieda Banri, testimony before the Diet
Investigation Commission, Minutes No. 14, May 17, 2012; Tetsuro Ito, interview,
April 9, 2012.

6. "Great East Japan Earthquake: TEPCO President on Private Trip on the Day
of the Quake—Suspicions of False Explanation of 'Official Business Trip,'" *Mainichi
Shimbun*, May 28, 2011; "TEPCO's Mortal Sin," *Shukan Bunshun Extraordinary
Supplement*, July 27, 2011, 24.

7. Interview with an Emergency Operation Team member, October 10, 2012.

8. Interview with a senior official of the Ministry of Defense, November 9, 2011.

9. Ibid., November 18, 2011.

10. Takahiro Takino, *The SDF and the Great East Japan Earthquake* (Tokyo:
Poplar Publishing, 2012), 17, 84.

11. Hiroshi Takashima, "The Realities and Challenges of the Self-Defense Force

Disaster Relief," National Defense Academy, Japan Society of Defense Studies 2011 Research Conference symposium, November 25, 2011.

12. Toshimi Kitazawa, *Why Japan Needs the SDF* (Tokyo: Kadokawa Shoten, 2012), 34.

13. Interview with a senior official of the Ministry of Defense, November 9, 2011; "Investigation of the Great Quake: Operation Tomodachi—U.S. Asia Pacific Strategy Clear," *Mainichi Shimbun*, December 31, 2011; Ryoichi Oriki, interview, March 6, 2012; Tetsuro Ito, interview, April 9, 2012; Military of Defense, 2010 Defense white-paper; Third Meeting of the Nuclear Emergency Response Headquarters, Summary Minutes, March 12, 2011; Naoto Kan, *The TEPCO Fukushima Nuclear Accident: My Thoughts as Prime Minister* (Tokyo: Gentosha Shinsho, 2012), 49.

14. "Investigation of the Great Quake: Operation Tomodachi—U.S. Asia Pacific Strategy Clear," *Mainichi Shimbun*, December 31, 2011.

15. Toshimi Kitazawa, interview, March 15, 2011.

16. Bruce A. Elleman, *Waves of Hope: The U.S. Navy's Response to the Tsunami in Northeastern Indonesia* (Newport, R.I.: Naval War College Press, 2007), 103–05.

17. Kan, *The TEPCO Fukushima Nuclear Accident*, 62.

18. The police also helped with the identification of bodies. In a meeting of NERHQ on April 11, Kansei Nakano, chairman of the National Public Safety Commission, remarked, "We have 1,000 officers patrolling within the thirty-kilometer zone. We have another 1,200 identifying bodies, and have identified 84 percent of the deceased in our care." This also included those drowned.

19. Eiji Kimizuka, "The Realities and Challenges of the Ground Self-Defense Force Disaster Relief," National Defense Academy, Japan Society of Defense Studies 2011 Research Conference symposium, November 25, 2011; Ryoichi Oriki, interview, March 6, 2012; interview with a senior official of the Ministry of Defense, September 12, 2011.

20. Koichi Isobe, The Frontline of Operation Tomodachi: Lessons Learned from the Fukushima Nuclear Accident for Improving Japan-U.S. Cooperation (Tokyo: Sairyusha, 2019), 34–38.

21. "Inside the Meltdown," *BBC*, February 23, 2012; "The Nuclear Crisis Episode 1: Why Did the Accident Become So Serious?" *NHK Special*, June 5, 2011; "TEPCO's Mortal Sin," *Shukan Bunshun Extraordinary Supplement*, July 27, 2011, 36; interview with a senior official of the Ministry of Defense, August 9, 2011; Shinji Iwakuma, interview, December 10, 2012; Shinji Iwakuma, "An Outline of Central Special Weapons Protection Corps Activities on Nuclear Disaster Deployment," Japan Society for Defense Studies, 2011 Research Conference Proceedings, November 25–26, 2011; Takino, *The SDF and the Great East Japan Earthquake*, 17, 75; Toshinobu Miyajima, interview, July 11, 2012; Isobe, The Frontline of Operation Tomodachi, 41.

22. "Arrested on Suspicion of Car Theft: 'Fukushima Daiichi Station, I Was Scared and Ran,'" *Asahi Shimbun*, April 19, 2011.

23. Yuki Imaura, interview, March 17, 2012.

24. Interview with a senior official of the Nuclear and Industrial Safety Agency, September 29, 2011.

25. Haruki Madarame, testimony before the Independent Investigation Commission, December 17, 2011.

26. Goshi Hosono, interview, January 13, 2012.

27. Kitazawa, *Why Japan Needs the SDF*, 80–81.

28. Interview with a senior METI official, September 30, 2011.

29. Interview with a senior JNES officer, September 3, 2012.

30. Tetsuro Ito, interviews, April 9, 2012, and September 25, 2012.

31. Interview with a senior official of the Ministry of Defense, November 17,

2011; Ryoichi Oriki, interview, March 6, 2012; interview with a senior SDF officer, October 29, 2012; Kan, *The TEPCO Fukushima Nuclear Accident*, 126.

32. Rebuild Japan Initiative Foundation (RJIF), *Independent Investigation Commission on the Fukushima Nuclear Accident* (Discover Twenty-One, 2012), 29. (Only included in the Japanese version.)

33. Government Investigation Commission on the Accident at the Fukushima Nuclear Power Stations of Tokyo Electric Power Company, Interim Report, December 26, 2011, 22.

34. Ibid., 248.

35. Ibid.

36. Ibid., 247–48.

37. Asahi Shimbun, *Investigation: The TEPCO Videoconferences* (Tokyo: Asahi Shimbun Press, 2012), 136.

38. TEPCO videoconference participant memo shown to the author, September 21, 2012.

39. NHK Special Meltdown Report Crew, *Meltdown: The Truth About the Chain Reaction* (Tokyo: Kodansha, 2013), 213.

40. Ibid., 215; NISA internal memo, 7.

41. Ninth Meeting of the Nuclear Emergency Response Headquarters, Summary Minutes.

42. NISA internal memo, 17; interview with a senior official of the Ministry of Defense, November 1, 2012; Kan, *The TEPCO Fukushima Nuclear Accident*, 128.

43. Hirokazu Kanai, interview, August 30, 2012; September 4, 2012; Koichi Kataoka, interview, September 20, 2012; interview with a senior SDF officer, October 29, 2012; Noriichi Yamashita, interview, May 19, 2020.

44. Government Investigation Commission, *Masao Yoshida, Hearing Results Report*, "J-Village, August 8, 2011," August 16, 2011, 4.

45. NISA internal memo, 17; TEPCO videoconference participant memo shown to the author, September 21, 2012.

46. Kitazawa, *Why Japan Needs the SDF*, 85; Goshi Hosono, interview, March 15, 2012; Goshi Hosono and Shuntaro Torigoe, *Testimony: Shuntaro Torigoe Closes In on the Truth About "The 500 Days of Nuclear Crisis"* (Tokyo: Kodansha, 2012), 123; Banri Kaieda, *The Kaieda Notes—A Record of the 176-Day Nuclear Struggle* (Tokyo: Kodansha 2012), 74.

47. Interview with a senior official of the Ministry of Foreign Affairs, April 5, 2012; interview with a senior official of the Ministry of Defense, September 22, 2011.

48. Interview with a senior official of the Joint Staff Office, March 10, 2012.

49. Interview with a senior official of the Ministry of Defense, November 9, 2011.

50. Ibid., August 9, 2011.

51. Kozo Oikawa, interview, July 23, 2012.

52. Isobe, *The Frontline of Operation Tomodachi*, 41.

53. Kitazawa, *Why Japan Needs the SDF*, 82.

54. Toshinobu Miyajima, interview, July 11, 2012.

55. Yoshifumi Hibako, "The Realities and Challenges of the Ground Self-Defense Force Disaster Relief," National Defense Academy, Japan Society of Defense Studies 2011 Research Conference symposium, November 25, 2011.

56. Ryoichi Oriki, interview, February 29, 2012.

57. Toshihiko Miyajima, interview, July 11, 2012.

58. Nuclear Safety Commission whiteboard paper, March 17, 2011, 1:15 a.m.

59. Interview with a senior official of the Joint Staff Office, March 10, 2012; interview with a senior SDF officer, June 17, 2012; interview with a senior official of the Ministry of Defense, October 15, 2012.

60. Katsutoshi Kawano, interview, May 8, 2012.

61. Interview with a senior official of the Ministry of Defense, October 15, 2012.

62. " 'Decided': 7,500 Litres at Once, Water Drop Operations into the Nuclear Reactor," *Nihon Keizai Shimbun Online*, March 11, 2016; "Inside the Meltdown," *BBC*, February 23, 2012; Yoshiyuki Yamaoka, interview, May 12, 2012; Takino, *The SDF and the Great East Japan Earthquake*, 32.

63. Toshimi Kitazawa, interview, February 29, 2012; interview with a senior official of the Joint Staff Office, March 10, 2012; interview with a senior SDF officer, June 18, 2012.

64. Interview with a senior official of the Ministry of Defense, November 9, 2011.

65. Charles Casto, *Station Blackout: Inside the Fukushima Nuclear Disaster and Recovery* (New York: Radius Book Group, 2018), 118.

66. "Stocks To and Fro," *Nihon Keizai Shimbun*, March 16, 18, 19, 2012; "Great Quake Investigation: Kan's Testimony," *Mainichi Shimbun*, September 7, 2011.

67. Kevin Maher, *The Japan That Can't Decide* (Tokyo: Bunshun Shinsho, 2011), 36.

68. Interview with a senior official of the Ministry of Foreign Affairs, March 29, 2012.

69. Ryoichi Oriki, interview, February 29, 2012.

70. Interview with a senior SDF officer, July 20, 2011.

71. Interview with a senior officer of the Joint Staff Office, June 18, 2012.

72. RJIF, *Independent Investigation Commission on the Fukushima Nuclear Accident*, 32–33. (The Japanese version is more in-depth, on 161.)

73. Naoto Kan, interview, August 7, 2012.

74. Goshi Hosono, interview, March 15, 2012.

75. Nuclear Regulatory Commission, Official Transcript of Proceedings: Japan's Fukushima Daiichi ET Audio File, March 16, 2011, 252, 344.

76. Kan, *The TEPCO Fukushima Nuclear Accident*, 132.

77. Hideo Suzuki, interview, February 17, 2012; Goshi Hosono, interview, March 15, 2012.

78. Tenth Meeting of the Nuclear Emergency Response Headquarters, Summary Minutes.

79. Tetsuro Ito, interview, September 25, 2012.

80. Yoshitsugu Oigawa, interview, March 8, 2013.

81. Interview with a senior SDF officer, October 10, 2012.

82. Interview with a senior official of the National Police Agency, February 28, 2013; Yoshitsugu Oigawa, interview, March 8, 2013.

83. Yoshifumi Hibako, interview, July 12, 2012.

84. Yoshitsugu Oigawa, interview, March 8, 2013.

85. Interview with a senior official of the Ministry of Foreign Affairs, April 5, 2012.

86. Hiroshi Ikukawa, interview, December 12, 2011.

87. Yoshitsugu Oigawa, interview, March 8, 2013.

88. Interview with a high-ranking official at the Kantei, February 23, 2012.

89. Nuclear Regulatory Commission, "Official Transcript of Proceedings," 427.

90. Interview with a senior official of the Ministry of Defense, July 20, August 9, 2011; Goshi Hosono, interview, September 5, 2012.

91. Interview with a senior official of the Joint Staff Office, March 14, 2012; Toshinobu Miyajima, interview, July 11, 2012; interview with a senior SDF officer, October 29, 2012.

92. Toshinobu Miyajima, interview, July 11, 2012; interview with a senior official of the Joint Staff Office, October 10, 2012.

93. Toshinobu Miyajima, interview, July 11, 2012.

Chapter 9

1. Tetsuro Ito, interview, September 25, 2012; Tatsuya Kabutan, interview, October 3, 2012.

2. Yuji Arai, interview, October 23, 2012.

3. Nobuyasu Kubo, interview, October 13, 2012.

4. Nobuyasu Kubo, interview, October 13, 2012.

5. Yuji Arai, interview, October 23, 2012.

6. Naoto Kan, *The TEPCO Fukushima Nuclear Accident: My Thoughts as Prime Minister* (Tokyo: Gentosha Shinsho, 2012), 133.

7. Nobuyasu Kubo, interview, October 13, 2012.

8. Ibid.; Kan, *The TEPCO Fukushima Nuclear Accident*, 132.

9. Nobuyasu Kubo, interview, August 10, 2012.

10. Yoshihiro Katayama, interview, August 1, 2011; Yuji Arai, interviews, August 5, 2011 and October 23, 2012; Nobuyasu Kubo, interview, October 13, 2012.

11. Banri Kaieda, interview, June 10, 2011; Rebuild Japan Initiative Foundation (RJIF), *Independent Investigation Commission on the Fukushima Nuclear Accident* (Tokyo: Discover Twenty-One, 2012), 162–63 (only included in the Japanese version); Goshi Hosono, interview, March 15, 2012; Hideo Suzuki, interview, June 6, 2012; Toshinobu Miyajima, interview, July 11, 2012; Takahiro Takino, *The SDF and the Great East Japan Earthquake* (Tokyo: Poplar Publishing, 2012), 61; Banri Kaieda, *The Kaieda Notes—A Record of the 176-Day Nuclear Struggle* (Tokyo: Kodansha, 2012), 90–91.

12. Narumi Suzuki, interview, November 10, 2011.

13. Ibid.; "Special Extended Report on the Nuclear Crisis: The Battle to Overcome, Mr. Sunday," *Fuji Television*, April 17, 2011; Yuji Arai, interviews, August 5, 2011 and October 13, 2012; Takino, *The SDF and the Great East Japan Earthquake*, 61; Takeyuki Inagaki, interview, December 10, 2013.

14. Nobuyasu Kubo, interview, October 13, 2012; Yuji Arai, interview, October 23, 2012; Shingo Akashi, interview, November 5, 2012; Yoshihiro Yamaguchi, interview, November 6, 2012.

15. Interview with a senior officer of the Joint Staff Office, October 10, 2012.

16. Goshi Hosono, interviews, October 6, 2011 and March 15, 2012; Yoshifumi Hibako, *Acting Immediately and Tenaciously, Complete the Mission: The Great East Japan Earthquake and the Records of Chief of Staff of Ground Self-Defense Force* (Tokyo: Manejimento-sha, 2015), 113–14; interviews with a senior official of the Ministry of Defense, December 2, 2011 and August 7, 2012; interview with a senior official of the National Police Agency, March 8, 2012; Tetsuro Ito, interview, April 9, 2012; Toshinobu Miyajima, interview, July 11, 2012.

17. Satoshi Maeda, interview, December 16, 2011; Akihisa Nagashima, interview, February 9, 2012; Yasunari Umezu, interview, February 20, 2012; Masayuki Hironaka, interview, March 10, 2012; Goshi Hosono, interview, March 15, 2012.

18. Masayuki Hironaka, interview, March 14, 2012; interview with a senior SDF officer, June 18, 2012.

19. Yuji Arai, interview, August 5, 2011; interview with a senior official of the Ministry of Defense, October 7, 2011; interview with a senior official of the Ministry of Defense, November 9, 2011; Akihisa Nagashima, interview, February 9, 2012; Ryoichi Oriki, interview, March 6, 2012; Goshi Hosono, interviews, March 15, 2012 and September 5, 2012; Tatsuya Kabutan, interview, October 3, 2012; interview with a Kantei parliamentary secretary, October 28, 2012.

20. Interview with a senior official of the Ministry of Defense, November 9, 2011; interview with a senior official of the Joint Staff Office, March 10, 2012; Toshinobu Miyajima, interview, July 11, 2012; Ryoichi Oriki, interview, August 4, 2012; Toshimi Kitazawa, *Why Japan Needs the SDF* (Tokyo: Kadokawa Shoten, 2012), 89.

21. TEPCO, "Fukushima Nuclear Accident Report," June 20, 2012, 301.

22. Haruki Madarame, testimony before the Government Investigation Commission, February 15, 2012; Koji Okamoto, *Testimony: Haruki Madarame—Where NISA Went Wrong* (Tokyo: Shinchosha, 2012), 94.

23. Shiro Yamazaki, interview, December 15, 2011.

24. Akihisa Nagashima, interview, February 9, 2012.

25. Government Investigation Commission on the Accident at the Fukushima Nuclear Power Stations of Tokyo Electric Power Company, Final Report, July 23, 2012, 285.

26. Interview with a senior official of the Ministry of Defense, February 17, 2012.

27. Ryoichi Oriki, interview, March 6, 2012.

28. Makoto Akashi, interviews, November 24, 2011 and November 5, 2012. TEPCO official, interview, October 24, 2017.

29. ICRP, "The 2007 Recommendations of the International Commission on Radiological Protection," ICRP Publication 103, Ann., ICRP 37, nos. 2–4, 2007.

30. Kazuo Sakai, interview, December 26, 2012.

31. Goshi Hosono, interview, January 13, 2012; interview with a Kantei parliamentary secretary, December 15, 2011.

32. Interview with a senior official of the Ministry of Defense, December 2, 2011.

33. Kimito Nakae, interview, November 1, 2012.

34. Kan, *The TEPCO Fukushima Nuclear Accident*, 130.

35. Interview with a senior official of the Ministry of Defense, November 9, 2011; Nakae Kimito, interview, November 17, 2011.

36. Interview with a senior SDF officer, July 28, 2011.

37. Interview with a Kantei parliamentary secretary, January 6, 2012.

38. Interview with an ex-police Kantei staff member, November 22, 2011.

39. Interview with a Kantei staff member, August 18, 2011; Goshi Hosono, interview, January 13, 2012; interview with a Kantei parliamentary secretary, January 6, 2012.

40. Interview with a senior official of the Joint Staff Office, March 10, 2012; Toshimi Kitazawa, interview, February 29, 2012.

41. Ryoichi Oriki, interview, February 29, 2012.

42. Interview with a senior official of the Joint Staff Office, March 10, 2012.

43. Ibid., May 8, 2012; interviews with a senior SDF officer, June 18, 2012 and October 29, 2012.

44. Kiyohiko Toyama, interview, April 23, 2012; Tetsuro Fukuyama, interview, September 26, 2012; Kiyohiko Toyama, *The Politics of Aspiration: Japan's Road Back to Recovery* (Tokyo: Ronsosha, 2012), 5–9.

45. Kiyohiko Toyama, interview, April 23, 2012.

46. Hiroshi Suzuki, interview, May 31, 2012.

47. Goshi Hosono, interviews, September 5, 2012 and November 1, 2012.

48. Government Investigation Commission on the Accident at the Fukushima Nuclear Power Stations of Tokyo Electric Power Company, Interim Report, December 26, 2011, 272.

49. Atushi Oshima, interview, December 26, 2011; Yojiro Hatakeyama, interview, February 23, 2012; Goshi Hosono, interview, March 15, 2012; Yoshihiro Katayama, interview, July 18, 2012.

50. Hiroshi Suzuki, interview, May 31, 2012.

51. Eleventh Meeting of the Nuclear Emergency Response Headquarters, Summary Minutes.

52. Haruaki Yasui, interview, May 21, 2020.

53. Kaieda, *The Kaieda Notes*, 99.

54. Hiroshi Ikukawa, interview, December 21, 2011; Haruaki Yasui, interview, May 21, 2020.

55. Hiroshi Suzuki, interview, May 31, 2012. Keil explained as such, but the actual scale of casualties at Chernobyl still remains to be unknown. An authoritative research on the topic describes the case as follows: The firefighters based onsite or in the local community were the first ones to rush to the reactor immediately after the Chernobyl nuclear explosion. They quickly tended to extinguishing the fire without sufficient protective wear, despite high levels of radiation. As a result, many of the fire-fighters received extreme doses and passed away. The military's helicopter squad was then brought to the site. Forty hours after the accident happened, the workers started dumping sand and boron from the air toward the reactor, which soon amounted to five thousand tons by May 8. Many of the pilots were highly skilled from having fought in Afghanistan. It was the draftees, the reserve officers, the engineering unit, and the civilian defense force who were in charge of the cruelest tasks that involved removing contaminated debris and creating the sarcophagus around the plant. Many of the young draftees were from Central Asia—they were unable to speak Russian fluently and lacked knowledge of radioactive protection. They were dubbed "bio-robots." Nearly 600,000 of them were involved in these fierce tasks. Three months after the accident, the number of fatalities included 2 who died instantly from the explosion and 29 who died from acute exposure to radiation. A total of 134 out of the 237 personnel who were flown from Moscow for the sarcophagus operation showed symptoms of acute exposure to radiation. Later, a total of 50 people died of acute exposure. Estimated numbers for projected fatalities from exposure to radiation at Chernobyl range from 4,000 (U.N.) to 90,000 (Greenpeace International). In Serhii Plokhy, *Chernobyl: History of a Tragedy* (Allen Lane, 2018), 339–40.

56. Government Investigation Commission, "J-Village, August 8–9," Masao Yoshida, Hearing Results Report, August 16, 2011, 5–8.

57. "NHK Special: Linked Project—Fate's Unit 1: The Truth the '30,000 Conversation' Reveals—TEPCO Teleconference, the Latest Science Analyzes," https://www3.nhk.or.jp/news/special/shinsai6genpatsu/index.html.

58. Haruaki Yasui, interview, May 21, 2020.

Chapter 10

1. Jeffrey Bader, interview, June 28, 2012.
2. Richard Reed, interview, June 25, 2012.
3. Interview with a high-ranking U.S. administration official, May 21, 2012.
4. Richard Reed, interview, June 25, 2012.
5. Interview with a high-ranking U.S. administration official, March 30, 2012.
6. "EAP Assistant Secretary Kurt Campbell's Meetings with MOFA DG Akitaka Saiki," https://wikileaks.org/plusd/cables/09TOKYO2197_a.html; "MOFA Bureaucrat: 'The Democratic Party Request for Equal U.S.-Japan Relations Is Stupid'—Translation of an Official U.S. Telegram," *Asahi Shimbun,* May 7, 2011.
7. James Zumwalt, interview, August 21, 2013.
8. Joseph Donovan, interview, June 29, 2012; Ayako Kimura, interview, November 7, 2012.
9. Interview with a high-ranking U.S. government official, June 26, 2012; Kevin Maher, *The Japan That Can't Decide* (Tokyo: Bunshun Shinsho, 2011), 22–24.
10. Michael Schiffer, interview, June 27, 2012; interview with a senior official of the Defense Department, June 28, 2012.
11. Richard Reed, interview, June 25, 2012.
12. Ibid.; interview with a high-ranking U.S. administration official, June 29, 2012.
13. "We See No Radiation at Harmful Levels Reaching U.S. from Damaged Japanese Nuclear Power Plants," *NRC News,* March 13, 2011; Gregory B. Jaczko, interview, April 22, 2013.

14. Gregory B. Jaczko, *Confessions of a Rogue Nuclear Regulator* (New York: Simon & Schuster, 2019), 76.

15. Interview with a senior official of the Defense Department, June 28, 2012.

16. "Investigation of the Great Quake: Operation Tomodachi—U.S. Asia Pacific Strategy Clear," *Mainichi Shimbun*, December 31, 2011; interview with a high-ranking U.S. naval officer, June 27, 2012.

17. "The U.S.-Japan Navy Friendship Association, Special Contribution: Operation Tomodachi," *U. S.-Japan Navy Friendship Association Bulletin*, no. 40, July 1, 2011.

18. Interview with a senior official of the Ministry for Foreign Affairs, July 27, 2012.

19. Nuclear Regulatory Commission, Official Transcript of Proceedings: Japan's Fukushima Daiichi ET Audio File, March 13, 2011, 81–89.

20. Kevin Maher, interview, August 18, 2011; "Investigation of the Great Quake: Operation Tomodachi—U.S. Asia Pacific Strategy Clear," *Mainichi Shimbun*, December 31, 2011.

21. Jeffrey Bader, interview, June 28, 2012.

22. Interview with a senior official of the Ministry for Foreign Affairs, March 7, 2012; April 9, 2012; interview with a senior U.S. embassy official, August 28, 2012.

23. Matsumoto Takeaki, interview, September 19, 2012.

24. Interview with a senior U.S. embassy official, August 28, 2012.

25. Interview with a high-ranking official of the Ministry for Foreign Affairs, March 7, 2012.

26. Charles Casto, *Station Blackout: Inside the Fukushima Nuclear Disaster and Recovery* (New York: Radius Book Group, 2018), 102.

27. Interview with a senior U.S. embassy official, August 28, 2012.

28. Gregory B. Jaczko, interview, August 23, 2013; to the contrary, Jaczko himself has no recollection of receiving an e-mail from Sogabe. There seems to be a very good chance that it did not reach as far as Jaczko.

29. Rebuild Japan Initiative Foundation (RJIF), *Independent Investigation Commission on the Fukushima Nuclear Accident* (Abingdon: Routledge, 2014), 162–63.

30. Nuclear Regulatory Commission, Official Transcript of Proceedings: Japan's Fukushima Daiichi ET Audio File, March 12, 2011, 30.

31. "Investigation of the Great Quake: Largest Operation in History—100,000 SDF Troops," *Mainichi Shimbun*, April 22, 2011.

32. Interviews with a high-ranking U.S. administration official, June 26, and August 22, 2012.

33. Interview with a senior official of the Department of Defense, June 28, 2012.

34. Interview with a high-ranking U.S. administration official, June 29, 2012.

35. Interview with a senior official of the Ministry of Defense, November 9, 2011; Shunsuke Kondo, interview, April 30, 2012.

36. Takeaki Matsumoto, interview, September 19, 2012.

37. Nei himself, however, has "absolutely no recollection" of saying, "We're preparing to withdraw." Hisanori Nei, interview, February 27, 2012.

38. Charles Casto, *Station Blackout: Inside the Fukushima Nuclear Disaster and Recovery* (New York: Radius Book Group, 2018), 129.

39. Interview with a senior U.S. embassy official, September 12, 2011; interview with a senior official of the Ministry of Defense, May 24, 2012.

40. "Investigation of the Great Quake: Operation Tomodachi—U.S. Asia Pacific Strategy Clear," *Mainichi Shimbun*, December 31, 2011; Key Kantei official, chronological memo.

41. Interview with a senior official of the Ministry for Foreign Affairs, April 9, 2012.

42. Interview with a senior official of the Joint Staff Office, May 8, 2012.

43. Tetsuro Fukuyama, interviews, May 19, 2011, and September 6, 2011; Tetsuro Fukuyama, *The Nuclear Crisis: Testimony from the Kantei* (Tokyo: Chikuma Shinsho, 2012), 114; Yukio Edano, testimony before the Diet Investigation Commission, Minutes No. 15, May 27, 2012; interview with a high-ranking official of the Ministry for Foreign Affairs, June 27, 2012; Key Kantei official, chronological memo; interview with a high-ranking U.S. administration official, May 21, 2012.

44. Interview with a high-ranking Kantei official, September 15, 2011; Fukuyama Tetsuro, interview, September 27, 2011; "Investigation of the Great Quake: Operation Tomodachi—U.S. Asia Pacific Strategy Clear," *Mainichi Shimbun*, December 31, 2011; Key Kantei official, chronological memo; Fukuyama, *The Nuclear Crisis*, 130.

45. Interview with a high-ranking U.S. administration official, August 22, 2012.

46. Ibid., May 21, 2012.

47. Charles Casto, *Station Blackout: Inside the Fukushima Nuclear Disaster and Recovery* (New York: Radius Book Group, 2018), 125.

48. Ibid.

49. Interviews with a high-ranking official of the Ministry for Foreign Affairs, April 21, 2011, March 13, 2012, and April 9, 2012; interview with a high-ranking U.S. administration official, August 22, 2011; Takeaki Matsumoto, interview, September 19, 2012.

50. James Steinberg, interview, May 21, 2011.

51. James Steinberg, interview, June 26, 2011; interview with a senior official of the Ministry for Foreign Affairs, April 9, 2012.

52. Matthew L. Wald, "Confusion in U.S. at Start of Japan's Atomic Crisis," *New York Times*, February 21, 2012; Nuclear Regulatory Commission, Official Transcript of Proceedings: Japan's Fukushima Daiichi ET Audio File, March 14, 2011, 59.

53. Interview with a Kantei parliamentary secretary, February 14, 2012; interview with a senior official of the Department of Defense, February 15, 2012; interview with a high-ranking U.S. administration official, June 26, 2011.

54. Interview with a senior official of the Ministry for Foreign Affairs, July 5, 2011; interviews with a high-ranking official of the Ministry for Foreign Affairs, August 30, 2011 and March 7, 2012.

55. The Imperial Household Agency, "A Message from His Majesty the Emperor," March 16, 2011.

56. Maher, *The Japan That Can't Decide*, 34–35.

57. Yutaka Kawashima, "The Prayers of the Emperor and Empress: A Week from the Nuclear Power Station," *Bungei Shunju* (May 2011).

58. Kawashima, "The Prayers of the Emperor and Empress"; Yutaka Kawashima, interview, July 31, 2013.

59. Interview with Fujisaki's aide, November 5, 2011.

60. Interview with a senior Japanese embassy official, May 5, 2011; interviews with a senior State Department official, November 17, 2011 and October 5, 2012; interview with a high-ranking official of the Ministry for Foreign Affairs, June 27, 2012; interview with a high-ranking U.S. administration official, June 26, 2012; interview with a senior official of the Ministry for Foreign Affairs, August 2, 2012.

61. Interview with an official of the Ministry for Foreign Affairs, April 5, 2018.

62. Peter Behr, "Fukushima Crisis Worsens as U.S. Warns of a Large Radiation Release," *New York Times*, March 17, 2011.

63. NRC News, "NRC Provides Protective Action Recommendations Based on U.S. Guidelines," March 16, 2011.

64. Gregory B. Jaczko, interview, April 22, 2013.

65. Tetsuro Fukuyama, interview, September 27, 2011; interviews with a high-ranking U.S. administration official, April 26 and May 21, 2012; Goshi Hosono, interview, May 30, 2012.

66. Interview with a senior Japanese embassy official, August 2, 2012.

67. Interview with a senior Japanese embassy official, February 20, 2012; interview with a senior official of the Joint Staff Office, March 10, 2012; interview with a senior SDF officer, June 17, 2012; interview with a senior official of the Ministry of Defense, October 15, 2012.

68. Interview with a senior official of the Ministry for Foreign Affairs, July 5, 2011; interview with a senior official of the Ministry of Defense, November 9, 2011; Ryoichi Oriki, interviews, February 29, 2012 and March 6, 2012; interview with a high-ranking official of the Ministry for Foreign Affairs, June 27, 2012.

69. Charles Casto, interview, July 26, 2013.

70. Charles Casto, *Station Blackout: Inside the Fukushima Nuclear Disaster and Recovery* (New York: Radius Book Group, 2018), 24.

71. Nuclear Regulatory Commission, Official Transcript of Proceedings: Japan's Fukushima Daiichi ET Audio File, March 14, 2011, 228–29.

72. Interview with a high-ranking U.S. administration official, August 22, 2012.

73. Charles Casto, *Station Blackout: Inside the Fukushima Nuclear Disaster and Recovery* (New York: Radius Book Group, 2018), 24.

74. Ibid.

75. Charles Casto, interview, August 24, 2011; Julie Wernau, "Executive Profile: Chuck Casto, Regional Administrator, Nuclear Regulatory Commission, Region III," *Chicago Tribune*, July 2, 2012; interview with a high-ranking U.S. administration official, August 22, 2012.

76. Charles Casto, interview, August 26, 2019.

77. Charles Casto, interview, July 23, 2013; interview with a high-ranking U.S. administration official, August 26, 2011.

78. Gregory B. Jaczko, *Confessions of a Rogue Nuclear Regulator* (New York: Simon & Schuster, 2019), 13.

79. Gregory B. Jaczko, interview, April 22, 2013.

80. Ibid.

81. Nuclear Regulatory Commission, Official Transcript of Proceedings: Japan's Fukushima Daiichi ET Audio File, March 16, 2011, 29; March 17, 2011, 78; interview with a manager of a U.S. nuclear power manufacturer, May 4, 2011; interview with a senior officer of the National Police Agency, August 11, 2011; Matthew L. Wald, "Records Show Conflicts in U.S. at Start of Japan's Atomic Crisis," *New York Times*, February 21, 2012; Charles Casto, interview, June 25, 2012.

82. Charles Casto, *Station Blackout: Inside the Fukushima Nuclear Disaster and Recovery* (New York: Radius Book Group, 2018), 134.

83. Ibid., 135.

84. Ibid.

85. Ibid.

86. Ibid., 136.

87. Ibid., 137.

88. Ibid.

89. Ibid.

90. Nuclear Regulatory Commission, Official Transcript of Proceedings: Japan's Fukushima Daiichi ET Audio File, March 18, 2011, 280–91; Charles Casto, interviews, August 10, 2011, August 24, 2012, and July 26, 2013.

91. Nuclear Regulatory Commission, Official Transcript of Proceedings: Japan's Fukushima Daiichi ET Audio File, March 14, 2011, 274, 278–79, 281.

92. Government Investigation Commission on the Accident at the Fukushima Nuclear Power Stations of Tokyo Electric Power Company, Interim Report, December 26, 2011, 249–50.

93. Nuclear Regulatory Commission, Official Transcript of Proceedings: Japan's Fukushima Daiichi ET Audio File, March 14, 2011, 291.

94. Ibid., March 16, 2011, 216.

95. Ibid., 162.

96. The NRC issued a statement on March 16, 2011, that "Hawaii, Alaska, the U.S. territories, and the U.S. West Coast are not expected to experience any harmful levels of radioactivity." In Nuclear Regulatory Commission, Official Transcript of Proceedings: Japan's Fukushima Daiichi ET Audio File, March 16, 2011, 159.

97. Toshihiro Okuyama, *Report: A Month of TEPCO's Nuclear Accident* (Tokyo: Asahi Shinsho, 2011), 106.

98. TEPCO, "Fukushima Nuclear Accident Report," June 20, 2012, 328.

99. Osamu Maekawa, interview, January 5, 2012; Masaya Yasui, interviews, February 9, 2012, and May 27, 2012; "Unit 4 Deep Scars," *Asahi Shimbun*, May 27, 2012, and Norikazu Yamashita, interview, May 19, 2020.

100. Masaya Yasui, interview, September 30, 2011.

101. Nuclear Regulatory Commission, Official Transcript of Proceedings: Japan's Fukushima Daiichi ET Audio File, March 17, 2011, 55.

102. Goshi Hosono and Shuntaro Torigoe, *Testimony: Shuntaro Torigoe Closes In on the Truth About "The 500 Days of Nuclear Crisis"* (Tokyo: Kodansha, 2012), 196.

103. Masaya Yasui, interview, September 30, 2011.

104. NISA internal memo, no. 18.

105. Naoto Kan, interview, September 20, 2012.

106. Banri Kaieda, *The Kaieda Notes—A Record of the 176-Day Nuclear Struggle* (Tokyo: Kodansha, 2012), 75.

107. The Atomic Energy Society of Japan, "The Fukushima Daiichi Nuclear Accident: Final Report of the AESJ," March 2014, 30.

108. Hiroshi Ikukawa, interview, July 12, 2012.

109. Charles Casto, interview, July 26, 2013.

110. David Sanger and others, "U.S. Calls Radiation 'Extremely High'; Sees Japan Nuclear Crisis Worsening," *New York Times*, March 16, 2011.

Chapter 11

1. Interview with a high-ranking U.S. administration official, August 22, 2012.

2. Kevin Maher, *The Japan That Can't Decide* (Tokyo: Bunshun Shinsho, 2011), 31–32.

3. Charles Casto, interview, August 24, 2011.

4. Ibid., August 10, 2011.

5. Michael Schiffer, interview, June 27, 2012.

6. Interviews with a high-ranking government official, April 26, 2013, and August 16, 2013.

7. Interview with a high-ranking U.S. administration official, March 30, 2012; Richard Danzig, interview, August 23, 2012.

8. Nuclear Regulatory Commission, Official Transcript of Proceedings: Japan's Fukushima Daiichi ET Audio File, March 16, 2011, 50.

9. Gregory B. Jaczko, interview, April 22, 2013.

10. Nuclear Regulatory Commission (NRC) News, "NRC Sees No Radiation at Harmful Levels Reaching U.S. from Damaged Japanese Nuclear Power Plants," March 13, 2011.

11. Gregory B. Jaczko, *Confessions of a Rogue Nuclear Regulator* (New York: Simon & Schuster, 2019), 85.

12. Gregory B. Jaczko, interview, August 16, 2013.

13. Gregory B. Jaczko, *Confessions of a Rogue Nuclear Regulator* (New York: Simon & Schuster, 2019), 87.

14. Nuclear Regulatory Commission, Official Transcript of Proceedings: Japan's Fukushima Daiichi ET Audio File, March 16, 2011, 112–15, 140–43.

15. Ibid., March 16, 2011, 156–58.

16. Ibid., March 17, 2011, 414.

17. Ibid., March 16, 2011, 223–25.

18. Ibid., March 16, 2011, 41, 231, 293–94; National Diet of Japan Fukushima Accident Independent Investigation Commission, Official Report, July 5, 2012, ch. 2, 31–32; "Investigation: The Fukushima Daiichi NPS Accident Investigation Commissions," *Asahi Shimbun*, May 1, 2012.

19. "Pentagon Preparing for a Nuclear Worst-Case Scenario at Fukushima," *Stars and Stripes*, March 16, 2011.

20. Jeffrey Bader, interview, June 26, 2012; Jeffrey Bader, *Obama and China's Rise: An Insider's Account of America's Asia Strategy* (Washington: Brookings Institution Press, 2012), 138.

21. Gidget Fuentes and Sam Fellman, "Roughead Downplays Odds of Forced Evacuations," *Navy Times*, March 23, 2011.

22. Interview with a high-ranking U.S. administration official, March 30, 2012.

23. Ibid.

24. Interviews with a high-ranking U.S. administration official, March 30, 2012, April 26, 2012, May 21, 2012, June 26, 2012, and August 22, 2012; interview with a high-ranking official of the Department of State, June 26, 2012.

25. Ibid.

26. Interview with a high-ranking U.S. administration official, May 21, 2012.

27. Jeffrey Bader, interview, June 26, 2012.

28. Ibid.; Richard Reed, interview, June 25, 2012.

29. Richard Reed, ibid.

30. Interview with a senior NRC official, June 25, 2012.

31. Jeffrey Bader, "Inside the White House During Fukushima," *Foreign Affairs*, March 8, 2012.

32. Interview with a high-ranking U.S. administration official, May 21, 2012; Jeffrey Bader, interview, June 26, 2012.

33. Richard Reed, interview, June 25, 2012.

34. Interview with a high-ranking U.S. administration official, March 30, 2012.

35. Ibid., April 26, 2012.

36. Ibid., April 22, 2013.

37. Interview with a high-ranking official of the Department of Defense, June 26, 2012.

38. Interview with a high-ranking official of the Department of State, June 29, 2012.

39. Richard Reed, interview, June 25, 2012.

40. Interview with a high-ranking White House official, March 30, 2012.

41. Bader, *Obama and China's rise*, 138.

42. Gregory B. Jaczko, *Confessions of a Rogue Nuclear Regulator* (New York: Simon & Schuster, 2019), 90.

43. Ibid.

44. Gregory B. Jaczko, interview, April 22, 2013.

45. Core parliamentary member of the Kantei, chronological memo.

46. Amanda Cox and others, "The Evacuation Zones Around the Fukushima Daiichi Nuclear Plant," *New York Times*, March 25, 2011.

47. Interview with Jeffrey Bader.

48. Bader, *Obama and China's rise*, 139.

49. Maher, *The Japan That Can't Decide*, 32–33.

50. David E. Sanger and others, "U.S. Sees 'Extremely High' Radiation Level at Plant, Focusing on Spent Fuel's Impact," *New York Times*, March 17, 2011; Nuclear Regulatory Commission, 582nd Meeting, Advisory Committee on Reactor Safeguards, April 7, 2011.

51. Interview with a high-ranking U.S. administration official, August 28, 2013.

52. Charles Casto, interview, July 26, 2013.

53. NEA participant presentation outline, received June 9, 2012.

54. NRC transcript, March 15, 2011, 177.

55. Interview with a senior official of the Department of State, November 17, 2011.

56. Gregory B. Jaczko, interview, April 22, 2013.

57. Interviews with a high-ranking U.S. administration official, August 26, 2011, April 26, 2012, and October 10, 2012; interview with a senior official of the Department of Defense, February 15, 2012; interviews with a high-ranking official of the Ministry for Foreign Affairs, March 7, 2012 and April 11, 2012; Tetsuro Ito, interview, September 25, 2012; interview with a Kantei parliamentary secretary, October 10, 2012.

58. Richard Reed, interview, June 25, 2012.

59. Takashi Noda, interview, September 14, 2012.

60. Takanori Nakata, interview, October 5, 2012.

61. Nuclear Regulatory Commission, Official Transcript of Proceedings: Japan's Fukushima Daiichi ET Audio File, March 14, 2011, 245–47.

62. Ibid., 258.

63. Ibid., 263–64.

64. Interview with a senior officer of the Joint Staff Office, March 10, 2012.

65. Ibid.

66. Ibid., June 16, 2012.

67. Interview with a senior SDF officer, June 18, 2012.

68. "No Exit for DODEA Workers Hired in U.S.," *Stars and Stripes*, March 19, 2011.

69. "Evacuation: Willard Sets Out to Clear Up Conflicting Reports at Yokosuka," *Stars and Stripes*, March 23, 2011.

70. Interview with a high-ranking officer of the U.S. Navy Yokosuka Headquarters, June 27, 2012; interview with a high-ranking officer of the U.S. Joint Chiefs of Staff, January 6, 2016.

71. Interview with a senior SDF officer, June 18, 2012; interview with a high-ranking officer of the U.S. Navy Yokosuka Headquarters, October 5, 2012.

72. Interview with a senior official of the Department of State, April 27, 2013.

73. Ibid., June 28, 2012.

74. Interview with a senior SDF officer, August 3, 2012; interview with a senior officer of the Joint Staff Office, August 4, 2012.

75. Interview with a high-ranking officer of the U.S. Navy Yokosuka Headquarters, June 27, 2012; interview with a senior officer of the Joint Staff Office, July 20, 2011; interview with a senior SDF officer, August 4, 2012.

76. Interview with a high-ranking U.S. administration official, August 22, 2012.

77. Nuclear Regulatory Commission, Official Transcript of Proceedings: Japan's Fukushima Daiichi ET Audio File, March 17, 2011, 75–77; interview with a senior official of the Ministry of Defense, August 9, 2011; interview with a senior NRC officer, June 25, 2012; ibid.

78. Takashi Noda, interview, September 14 and 15, 2012; interview with a senior official of the Department of Defense, June 28, 2012; interview with a high-ranking U.S. administration official, August 22, 2012; interview with a senior U.S. embassy official, August 28, 2012.

79. Interview with a high-ranking U.S. administration official, April 26, 2012.

80. Ibid., August 22, 2012.

81. Richard Reed, interview, June 25, 2012.

82. Interview with a high-ranking U.S. administration official, August 16, 2013.

83. Interview with a U.S. administration official, August 14, 2013.

84. Interview with a senior official of the Ministry for Foreign Affairs, March 13, 2012.

85. Interview with a senior official of the Ministry of Defense, November 9, 2011.

86. Burton Field, interview, August 21, 2013.

87. Interview with a senior Self-Defense Forces officer, September 14, 2012; Kenneth Glueck, interview, June 27, 2013.

88. Kenneth Glueck, interview, June 27, 2013; Burton Field, interview, August 21, 2013.

89. Interview with a U.S. administration official, August 14, 2013.

90. Ibid., April 27, 2013.

91. Kenneth Glueck, interview, June 27, 2013.

92. Interview with a U.S. administration official, August 14, 2013.

93. Interview with a high-ranking officer of the U.S. Navy Yokosuka Headquarters, June 27, 2012.

94. Interview with a U.S. administration official, April 27, 2013.

95. Interview with a high-ranking officer of the U.S. Navy Yokosuka Headquarters, June 27, 2012.

96. YouTube, "Admiral Robert F. Willard Addresses Yokosuka," Fleet Activities Yokosuka—Town Hall Meeting, March 22, 2011; interview with a senior maritime SDF officer, July 5, 2012; interview with a senior SDF officer, September 14, 2012.

97. Ibid.; Kenneth Glueck, interview, June 27, 2013.

98. "Pacific Commander Says Mandatory Evacuation Is Unlikely," *Stars and Stripes*, March 22, 2011.

99. Interview with a senior SDF officer, September 14, 2012.

100. Katsutoshi Kawano, interview, October 10, 2012.

Chapter 12

1. Ministry of Foreign Affairs telegraph, "Telephone Conversation between President Obama and Prime Minister Kan [Tohoku-Pacific Ocean Earthquake]," information disclosure based on the Freedom of Information Act, October 7, 2013.

2. Interview with a senior official of the Ministry of Foreign Affairs, March 13, 2012.

3. Interview with a Kantei parliamentary secretary, November 20, 2012.

4. "Fukushima Daiichi Nuclear Power Station Inspection," *Asahi Shimbun*, April 10, 2011; "U.S. Leaders 'No Policy, Then Mandatory Evacuation': U.S. and Japan Coping with the Fukushima Daiichi Disaster Behind the Scenes," *Asahi Shimbun*, May 15, 2011); interview with a senior official of the Ministry of Defense, November 18, 2011; interview with a senior official of the Ministry of Foreign Affairs, March 12, 2012; "U.S. Army, Full-Scale Support List: Mass Pollution Expected After Fukushima Explosion," *Asahi Shimbun*, May 22, 2011.

5. "U.S. Leaders 'No Policy, Then Mandatory Evacuation': U.S. and Japan Coping with the Fukushima Daiichi Disaster Behind the Scenes," *Asahi Shimbun*, May 15, 2011); prime minister of Japan and his cabinet, speeches and statements, "Telephone Conversation with President Barack Obama of the United States," March 12, 2011; prime minister of Japan and his cabinet, speeches and statements, "Telephone Conference between Prime Minister Kan and U.S. President Obama," March 17, 2011.

6. YouTube, ShareAmerica, "President Obama's Condolences for Japan" (English and Japanese), March 24, 2011; White House, President Barack Obama, "President Obama Offers Condolences and Support for Japan," March 17, 2011.

7. Interview with a high-ranking U.S. administration official, March 30, 2012; Daniel Russel, interview, January 24, 2017; White House, President Barack Obama, "President Obama: 'We Will Stand with the People of Japan,'" March 17, 2011.

8. Interview with an official of the Ministry of Defense, August 9, 2011; Toshimi Kitazawa, *Why Japan Needs the SDF* (Tokyo: Kadokawa Shoten, 2012), 91.

9. Interview with a high-ranking official of the Ministry of Defense, November 17, 2011; Ryoichi Oriki, interview, March 6, 2012.

10. Ayako Kimura, interview, August 9, 2011.

11. Ayako Kimura, interview, November 7, 2012.

12. Interview with a senior NRC officer, June 25, 2012; Ayako Kimura, interview, August 9, 2011.

13. Charles Casto, *Station Blackout: Inside the Fukushima Nuclear Disaster and Recovery* (New York: Radius Book Group, 2018), 119.

14. Nuclear Regulatory Commission, Official Transcript of Proceedings: Japan's Fukushima Daiichi ET Audio File, March 17, 2011, 408.

15. Charles Casto, *Station Blackout: Inside the Fukushima Nuclear Disaster and Recovery* (New York: Radius Book Group, 2018), 101.

16. Ibid., 99.

17. Ibid., 100.

18. Interview with a senior official of the Ministry of Defense, October 15, 2012; key Kantei official, chronological memo.

19. Charles Casto, *Station Blackout: Inside the Fukushima Nuclear Disaster and Recovery* (New York: Radius Book Group, 2018), 104.

20. Akihisa Nagashima, interview, May 20, 2011.

21. Interview with a senior official of the Ministry of Defense, September 2, 2011; Hideo Suzuki, interview, September 22, 2011; interview with a senior official of the Ministry for Foreign Affairs, February 20, 2012.

22. Interview with a Kantei parliamentary secretary, October 10, 2012.

23. Interview with a senior official of the Ministry of Defense, October 7, 2011; interview with a senior official of the Ministry of Economy, Trade, and Industry, November 17, 2011.

24. Goshi Hosono, interview, May 30, 2012.

25. Goshi Hosono, interview, May 16, 2011; Akihisa Nagashima, "Dealing with the Nuclear Emergency: Behind the Scenes of U.S.-Japan Cooperation," *VOICE*, July 2011, 136; Akihisa Nagashima, interview, February 9, 2012.

26. Akihisa Nagashima, interview, February 9, 2012; interview with a senior official of the Ministry of Defense, November 9, 2011; Kimito Nakae, interviews, November 17, 2011, and November 1, 2012; interview with a Kantei parliamentary secretary, December 16, 2011; Goshi Hosono, interview, May 30, 2012; Toshimi Kitazawa, interview, June 14, 2012.

27. Banri Kaieda, interview, July 10, 2012.

28. Interview with a senior official of the Ministry of Defense, May 24, 2012.

29. Tetsuro Ito, interview, April 9, 2012; interview with a high-ranking U.S. administration official, August 22, 2012.

30. Interview with a high-ranking U.S. administration official, August 22, 2012.

31. Tetsuro Fukuyama, *The Nuclear Crisis: Testimony from the Kantei* (Tokyo: Chikuma Shinsho, 2012), 134.

32. Interview with a high-ranking U.S. administration official, August 22, 2012.

33. Ibid.

34. Interview with a senior official of the Ministry of Defense, October 7, 2011; interview with a senior official of the Ministry of Economy, Trade, and Industry, June 30, 2011; Goshi Hosono, interview, February 13, 2012; interview with a Kantei parliamentary secretary, October 28, 2012.

35. Akihisa Nagashima, interview, February 9, 2012; interview with a senior official of the Ministry of Foreign Affairs, March 13, 2012; Goshi Hosono, interview, August 9, 2012.

36. Government internal memo, Joint Crisis Management Coordination Group

on the Nuclear Emergency, 4th Meeting: 8:00 p.m.–9:30 p.m., Cabinet Annex, March 24, 2011.

37. Interview with a high-ranking U.S. administration official, August 26, 2011.

38. Interview with a high-ranking U.S. government official, August 26, 2011.

39. Kevin Sullivan and Mary Jordan, "Japan to Compensate for Tainted Blood," *Washington Post*, March 16, 1996, www.washingtonpost.com/archive/politics/1996/03/16/japan-to-compensate-for-tainted-blood/614f2498-914f-4afc-9432-627f9005fc0e/.

40. Government internal memo, Joint Coordination Group on the Nuclear Emergency, 4th Meeting: 8:00 p.m.–9:30 p.m., Cabinet Annex, March 24, 2011; interview with a senior official of the Ministry of Economy, Trade, and Industry, November 17, 2011; interview with a senior official of the Ministry of Economy, Trade, and Industry, June 30, 2011; Tetsuro Ito, interview, September 25, 2012; interview with a senior official of the Ministry of Health, Labor, and Welfare, October 11, 2012; interview with a senior official of the Nuclear and Industrial Safety Agency, October 25, 2012.

41. Charles Casto, *Station Blackout: Inside the Fukushima Nuclear Disaster and Recovery* (New York: Radius Book Group, 2018), 157.

42. Ibid., 153.

43. Ibid., 117.

44. Gregory B. Jaczko, *Confessions of a Rogue Nuclear Regulator* (New York: Simon & Schuster, 2019), 93.

45. Charles Casto, *Station Blackout: Inside the Fukushima Nuclear Disaster and Recovery* (New York: Radius Book Group, 2018), 116.

46. Nuclear Regulatory Commission, Official Transcript of Proceedings: Japan's Fukushima Daiichi ET Audio File, March 16, 2011, 407–12, 414.

47. Gregory B. Jaczko, *Confessions of a Rogue Nuclear Regulator* (New York: Simon & Schuster, 2019), 93.

48. Charles Casto, *Station Blackout: Inside the Fukushima Nuclear Disaster and Recovery* (New York: Radius Book Group, 2018), 116.

49. Rebuild Japan Initiative Foundation (RJIF), *Independent Investigation Commission on the Fukushima Nuclear Accident* (Abingdon: Routledge, 2014), 165; "Energy Secretary Chu Says Reactor Core Is Damaged," *Wall Street Journal*, April 1, 2011.

50. Interview with a high-ranking U.S. government official, November 4, 2011; Goshi Hosono and Shuntaro Torigoe, *Testimony: Shuntaro Torigoe Closes In on the Truth About "The 500 Days of Nuclear Crisis"* (Tokyo: Kodansha, 2012), 197–200.

51. Government internal memo, Joint Crisis Management Coordination Group on the Nuclear Emergency, 4th Meeting: 8:00 p.m.–9:30 p.m., Cabinet Annex, March 24, 2011.

52. Interview with a senior official of the Ministry of Economy, Trade, and Industry, June 30, 2011; interview with a senior official of the Ministry for Foreign Affairs, July 5, 2011; Ryoichi Oriki, interview, March 6, 2012.

53. Interview with an SDF staff member, June 18, 2012.

54. Government internal memo, Joint Crisis Management Coordination Group on the Nuclear Emergency, 5th Meeting: 8:00 p.m.–9:30 p.m., Cabinet Annex, March 25, 2011.

55. RJIF, *Independent Investigation Commission on the Fukushima Nuclear Accident*, 158.

56. Tetsuro Fukuyama, interview, September 6, 2011.

57. Interview with a senior official of the Ministry for Foreign Affairs, July 5, 2011; interview with a senior official of the Department of Defense, June 28, 2012; interviews with a high-ranking U.S. administration official, August 26, 2011, August 22, 2012.

58. Ministry of Foreign Affairs telegraph, "Telephone Conversation between President Obama and Prime Minister Kan [Tohoku-Pacific Ocean Earthquake]," information disclosure based on the Freedom of Information Act, October 7, 2013.

59. Kevin Maher, *The Japan That Can't Decide* (Tokyo: Bunshun Shinsho, 2011), 42; Akihisa Nagashima, "Dealing with the Nuclear Emergency: Behind the Scenes of U.S.-Japan Cooperation," *VOICE*, July 2011, 137; interview with a senior official of the Department of Defense, June 28, 2012.

60. Burton Field, interview, August 21, 2013.

61. Interview with a high-ranking official of the Department of Defense, June 28, 2012.

62. Interview with a high-ranking U.S. administration official, March 30, 2012.

63. Interview with a Kantei parliamentary secretary, August 9, 2012.

64. Maher, *The Japan That Can't Decide*, 41.

65. Goshi Hosono, interview, February 13, 2012.

66. Interview with a Kantei staff member, August 17, 2011.

67. NISA internal memo no. 14.

68. Interview with a senior official of the Ministry of Defense, May 24, 2012.

69. Implementation request items to the U.S. Army and implementation request items to the Ministry of Defense.

70. Interview with a senior official of the Ministry of Defense, May 24, 2012; Ryoichi Oriki, interview, March 6, 2012; interview with a senior officer of the Joint Staff Office, March 10, 2012; Hosono and Torigoe, *Testimony*, 185–89.

71. Interviews with a senior official of the Ministry of Defense, August 9, 2011; October 11, 2011; interview with a senior officer of the Joint Staff Office, March 10, 2012; interview with a senior SDF officer, June 18, 2012. Kan denies having said "perhaps we'd better leave it up to America." He states, "I never thought of getting someone from outside Japan to clean up an accident that Japan had caused, and in the most dangerous frontlines at that. It would be impossible to ask someone to do what the SDF couldn't do, or wouldn't do even though they could." In Naoto Kan, interview, November 14, 2012; Ryoichi Oriki, interview, July 29, 2017.

72. Interview with a senior official of the Ministry of Defense, October 7, 2011; Yoshifumi Hibako, "The Realities and Challenges of the Ground Self-Defense Force Disaster Relief," National Defense Academy, Japan Society of Defense Studies 2011 Research Conference symposium, November 25, 2011; Ryoichi Oriki, interview, March 6, 2012; interview with a senior officer of the Joint Staff Office, May 12, 2012.

73. Interview with a senior SDF officer, August 3, 2012, and August 30, 2012.

74. Burton Field, interview, August 21, 2013; Masayuki Hironaka, interview, March 10 2012.

75. Nuclear Regulatory Commission, Official Transcript of Proceedings: Japan's Fukushima Daiichi ET Audio File, March 16, 2011, 382–84; interview with a high-ranking U.S. administration official, August 22, 2012.

76. Interview with a Department of State official, August 14, 2013.

77. Interview with a high-ranking maritime SDF officer, July 20, 2011.

78. Interview with a senior official of the Ministry of Defense, August 9, 2011.

79. Interview with a U.S. embassy staff member, August 9, 2011.

80. Charles Casto, interview, June 25, 2012.

81. Interview with a high-ranking U.S. administration official, May 21, 2012.

82. Ibid.

83. Richard Reed, interview, June 25, 2012.

84. Interview with a high-ranking U.S. administration official, May 21, 2012.

85. Interview with a senior official of the Joint Staff Office, March 10, 2012.

86. Interview with a high-ranking White House official, March 30, 2012; Jeffrey Bader, *Obama and China's Rise: An Insider's Account of America's Asia Strategy*, (Washington: Brookings Institution Press, 2012), 139.

87. Interview with a high-ranking U.S. administration official, March 30, 2012.

88. Ibid., May 21, 2012.

89. Department of Energy, "Joint EPA/DOE Statement: Radiation Monitors Confirm that No Radiation Levels of Concern Have Reached the United States," March 18, 2011.

90. Edward N. Luttwak, *The Rise of China vs. the Logic of Strategy* (Cambridge, Mass.: Belknap Press of Harvard University Press, 2011), 135.

91. Interview with a senior maritime SDF officer, May 8, 2012.

92. Interview with a senior ground SDF officer, July 28, 2011. De Gaulle said the following in a press conference in January 1963: ". . . for a great people the free determination of its destiny and the possession of means to preserve this self-determination are an absolute imperative, because alliances have no absolute virtues, whatever may be the sentiments on which they rest." De Gaulle condensed into these words the French logic for having nuclear weapons. See, Wladyslaw W. Kulski, *De Gaulle and the World: The Foreign Policy of the Fifth French Republic* (New York: Syracuse University Press, 1966), 95.

Chapter 13

1. Goshi Hosono, interview, January 13, 2012; Government Investigation Commission on the Accident at the Fukushima Nuclear Power Stations of Tokyo Electric Power Company, Interim Report, December 26, 2011, 256–57.

2. Goshi Hosono, interview, February 5, 2012.

3. Interview with Haruki Madarame, December 14, 2011.

4. Haruki Madarame, interview, December 14, 2011.

5. Akihiro Ohata, interview, May 11, 2012; Koichiro Genba, interview, July 16, 2012.

6. Koichiro Genba, interview, July 16, 2012.

7. Shunsuke Kondo, interviews, April 30, 2012 and October 26, 2012; Koichiro Genba, interviews, July 16, 2012 and July 24, 2012; Government Investigation Commission on the Accident at the Fukushima Nuclear Power Stations of Tokyo Electric Power Company, Final Report, July 23, 2012, 333.

8. Koichiro Genba, interview, July 24, 2012.

9. Seventeenth Meeting of the Nuclear Emergency Response Headquarters, summary minutes.

10. Nuclear Safety Commission, whiteboard memo, Appendix 1–24/36–38.

11. Ryusho Kadota, *The Man Who Went to the Brink of Death—Masao Yoshida and His 500 Days at the Fukushima Daiichi Nuclear Station* (Kyoto: PHP, 2012), 31, 356.

12. Yukio Edano, testimony before the Independent Investigation Commission, December 10, 2011.

13. Tetsuro Fukuyama, interview, January 21, 2012.

14. Tetsuro Ito, interview, April 9, 2012.

15. Ibid.

16. Soramoto Seiki, interview, September 26, 2012.

17. Akihiro Ohata, interview, May 11, 2012; Seiki Soramoto, interview, September 20, 2012.

18. Interview with a senior official of the Ministry of Education, Culture, Sports, Science, and Technology, June 7, 2012.

19. Interview with a senior official of the Japan Atomic Energy Agency, January 31, 2012.

20. Akira Omoto, interview, April 19, 2012.

21. Seiki Soramoto, interview, September 20, 2012; "The Truth About the Shadow Warriors: The 3/11 Advisory Team," *Tokyo Shimbun*, May 25, 2012.

22. Akira Omoto, interview, October 24, 2012.

23. Interview with a Kantei staff member, August 18, 2011.

24. Advisory Team, Issues to Be Considered/Implemented, as of 11:00 p.m., March 16, 2011; Shunsuke Kondo, interview, April 30, 2012.

25. TEPCO videoconference participant memo shown to the author, September 21, 2012.

26. Yoshikatsu Nakayama, interview, May 16, 2012.

27. Mitsumasa Hirano, interview, September 19, 2012.

28. Items for consideration and implementation in Advisory Team to the Minister for Economy, Trade, and Industry and the Prime Minister (2) proposal, March 17, 2011.

29. Yoshikatsu Nakayama, interview, May 16, 2012.

30. Interviews with several participants, January 31, 2012, October 24, 2012, and November 7, 2012.

31. Toshimitsu Homma, interview, June 1, 2012.

32. TEPCO videoconference participant memo shown to the author, September 21, 2012.

33. Kondo Shunsuke, interviews, April 30, 2012 and October 26, 2012; Akira Omoto, interviews, April 19, 2012 and October 24, 2012; Toshimitsu Homma, interviews, January 31, 2012 and June 1, 2012.

34. Toshimitsu Homma, interview, January 31, 2012.

35. Goshi Hosono, interview, February 3, 2012.

36. Masaya Yasui, interview, June 20, 2012.

37. Yutaka Kukita, interview, January 20, 2012.

38. Akira Omoto, interview, October 24, 2012.

39. The Eleventh Meeting of the Nuclear Emergency Response Headquarters, summary minutes.

40. Shunsuke Kondo, interview, February 1, 2012.

41. Government Investigation Commission on the Accident at the Fukushima Nuclear Power Stations of Tokyo Electric Power Company, Final Report, July 23, 2012, 333.

42. Seiki Soramoto, interview, September 21, 2012; Haruki Madarame, interview, October 4, 2012; Shunsuke Kondo, interview, October 26, 2012.

43. Mitsuhiro Kajimoto, interview, September 3, 2012; Mitsumasa Hirano, interview, September 19, 2012.

44. Masaya Yasui, interview, February 9, 2012.

45. Toshimitsu Homma, interview, June 1, 2012.

46. Interviews with several participants, June 1, 2012, September 3, 2012, and October 24, 2012.

47. Government Investigation Commission, Final Report, 334.

48. Tetsuro Fukuyama, interview, January 21, 2012; Shunsuke Kondo, interview, February 1, 2012; Goshi Hosono, interview, February 5, 2012.

49. Goshi Hosono, interview, February 3, 2012.

50. Ibid., February 13, 2012.

51. "Investigation: Investigation Commission on Fukushima Daichi NPS," *Asahi Shimbun*, May 1, 2012; Nuclear Regulatory Commission, Official Transcript of Proceedings: Japan's Fukushima Daiichi ET Audio File, March 14, 2011, 37.

52. Ibid., March 14, 2011, 37, and March 16, 2011, 157, 160.

53. Shunsuke Kondo, interview, April 30, 2012.

54. Mitsumasa Hirano, interview, September 19, 2012.

55. Shunsuke Kondo, interview, October 26, 2012.

56. Charles Casto, *Station Blackout: Inside the Fukushima Nuclear Disaster and Recovery* (New York: Radius Book Group, 2018), 160.

57. Goshi Hosono, interview, May 30, 2012; Charles Casto, interviews, June 25, 2012 and July 26, 2013; interviews with a Kantei parliamentary secretary, October 28, 2012 and November 3, 2012.

58. The Nuclear Regulatory Commission, Interim Comprehensive Assessment of Fukushima Event, June 29, 2012; Gregory B. Jaczko, interview, August 16, 2013.

59. Gregory B. Jaczko, interviews, April 22, 2013, and August 16, 2013.

60. Gregory B. Jaczko, *Confessions of a Rogue Nuclear Regulator* (New York: Simon & Schuster, 2019), 97.

61. Ibid., 103.

62. Interview with a senior official of the Joint Staff Office, June 17, 2012.

63. NISA internal memo, 15.

64. Interview with a senior official of the Joint Staff Office, October 10, 2012.

65. Toshinobu Miyajima, interview, July 11, 2012.

66. Interview with a senior official of the Joint Staff Office, October 10, 2012.

67. Takahiro Takino, *The SDF and the Great East Japan Earthquake* (Tokyo: Poplar Publishing, 2012), 41; Yoshifumi Hibako, interview, August 7, 2012.

68. Interview with a senior official of the Ministry of Defense, July 9, 2012.

69. Masayuki Hironaka, The Real Reason Why Soldiers Should Not Be Politicians: Considering Civil-Military Relations (Tokyo: Bungei Shunju, 2017), 32.

70. Interview with a senior official of the Ministry of Defense, August 9, 2011.

71. Interview with a senior officer of the Self-Defense Forces, May 8, 2012; Toshimi Kitazawa, interview, June 14, 2012; interview with a senior official of the Ministry of Defense, July 9, 2012; interview with a senior official of the Joint Staff Office, July 13, 2012.

72. Toshimi Kitazawa, *Why Japan Needs the SDF* (Tokyo: Kadokawa Shoten, 2012), 78.

73. "The Great East Japan Earthquake: Former GSDF Commander, 'I Thought Japan Was Finished,'" *Mainichi Shimbun*, December 31, 2011; interview with a senior official of the Joint Staff Office, June 17, 2012; Toshinobu Miyajima, interview, July 11, 2012; Takino, *The SDF and the Great East Japan Earthquake*, 70–71.

74. Interview with a senior official of the Ministry of Defense, July 9, 2012; interview with a senior official of the Joint Staff Office, July 13, 2012.

75. Interview with a high-ranking official of the Ministry of Defense, April 1, 2015.

76. Oriza Hirata, interview, August 7, 2012; Ekou Yagi, interview, November 8, 2012.

Chapter 14

1. Government Investigation Commission on the Accident at the Fukushima Nuclear Power Stations of Tokyo Electric Power Company, Interim Report, December 26, 2011, 286.

2. Ibid., 283.

3. Ibid., 284; National Diet of Japan Fukushima Nuclear Accident Independent Investigation Commission, Official Report, July 5, 2012, ch. 3, 42; Nuclear Safety Commission staff, October 9, 2012.

4. Government Investigation Commission, Interim Report, 284.

5. Interview with a senior official of the Ministry of Education, Culture, Sports, Science, and Technology, July 5, 2012; interview with a Nuclear Safety Commission staff member, October 9, 2012.

6. Hirohiko Izumida, interview, May 7, 2012.

7. Government Investigation Commission, Interim Report, 284; National Diet Commission, Official Report, ch. 3, 42.

8. Shigeharu Kato, interview, November 5, 2012.

9. National Diet Commission, Official Report, ch. 3, 42.

10. Tetsuro Fukuyama, interview, September 26, 2012.

11. The Eleventh Meeting of the Nuclear Emergency Response Headquarters, summary minutes.

12. Ministry of Education, Culture, Sports, Science, and Technology (MEXT), "Recovery and Reconstruction from the Great East Japan Earthquake: An Overview of the Investigative Results on MEXT's Approach," July 27, 2012, 23.

13. Interview with a Kantei staff member, October 12, 2011; interview with a senior official of the Ministry of Economy, Trade, and Industry, November 6, 2011.

14. Government Investigation Commission on the Accident at the Fukushima Nuclear Power Stations of Tokyo Electric Power Company, Final Report, July 23, 2012, 244; "March 12: Couldn't Measure Radiation Dispersal, Helicopter and Crew Fail to Meet Up, Fukushima Nuclear Accident," *Asahi Shimbun*, February 24, 2012; MEXT, "Recovery and Reconstruction from the Great East Japan Earthquake," 27; interview with a Nuclear Safety Commission staff member, October 9, 2012; interview with a senior officer of the Nuclear Safety Technology Center, October 11, 2012.

15. Government Investigation Commission, Interim Report, 290; MEXT, "Recovery and Reconstruction from the Great East Japan Earthquake," 28.

16. Hiroto Ishida, interview, August 1, 2012.

17. Nuclear and Industrial Safety Agency website.

18. "MEXT Radiation Team Memo, March 19, 2012, Level 2 Confidentiality (To Be Handled with Care); Level 7/Extra Edition: Examining SPEEDI," *Tokyo Shimbun*, March 10, 2012; Koji Okamoto, *Testimony: Haruki Madarame—Where NISA Went Wrong* (Tokyo: Shinchosha, 2012), 125. MEXT takes the position, however, that including this point: "There was a consensus between the three top political officers and others that monitoring data would be made quickly available, as it was, that it would be reported as soon as possible to the Emergency Operation Team at the Kantei, and that they had endeavored to share information with the government authorities, including the Kantei." In MEXT, "Recovery and Reconstruction from the Great East Japan Earthquake," 23–24. In addition, MEXT Deputy Director General Yasutaka Moriguchi claims, "There are inaccuracies in the internal memo of the radiation team. In the conversation on March 15, we did not discuss the pros and cons of going public with SPEEDI, and the discussion was continued as noted in the Interim Report of the Government Investigation Commission." In Tokyo Shimbun Editorial Board, *Reporting on the Nuclear Power Plant: How Tokyo Shimbun Covered It* (Tokyo Shimbun, 2012), 54.

19. MEXT, "Recovery and Reconstruction from the Great East Japan Earthquake," 24.

20. "Level 7/Extra Edition: Examining SPEEDI," *Tokyo Shimbun*, March 10, 2012; Makio Watanabe, "A Week of the Great East Japan Earthquake," recorded March 11–19, 2011; Makio Watanabe, interviews, September 7, 2012 and September 17, 2012; Takayuki Amaya, interviews, July 7, 2012 and July 31, 2012. Amaya had said, "Akougi," but the actual measurement point was Kawafusa in Namie Town, a little away from there. See Government Investigation Commission, Final Report, 245.

21. Makio Watanabe, interview, September 7, 2012.

22. Shoji Ozawa, *Iitate Village: Six Thousand People Chased Out of Their Beautiful Village* (Tokyo: Nanatsumori Shokan, 2012), 84–85.

23. Yoshitomo Shigihara, interview, November 2, 2012.

24. Yukio Edano, *What Has to Be Said Even If Not Popular: "De-modernization" and "Negative Redistribution"* (Tokyo: Toyo Keizai Shinposha, 2012), 234–35; Makio Watanabe, "A Week of the Great East Japan Earthquake," recorded March 11–19, 2011; Makio Watanabe, interview, September 10, 2012.

25. Makio Watanabe, interview, September 10, 2012.

26. Takayuki Amaya, interview, September 10, 2012.

27. Yukio Edano, testimony before the Diet Investigation Commission, Minutes No. 15, May 27, 2012.

28. Edano, *What Has to Be Said Even If Not Popular*, 212.

29. Akihiko Iwahashi, interview, August 2, 2012.

30. Tetsuro Ito, interview, April 9, 2012.

31. Interview with a Kantei parliamentary secretary, October 10, 2012.

32. Government Investigation Commission, Final Report, 246, 259; Akira Fukushima, interview, July 26, 2012; interviews with a senior official of the Nuclear Safety Commission, July 27, 2012, and September 24, 2012; interview with a senior official of the Ministry of Education, Culture, Sports, Science, and Technology, July 31, 2012; Kan Suzuki, interview, August 2, 2012; Akihiko Iwahashi, interview, August 2, 2012; Shizuyo Kusumi, interview, August 28, 2012; Tetsuro Fukuyama, interview, September 26, 2012; interview with a senior official of the Ministry of Education, Culture, Sports, Science, and Technology, November 5, 2012.

33. "Level 7/Extra Edition: Examining SPEEDI," *Tokyo Shimbun*, March 10, 2012; Nuclear Safety Commission internal document, "Regarding SPEEDI: Exchanges Between SPEEDI Officers from March 16," July 26, 2012; interview with a senior official of the Nuclear Safety Commission, July 27, 2012; Akihiko Iwahashi, interview, August 2, 2012.

34. Haruki Madarame, interview, October 4, 2012; Hideaki Tsuzuki, interview, July 4, 2012; interview with a Kantei parliamentary staff, July 12, 2012; interview with a senior official of the Nuclear Safety Commission, July 27, 2012.

35. Ministry of Education, Culture, Sports, Science, and Technology, "Recovery and Reconstruction from the Great East Japan Earthquake: An Overview of the Investigative Results on MEXT's Approach" (draft), May 18, 2012, 7–8; Haruki Madarame, Nuclear Safety Commission Press Conference, Joint Government Office Building No. 4, June 9, 2011; interview with a senior official of the Nuclear Safety Commission, July 27, 2012; Akihiko Iwahashi, interview, August 2, 2012.

36. Ryuzo Sasaki, MEXT press conference, March 16, 2011.

37. Interview with a senior official of the Ministry of Education, Culture, Sports, Science, and Technology, April 6, 2012; Shizuyo Kusumi, interviews, May 23, 2012, and August 28, 2012; Hideaki Tsuzuki, interview, July 24, 2012; Tetsuro Fukuyama, interview, September 26, 2012; Okamoto, *Testimony*, 125.

38. ERC Residents Safety Team, "Concerning the Thinking behind Evacuation Zones," sent from the ERC Coordinating Team to the Nuclear Safety Commission, March 18, 2011.

39. Toshiso Kosako, interview, November 11, 2011.

40. Ibid., November 5, 2012; Yoshikatsu Nakayama, interview, May 16, 2012.

41. Seiki Soramoto, interview, September 20, 2012; Toshiso Kosako, interview, November 5, 2012.

42. Interview with a Kantei parliamentary secretary, January 12, 2012; Hideaki Tsuzuki, interview, July 24, 2012.

43. Interview with a senior official of the Nuclear and Industrial Safety Agency, June 20, 2012.

44. Tetsuro Ito, interview, April 9, 2012.

45. Yutaka Kukita, interview, November 30, 2012.

46. Masamichi Chino, interview, September 9, 2011.

47. Ibid.

48. Ibid., August 1, 2012; Yutaka Kukita, interview, November 30, 2012.

49. National Diet Commission, Official Report, ch. 4, 59–60.

50. Interview with a senior official of the Nuclear Safety Commission, August 2, 2012; Yutaka Kukita, interview, November 30, 2012.

51. Hideaki Tsuzuki, interview, July 24, 2012; Masamichi Chino, interview, August 1, 2012.

52. Masamichi Chino, interview, August 1, 2012.

53. Interview with a Nuclear Safety Commission staff member, July 18, 2012; Masamichi Chino, interview, August 1, 2012.

54. Nuclear Safety Commission, "The Emergency Rapid Radiation Impact Predic-

tion Network System (SPEEDI) Calculations," March 23, 2011; Tetsuro Fukuyama, *The Nuclear Crisis: Testimony from the Kantei* (Tokyo: Chikuma Shinsho, 2012), 145.

55. Masamichi Chino, interview, August 1, 2012.

56. Section 13, Budget Committee Minutes No. 7, House of Councilors, March 22, 2011.

57. Toshiso Kosako and Seiki Soramoto, "Bringing the Nuclear Disaster to an End," April 10, 2011, amended April 17, 2011.

58. Toshiso Kosako, interview, November 1, 2011.

59. Seiki Soramoto, interview, September 26, 2012.

60. Tetsuro Fukuyama, testimony before the Independent Investigation Commission, October 29, 2011.

61. Seiji Shiroya, interview, September 6, 2012.

62. Yasutaka Moriguchi, interview, December 22, 2011.

63. Interview with a senior official of the Nuclear and Industrial Safety Agency, February 9, 2012.

64. Banri Kaeda, testimony before the Independent Investigation Commission, October 5, 2011.

65. Interview with a senior official of the Nuclear and Industrial Safety Agency, June 20, 2012.

66. House of Representatives' Special Committee on Promoting Scientific and Technological Innovation Meeting, May 25, 2011.

67. Toshiso Kosako, interview, November 1, 2012.

68. Akihiko Iwahashi, interview, August 2, 2012.

69. Goshi Hosono, Government and TEPCO joint press conference, May 2, 2011.

70. Akihiko Iwahashi, interview, August 2, 2012.

71. Masamichi Chino, interview, September 9, 2011.

72. Ibid., August 1, 2012.

73. Tetsuro Fukuyama, interviews, January 21, 2012, and September 26, 2012.

74. Rebuild Japan Initiative Foundation (RJIF), *Independent Investigation Commission on the Fukushima Nuclear Accident* (Abingdon: Routledge, 2014), 72, 180.

75. Nobuyuki Fukushima, interview, September 27, 2011.

76. Yukio Edano, testimony before the Independent Investigation Commission, December 10, 2011.

77. Akihiko Iwahashi, interview, August 2, 2012.

78. Yutaka Kukita, interview, August 7, 2012.

79. Kohta Juraku and Shinetsu Sugawara, "What Is 'SPEEDI'? In What Way Can It Be Used in Nuclear Disaster Prevention?" Social Science Research Support Project on Nuclear Power and Communities, 2016 Research Results Report, March 2017.

80. RJIF, *Independent Investigation Commission on the Fukushima Nuclear Accident*, 180.

81. Juraku and Sugawara, "What Is 'SPEEDI'?" Social Science Research Support Project. There is still no convergence in discussions on what sort of lessons should be taken from SPEEDI not being used at the time of the resident evacuation. For example, the government, which received the proposal from the National Governors' Association that "it should be used effectively," determined that "we won't prevent each regional body from having their own responsibility over its use." The Nuclear Regulatory Commission (NRC) showed their policy direction of "it can't be used, so shouldn't be used." It remains such that common understanding has not been reached among the various relevant bodies. See Juraku and Sugawara, "What Is 'SPEEDI'?" Social Science Research Support Project.

Chapter 15

1. Shizuyo Kusumi, interview, August 28, 2012.

2. MEXT, "Recovery and Reconstruction from the Great East Japan Earthquake," 10; Masamichi Chino, interview, August 1, 2012; Akihiko Iwahashi, interview, August 2, 2012.

3. Tetsuro Ito, interview, April 9, 2012; Shizuyo Kusumi, interview, May 23, 2012; Goshi Hosono, interviews, October 6, 2011, and August 9, 2012; interview with a Kantei parliamentary secretary, September 28, 2012.

4. Interviews with a Kantei parliamentary secretary, September 28, 2012, and October 10, 2012; Shizuyo Kusumi, interview, August 30, 2012.

5. Haruki Madarame, interview, October 4, 2012.

6. Ibid.

7. Goshi Hosono, interview, August 9, 2012; Shizuyo Kusumi, interview, August 28, 2012.

8. Kazuo Sakai, interview, December 26, 2011; Seiki Soramoto, interview, September 21, 2012; Masamichi Chino, interview, August 1, 2012; Nuclear Safety Commission internal memo, "Discussions in the Kantei, Prime Minister's Office," March 23, 2011; Toshiso Kosako, interview, November 5, 2012.

9. Shizuyo Kusumi, interview, August 28, 2012; Seiki Soramoto, interview, September 21, 2012; interview with a senior official of the Nuclear and Industrial Safety Agency, July 31, 2012; Toshiso Kosako, interview, November 5, 2012.

10. Tetsuro Ito, interviews, April 9, 2012, and September 25, 2012; Shizuyo Kusumi, interview, August 28, 2012; Masamichi Chino, interview, August 1, 2012; Kazuo Sakai, interview, October 15, 2011.

11. ICRP is an international NGO closely related to the IAEA. The ICRP has been criticized as covertly pro-nuclear. For more details, see Nakagawa Yasuo, *A History of Radiation Exposure: From the American Atomic Bomb to the Fukushima Nuclear Power Station Accident* (Tokyo: Akashi Shoten, 2012). However, the recommendations of its publication have become the international de facto standard and are respected by experts around the world.

12. Tetsuro Ito, interviews, April 9, 2012, and September 25, 2012; Hiroyuki Fukano, interview, August 9, 2012; interview with a Kantei parliamentary secretary, October 2, 2012; Manabu Terada, interview, October 17, 2012; Tetsuro Fukuyama, *The Nuclear Crisis: Testimony from the Kantei* (Tokyo: Chikuma Shinsho, 2012), 146; Haruki Madarame, interview, October 4, 2012.

13. Masamichi Chino, interview, August 1, 2012; Nuclear Safety Commission internal memo, August 29, 2012; Shizuyo Kusumi, interviews, August 28, 2012, and August 30, 2012; Seiji Shiroya, interview, September 6, 2012.

14. Eiji Hiraoka, interview, August 9, 2012; Seiki Soramoto, interview, September 26, 2012; Tetsuro Fukuyama, interview, September 26, 2012; Toshiso Kosako, interview, November 5, 2012.

15. Akihiko Iwahashi, interview, August 2, 2012; Yutaka Kukita, interview, August 7, 2012; Tetsuro Ito, interview, September 25, 2012; Tetsuro Fukuyama, interview, September 26, 2012.

16. Goshi Hosono, interview, August 9, 2012; interview with a Kantei parliamentary secretary, September 28, 2012.

17. Koji Okamoto, *Testimony: Haruki Madarame—Where NISA Went Wrong* (Tokyo: Shinchosha, 2012), 132.

18. Akihiko Iwahashi, interview, August 2, 2012; Haruki Madarame, interview, October 4, 2012; Government Investigation Commission on the Accident at the Fukushima Nuclear Power Stations of Tokyo Electric Power Company, Interim Report, December 26, 2011, 76–77.

19. Akihiko Iwahashi, interview, August 2, 2012.

20. Kenkichi Hirose, interview, October 9, 2012.

21. Tetsuro Fukuyama, interview, September 26, 2012.

22. Tetsuro Ito, interview, September 25, 2012.

23. National Diet of Japan Fukushima Nuclear Accident Independent Investigation Commission, Official Report, July 5, 2012, ch. 4, 26.

24. Tetsuro Fukuyama, interview, September 26, 2012; Fukuyama, *The Nuclear Crisis*, 163.

25. Tetsuro Fukuyama, interview, September 26, 2012.

26. Manabu Terada, interview, July 26, 2012.

27. Hiroyuki Fukano, interview, August 9 2012.

28. Haruki Madarame, interview, October 4, 2012.

29. Akihiko Iwahashi, interview, August 2, 2012.

30. Yutaka Kukita, interview, August 7, 2012; Hiroyuki Fukano, interview, August 9, 2012.

31. Norio Kanno, *Radiation Fell on a Beautiful Village: Iitate Mayor's 120 Days of Decision and Resolve* (Tokyo: Wani Books PLUS Shinsho, 2011), 30–31.

32. Office of the Prime Minister, "On Establishing the Planned Evacuation Areas and the Emergency Evacuation Preparation Area," METI, April 22, 2011; Kenkichi Hirose, interview, October 9, 2012.

33. Tetsuro Ito, interview, September 25, 2012.

34. Manabu Terada, interview, July 26, 2012.

35. Tadahiro Matsushita, interview, November 8, 2011.

36. Kazuo Matsunaga, interview, October 25, 2012; interview with a senior official of the Ministry of Economy, Trade, and Industry, October 9, 2012.

37. Interview with a senior official of the Ministry of Economy, Trade, and Industry, January 4, 2012; Tadahiro Matsushita committed suicide on September 10, 2012. At the time, he was cabinet office minister extraordinary (monetary affairs).

38. Kanno, *Radiation Fell on a Beautiful Village*, 155–56; Norio Kanno, interview, September 4, 2012. On the afternoon of April 13, Kenichi Matsumoto, cabinet secretariat adviser, told this to reporters as something Kan had said. Kan immediately denied it. Three hours later, Matsumoto withdrew his previous statement, saying it was he himself, and not the prime minister, who had said, "It will be uninhabitable for twenty or thirty years." In "Kan Administration: Loose Words 'Plant Vicinity Uninhabitable for Ten, Twenty Years' Explained in PM Statement, Withdrawn in Three Hours," *Asahi Shimbun*, April 15, 2011.

39. Fukuyama, *The Nuclear Crisis*, 162.

40. Nuclear Safety Commission, Transcript of the Second Meeting of the Working Group to Review the Regulatory Guide for Emergency Preparedness for Nuclear Facilities, August 12, 2011, 31.

41. Hiroshi Tada, interview, September 27, 2012.

42. Akihiko Iwahashi, interview, August 2, 2012; Yutaka Kukita, interview, August 7, 2012; Tetsuro Fukuyama, interview, September 24, 2012; interview with a Nuclear Safety Commission staff member, October 9, 2012; Haruki Madarame, interview, October 4, 2012.

43. Interview with a senior official of the Nuclear Safety Commission, July 4, 2012.

44. Nuclear Safety Commission Secretariat, "Events Leading Up to the Proposition and Opinions of the Nuclear and Industrial Safety Agency During the 2006 Revision of Disaster Guidelines for PAZ," March 15, 2012; Shizuyo Kusumi, "May 23, 2012; Priority Disaster Areas: NISA Chairman Instructs Putting Off 'Keep Existing System for Ten Years'—Internal Discussions with Top Officers 2006," *Tokyo Shimbun, Evening Edition*, June 5, 2012; "Neutralizing Pressure at NISA: Anxious about Delays in Pulsamar—Disaster Prevention Areas Extended, Adverse Trends Excluded," *Tokyo Shimbun, Evening Edition*, June 5, 2012; Government Investigation Commission on the Accident at the Fukushima Nuclear Power Stations of Tokyo

Electric Power Company, Final Report, July 23, 2012, 392–93; Kiyohru Abe, interview, August 26, 2012; "A Request for Discussion Topics at Lunch with the NSC on March 24," e-mail from Kiyoharu Abe to Hidehiko Nishiyama, May 24, 2006.

45. Interview with a Nuclear Safety Commission staff member, October 9, 2012; Goshi Hosono, interview, November 1, 2012.

Chapter 16

1. Shunsuke Kimura, "In the Midst of Chaos—Scenes from the TEPCO Videoconference: (4) Lend Me Your Car Battery," *Asahi Shimbun, Fukushima Edition*, September 17, 2012.

2. TEPCO, "Fukushima Nuclear Accident Report," June 20, 2012, 237.

3. INPO, "Lessons from the Nuclear Accident at the Fukushima Daiichi Nuclear Power Station (Special Report)," August 2012, 19.

4. TEPCO videoconference participant memo shown to the author, September 21, 2012.

5. Interview with a senior associate company manager, September 4, 2012.

6. NHK Special Meltdown Report Crew, *Meltdown: The Truth About the Chain Reaction* (Tokyo: Kodansha, 2013), 284.

7. Interview with a Kantei staff member, October 12, 2011; Hiroshi Ikukawa, interview, December 21, 2011.

8. Makio Miyagawa, interview, July 5, 2011.

9. Interview with a Kantei staff member, October 12, 2011.

10. "TEPCO Videoconferences Released: Stopgap Response, Kantei Out of Step," *Mainichi Shimbun*, August 7, 2012.

11. Shunsuke Kimura, "In the Midst of Chaos—Scenes from the TEPCO Videoconference: (1) High Radiation Dosage, in Paralysis Onsite," *Asahi Shimbun, Fukushima Edition*, September 14, 2012.

12. INPO, Special Report, 24.

13. Ibid., 25.

14. Interview with a senior executive at NISA, September 26, 2012.

15. "Radiation—'I Can't Let My Subordinates Undergo Any More Exposure'—Seven Days After the Accident, Site Superintendent Resists HO, TEPCO Videoconference Released," *Asahi Shimbun*, December 1, 2012.

16. Letter from Yamaguchi Yoshihiro to President Tohru Aruga, Japan Organization of Occupational Health and Safety, March 24, 2011.

17. Banri Kaieda, *The Kaieda Notes—A Record of the 176-Day Nuclear Struggle* (Tokyo: Kodansha, 2012), 117.

18. "Government-TEPCO Integrated Response Office—Former Integrated Response Centre—Proceedings Summary," *Yomiuri Shimbun*, March 10, 2012.

19. Ibid.

20. Nuclear Regulatory Commission, Official Transcript of Proceedings: Japan's Fukushima Daiichi ET Audio File, March 16, 2011, 348–51.

21. Ibid., 373.

22. Interview with Toshiba engineering team, August 30, 2012.

23. Interview with a Kantei staff member, August 18, 2011.

24. National Diet of Japan Fukushima Nuclear Accident Independent Investigation Commission, Official Report, July 5, 2012, ch. 3, 17.

25. Ibid., 66.

26. Ibid., 10.

27. Takeyuki Inagaki, interview, December 10, 2013.

28. Goshi Hosono, interview, March 15, 2012.

29. Ibid.

30. Naoto Kan, interview, September 14, 2011.

31. Goshi Hosono, interview, March 15, 2012; *Super News Special Report*, Fuji Television, March 21, 2011.

32. Shigetoshi Kai, interview, August 6, 2012.

33. Yasuhiko Sakane and Shigetoshi Kai, interview, August 6, 2012.

34. Charles Casto, interview, August 24, 2011.

35. Ibid., August 10, 2011.

36. Interview with a high-ranking U.S. government official, August 26, 2011.

37. Goshi Hosono, interview, October 6, 2011.

38. Government Investigation Commission on the Accident at the Fukushima Nuclear Power Stations of Tokyo Electric Power Company, Interim Report, December 26, 2011, 392–98.

39. Interview with a senior official of the Nuclear and Industrial Safety Agency, October 14, 2012; Kazuo Sakai, interview, October 15, 2012.

40. "TEPCO Videos Released: Head Office Late with Contaminated Water Measures: Site Superintendent Repeatedly Calls for a Week," *Tokyo Shimbun*, December 1, 2012.

41. Akira Omoto, interview, October 24, 2012.

42. Toshiso Kosako, interview, November 5, 2012.

43. Interview with a Kantei parliamentary secretary, October 28, 2012.

44. Goshi Hosono, interview, November 1, 2012.

45. Kaieda, *The Kaieda Notes*, 143; "TEPCO Videos Released: Head Office Late with Contaminated Water Measures: Site Superintendent Repeatedly Calls for a Week," *Tokyo Shimbun*, December 1, 2012; "Detailed Account of Additional TEPCO Videoconference Release," *Yomiuri Shimbun*, December 1, 2012.

46. Kaieda, *The Kaieda Notes*, 144.

47. Toshiso Kosako, interviews, November 1, 2011, and November 5, 2012; Toshiso Kosako memo, "Concerning the Emergency Release of Seawater from Buildings Flooded with Seawater by the Tsunami," April 2, 2011.

48. Goshi Hosono, interview, November 1, 2012.

49. "Detailed Account of Additional TEPCO Videoconference Release," *Yomiuri Shimbun*, December 1, 2012; "TEPCO Videoconference Released: Worst-Case Contaminated Water Ocean Release," *Mainichi Shimbun*, December 1, 2012.

50. "TEPCO Videos Released: Head Office Late with Contaminated Water Measures: Site Superintendent Repeatedly Calls for a Week," *Tokyo Shimbun*, December 1, 2012; "Detailed Account of Additional TEPCO Videoconference Release," *Yomiuri Shimbun*, December 1, 2012.

51. Interviews with a Kantei parliamentary secretary, October 7, 2012, October 10, 2012, and November 3, 2012; Goshi Hosono, interview, November 1, 2012; Naoto Kan, interview, November 1, 2012.

52. Interview with a senior official of the Nuclear and Industrial Safety Agency, October 14, 2012.

53. Hideaki Tsuzuki, interview, October 8, 2012.

54. Kaieda, *The Kaieda Notes*, 153.

55. "Detailed Account of Additional TEPCO Videoconference Release," *Yomiuri Shimbun*, December 1, 2012.

56. "Savior to Stop Contaminated Water Is 'Water Glass' at ¥70 a Kilo," *Tokyo Shimbun*, April 7, 2011.

57. Goshi Hosono, interview, November 1, 2012.

58. Gerald Rondoe, interview, October 6, 2011; Ichiro Yamaguchi, interview, October 6, 2011.

59. Ken Nakajima, interview, November 5, 2012.

60. Government internal memo, Joint Coordination Group on the Nuclear Emergency, Cabinet Secretariat Annex, March 22, 2011.

61. Gerald Rondoe, interview, October 1, 2011; Ichiro Yamaguchi, interview, October 6, 2011.

62. Eiji Koyanagi, "Using Scientific Technology and Consequence Management in a Large-Scale Complex Disaster: Toward the Effective Use of Robots and Unmanned Technology," *Japan Institute of International Affairs*, July 25, 2011.

63. Ichiro Yamaguchi, interview, October 6, 2011.

64. Interview with a senior TEPCO manager, May 10, 2012; Ichiro Yamaguchi, interview, October 6, 2011.

65. Gerald Rondoe, interview, October 1, 2011.

66. Yasuyuki Sakai, "Japan's Decline as a Robotics Superpower: Lessons from Fukushima," *Asia Pacific Journal*, vol. 9, no. 2 (June 2011).

67. "Elusive National Nuclear Disaster Robots," *Nihon Keizai Shimbun*, April 11, 2011; Seiji Iwata and Shintaro Kajimoto, "Putting the Kingdom on the Line . . . Nationally Manufactured Robots Sent into Fukushima NPS," *Asahi Shimbun*, April 22, 2011; interview with a senior official of the Ministry of Defense, August 9, 2011; interview with a senior official of the Ministry of Education, Culture, Sports, Science, and Technology, August 18, 2011; Shigeo Hirose, interview, October 26, 2012; Toshiso Kosako, interview, November 5, 2012.

68. Okuyama, *Report*, 144.

69. Kaieda, *The Kaieda Notes*, 125–26.

70. "Following Failure: Mr. Tsunehisa Katsumata (TEPCO Chairman) TEPCO's Don Falls with Nuclear Accident," *Nikkei Business*, June 18, 2012.

71. Conversation with Masataka Shimizu, January 6, 2010.

72. Interview with a Kantei staff member, September 14, 2011.

73. National Diet Commission, Official Report, ch. 3, 25.

74. Interview with a senior official of the Nuclear and Industrial Safety Agency, February 27, 2012.

75. Okuyama, *Report*, 169.

76. Interview with a senior official of the Ministry of Economy, Trade, and Industry, June 30, 2011.

77. "Great East Japan Earthquake: Fukushima Daiichi Nuclear Accident—Fukushima Governor 'Never Operate Again'—First TEPCO President Apology After Accident," *Mainichi Shimbun, Evening Edition*, April 22, 2011.

78. The first time the phrase "Fukushima 50" appeared on the Internet was when the *New York Post* tweeted: "Nuclear Update. Fukushima 50 Brave Japanese Remain Fighting the Overheating Cores #prayforjapan" on their official Twitter account at 10:40 p.m. (EST) on March 14, 2011. An hour later, at 11:46 p.m., the guitarist Brian Ray tweeted, "the #Fukushima50 Absolutely . . . New Heroes of Japan, for reals." In addition, an article by Tania Branigan and Justin McCurry, titled "Fukushima 50 Battle Radiation Risks as Japan Nuclear Crisis Deepens" and published by *The Guardian* at 1:59 p.m. (EST) on March 15, 2011, popularized the phrase. The article stated: "Fifty to seventy workers are left on site and combating the crisis." The story of the TEPCO workers who remained in the Anti-Seismic Building when Yoshida ordered workers to evacuate from Fukushima Daini during the early morning hours on March 15 was tweeted in the United States a couple of hours later, and was the story that spread throughout the world the following day.

79. Government Investigation Commission, Interim Report, 83–84; TEPCO, "Fukushima Nuclear Accident Report," 75–77.

80. Fukushima Nuclear Power Accident Record Team, Tomomi Miyazaki and Hideaki Kimura, *A Record of Forty-Nine Hours of TEPCO's Fukushima Nuclear Accident Videoconference* (Tokyo: Iwanami Shoten, 2013), 327.

81. National Diet Commission, Official Report, ch. 3, 24; "Fukushima Daiichi NPS: TEPCO Videoconference Exchanges," *Asahi Shimbun*, September 5, 2012; Fu-

kushima Nuclear Power Accident Record Team and others, *A Record of Forty-Nine Hours of TEPCO's Fukushima Nuclear Accident Videoconfe*rence, 348, 353, 357.

82. Masatoshi Fukura, interview, December 2, 2014.

83. Government Nuclear Investigation Committee, "J-Village, August 9, 2011," *Masao Yoshida, Hearing Results Report*, August 16, 2011, 50.

84. Fukushima Nuclear Power Accident Record Team and others, *A Record of Forty-Nine Hours of TEPCO's Fukushima Nuclear Accident Videoconfe*rence, 358.

85. Interview with a member of the TEPCO management team, January 11, 2012.

86. "Politician Hearings Outline," *Asahi Shimbun*, September 12, 2014.

87. Government Nuclear Investigation Committee, "J-Village, July 29, 2011," *Masao Yoshida, Hearing Results Report*, August 16, 2011, 54.

88. Masatoshi Fukura, interview, December 2, 2014.

89. Government Nuclear Investigation Committee, "J-Village, November 6, 2011," *Masao Yoshida, Hearing Results Report*, November 25, 2011.

90. Ibid.

91. Government Nuclear Investigation Committee, "J-Village, August 8, 2011," *Masao Yoshida, Hearing Results Report*, August 16, 2011, 53.

92. Interview with a senior TEPCO manager, January 11, 2012.

93. Haruki Madarame, interview, December 17, 2011.

94. "Politician Hearings Outline," *Asahi Shimbun*, September 12, 2014.

95. Keith Bradsher and Hiroko Tabuchi, "Last Defense at Troubled Reactors: Fifty Japanese Workers," *New York Times*, March 15, 2011; Tania Branigan and Justin McCurry, "Fukushima 50 Battle Radiation Risks as Japan Nuclear Crisis Deepens," *Guardian*, March 15, 2011.

96. "Fukushima Daiichi NPS, All Videoconference Statements by Superintendent Yoshida," *Mainichi Shimbun News Bulletin*, August 11, 2012; National Diet Commission, Official Report, ch. 3, 24.

97. "Fukushima Daiichi NPS, All Videoconference Statements by Superintendent Yoshida," *Mainichi Shimbun News Bulletin*, August 11, 2012.

98. Interview with a Toshiba engineer, August 30, 2012.

99. Interview with a senior official of the Department of Defense, May 19, 2011.

100. Gregory B. Jaczko, interview, August 16, 2013.

101. Shiro Yamazaki, interview, January 6, 2012.

102. Interview with a senior associate company manager, September 4, 2012.

Epilogue

1. Manabu Terada, interview, October 17, 2012.

2. Mure Dickie and Lionel Barber, "Japanese Ready for Return to Normalcy," *Financial Times*, March 31, 2011.

3. Manabu Terada, interview, November 10, 2011; Naoto Kan, *The TEPCO Fukushima Nuclear Accident: My Thoughts as Prime Minister* (Tokyo: Gentosha Shinsho, 2012), 142.

4. Kan, *The TEPCO Fukushima Nuclear Accident*, 68.

5. Tetsuro Ito, interview, April 9, 2012.

6. Haruki Madarame, interview, October 4, 2012.

7. Ibid., December 17, 2011.

8. TEPCO estimated in a later study that water had flowed from the adjacent reactor well into the fuel pool of Unit 4, keeping the water level constant. The reactor well and fuel pool were separated by a partition called the pool gate, but when the water pressure on the reactor well side increased, it was structured so that a gap in the pool gate junction would be opened and water would flow into the fuel pool side. It was believed that when the fuel pool lost power, the water temperature climbed to an abnormal height and the water level dropped, but every time the water level fell, water would flow in from the reactor well side, keeping the water constant. At the

time, Unit 4 was undergoing periodic inspection, and the reactor well and adjacent equipment storage were almost full with almost the same 1,400 tons of water as the fuel pool. Usually water was not held there, but it had been left full of water because shroud replacement work scheduled for March 7, 2011, just before the earthquake, was postponed due to a size difference in the jig. This, too, was "fortunate." See, NHK Special Meltdown Report Crew, *Meltdown*, 222.

9. Masaya Yasui, interview, February 9, 2012; interview with a high-ranking U.S. government official, May 21, 2012; Tatsuo Hirano, interview, June 16, 2012; Nobushige Takamizawa, interview, August 16, 2011; Kan, *The TEPCO Fukushima Nuclear Accident*, 119; Gregory B. Jaczko, interview, August 16, 2013; Takeyuki Inagaki, interview, December 10, 2013; Akira Ono, interview, December 18, 2015.

10. TEPCO estimated in a later investigation that a certain level of water was maintained in the Unit 4 fuel pool, since water was pouring in from the reactor well on the right side of the spent fuel pool (the pool's top level is located next to the reactor well's top level). The fuel pool and the reactor well were divided by a board called the pool gate. When the water pressure of the reactor well rises, the gap in the connecting section of the pool gate opens and water pours into the fuel pool. The water temperature of the fuel pool, which lost power, shot up dramatically and the water level decreased, but when the amount of water decreases, it appears that the water level was maintained at a constant as water came in from the nuclear well. Unit 4 was undergoing a routine check then. The nuclear well and the equipment storage pool right next to it was filled with 1,400 tons of water, which was the same amount as the fuel pool. There usually is no water there, but it was there, since the shroud replacement work was postponed due to a mismeasurement of one of the pieces of equipment on March 7, 2011, right before the great earthquake. This may also have been "luck." Shroud is a cylindrical stainless-steel container that holds fuel assemblies and control rods. NHK Special Meltdown Report Crew, *Meltdown: The Truth About the Chain Reaction* (Tokyo: Kodansha, 2013), 222; Kan, *The TEPCO Fukushima Nuclear Accident*, 37.

11. Kiyoharu Abe, interview, August 26, 2012.

12. Sixth Meeting of the Nuclear Emergency Response Headquarters, summary minutes.

13. Charles Casto, interview, August 10, 2011.

14. Government Investigation Commission on the Accident at the Fukushima Nuclear Power Stations of Tokyo Electric Power Company, Final Report, July 23, 2012, 498.

15. National Diet of Japan Fukushima Nuclear Accident Independent Investigation Commission, Official Report, July 5, 2012, ch. 3, 71.

16. Rebuild Japan Initiative Foundation (RJIF), *Independent Investigation Commission on the Fukushima Nuclear Accident* (Abingdon: Routledge, 2014), 190–91.

17. Interview with an ex-official of the Ministry of Economy, Trade, and Industry, May 7, 2012.

18. Interview with a Kantei parliamentary secretary, December 16, 2011.

19. Banri Kaieda, testimony before the Diet Investigation Commission, Minutes No. 14, May 17, 2012.

20. Goshi Hosono, interview, February 13, 2012.

21. Goshi Hosono, testimony before the Independent Investigation Commission, November 19, 2011.

22. "Great Earthquake Investigation: Ex-PM Kan's Testimony," *Mainichi Shimbun*, September 7, 2011; Naoto Kan, interview, November 14, 2012.

23. Naoto Kan, interview, November 14, 2012.

24. Government Investigation Commission, "J-Village, August 8, 2011," *Masao Yoshida, Hearing Results Report*, August 16, 2011, 52.

25. Naoto Kan, Testimony for the Diet Investigation Commission, Conference Note No. 6, May 28, 2012.

26. Eighteenth and Nineteenth Meeting of the Nuclear Emergency Response Headquarters, Sixth Meeting of the Eastern Japan Earthquake Recovery Headquarters, summary minutes, August 26, 2011.

27. "Fukushima Daiichi NPS: Ex-Site Superintendent Yoshida, Entire Video Statements," *Mainichi News Bulletin*, August 11, 2012.

28. Interview with an engineer acquainted with Yoshida for close to thirty years, October 14, 2011.

29. Kunio Yanagida, "My Final Report on the Nuclear Plant Accident 2, Reactor Meltdown, Superintendent Yoshida's Failure," *Bungeishunju* (October 2012), 360.

30. INPO, "Lessons Learned from the Nuclear Accident at the Fukushima Daiichi Nuclear Power Station," August 2012, 22.

31. Ibid., 31.

32. National Diet Commission, Official Report, ch. 3, 66.

33. Fukushima Nuclear Accident Record Team, *Forty-Nine Hours of the Fukushima Nuclear Accident TEPCO Videoconference Records,* edited by Tomomi Miyazaki and Hideaki Kimura (Tokyo: Iwanami Shoten, 2013), 59–60.

34. According to a subsequent analysis of the reactor status by TEPCO, the distance between the steel of the reactor containment vessel and the erosion extent of the molten fuel was estimated at a mere 37 centimeters. Professor Tsuneo Futami of Tokyo Institute of Technology (Department of Nuclear Engineering) pointed out that, if they had interrupted the injection of seawater on the night of March 12, 2011, the molten fuel would have dropped down and the so-called core concrete reaction would have had to have been more advanced. Futami was Yoshida's senior at both the Tokyo Institute of Technology and TEPCO, and he shared Yoshida's and the site's concern that "once you stopped water injection in a harsh working environment like this, it might not be possible to restart it," writing, "I can only take my hat off to the courageous decision and life-threatening efforts of the people in the field." In Tsuneo Futami, interview, November 22, 2012; Tsuneo Futami, *Nuclear Power Plant Accidents/Trouble: Analysis & Lessons* (Tokyo: Maruzen Publishing, 2012), 104–05.

35. Ibid.

36. Interview with an engineer from an associate company, September 4, 2012.

37. NHK Special Meltdown Report Crew, *Meltdown: The Truth About the Chain Reaction* (Tokyo: Kodansha, 2013), 279.

38. Rebuild Japan Initiative Foundation (RJIF), *Anatomy of the Yoshida Testimony* (Tokyo: Toyo Publishing, 2015), 67.

39. Government Investigation Commission on the Accident at the Fukushima Nuclear Power Stations of Tokyo Electric Power Company, Interim Report, December 26, 2011, 473.

40. Ryusho Kadota, *The Man Who Went to the Brink of Death—Masao Yoshida and His 500 Days at the Fukushima Daiichi Nuclear Station* (Kyoto: PHP, 2012), 71.

41. Masaya Yasui, interview, September 30, 2011.

42. Toshimi Kitazawa, interview, February 29, 2012; Toshimi Kitazawa, *Why Japan Needs the SDF* (Tokyo: Kadokawa Shoten, 2012), 75.

43. Kan, *The TEPCO Fukushima Nuclear Accident*, 77.

44. Charles Casto, interview, August 10, 2011.

45. Ibid.

46. Tadahiro Matsushita, interview, November 8, 2011; Masato Taura, interview, November 13, 2012; Takahiro Takino, *The SDF and the Great East Japan Earthquake* (Tokyo: Poplar Publishing, 2012), 77.

47. Interview with a senior associate company officer, October 14, 2011.

48. "Meltdown File 6: Nuclear Reactor Cooling, the Overlooked Crisis Twelve Days In," *NHK Special*, March 12, 2017.

49. Interview with a senior associate company officer, September 4, 2012.

50. On November 16, 2011, Yoshida was told he had esophageal cancer. In Feb-

ruary 2012, he underwent surgery for the cancer, but suffered a brain hemorrhage in July of the same year. He passed away on July 10, 2013. He was fifty-eight years old. On his death, the emperor sent his condolences to Mrs. Yoshida. The emperor had been looking forward to Masao Yoshida's imperial lecture, which had been scheduled for the end of 2012, but this was not to be.

51. Interview with a senior TEPCO officer, December 12, 2012.

52. Naohiro Masuda, interview, May 27, 2013.

53. Ibid.

54. Ibid.

55. INPO, "Lessons Learned from the Nuclear Accident," 29.

56. Naohiro Masuda, interview, July 17, 2013.

57. Ibid.

58. Akio Miyashita, interview, June 6, 2013; Naohiro Masuda, interview, May 27, 2013.

59. Ikuo Izawa, interview, August 8, 2013; Naohiro Masuda, interview, May 27, 2013.

60. Naohiro Masuda, interview, May 27, 2013.

61. Ibid.

62. Shunsuke Kimura, "In the Midst of Chaos—Scenes from the TEPCO Video-conference: (4) Lend Me Your Car Battery," *Asahi Shimbun, Fukushima Edition,* September 17, 2012.

63. Fukushima Nuclear Accident Record Team and others, *Forty-Nine Hours of the Fukushima Nuclear Accident TEPCO Videoconference Records,* 376.

64. Naohiro Masuda, interview, May 27, 2013.

65. Government Investigation Commission on the Accident at the Fukushima Nuclear Power Stations of Tokyo Electric Power Company, Final Report, July 23, 2012, 200–01, 213.

66. "Reactor Meltdown 'A Fine Line,' Fukushima Daini Site Superintendent," *Yomiuri Shimbun,* February 9, 2012.

67. Nuclear Safety Commission, whiteboard memo, Appendix 1–9/38.

68. TEPCO, "Fukushima Nuclear Accident Report," June 20, 2012, 248; TEPCO videoconference participant memo, released September 21, 2012.

69. Takafumi Anegawa, interview, May 27, 2013.

70. Interview with a Toshiba engineer, August 30, 2012.

71. Masaya Yasui, interview, February 9, 2012.

72. Interview with a Toshiba engineer, August 30, 2012.

73. Charles Casto, interview, August 24, 2011.

74. INPO, "Lessons Learned from the Nuclear Accident," 29.

75. Government Investigation Commission, "J-Village, July 29, 2011," *Masao Yoshida, Hearing Results Report,* August 16, 2011, 57.

76. Takafumi Anegawa, interview, November 27, 2014.

77. Naohiro Masuda, interview, May 27, 2013.

78. Charles Casto, interview, August 24, 2011.

79. Mari Sato, interviews, January 15, 2016, and April 21, 2017.

80. Ikuo Izawa, interview, August 8, 2013; Ikuo Izawa's lecture at Japan Nuclear Safety Institute's Duty Manager Training, February 12, 2014.

81. TEPCO official, interview, October 24, 2017.

82. Ryuta Edogawa, interview, August 10, 2018.

Interviewee List

(*Association true as of March 2011*)

Prime Minister's Office (Kantei)
Yukio Edano, Tetsuro Fukuyama,
Hirohisa Fujii, Shigeki Habuka,
Yojiro Hatakeyama, Goshi Hosono,
Keiichi Ichikawa, Koji Inoue,
Tetsuro Ito, Koichi Kato, Naoto Kan,
Motohiko Oka, Tetsu Okumura,
Noriaki Ozawa, Satoshi Maeda,
Sumio Mabuchi, Hideshi Mitani,
Keiichiro Naito, Itaru Nakamura,
Tetsuya Nishikawa, Keisuke Sadamori,
Yoshito Sengoku, Noriyuki Shikata,
Naohisa Shibuya, Kenichi Shimomura,
Manabu Terada, Shiro Yamasaki

Cabinet Office (CAO)
Koichiro Genba, Tatsuo Hirano,
Ryu Matsumoto, Futoshi Matsumoto,
Takashi Yanagi

*Special Advisers to the
Cabinet Secretary*
Oriza Hirata, Kenkichi Hirose,
Toshiso Kosako, Harufumi Mochizuki,
Hiroshi Tasaka, Noboru Yamaguchi

Nuclear Safety Commission (NSC)
Makoto Hashimoto, Akihiko Iwahashi,
Kaoru Kohara, Yutaka Kukita,
Shizuyo Kusumi, Kiyoshi Kurihara,
Haruki Madarame, Hideki Mizuma,
Kazuaki Sakamoto, Seiji Shiroya,
Hideaki Tsuzuki

*Japan Atomic Energy
Commission (JNES)*
Akira Omoto, Shunsuke Kondo,
Tatsujiro Suzuki

*Ministry of Economy, Trade,
and Industry (METI)*
Hiroyuki Fukano, Tetsuro Fukunaga,
Koichi Hamano, Motohisa Ikeda,
Takaya Imai, Banri Kaieda,
Hirobumi Kayama, Kazuo Matsunaga,
Tadahiro Matsushita, Takatoshi Miura,
Yoshikatsu Nakayama,
Kiyoshi Sawaki, Takashi Shimada,
Kaname Tajima, Yoshihisa Yamano,
Mitsuyoshi Yanagisawa, Tadao Yanase,
Masaya Yasui

*Nuclear and Industrial
Safety Agency (NISA)*
Eiji Hiraoka, Shuichi Kaneko,
Hiromu Katayama, Masaru Kobayashi,
Shinchi Kuroki, Akio Miyashita,
Koichiro Nakamura,
Hisanori Nei, Harushige Ogoshi,
Nobuaki Terasaka, Tomoho Yamada,

Tetsuya Yamamoto, Ryuichi Yamashita,
Naohiko Yokoshima, Kazuma Yokota,
Masataka Yoshizawa

*Japan Nuclear Energy Safety
Organization (JNES)*
Kiyoharu Abe, Akira Fukushima,
Mitsumasa Hirano,
Mitsuhiro Kajimoto,
Masaki Nakagawa,
Yoshihiro Nakagome, Masao Ogino,
Shohei Sato, Hitoshi Sato

*Ministry of Education, Culture, Sports,
Science, and Technology (MEXT)*
Yoshinari Akeno, Takayuki Amaya,
Kanji Fujiki, Kazuko Goto,
Hiroshi Ikukawa, Takashi Inutsuka,
Shigeharu Kato, Naohito Kimura,
Yasutaka Moriguchi,
Yoshihisa Nagayama,
Motoshi Shinozaki, Kan Suzuki,
Yoshiaki Takagi, Atsuo Tamura,
Satoshi Tanaka, Itaru Watanabe,
Makio Watanabe, Tomoki Yamaguchi

Japan Atomic Energy Agency (JAEA)
Masamichi Chino, Toshimitsu Homma,
Yosuke Naoi, Hideaki Yokomizo

Nuclear Safety Technology Center
Hiroto Ishida, Tominori Suzuki,
Masahiro Yoshida

*National Institute of Radiological
Sciences (NIRS)*
Makoto Akashi, Kazuo Sakai,
Takako Tominaga

Ministry of Defense (MOD)
Yoshitaka Akiyama, Koji Kano,
Toshimi Kitazawa, Keiichi Kuno,
Kazunori Inoue, Shigeki Ito,
Kimito Nakae, Masanori Nishi,
Kazuya Ogawa, Kozo Oikawa,
Shuichi Sakurai, Tatsuro Sasaki,
Atsuo Suzuki, Hideo Suzuki,
Nobushige Takamizawa,
Takahiro Yoshida

Self-Defense Forces (SDF)
Koichiro Bansho, Katsuro Fukaya,
Hideki Hayashi, Yoshifumi Hibako,

Masayuki Hironaka,
Hidetoshi Horiguchi, Koichi Isobe,
Yuki Imaura, Shinji Iwakuma,
Seiji Karaki, Koichi Kataoka,
Katsutoshi Kawano,
Takashi Kimizuka, Shigeru Kobayashi,
Toshinobu Miyajima,
Katsumi Nakamura, Mitsuru Nodomi,
Sadamasa Oue, Ryoichi Oriki,
Takashi Saito, Hiromi Takashima,
Masato Taura, Takeo Yamaoka,
Yoshiyuki Yamaoka, Masanori Yoshida,
Yoshihide Yoshida, Shunji Yosihino

*National Public Safety
Commission (NPSC) and
National Police Agency (NPA)*
Shigeru Kitamura, Kansei Nakano,
Noritsugo Oigawa, Kiyotaka Takahashi

Ministry of Foreign Affairs (MOFA)
Takeo Akiba, Ichiro Fujisaki,
Kenji Goto, Takeaki Matsumoto,
Makio Miyagawa, Hiroyuki Namazu,
Ichiro Ogasawara, Kenichiro Sasae

*Ministry of Internal Affairs and
Communications (MIC)*
Yoshihiro Katayama,
Masakatsu Okamoto

Fire and Disaster Management Agency
Tatsuya Kabutan, Nobuyasu Kubo

*Ministry of Agriculture, Forestry,
and Fisheries (MAFF)*
Takashi Shinohara, Yosei Umetsu

Tokyo Fire Department
Yuji Arai, Hiroyuki Kawamura,
Narumi Suzuki, Junichi Yamazaki

*Ministry of Health, Labour,
and Welfare (MHLW)*
Takeshi Karasawa,
Takahisa Nishikawa, Kohei Otsuka,
Masayoshi Shibatsuji

*Ministry of Land, Infrastructure,
Transport, and Tourism (MLIT)*
Shigetoshi Kai, Akihiro Ohata,
Yasuhiko Sakane

Okuma Town
Jin Ishida, Ichiro Suzuki

Minamisoma City
Sadayasu Abe, Takashi Murata,
Katsunobu Sakurai

Namie Town
Tamotsu Baba, Shinpei Ueno

Iitate Village
Norio Kanno, Yoshitomo Shigihara,
Hiroshi Tada

Miharu Town
Kuniharu Hashimoto, Hiroyuki Kudo,
Yoshinori Suzuki, Chisato Takenouchi

Niigata Prefecture
Hirohiko Izumida

Yokosuka City
Aiichiro Nakano, Takanori Nakata,
Takashi Noda, Kazuaki Onuki,
Koji Tomioka, Naoki Uehara,
Yuto Yoshida

Politicians
Hiroyuki Arai, Nobuyuki Fukushima,
Yasukazu Hamada, Hiroshi Kawauchi,
Seiji Maehara, Teruhiko Mashiko,
Akihisa Nagashima, Atsushi Oshima,
Seiki Soramoto, Makiko Tanaka,
Kiyohiko Toyama

*Tokyo Electric Power
Company (TEPCO)*
Takafumi Anegawa, Toshihiko Fukuda,
Masatoshi Fukura, Shiro Hikida,
Ryuta Idogawa, Ikuo Izawa,
Takeyuki Inagaki, Masanori Kanei,
Shinichiro Kengaku, Shunichi Kimura,
Mitsuru Komemasu, Naohiro Masuda,
Akiyoshi Minematsu, Hiroyuki Ogawa,
Akira Ono, Mari Sato, Fumio Sudo,
Akio Takahashi, Shizuo Takahashi,
Kazuhiro Takei, Ichiro Takekuro,
Kenji Tateiwa, Noriichi Yamashita,
Tadayuki Yokomura

Toshiba Corporation
Kazuo Aoki, Mamoru Hatazawa,
Tetsuo Kadoya, Hirokazu Kanai,

Osamu Maekawa, Atsutoshi Nishida,
Norio Sasaki, Akihiro Takubo

Hitachi
Masayuki Ishiwata, Hideo Kawai,
Hiroaki Nakanishi, Keisaku Shibatani

*Other Associate Companies
and Manufacturers*
Tatsuo Haga, Yasuo Hibi,
Akihide Kugo, Kosuke Suzuki,
Hiroshi Minami, Keisuke Saito,
Hiroshi Suzuki

Others
Nobuyasu Abe, Tsuneo Futami,
Ryugo Hayano, Shigeo Hirose,
Shinji Iwaba, Akihide Kugo,
Yoichiro Matsumoto, Ken Nakajima,
Takeshi Noda, Kazuhiko Noguchi,
Kensuke Okoshi, Yukinobu Okamura,
Keiko Takahashi, Mitsuhiko Tanaka,
Shunichi Tanaka, Taketoshi Taniguchi,
Tomoko Tsuchiya, Akira Watanabe,
Toshio Yamagata, Ekou Yagi,
Yoshihiro Yamaguchi,
Yoshimitsu Yamazaki, Yoshiaki Yano

*International Atomic
Energy Agency (IAEA)*
Yukiya Amano, Nobuhiro Muroya,
Tomihiro Taniguchi

U.S. Federal Government
Jeffrey Bader, Suzanne Basalla,
Kurt Campbell, Charles Casto,
Joseph R. Donovan Jr.,
Robert D. Eldridge,
Burton M. Field, Raymond Greene,
Wallace "Chip" Gregson,
Kenneth Glueck, Gregory Jaczko,
Christopher B. Johnstone,
Ayako Kimura, Yuji Kumamaru,
Karl King, Jeffrey Miller,
Michael Mullen, John P. Niemeyer,
Richard Reed, Daniel Russel,
John V. Roos, Michael Schiffer,
James B. Steinberg, James P. Zumwalt

Overseas Private Sector
Lake H. Barrett, Theodore C. Bestor,
David Carlson, Richard Danzig,
Evan Osnos, Roy Rondoe

Index

Saito, Tetsuo, 112
Sakai, Kazuo, 437, 438, 440
Sakashita Dam, 360–61
Sakurai, Katsunobu, 197–202, 452
Sakurai, Shuichi, 31, 181, 217, 257–58
Sasae, Kenichiro, 287, 294–95, 328, 352–53
Sasaki, Norio, 107–09, 113
Sasaki, Ryuzo, 418–19
Sato, Mari: disaster response by, 512–13; evacuation of plant and, 149–50; evacuation of residents and, 184, 193; TEPCO leadership and, 488; Unit 1 explosion and, 76; water injection operations and, 89–94
Sato, Yuhei, 114, 193, 200, 482
Sawaki, Kiyoshi, 125, 128, 155
SC. *See* Suppression chamber
Schiffer, Michael, 283
Science and Technology Agency (STA): evacuation of residents and, 192, 454; Integrated Response Office and, 162, 166–68, 179; SPEEDI monitoring data and, 417, 424, 429–30, 432; station blackout and, 22, 24; worst-case scenario planning and, 378
SDF. *See* Self-Defense Forces
Seawater: Hyper Rescue Squad and, 246, 261, 277; isolation condenser and, 9, 10; nuclear emergency declaration and, 46; SDF and, 230, 233, 236, 241–42, 244; station blackout and, 20; tsunami waves, 3–6, 501–02; worst-case scenario planning and, 380, 383, 387. *See also* Water discharge operations; Water injection operations
Security police (SP), 29–30, 32, 61, 143–44, 152, 168
Seino, Satoshi, 39
Self-Defense Forces (SDF), 215–45; aircraft, 176, 284–85, 340, 373, 402, 405; disaster response operations, 215–26; evacuation of plant and, 138; evacuation of residents and, 189, 191, 193, 198–99, 210, 440; Hyper Rescue Squad and, 246, 256–60; Integrated Response Office and, 154, 164, 175, 178, 180–81; Kan's leadership and, 496–98; Masuda's leadership and, 508; nuclear emergency declaration and, 31, 38, 41–44, 221–22; offsite center relo-

cation and, 130, 134; Operation Tomodachi and, 284–85, 291, 298–99, 301–02; riot police, 240–44, 249, 278–79; SPEEDI monitoring data and, 404–05; station blackout and, 22–23, 25–26; Unit 3 explosion and, 223; U.S.-Japan relations and, 345, 350–51, 353, 355–56, 364–69, 373; water bombing operations, 226–38, 240; worst-case scenario planning and, 383, 391–96; Yokosuka naval base and, 340; Yoshida's leadership and, 504. *See also* Ground Self-Defense Forces; Maritime Self-Defense Forces; *specific units*
Sengoku, Yoshito, 258, 301, 351–52
Senkaku Shock (2010), 220–21, 287
SFP. *See* Spent-fuel pools
Shadow evacuations, 189
Shigihara, Yoshitomo, 410–11
Shiina, Etsusaburo, 66
Shikoku Electric Power Ikata Nuclear Power Station, 458
Shimizu, Masataka: evacuation of plant and, 124–25, 128–29, 137, 139–45, 147, 149–51; Fukushima 50 and, 483–87; ice drop operation and, 105; Integrated Response Office and, 154–55; nuclear emergency declaration and, 41, 49–50, 51; removal from TEPCO leadership, 480–82; SDF and, 216, 217–18, 227; TEPCO leadership and, 462, 480–82, 483, 486, 489; Unit 1 explosion and, 85–86; Unit 2 crisis and, 114, 117–18; venting decisions and operations, 73–74; water injection operations and, 98
Shimodaira, Koji, 230
Shimomura, Kenichi: Integrated Response Office and, 161; Kan's site inspection and, 61, 63, 65, 67; nuclear emergency declaration and, 33, 35
Shin Nippon Helicopters, 105–06
Shiozaki, Makoto, 105
Shirasu, Jiro, 364
Social Democrats of Japan, 66
Sogabe, Katsuhiro, 288
Son, Masayoshi, 351
Soramoto, Seiki, 377–79, 384, 421, 438, 443
Southern Tohoku General Hospital, 211
SP. *See* Security police